Union and Empire

The making of the United Kingdom in 1707 is still a matter of significant political and historical controversy. Allan Macinnes here offers a major new interpretation that sets the Act of Union within a broad European and colonial context and provides a comprehensive picture of its transatlantic and transoceanic ramifications which ranged from the balance of power to the balance of trade. He reexamines English motivations from a colonial as well as a military perspective and assesses the imperial significance of the creation of the United Kingdom. He also explores afresh the commitment of some determined Scots to secure Union for political, religious and opportunist reasons and shows that, rather than an act of statesmanship, the resultant Treaty of Union was the outcome of politically inept negotiations by the Scots. *Union and Empire* will be a major contribution to the history of Britain, empire and early modern state formation.

ALLAN I. MACINNES is Professor of Early Modern History at the University of Strathclyde. He has published extensively on covenants, clans and clearances, British state formation and Jacobitism. His previous publications include *Clanship, Commerce and the House of Stuart, 1603–1788* (1996) and, as co-editor with A. H. Williamson, *Shaping the Stuart World, 1603–1714: the American Connection* (2006).

Union and Empire
The Making of the United Kingdom in 1707

Allan I. Macinnes
University of Strathclyde

CAMBRIDGE UNIVERSITY PRESS
Cambridge, New York, Melbourne, Madrid, Cape Town, Singapore, São Paulo, Delhi

Cambridge University Press
The Edinburgh Building, Cambridge CB2 8RU, UK

Published in the United States of America by Cambridge University Press, New York

www.cambridge.org
Information on this title: www.cambridge.org/9780521616300

© Allan I. Macinnes 2007

This publication is in copyright. Subject to statutory exception
and to the provisions of relevant collective licensing agreements,
no reproduction of any part may take place without
the written permission of Cambridge University Press.

First published 2007

Printed in the United Kingdom at the University Press, Cambridge

A catalogue record for this publication is available from the British Library

ISBN 978-0-521-85079-7 hardback
ISBN 978-0-521-61630-0 paperback

Cambridge University Press has no responsibility for the persistence or
accuracy of URLs for external or third-party internet websites referred to
in this publication, and does not guarantee that any content on such
websites is, or will remain, accurate or appropriate.

To Cathie and Donald

Contents

Acknowledgements	*page* ix
List of abbreviations	xii

Part I Setting the Scenes

1	Introduction	3
2	The historiography	12

Part II Varieties of Union, 1603–1707

3	Precedents, 1603–1660	53
4	Projects 1661–1703	80
5	The Irish dimension	106

Part III The Primacy of Political Economy, 1625–1707

6	The transatlantic dimension	137
7	The Scottish question	172
8	Going Dutch?	201

Part IV Party Alignments and the Passage of Union

9	Jacobitism and the War of the British Succession, 1701–1705	243
10	Securing the votes, 1706–1707	277

Part V Conclusion

   11 The Treaty of Union   313

Appendix   327
Bibliography   328
Index   368

Acknowledgements

Unstinting support and assistance from a variety of individuals and institutions made this book possible. My researches into the making of the United Kingdom were originally facilitated by a series of major research grants from the British Academy that sponsored access to the archives at Dumfries House in Ayrshire, at Mount Stuart House on the Isle of Bute, at Inveraray Castle in Argyllshire, and at Buckminster, Grantham, in Lincolnshire. For permission to work in these archives I am indebted to the late Marquess of Bute, the Trustees of the 10th Duke of Argyll, and the Tollemache family. I deeply appreciate the diligence and organisational flair of my former research assistant Linda Fryer in the collation and structuring of this material. My researches into the Atlantic dimension and into the importance of political economy in shaping the Treaty of Union was made possible by a generous research grant for a project, 'American Colonies, Scottish Entrepreneurs and British State Formation in the Seventeenth Century', which was part of the Arts & Humanities Research Council's funding for the Research Institute for Irish and Scottish Studies as a research centre of excellence at Aberdeen University. My colleague on this project was Esther Mijers, to whom I am indebted for her forensic knowledge of Batavian–Caledonian relations in the seventeenth century. I am also greatly indebted to Alexia Grosjean and Steve Murdoch who ran an associated project on 'Scottish Networks in Northern Europe', which has proved pathbreaking, highly productive and a model of good research practice. I am further indebted to the Arts & Humanities Research Council for funding four months' study leave in 2006, which allowed me time to bring my researches to fruition. In this context, I am also grateful to Robert Frost, the current head of the School of Divinity, History and Philosophy at Aberdeen, not only for authorising my sabbatical from teaching duties in 2005–6, but also for his sage advice on continental European developments around the time of Union in 1707.

My work on the American dimension was aided by a renewed research fellowship (as Andrew W. Mellon Foundation Fellow) at the Huntington

Library in 2005 and the accustomed generosity and assistance from Roy Ritchie (W. M. Keck Foundation Director of Research) and Mary Robertson (William A. Moffet Chief Curator of Manuscripts). Over the years, I have also been able to draw on the expertise, guidance and new pathways opened up by Bob and Barbara Cain, now retired from the North Carolina State Archives. My researches in the United States have been further aided by helpful assistance from the staff in the Newberry Library in Chicago, in the Folger Library and the Library of Congress in Washington DC, in the New York Public Library and in the New England Historic Genealogical Society in Boston. The Rigsarkivet in Copenhagen remains a pleasure to work in, while the Centre historique des Archives Nationales in Paris offers an undoubtedly interesting experience. I have been immensely heartened that George MacKenzie, as Keeper of the Records, has introduced positive changes in the support offered to researchers from beyond the central belt in the National Archives of Scotland. The staff there as always continue to be helpful, as is manifestly the case in the British Library, the Public Record Office (now the National Archives) and the National Library of Scotland. I have also appreciated the assistance received whenever I had the opportunity to work in the city and local archives in Aberdeen, Berwick-upon-Tweed, Dundee, Edinburgh, Glasgow, Orkney and Shetland, as in the university archives at the Bodleian in Oxford and, above all, in the Special Collections at Aberdeen where the staff are quite simply immense, if addicted to chocolate!

I have derived much appreciated intellectual sustenance from the work of my graduate students at Aberdeen, notably Linas Eriksonas, Jeffrey Stephen and James Vance. I have also been privileged to read the ongoing research endeavours of Gerry Sarney, Abbey Swingen and James Vaughn, who were postgraduates at the University of Chicago during my stint as Visiting Professor in British History in 2003. My evolving ideas on the making of the United Kingdom in 1707 have also been tried out at undergraduate level in my special subject on the Treaty of Union as on dissertation students studying this topic at Aberdeen. I must acknowledge my debt for supportive argument, blatant disagreement and relentless wit to the usual suspects – Sarah Barber, Mike Broers, Ali Cathcart, Tom Devine, Steven Ellis, Tim Harris, Roger Mason, Steve Pincus, Thomas Riis, Kevin Sharpe, Dan Szechi, Art Williamson, Kariann Yokota and John Young. I also have received particularly illuminating insights from Karen Kupperman, Andrew Mackillop, Edward Opalinski and Bill Speck. My researches have also been aided by the intellectual generosity of Bob Harris, Jason Peacey and Justine Taylor. In this context, special mention must be accorded to David Dobson for his encyclopedic knowledge of Scots in America as in Dutch service. Jean-Frédéric Schaub has also to be thanked for his intellectual input as for his sponsoring of a research fellowship at the École des Hautes Études en Sciences Sociales that brought Nicholas Canny and me together in Paris for a month of productive discussion in 2005.

Spiritual sustenance has been provided, on the one hand, by my good friend Revd Canon Emsley Nimmo of St Margaret's in the Gallowgate, Aberdeen, and, on the other, by the lads in the Potterton local of the Scotch malt whisky appreciation society. I must also thank Michael Watson of Cambridge University Press for his encouragement, forbearance and relaxed negotiating style, and Leigh Mueller for her meticulous diligence and her constructive copy-editing. However, I shall lay sole claim to the sins of omission and commission in the production of this book. Last, but by no means least, I thank my wife Tine Wanning for her love and support, stress counselling, and final preparation of the typescript.

Abbreviations

ACA	Aberdeen City Archives
ACS	*Annals and Correspondence of the Viscount and the First and Second Earls of Stair*, ed. J. M. Graham, 2 vols. (Edinburgh, 1875)
AHR	*American Historical Review*
APC, Colonial	*Acts of the Privy Council Colonial Series*, ed. W. L. Grant & J. Munro, 2 vols. (London, 1908–10).
APS	*Acts of the Parliament of Scotland*, ed. T. Thomson & C. Innes, 12 vols. (Edinburgh, 1814–72)
AUL	Aberdeen University Library
BL	British Library, London
BOU	Bodleian Library, Oxford University
Bruce, *REC*	John Bruce, *Report on the Events and Circumstances which produced the Union of England and Scotland*, 2 vols. (London, 1799).
Buccleuch	HMC, *Report on the Manuscripts of the Duke of Buccleuch & Queensberry preserved at Montague House, Whitehall*, vol. II, part 2 (London, 1903)
Burnet's HHOT	*Bishop Burnet's History of His Own Time: from the Restoration of King Charles the Second to the Treaty of Peace at Utrecht, in the reign of Queen Anne* (London, 1857)
CBJ	*Correspondence of George Baillie of Jerviswood, 1702–1708*, ed. George Elliot, Earl of Minto (Edinburgh, 1842).
Crossrigg, *DPP*	Sir David Hume of Crossrigg, *A Diary of the Proceedings in the Parliament and Privy Council of Scotland, 1700–1707*, ed. J. Hope (Edinburgh, 1828).
CSP, Colonial	*Calendars of State Papers, Colonial: America and the West Indies*, ed. W. M. Sainsbury, J. W.

	Fortescue & C. Headlam, 17 vols. (London, 1880–1916).
CTB	*Calendar of Treasury Books (1706–1708)*, ed. W. A. Shaw, vols. XXI–XXII (1950–2).
DCA	Dundee City Archives
Defoe, *HUGB*	Daniel Defoe, *The History of the Union of Great Britain* (Edinburgh, 1709)
DH	Dumfries House, Cumnock, Ayrshire
EHR	*English Historical Review*
Fountainhall, *HNS*	Sir John Lauder of Fountainhall, *Historical Notices of Scottish Affairs (1661–1688)*, 2 vols. (Edinburgh, 1848)
GCA	Glasgow City Archives
HJ	*Historical Journal*
HL	Huntington Library, San Marino, California
HMC	Historical Manuscripts Commission
ICA	Inveraray Castle Archives, Inveraray, Argyllshire
IHS	*Irish Historical Studies*
ISL	*Intimate Society Letters of the Eighteenth Century*, ed. Duke of Argyll, 2 vols. (London, 1910).
JHC	*Journal of the House of Commons*
JHL	*Journals of the House of Lords*
Laing	HMC, *Report on the Laing Manuscripts preserved in the University of Edinburgh*, vol. II, ed. H. Paton (London, 1925)
LDD	*The Letters of Daniel Defoe*, ed. G. H. Healey (Oxford, 1955).
LDN	*The London Diaries of William Nicolson, Bishop of Carlisle 1702–1718*, ed. C. Jones & G. Holmes (Oxford, 1985).
Lords	HMC, *Manuscripts of the House of Lords*, original series, 3 vols. (1689–93), ed. E. F. Taylor & F. Skene (London, 1889–94); new series, 7 vols. (1693–1708), ed. C. L. Anstruther, J. P. St John, C. Headlam, J. B. Hotham, F. W. Lascelles & C. K. Davidson (London, 1900–21).
LP	*The Lockhart Papers: Memoirs and Correspondence upon the Affairs of Scotland from 1702 to 1715*, ed. A. Aufrere, 2 vols. (London, 1817).

LQA	*The Letters and Diplomatic Instructions of Queen Anne*, ed. B. C. Brown (London, 1968)
LRS	*Letters Relating to Scotland in the Reign of Queen Anne by James Ogilvy, First Earl of Seafield and others*, ed. P. H. Brown (Edinburgh, 1915).
Macpherson, *OP*	James Macpherson, *Original Papers, containing the secret history of Great Britain from the Restoration, to the accession of the House of Hanover*, 2 vols. (London, 1775).
Mar & Kellie	HMC, *Report on the Manuscripts of the Earl of Mar and Kellie preserved at Alloa House*, ed. H. Paton (London, 1904)
Marchmont	HMC, *The Manuscripts of the Duke of Roxburghe; Sir H. H. Campbell, bart.; the Earl of Strathmore; and the Countess Dowager of Seafield* (London, 1894)
MGC	*The Marlborough–Godolphin Correspondence*, ed. H. L. Snyder, 3 vols. (Oxford, 1975).
MLP	*Memoirs of the Life of Sir John Clerk of Penicuik*, ed. J. M. Gray (Edinburgh, 1892)
MSH	Mount Stuart House, Rothesay, Isle of Bute
MSSM	*Memoirs of the Secret Services of John Macky, esq., during the reign of King William, Queen Anne and King George I*, ed. J. M. Gray (London, 1895).
NAS	National Archives of Scotland, Edinburgh
NLC	Newberry Library, Chicago
NLS	National Library of Scotland, Edinburgh
NROB	Northumberland Record Office, Berwick-upon-Tweed
Ormonde	HMC, *Calendar of the Manuscripts of the Marquess of Ormonde K. P. preserved at Kilkenny Castle*, new series, vol. VIII (London, 1920)
PEM	*A Selection from the Papers of the Earls of Marchmont illustrative of events from 1685–1750*, ed. G. H. Rose, 3 vols. (London, 1831).
Penicuik, *HUSE*	Sir John Clerk of Penicuik, *History of the Union of Scotland and England*, ed. D. Duncan (Edinburgh, 1993)
PH	*Parliamentary History*
Portland	HMC, *The Manuscripts of His Grace the Duke of Portland, preserved at Welbeck Abbey*, vol. IV, ed.

	J. J. Cartwright (London, 1897) and vol. VIII, ed. S. C. Lomas (London, 1907).
PRO	Public Record Office, London (now National Archives)
RC	Rigsarkivet, Copenhagen
Ridpath, *PPS*	[George Ridpath], *The Proceedings of the Parliament of Scotland begun at Edinburgh 6 May 1703* (Edinburgh, 1704)
RPCS	*Registers of the Privy Council of Scotland*, first series, ed. D. Masson, 14 vols. (Edinburgh, 1877–98); second series, ed. D. Masson & P. H. Brown, 8 vol. (Edinburgh, 1899–1908); third series, ed. P. H. Brown, H. Paton & E. W. M. Balfour-Melville, 16 vol. (Edinburgh, 1908–70).
RSCHS	*Records of the Scottish Church History Society*
SC	*Seafield Correspondence from 1685 to 1708*, ed. J. Grant (Edinburgh, 1912).
SHR	*Scottish Historical Review*
SPC	*State Papers and Letters addressed to William Carstares, Secretary to King William*, ed. J. McCormick (Edinburgh, 1774).
SR	'*Scotland's Ruine*': *Lockhart of Carnwath's Memoirs of the Union*, ed. D. Szechi (Aberdeen, 1995).
TFA	Tollemache Family Archives, Buckminster, Grantham, Lincolnshire
TKUA	Tyske Kancellis Udenrigske Afdeling

Part I

Setting the Scenes

1 Introduction

The joining of Scotland and England to form the United Kingdom through the Treaty of Union in 1707 is still a matter of controversy. And as long as the Union endures, it is likely to remain so. Of course, this controversy plays more strongly in Scotland than England, since the former country clearly lost its political independence. In the latter country, the Union has tended to be viewed as an expeditious constitutional adjustment to lay a secure basis for the expansion of Empire.[1] This controversy is not just political; it is also historiographic.[2] Much ink has been spilt in claiming, on the one hand, that the Union was a farsighted act of statesmanship that laid the basis not just for the British imperial expansion on a global scale, but also the modernising of Scotland. On the other hand, the Union has from its inception been castigated as a sordid political exercise in which avaricious Scottish parliamentarians betrayed their country for English gold and, in the process, eradicated Scotland's capacity to determine its own course towards modernity.

Although Scottish animation on the subject of Union has often stood in marked contrast to English indifference, the advent of devolution in 1999 has sharpened English awareness of ongoing constitutional issues from 1707. Indeed, the United Kingdom is undergoing a constitutional transition from a unitary state that is a continuous, but not necessarily a conciliatory, process in which an incorporating union can no longer be taken for granted. British state formation, transformation and perhaps even disintegration constitute a heady intermingling of perception and reality that requires some preliminary sketching.

---

[1] See that the Treaty of Union does not even in feature in E. N. Williams, *The Eighteenth Century Constitution: Documents and Commentary* (Cambridge, 1960), while it merits a separate section in *A Source Book of Scottish History*, vol. III, ed. W. C. Dickinson & G. Donaldson (Edinburgh, 1961), pp. 469–95.
[2] See A. I. Macinnes, 'Early Modern History: The Current State of Play', *SHR*, 53 (1994), pp. 30–46.

The formation of early modern states was achieved usually by association and coalescence or by annexation and conquest.[3] The political incorporation of Great Britain accomplished in 1707 involved only two of the three kingdoms held by the British monarchy. Ireland was not included. England had absorbed Wales (and Cornwall) by 1543 through parliamentary incorporation, administrative cohesion in church and state, and the political if not the cultural integration of the ruling elites. However, Ireland, despite being declared a dependant kingdom in 1541, was not incorporated into a composite English kingdom. Successive Tudor monarchs failed to effect conquest and achieved little integration outwith Dublin and the surrounding Pale. The limited advent of the Protestant Reformation in Ireland further compounded this failure. This uneasy relationship was aggravated by plantation and large-scale migration to Ireland from Scotland as well as England in the seventeenth century.[4]

Nevertheless, the current narrative of state formation casts the multiple kingdoms of England, Scotland and Ireland on a transitional stage in the course of the seventeenth and eighteenth centuries; from a composite English kingdom in 1603 to a unified kingdom for Britain in 1707 and then for Britain and Ireland in 1800.[5] Did the accession of James VI of Scotland to the English throne in 1603 inevitably pave the way for the United Kingdom of Great Britain in 1707, to which Ireland was added in 1800?[6] The move from regal or dynastic union to parliamentary union was not seamless. The English parliament rejected full union with Scotland in 1607 and 1670, and Irish overtures for political incorporation in 1703, 1707 and 1709. A proposal for union in the House of Lords in 1695 never got off the ground and another at the outset of 1700 was rejected in

---

[3] J. H. Elliot, 'A Europe of Composite Monarchies', *Past & Present*, 137 (1992), pp. 48–71; M. Greengrass, 'Introduction: Conquest and Coalescence' in M. Greengrass, ed., *Conquest and Coalescence: The Shaping of the State in Early Modern Europe* (London, 1991), pp. 1–24.

[4] C. Brady, 'The Decline of the Irish Kingdom' in Greengrass, ed., *Conquest and Coalescence*, pp. 94–115; S. G. Ellis, 'Tudor State Formation and the Shaping of the British Isles" in S. G. Ellis & S. Barber, eds., *Conquest and Union: Fashioning a British State, 1485–1725* (London, 1995), pp. 40–63.

[5] See A. Murdoch, *British History, 1660–1832: National Identity and Local Culture* (Basingstoke, 1998); J. Smyth, *The Making of the United Kingdom, 1660–1800* (Harlow, 2001).

[6] See B. P. Levack, *The Formation of the British State: England, Scotland and the Union, 1603–1707* (Oxford, 1987); K. M. Brown, *Kingdom or Province? Scotland and the Regal Union, 1603–1715* (Basingstoke, 1992); D. L. Smith, *A History of the Modern British Isles, 1603–1707: the Double Crown* (Oxford, 1998); M. Kishlansky, A *Monarchy Transformed: Britain 1603–1714* (London, 1996); J. Morrill, 'The British Problem, c.1534–1707' in B. Bradshaw & J. Morrill, eds., *The British Problem, c.1534–1707: State Formation in the Atlantic Archipelago* (Basingstoke, 1996), pp. 1–38.

the House of Commons. For their part, the Scottish Estates favoured a federative union[7] in 1641 and 1643, split over incorporating union in 1648 and resisted incorporating overtures in 1689 and 1702 – albeit, like the Irish parliament, they were forced into an unwanted union at the behest of the English Commonwealth in 1651, repackaged as the Protectorate from 1654. During the Restoration era, Scottish moves towards commercial union initiated in 1664 were rebuffed in 1668. A similar English initiative never got off the drawing board in 1674 or in 1685.[8] Not only must the inevitability of Union be questioned, but also whether the Treaty of 1707 represented an equitable accommodation of English and Scottish interests.

As England's wealth and resources were as much as ten times greater than those of Wales, Ireland and Scotland combined, the adjustment from England to Great Britain could be viewed essentially as a cosmetic exercise to appease the Scots. Indeed, the terms 'England' and 'Britain' or 'English' and 'British' continue to be viewed as interchangeable, not just by Scotland's southern neighbours but also by foreign powers, peoples and institutions, until the present day. Undoubtedly, political power from 1707 was centred in England, albeit this power was exercised imperially through the British Empire until its demise in the twentieth century. Thus, governance was viewed as English, but the dominions ruled from London were British. From an anglocentric perspective, England was a global power prior to 1707 and for over two centuries thereafter. The British appellation to the Empire courteously recognised the supplementary endeavours of the other peoples from the British Isles.

For the Scots, however, there was clearly a major step up from a Scottish kingdom to a British Empire. At the same time, incorporation with England did not fundamentally alter their separate Kirk, their distinctive legal system and particular forms of local government until state intervention became the norm rather than the exception from the mid nineteenth century. Incorporation, therefore, could be viewed initially as a partnership, albeit not necessarily an equal partnership given the disparity of wealth and resources. This partnership had particular force

---

[7] The term 'federative' denotes a relationship that can be either confederal or federal. A federative union can be viewed as an association or confederation of executive powers authorised by the Scottish and the English parliaments that did not involve the subordination or incorporation of these separate constitutional assemblies. A federalist position would have subordinated the Scottish and the English Parliaments to a British assembly. Full parliamentary union, as achieved in 1707, required the incorporation or merger of the Scottish parliament with the English.

[8] A. I. Macinnes, 'Politically Reactionary Brits?: The Promotion of Anglo-Scottish Union, 1603–1707' in S. J. Connolly, ed., *Kingdoms United? Great Britain and Ireland since 1500: Integration and Diversity* (Dublin, 1999), pp. 43–55.

within the British Empire. New territorial acquisitions in the West and East Indies in the eighteenth century and in Africa in the nineteenth, created a level playing field for enterprise and endeavour that ranged from venture capitalism to missionary work, through colonial administration and military careerism. For the Scots, the Empire cemented their commitment to the British adventure.[9] From a non-anglocentric perspective, the British Empire was manifestly a greater entity than the English, no less than the Scottish, kingdom.

Although the Empire in the course of the twentieth century was transformed into a Commonwealth of independent states, not all of whom have retained the monarchy, the Union of 1707 is now entering its fourth century. At the same time, devolution, particularly in Scotland, has tended to be viewed as a process. However, the making of the Treaty is no more an issue devolved to Scottish historians than a reserved matter for British history. Indeed, the Union of 1707, which brought together two sovereign kingdoms with their own representative assemblies, established churches and legal systems, was accomplished through an international treaty. The Treaty was negotiated and concluded in the midst of a war being waged in Europe and the Americas. Commercial no less than constitutional relationships were to be resolved. Thus, the Union of 1707 had not only transatlantic but transoceanic ramifications that ranged from the balance of power to the balance of trade.

In attempting to understand and unravel the complexities involved in the making of the Treaty of Union, a holistic rather than a particularist approach is required, to examine forensically and then to challenge fundamentally why England and Scotland negotiated an incorporating union. There are in fact six guiding principles for avoiding insularity and introspection, for integrating policy and process, and for connecting domestic and imperial history. The first two principles relate to state formation. In promoting a non-anglocentric view of union, the process of state formation will take account of the Irish as well as the English and Scottish situations: in the first case, union failed; in the second, union was accomplished. At the same time, union with England was not the sole issue on the Scottish political agenda at the outset of the eighteenth century. Scotland's formative relationships with not just the English, but also the Dutch, will be examined in terms of transoceanic associations. Two other key principles emerge in relation to the actual

---

[9] T. M. Devine, *Scotland's Empire, 1600–1815* (London, 2003), and M. Fry, *The Scottish Empire* (Edinburgh, 2001), who have fundamentally different interpretations of Scottish engagement with the British Empire, at least agree on this point. A constructive précis of the importance of this imperial engagement can be found in D. Allan, *Scotland in the Eighteenth Century: Union and Enlightenment* (Harlow, 2002), pp. 165–85.

making of Union. Issues of political economy will be rehabilitated, as will divisions of substance between proponents and opponents of Union. To this end, the debates on Union, which were conducted through the press and the pulpit, will be rigorously analysed with respect to parliamentary votes and extra-parliamentary protests. The final two principles relate to English and British interests. English motivation for Union will be reappraised from a colonial, as well as the traditional military, perspective, and a summative assessment will be offered on the imperial significance of the creation of the United Kingdom.

An immense advantage for any holistic study of the making of the Anglo-Scottish Union is the richness of the published and manuscript sources. There is a plethora of official records for the English and Scottish parliaments, as for the executive and judicial agencies of government within the British Isles and the colonies. Antiquarian societies and historical clubs have sponsored published commentaries by players in and observers of the political process that culminated in the Treaty of 1707.[10] In this respect, Scotland has been particularly well served, with such publication being instigated as an aspect of civic patriotism in the nineteenth century and further stimulated by the Disruption within Scottish Presbyterianism in 1843. With the breakaway Free Kirk contesting the claims of the Established Kirk to speak for Scotland at home and abroad, their rivalry extended to historical issues no less than to matters of faith, and to social welfare and education as to urban and overseas missions.[11] The call for Home Rule from the later nineteenth century sustained the momentum for eclectic issuing of source material on Scottish history in which the Treaty of Union continued to feature prominently. At the same time, the publication of sources has been further enhanced by the comprehensive identification of pamphlets relating to Union that have now been catalogued systematically, with the relevant texts largely made available electronically either by Early English Books Online (EEBO) or by Eighteenth Century Collections Online (ECCO).[12]

Technological advance through the computerising of abstracts and the digitisation of documents has further facilitated archival research, continuously offering up exciting discoveries of material pertinent to Union. In addition to examining selectively the vast array of primary sources on

---

[10] See D. Stevenson & W. B. Stevenson, *Scottish Text and Calendars: An Analytical Guide to Serial Publications* (Edinburgh, 1987).
[11] L. Eriksonas, *National Heroes and National Identities: Scotland, Norway and Lithuania* (Brussels, 2004), pp. 147–60; M. Ash, *The Strange Death of Scottish History* (Edinburgh, 1980), pp. 59–86.
[12] W. R. McLeod & V. B. McLeod, *Anglo-Scottish Tracts, 1701–1714* (Kansas, 1979); http://eebo.chadwyck.com/home?ath; http://galenet.galegroup.com/servlet/ECCO.

this topic in such major depositories as the British Library, the Public Records Office (now National Archives), the National Library of Scotland, National Archives of Scotland and the Aberdeen University Special Collections, this book has been grounded in three archival collections – firstly the Loudon Papers, dispersed between Dumfries House in Ayrshire, Mount Stuart House on the Isle of Bute and the Huntington Library, San Marino, California; secondly, the Bridgewater & Ellesmere Manuscripts and the Blathwayt Papers also at the Huntington Library; and thirdly, the section among the Tyske Kancellis Udenrigske Afdeling [TKUA] in the Rigsarkivet, Copenhagen, marked as relating to England, but dealing with Britain.

Pre-eminent among the papers relating to the political activities of Hugh Campbell, 3rd Earl of Loudoun, and his associates, from the accession of Queen Anne in 1702 until the conclusion of the Treaty in 1707, are the detailed correspondence of Sir David Nairn and the diaries of Colonel William Dalrymple of Glenmure, covering the last two sessions of the Scottish and the first of the British parliaments, 1705–8.[13] Sir David Nairn was based in London where he maintained a watching brief over the English ministries and reported regularly to Loudoun, a politician usually overlooked in narratives of Union even though he was Secretary of State for Scotland before and after the Treaty. Nairn also served as secretary to the Scottish commissioners when the details of the Treaty were negotiated with their English counterparts from April to July 1706. His finger on the pulse of English politics was complemented by his concern for the nuts and bolts of the political process as the Union progressed through the final session of the Scottish Estates from October 1706 to January 1707. His letters to Loudoun complement rather than replicate

---

[13] Dumfries House, Ayrshire, Loudoun Papers A 817/1–3. The correspondence with Sir David Nairn is split between deed boxes in Dumfries House and in Mount Stuart House. The Earl of Loudoun's correspondence is spread over forty-seven volumes in the Loudoun Scottish Collection at the Huntington Library, San Marino, California. Two other unpublished diaries deal with the political circumstances and proceedings of the last session of the Scottish Estates in 1706–7. The one more focused on parliament is probably by Walter Stewart of Pardovan, burgh commissioner for Linlithgow, although it has also been ascribed to two others, both Presbyterian ministers, the antiquarian Robert Wodrow and the radical leader Robert Wyllie (NLS, Wodrow MS, quarto lxxv, 'Ane Short Account of the proceedings of the Last Session of the Scottish Parliament. With some necessary reflections thereupon', fols.138–60). All three putative authors were opponents of Union, but Stewart of Pardovan, who was a burgh commissioner from 1700, is the more likely as the writer claims to have attended the last and the proceeding parliament. His reflections were drawn up no earlier than 1713. The other diary by J. B., almost certainly John Bell, Presbyterian minister of Gladsmuir in East Lothian, is concerned mainly with the affairs of the Kirk of Scotland as they impinged upon parliament (NLS, Wodrow MS, quarto lxxxii, 'The IInd Part of the Most Remarkable Passages of the Life and Times of Mr J. B., written with his own Hand', ff. 49–96).

his published correspondence with the other Scottish Secretary of State, John Erskine, 6th Earl of Mar.[14]

Dalrymple of Glenmure was a commissioner for the shire of Ayr and a supporter of Union. Nevertheless his diaries reveal that political incorporation with England was neither a foregone conclusion nor an unsophisticated exercise in political management. At the same time, his diaries disclose that issues of principle were not sidelined by the manipulative political influences that purportedly dominated the last session of the Scottish Estates. Indeed, his diaries demonstrate how the extra-parliamentary polemical debates fed into the parliamentary proceedings, and thereby seriously question the concession, by historians of ideas, that speeches, like pamphlets, 'made little impression on the actions of Scottish parliamentarians'.[15] This concession, made to the proponents of the supremacy of a parliamentary process governed by political pragmatism, is further undermined methodologically by historical computing. Analysis of accumulated data with respect to voting patterns and other measurable political influences has suggested that issues of principle inspired proponents no less than opponents of Union. In turn, a relatively high incidence of cross-party voting suggests issues were debated on their merits, as affirmed by Dalrymple of Glenure and other contemporary reports of parliamentary proceedings which acknowledge that players in the making of Union were both polemicists and politicians.[16]

The extensive materials at the Huntington Library on English diplomats, policy makers and colonial officials who reported regularly to the Board of Trade and Plantations concerning Scottish engagement with the American colonies as entrepreneurs and planters, and occasionally as preferred associates of the Dutch, reveal unexpected insights into English commercial motivation for Union.[17] Their reports echo the warnings and vociferous complaints from English merchants on both sides of the Atlantic, about Scottish competition in Ireland, Scandinavia and continental Europe as well as the Americas. In turn, if the Union is to be viewed as creating a structure for sustainable economic growth,[18]

---

[14] *Mar & Kellie*, pp. 273–387.
[15] C. Kidd, *Subverting Scotland's Past: Scottish Whig Historians and the Creation of an Anglo-British Identity, 1689 – c.1830* (Cambridge, 1993), pp. 36–7.
[16] A. I. Macinnes, 'Influencing the Vote: The Scottish Estates and the Treaty of Union, 1706–07', *History Microcomputer Review*, 2 (1990), pp. 11–25.
[17] In addition to the Bridgewater & Ellesmere MSS and Blathwayt Papers, other relevant material is also found at the Huntington Library, primarily in the miscellaneous Huntington Manuscripts (HM) series, the Stowe Collection and the Hastings Irish Papers.
[18] T. C. Smout, 'Introduction' in T. C. Smout, ed., *Anglo-Scottish Relations from 1603 to 1900* (Oxford, 2005), pp. 1–12.

this structure was devised primarily in the interests of England not of Scotland. Innovatory insights can thus be offered on imperial, manufacturing and demographic considerations influencing England to press for political incorporation in the reign of Queen Anne.

Among the vast range of papers classified under TKUA are copybooks of diplomatic letters from the British Court from the accession of Queen Anne to the Union. In particular, Iver Rosenkrantz, as envoy extraordinary between 1702 and 1705, wrote a detailed diplomatic letter at least once a week as a close confidant of Prince George of Denmark, Queen Anne's consort, as well as an assiduous cultivator of leading members of the English and Scottish ministries. His perspective from the Court on the making of Union is not only candid and absorbing but also revelatory. Seemingly, the outstanding issue for the credibility of Scottish and English politicians serving the queen as ministers was their commitment to the royal prerogative, specifically to its conservation, rather than to the furtherance of the Revolution Settlements of 1688–91 which had imposed permanent checks on the monarchy in England, Scotland and Ireland as well as replacing James II of Great Britain (& VII of Scotland) with his Dutch son-in-law, William of Orange. William had subsequently been succeeded by his sister-in-law Anne (the daughter of James II by his first marriage). However, Anne's children having all predeceased her by her accession, the succession to the three kingdoms lay with either the closest Protestant heir from the electoral house of Hanover or a return to the direct line of the Stuarts, now in exile at Saint-Germain outside Paris. The former was certainly favoured by the Whigs and, more equivocally, by the Tories, who had effected the Revolution Settlements; the latter, by the Jacobites who had opposed them. The Hanoverian Succession, promoted in England in 1701 and accepted in Ireland by 1703, was only secured in Scotland by the Union. At the same time, the ongoing War of the Spanish Succession threatened to become the War of the British Succession once Louis XIV of France recognised Anne's Roman Catholic half-brother as James III (& VIII). In this light, the Union was less relevant to perpetuating the Revolution than to securing a Protestant Succession in which, as Rosenkrantz makes clear, Anne was not a cipher who waited upon events but a determined and proactive player.[19]

If English interests can be said to be driven by the primacy of political economy in war and peace and if Queen Anne was pre-eminently

---

[19] RC, TKUA England, Akter og Dokumenter nedr Sofart og Handel: Order med Bilag, 1702–7, A.III/ 207–10, /214–17. Rosenkrantz as envoy extraordinary from 1702 to 1705 was succeeded for 1706–7 by Malthias Balthazar. In the interim, the reports were filed by diplomatic secretary Jens Elling.

motivated by the desire to conserve the royal prerogative, the making of the Treaty of Union also required a core group of determined Scottish politicians intent on political incorporation to secure the royal prerogative, the Presbyterian establishment in the Kirk and, ultimately, the Protestant Succession at the expense of an independent Scottish parliament no less than the exiled Catholic house of Stuart. The political resolve of this core grouping of Unionists made the accomplishment of the Treaty of 1707 an act of managerial sophistication, not a crude exercise in political influence. Conversely, accompanying polemical claims that political incorporation was the only realistic means of securing economic stability and growth in Scotland must be treated with caution. The institutional perspectives of government, incorporated burghs, colonial companies and even merchant houses present a far from complete and an overly pessimistic picture. Journals, letter and account books detailing the operation of Scottish commercial networks from the Baltic to the Mediterranean and on to the Caribbean reveal a burgeoning entrepreneurship that could certainly be enhanced by closer political collaboration; but not necessarily with England nor exclusively by the Treaty of Union.[20]

However, before we bring these fresh political, economic and diplomatic perspectives together to construct a holistic analysis of the making of the Anglo-Scottish Union, we must first deconstruct the historiography arising from the Treaty of 1707. At the same time, we must take cognisance of the historian's craft as outlined by a leading figure of the Scottish Enlightenment, Adam Ferguson, in *An Essay on the History of Civil Society* (1767):

If conjectures and opinions formed at a distance, have not sufficient authority in the history of mankind, the domestic antiquities of every nation, must for this very reason, be received with caution. They are, for most part, the mere conjectures or the fiction of subsequent ages; and even where at first they contained some resemblance of truth, they still vary with the imagination of those by whom they are transmitted, and in every generation receive a different form.[21]

---

[20] See NAS, Journal of William Fraser, merchant, London, 1699–1711, CS 96/524; Letter and account book of John Watson, younger, merchant, Edinburgh, 1696–1713, CS 96/3309; Memorandum, account and letter book of William and John Cowan, merchants, Stirling, 1697–1754, CS 96/1944; Letter book of John Swinton of that Ilk, merchant, London, 1673–1677, CS 96/3264; Letter book of Gilbert Robertson, merchant, Edinburgh, 1690–1694, CS 96/1726; Commission book, James Ramsay, merchant, Rotterdam, 1691–1694, CS 96/1337; and Account book of James Lawson, merchant, Anstruther Easter, 1688–1698, CS 96/3263. AUL, Account books of George Ross of Clochcan, merchant in Aberdeen, 1679–1703, Leith Ross MS 3346/12/7–8; Letter book of Robert Gerard, senior and junior, merchants in Aberdeen, 1677–1702, Duff House (Montcoffer Papers) MS 3175/Z/156.

[21] Adam Ferguson, *An Essay on the History of Civil Society 1767*, ed. D. Forbes (Edinburgh, 1966), p. 76.

2 The historiography

The historiography of the Treaty of Union reflects the changing and interchanging domestic and imperial perspectives. In the process, it tells us much about the reception and perception of Union, without necessarily coming to grips with its conception and delivery. Indeed, the historiography has three pronounced features – its longevity, its partisanship and its ideological fragmentation. It is long on emphatic pronouncements but short on scientific rigour and academic detachment as the Union has been challenged but never broken over the last 300 years, neither by Jacobitism in the eighteenth century nor by Home Rule movements from the nineteenth century. Commentators on the Union have ranged from players and spectators at the outset, through the intellectuals and improvers of the Enlightenment, to professional academics in history and cognate disciplines. Along the way, novelists, clergymen, lawyers, journalists and diplomats have made contributions that were no less significant or informed. Their diverse offerings set the scenes for a wider contextualising that will extend far beyond the confines of Anglo-Scottish relations.

Jacobites and Whigs

Partisans and activists who were far from averse to self-serving observations provided the initial commentaries on Union. First up was Daniel Defoe, novelist, polemicist and spy, who was sent to Scotland by the English ministry in 1706 to facilitate the passage of Union. His unattributed *The History of England from the beginning of the reign of Queen Anne, to the conclusion of the Glorious Treaty of Union between England and Scotland*, which was rushed out in 1707, placed the Union as the culmination of a series of battles, sieges, victories and turns of fortune by land and sea that characterised the allied endeavours under John Churchill, 1st Duke of Marlborough, against the forces of Louis XIV of France during the War of the Spanish Succession. However, he does deal painstakingly with the how, when and where of political incorporation which is the primary focus of his more reflective and attributed *The History of the*

Union of Great Britain (1709). Greater attention was given to the passage of Union through the unicameral Scottish parliament, consisting of the three estates of the nobility, the gentry and the burgesses; the former being individually summoned and the latter two estates represented respectively by shire and burgh commissioners. The ratification of Union through the bicameral English parliament was more noted than analysed, with respect to both the unelected House of Lords and the elected House of Commons.[1]

A partial answer as to why Union was accomplished was provided by *Memoirs concerning the Affairs of Scotland from Queen Anne's accession to the Throne, to the Commencement of the Union* (1714), attributed to George Lockhart of Carnwath and published in the year of the Hanoverian Succession. An avid adherent of the exiled house at Saint-Germain, outside Paris, for whose Jacobite cause he was a paramilitary organiser, Lockhart of Carnwath had also served as a commissioner who negotiated Union at Whitehall in 1706, and subsequently as a member of the British parliament. In this latter capacity, he established in 1711 that the English ministry had despatched £20,000 sterling (£240,000 Scots) to shore up support for Union prior to its passage through the Scottish parliament. Lockhart also offered a more sophisticated analysis of party influences, particularly within Scotland. The original divisions in both England and Scotland were based on the Revolution, which had not only exiled James II & VII, but also imposed constitutional checks on monarchy that the Whigs supported, the Tories acquiesced in and the Jacobites opposed. However, the reign of William of Orange post-Revolution witnessed a growing polarity between Court and Country. In Scotland, where the Jacobite presence was more obvious than in England, there was a further division on religious grounds. The Revolution, which had consolidated the Anglican ascendancy in the Church of England, had led to a change in the established Kirk of Scotland. Episcopalianism, as a church run by bishops, was replaced by Presbyterianism, a church run by a hierarchy of ecclesiastical courts. Moreover, from the outset of the reign of Queen Anne in 1702, mounting resentment about direct interference in Scottish affairs by English ministries further refined party divisions. Lockhart was particularly forthright in his characterisation of the principal politicians and their party affiliations. Statesmanship did not figure prominently in the leadership offered to the Court Party by James Douglas, 2nd Duke of Queensberry, nor that offered to the Country Party – led

---

[1] [Daniel Defoe], *The History of England from the beginning of the reign of Queen Anne, to the conclusion of the Glorious Treaty of Union between England and Scotland* (London, 1707), and Daniel Defoe, *The History of the Union of Great Britain* (Edinburgh, 1709).

nominally by James Douglas-Hamilton, 4th Duke of Hamilton – which included not only the Jacobites grouped around John Murray, 1st Duke of Atholl, but also constitutional reformers led by Andrew Fletcher of Saltoun, who wished to extend the constitutional limitations achieved at the Revolution from the monarchy to the aristocracy. Lockhart's scorn was especially directed at the expedient behaviour of the New Party or Squadrone Volante (Flying Squadron), led by John Hay, 2nd Marquis of Tweeddale, whose shift away from the Country to the Court was critical to the delivery of Union through the Scottish Estates from October 1706 to January 1707.[2]

Abel Boyer, whose trade was effectively that of a lobby journalist at Westminster, produced *The History of the Life and Reign of Queen Anne* in 1722, which was a digest of the voluminous annual reports that he had published studiously between 1703 and 1713. He set the Union firmly within the context of the two defining and enduring issues of Anne's reign; the War of the Spanish Succession in which English forces were aligned against France to maintain the balance of power in Europe, and the endeavours of the partisans of the exiled house of Stuart to set aside the Hanoverian Succession. Although he was a staunch supporter of the Union and attributed political discontent during Anne's reign primarily to the Jacobites, he relied unapologetically on Lockhart's political characterisations for their vitality if not their accuracy. At the same time, in his determination to transcend the 'story-telling' of gazettes, newspapers and state reports, he offered the first detailed insight into the passage of the Union through the Lords and Commons from February to April 1707, basing his work on manuscript journals, reports of speeches and eye-witnessing of proceedings.[3]

Gilbert Burnet, Bishop of Salisbury, an Anglo-Scot and prominent Whig polemicist, who actually (at times despairingly) sat in, and even chaired, proceedings in the House of Lords as the Union passed through the English parliament, offered more varied motivation. In the second

---

[2] [George Lockhart of Carnwath], *Memoirs concerning the Affairs of Scotland, from Queen Anne's Accession to the Throne, to the Commencement of the Union of the Two Kingdoms of Scotland and England in May 1707* (London, 1714). The seemingly corrupt nature of Union politics was further underlined by the publication of the wholly unreliable memoirs in 1726–7 of John Ker of Kersland, a double, if not a triple, agent ([John Ker], *The Memoirs of John Ker of Kersland in North Britain, Esq., Relating Politicks, Trade and History* (London, 1727)). Alternative and more rounded British characterisation was provided by another Scottish spy, John Macky, in *Memoirs of the Secret Services of John Macky, esq., during the reign of King William, Queen Anne and King George I*, ed. J. M. Gray (London, 1895). His characterisations of English and Scottish politicians, diplomats and military men were drawn up around 1704 but not finalised until 1723 and not prepared for publication until 1732.

[3] Abel Boyer, *The History of the Life and Reign of Queen Anne* (London, 1722).

volume of *Bishop Burnet's History of His Own Time*, which appeared posthumously in 1734, he affirmed that England had generously conceded Union in order to shut the back door to invasion from France, whose king, Louis XIV, was backing the Jacobites. In addition, the Union offered the Scots redress for their failed colonial venture, the Darien Scheme on the Panama Isthmus, which William of Orange had signally failed to support in the late 1690s. At the same time, the Scots were liberated from an oppressive and corrupt ministry who had governed their country with partiality and venality since the Revolution. The firm commitment of Queen Anne in favour of Union was also decisive, as was the low state of France, which could spare neither men nor money to support a Jacobite rising that would have turned the ongoing War of the Spanish Succession into that of the British Succession.[4]

These texts became the basic sources for the making of the Anglo-Scottish Union for the next two centuries. As Jacobitism, which was committed to the abrogation of the Treaty of Union,[5] was far more vibrant in Scotland than in England, Scottish commentators were initially more muted in their comments.[6] In England, John Oldmixon, an unapologetic Francophobe, a Whig polemicist and virulent anti-Jacobite, considered the Union as no more than a constitutional adjustment in English history that happened to occur in the midst of the War of the Spanish Succession. *The History of England* (1735), which commenced with his glorification of the Revolution instigated by the invasion of William of Orange from the Netherlands, continued through the reigns of Queen Anne and that of the first Hanoverian, George I. Scottish affairs, which were no more than an interruption to his narrative, were reported with disparagement.

---

[4] Gilbert Burnet, *Bishop Burnet's History of His Own Time*, 2 vols. (London, 1724–34), and *Bishop Burnet's History of His Own Time: from the Restoration of King Charles the Second to the Treaty of Peace at Utrecht, in the reign of Queen Anne* (London, 1857).
[5] *Historical Papers relating to the Jacobite Period, 1699–1750*, ed. J. Allardyce, 2 vols. (Aberdeen, 1895), I, pp. 177–92; *The Jacobite Threat: A Source Book*, ed. B. P. Lenman & G. S. Gibson (Edinburgh, 1990), pp. 122–6.
[6] James Wallace, *History of the Lives and Reigns of the Kings of Scotland from Fergus the first King, continued to the commencement of the Union of the Two Kingdoms of Scotland and England in the year of the reign of our late Sovereign Queen Anne, Anno Domini, 1707* (Dublin, 1722), was concerned more with the failed union of 1702 at the commencement of Queen Anne's reign. As befitting a Presbyterian not entirely convinced about the merits of Union, but not wishing to be identified with Jacobitism, Wallace concluded his discourse with a note of regret that the ancient nation which had been reputedly known to the world for the past 2,037 years as 'Scotland', was now to be called 'North-Britain'. Another Presbyterian author, George Craufurd, *The Lives and Characters, of the Officers of the Crown, and of the State in Scotland, from the beginnings of the reign of King David I to the Union of the Two Kingdoms* (London, 1726), made little of the actual accomplishment of Union other than to commend the officers cited for their public service in securing a Protestant Succession through the House of Hanover.

Thus, Lockhart of Carnwath was villainous, the Scottish parliament was more prone to violent exchanges than reasoned debate, and association with Saint-Germain tainted all leaders of the opposition.[7]

Nicholas Tindal covered the same chronological span in his voluminous history of England (1744–6). This Anglican clergyman offered a more measured, but nonetheless unashamedly pro-Whig and anti-Jacobite, scrutiny of the Union, as befitting an endeavour accomplished in time for the last great rising in favour of the exiled house of Stuart. Again the Union, though characterised as one of the distinguishing glories of Queen Anne's reign, was no more than a constitutional adjustment in an English narrative. Nevertheless, Tindal's sophisticated appreciation of party interests within the Scottish parliament transcended his heavy borrowing from Burnet. Although he did not discount the politics of influence and the judicious use of money to facilitate its passage, Union was carried in Scotland in the teeth of opposition from Jacobites and some Presbyterian clergymen because those members of the Scottish gentry who had visited England frequently had come to admire the protection the House of Commons offered to civil liberties and from partial judges. The commercial opportunities for unfettered access to the American colonies guaranteed by Union and secured by the Royal Navy was also a significant inducement. But the principal factor in accomplishing Union was reputedly the unselfish behaviour of the party of nobles and gentry known as the Squadrone Volante who held the balance of power between the Court party, under Queensberry, and the Country party, under Hamilton. Union would have foundered without their timely casting in their lot with the Court.[8]

The contribution of the Anglo-Scottish novelist Tobias Smollett marked a distinctive shift from an anglocentric to Anglo-Britannic perspective; a perspective much associated with Scotsmen on the make in England, where it had considerably greater resonance in London than in the author's ancestral surrounds of Dumbarton Rock on the River Clyde. Smollet's voluminous *History of England* (1757–60), which extended from the Revolution until the close of the reign of George II, again treated the Union as a constitutional adjustment. However, he was prepared to

---

[7] John Oldmixon, *The History of England, during the reigns of King William and Queen Mary, Queen Anne, King George I* (London, 1735). Oldmixon would appear to be the first historical commentator to use the term 'British Empire' in print after the Union: *The British Empire in America, containing The History of the Discovery, Settlement, Progress and present State of all the British Colonies on the Continent and Islands of America*, 2 vols. (London, 1708).

[8] Nicholas Tindal, *The History of England, by Mr Rapin de Thoyras; continued from the Revolution to the Accession of King George II*, 10 vols. (London, 1744–6). Tindal was rector of Alverstoke in Hampshire and chaplain to the Royal Hospital at Greenwich.

acknowledge the murky workings of the politics of influence and intimidation in ensuring that the Union passed through the Scottish parliament. Fletcher of Saltoun stood out as 'a man of undoubted courage and integrity' whose republican principles' more natural home was 'in some Grecian commonwealth' rather than in the Scottish Estates. He was no less adamant that the Union was carried in the teeth of public opinion in Scotland. As he noted, its formal implementation on 1 May 1707 was marked silently in Scotland while celebrated in England. But he was no less certain that association with Saint-Germain tainted the principal leaders of the opposition and that the Scottish politicians who carried the Union acted heroically where necessary, and with prudence and resolution in equal measure. The Union was a great project which had prevented violent convulsions between both nations and was so fit for purpose that, since 1707, no difficulty in the body politic had proved insurmountable:[9] an interpretation which conveniently glossed over two major Jacobite rebellions in 1715–16 and 1745–6, and two minor ones in 1708 and 1719.

Patriotism and *belles lettres*

Whig triumphalism, which glorified the Revolution for securing Protestantism, property and progress, ran into a formidable Scottish challenge that was intellectual as well as military in the wake of Union. On the one hand, an exiled Stuart dynasty sought restoration to all three kingdoms of England, Scotland and Ireland; on the other, their military support was overwhelmingly Scottish and intent on reversing the Union in a patriotic endeavour to restore national independence. However, these tensions between British dynasticism and Scottish patriotism were part of the continuous process of redefinition of Jacobitism in Scotland. This process, which accorded precedence to Scottish patriotism, was based on the concept of *patria* that was founded on humanist teaching, specifically neo-Stoicism as received in Marischal College, Aberdeen, in the wake of the regal union of 1603, after James VI of Scotland established the Stuarts as a British dynasty. The identity of the Scottish people was expressed through the momentous attainments of scholars, soldiers and adventurers no less than monarchs, an identity that was energised by the epic heroism of the likes of William Wallace, the leader of the Scottish community of the realm during the Wars of Independence from England in the late thirteenth and early fourteenth century. Patrick Abercromby and George Mackenzie

---

[9] Tobias Smollett, *The History of England from the Revolution to the death of George the Second*, 4 vols. (London, 1758–60); and new edition, London, 1841).

articulated the concept of the *patria* in the immediate aftermath of the parliamentary union to signal that territorial nationhood should take precedence over dynastic statehood.[10] Certainly, strong monarchy was to be commended for liberating Scotland from the dominance of baronial interests, but the nation was now considered as having moved beyond the provenance of the political elite to a shared cultural, literary and territorial heritage of its people. Thus, this Scottish *patria* transcended contemporaneous discussion on how Scots should contribute to Britain and wholly rejected an Anglo-British perspective in which Scotland was absorbed into a British identity created from England.[11]

Nevertheless this shared heritage cannot be viewed as the exclusive property of Jacobitism. As evident from the subscription lists to the relevant works of both Abercromby and Mackenzie, the *patria* appealed across the political divide between Jacobites and Whigs and became embedded in a common Scottish culture, when loyalty to the territorial nation became a more pressing concern than allegiance to the exiled house of Stuart or the incoming house of Hanover. To underscore that Scottish Jacobitism did not have exclusive copyright on the *patria*, David Scott produced a historical riposte, with comparable subscribers to the works of Abercromby and Mackenzie, which rebranded the *patria* with a British identity.[12] Scott himself was a Presbyterian whose reluctant acceptance of Union was borne more out of pragmatism than principle in the wake of the failure of the first major rising in 1715–16. Nonetheless, the Scotto-British identity could lay claim to an intellectual tradition that can be traced back to the civic humanism of George Buchanan in the sixteenth century, a tradition that also advocated British Union to secure the Protestant Reformation in both Scotland and England.[13] In turn, pro-Hanoverian figures of the Scottish Enlightenment, such as Adam Ferguson, famed for his sociological approach to politics, sought to infuse British patriotism among fellow Highlanders serving in the Black Watch regiment at the outset of the last major rising in 1745. Ferguson's

---

[10] Patrick Abercromby, *The Martial Achievements of the Scottish Nation*, 2 vols. (Edinburgh, 1711–15); George Mackenzie, *The Lives and Characters of the Most Eminent Writers of the Scottish Nation*, 3 vols. (Edinburgh, 1708–22); L. Eriksonas, *National Heroes and National Identities: Scotland, Norway and Lithuania* (Brussels, 2004), pp. 87–107.

[11] Kidd, *Subverting Scotland's Past*, pp. 6–7, 98–9.

[12] David Scott, *The History of Scotland: Containing All the Historical Transactions of the Nation, from the Year of the World 3619, to the Year of Christ 1726* (Westminster, 1728).

[13] R. A. Mason, 'Imagining Scotland: Scottish Political Thought and the Problem of Britain 1560–1650' in R. A. Mason, ed., *Scots and Britons: Scottish Political Thought and the Union of 1603* (Cambridge, 1994), pp. 3–13; P. McGinnis & A. H. Williamson, 'Britain, race, and the Iberian world empire' in A. I. Macinnes & J. Ohlmeyer, eds., *The Stuart Kingdoms in the Seventeenth Century: Awkward Neighbours* (Dublin, 2002), pp. 70–93.

endeavours to align Scottish Presbyterianism with British patriotism were certainly shared overwhelmingly among the ministers and elders of the established Kirk who served as the Whig interest at prayer.[14]

The most problematic intellectual figure among the Whig interest at prayer was William Robertson, Principal of Edinburgh University and the dominant power broker in the general assembly of the Kirk of Scotland between the 1760s and the 1780s. Robertson's *History of Scotland* (1759) from the Reformation had ended effectively with the regal union in 1603 when, he argued, Scotland ceased to be a fully independent kingdom. The seventeenth century was largely a British engagement in which Scotland was rescued from absolute monarchy at the Revolution and freed from the dominance of its feudal aristocracy at the Union.[15] This has led to Robertson being viewed as the most prominent spokesman for a Scotland freed from its feudal shackles by the Union, an accomplishment which enabled the country not only to participate in the onward march of civilisation but also to establish itself as a nation of Enlightenment.[16] This Anglo-British perspective has the same degree of credibility as the notion that Robertson's *History of Scotland* set the pattern for a Scottish historical narrative of theology interspersed with homicide and aggravated by binge drinking! Robertson's elegant exposition on the expunging of feudalism from the Union is primarily an exercise in *belles lettres*, not an accurate historical observation. For as long as he was writing and publishing history,

---

[14] Mr Adam Ferguson, *Chaplain to the Regiment, A Sermon preached in the Ersh Language to his Majesty's First Highland Regiment of Foot commanded by Lord John Murray at the Containment at Camberwell on 18 December 1745* (London, 1746). Ironically, Ferguson's Gaelic sermon, delivered in his capacity as regimental chaplain, stressed the shared rights and liberties of Britons to troops confined in Camberwell barracks near London, whose patriotism was still deemed more Scottish, and hence pro-Jacobite, than British, and therefore pro-Whig.

[15] William Robertson, *History of Scotland during the Reigns of Queen Mary and of King James VI till his accession to the throne of England*, 3 vols. (London, 1812 edition), III, pp. 185–200. Gilbert Stuart, *Observations concerning the Public Law, and the Constitutional History of Scotland: with occasional remarks concerning English antiquity* (Edinburgh, 1779), was to offer a more sophisticated critique of the move from a feudal to a commercial society. The feudal powers of the nobility were being undermined judicially by a strong monarchy from the fifteenth century, and fiscally by the introduction of customs and excise as taxes on trade and consumption rather than land in the seventeenth century. However, he did concur with Robertson in viewing the Union as securing the Revolution, but the people's liberation from aristocratic oppression actually had to await separate legislation in the wake of the last Jacobite rising.

[16] N. Philipson, 'Politics, Politeness and the Anglicisation of early Eighteenth-Century Scottish Culture' in R. A. Mason, ed., *Scotland and England, 1286–1815* (Edinburgh, 1987), pp. 226–46; D. Allan, *Virtue, Learning and the Scottish Enlightenment: Ideas of Scholarship in Early Modern History* (Edinburgh, 1993), pp. 5–6, 84–5, 157; J. Rendall, *The Origins of the Scottish Enlightenment* (London, 1978), pp. 1–27.

unchecked landed power was effecting the wholesale removal and relocation of people known as the Lowland and Highland Clearances.[17]

Other caveats must be borne in mind. Robertson was undoubtedly a leading proponent of a polite culture to which Scotland was certainly opened up in the wake of Union. However, he was not arguing that civilisation commenced with Union, merely that the Union was the complement to the Revolution, which restored Scotland on the pathway to civility. In the process, Robertson did pay tribute to the towering influence of George Buchanan, as a classicist par excellence if not as a civic humanist. But he wholly glossed over the Scottish intellectual contribution in the fields of jurisprudence, architecture, mathematics, astronomy, cartography and biology which can be associated with the European movement known as the 'republic of letters', which had a British pedigree as the 'commonwealth of letters' from 1661.[18] Indeed, a civic culture of learning, endeavour and attainment, which could be Jacobite as well as Scotto-British, had considerably greater claims to have lain the foundations of Enlightenment than that of a polite culture based on fashion, taste and manners.

Moreover, caution must be exercised in accepting a Whig interpretation of modernity through the triumphalist linking of Protestantism, property and progress with the 'Glorious' Revolution – a linkage that overplays the causal relationship of political revolution to commercial revolution and severely underplays the engagement of Tories and Jacobites in commercial enterprise.[19] For the Tories and Jacobites also had an alternative approach, which valued land over trade, mercantilist regulation and monopolistic companies over free enterprise. Like the Whigs, Tories and Jacobites were engaged in co-partneries to exploit manufactures, fisheries and colonies. A further complication was the ongoing national rivalries between Scotland and England, which actually cut across political

---

[17] See T. M. Devine, "The Great Landlords of Lowland Scotland and Agrarian Change in the Eighteenth Century", and A. I. Macinnes, 'Scottish Gaeldom from Clanship to Commercial Landlordism' in S. Foster, A. I. Macinnes & R. MacInnes, eds., *Scottish Power Centres from the Early Middle Ages to the Twentieth Century* (Glasgow, 1998), pp. 147–90.

[18] G. Donaldson, *Scotland: James V – James VII* (Edinburgh, 1978), pp. 394–5; J. I. Israel, *Radical Enlightenment: Philosophy and the Making of Modernity, 1650–1750* (Oxford, 2001) pp. 3–22, 72–3, 137–8, 472; Joshua Childrey, *Britannia Baconica: Or, the Natural Rarities of England, Scotland and Wales as they are to be found in every shire* (London, 1661), preface.

[19] R. Saville, 'Scottish Modernisation Prior to the Industrial Revolution, 1688–1763' in T. M. Devine & J. R. Young, eds., *Eighteenth Century Scotland: New Perspectives* (East Linton, 1999), pp. 6–23; D. Armitage, 'The Political Economy of Britain and Ireland after the Glorious Revolution' in J. H. Ohlmeyer, ed., *Political Thought in Seventeenth-Century Ireland: Kingdom or Colony* (Cambridge, 2000), pp. 221–43.

allegiances among Whigs, Tories and Jacobites.[20] Scottish commercial endeavours post-Revolution under William of Orange in the 1690s were looked upon no more favourably by English Tories and Jacobites than by the Whigs – a situation not immediately laid to rest by the Union as the persistence of Jacobitism in Scotland was not conducive to either political or economic stability. Robertson, who had fought (and lost) against the Jacobites in 1745, was very much aware of this discordant message from North Britain which led Scottish Whigs, in the aftermath of the rising, to promote new banking and manufacturing ventures (as, later, town planning) in Scotland as British. Thus, they demonstrated their unswerving commitment to patriotism through commercial and cultural improvement.[21]

This Scotto-British perspective had three further important manifestations. Firstly, Robertson, as the ecclesiastical power broker par excellence, ensured that the general assembly of the Kirk, attended by select ministers and members of the landed and commercial elite in their capacity as elders, became an enlightened forum for the annual debate of issues of Scottish, British and imperial significance. Indeed, from the 1760s to the 1780s, the general assembly was the corporate voice of the progressive Whig influence within Scotland.[22] Secondly, as pointed out by Sir John Dalrymple, whose family had been intimately involved as advocates of Union, the Revolution in Scotland, unlike that in England, was uncompromised by any accommodation with Tories and was more purposefully anti-Jacobite. Accordingly, James VII was deposed in Scotland whereas he was deemed, as James II, to have abdicated in England. Scottish Whigs could thus claim the flame of political purity without regretting the demise of a parliament more marked for indulging in licentiousness than in upholding liberty.[23] Certainly, leading figures of the Scottish

---

[20] S. Pincus, 'From holy cause to economic interest: the study of population and the invention of the state' in A. Houston & S. Pincus, eds., *A Nation Transformed: England after the Restoration* (Cambridge, 2001), pp. 277–98.

[21] C. Whatley, *Scottish Society, 1707–1830: Beyond Jacobitism Towards Industrialisation* (Manchester, 2000), pp. 116–24; S. G. Checkland, *Scottish Banking: A History, 1695–1973* (Glasgow and London, 1975), pp. 92–7.

[22] I. D. L. Clark, 'From Protest to Reaction: The Moderate Regime in the Church of Scotland, 1752–1805' in N. T. Philipson & R. Mitchison, eds., *Scotland in the Age of Improvement* (Edinburgh, 1970), pp. 200–24; R. Sher, *Church and University in the Scottish Enlightenment: The Moderate Literati of Edinburgh* (Edinburgh, 1985), pp. 120–47.

[23] Sir John Dalrymple, *Memoirs of Great Britain and Ireland from the dissolution of the last Parliament of Charles II until the sea-battle of La Hogue*, 2 vols. (London, 1771–88). Dalrymple demonstrated the enduring vitality of Scottish patriotism when he reported the alleged words spoken on behalf of the mutineers among two Scottish regiments, whom William of Orange intended to send to Flanders in the spring of 1689: 'They were part of a free

Enlightenment adhered to a stadial view of man's social development from hunter–gatherer to a commercial state in which English institutions were classified as being manifestly in the vanguard of progress.[24] Nevertheless, Adam Ferguson, the foremost thinker on the sociology of politics, remained sceptical about the perfectibility of the English constitution and, indeed, about equating change with progress and about accepting improvement as a material benefit for all.[25] Ferguson and his fellow members of the Poker Club, formed to agitate against Scotland being excluded from the Militia Act of 1757, came to view themselves as the moral guardians of the British constitution established at the Revolution and consolidated by the Treaty of 1707, an intellectual position that required the Scots to be treated as equal partners in Union. Despite grievances about English distrust provoked by Scotland repeatedly being denied a militia in 1760, 1762, 1776 and 1782, British national identity was promoted assiduously from Scotland as patriotism and prosperity imbued by a common commitment to liberty and Protestantism.[26]

Thirdly, part of this guardianship was a reawakening interest in union all round, which harmonised with contemporaneous British critiques of mercantilism that argued forcefully for the repeal of commercial restrictions on Ireland and even on the American colonies. Such transatlantic extensions of union appeared initially no more than kite-flying by the maverick improver Sir Alexander Murray of Stanhope in 1742, who was attempting to expedite the pace of commercialism in the West Highlands through mines and canals on the estates forfeited by Jacobites. Nevertheless, the imperial dimension to union was given added force by Malachy Postelthwayt at the outset of the Seven Years' War in 1757. He argued from an Anglo-Irish perspective that the beneficence England had bestowed on Scotland since 1707 should be extended for Ireland through the concession of full union. Writing prior to the American Revolution, John

---

people, independent of the government of England and of its laws. Their national assembly had not as yet renounced allegiance to King James. By the law of nations, they were not subject to the orders of any King, but of one acknowledged in Scotland, the King of their country. Their ancestors had transmitted the independence of their kingdom safe to them. It was their duty to convey it inviolated to posterity. They had arms, the marks and honours of freemen, in their hands. And, while they had these, to submit and suffer transportation like felons was unworthy of their own character, or that of their nation' (*ibid.*, I, pp. 277–8).

[24] C. Kidd, 'North Britishness and the Nature of Eighteenth-Century British Patriotisms', *HJ*, 39 (1996), pp. 361–82.
[25] Adam Ferguson, *An Essay on the History of Civil Society 1767*, pp. 8–9, 24–5, 76–7, 166–7, 200–1, 218–19, 250–1.
[26] J. Robertson, *The Scottish Enlightenment and the Militia Issue* (Edinburgh, 1985), pp. 98–199; L. McIlvanney, *Burns the Radical: Poetry and Politics in Late Eighteenth-Century Scotland* (East Linton, 2002), pp. 14–37.

Campbell reclaimed the moral high ground for the Scottish contribution to Union. His surveys of Empire highlighted the integral contribution of Scotland in partnership with England in contrast to the restricted access and impact made by Ireland.[27] Adam Smith in his magisterial *Wealth of Nations* (1776) called, on the one hand, for either a full union with the colonies or British disengagement from America, and, on the other, for a British union with Ireland building on the Union of 1707.[28] However, his assertion that this precedent would involve not only free trade, but also the freeing of the Irish people from aristocratic oppression,[29] was a fanciful as well as an elegant exercise in *belles lettres*.

Revolution and reaction

Issues of representation and taxation, and the subsequent questioning of constitutional relationships provoked by the American Revolution, stimulated fresh thinking on the Anglo-Scottish Union. To the fore was James Macpherson. His rich embellishment of Gaelic oral tradition relating to the classical heroes of Celtic mythology had instigated the 'Ossianic controversy' and provided an exemplar for Romanticism, where fascination with the primitive and the irrational fundamentally questioned the Enlightenment as the tempering of reason with emotion. Macpherson, however, was far from romantic in his approach to Union as articulated in his *History of Great Britain* (1775), which ranged from the Restoration of the Stuart monarchy in 1660 to the Hanover Succession in 1714, and drew on original papers from the archives of both royal houses.[30] A member

---

[27] Sir Alexander Murray, *The true interest of Great Britain, Ireland and our plantations: or, A proposal for making such an union between Great Britain and Ireland, and all our plantations, as that already made betwixt Scotland and England* (London, 1740); Malachy Postelthwayt, *Britain's commercial interest explained and improved, in a series of dissertations on several important branches of her trade and police . . . Also the great advantage which would accrue to this kingdom from an union with Ireland* (London, 1757); John Campbell, *A Political Survey of Britain: Being a Series of Reflections on the Situation, Lands, Inhabitants, Revenues, Colonies and Commerce of this Island*, 2 vols. (London, 1774).

[28] Adam Smith, *An Inquiry into the Nature and Causes of the Wealth of Nations*, ed. R. H. Campbell & A. S. Skinner (Indianapolis, 1981), pp. 944–7. Smith was not averse to a whimsical Scottish exercise in logic in suggesting that the centre of the British Empire would eventually move (from London to New York) should union be concluded with the American colonies, the precedent for this stadial development being the shift of the Scottish court from Edinburgh to London in 1603 (*ibid.*, pp. 624–5).

[29] C. Kidd, 'Eighteenth Century Scotland and the Three Unions' in Smout, ed., *Anglo-Scottish Relations*, pp. 171–87.

[30] James Macpherson, *The History of Great Britain, from the Restoration to the Accession of Power of the House of Hannover* (London, 1775). Macpherson, who was also a trenchant critic of the commercial monopoly and the political autonomy of the East India Company, published his source material as *Original Papers, containing the secret history of Great Britain from the Restoration to the Accession of the House of Hannover* (London, 1776).

of a Highland clan more than tainted with Jacobitism, Macpherson was particularly concerned about the clandestine manoeuvres that had influenced the accomplishment of Union. On the one hand, he welcomed the Union for bringing an end to the fractious and scheming Scottish parliament. On the other hand, Macpherson recognised that the Revolution and the imposition of constitutional limitations on the monarchy had opened up opportunities for sophisticated parliamentary development in Scotland, opportunities that were lost in 1707. He was adamant that the Scottish commissioners charged to negotiate Union with their English counterparts from April to July 1706 had failed to secure the best deal available politically or commercially. With the restoration of the Scottish Estates out of the question, the pressing issue was how the Union could be made to work more equitably to serve the interests of Scotland within Empire.

John Knox, an enthusiastic improver, provided an innovative proposal in this direction, principally by the development of the fishing resources around the British Isles and especially in the Highlands and Islands of Scotland. Knox argued that there were strong moral and commercial grounds for the special promotion of Scottish economic development within the framework of Union. His commercial analysis, which mirrored and complemented the political analysis of William Robertson on the deleterious impact of regal union from 1603, viewed the seventeenth century as a black hole for Scotland. The Union had represented the annihilation of all prospects of separate Scottish commercial activity at home or abroad in return for the Scots subjecting themselves to higher taxes and commercial restrictions unknown before 1707. Gradual commercial recovery brought about by direct involvement in the tobacco trade with the American colonies, bounties for linen manufacture and fishing and, above all, by the spirit of improvement, industry and commerce stimulated in the generation after the Union had been seriously disrupted by the American Revolution. Yet, Scotland remained England's most reliable and reliant trading partner. Recovery was to be achieved by the creation of a Commercial Parliament or College of Commerce that would involve the landed and commercial elite and incorporate the existing annual Convention of the Royal Burghs to promote the prosperity of the kingdom and the happiness of the people.[31]

At the same time, the spread of the county movement for parliamentary reform from England to Scotland and resurgent desires for burgh

---

[31] John Knox, *A View of the British Empire, more especially Scotland; with some proposals for the improvement of that country, the extension of its fisheries, and the relief of the people* (London, 1784).

reform during the 1780s sought distinctively to make the Union work more equitably in Scottish interests, hitherto neglected or treated cursorily at Westminster. Again the Union was not to be threatened but improved by annual conventions to promote or review legislation prior to its passage through the imperial parliament. However, the main stimulus to reappraising the Union was not immediately attributable to the American Revolution so much as to the latter's impact on the constitutional relationship between Great Britain and Ireland. For Irish radicalism and constitutional instability were now perceived as a threat to England. The Anglican ascendancy that had dominated Irish affairs since the Revolution, essentially as the English interest in Ireland, was no longer content with a position of political dependency and was no longer prepared to tolerate economic discrimination which denied Ireland direct access to the American and colonial trades. Moreover, the Anglican ascendancy's assertion of political and commercial independence within the Crown's British dominions was reinforced by the military practice of volunteering, which spread across the Protestant community to the Presbyterian dissenters among whom the large Scottish presence in Ulster figured prominently.

Union all round was the response from Westminster, albeit whether this union was to be federal or incorporating remained initially an open question. At the prompting of William Cavendish-Bentinck, 3rd Duke of Portland, erstwhile lord lieutenant of Ireland and future prime minister of Great Britain, the Scot William Ogilvie promoted a scheme for Union along federal lines in 1782, which received little encouragement from Irish parliamentarians.[32] Four years later, Daniel Defoe's highly partial history of the making of the Treaty of 1707 was reissued with an introduction by the English advocate John Lewis de Lolme in which the consequences and probability of a like union between Britain and Ireland were considered.[33] The following year, de Lolme issued a commentary on *The British Empire in Europe* in which Scotland was rather despairingly recognised as a distinct nation and kingdom eventually liberated as a people by the Union. The closing of the door to French invasion, the permanent exclusion of the Stuarts and the avoidance of civil war had advantaged England. Despite higher taxes, Scotland had benefited from English trade and from perpetual peace throughout Great Britain. Defoe's reissued volume was

---

[32] J. Vance, 'Constitutional Radicalism in Scotland and Ireland in the era of the American Revolution, c.1760–1789' (Aberdeen University, Ph.D. thesis, 1998); N. T. Philipson, 'Scottish Public Opinion and the Union in the Age of Association' in Philipson & Mitchison, eds., *Scotland in the Age of Improvement*, pp. 125–47; J. Kelly, *Prelude to Union: Anglo-Irish Politics in the 1780s* (Cork, 1992), pp. 21–92.

[33] Daniel Defoe, *The history of the union between England and Scotland* (London, 1786).

prefixed with a complementary gloss on his life by the Scottish historian George Chalmers, who concurred with de Lolme that a spirit of national struggle and opposition was counter-productive to the happiness of the people. Chalmers subsequently extolled the expunging of fractious separate parliaments that compromised the political integrity of the imperial parliament at Westminster.[34]

As part of the cultural conditioning for eventual union, a manuscript history of Great Britain from 1688 to 1714 was translated from Latin and published in 1782. The author was Alexander Cunningham, diplomat and spy, who was well connected to Scottish commercial networks in the Netherlands and had served on a Scottish trading mission to France prior to the Union. Subsequently, he served as British resident in the Venetian Republic at the behest of George I between 1715 and 1720. Cunningham's account of the Treaty of Union is both remarkable and innovative. He was the first author to argue that England as well as Scotland had commercial advantages to gain from association through Union. He was also the first to cite the Dutch (though allies) as well as the French as having vested interests and, if necessary, the cash to encourage the Scots to oppose Union. As a political fixer as well as a closet adviser to the English ministry on the conduct of Scottish affairs, he viewed the Union as a Whig accomplishment, with Robert Harley, as Secretary of State, no less influential than Sidney Godolphin, 1st Earl of Godolphin, as Treasurer. He was particularly supportive of the political career of John Campbell, 2nd Duke of Argyll, who was of vital assistance to Queensberry in securing the passage of Union through the Scottish Estates and later ensured the military frustration of the Jacobite rising of 1715–16. Most importantly, Cunningham was the first to suggest that issues of principle affected the decisions of both proponents and opponents of Union in Scotland. Indeed, while he makes no attempt to disregard the impact of corruption in effecting Union, his principal concern was with the extra-parliamentary activity that appeared to threaten its accomplishment. However, his take on such activity was no less original. Queensberry was recognised for his political astuteness in his employment of agents provocateurs to pre-empt armed resistance. His use of the £20,000 sent from the English treasury was deemed so prudent that he reportedly had to lay up £12,000 as unspent![35]

---

[34] John Lewis de Lolme, *The British Empire in Europe* (London, 1787); George Chalmers, *Caledonia, or, A Historical and Topographical Account of North Britain, from the most ancient to the present times*, 8 vols. (Paisley, 1887–1902), II, pp. 865–8.

[35] Alexander Cunningham, *The History of Great Britain from the Revolution in 1688 to the Accession of George the First*, ed. T. Hollingbery, 2 vols. (London, 1787).

The representation of Scotland as an exemplar for Ireland entering an incorporating union gained a renewed sense of political urgency during the 1790s. Whereas the United States of America had posed no threat to the security of Britain in the 1780s, the same could not be said of France following the Revolution of 1789. By 1793, the series of military campaigns that became known as the Napoleonic Wars had commenced and were to endure until 1815. A separate Ireland, like a separate Scotland before 1707, was seen as the back door to invasion from France. However, it was not until moves commenced in Westminster in support of Catholic emancipation that the Anglican ascendancy was convinced that incorporating Union was a more attractive option than power sharing in Ireland. The 3rd Duke of Portland again promoted a Scottish contribution, when John Bruce, as keeper of the state papers, was commissioned to prepare a two-volume report on the Anglo-Scottish Union in order to establish favourable precedents for the political union of Britain and Ireland. His report, which was published in 1799, dealt not only with the accomplishment of Union in 1707, but also with the documentation for unsuccessful attempts at union in 1604–7, 1668–70, 1689 and 1702–3; the Cromwellian forced union of Scotland and Ireland into the English Commonwealth in the 1650s was diplomatically glossed. However, the main purpose of his recalling the successful passage of Union through the Scottish and English parliaments was to demonstrate that political incorporation had proved the source of British national strength and prosperity. The Union, in which England communicated its privileges of trade to Scotland in return for Scotland's acceptance of the Hanoverian Succession, was the perfecting of the constitutional settlements established in both countries at the Revolution. Not only was the British Empire consolidated through a happy accommodation of reciprocal interests, but the balance of power in Europe was also preserved through British political and commercial influence.[36]

Notwithstanding Bruce's positive spin on political incorporation as the source of civilisation and prosperity, the relevance of the Scottish experience to the Irish situation remained a subject of contention. Scottish pretensions to a partnership with England in the British Empire were thrown into sharp relief by the main thrust of debate inspired by considerations of motherhood – whether England's treatment of Scotland since 1707 had manifest 'the fostering hand of a natural parent, or the cold neglect of a step-mother'. Proponents of Union made much of Scottish commercial

---

[36] J. Bruce, *Report on the Events and Circumstances, which produced the Union of the Kingdoms of England and Scotland*, 2 vols. (London, 1799); Smyth, *The Making of the United Kingdom*, pp. 194–220.

advance since 1707, as measured by revenues, shipping capacity, textile manufacturing and demographic growth. Malignant Irish supporters of the French Revolution were castigated as Irish Jacobins who posed as much a threat to Union as the Scottish Jacobites during the War of the Spanish Succession.[37] However, the opponents of political incorporation were not convinced that the events surrounding the 'Scotch Union' of 1707, when the Scottish Estates were 'merged in the Vortex of English Power', were any more than a warning to Ireland. That Scotland's economic potential had been blunted rather than fulfilled by Union was a theme taken up by Ulster critics. Robert Orr, an avowed associate of the United Irishmen, the embodiment of the Irish Jacobins, sympathised 'with the injuries of Scotland'. An admirer of its commercial enterprise, and its classical and scientific learning which long predated the Union, Orr cited the unfulfilled reforming agenda of Fletcher of Saltoun to critique political incorporation as regressive.[38]

The Scottish response to the French Revolution, while less nationalist than the Irish, was arguably no less radical. The Scottish Friends of the People and their later offshoot the United Scotsmen maintained fraternal links with the United Irishmen, which made them subject to oppressive reprisals by a reactionary British state which deployed show trials, selective executions and transportation to Australia. Prominent in this British reaction was Henry Dundas (later Viscount Melville), the supreme political manager of Scotland who, with William Pitt the younger, had recreated the Tory Party as an effective party of government as a result of Whig disarray in the wake of the American Revolution. Dundas, who used British patriotism as a means to curtail civil liberties, promote state power and crush radical aspirations, was an assiduous parliamentary promoter of legislative union with Ireland from 1799. His political clients and associates were to the fore among Scots arguing this case, both at Westminster and in the country, based on the reputedly advantageous experience that Scotland had enjoyed since 1707, notwithstanding numerous breaches in the spirit if not the letter of the Treaty and vicious reprisals against Jacobites, particularly in the Highlands and Islands in the aftermath of

---

[37] J. Kelly, 'The Act of Union: Its Origin and Background' in D. Keogh & K. Whelan, eds., *Acts of Union: The Causes, Contexts and Consequences of the Act of Union* (Dublin, 2001), pp. 46–66; [Edward Cooke], *Arguments for and against an union, between Great Britain and Ireland, considered* (Dublin, 1798); Colonel Tittler, *Ireland profiting by example: or, the question, whether Scotland has gained, or lost, by an union with England, fairly discussed. In a letter, from a gentleman in Edinburgh, to his friend in Dublin* (Dublin, 1799); William Johnson, *Reasons for adopting an union, between Ireland and Great Britain* (Dublin, 1799).

[38] Sir John Jervis White Jervis, *A letter addressed to the gentlemen of England and Ireland, on the inexpediency of a federal union between the two kingdoms* (Dublin, 1798); Robert Orr, *An address to the people of Ireland, against an union* (Dublin, 1799).

the last rising in 1745–6. In this light, the eventual accomplishment of union for Ireland within two years can be seen as a reactionary British endeavour.[39]

Partnership in Empire

The French Revolution, the Irish situation and the British reaction impacted directly on Scottish retrospectives of the Union of 1707. Scottish Jacobins and other initial sympathisers with the French Revolution adopted the Jacobite canon, whereby Union was accomplished primarily by the perfidy of a usurping monarchy and by the bribery of corrupt Scottish politicians greedy for English gold.[40] Robert Burns, Scotland's iconic poet, contended that the Union had been bought and sold by a parcel of rogues in the Scottish Estates. Scottish radicals, like the reformers in shire and burgh in the 1780s, saw constitutional conventions as integral both to the improvement of Union and to the improved accountability of parliament.[41] Notwithstanding the crushing of radicalism in Scotland as in Ireland by the British reaction, Scottish commentaries on the Union throughout the 1790s tended to stress the importance of the imperial context for securing a lasting partnership. Sir John Sinclair of Ulbster, a Caithness landowner and member of parliament specialising in the scrutiny of public accounts, had stated such an expectation at the

---

[39] Henry Dundas, *Substance of the speech of the Right Hon. Henry Dundas, in the House of Commons, Thursday, February 7, 1799, on the subject of legislative union with Ireland* (London, 1799); Gilbert Elliot, Earl of Minto, *The speech of the Lord Milton, in the House of Peers, April 11, 1799, on a motion for an address to His Majesty, to communicate the resolution of the two houses of Parliament, respecting an union between Great Britain and Ireland* (London, 1799); Sylvester Douglas of Glenbervie, *Speech of the Right Honourable Sylvester Douglas: in the House of Commons on Tuesday, April 23, 1799; on seconding the motion of the Right Honourable Chancellor of the Exchequer, for the House to agree with the Lords in an address to His Majesty, relative to a Union with Ireland* (Dublin, 1799); Captain Charles Kerr, *Strictures upon the union betwixt Great Britain and Ireland . . . Particularly detailing the advantage derived to Scotland from her union with England* (Dublin, 1799). For a flavour of Jacobite repression, see A. I. Macinnes, 'The British Fiscal-Military State and the Gael: New Perspectives on the "45"' in C. Ó Baoill & N. R. McGuire, eds., *Rannsachadh na Gàidhlig 2000* (Aberdeen, 2002), pp. 257–69.

[40] See *Orain Iain Luim: Songs of John MacDonald, Bard of Keppoch*, ed. A. M. MacKenzie (Edinburgh, 1973), pp. 222–9; [William Meston], *The Poetical Works of the Ingenious and Learned William Meston: sometime Professor of Philosophy in the Marshal College of Aberdeen* (Edinburgh, 1767), pp. 225–6, and *Old Mother Grim's Tale: Decade I* (London, 1737), pp. xi–xii, 7–12; Alexander Robertson of Struan, *Poems on Various Subjects and Occasions* (Edinburgh, 1749), pp. 112–20, 188–92, 208–11, 291–5; T. Crawford, 'Political and Protest Songs in Eighteenth century Scotland, II: Songs of the Left', *Scottish Studies*, 14 (1971), pp. 105–31.

[41] Robert Burns, *The Canongate Burns*, ed. A. Noble & P. S. Hogg (Edinburgh, 2001), pp. 393–4; W. Ferguson, *Scotland: 1689 to the Present* (Edinburgh, 1978), pp. 248–65; McIlvanney, *Burns The Radical*, pp. 189–219.

outset of the French Revolution. Sinclair was adamant that Scotland more than paid its way as a partner in Empire. England, no less than Scotland, had been advantaged by Union which had not so much created as accelerated entrepreneurial activity and the general course of improvement in town and country.[42]

In his *History of Great Britain during the reign of Queen Anne* (1798), Thomas Sommerville appeared to hark back to his fellow Presbyterian cleric, William Robertson, in viewing Scotland in the seventeenth century as a country in which science and literature languished, and commerce, manufacturing and population declined. Scotland was no more than a political satellite and its much-vaunted political sovereignty 'was nothing more than an empty phantom'. The liberation of Scotland, through 'the happy effect' of the Union was not, however, from aristocratic oppression, but from 'the unkind interference and over-ruling influence of English counsels'. Darien was but the last in a long line of Scottish schemes thwarted by English ministries and parliaments. Union, however, had not only redressed such prejudicial action but also created a partnership for civil liberty, political security and commercial growth, which the Irish should seriously consider joining in order to exalt the British Empire 'to its utmost pitch of power and glory'.

Somerville was the first commentator to recognise England as a fiscal–military state prior to the Union, as personified by the political power exercised jointly by Marlborough as commander-in-chief of the armed forces and by Godolphin as lord treasurer. At the same time, he recognised that the failed negotiations between the English and Scottish commissioners in 1702–3 laid the basis for the successful negotiations between the commissioners for both kingdoms in 1706. This observation was based partly on the continuity of personnel between both negotiations, but primarily on his access to the then unpublished papers of the Scottish parliament and of Sir John Clerk of Penicuik, one of the Scottish commissioners in 1706 and a member of the burgess estate (representing Whithorn).[43] Sommerville attributed the achievement of

---

[42] Sir John Sinclair, *The History of the Public Revenue of the British Empire* (London, 1790), pp. 332–59. Sinclair was the instigator and promoter of the *Statistical Accounts*, a qualitative and quantitative survey of all measurable aspects of environment, history and culture in every parish in every county of Scotland, which composed an impressive practical exercise in Enlightenment during the 1790s.

[43] The acts, overtures and minutes of the Scottish parliament were eventually published in the course of the nineteenth century as *Acts of the Parliament of Scotland*, ed. T. Thomson & C. Innes, 12 vols. (Edinburgh, 1814–72). Sir John Clerk of Penicuik's extensive papers relevant to the making of Union have been published in part by the Scottish History Society in its first series as *Memoirs of the life of Sir John Clerk of Penicuik,*

Union to six factors favourable to the Whig interest: The lack of cohesion among the opponents of Union in Scotland; the disappointment of hopes for a domestic insurrection backed by French forces severely weakened by Marlborough's victory at Ramillies in 1706, which complemented that at Blenheim two years earlier; the uncommonly rainy and tempestuous season which made roads impassable and inhibited public demonstrations against and assaults on the Scottish parliament; the ineffectiveness of the English Tories in preventing Whig ministers offering highly favourable terms for political incorporation which were secured by Queensberry's adroit and assiduous, if highly partial, management of the Scottish Estates; the prudence and moderation of the Kirk's Presbyterian ministers bridled popular violence and facilitated the progress of the Treaty; finally, the force of argument reinforced by sagacious and disinterested patriotism ensured the passage of Union through both parliaments.[44]

Somerville's fellow Presbyterian minister, Ebenezer Marshal, laid claim to writing the first designated *History of the union of Scotland and England* in 1799. Marshal associated himself with the Scottish advocates of parliamentary reform through the elimination of corruption and the curtailment of ministerial influence who were regrouping around the Whig opponents of Henry Dundas. Marshal duly reasserted the Whig belief that the Union was a progressive constitutional accomplishment that rescued Scotland from the irregular and factious government of over-mighty nobles and 'the shock of party'. Simultaneously, the Union improved the commerce and wealth of Scotland. The Union was also providential for the preservation of the religion and liberty of the British Isles then under threat from Jacobitism. As befitting his denominational commitment,

---

baronet, baron of the Exchequer. Extracted by himself from his own journals, 1676–1755, ed. J. M. Gray (Edinburgh, 1892), and again in the fifth series as Sir John Clerk of Penicuik, *History of the Union of Scotland and England*, ed. D. Duncan (Edinburgh, 1993).

[44] Thomas Somerville, *The History of Great Britain during the reign of Queen Anne* (London, 1798). Without launching an *ad hominem* attack, Sommerville, minister in the border town of Jedburgh, drew on his expertise in archival resources to rebut the conspiracy claims forwarded by Charles Hamilton, *Transactions during the reign of Queen Anne: from the union to the death of the princess* (Edinburgh, 1790). Hamilton, as the grandson of the 4th Duke of Hamilton, claimed that both parliamentary and extra-parliamentary opposition to the Union was effectively neutralised when his ancestor received a directive from Saint-Germain to let the Treaty pass in order to secure peace for France on terms communicated to the Jacobite court in exile by Marlborough and Godolphin, who duly reneged on their promise once the Union was secured. The key correspondence, however, could not be produced, other than a claim that the 4th Duke had burned the critical letter from Saint-Germain in the spring of 1707. More pertinently, Hamilton's inept leadership of the opposition pre-dated the letter by more than twelve months.

he vigorously defended the conduct of the Presbyterian clergy who had avoided anti-Union rhetoric and deployed the ecclesiastical courts as the natural guardians of the privileges of the Kirk. He drew heavily on Burnet and, like Cunningham, played up the Union as a Whig achievement. But, Marshal did not neglect the characterisation and corruption castigated by Lockhart. His focus, like that of Defoe, was clearly on the process and passage of Union through the Scottish and English parliaments. However, he also affirmed the Scottish expectation of being treated as an enduring partner in Empire, having maturely and decisively voted in favour of Union: 'a great work' achieved through the courageous, firm and intrepid direction of Queensberry and the steady, extensive and vigorous support from the previously maligned Scottish nobility.[45]

The Whig belief in progress through Union was tied more closely to a reform agenda achieved through parliamentary legislation. Religious impediments to full citizenship were removed through the repeal of the Test and Corporation Acts (1828) and the passing of the Catholic Emancipation Act (1829). The franchise for parliament and municipal corporations was expanded, to ensure a wider representation for and accountability to the propertied interests from commerce and industry as well as land, by the First or Great Reform Acts (1832) and the Burgh Reform Acts (1833). Before this legislative programme commenced, Daniel Macintosh published a *History of Scotland* from the Roman invasions until the last Jacobite rising in 1745–6, which made much of the Union continuing the work of the Revolution in liberating the Scottish people from the neglect of an absentee monarchy and from the oppressive power of the nobility. Their commerce had been extended, their manners refined and their quality of life improved by their dignified adoption of a more liberal constitution. At the same time he regarded the opponents of Union as acting from principles of pure patriotism and claimed that extra-parliamentary opposition was more widespread than localised. In addition to the covert money specified by Lockhart, he also claimed that the

---

[45] Ebenezer Marshal, *The history of the union of Scotland and England: Stating the circumstances which brought it to a conclusion, and the advantages resulting from it to the Scots* (Edinburgh, 1799). Marshal was minister of Cockpen parish in Mid-Lothian. Interest in the role of the Kirk in the making of Union had undoubtedly been stimulated by the publication of *State Papers and Letters addressed to William Carstares, Secretary to King William, relating to public affairs in Great Britain, but more particularly in Scotland, during the reign of K[ing] William and Q[ueen] Anne*, ed. J. McCormick (Edinburgh, 1774). As well as being a political fixer of Scottish ministries, Carstares anticipated William Robertson in being both Principal of Edinburgh University and manager of the general assemblies of the Kirk. An academic meddler par excellence, Carstares was a strong supporter of Union and used his considerable influence in the Kirk to curtail opposition to political incorporation.

English ministry had secured the passage of Union through the Scottish Estates by their overt concession of Equivalents – the sums granted as reparations for Darien, for liquidating public debts, for equalising the customs and excise, for standardising the coinage and for promoting the woollen industry.[46]

In a more focused *History of Scotland* (1827–8) from 1707 to the aftermath of the rising of 1745–6, John Struthers claimed that the management of the Union through the Scottish Estates was carried by money and influence rather than by the force of reason and truth. Statesmanship was the preserve of the English ministry who demonstrated consummate wisdom and great liberality. Scottish politicians favoured Union as much for their own interests as for Revolution principles. The opponents of Union, with the exception of the Jacobites, were viewed as strenuous advocates of liberty and independence, albeit Hamilton was compromised by his endeavours to secure funding from Saint-Germain. Much was made of the apocalyptical eloquence of John Hamilton, Lord Belhaven, who had argued forcibly in the opening debates on the Treaty that 'None can destroy Scotland, save Scotland's self.' Reiterating an aspect first raised by Macpherson fifty years earlier, Struthers was far from convinced that the Scots had obtained the best available deal, having too easily given up prospects for a federal union and being too compromising in agreeing to the continuing Anglican establishment in the Church of England. Notwithstanding its accomplishment 'in direct opposition to the great body of the Scottish people', Struthers considered the Union a great work, almost unrivalled among constitutional treaties, for the many permanent and universal blessings it had bestowed on Britain and Empire. Political changes of such magnitude that carried no more than local or transient evils were well worth bearing.[47]

Concerned with the revolutionary potential of class alienation through industrialisation and urbanisation, Scotland's pre-eminent novelist Sir

---

[46] Daniel Macintosh, *The History of Scotland from the invasion of the Romans till the Union with England, with a supplementary narrative of the rebellions in 1715 and 1745* (London, 1822). Accordingly, Macintosh raised the inducements on offer from £20,000 to about £500,000 – an overestimate of £67,000. Macintosh was undoubtedly influenced by the republication of a more comprehensive and attributable edition of Lockhart of Carnwath's memoirs and political correspondence as *The Lockhart Papers: Memoirs and Correspondence upon the Affairs of Scotland from 1702 to 1715*, ed. A. Aufrere, 2 vols. (London, 1817), which had underscored the seemingly inherent corruption within British government. The memoirs and relevant correspondence have been updated as *'Scotland's Ruine': Lockhart of Carnwath's Memoirs of the Union*, ed. D. Szechi (Aberdeen, 1995).

[47] John Struthers, *The History of Scotland from the Union to the abolition of the heritable jurisdictions*, 2 vols. (Glasgow, 1827–8). Struthers was a Presbyterian of evangelical persuasion having written off the Church of England as a 'system of avaricious superstition' (*ibid.*, pp. xlv–xlvi).

Walter Scott, a Presbyterian converted to Episcopalianism and a Jacobite by inclination if not by intellect, reworked the Tory position on the Union of 1707. Scott has been castigated, indeed caricatured, as a leading fabricator of spurious 'Highlandism' or kitsch 'Caledonianism', primarily because of his stage management of the royal visit of George IV to Scotland in 1822 as a tartan extravaganza – an event that was indeed a sad testimony to the lack of a Scottish fashion police. Scott, however, was not simply the prototype of a Hollywood director romanticising Scotland and its history. His historical purpose, as both a commentator and a novelist, was to restore an appreciation of the enduring validity of Scotland's essentially rural community values. In the process, he wished to rehabilitate the Highland clans that had been the military bedrock of Jacobitism but had become the most reliable light infantry in the service of the British Empire on a global scale, from the Seven Years' War (1756–63) through the American Revolutionary Wars (1776–83) to the Napoleonic Wars (1793–1815). Scott must also be exonerated from the anesthetising of the heroic tradition of William Wallace in which Scotland's liberator from the Wars of Independence was transformed into a figure who had prepared Scotland to enter the Union as a free and equal nation in partnership with England. This position is particularly associated with the monumentality and other visual imagery of 'unionist-nationalism', an oxymoron that offers an insular and introspective insight on an urban version of civic patriotism devoid of its imperial context.[48]

Scott, as is evident from his *Tales of a Grandfather* (1828), was offering a version of Scottish history from the Wars of Independence to the last Jacobite rising that was rooted in the civic humanism and belief in the *patria* associated particularly with a Scotto-British perspective on the Union. His scholarship was sound and distinctive. His informed coverage of the passage of Union through the Scottish and English parliaments was balanced and perceptive. With the exception of the contribution made by Godolphin, the foremost politician in the confidence of Queen Anne, he did not recognise the Union as an accomplishment of statesmanship. Instead he demonstrates that the Union mixed political sophistication in terms of procedural manoeuvres with undue influence and outright corruption to secure a favourable vote in the Scottish Estates. Notwithstanding bribery on the one hand and extra-parliamentary protest on the other, he welcomed the Union as validating Scotland as a partner in Empire.[49]

---

[48] T. M. Devine, *The Scottish Nation, 1700–2000* (London, 1999), pp. 241–5, 292–5; G. Morton, *Unionist-Nationalism: Governing Urban Scotland, 1830–1860* (East Linton, 1999), pp. 155–88; Kidd, *Subverting Scotland's Past*, pp. 263–7.

[49] Sir Walter Scott, *Tales of a Grandfather; being stories taken from Scottish History* (Edinburgh, 1828), and new edition, *The Tales of a Grandfather: being the History of Scotland from the earliest period to the close of the rebellion 1745–46* (London, 1898). Scott was intimately

The historiography 35

On no account, however, did the Union justify the provincial relegation of Scotland or the subordination of Scottish political, commercial and ecclesiastical interests to those of England. Scott had taken up the cudgels on behalf of the maintenance of separate Scottish banknotes in his *Letters of Malachi Malagrowther* (1826), his successful campaign being a practical application of the Scotto-British perspective, not the production of the first manifesto of modern Scottish nationalism that would lead to a sundering of Union.[50] His reworked Scotto-British standpoint was also the inspiration of the short-lived National Association for the Vindication of Scottish Rights, which campaigned not for separation but for recognition of equal partnership in Union and Empire during the 1850s. Industrialised Glasgow was now the second city of Empire, and Edinburgh was second only to London in the provision of financial services.[51] More enduringly, Sir Walter's reworked Scotto-British perspective remained the basis for the popular understanding of the Treaty of Union well into the twentieth century, while Anglo-British and academic commentators remained thirled to a progressive Whig interpretation in their specialist books and journal articles.

Whiggery reasserted

Thomas Babington Macaulay, whose Presbyterian grandfather, the Reverend Zachary Macaulay, was thrown out of the isle of Lewis for his Hanoverian sympathies in the Jacobite rising of 1745–6, articulated the classical Whig position on the glorious securing of Protestantism, property and progress by the Revolution Settlements. However, despite a stated intent to write the history of England from the accession of James II through the Union of 1707 and on, certainly, to the loss of the American colonies by 1783, and possibly to the union with Ireland in 1801, his voluminous *History of England* (1849–61) stopped with the death of William of Orange. His celebration of Union, and of an Empire that was far mightier and wealthier than the Spanish colonies to the west and more splendid

---

involved in a further aspect of civic patriotism, the publication of original material relating to Scottish history through a plethora of antiquarian and historical clubs – endeavours that resulted in further material on the Union being brought into the public domain, notably by the Bannatyne Club: Sir David Hume of Crossrigg, *A Diary of the Proceedings in the Parliament and Privy Council of Scotland, May 21 MDCC – March 7, MDCCVII*, ed. J. Hope (Edinburgh, 1828); *Correspondence of George Baillie of Jerviswood, MDCCII–MDCVIII*, ed. G. Elliot, Earl of Minto (Edinburgh, 1842); *The Darien Papers: being a selection of original letters and official documents relating to the establishment of a colony at Darien by the Company of Scotland trading to Africa and the Indies, 1695–1700*, ed. J. H. Burton (Edinburgh, 1849).

[50] Sir Walter Scott, *The Letters of Malachi Malagrowther*, ed. P. H. Scott (Edinburgh, 1981).
[51] National Association for the Vindication of Scottish Rights, *Address to the People of Scotland, and statement of grievances* (Edinburgh, 1853).

and durable than the classical conquests of Alexander the Great to the east, was left on the drawing board as he concentrated on the foundations of English global greatness between 1685 and 1702.[52]

With Macaulay's exposition on Union going by default, the reassertion of the Whig position was left to J. Hill Burton, who, in his *History of Scotland* (1853) from the Revolution to the last Jacobite rising, shifted the focus onto domestic politics, particularly onto the issues and party allegiances affecting the passage of the Treaty through the Scottish Estates from 1702 to 1707. Burton revived Marshal's interest in the irenicist conduct and institutional stance of the Kirk on Union, which he viewed as a necessity from the failure of the Darien venture. He also gave some pioneering, but by no means systematic, consideration to the polemical controversies integral to the process of Union in both Scotland and England, which he dismissed as a torrent of pamphlets. Although the accomplishment of Union was set within the context of the War of the Spanish Succession, the role of the English parliament was treated cursorily other than with respect to legislative disputes with the Scottish Estates. The English ministry as directed by Godolphin, who was deemed not averse from clandestinely using public money to attain his political objectives, were exonerated from all inferences of corruption or intimidation. The Union was manifestly a great work of statesmanship by politicians infused by practical sense and business habits, in Scotland no less than in England. Opponents of Union, when not dismissed as Jacobites, were damned with faint praise as a body of patriots who wished to sustain national independence. Union, however, demonstrated the fitness of both England and Scotland to combine in one British Empire.[53]

Macaulay's abandoned intent to deal integrally with Union and Empire not only contributed to the devolution of Scottish from British history, but also led to the fracturing of domestic and imperial history. The history of the reign of Queen Anne by Philip Stanhope, Earl of Stanhope, focused mainly on the War of the Spanish Succession as fought within Europe, devoid of its American theatre. His perspective on Union is memorable only for his observation that Glasgow was raised from 'a petty huckster town on the Clyde into a mart of manufacture'. Frederick Wyon

---

[52] T. B. Macaulay, Lord Macaulay, *The History of England from the Accession of James II*, 6 vols. (London, 1849–61).

[53] J. H. Burton, *History of Scotland, from the revolution to the extinction of the last Jacobite rebellion (1689–1746)*, 2 vols. (London, 1853). An alternative contemporary offering by Thomas Wright, *The History of Scotland from the earliest period to the present time*, 3 vols. (London, 1852–5), sought in its treatment of the Union in the third volume to provide an accurate narrative rather than a systematic analysis. Despite a frontpiece to Sir Walter Scott, Wright relied principally on Daniel Defoe.

endorsed Stanhope's one-dimensional view that English generosity at the Union liberated Scotland from the turbulence of party fuelled by polemicists, mainly of a Jacobite hue. But Wyon introduced an ethnic dimension with his claim that 'closer contact with a race of superior civilization' had undoubtedly imbued the Celtic areas of Scotland with wider theories of duty, order and government than they had hitherto possessed.[54] Clearly Wyon was influenced by contemporary literary criticism which held that the institutional and organisational supremacy of the Anglo-Saxons in politics and business made the assimilation of 'separate provincial nationalities' a necessity for modern civilisation.[55] This influence is also detectable in J. R. Seeley's work on *The Expansion of England* (1891), which became the trendsetter for imperial history. The Union of 1707 was deemed incidental to the shaping of Empire through the export of the glorious constitutional legacy of the English Revolution. Great Britain, both in terms of internal union and of Empire, was the extension of the English state.[56] Among his Whiggish fellow travellers in the celebration of Empire, little or no regard was paid to the Union as a precedent for state formation and constitutional modelling, even though dominions in Canada, Australia and South Africa were based on the federative (federal and confederal) principles that featured prominently in the polemical and parliamentary debates between 1702 and 1707.[57]

At a time of calls for Home Rule all round for Ireland, Scotland and Wales, two Scottish historians made important qualifications to the Whig position without ever challenging the orthodoxy of Protestantism, property and progress. In, *The Union of England and Scotland* (1896), James Mackinnon insisted that the Treaty of 1707 must be set within its international context. A sympathiser with Home Rule and of a new federal relationship with the imperial parliament within the British Isles, Mackinnon was particularly concerned to explore the interaction of polemics and politics and the extent to which federative alternatives to incorporation were compatible with the interests of Scotland. At the same time, he was favourably influenced by the writings of Defoe and ultimately deemed the opponents of Union as short-sighted. He vindicated its promoters from all charges of corruption, if not from moral laxity. The Union had

---

[54] P. H. Stanhope, Earl of Stanhope, *History of England, comprising the reign of Queen Anne until the peace of Utrecht, 1701–1713* (London, 1871); F. W. Wyon, *The History of Great Britain during the reign of Queen Anne* (London, 1876).

[55] See Matthew Arnold, *The Study of Celtic Literature* (London, 1867), pp. 1–23, 72–5, 94–111, 152–9, 174–81.

[56] Sir J. R. Seeley, *The Expansion of England: Two Courses of Lectures* (London, 1891).

[57] H. E. Eggerton, *Federations and Unions within the British Empire* (Oxford, 1911); E. G. Hawke, *The British Empire and its History* (London, 1911).

not guaranteed the general advance of Scotland. But Union in association with Empire, enterprise and invention were the keys to commercial reform, agricultural improvement and industrialisation in both England and Scotland. Notwithstanding his British engagement, Mackinnon set a trend for subsequent writing on the Treaty of 1707, which has looked at the relationships of Scottish politicians among themselves and with the English ministry but has largely ignored what English politicians thought, or debated and corresponded with each other on, regarding Union and Empire.[58] William Mathieson expanded the role of the Kirk as brought to prominence by Burton. The making of Union was treated as a further extension of the Kirk–State controversy that had dominated Scottish history from the Reformation in 1560 to the Revolution Settlement of 1689–90. However, Mathieson gave more concentrated focus than Mackinnon to the polemical debates between 1702 and 1707. His instructive analysis ranged from issues of sovereignty and state formation, through confessionalism and religious establishments, to the formative role of political economy in shaping modernity. But Mathieson made little or no attempt to demonstrate how pamphleteering shaped political debates, a deficiency that has become an accepted tenet of Union historiography.[59]

While making no attempt to challenge the Whig canon that the Union of 1707 was an economic necessity for Scotland and a political necessity for England, Theodora Keith constructively explored Scotland's engagement with the Americas, in terms of mercantile enterprise as well as colonial settlement. Indeed, her work on the *Commercial Relations of England and Scotland, 1603–1707* (1910), though over-reliant on official records and in assessing trade from customs and fiscal dues, did suggest that both kingdoms had economic grounds for seeking union that ranged beyond conflict resolution in the wake of the Darien fiasco. She was little concerned with the debate on issues of political economy, however, preferring to concentrate on the resolution of commercial differences and future arrangements for fiscal regulation after 1707, which she found to be impartial and fair.[60]

---

[58] J. Mackinnon, *The Union of England and Scotland: a study of international history* (London, 1896).
[59] W. L. Mathieson, *Scotland and the Union: a history of Scotland from 1695 to 1747* (Glasgow, 1905).
[60] T. Keith, *Commercial Relations of England and Scotland, 1603–1707* (Cambridge, 1910), and 'The Economic Case for the Scottish Union', *EHR*, 21 (1909), pp. 44–66. The case for commercial necessity no less than political realism was also taken up by W. R. Scott, *The Constitution and Finance of English, Scottish and Irish Joint-Stock Companies to 1720*, 3 vols. (Cambridge, 1911–12), based on his examination of the performance of joint-stock companies or commercial co-partneries whose activities ranged from manufacturing and fisheries to banking and colonial endeavours. The possibility that colonial enterprise gave

By the outbreak of the First World War, P. Hume Brown had reshaped the Whig domestic canon in terms of political realism in a notably scholarly and research-led direction. *The Legislative Union of England and Scotland* offered an unusually nuanced appreciation of party loyalties and divisions in the Scottish Estates as he shifted the historiographic debate towards the detailed consideration of the legislative war between the English and Scottish parliaments. In response to the English Act of Settlement in 1701, which unilaterally laid down a Hanoverian Succession, the Scottish Estates passed retaliatory measures in 1703, most notably the Act of Security which stated that Scotland would not accept the same succession as England unless her parliament, Kirk and commerce were guaranteed to be free from interference by the English ministry. This measure, which was denied royal assent until 1704, was supplemented by the Act anent Peace and War which stated that the Scottish parliament, on the death of Queen Anne, had the exclusive right to decide the terms on which Scotland would be committed to or withdrawn from foreign conflict. However, this conditional assertion of independence was trumped by the English parliament passing the Alien Act in 1705, which offered the Scots the stark choice of treating for an incorporating union or being designated as aliens subject to commercial restrictions over access to markets in England and the colonies. The actual passage of the Union through the Scottish Estates was not a major part of Brown's narrative. Little consideration was given to issues of political management other than to dismiss charges of pensions and offices being awarded as inducements to secure Union, lauded as a sincere accomplishment by political realists. In like manner, because the Union was deemed more acceptable to England than to Scotland, Brown treated its ratification through the Lords and Commons as a formal rather than a contested measure. Union was necessary and desirable to secure Scotland's due share of prosperity and to ensure its development as a modern nation. At the same time, England united with Scotland laid a secure basis for imperial expansion, though the global range of such expansion was not deemed an appropriate concern for Scottish history.[61]

England a vested interest in securing Scotland as an incorporated partner was first raised by the Revd Alexander MacRae in what was essentially a Whig reader for introducing modern Scottish history to schools: *Scotland from the Treaty of Union with England to the present time (1707–1907)* (London, 1908). His work was essentially supplementary to that of Andrew Lang, *History of Scotland from the Roman Occupation*, 4 vols. (New York, 1907), whose last volume, from the Revolution to the last Jacobite rising, was more than tinged with Jacobite romanticism.

[61] P. H. Brown, *The Legislative Union of England and Scotland: The Ford Lectures Delivered in Hilary Term, 1914* (Oxford, 1914).

Didactic inferences drawn principally from Brown's researches were the basis of the *Thoughts on the Union between England and Scotland* (1920) by Albert Dicey and Robert Rait, which brought together the perspectives of a constitutional lawyer and a parliamentary historian. Although they were not concerned to pass judgement on the calibre or personal motivation of Scottish politicians, they were adamant that the Union was the accomplishment of statesmanship, Protestantism and the pressing Scottish necessity for material prosperity. Their work had three distinctive themes. Firstly, the Scottish parliament since the Revolution had proved an effective check on ministerial government and had developed a procedural sophistication that was further honed in the legislative sparring with the English parliament prior to Union. However, this development was viewed as a recent novelty – largely by disregarding the constitutional attainments of the Covenanting Movements in the 1640s (to which Burnet had drawn attention in his account of the Union in 1734). Nevertheless, the Scottish parliament shared credit with the Kirk in facilitating the passage of Union that absorbed Scotland into a fully sovereign parliamentary system now transposed from England to Britain. Secondly, after scrutinising the negotiations between the commissioners for England and Scotland from April to July 1706, the Union was deemed a contractual and consensual act – that is, a real treaty beneficial to both parties that also carried continuing obligations on both sides. Scotland, firmly wedded to Union and Empire, remained a distinctive entity – albeit as a stateless nation – through its Kirk, its law and its local government. Thirdly, the joint authors were determined to overcome ignorance and forgetfulness about the enduring importance of Union, particularly on the part of Englishmen who had taken the political and moral unity of Great Britain for granted.[62]

One Englishman who certainly took up this challenge to review the Union as a progressive and enduring development was George Macaulay Trevelyan, perhaps the doyen of Whig historians in the twentieth century. In an innovative radio programme for the British Broadcasting Corporation in 1929, Trevelyan pronounced the Union to be a work of consequence, compromise and consensus that was a worthy model for the League of Nations set up in the aftermath of the First World War. Formed in the spirit of equity and justice, the Union respected differences, especially in religion, between Scotland and England and had also averted the real danger of war, occasioned by Scottish provocation as much as English

---

[62] A. C. Dicey & R. S. Rait, *Thoughts on the Union between England and Scotland* (London, 1920).

intimidation. Fletcher of Saltoun was commended for his endeavours to retain a Scottish parliament with a potential for, rather than a proven record of, constitutional development. More celebrated, however, were the Presbyterians for their determination to retain their separate national Kirk rather than a separate national parliament. The principal protagonists for Union in both Scotland and England were not remarkably high-minded or idealistic politicians; rather they were courageous yet wary statesmen who acted on the basis of sound information and political calculation in furthering the glorious attainments of the Revolution. Above all, the Union had made possible the British Empire, 'one of the greatest and happiest feats in our island history' and this encomium would remain even if the Treaty of 1707 were further modified by a measure of Home Rule in the course of the twentieth century.[63]

Following the conclusion of the Second World War, George S. Pryde, a sceptic about any measure of devolution for Scotland, produced the final reworking of the classic Whig interpretation of Union from a Scottish historical perspective. Pryde placed as much emphasis on explaining the text as in exploring the context of the Treaty of 1707. He shared Brown's concern for a nuanced interpretation of party affiliations and the signal importance of the legislative war of 1701–5. He also endorsed the focus of Dicey and Rait on the relative novelty of Scottish parliamentary development and on the making of Union through a definite tender of contract as negotiated by the commissioners of both kingdoms in 1706. He also concurred with Trevelyan that the Scottish path to true prosperity commenced with the Union and full participation in the British Empire. Notably influenced by pro-Unionist commentaries on the passage of the Treaty through the Scottish Estates, Pryde commended the Court and Squadrone for the tact and success with which they set aside Scotland's illusory independence. They had realised that the choice was not between a federative or an incorporating union, but whether Scotland would continue to be subject to an English ministry, yet denied access to colonial trade, or accept subjection to an English parliament as the price of that access. The Scottish nobility, the political estate most pronouncedly in

---

[63] G. M. Trevelyan, *The Parliamentary Union of England and Scotland 1707* (London, 1929). This broadcast essentially anticipated his more developed historical narrative 'Ramillies and the Union with Scotland', the second of the three volumes in his *England under Queen Anne* (London, 1930–2). G. N. Clark, *The Later Stuarts, 1660–1714* (Oxford, 1934), was no less eulogistic about the negotiations accomplished by the commissioners for England and Scotland – who included on both sides men of the highest legal and political ability – which ensured that the Union as an accomplished fact was a very great feat of constructive statesmanship, even if members of the Scottish Estates were partial to occasional inducements to stiffen their sense of purpose.

favour of Union, were commended for their courage, intelligence and ability in resisting public opinion and extra-parliamentary opposition to the Treaty. In the process, he explained the £20,000 advanced from the English Treasury not as bribery but as a legitimate subvention to meet arrears of pensions and salaries for officials and other leading Scottish politicians.[64]

Whiggery fragmented?

By the 1960s, as British identification with Empire and enterprise gave way to that with the National Health and welfare services, a Whig historiography that placed greater emphasis on narrative rather than theory had seemingly fragmented under pressure from the social sciences, as well as from alternative radical, revisionist, ideological and methodological approaches. As early as 1955, A. M. Carstairs, echoing Mathieson fifty years earlier, had called for greater attention to be given to issues of political economy, in relation to both the polemical debates and the eventual passage of Union.[65] This call was taken up systematically by Christopher Smout, *Scottish Trade on the Eve of Union, 1660–1707* (1963), which clearly demonstrated that Scottish commerce, after a period of relative expansion in the Restoration era, had come under increasing pressure from the muscular mercantilism of the major European powers who implemented protectionist policies to balance trade, attract and retain money – whether as bullion or specie – and promote navigation and manufactures. A growing commercial dependence on England from the Revolution was compounded by four disasters – the disruption to trade occasioned by wars with France from 1688 to 1697 and from 1701 through the Union; the famine of 1695 to 1699; the loss of markets through tariff restrictions, including reaffirmed Navigation Laws that curtailed trade with England and the colonies; and, the failure of the Darien scheme to establish a Scottish colony on the Panama Isthmus by 1700. Based primarily on evidence drawn from customs records and bullion supplies, supplemented by the correspondence of Scottish merchants operating in the Netherlands as well as England and Scotland, Smout contended that the whole period from the Revolution to the Union was characterised by 'economic stagnation punctuated by crisis and decline'. An incorporating union offered the only clear prospect for Scottish recovery – albeit

---

[64] *The Treaty of Union of Scotland and England 1707*, ed. G. S. Pryde (London, 1950).
[65] A. M. Carstairs, 'Some Economic Aspects of the Union of Parliaments', *Scottish Journal of Political Economy*, 2 (1955), pp. 64–72.

the prospect that English motivation for Union was economic as well as political largely went without saying.[66]

Roy Campbell consolidated Smout's arguments for the economic motive in a Unionist direction, assuredly and deliberatively.[67] Rosalind Mitchison enthusiastically, if not evangelically, viewed the Union as marking the advent of social and cultural civility in Scotland. In particular, she made the telling point that reliance on political correspondence seriously underplays issues of political economy.[68] However, the radical reappraisal by economic and social historians can also be viewed as underscoring as much as qualifying the Whig view that Union was an inevitable as well as a progressive development in Scotland. Indeed, while he endorsed a Unionist view of Scotland's exposure to a civilising culture from 1707, David Daiches was nevertheless concerned to provide depth and perspectives to contemporary arguments for devolution stimulated by the rise of Scottish nationalism. Through sample illustrations, Daiches explored the full range of issues in the parliamentary as well as the polemical debates as Union dominated the agenda in the Scottish Estates between 1702 and 1707. He was particularly respectful of the intellectual vision, the civic engagement and the polemical advocacy of a federation offered by Andrew Fletcher of Saltoun.[69]

William Ferguson adopted a more trenchant, acerbic and uncompromising standpoint. His forensic work of revisionism, *Scotland's Relations with England: A Survey to 1707* (1977), lambasted all who did not accord primacy to politics in the making of Union. The key feature of his attack upon Smout and those of a Unionist persuasion is that economic determinism does not explain why Union was rejected by the Scottish Estates in 1702 but accepted in 1707. The Union was unequivocally an accomplishment of political jobbery, a result of management and influence exercised on behalf of the Court by the Duke of Queensberry; the shifting stance

---

[66] T. C. Smout, *Scottish Trade on the Eve of Union, 1660–1707* (Edinburgh and London, 1963). Smout's arguments for economic motivation were also furthered in 'The Anglo-Scottish Union of 1707. I: The Economic Background', *Economic History Review*, new series 16 (1964), pp. 498–527, and 'The Road to Union' in G. Holmes, ed., *Britain After the Glorious Revolution* (London, 1969), pp. 455–67.

[67] R. H. Campbell, 'The Anglo-Scottish Union of 1707. II: The Economic Consequences', *Economic History Review*, new series 16 (1964), pp. 468–77, and *Scotland Since 1707: The Rise of an Industrial Society* (Oxford, 1965), pp. 38–42, 54–63.

[68] R. Mitchison, *Lordship to Patronage: Scotland, 1603–1746* (London, 1983), pp. 93–160, and *A History of Scotland* (London, 1977), pp. 291–317. For Mitchison, a fatuous Darien scheme, the famine of the late 1690s and the trade depression of 1704 demonstrated that Scottish independence could not be sustained politically or economically.

[69] D. Daiches, *Scotland and the Union* (London, 1977); *Andrew Fletcher of Saltoun: Selected Political Writings and Speeches*, ed. D. Daiches (Cambridge, 1979).

of the Squadrone Volante; interference and intimidation on the part of the English ministry; the selective payments of arrears of pensions and salaries to secure affirmative voting; and the Duke of Hamilton's weak leadership of the loosely confederated opposition. Other than on issues of sovereignty, the polemical debate was of little relevance. Where principle was to be found, it was only among the parliamentary opponents of Union, and even there among the distinctive minority grouping of constitutional reformers, the reputedly anti-aristocratic followers of Fletcher of Saltoun.[70]

Although Ferguson gave little regard to the 'easy passage' of Union through the English parliament, his revisionist approach was reinforced by P. W. J. Riley who viewed British politics since the Revolution primarily in terms of how governments operated and ministries were formed. Such an emphasis on the politics of patronage and influence gives undue prominence to such political brokers as the meddling academic William Carstares, Principal of Edinburgh University – who was seemingly stitched into the fabric of William of Orange's court – or James Ogilvie, 1st Earl of Seafield, whose corruption was the watchword for his actions as for the pursuit of place and profit by aristocratic factions. In recognising that the Union was an important episode in English politics, Riley essentially projected Sir Lewis Namier's approach to politics in the reign of George III, in the later eighteenth century, back into the reign of Queen Anne. Accordingly, patronage and influence were favoured over party and principle. Indeed, Riley goes so far as to assert in his preface to *The Union of England and Scotland* (1978) that 'The Union was made by men of limited vision for very short-term and comparatively petty, if not squalid, aims.' National interests of both Scotland and England were peripheral considerations.[71] The prevalence of jobbery and the absence of statesmanship were carried further in a nationalist direction by Paul Scott, who revitalised Lockhart of Carnwath's claims that the Scottish Estates were suborned by bribery and that the Union was secured by intimidation. Simultaneously, Fletcher of Saltoun was eulogised as a Scottish patriot and classical republican. The central tenet of Whig orthodoxy that the Union was an admirable and enlightened transaction was dismissed

---

[70] W. Ferguson, *Scotland's Relations with England: A Survey to 1707* (Edinburgh, 1977); 'The Making of the Treaty of Union of 1707', *SHR*, 43 (1964), pp. 89–110; 'Imperial crowns: a neglected facet of the background to the Treaty of Union of 1707', *SHR*, 53 (1974), pp. 22–44.

[71] P. W. J. Riley, *The Union of England and Scotland: A Study in Anglo-Scottish Politics of the Eighteenth Century* (Manchester, 1978); *King William and the Scottish Politicians* (Edinburgh, 1979); 'The Union of 1707 as an Episode in English Politics', *EHR*, 84 (1969), pp. 498–527.

as a historiographic conspiracy. Keenly anticipating the dissolution or drastic modification of Union, about whose advantaging of Scotland he remained deeply sceptical, Scott further contended that the contemporary usage of such words as 'union' and 'federal' in relation to the Treaty of 1707 had been misunderstood not only by economic determinists but also by historians of ideas.[72]

However, intellectual historians, especially John Robertson and David Armitage, brought fresh and persuasive insights into the making of Union by exploring alternative ideas of state formation and Empire. Robertson convincingly recontextualised the polemical debates in relation to federative alternatives to political incorporation, particularly in terms of European comparators as well as classical and imperial models of union. Fletcher of Saltoun was demonstrably an upholder of European as well as British federation.[73] Armitage lucidly demonstrated that the Scots were no less concerned players than the English in the transatlantic pursuit of Empire before 1707. Scottish entrepreneurial engagement with the Americas was as much inspired by the Dutch as by the English. Indeed, as evident from the Darien fiasco, Scottish aspirations were not necessarily complementary to the English. Since the Restoration era, colonial endeavour was viewed as an alternative to Union and considerably less draining on commercial resources than the fiscal demands for the support of a large standing army, which became a pronounced feature of post-Revolutionary England.[74] However, historians of ideas have tended to concentrate on policy at the expense of process. Thus, Fletcher of Saltoun continues to be eulogised while his incapacity to work purposefully and co-operatively in the Scottish Estates has been glossed over. Likewise, George MacKenzie, 1st Earl of Cromartie, has been commended for his principled advocacy of incorporating union, but his manifest political opportunism as a career politician has been understated. William Paterson, the leading proponent of a Scottish colony at Darien, whom Lord Macaulay memorably deemed as having acquired an

---

[72] P. H. Scott, *Andrew Fletcher and The Treaty of Union* (Edinburgh, 1992), 'The Boasted Advantages': *The Consequences of the Union of 1707* (Edinburgh, 1999) and *1707: The Union of Scotland and England in Contemporary Documents with a Commentary* (Edinburgh, 1979).
[73] J. Robertson, 'Empire and Union: Two Concepts of the Early Modern European Political Order', and 'An Elusive Sovereignty. The Course of the Union Debate in Scotland 1698–1707' in J. Robertson, ed., *A Union for Empire: Political Thought and the British Union* (Cambridge, 1995), pp. 3–36, 198–277; 'Union, State and Empire: The Britain of 1707 in its European Setting' in L. Stone, ed., *An Imperial State at War: Britain from 1689–1815* (London, 1994), pp. 224–57; 'Andrew Fletcher's Vision of Union' in Mason, ed., *Scotland and England, 1286–1815*, pp. 203–25.
[74] D. Armitage, *The Ideological Origins of the British Empire* (Cambridge, 2000).

influence resembling that of a founder of a new religion,[75] has not been fully recognised for his consummate abilities as a spin-doctor, which were deployed prior to the last session of the Scottish Estates in 1706–7 at the behest of the English ministry. Historians of ideas, moreover, still appear more comfortable in dealing with issues of sovereignty and confessionalism than with political economy, notwithstanding its centrality to the debate on the national interest in England and to national survival in Scotland (and Ireland) since the mid seventeenth century.[76]

In the run-up to the successful attainment of Scottish devolution in 1997, Christopher Whatley was instrumental in refocusing the historiographic debate on the importance of economic no less than political issues, in both the making and the accomplishment of Union. In offering a measured, structured and perceptive view that endorsed qualitative decision making over political jobbery, Whatley nonetheless takes a rather pessimistic view about Scotland's prospects as a notionally independent nation. He largely reinforces the view of Smout that Scotland was rescued from economic ruin by a Union achieved by realistic rather than corrupt politicians: a situation which appears to make the Union an unprecedented act of political altruism on the part of the English ministry.[77]

The counter to this somewhat 'pessimistic' view of Scottish prospects has been led by Tom Devine, who has focused on the basic resilience of the Scottish economy, on native entrepreneurship and its global outreach, and on an integrated landed and commercial elite which ensured that Scottish recovery was well underway by Union. The Treaty of 1707 was an accomplishment that created a favourable climate for economic growth and engagement with Empire, but by no means guaranteed Scottish commercial expansion, agricultural improvement or industrialisation in the course of the eighteenth century.[78]

---

[75] Macaulay, *The History of England from the Accession of James II*, v, pp. 212–13.

[76] S. Pincus, 'Neither Machiavellian Moment nor Possessive Individualism: Commercial Society and the Defenders of the English Commonwealth', *AHR*, 103 (1998), pp. 705–36; A. I. Macinnes, *The British Revolution, 1629–1660* (Basingstoke, 2004), pp. 219–23.

[77] C. A. Whatley, *Bought and Sold for English Gold? Explaining the Union of 1707* (East Linton, 1994, with second edition in 2001); 'Economic Causes and Consequences of the Union of 1707', *SHR*, 68 (1989), pp. 150–81; 'Taking Stock: Scotland at the End of the Seventeenth Century' in Smout, ed., *Anglo-Scottish Relations*, pp. 103–25. In an otherwise commendably balanced contribution on Union and Scottish economic development, Ian D. Whyte (*Scotland's Society and Economy in Transition, c. 1500 – c. 1760* (Basingstoke, 1977), pp. 154–65) further questions the credibility of economic causation by asserting, on the one hand, that English ministers acted purely from political motives, having little interest in a backward Scottish economy, and, on the other, that the Scots were concerned with access to English domestic not colonial markets.

[78] Devine, *The Scottish Nation, 1700–2000*, pp. 3–30, 49–63. This perspective has been wholly ignored by Neil Davidson, *Discovering the Scottish Revolution, 1692–1746* (London, 2003),

Notwithstanding the undoubted structural weaknesses in the Scottish economy, its relative lack of depth and diversity and its vulnerability to mercantilist policies applied by the leading European states, trade and commerce was neither stagnant nor on an irreversible downward spiral by the Union of 1707. Considerable caution must be exercised before accepting official reports, customs records, fiscal returns and unfulfilled commitments to military and civil expenditure as accurate indicators of the Scottish economy. Notwithstanding the frequent imposition of Navigation Laws in England since the Restoration, Scots had become adept at circumventing them through privateering, disguised ownership of shipping, smuggling, tax evasion and other illicit commercial practices that facilitated trade between Scotland and the American colonies. Moreover, the transfer of the distinctive Scottish trading practice of tramping from the Baltic to the Caribbean and subsequently on to the Indian Ocean and the China Seas in the eighteenth century ensured that illicit trading, customs evasion and smuggling continued well beyond the Treaty of Union's concession of free trade with the colonies.[79] Steve Murdoch has introduced a vital new awareness of the integrated, but expansive, transoceanic activities of Scottish commercial networks in the seventeenth century. Scottish entrepreneurs were notably prominent in the development of textile manufacturing and the industrial production of iron and steel in Sweden. The new questions his work raises about the flow of inward and outward investment through these thriving networks on the eve of Union await further research, however.[80]

---

who offers a Marxist interpretation based on three propositions: that the 1690s represented a crisis of feudalism; that the Union of 1707 offered a capitalist solution to this crisis; and that the British state demonstrated its capacity to consolidate revolutionary change by the abolition of heritable jurisdictions in the wake of the last Jacobite rising in 1747. Notwithstanding the fact that he is effectively reiterating the common currency of the Enlightenment in attesting that the Union brought about the demise of Scottish feudalism, the abolition of heritable jurisdictions and of feudal ward holdings in 1747 was essentially a sop to public opinion in England which sought an institutional solution to the essentially personal authority exercised by Jacobite clan chiefs. Indeed, the main purpose of the legislation was to reward the Scottish landed elite who had remained loyal to the British state, to the tune of £493,000 – the largest injection of political capital into Scotland since the Treaty of Union (A. I. Macinnes, *Clanship, Commerce and the House of Stuart, 1603–1788* (East Linton 1996 and 2000), pp. 225–6). Davidson's analysis, which takes its polemical inspiration from the latter-day *belles lettres* of Hugh Trevor-Roper, Lord Dacre (H. R. Trevor-Roper, 'The Anglo-Scottish Union', *From Counter-Reformation to Glorious Revolution* (London, 1992), pp. 282–303), clearly makes William Robertson an intellectual mentor of Leo Trotsky. For 'New Marxist' read 'Old Whig'.

[79] A. I. Macinnes, 'Circumventing State Power – Scottish Mercantile Networks and the English Navigation Laws, 1660–1707' in P. Borschberg & M. Krieger, eds., *Water and State in Europe and Asia*, (Delhi, 2007) forthcoming

[80] S. Murdoch, *Network North: Scottish Kin, Commercial and Covert Associations in Northern Europe, 1603–1746* (Leiden and Boston, 2006).

New British perspectives

For historians not actively engaged in or pre-occupied by Scottish history, the view of the Union as a constitutional adjustment to an essentially English political narrative has been replaced by the general acceptance of the apparent Scottish consensus that the accomplishment of the Treaty of 1707 can be attributed to various influences. Diplomatic brinkmanship, military intimidation and political manipulation on the part of the English ministry at the Court of Queen Anne were compounded by economic defeatism, financial chicanery and, above all, political ineptitude on the part of the Scottish Estates which remained immune to an overwhelmingly hostile public reception in the country.[81] However, this tendency to offer a synthesis rather than an original analysis has three important exceptions.

Firstly, John Brewer has led the challenge to the proclaimed Whig achievement of constitutional monarchy in place of autocracy at the Revolution that purportedly laid the foundations of British imperial power and nationhood. This prevailing orthodoxy had glossed over the continuation of the fiscal–military state instigated in the Stuarts' dominions outwith England in the Restoration era. Ostensibly under parliamentary control from the Revolution, British imperialism was moderated, not contained, by votes of supply and fructified by the creation of the National Debt in 1693 that was financed through the Bank of England from 1694.[82] The Jacobite threat, more perceived than actual, disrupted the political process that sustained British state formation fiscally and militarily. John Young has duly identified the fiscal–military pressures from England as an essential component in the making of Union. At the same time, he has turned around the alleged inferiority of parliamentary tradition in Scotland, to trace back the inspirational precedents for Fletcher of Saltoun's endeavours to impose permanent limitations on monarchy, in the course of the Union debates, not just to the Revolution

---

[81] See G. Holmes, *The Making of a Great Power: Late Stuart and Early Georgian Britain, 1660–1722* (Harlow, 1993), pp. 307–21; F. O'Gorman, *The Long Eighteenth Century: British Political & Social History, 1688–1832* (London, 1997), pp. 43–64; J. Hoppit, *A Land of Liberty? England 1689–1727* (Oxford, 2000), pp. 242–57; D. Hayton & D. Szechi, 'John Bull's Other Kingdoms: The English Government of Scotland and Ireland' in C. Jones, ed., *Britain in the First Age of Party, 1680–1750: Essays Presented to Geoffrey Holmes* (London, 1987), pp. 241–80; D. Hayton, 'Constitutional Experimentation and Political Expediency, 1689–1725' in Ellis & Barber, eds., *Conquest and Union*, pp. 276–305.

[82] J. Brewer, *The Sinews of Power: War, Money and the English State, 1688–1783* (London, 1989), pp. 25–161; S. S. Webb, *The Governors-General: The English Army and the Definition of Empire, 1569–1681* (Chapel Hill, 1979), pp. 329–466; M. J. Braddick, *The Nerves of State: Taxation and the Financing of the English State, 1558–1714* (Manchester, 1996), pp. 27–45.

but to the constitutional attainments of the Covenanting Movement in 1640–1.[83]

Secondly, Bill Speck, in a year-by-year approach to the first decade of the eighteenth century, has reasserted the importance of Union to both England and Scotland, with respect to its military and commercial as well as its political context. He has also suggested perceptively that more research was required on the influence of Prince George of Denmark who, as consort of Queen Anne, was an understated but demonstrable player in the making of Union.[84] While the correspondence of Prince George home to the Danish Court has not proved particularly rewarding, the Rigsarkivet in Copenhagen possesses an extensive series of letter books written by Danish diplomats between 1702 and 1707, whose stunning and novel insights on how the progress of Union was actually viewed at the Court of Queen Anne have been mentioned already in the Introduction.

Thirdly, and most problematically, there is the call from John Pocock for new British histories stimulated by his opposition to the entry of Britain and Ireland into the European Community (now the European Union) in 1973. Notwithstanding his lament for the inevitable decline of the British Commonwealth, Pocock made an incisive appeal for historical integration not only between England, Scotland and Ireland, but also between domestic and imperial history. This remains the ideal, not the actuality.[85] Indeed, the primacy accorded to national identities, civil wars and, above all, state formation seriously questions whether the 'New British Histories' have marked a distinctive shift in focus away from Whiggish concerns with nation building.[86] A case can certainly be made for the simultaneous intensification of state authority within the British Isles and its extension into the Stuarts' American dominions.[87] However, the creation of a common elite identity based on shared notions of authority and civility is a far more suspect proposition, particularly as

---

[83] J. R. Young, 'The Parliamentary Incorporating Union of 1707: Political Management, Anti-Unionism and Foreign Policy' in Devine & Young, eds., *Eighteenth Century Scotland*, pp. 24–52; 'The Scottish Parliament and the Covenanting Heritage of Constitutional Reform' in Macinnes & Ohlmeyer, eds., *The Stuart Kingdoms*, pp. 226–50; 'The Scottish Parliament in the Seventeenth Century: European Perspectives' in A. I. Macinnes, T. Riis & F. G. Pedersen, eds., *Ships, Guns and Bibles in the North Sea and Baltic States, c.1350–c.1700* (East Linton, 2000), pp. 139–72.

[84] W. A. Speck, *The Birth of Britain: A New Nation, 1700–1710* (Oxford, 1994), pp. 3–21.

[85] J. G. A. Pocock, 'The Limits and Divisions of British History: In Search of an Unknown Subject', *AHR*, 87 (1982), pp. 311–36.

[86] A. I. Macinnes, 'The Multiple Kingdoms of Britain and Ireland: the "British problem"' in B. Coward ed., *The Blackwell Companion to Stuart Britain* (Oxford, 2002), pp. 3–25.

[87] M. J. Braddick, *State Formation in Early Modern England, c. 1550–1700* (Cambridge, 2000), pp. 340–419.

full integration was never achieved with respect to the church, the law and local government.[88] The British nature of the Empire was reasserted predominantly through Scottish commercial networks within an English governmental framework.[89] Yet, as Andrew Mackillop has recently demonstrated, the Union actually constricted Scottish participation in the East Indies, when the Company trading to Africa and the Indies, under whose auspices the Darien scheme had been implemented, was actually wound up as part of the final Treaty of 1707. Indeed, negotiations for a merger between the Old and New English East India companies, which commenced in 1702, were not actually concluded until 1709, and were arguably of no less concern to the English landed and commercial elite than the Anglo-Scottish Union.[90]

[88] D. Szechi, 'The Hanoverians and Scotland' in Greengrass, ed., *Conquest and Coalescence*, pp. 116–33; K. M. Brown, 'The Scottish Nobility and the British Multiple Monarchy (1603–1714)' in R. G. Asch, ed., *Der europäische Adel im Ancien Régime: Von der Krise der ständischen Monarchien bis zur Revolution (ca.1600–1789)* (Böhlau, 2001), pp. 363–84.

[89] A. I. Macinnes, 'Introduction: Connecting and Disconnecting with America' in A. I. Macinnes & A. H. Williamson, eds., *Shaping the Stuart World, 1603–1714: The American Connection* (Leiden and Boston, 2006), pp. 1–30.

[90] A. Mackillop, 'Accessing Empire: Scotland, Europe, Britain and the Asia Trade, 1695 – c. 1750', *Itinerario*, 19 (2005), pp. 7–30.

Part II

Varieties of Union, 1603–1707

3 Precedents, 1603–1660

The territorial acquisitiveness of Edward I of England and of his grandson Edward II instigated and perpetuated the Scottish Wars of Independence from the late thirteenth century through most of the fourteenth. For much of the fifteenth century, the Border district of southern Scotland remained under English occupation. There was a more ambivalent English approach under the Tudors in the sixteenth century. On the one hand, Scotland was faced with a renewed threat of conquest and occupation, particularly during the 1540s and 1550s. On the other hand, the 'Rough Wooing' opened up the prospect of not only a regal but also an institutional union should the future Edward VI of England marry Mary, Queen of Scots. Although the Scots initially preferred a French match for their young queen, armed intervention authorised by Elizabeth Tudor secured the Scottish Reformation in the teeth of French-backed opposition. The confirmation that Berwick-upon-Tweed would continue in English hands was the only territorial adjustment of any significance on the restored Anglo-Scottish Borders. Although Elizabeth was notoriously reluctant to name her successor, the marriage of Margaret Tudor to James IV of Scotland in 1503 paved the way for their great-grandson, James VI of Scotland, to become James I of England in 1603.[1] The prospect of a forced or a negotiated union between the Tudor and Stuart dynasties had stimulated considerable debate on the topic of British state formation in the course of the sixteenth century.[2] This wideranging debate, which was marked by a heady mixture of myth, humanism and providentialism, was hugely influential in the determination of the new king of Scotland and England to be viewed, from 1603, as James I of Great Britain. His resolve

---

[1] Donaldson, *Scotland: James V – James VII*, pp. 16–30; M. Merriman, *The Rough Wooings: Mary Queen of Scots, 1542–1551* (East Linton, 2001), pp. 111–63, 232–64.
[2] J. H. Burns, *The True Law of Kingship: Concepts of Monarchy in Early Modern Scotland* (Oxford, 1996), pp. 54–92, 185–221; R. A. Mason, *Kingship and the Commonweal: Political Thought in Renaissance and Reformation Scotland* (East Linton, 1998), pp. 242–69; A. H. Williamson, 'Education, Culture and the Scottish Civic Tradition' in Macinnes & Williamson, eds., *Shaping the Stuart World*, pp. 33–54.

to foster a new British dynasty under the Stuart appellation was complemented by his commitment to a British state that would harmonise differing Scottish and English perceptions about union.[3]

Rival perceptions

There were three rival perceptions of Great Britain that emanated from Scotland and England – the Britannic, the Scottish and the Gothic. These are normative, not just descriptive, labels as they prescribe both inclusive and exclusive perceptions of state formation. The Britannic, which extolled imperial monarchy, was inclusive in its promotion of full union through incorporation, yet exclusive in claiming unfettered sovereignty within the British Isles. James I saw himself as the founder of a Britannic Empire not just as a ruler of multiple kingdoms, a vision that had firm intellectual roots in his ancient and native kingdom, not least because tangible British harmony enabled the Scots to counter English claims to overlordship. The Scottish perspective, which upheld aristocratic republicanism as the ideal of civic humanism, was inclusive in seeking federative union, a Scotto-Britannic variant that had been given a particular fillip by Protestant Reformation in both Scotland and England. The Gothic, which upheld the supremacy of the English parliament and the common law, was exclusive in threatening to reduce Scotland (like Ireland) to a political dependency of England.

The anglocentric dominance of the Britannic perspective rested on Welsh myth-making of the twelfth century that was eventually rationalised into a territorially expansive construct by the antiquarian William Camden, in his final version of *Britannia* prepared in 1607. Camden's concept of Britain underwrote English claims to be an exclusive empire. The English were an elect Protestant nation with a Christian tradition under an episcopacy unbeholden to Rome but deemed erastian through its close ties to the monarchy. England's civilising mission had been refined by conquest and invasion. Thus, London, the old Roman foundation, was now the metropolitan capital of a composite British Empire whose territories encompassed the Anglo-Saxon heptarchy as well as Wales and Cornwall. This composite Empire could lay claim not only to Ireland but also to that part of Scotland formerly held by the Picts. Though barbarians, they were not, like the Irish and the Scots, of irredeemable Gothic stock, but actually Britons who had lived outwith the boundaries of Roman civilisation: the classical demarcation which ensured that such redeemable Gothic influences as the Saxons, Danes and

---

[3] Macinnes, *The British Revolution*, pp. 8–39.

Normans were deemed to have enriched rather than destroyed Britain. These northern boundaries, which were settled at the Forth–Clyde division of Scotland, conformed to the division between the ancient Scottish kingdom of Alba and the Saxon kingdom of Northumbria. Following his accession to the English throne, the founder of the Stuart dynasty's imperial vanity was certainly enhanced by the notion that he was the fabled heir to Emperor Constantine the Great and King Arthur as well as the more prosaic Tudors. At the same time, the repeated print runs of Camden's *Britannia* throughout the seventeenth century fuelled rather than dispelled English claims to superiority over the British Isles.[4]

That Scotland, England and Ireland were actually an imperial composite was illustrated graphically by the cartographer John Speed, whose *The Theatre of the Empire of Great Britain*, first published in 1611, remained the template for the subsequent mapping of the British Isles for much of the seventeenth century. Subsequent abridged versions of his maps, though purportedly depicting multiple kingdoms, adhered to the basic structure of a composite empire. Romans, Saxons, Danes and Normans in the guise of classical heroes refined the barbarous, if noble, representation of a male Britannia. Speed thus illustrated the importance of progressive civility to the Stuart dynasty's imperial project. The composite representation of Camden and Speed, which effectively appended Scotland and the rest of the British Isles on to detailed topographical descriptions of the English and Welsh shires, was accorded international recognition by the leading Dutch cartographer, Wilhelm Blaeu. His map of *Britannia* was published posthumously in 1645.[5]

---

[4] William Camden, *Britain, or A Chronological description of the most flourishing kingdomes, England, Scotland and Ireland, and the islands adjoining, out of the depth of antiquity* (London, 1610 and 1637). The construct of Britain was derived from Brut, the epic Trojan hero who moved to Rome before progressing through Gaul from where he and his followers settled the whole of the British Isles. Although Britain was divided up among the successors of Brut during the first millennium BC, anglocentric dominance was reasserted under Roman occupation. Constantine the Great, who spread Christianity throughout the Roman Empire and transferred the capital from Rome to Byzantium at the outset of the fourth century AD, was both born and acclaimed emperor in Britain. Following the fall of Rome, the Britons were subject to invasions by Picts, Scots and Saxons that forced them to the margins in Wales and Cornwall. Successive conquests by the Saxons, Danes and Norsemen contributed to the march of civility as institutionalised through kingship, the common law and post-Reformation Protestantism. This mythical perception of Britain was reinforced by Welsh antiquarians, keen to identify Wales as the enduring heartland of the original Britons, as well as by English chroniclers like Raphael Holinshed and mercantile adventurers like John Dee during the sixteenth century (D. R. Woolf, *The Idea of History in Early Stuart England: Erudition, Ideology, and 'The Light of Truth' from the Accession of James I to the Civil War* (Toronto, 1990), pp. 55–64, 115–27).

[5] John Speed, *The Theatre of the Empire of Great Britain: presenting an exact geography of the kingdomes of England, Scotland, Ireland and the isle adjoyning* (London, 1616 and 1627);

Although James I glorified in portraying himself as Emperor Constantine *redivivus*, his main preference was for biblical rather than classical analogies, and most notably for his idealisation as Great Britain's Solomon. As a firm advocate of monarchy being divinely interposed between God and civil society, James viewed dynastic consolidation as the first step towards perfect union under an imperial monarchy. Such a union opened up the prospect of British leadership in a Protestant Europe battling to resist the Anti-Christ in the form of the papacy and the whole panoply of the Counter-Reformation. For his vision of godly monarchy, James drew demonstrably on traditional English claims to be an empire free from papal control. Simultaneously, he rebutted Presbyterian claims to the autonomy of the Scottish Kirk.[6] With varying degrees of enthusiasm, the Protestant episcopate in Scotland, England and Ireland endorsed his imperial concept of British union.

John Thornborough, Bishop of Bristol, viewed the providential reunification of the British Empire under a godly monarch as an occasion of great happiness that would be perfected by the eventual merging of the constituent identities of Scotland and England into a composite British nation.[7] James himself had sponsored the publication of two works in Scotland that sought to ally providence and prophecy to his Britannic project. The claims of an anonymous English apologist that the miraculous and happy union between England and Scotland would prove expeditious and profitable to both nations, and stop unnecessary wars, were reprinted in Edinburgh in 1604. The Scottish Estates should participate, without equivocation, in the creation of 'the moste opulent, strong and entire Empire of the worlde', capable of transatlantic confrontation with Spain and the papacy.[8] With the second of these works, James was also determined to demonstrate that his accession to the English throne was

---

C. Moreland & D. Bannister, *Antique Maps* (London, 2000), pp. 209, 213–16. In like manner, when the work of the earlier great Dutch cartographer, Gerard Mercator, was 'Englished' in 1635, his map of England, Scotland and Ireland first published in 1595 was retitled as 'the Isles of Britain' ([Wye Saltonstall], *Historia Mundi: Or Mercator's Atlas* (London, 1635), pp. 38–43, 68–87).

[6] J. H. Burns, *The True Law of Kingship*, pp. 222–54; J. Wormald, 'James VI and I, *Basilikon Doron* and *The Trew Law of Free Monarchies*: The Scottish Context and the English Translation' in L. L. Peck, ed., *The Mental World of the Jacobean Court* (Cambridge, 1991), pp. 36–54. The Authorized Version of the Bible produced in 1611 upheld King James's vision of godly monarchy and his resolve that English should be the language of Reformed civility throughout his British dominions.

[7] John Thornborough, Bishop of Bristol, *A Discourse Shewing the Great Happiness that hath and may still accrue to his Majesties Kingdomes of England and Scotland By re-Uniting them into ane Great Britain* (London, 1604 and 1641). Thornborough's plea for a composite British nation was reissued in 1641 to serve the Royalist cause of Charles I.

[8] Anon., *The Miraculous and Happie Union of England & Scotland* (Edinburgh, 1604).

the peaceful fulfilment of British unification not only predicted by the likes of Merlin, Bede and Thomas the Rhymer, but also endorsed from French and Danish sources. Printed in 1617 in both Latin verse and Scots metre, this text gained notable British currency throughout the 1640s; for the prophecies favouring union and concerted action against the papal Anti-Christ were also reinterpreted to uphold the claims of Scottish Covenanters against the absentee Stuart monarchy, to secure Scottish deliverance from dependence on England, their recovery of Berwick-upon-Tweed and the imposition of a federative union of Britain from the north.[9]

The shaping of a composite British Empire had to contend with Scottish origin myths. Largely the product of the Wars of Independence in the late thirteenth and fourteenth centuries, these Scottish myths borrowed heavily from the Irish origin mythology, the first to be articulated within the multiple kingdoms from the eleventh century. In contrast to the Roman imperial element, which the English shared with other aggressive northern powers in early modern Europe, the Scottish myths stressed civic origins through Greece and Egypt.[10] Fergus MacEarc, who actually ruled around 500 AD, was the first authentic King of Scots. His designation as fortieth in line from Fergus MacFerchar was a fabrication notably embellished by Hector Boece in his *Scotorum Historiae* (1527), when Anglo-Scottish relations had degenerated towards the real prospect

---

[9] *The Whole Prophecies of Scotland, England, France, Ireland and Denmarke* (Edinburgh, 1617).

[10] R. A. Mason, 'Scotching the Brut: Politics, History and National Myth in Sixteenth-Century Britain' in Mason, ed., *Scotland and England, 1286–1815*, pp. 60–84; S. C. Rowell, 'The Grand Duchy of Lithuania and Baltic Identity, c. 1500–1600' in Macinnes, Riis & Pedersen, eds., *Ships, Guns and Bibles*, pp. 65–92. Gathelus of Athens, having sojourned in Egypt, married Scota, daughter of the Pharaoh, shortly before Moses led the Israeli exodus. In the wake of the Pharaoh's destruction in the Red Sea, Gathelus and Scota wandered to Iberia from whence their heirs moved to Ireland and then to Scotland, where an autonomous kingdom was established in 330 BC under Fergus, son of Ferchar, a contemporary of Alexander the Great. Around 403 AD, having overcome an alliance of the Romans and the Picts, which temporarily forced their return to Ireland, Fergus, son of Earc, re-established the kingdom of the Scots that was expanded under Kenneth MacAlpine in 843 to include that of the Picts. Despite continuing English hostility, their descendants went on to consolidate the borders of Scotland from the Solway to the Tweed in the eleventh century. This legend not only underwrote Scottish pretensions to the longest unbroken line of kings in Europe, but also the imperial aspirations of their Stewart monarchy. For Achaius, the sixty-fifth King of Scots was leagued in friendship, not clientage, with Charlemagne, the Holy Roman Emperor, around 790 – a league which had laid the foundation of the 'auld alliance' between Scotland and France that was consolidated by the Wars of Independence. The advent of Reformation gave added significance to the legend, for the propagation of Christianity from the Scots to the Picts by Columba and his followers during the sixth century was viewed as proto-Presbyterianism untrammelled by an erastian episcopate or by Rome.

of English conquest of Scotland. Six years earlier, Boece's fellow countryman John Mair had proposed an alternative strategy offering permanent resolution for Anglo-Scottish conflict. His *Historia Maioris Britannia* discounted the mythical origins of both countries, rejected English claims to superiority and distanced him from his country's xenophobia towards England. Mair was an eloquent advocate of British union through dynastic alliance such as that between James IV of Scotland and Margaret Tudor of England in 1503. James VI & I was notably indebted to Mair's imperial vision of Great Britain. But this vision requires wider international contextualising, especially as the Spanish monarchy had already established an Iberian world Empire when the Stuarts commenced their imperial project for British Union.[11]

Mair was the principal Iberian apologist within the British Isles. However, the main opponents of world Empire within these Isles were also Scots, notably John Knox from a biblical and apocalyptic British perspective and George Buchanan as an exponent of aristocratic republicanism. Both viewed post-Reformation Scotland as a virtuous commonwealth that should be open to wider federative arrangements to counter universal monarchy. Buchanan had firmed up Boece's fabricated line of kings in order to demonstrate the capacity of the Scottish commonwealth to remove tyrannical monarchs. In marked contrast to Camden's imperial perception of continuity and stability through virtuous monarchy, Buchanan stressed that an elective kingship depended on the consent of the political community. Buchanan's advocacy of the right of resistance to monarchy, which upheld trusteeship over sovereignty in *De Iure Regnis apud Scotus dialogus* (1579), made the book a ready target for proscription by successive Stuarts during the seventeenth century.[12]

The fundamental reconfiguration of Britain was also a prime concern of Andrew Melville, humanist, educational reformer and founder of Scottish Presbyterianism. Melville viewed the constituent parts of the British Isles as distinctive but mutually supportive elements in the great war against the Iberian world Empire. It was Melville who first suggested the merging of the two rival formulations of Britain. In 1594, he anticipated the future regal union would join Scotland and England in a united commonwealth of the Scoto-Britannic people. This new commonwealth, however, was but the first step in a grand confederation of free Protestant states. David Hume of Godscroft, the leading Presbyterian intellectual in Jacobean

---

[11] A. H. Williamson, 'Scots, Indians and Empire: The Scottish Politics of Civilization, 1519–1609', *Past & Present*, 150 (1996), pp. 46–83.

[12] Burns, *The True Law of Kingship*, pp. 283–95; Mason, *Kingship and the Commonweal*, pp. 165–86.

Britain, was no less committed to the full integration of Britain. In 1605, he promoted a complete political and religious union that would lead to the fusion of British peoples.[13] Seven decades before William Petty advocated a similar policy for Ireland, Hume proposed that English 'colonia' be implanted in the less developed regions of Scotland. In essence, these were to be exemplary plantations, drawing on the medieval practice of planting towns in devastated districts, to promote the improvement not the subjugation of native peoples.[14] Nonetheless, the creation of a universal British Commonwealth under the Stuart dynasty to challenge Spain and the papacy sat awkwardly with the aristocratic republic that he, like Buchanan, idealised. The Iberian menace pointed to new political directions that were not necessarily liberating. Reluctant to condone outright resistance to monarchy, Hume had no clear alternative should the Stuart dynasty choose not to co-operate with his vision. Buchanan, on the other hand, had afforded an incisive and unequivocal critique of imperial kingship that was to prove attractive to Scottish Covenanters and British Whigs as the seventeenth century unfolded.

At the same time, Dutch typographers and cartographers turned to Buchanan, supplemented by Boece, when seeking a distinctive counterpoint to the composite delineation of Great Britain by Camden and Speed. In 1627, Bonaventure and Abraham Elzevirus published at Leiden a topographical compilation, *Respublica, sive Status Regni Scotiae et Hiberniae*. Their selective representation, together with a summative history of the 'auld alliance' with France, underlined Scotland's status as a classic commonwealth independent of England. For Ireland, however, the evidence drawn predominantly from Camden and Speed was loaded in favour of its status as an English dependency. This differentiation was sustained by the publication in Amsterdam of Johannes Blaeu's *Grand Atlas* in 1654.[15]

---

[13] *The British Union: A Critical Edition and Translation of David Hume of Godscroft's De Unione Insulae Britannicae*, ed. P. J. McGinnis & A. Williamson (Aldershot, 2002), pp. 1–53; D. Allan, *Philosophy and Politics in Later Stuart Scotland* (East Linton, 2000), pp. 47–58, 116–21.
[14] Sir William Petty, *The Political Anatomy of Ireland, 1672* (Dublin, 1691); M. Beresford, *New Towns of the Middle Ages: Town Plantation in England, Wales and Gascony* (London, 1967), pp. 76–85.
[15] [Bonaventure & Abraham Elzevirus], *Respublica, sive Status Regni Scotiae et Hiberniae* (Leiden, 1627); Johannes Blaeu, *Scotiae Quae Est Europae, Liber XII* (Amsterdam, 1654 and 1662); J. Goss, *World Historical Atlas, 1662* (London, 1990), pp. 84–5. Scotland was covered in book 12 of Blaeu's first edition. Ireland, though recognised as a distinct European entity in book 13, was treated in a supplement. The accompanying topographical sections were prepared primarily by Sir Robert Gordon of Stralloch, an Aberdeenshire laird firmly wedded to the Graeco-Egyptian origins of the Scots, to the antiquity of the Scottish kingdom and to the emphatic rebuttal of Camden.

Notwithstanding their antithetical perceptions on the role of monarchy in British Union, the Britannic and Scottish perspectives were both challenged by Gothic anglocentricism. The endeavours of James I to effect the full integration of his British dominions provoked an English backlash. The formative role of the Anglo-Saxons in the constitutional history of England led Camden's antiquarian associates, Sir Henry Spelman and John Selden, to play down British continuity from the Romans to the Normans. Spelman and Selden argued for the foundations of common law in the transmission of the immemorial, Gothic predilection for liberty and constitutional assemblies during the Anglo-Saxon incursions of the fifth century. Institutional and cultural continuity in English life had been preserved despite Danish incursions in the ninth century and the Norman Conquest of 1066. Notwithstanding the stress on hereditary and authoritarian monarchy associated with this conquest, the Normans had facilitated the refinement of constitutional assemblies into the parliaments that guaranteed English laws and liberties.[16] The rehabilitation of the Anglo-Saxon contribution, through their positive identification with Gothic virtues, which could be represented chronologically rather than mythologically, has been attributed primarily to Richard Verstegan. His work on the *Restitution of Decayed Intelligence* (1605) was dedicated to James I in terms which excluded any Britannic or Scottish perspective: 'as descendant of chiefest blood royal or our ancient English-Saxon kings'. Verstegan solidified the association of the Gothic virtues of the Germanic peoples with the migration of the Anglo-Saxons, which was the formative influence in fashioning the English nation.[17]

---

[16] C. Kidd, *British Identities before Nationalism: Ethnicity and Nationhood in the Atlantic World, 1600–1800* (Cambridge, 1999), pp. 77–87; G. Burgess, *The Politics of the Ancient Constitution: An Introduction to English Political Thought, 1603–1641* (University Park, PA, 1992), pp. 58–78.

[17] S. Kliger, *The Goths in England: A Study in Seventeenth and Eighteenth Century Thought* (New York, 1952), pp. 111–12; Richard Verstegan, *Restitution of Decayed Intelligence* (Antwerp, 1605). Verstegan claimed Tacitus as a primary source for Gothic antiquity. For this Stoic had identified the distinctive moral virtue of the Germanic peoples, whose aversion to arbitrary and hereditary government contrasted starkly with the duplicity, corruption and tyranny among the political elite prior to the fall of imperial Rome. However, the humanist rehabilitation of Gothic civility was actually instigated in the mid sixteenth century by Joannus and Olaus Magnus, and aided visually by the latter's *Carta Marina* (1539). The Magnus brothers, who served successively as the Roman Catholic bishops of Uppsala in exile on account of the Lutheran Reformation in Sweden, built upon the claims of Jordanes in the sixth century and Isidore of Seville in the seventh – that the Goths were direct descendants of Noah; that, as the aboriginal people from Scandza, they spread over Europe and Asia; and that Sweden constituted the true heartland of the Goths, a people associated with a heroic civilisation that predated that of either Greece or Rome. The moral and physical superiority of the Goths was confirmed by their formative role in the destruction of the Roman Empire in the fifth century. The

The Gothic proponents of English greatness through the supremacy of the common law placed contractual emphasis on rights, liberties and privileges which were applicable to all freeborn Englishmen, but which were exclusively English at the expense of differing Scottish legal traditions or Gaelic customs. Where the Anglo-Saxon invasion was held to be qualitatively different from that of the Romans, Danes and Normans was in that the civilisation of England was advanced through the expulsion of the Britons. Thus the Welsh, the inspirational proponents of the Britannic perspective, were written out of the Gothic. The Welsh could be held to have acquired civility through assimilation into the expanding English state in the sixteenth century (an argument that also underwrote displacement and plantation in Ireland). Scotland's past was not endorsed by institutional development comparable to that of England.[18] Where the Gothic unashamedly borrowed from the Scottish and Britannic perspectives was in the use of prophesying in relation to state formation. Scottish prophesying in the guise of Merlin Caledonicus had facilitated the refashioning of the regal union into British confederation through the Solemn League and Covenant of 1643. Nonetheless, the foretelling of a return to peace in the British Isles, after the cathartic impact of war on all three kingdoms which had been instigated from the north during the 1640s, was utilised also from a Gothic perspective. Thus, the prediction of the English triumphing over internal foes as well as external enemies countenanced the forcible conquest of Ireland and occupation of Scotland in 1649–51.[19]

Regal union and *ius imperium*

The extent to which non-anglocentric interests could be accommodated within the English body politic was the historic nub of the British problem.[20] In formulating his Britannic concept of empire as his *ius imperium*, James I drew a cardinal distinction between the theoretically absolute powers of an imperial monarch and the empirical exercise of political

---

brothers' work in Latin, which was composed during the 1530s but not published for another two decades, first in Rome, then Paris, Antwerp and Basle, had a reported currency in England by 1559 (E. Van Mingroot & E. Van Ermen, *Scandinavia in Old Maps and Prints* (Knokke, 1987), pp. 8–9; Joannus & Olaus Magnus, *De Omnibus Gothorum Sic Numque Regibus, qui unquam ab initio nationis extitere* (Rome, 1554 and 1567), especially books XX and XXIII). England and Scotland were both identified as nations created from the Gothic diaspora.

[18] Kliger, *The Goths in England*, pp. 1–21, 65; Burgess, *The Politics of the Ancient Constitution*, pp. 101–2.
[19] H. Rusche, 'Prophecies and Propaganda, 1641 to 1651', *EHR*, 84 (1969), pp. 752–70.
[20] A. I. Macinnes, 'The Multiple Kingdoms of Britain and Ireland: "The British Problem"' in B. Coward, ed., *The Blackwell Companion to Stuart Britain* (Oxford, 2002), pp. 3–25.

entente through personal forbearance. On the one hand, James upheld the common law of England whose tradition was based on precedent and case law reinforced by parliamentary enactment. On the other hand, James also drew on the Scottish tradition of civil (or Roman) law, based on principles of jurisprudence as perceived practically, though not always systematically, through 'practicks' into which were incorporated decisions by privy and judicial councils as well as by conventions of the political Estates meeting in lieu of a parliament. In the former tradition, the English parliament was the supreme and sole legislature for matters of state. In the latter tradition, the Scottish parliament was the supreme, but not the sole, legislative body. Civil law as received in Scotland made an integral distinction between *ius regis*, as a universal concept relating to the whole framework of government, and *lex regis*, as a relative concept covering the specific acts, statutes or customs implemented in different societies by magistrates or rulers. Whereas *lex* was alterable when required for the common welfare, *ius* was a permanent feature of the fundamental law that not only governed the succession of the Stuarts, but was maintained usually with the consent of the political nation or sustained by immemorial custom. Without *ius*, the key to civility that naturally bonded human society, Scotland could not be an independent kingdom or Britain a true Empire.[21]

The principal propagator of this distinction between *ius* and *lex* was Sir Thomas Craig of Riccarton, the leading Scottish jurist and one of the joint-parliamentary commissioners charged by James I to negotiate full and complete union from 1604.[22] As close agreement was apparent on the fundamentals of *ius* in both Scotland and England, Riccarton contended that there should be no insurmountable obstacle to harmonising civil and common laws. James had admonished the English parliament in 1607 that the civil government in Scotland should not be sacrificed to an imperial construct in which English common law would invariably predominate. However, perfect union tended to be interpreted on the English side as the full integration of both government and laws. The more gradualist position in favour of political and commercial integration also came

---

[21] J. H. Burns, *The True Law of Kingship*, pp. 255–81; A. I. Macinnes, 'Regal Union for Britain, 1603–38' in G. Burgess, ed., *The New British History: Founding a Modern State, 1603–1715* (London, 1999), pp. 33–64.

[22] After the bill for appointing commissioners was passed in the English parliament in June 1604, forty-four members of the Lords and Commons, as well as merchants in the city of London, went on to represent England, while the Scottish Estates appointed thirty commissioners to serve throughout the three years of negotiations (Dicey & Rait, *Thoughts on the Union*, pp. 376–8).

under sustained attack in the English parliament. Fitful negotiations by the joint commissioners over three years eventually foundered on the back of English concepts of political hegemony and parliamentary supremacy. By the autumn of 1607, there was a marked aversion to accepting any arrangement for union that neither accorded supremacy nor deferred ultimately to common law, the quintessentially Gothic basis of the English parliamentary privileges, religious liberties and rights of property.[23]

The English preference for establishing nationality on the basis of case law rather than legislation led to Colvin's Case in June 1608, whose strained resolution accorded common nationality to all born within Britain since the regal union.[24] In promoting this objective as attorney-general for England, Sir Francis Bacon argued before the House of Commons that the benefit of conceding naturalisation to the Scots was the undoubted association of both kingdoms on English terms: that is, by assimilation through the spread of the common law rather than an accommodation with the civil law of Scotland. Bacon, who had been an English commissioner in the abortive union negotiations, was arguing for an expansion of the composite English kingdom that had absorbed Wales and Cornwall in the sixteenth century, not the creation of a composite British Empire. The spread of the common law to Scotland would enhance the security of England by making permanent the sundering of the 'auld alliance' with France. Indeed, for Bacon, having Scotland united through the common law was the constitutional bedrock of English greatness as an elect kingdom capable of global expansion – a viewpoint that was to be reaffirmed in the course of future union debates.[25]

---

[23] B. Levack, 'Law, Sovereignty and the Union' in Mason, ed., *Scots and Britons*, pp. 213–40; B. Galloway, *The Union of England and Scotland 1606–1608* (Edinburgh, 1986), pp. 103–30; *De Unione Regnorum Britanniae Tractatus by Sir Thomas Craig*, ed. C. S. Terry (Edinburgh, 1909); L. L. Peck, 'Kingship, Counsel and Law in Early Stuart Britain' in J. G. A. Pocock, ed., *The Varieties of British Political Thought, 1500–1800* (Cambridge, 1996), pp. 80–115.

[24] Burgess, *The Politics of the Ancient Constitution*, p. 127; *A Source Book of Scottish History*, III, p. 461. Colvin's or Calvin's Case was actually instigated by a Scottish noble, James Colville, Lord Colville, who wished to ensure that his son Robert, then an infant who had been born in Edinburgh, could succeed to lands in England. However, doubts remained as to whether Scottish landowners in England could freely dispose of the produce of their estates (Bruce, *REC*, pp. 101–8).

[25] B. H. G. Wormald, *Francis Bacon: History, Politics and Science, 1561–1626* (Cambridge, 1993), pp. 154–8; [Sir Francis Bacon], *Three speeches of the Right Honourable, Sir Francis Bacon Knight, then his Majesties Sollicitor Generall, after Lord Verulam, Viscount Saint Alban. Concerning the post-nati naturalization of the Scotch in England, Union of the lawes of the kingdomes of England and Scotland* (London, 1641). In arguing that British civility was tied strategically to English security, he was underscoring the case made by Sir John Davies, an antiquarian associate of Camden as well as the king's solicitor in Ireland. The imposition of the common law would not only reduce Ireland to obedience, but also cut

Although the failure of the first plenary negotiations for union apparently contributed to a 'ramshackle' if highly personalised regal union, three matters arising require more measured comment.[26] Firstly, the Scottish Estates, which had conditionally accepted integration in deference to James, were more than relieved that a wrecking motion in the House of Commons terminated the projected union in September 1607 that would have threatened Scotland's favourable trade relations with France and with Holland and Zeeland in the United Provinces.[27] Secondly, notwithstanding trenchant defences from the practitioners of English common law, proponents of English commercial superiority were somewhat apprehensive about the potential impact of the Scottish carrying trade, which carried a competitive edge through its association with Dutch shipping.[28] Thirdly, the regal union consolidated the absence of military confrontation for over three decades prior to 1603 and furthered amicable relations for well over another three decades, especially as James instigated a range of policies to promote his inclusive British agenda in the absence of full union.[29]

James I was determined to demonstrate the sovereign independence of Great Britain and Ireland under imperial monarchy. Accordingly, he promoted an international British agenda as manifest in foreign policy through espionage, embassies and military intervention in the Thirty Years' War (1618–48), a policy continued by his son Charles I on his accession in 1625. At the same time, the early Stuarts' Britannic version of *ius imperium* gave territorial as well as ideological integrity to the unity of Scotland, England and Ireland as multiple kingdoms, a perspective which also sought to demonstrate the interdependence of the

---

off the threat of invasion from Spain. However, because Bacon argued for gradual rather than forced assimilation to the common law he was to be lauded during the Scottish Enlightenment for maintaining that a general union of laws was unnecessary and that only those laws which 'immediately concerned the good of the state' should be the same in both parts of the United Kingdom (Alexander Wright, *A Treatise on the Laws concerning the Election of the Different Representatives sent from Scotland to the Parliament of Great Britain* (Edinburgh, 1773), pp. 85–6).

[26] J. Wormald, 'O Brave New World? The Union of England and Scotland in 1603' in Smout, ed., *Anglo-Scottish Relations*, pp. 13–35.

[27] E. J. Cowan, 'The Union of the Crowns and the Crisis of the Constitution in 17th-century Scotland' in S. Dyrvik, K. Mykland & J. Oldervoll, eds., *The Satellite State in the 17th and 18th Centuries* (Oslo, 1979), pp. 121–40; Bruce, *REC*, pp. 74–5.

[28] T. M. Devine & S. G. E. Lythe, 'The Economy of Scotland under James VI: A Revision Article', *SHR*, 50 (1971), pp. 91–106; Bruce, *REC*, pp. 66–8.

[29] K. M. Brown, 'A Blessed Union? Anglo-Scottish Relations before the Covenant' in Smout, ed., *Anglo-Scottish Relations*, pp. 37–55; A. D. Nicholls, *The Jacobean Union: A Reconsideration of British Civil Policies under the Early Stuarts* (Westport, CT, 1999), pp. 23–46.

three kingdoms at home and abroad.[30] Thus, James implemented civilising projects designed to bring order throughout his exclusive Britannic Empire – namely, the cross-Border policing of the Middle Shires, the plantation of Ulster, and the military and legislative offensive against the West Highlands and Islands. The annexation of Orkney and Shetland was partly an extension of such a frontier policy, but primarily the consolidation of the territorial waters around the British Isles into the Stuarts' *ius imperium*. His projection of the Stuarts as the first composite British dynasty impacted significantly on colonial policy (see Chapter 6).

However, the Britannic perspective faced several obstacles. The rejection of full union meant that there was no formal British executive or legislature for Scotland, England and Ireland. The English parliament manifested a continuing Gothic hostility to the use of the designation 'Great Britain' in its dealings with the Crown.[31] Likewise, once political and commercial integration had been rejected, the Scottish Estates reverted to the practice of not using the term 'Great Britain'. Nonetheless, the Scots were foremost amongst the peoples of the three kingdoms in accepting the British internationalism of their native dynasty. Scots played significant roles in the military, diplomatic and colonial affairs concerted from the British Court. Some Scots, as proponents of Britannic Empire, used the appellation 'Britanno-Scotus'. Others preferred the more ambivalent 'Scoto-Britannus', which sustained Scottish perceptions of aristocratic republicanism and federative rather than incorporating union.[32]

Charles I was intent on pushing his father's British agenda. For Scots, however, his promotion as King of Great Britain had different resonances internationally and domestically that proved politically critical during

---

[30] Burgess, *The Politics of the Ancient Constitution*, pp. 129–30; J. H. Burns, *The True Law of Kingship*, pp. 267–8; S. Murdoch, *Britain, Denmark-Norway and the House of Stuart, 1603–1660* (East Linton, 2000), pp. 44–63.

[31] HL, Bridgewater & Ellesmere MSS, EL 6931, 6952, and Huntington Manuscripts, HM 102.

[32] See John Gordon, *Elizabethae Reginae Manes De Religione Et Regno Ad Iacobum Magnum Brittaniarum Regem, Per Ionnem Gordonium Britanno-Scotum* (London, 1604); Sir David Murray, *The Tragicall Death of Sophinisba. Written by David Murray, Scoto-Brittaine* (London, 1611); Alexander Craig, *The Political Recreations of Mr Alexander Craig of Rose-Craig, Scoto-Britan* (Aberdeen, 1623). Conversely, the use of the term 'Anglo-Britannus' is a rarity. It was used by Charles Howard, 1st Earl of Nottingham, the veteran naval commander who led the English forces against the Spanish Armada in 1588, when petitioning Christian IV of Denmark-Norway for the liberation of a suspect pirate in 1616. The term did not survive the reign of James I (RC, TKUA, England A II, 12, Breve fra forskellige engelske Stats og Hofembedsumamd til Kong Christian IV, 1588–1644).

the 1630s. The placing of Scotland in a posture of defence from 1625 and the recurrent cost of maintaining British fortifications against Spain had promoted tensions between the Court and the Country that were not abated when Charles struck at the 'auld alliance' by declaring war against France in 1626. These tensions paled into insignificance, however, when set against the national outcry over the king's use of his Britannic imprimatur to push through his scheme for a common fishing. This initiative abrogated the Scottish accommodation with the Dutch negotiated by James VI in 1594, whereby Dutch herring busses had access to Scottish deep-sea waters, but the inshore fishing was reserved for the Scots. While reluctantly accepting its implementation, the Scottish Privy Council vigorously rebuffed its promotion as a British policy in 1630. Particularly prejudicial was the suppression of Scottish authorisation in all warrants in favour of 'the name of great Britane, altho ther be no unioun as yit with England'.[33]

The common fishing was but the first step in a policy of British uniformity associated with the promotion of 'thorough' in Church and state by William Laud, Archbishop of Canterbury, and Thomas Wentworth (later Earl of Strafford), Lord-Deputy of Ireland. Scotland, like Ireland, was being used as a political laboratory prior to the more rigorous enforcement of centralised royal power in England. The authorisation of uniformity by Charles unleashed pent-up dissatisfaction in Scotland that culminated in the termination of his rule by prerogative in all three kingdoms. Religious and constitutional protest, reinforced by economic recession, was propagated as a reaction against the perceived imposition of anglicisation, Counter-Reformation and authoritarianism. A comparison of Charles I with his father James VI & I, who also endorsed Episcopalianism and liturgical reform, is particularly instructive at this juncture. James had grafted Episcopalianism onto the Presbyterian polity in the Kirk by retaining the kirk-sessions in the parishes, the presbyteries in the districts and the synods in the regions under the diocesan control of the bishops. He had introduced liturgical innovations to move the Kirk in the direction of Anglicanism. But he had realised the limits to the changes he could effect when confronted by concerted Scottish opposition in Kirk and state. Charles sought to eradicate Presbyterianism from the Kirk. He promoted liturgical innovations along Anglican lines, which were handled in such an authoritarian manner that they left him and Laud open to charges of insinuating Roman Catholicism. He was not prepared to

---

[33] *RPCS*, second series, IV, pp. 56–7; A. I. Macinnes, *Charles I and the Making of the Covenanting Movement, 1625–41* (Edinburgh 1991 and 2003), pp. 108–17.

countenance any expressions of Scottish dissent through constitutional assemblies or grass-roots petitioning from the parishes and presbyteries. Charles I's unbending endorsement of British uniformity provoked the National Covenant of 1638, which offered a radical Scottish corrective to imperial monarchy and led to the replacement of regal by federative union.[34]

Confession confederation

The National Covenant, which bound the Scottish people by social compact to justify and consolidate revolt against Britannic monarchy, was an important political milestone in seventeenth-century Anglo-Scottish relations for three reasons. Firstly, it established a written constitution that was not concerned with the details of how power should be exercised or who should fill offices or places on councils and committees. Instead, priority was accorded to parliamentary supremacy within the fundamental context of a religious and constitutional compact between God, king and people. Secondly, its clear distinction between the office of the monarch and the person of the king sustained loyalty to the house of Stuart but not necessarily to Charles I. Thirdly, Buchanan's anti-imperial notions of an aristocratic republic were given force by the most radical aspect of the National Covenant – the oath of allegiance and mutual association. This oath was a positive act of defiance in reserving loyalty for a covenanted king – that is, one who accepted the contractual nature of his rule. In so far as the king was to accept the religious and constitutional imperatives of the National Covenant, then he was to be defended. The oath further upheld the corporate right of the people to resist a lawful king who threatened to become tyrannical. Such resistance was to be exercised by the natural leaders of society: not the nobles exclusively but the Tables – the revolutionary organisation promoting the Covenanting Movement – as the corporate embodiment of the divinely warranted custodians of the national interest. Each political estate constituted a legislative Table with an executive fifth Table, dominated by the nobility but including representatives from the gentry, burgesses and clergy: a governmental structure that operated in an oligarchic rather than aristocratic manner in exacting unprecedented demands for ideological conformity, financial supply and military recruitment.[35]

[34] A. R. MacDonald, *The Jacobean Kirk, 1567–1625: Sovereignty, Polity and Liturgy* (Aldershot, 1998), pp. 179–87; Macinnes, *The British Revolution*, pp. 74–110.
[35] *APS*, v, pp. 272–6; D. Stevenson, *The Covenanters: The National Covenant and Scotland* (Edinburgh, 1988), pp. 35–44; A. I. Macinnes, 'Covenanting Ideology in

A general assembly of the Kirk, authorised by Charles I but rigorously managed by the Tables, had abolished episcopacy by the close of 1638. Simultaneously, the Tables had encouraged the return of veterans of the Thirty Years' War, primarily in the service of Sweden and the United Provinces, to provide a professional backbone for the Covenanting army raised by subscription and funded by national levies of taxation. After an inconclusive First Bishops' War fought within Scotland in 1639, the fifth Table, now reconstituted as the Committee of Estates by a Covenanter parliament, won the Second Bishops' War of 1640 by invading the north of England, defeating the Royalist forces of Charles I at Newburn and occupying the counties of Northumberland and Durham. The Covenanting stranglehold on the coal supply from Newcastle to London pressurised Charles I into suing for peace.[36] Prior to the invasion of England, the Covenanter parliament instituted a constitutional revolution in the state to complement the abolition of episcopacy in the Kirk. Indeed, this revolution demonstrated the political vitality of the Scottish Estates in a comparative European context. The clerical estate in parliament was abolished and the gentry had their voting powers effectively doubled. Instead of one composite vote being cast for each shire, gentry summoned as shire commissioners were accorded the same individual voting rights enjoyed by the nobles and burgesses. Subscription to the National Covenant was made compulsory for all holding public office. The committee of articles, which the early Stuarts had used to manage parliamentary proceedings and constrict discussions on controversial topics, was declared an optional procedure. If deployed, it was to be elected by and answerable to the reconstituted three estates. A Triennial Act specified that parliament should meet every three years regardless of a royal summons. The scope of treason was extended to cover all who advised or assisted policies destructive of the Covenanting Movement.[37]

Seventeenth-Century Scotland' in Ohlmeyer, ed., *Political Thought in Seventeenth-Century Ireland*, pp. 191–220. Given the Covenant's clear distinction between the royal office and the person of the king, the Covenanters found no necessary incompatibility in promising to defend royal authority in the abstract while simultaneously promoting policies contrary to the professed interests and intentions of the man, Charles I. Hence the paradox: resistance to Charles the man was in the long-term interests of monarchy and people, a necessary curative if the kingdom were to be restored to godly rule.

[36] A. Grosjean, *An Unofficial Alliance: Scotland and Sweden, 1569–1654* (Leiden, 2003), pp. 165–90; J. Scally, 'Counsel in Crisis: James, Third Marquis of Hamilton and the Bishops' Wars, 1638–1640' in J. R. Young, ed., *Celtic Dimensions of the British Civil Wars* (Edinburgh, 1997), pp. 18–34; S. Murdoch, 'Scotland, Scandinavia and the Bishops' Wars, 1638–40' in Macinnes & Ohlmeyer, eds., *The Stuart Kingdoms*, pp. 113–34.

[37] J. R. Young, 'The Scottish Parliament in the Seventeenth Century: European Perspectives' in *Ships, Guns and Bibles*, pp. 139–72.

The Covenanters were not content with constitutional revolution in Scotland, however. As victors in the Bishops' Wars, they insisted that Charles summon an English parliament to guarantee the maintenance of a negotiated peace. At the same time, the summoning of what became known as the Long Parliament provided a forum for the airing of English grievances and the calling of Charles I's rule by prerogative to account. From the outset of the peace negotiations, which commenced in Ripon, Yorkshire, in October 1640 and concluded in London ten months later, the Covenanting Movement was able to retain the political initiative in Britain, which they had first asserted in 1638. Central to this Scottish Moment was a programme of confessional confederation to establish a godly monarchy in association with godly commonwealths in all three Stuart kingdoms.[38]

In their negotiations for the Treaty of London, unity in religion and uniformity in church government were seemingly accorded priority by the Covenanters. However, the main thrust of their remit was to strengthen the bond of union between both kingdoms professed since the first sustained appeal to British public opinion in the prelude to the Bishops' Wars. A lasting alliance was to be secured by a defensive and offensive league between Scotland and England – that is, by confederation, not incorporating parliamentary union. The only institutional innovation was to be the appointment of parliamentary commissioners in both kingdoms, charged to conserve the peace and redress any breaches in the intervals between parliaments. In ratifying the Treaty, the Long Parliament reserved its right to determine the nature of the English Reformation, but duly conceded that the waging of war and the stopping of trade within the king's dominions required parliamentary approval in both countries. Charles I assented formally to the Long Parliament's recognition of the sovereign and independent power of the Scottish Estates as a 'free parliament', the first English recognition of Scotland as an independent nation since the treaty of Northampton of 1328, which had concluded the first phase of the Scottish Wars of Independence. More immediately, the spectre of provincialism that had haunted Scotland since the regal union was laid to rest.[39] The Covenanters were not exclusively concerned with such a bipartisan approach. At the same time as the Scottish commissioners were presenting their proposals for union to their English counterparts, the Covenanting leadership was actively, but fruitlessly, promoting an

---

[38] A. I. Macinnes, 'The Scottish Moment, 1638–1645' in J. Adamson, ed., *The Civil Wars: Rebellion and Revolution in the Kingdoms of Charles I* (London, 2007) forthcoming.
[39] Levack, *The Formation of the British State*, pp. 110, 130–1; C. L. Hamilton, 'The Anglo-Scottish Negotiations of 1640–41', *SHR*, 41 (1962), pp. 84–6.

expanded confederation that would involve initially the United Provinces and then Sweden.[40]

The conclusion of the Treaty of London also afforded the Covenanters time to conclude the constitutional revolution instigated in 1640. Accordingly, at a recalled parliament in the autumn of 1641, the Scottish Estates secured an effective veto over the executive and judiciary when Charles I, then attending in person, gave a binding commitment that officers of state, privy councillors and judges would henceforth be chosen with their advice and consent. Charles was thus obliged to accept permanent restrictions on the royal prerogative that fulfilled his own prophecy, in the spring of 1638, that the triumph of the Covenanting Movement would leave him no more power than the Doge of Venice: a situation subsequently rationalised by the Scottish ideologue Samuel Rutherford in *Lex Rex* (1644).[41] Political power was now firmly exercised by a radical mainstream within the Covenanting Movement led by Archibald Campbell, Marquess of Argyll, with a conservative grouping coalescing pragmatically around James Hamilton, 3rd Marquess (later 1st Duke) of Hamilton. The outbreak of Irish rebellion in October 1641, and the descent to civil war between Royalists and Parliamentarians in England by August 1642, caused tension between radical and conservative Covenanters. Having already committed themselves to military engagement in Ireland from the spring of 1643, Argyll and the radicals promoted further intervention on the side of the Parliamentarians while Hamilton and the conservatives held out for aid to the Royalists. Radical control over the executive committees as well as the Estates ensured that a formal alliance with the English parliament was cemented by the Solemn League and Covenant of 1643 and followed up by military engagement in England from January 1644.[42]

---

[40] J. R. Young, 'The Scottish Parliament and European Diplomacy 1641–47: The Palatine, the Dutch Republic and Sweden' in S. Murdoch, ed., *Scotland and the Thirty Years' War, 1618–1648* (Leiden, 2001), pp. 77–106; Grosjean, *An Unofficial Alliance*, pp. 200–10.

[41] J. R. Young, *The Scottish Parliament 1639–1661: A Political and Constitutional Analysis* (Edinburgh, 1996), pp. 30–53; Gilbert Burnet, *The Memoirs of the Lives and Actions of James and William, Dukes of Hamilton and Castleherald* (London, 1838), pp. 46, 184–7; Samuel Rutherford, *Lex Rex or the Law and the Prince* (Edinburgh, 1848), pp. 56, 143–8, 199.

[42] A. Woolrych, *Britain in Revolution, 1625–1660* (Oxford, 2002), pp. 268–95; Young, *The Scottish Parliament*, pp. 54–70; A. I. Macinnes, 'The Scottish Constitution, 1638–1651: The Rise and Fall of Oligarchic Centralism' in J. Morrill, ed., *The Scottish National Covenant in its British Context, 1638–51* (Edinburgh, 1990), pp. 106–34. John Pym (*A Most Learned and Religious Speech spoken by Mr. Pym, at a Conference of both Houses of Parliament the 23 of . . . September. Declaring unto them the Necessity and Benefit of the Union of his Majesties three kingdomes, England, Scotland, and Ireland in matters of Religion and Church-Government* (London, 1642)) was instrumental in pushing for a military and religious

In promoting confederation for Britain, the Covenanters were adopting their Scottish perspective to the confrontations between the Austrian Habsburgs and the constituent assemblies within the Holy Roman Empire. The reinvigoration of confederation for confessional and constitutional purposes by Protestant Estates was attempted first in Moravia, Austria and Hungary against imperial power in 1608, then in Bohemia, Moravia, Silesia and the two Lusatias against territorial integration in 1619. It was within this international context that the Solemn League and Covenant was welcomed in England, having already been endorsed by the Protestants of Zealand, as 'a seasonable engagement'.[43] However, the association of a solemn league with a perpetual confederation had been explicitly laid out in the incorporating articles of the United Colonies of New England, subscribed by four Puritan plantations for common defence against the Dutch, the French and the Indians in May 1643 – three months before the Anglo-Scottish treaty. Despite a common tradition of providential banding by English Puritans and Scottish Presbyterians, any ideological connection between the confederal formulations for New England and for Britain was purely coincidental. But this transatlantic context, which allowed greater scope for congregational autonomy, was more suited to the mix of Presbyterians and Independents that characterised the English Parliamentarians and more readily adaptable to a Gothic perspective.[44]

Notwithstanding the political incompatibilities soon magnified on the battlefield and in government between the Scottish and the Gothic perspectives, the Covenanting leadership was certainly determined to accomplish a federative, not a federalist,[45] reconfiguration of the

---

alliance with the Scottish Covenanters that opened up the prospect of confederal and confessional union. In order to revitalise Britannic monarchy, prevent further recourse to war within the British Isles and resolve the Irish situation through closer association with England, Henry Parker (*The Generall Junto, or The Councell of Union: chosen equally out of England, Scotland and Ireland, for the Better Compacting of Three Nations into One Monarchy* (London, 1642)) was arguing for a confederal executive or 'general junto' drawn equally out of the three kingdoms.

[43] G. Schramm, 'Armed Conflict in East-Central Europe: Protestant Noble Opposition and Catholic Royalist Factions, 1604–20', and I. Auerbach, 'The Bohemian Opposition, Poland-Lithuania, and the Outbreak of the Thirty Years War', successively in R. J. W. Evans & T. V. Thomas, eds., *Crown, Church and Estates: Central European Politics in the Sixteenth and Seventeenth Centuries* (London, 1991), pp. 176–225; Edward Bowles, *The Mysterie of Iniquity, Yet Working in the Kingdomes of England, Scotland, and Ireland, for the Destruction of Religion Truly Protestant* (London, 1643).

[44] *The Journal of John Winthrop, 1630–1649*, ed. R. S. Dunn, J. Savage & L. Yeandle (Cambridge, MA, 1996), pp. 429–40; E. Vallance, *Revolutionary England and the National Covenant: State Oaths, Protestantism and the Political Nation, 1553–1682* (Woodbridge, 2005), pp. 102–29.

[45] D. Stevenson, 'The Early Covenanters and the Federal Union of Britain' in Mason, *Scotland and England, 1286–1815*, pp. 163–81; M. Lee Jr, 'Scotland, the Union and the

three kingdoms. In effect, the Solemn League promoted confessional confederation to achieve common spiritual and material aims while maintaining distinctive national structures in Church and state. Confederal union was to replace regal union. The right to resist the Crown was specifically exported in Clause 3, which incorporated the Covenanting oath of allegiance and mutual association.[46] Although the export of Covenanting ideology from Scotland was characterised by the language of religious revelation, negotiations had been founded and were welcomed primarily on the grounds of political pragmatism and military experience. Thus, the Solemn League and Covenant signposted a British confederal commitment to war not just among, but for, the three kingdoms.[47]

Tensions among English Parliamentarians over the Scottish alliance were partly checked so long as the Covenanting army contributed to the winning of the war against the Royalists, most notably in the combined victory at Marston Moor, Yorkshire, in July 1644. But tensions were also partly inflamed by the key role of the Scots in the Committee for Both Kingdoms, which co-ordinated the war effort against the Royalists, channelled political dealings between the Covenanters and the Parliamentarians, and secured international recognition for British confederation. The latter task was achieved by the diplomatic projection of the Committee as 'Concilium Amborum Magnae Britanniae'. The Committee, which was the one British institution to arise out of the Solemn League and Covenant, widened the fault lines between the Scottish and the Gothic perspectives. Operating from February 1644 until October 1646, the Committee was viewed within Parliamentary circles as an executive agency. But final decisions on the making of war and peace were never ceded to it. To effectively carry out its diplomatic functions and oversee the war effort by land and sea, against not only the English Royalists in England but also the Irish rebels now constituted as the Catholic Confederation, the Committee would have needed to operate as a federal

---

Idea of a General Crisis' in Mason, ed., *Scots and Britons*, pp. 41–87; K. M. Brown, *Kingdom or Province*, pp. 81–3; J. Morrill, 'The Britishness of the English Revolution, 1640–1660' in R. G. Asch, ed., *Three Nations – A Common History? England, Scotland, Ireland & British History, c. 1600–1920* (Bochum, 1920), pp. 83–115. Federalism did not feature in contemporary British political vocabulary until the debates on union in the reign of Queen Anne.

[46] *APS*, VI (i) (1641–7), pp. 41–3, 47–9; J. Coffey, 'Samuel Rutherford and the Political Thought of the Scottish Covenanters' in Young, ed., *Celtic Dimensions*, pp. 75–95.

[47] J. G. A. Pocock, 'The Atlantic Archipelago and the War of the Three Kingdoms' in Bradshaw & Morrill, eds., *The British Problem*, pp. 184–9; E. J. Cowan, 'The Solemn League and Covenant' in Mason, ed., *Scotland and England, 1286–1815*, pp. 182–202.

executive: not a step contemplated by the Long Parliament. For their part, the Covenanting leadership viewed the Committee as a co-ordinating confederal council, the prime but not the sole agency for preserving the interests of Scotland in the management of the affairs of both kingdoms.[48]

The Covenanting army of intervention remained the largest in the field in Parliamentary service. Furthermore, Scotland effectively expanded its territorial bounds to an unprecedented extent through the Covenanting armies of occupation, south from the Tweed to the Tees and on to the Humber and west from the Solway Firth to Lough Neagh. This expansion, which was the greatest by any army prior to the Cromwellian occupations of Ireland and Scotland in 1649–51, provoked genuine if unfounded fears of Scottish imperialism in both England and Ireland throughout the 1640s.[49] However, the Parliamentary forces, regrouped from 1645 under the New Model Army in which Oliver Cromwell was a prominent commander, began to defeat Royalist forces. The decisive Parliamentary victory at Naseby, Northamptonshire, in June 1645 instigated the break-up of British confederation, which was compounded in May 1646, when Charles I walked into the Scottish camp at Newark-on-Trent to become an unwanted detainee. Political tensions between Covenanters and Parliamentarians were further aggravated when the Scots, on withdrawing from England, handed over Charles at Newcastle for a transfer fee of £400,000 in January 1647.

Britannic engagement

Civil war between Royalists and Covenanters within Scotland had been concluded on the battlefield to the advantage of the latter at Philiphaugh, Selkirkshire, in September 1645. The radical Covenanters led by Argyll had insisted upon purging nobles and other conservatives tainted with Royalist sympathies from public office in 1646. At the same time, Argyll steadfastly maintained that Covenanters and Parliamentarians should maintain British unity based on confederation. The sale of the king, however, revived the conservative element under Hamilton. Bolstered by the move of John Maitland, 2nd Earl (later Duke) of Lauderdale, from the

---

[48] J. Adamson, 'The Triumph of Oligarchy: The Management of War and the Committee of Both Kingdoms, 1644–1645' in C. R. Kyle & J. Peacey, eds., *Parliament at Work: Parliamentary Committees, Political Power & Public Access in Early Modern England* (Woodbridge, 2002), pp. 101–27; Macinnes, *The British Revolution*, pp. 152–73.

[49] M. Perceval-Maxwell, 'Ireland and Scotland 1638–1648' in Morrill, ed., *The Scottish National Covenant*, pp. 193–211; D. Scott, *Politics and War in the Three Stuart Kingdoms, 1637–49* (Basingstoke, 2004), pp. 68–129.

radical caucus, the conservatives covertly concluded with Charles I, then imprisoned on the Isle of Wight, the Engagement to defend and restore the authority of Britannic monarchy, in December 1647. The Britannic Engagement, which was the first Scottish-instigated effort to promote incorporating union, linked political restoration to commercial recovery. The Engagers consciously endeavoured to accomplish the 'complete union of the kingdoms' which James I had initiated in 1604. Charles was not obliged to subscribe to the Covenants, and Presbyterianism was to be imposed on England for no more than a trial period of three years. The Engagement not only conceded that the Covenanting Movement had lost the political initiative within the British Isles, but also represented a reactionary effort to reassert aristocratic dominance over Scottish affairs. Scottish Royalists, who castigated the venture as a Tory or bandit endeavour, withheld their support. Oliver Cromwell terminated the ensuing and disastrous armed intervention in England, at Preston, Lancashire, in September 1648. Once the news of Preston filtered back to Scotland, the radicals in western districts staged a successful revolt, which commenced with the Whiggamore Raid on Edinburgh and, with the support of Oliver Cromwell, culminated in the exclusion of the Engagers from public office. The intentions of Argyll and his supporters to initiate a radical programme of social restructuring was overtaken by news of the execution of Charles I on 30 January 1649, a unilateral act by Cromwell and his fellow regicides.[50]

The Covenanters' proclamation of Charles II, not just as King of Scots but as King of Great Britain, on 5 February, was a reassertion of the international identity of the house of Stuart within the context of confederal union. However, this proclamation and the subsequent opening up of negotiations in March with Charles II, then in exile at Breda in the United Provinces, for his return as a covenanted monarch were also unilateral acts that provoked profound indignation in England, where Charles II was deemed only as King of Scots. The Gothic free state was proclaimed internationally on 14 May as the English Commonwealth (*Res Publica Anglicae*), untrammelled by any bilateral commitment to the Solemn League and Covenant that the Scots had breached by their Britannic Engagement. Damaging splits within the Covenanting Movement, not only between radicals and conservatives, but also among radicals on the issue of the trustworthiness of Charles II, enabled Cromwell

---

[50] *A Source Book of Scottish History*, III, pp. 134–9; J. Scally, 'Constitutional Revolution, Party and Faction in the Scottish Parliaments of Charles I' in C. Jones, ed., *The Scots and Parliament* (Edinburgh, 1996), pp. 54–73; A. I. Macinnes, 'The First Scottish Tories?' *SHR*, 67 (1988), pp. 56–66; Young, *The Scottish Parliament*, pp. 189–227.

to occupy Scotland south of the Forth–Clyde after the battle of Dunbar, East Lothian, on 3 September 1650. This battle, in which the Covenanters snatched defeat from the jaws of victory, caused a profound shock to radicals and conservatives alike, which not only questioned the godliness of the Covenanting cause but inculcated a sense of defeatism that reverberated to the Union of 1707 and beyond. The Scottish Moment in British politics was well and truly over.[51]

A patriotic accommodation of radicals, former Engagers and Royalists was consolidated in fundamentalist terms by the coronation of Charles II at Scone, Perthshire, as King of Great Britain and Ireland on 1 January 1651. However, the erroneous British military strategy of the new king, who pushed for further Scottish intervention in England without assurances of support from Presbyterians and Royalists disaffected with the Commonwealth, came to grief at Worcester on 3 September 1651. Scottish independence was fatally undermined, albeit the Cromwellian occupation of the whole country took another twelve months to complete. The incorporation of Scotland within the English Commonwealth laid to rest any prospect of a Britain united by confessional confederation, as pursued from a Scottish perspective, or by an Engagement consistent with a Britannic perspective.[52]

Imposed incorporation

The separate incorporations of first Ireland and then Scotland with England did not create a triple alliance of equal states. Although this incorporative process lacked formal parliamentary warrant other than for two years between April 1657 and May 1659, the prevailing Gothic perspective was marked by a desire to reach an accommodation that would appease distinctive religious and civic traditions. Notwithstanding Cromwell's personal vexation that Scotland remained attached to the exiled Stuart dynasty, Scotland, unlike Ireland, was not annexed to the Commonwealth. Consent was sought through the tender of incorporation. Commissioners from the English parliament – that is, from the rump not purged by the regicides – and from the occupying army, who were charged to order and manage the affairs of Scotland, arrived

---

[51] Woolrych, *Britain in Revolution, 1625–1660*, pp. 480–501; Macinnes, *The British Revolution*, pp. 184–92. I am indebted for this suggestion on the long-term impact of Dunbar to my former tutor, the late Dr Ronald G. Cant, Reader in Scottish History, St Andrew's University.

[52] *The Covenants and the Covenanters*, ed. J. Kerr (Edinburgh, 1896), pp. 348–98; D. Stevenson, *Revolution and Counter-Revolution in Scotland, 1644–1651* (London, 1977), pp. 180–210.

in January 1652. The English commissioners instructed the constituent shires and royal burghs of Scotland to elect two deputies to come to Dalkeith to give their assent to Union prior to their formal subscription of the tender at Edinburgh by March.[53] The Scottish deputies were certainly not negotiating from a position of equality. Yet these proceedings were not simply the imposition of an English settlement.[54]

Notwithstanding the reassertion of antiquarian Gothic claims for hegemony over Scotland, the English commissioners soon abandoned that aspect of their remit that required that the laws of England be put into execution in Scotland as in Wales and Ireland. Moreover, the authorisation granted to the Scottish deputies, as 'persons of integritie and good affection to the wealfaire and peace of this Island', allowed for a measure of latitude. Thus, the deputies for the shires of Argyll, Midlothian and Selkirk were instructed to 'treat, reason and debate, but not to conclude' until they reported back their proceedings at Dalkeith. This reservation of final consent to Union duly affected the formal subscription of the tender of incorporation at Edinburgh.[55] In the event, less than half the shires and burghs fully subscribed to the process of Scottish incorporation into the Commonwealth. Albeit delayed by storms in reaching Edinburgh, the deputies for Orkney and Shetland were mandated to support incorporation. Recently annexed to the Scottish Crown by James I,

---

[53] BL, Collection of Historical and Parliamentary Papers 1620–60, Egerton MS 1048, fols. 142–8; Woolrych, *Britain in Revolution, 1625–1660*, pp. 500–1, 552–3, 567–73, 589–92; Macinnes, *The British Revolution*, pp. 199–205. Some Independents antipathetic to Scottish interests, and particularly wary that free trade would favour Scottish salt to the prejudice of the salt works on the Tyne, did suggest that precedence after England be accorded to Ireland, which was reputedly the better country and had been planted chiefly by the English.

[54] F. D. Dow, *Cromwellian Scotland, 1651–1660* (Edinburgh, 1979), pp. 30–6; K. M. Brown, *Kingdom or Province*, pp. 136–7. As the military balance swung in favour of the Commonwealth during the first Anglo-Dutch war of 1652–4, original English schemes for a union with the United Provinces based on a federation of equals gave way to plans for incorporation in which the Dutch were to be offered similar terms to the Scots (S. Pincus, *Protestantism and Patriotism: Ideologies and the Making of English Foreign Policy, 1650–1668* (Cambridge, 1996), pp. 51–79).

[55] DH, Loudoun Papers, bundle A15/2; ICA, Argyll Papers, bundles 13/18; NAS, Breadalbane Collection, GD 112/1/568; Anon., *The Antiquity of Englands Superiority over Scotland and The Equity of Incorporating Scotland or other Conquered Nations, into the Commonwealth of England* (London, 1652). Of the thirty-one Scottish shires, twenty-eight sent deputies to assent to Union at Dalkeith, but only twenty sent deputies to Edinburgh to subscribe the tender. No more than fifteen deputies signed the commission for twenty-one deputies (fourteen from the shires, seven from the burghs) to continue detailed negotiations at Westminster between October 1652 and April 1653. Of the fifty-eight royal burghs, forty-four sent deputies to Dalkeith, but only thirty-seven were represented at Edinburgh, where thirty-four deputies actually subscribed the tender. Only twenty-five signed the commission for the deputies to Westminster.

the northern isles were nonetheless insistent that Scottish law must be maintained within the Union. Conversely, only three shires (Renfrew, Ayr and Kirkcudbright) and three burghs (Renfrew, Ayr and Irvine) from the radical Covenanting south-west made no effort to participate in the process. For the majority of Scottish deputies who complied, their position varied from de facto acceptance to conditional acquiescence that reserved prior commitment to the Covenants. The twenty-one deputies summoned to England for further negotiations complied only after express permission had been attained from the exiled Charles II now back in the United Provinces.[56]

The deputies who attended at Westminster were made initially to feel as much supplicants as negotiators in their dealings with the English committee on Union. Leading politicians and army officers, most notably Lord General Oliver Cromwell, supplemented this committee, which included most of the leading commissioners sent to Scotland. Although they lacked the parity accorded in negotiating the Solemn League and Covenant, the Scots in the course of the negotiations duly gained a measure of recognition for their standing, not as political clients from a dependent state, but as junior partners in union. The desire of the deputies to be constituted as a standing committee for Scottish affairs was not conceded. Nevertheless, they did succeed in retaining Scots law unscathed – a situation unchanged by the advent of the Protectorate in 1654; but they were not able to establish that sixty MPs should represent Scotland in the reconstituted 'Rump Parliament'. Extensive consideration was given to their argument that the proportion of Scottish MPs should not be based solely on the monthly assessment or cess, but should take into account relative populations and their parochial distribution. The deputies' argument that proportional assessment should not be the sole basis for Scottish representation, while England continued with a traditional electoral system that over-represented Cornwall and under-represented Hereford, was accepted. Electoral standardisation throughout the Commonwealth followed. The end result was that Scotland, like

---

[56] HL, Loudoun Scottish Collection, box 32, LO 9054; BL, Hardwicke Papers, vol. DXVI, Add.MSS 35,864, fols.1–12; *Scotland and the Commonwealth 1651–53*, ed. C. H. Firth (Edinburgh, 1895), pp. 15–185. The absence of some deputies was explicable by illness, and special allowance was sought for the absence of deputies from small coastal burghs engaged in the herring fishing. Special pleading was also undertaken for smaller shires remote from Edinburgh which usually sent only one commissioner to the Scottish parliament, and likewise for smaller and distant burghs. The deputies sent to England were also mandated to pursue an equitable reduction and redistribution of the common burdens of the kingdom.

Ireland, was to be represented by thirty MPs, a proportion determined by assessment and population.[57]

Tensions between the army and the Rump Parliament led to the latter's replacement by the Nominated or 'Barebones Parliament' in April 1653, just after the committee on Union had concluded business. Only two of the twenty-one deputies were among the five Scottish nominees to a parliament that lasted nine months before further pressure from the army led to Cromwell assuming executive power as Lord Protector. Although the union of Scotland and Ireland with England did receive legislative sanction under an ordinance of the Protectorate in April 1654, another three years were to elapse before the union was embedded in statute. Only twenty-one constituencies actually returned members to serve for Scotland in September 1654, of whom nine were non-Scottish military or civil administrators.[58]

Active collaboration with the Cromwellian regime, though marginally more evident than in Ireland, was confined to a radical handful. They provided a minority Scottish presence on the Commission for the Administration of Justice, which had replaced the English commissioners as the civil government of Scotland from April 1652, and, subsequently, on the devolved Scottish Council instituted under the Protectorate in May 1655. Nevertheless, the majority of Covenanters, like former Engagers and Royalists, remained as opposed to the Protectorate as they had been to the Commonwealth, which they had resolutely refused to serve as either deputies or MPs. Indeed, the Scottish deputies, prior to the conclusion of their negotiations in April 1653, had attested that there were several assemblies, in Edinburgh and elsewhere in Scotland, of disaffected

---

[57] PRO, Anglo-Scottish Committee of Parliament appointed to confer with the deputies from Scotland: minute book, 1652, October 14 – 1653, April 8, SP 25/138, pp. 3–64; BL, Letters and State Papers: Birch Collection, Add.MSS 4158, fols. 101–3; *The Cromwellian Union 1651–52*, ed. C. S. Terry (Edinburgh, 1902), pp. 11–184. Although English dominance with 400 MPs was not endangered, the quorum of 60 proposed for the reconstituted 'Rump Parliament' technically allowed parliament to function without English MPs. Despite a proportional basis of representation being decided, the actual distribution of Scottish seats was not settled until June 1654, when the Scottish shires were grouped to provide twenty constituencies, and the burghs grouped into ten.

[58] Young, *The Scottish Parliament*, pp. 297–303; TFA, Papers, TD 3758–60; BL, Maitland and Lauderdale Papers, 1532–1688, Add.MSS 35,125, fo. 54. The Scottish MPs were rigorously vetted to ensure not only their current loyalty to the Protectorate, but that their past political activity had not been tainted by subscription to the Britannic Engagement. While a full complement of thirty MPs was returned at the next election in 1656, only fourteen constituencies were actually represented by Scots. Following the death of Oliver Cromwell in 1658, the election to the parliament called by his son Richard in 1659 returned another full complement. Merely ten were Scots, including the Marquess of Argyll who managed to get himself elected for Aberdeenshire despite the endeavours of the occupying forces to ensure only the return of pliable placemen.

persons, intent on 'keeping off the hearts of the people of Scotland from this Union'. The deliberate avoidance of 'Great Britain' for this incorporation denoted not only a chauvinistic disregard for traditional Scottish defences against English overlordship, but an emphatic Gothic rejection of both the Stuart vision of Britannic Empire and the Scottish confederal conception of a kingdom united by covenanting. In essence, the Commonwealth and Protectorate were labels of convenience for the concentration of power that reasserted England's intrusive hegemony in the guise of republicanism.[59]

With the Protectorate having imploded following the death of Oliver Cromwell in September 1658, the Restoration of Charles II in May 1660 formally concluded the Cromwellian precedent for political incorporation. However, the return to regal union did not bring an end to federative and incorporative projects for uniting Scotland and England.

---

[59] PRO, Anglo-Scottish Committee of Parliament, SP 25/138, pp. 62–3; DH, Loudoun Deeds, bundle 2/6; A. H. Williamson, 'Union with England Traditional, Union with England Radical: Sir James Hope and the Mid-Seventeenth Century British State', *EHR*, 110 (1995), pp. 303–12; D. Hirst, 'The English Republic and the Meaning of Britain' in Bradshaw & Morrill, eds., *The British Problem*, pp. 192–219.

4 Projects 1661–1703

Formally restored to independence in 1660, Scotland continued to operate as a junior political partner to England, albeit with greater participation of Scots in the process of government than in the 1650s. The Scottish Council at Whitehall, a devolved committee of the English Privy Council, demarcated Scotland's provincial standing while serving as a channel for the constitutional settlement in Scotland to follow English practice. Though not immediately required by Charles II, Presbyterianism was duly abandoned in favour of Episcopalianism. Notwithstanding the duplicitous dealings of leading clerics to secure themselves bishoprics, the driving force behind this change to the religious establishment was the Scottish nobility, led by former Britannic Engagers such as the future Duke of Lauderdale. Their dominance in the revived Scottish Privy Council was fortified by unflinching support from the restored judiciary. Although Lauderdale was not the foremost political influence within Scotland at the outset of the Restoration, he soon turned the mendacity, venality and chicanery rampant throughout the regime to his personal advantage. His ascendancy, which terminated the Scottish Council, led to his personal exercise of provincial government from 1667. Over the next decade, Scotland again served as a political laboratory. English fears that Lauderdale was using Scotland as a model for absolutism on the cheap were not groundless. Simultaneously, he exploited an exaggerated climate of religious dissent in the Lowlands and social disorder in the Highlands. He built up not only the standing forces but also a militia sustained by cess (as a monthly maintenance) and empowered to quell unrest anywhere within the king's dominions.[1] Within this authoritarian context, Lauderdale's dominance over the Scottish Estates was critical to federative and incorporative overtures for Union, both as political projects and in response to the muscular mercantilism of England and the other

---

[1] HL, Hastings Irish Papers, box 11/HA 14779, 14958, 15993; J. M. Buckroyd, 'Bridging the Gap: Scotland 1659–1660', *SHR*, 66 (1987), pp. 1–25; A. I. Macinnes, 'Repression and Conciliation: The Highland Dimension, 1660–1688', *SHR*, 65 (1986), pp. 167–95.

great European powers during the Restoration era.² The latter factor, as the central issue of political economy, continued to affect British state-formation through to the reign of Queen Anne. However, a unilateral explanation of Union projects between the 1660s and the 1700s, as the Scottish response to a series of trade crises, not only disregards overtures emanating from England, but also underplays the targeted pursuit of colonies by Scots as a commercial alternative to Union, an activity first encouraged by Lauderdale.³

Commercial confederation or political incorporation?

The Restoration of Charles II in 1660 produced constitutional settlements in all three kingdoms, as in his overseas dominions, which revived the Stuarts' *ius imperium* by land and sea. However, the extent to which the Restoration marked a return to Britannic monarchy as an organically inclusive construct for the three constituent kingdoms of the British Isles remains questionable. In particular, the continuing political dominance of England, which was confirmed rather than checked by the Restoration, threatened that Scotland, like Ireland, would become a permanent political satellite. With the Privy Council restored as the king's executive agency of government in England, with the city of London intimately involved in the permanent commissions of Trade and Plantations, and with the restored erastian episcopacy reinforcing the purity of the Anglican Church, the Restoration bolstered the anglocentric appropriation of Britain for England.⁴ Former revolutionaries as well as Royalists asserted the spiritual and temporal supremacy of the English monarchy throughout the British Isles.⁵ Notwithstanding the association of the Gothic perspective with civil war and popular insurrections during the 1640s and 1650s, the imposition of Navigation Acts by the English

---

² G. H. MacIntosh, 'Arise King John: Commissioner Lauderdale and Parliament in the Restoration Era' in K. M. Brown & A. J. Mann, eds., *The History of the Scottish Parliament*, vol. II: *Parliament and Politics in Scotland, 1567–1707* (Edinburgh, 2005), pp. 163–83; R. Lee, 'Retreat from Revolution: The Scottish Parliament and the Restored Monarchy, 1661–1663' in Young, ed., *Celtic Dimensions*, pp. 164–85.
³ M. Goldie, 'Divergence and Union: Scotland and England, 1660–1707' in Bradshaw & Morrill, eds., *The British Problem*, pp. 220–45.
⁴ T. Harris, *Restoration: Charles II and His Kingdoms, 1660–1685* (London, 2005), pp. 43–84, 104–35; R. Hutton, *The Restoration: A Political & Religious History of England and Wales, 1658–1667* (Oxford, 1985), pp. 125–84; Holmes, *The Making of a Great Power*, pp. 27–43.
⁵ William Prynne, *The first tome of an exact chronological vindication and historical demonstration of our British, Roman, Saxon, Danish, Norman, English kings supreme ecclesiastical jurisdiction, in, over all spiritual, or religious affairs, causes, persons, as well as temporal within their realms of England, Scotland, Ireland, and other dominions* (London, 1665); J. Smyth, *The Making of the United Kingdom*, pp. 77–87; N. H. Keeble, *The Restoration: England in the 1660s* (Oxford, 2002), pp. 109–31.

parliament in 1660, 1662–3, 1670–1 and 1673, and the rise of London to global significance, facilitated a Gothic mercantilism as well as further English appropriation, this time of the Britannic Empire by cartographers like Richard Burton (alias Nathaniel Crouch).[6]

Whereas the constitutional situation in England was effectively restored to the situation at the outset of the Long Parliament in 1640–1, all vestiges of the Covenanting Movement were swept away through the Act of Recissory in 1661. Scotland was returned to its constitutional standing at the coronation parliament of 1633. Although no effort was made to reimpose Charles I's liturgical innovations, the oath of allegiance now mandatory for all officeholders replaced the imperative of covenanting with an unreserved commitment to the royal prerogative. The Marquess of Argyll became the most prominent victim among the revolutionary politicians who actually witnessed the Restoration. Following trial and conviction, he was publicly beheaded at Edinburgh in May 1661. At the same time, the Solemn League and Covenant, the high-water mark of confessional confederation, was burned by the common hangman at Westminster and removed from all public places of record and from all churches in England and Wales. Though shorn of its political leadership, the Covenanting cause was not terminated – but it moved from being a movement of power to one of protest. The restoration of episcopacy in Scotland created the most sizeable element of Protestant dissent within the three kingdoms, which was led not just by radical, but by militant, Presbyterians, and sustained by conventicles (clandestine meetings) in house and field.[7]

In reality, restored Stuart rule in the Restoration era represented a compromise between Britannic and Gothic perspectives. The inclusive Britannic perspective of the monarchy was highlighted by the Dutch academic Rutgerius Hermannides, in his *Britannia Magna* of 1661, which nevertheless chronicled English hegemony over Scotland as over Ireland. The German jurist Samuel von Puffendorf, who came to view England as a composite monarchy with Scottish and Irish dependencies, forcibly articulated the exclusive Gothic perspective. Charles II was carrying on the mantle of Oliver Cromwell and his republican regime of the 1650s in maintaining English greatness through overseas dominions and the

---

[6] R[ichard] B[urton] *The English Empire in America: or a prospect of His Majesties dominions in the West-Indies* (London, 1685); John Seller, *Atlas Minimus or a Book of Geography showing all the Empires, Monarchies, Kingdomes, Regions, Dominions, Principalities and Countries in the whole World* (London, 1679); Greenville Collins, *Great Britain's coasting-pilot, being a new and exact survey of the sea-coast of England* (London, 1693).
[7] Macinnes, *The British Revolution, 1629–1660*, pp. 227–35.

promotion of commerce.[8] Yet an alternative Scottish perspective for a federative Britain was not entirely subliminal. The imposition of the English Navigation Acts switched the ongoing debate on Union away from confessional to commercial confederation. Indeed, the supplanting of confessional by commercial politics had been signposted already by a series of confederations – Denmark and the Netherlands in 1649, England and Denmark in 1654 (reaffirmed as Great Britain and Denmark 1661) and England and Sweden in 1658.[9]

Proposals for commercial confederation were instigated from Scotland in 1664. But parliamentary commissioners for both countries (twelve on each side nominated by the king) did not discuss them for four years, and then inconclusively. Negotiations from the outset of 1668, which foundered within six months, were concerned primarily with the termination of discriminatory tariffs not with the equalisation of customs and other fiscal dues. Indeed, the Houses both of Lords and of Commons regarded the negotiations as primarily discussions about balancing trade between England and Scotland. The Scots complained that the Navigation Acts, which denied them free commercial access to England and the American colonies, breached Colvin's Case of 1608. Their apprehensions about being treated as aliens within the dominions of Britannic monarchy ran up against English fears about the competitive edge enjoyed by the Scottish carrying trade, the close Scottish trading links with the Dutch and, above all, the perceived Scottish threat to vested coal and salt interests in the north-east of England. Nevertheless, support for commercial union was also an important power play by Lauderdale to establish his supremacy at Court as adviser on Scottish affairs.[10] His renewed promotion of Union in 1669, but now as political incorporation, and his subsequent wrecking of negotiations between commissioners for both parliaments in 1670, were even more cynical ruses to cover up secret negotiations between Charles II and Louis XIV of France.[11]

---

[8] Rutgerius Hermannides, *Britannia Magna* (Amsterdam, 1661); Samuel [von] Puffendorf, *An Introduction to the History of the Principal Kingdoms and States of Europe* (London, 1699).

[9] BL, Letters and State Papers: Birch Collection, Add.MSS. 4158 fols. 320–8; BL, T. Astle, Historical Collections, Add.MSS. 34,713 fols. 9–18; BL, Nicholas Papers, Egerton MS 2542 fols. 10, 55.

[10] E. Hughes, 'The Negotiations for a Commercial Union between England and Scotland in 1668', *SHR*, 24 (1927), pp. 30–47; BL, Leeds Papers, vol. XVII, Egerton MS 3340 fols. 1–10; HL, Stowe Papers: Temple Papers, STT, Miscellaneous Papers, 174, and STT, Parliamentary Box 3 (7); *JHL*, 12 (1666–75), pp. 161, 177–8; *JHC*, 9 (1667–87), pp. 5, 27, 33.

[11] W. Ferguson, *Scotland's Relations with England*, pp. 153–7; Penicuik, *HUSE*, pp. 78–81.

As a former Britannic Engager, Lauderdale deemed the resurrection of 'as close and strict an union as is possible' a fitting subject for negotiations between the parliaments, so long as the commissioners were appointed by the king in accordance with the English practice of 1604. Political incorporation would, on the one hand, emasculate the English Commons through a unicameral British parliament if necessary, and, on the other, wean Scotland away from commercial association and political sympathy with the Dutch, England's principal mercantilist adversary. The proposals for Union that Lauderdale drew up at Court sought fundamental safeguards for Scots law and the church, even though the re-establishment of episcopacy had been modelled along Anglican lines with little by way of accommodation for dissenting Presbyterians. In return, incorporation required the acceptance of a United Kingdom of Great Britain, commercial integration, fiscal equivalence and truncated Scottish representation – thirty members of parliament in the Commons and twelve (two of whom were to be bishops) in the Lords. Scottish representation, which was deemed proportional to fiscal burdens, consciously followed the precedent established in the parliament summoned by Richard Cromwell in 1658. Sir George MacKenzie of Rosehaugh articulated deep-rooted aversion to these proposals in the Scottish Estates. Yet this future lord advocate was firmly committed to the maintenance of royal authority and the stamping-out of dissent in Kirk and state.[12] The incumbent lord advocate, Sir John Nisbet of Dirleton, was no less resolute in opposing political incorporation during the actual negotiations, claiming that such a fundamental alteration in the constitution was potentially treasonable without a mandate from the Scottish electorate. But widespread antipathies among the Scottish nobility were mollified by selective payment of pensions and other salaries in arrears. Grossly inflated expenses were allowed for the twenty-five members of the estates appointed as parliamentary commissioners.

The 50 commissioners for both parliaments, whose nomination had been left to the king, did not meet until September 1670, four months after Charles II and Louis XIV had subscribed to the secret Treaty of Dover. Lauderdale, as head of the Scottish negotiators, played up to English concerns that European precedents for regal union – notably Portugal with Castille and Navarre with France – had not necessitated political incorporation. By 20 October, he created the stumbling block

---

[12] C. Jackson, *Restoration Scotland, 1660–1690: Royalist Politics, Religion and Ideas* (Woodbridge, 2004), pp. 25–31, 48–59, 82–90; T. Harris, 'Tories and the Rule of Law in the Reign of Charles II', *Seventeenth Century*, 8 (1993), pp. 9–27; W. Ferguson, *The Identity of the Scottish Nation: An Historic Quest* (Edinburgh, 1998), pp. 144–72.

that Scottish civil, criminal and ecclesiastical laws were to remain unaltered. By 1 November, negotiations were wrecked when he contrarily insisted upon equal Scottish representation in the joint parliament.[13] Although overtures for a commercial union emanated from the House of Lords in 1674, Charles II offered no public endorsement. Nor did he make any subsequent effort to revive proposals for incorporation. The Commons remained more concerned about the threat to regal union posed by Lauderdale's empowerment of the Scottish militia to march into England or Ireland.[14]

The colonial alternative

Bilateral discussions having failed to secure access to the English colonies in the Americas and the Indies, Lauderdale procured charters at Court in July 1671, licensing Scottish colonisation of lands then delineated as Georgia and Florida and of the Caribbean island of Dominica. His advocacy of colonialism was no more productive than that of unionism. Yet the Scots preference for colonial engagement was not an entirely fruitless pursuit over the next two decades. In 1681, the Committee for Trade reported to the Scottish Privy Council that the only effective way for the country to cope with mercantilism and growing dependence on English markets was either to seek closer union or to develop overseas colonies. James, Duke of York and Albany (the future James VII & II), had supported political incorporation in 1670. Nevertheless, having established his Court in Edinburgh during his retreat from the Exclusion Crisis in England, he duly authorised Scottish ventures to South Carolina in 1682 and East New Jersey from 1685 (see Chapter 6).[15]

The Exclusion Crisis in England was provoked by the prospect of Charles II being succeeded by his brother James, an avowed convert to Roman Catholicism. Undoubtedly, the Duke of York, both within the British Isles and in the Stuarts' overseas dominions, was committed to

---

[13] *APS*, VII, pp. 552, 565, and VIII, p. 6, c.1; *Journals of Sir John Lauder of Fountainhall with his observations on public affairs and other memoranda, 1665–1676*, ed. D. Crawford (Edinburgh, 1900), pp. 229–30; *The Cromwellian Union, 1651–52*, appendix, pp. 187–224; HL, Stowe Papers: Greville Papers, STG Parliamentary Box 1 (5); HMC, *10th Report, Appendix part iv*, ed. H. C. M. Lyte & F. H. B. Daniell (London, 1887), Lord Braye's MSS, pp. 180–1. There were twenty-five commissioners on each side (Dicey & Rait, *Thoughts on the Union*, pp. 378–80).

[14] BL, Leeds Papers, vol. XVII, Egerton MS 3340 fols. 11–13; *JHC*, 9 (1667–87), p. 307.

[15] NAS, Ogilvie of Inverquharity Papers, W.S., GD 205/40/13/3–4; *Aberdeen Council Letters, 1552–1681*, ed. L. B. Taylor, 6 vols. (Oxford, 1942–61), IV, pp. 152–7; *RPCS*, third series, I, pp. 89, 97–8, 114, 127, 158–9, 173, 182, 271, 315–16, and VII (1681–2), pp. 651–73; HMC, *Appendix to Third Report*, Manuscripts of John Webster, Esquire, advocate in Aberdeen, ed. J. Stuart (London, 1872), p. 421.

an inclusive Britannic agenda. However, his intended use of his prerogative powers to remove penal restrictions on his co-religionists played into the hands of Whigs committed to contractual limitations on monarchy but still fearful of the military threat from Scotland as a backdoor for the French absolutist, Louis XIV.[16] James marked his accession in 1685 by inviting the Scottish Privy Council, rather than the Scottish Estates, to constitute a Commission of Trade, to negotiate with commissioners from its English counterpart for 'the freedom and intercourse of trade and navigation between the tuo kingdoms of Great Britain'. Although the issue was raised in the king's letter to the Scottish parliament in 1686, no negotiations appear to have been held.[17] With his over-riding commitment to securing toleration for Roman Catholicism throughout the British Isles, James soon discovered that there was little political will at the Court, in the Scottish and English Privy Councils, or in both parliaments to sustain his Britannic agenda. This prospect was wholly sundered by the Revolution of 1689–91 when James was replaced by his elder daughter Mary and her husband William of Orange, the Stadholder of the United Provinces.

The Revolution in England can be glorified as a triumph of Gothic constitutionalism and mercantilism: the Anglican ascendancy was confirmed, limited monarchy was consolidated and the Navigation Acts were reasserted comprehensively and exclusively. In Scotland, William of Orange actively encouraged advocacy of an incorporating Union by a Convention of Estates in the spring of 1689. Such Scottish lobbying, ostensibly an ideological mark of Whig solidarity in Britain, was primarily driven by the military threat from Jacobitism that did not abate until 1691. Lobbying for Union effectively served as a device for the overwhelmingly Whiggish Convention to turn itself into a parliament, which had the exclusive power to commission bilateral negotiations. But the raising of the issue of Union did recognise that events in England had effectively committed Scotland to the Revolution to avert war between the kingdoms. Moreover, the debate on union served as an important precedent for the eventual incorporation of 1707 in that it raised issues of securing the succession as well as state-formation. If the succession of

---

[16] HL, Bridgewater & Ellesmere MSS, EL 84,422; Anon., *Britanniae Speculum: or a Short View of the Ancient and Modern State of Great Britain and the adjacent Isles, and of all other the Dominions and Territories, now in the actual possession of His present Sacred Majesty, King Charles II* (London, 1683).

[17] NAS, Supplementary Parliamentary Papers, PA 2/32 fols. 165–6; Jackson, *Restoration Scotland, 1660–1690*, p. 158. James II, in 1686, was prepared to countenance the drawing up of a list of Scottish ships in order that they may be exempt from the English Navigation Acts as requested in former negotiations between both kingdoms in 1668–70 (*RPCS*, third series, XII, p. 90).

William and Mary should be ratified before union, this could limit the prospects of attaining the latter and weaken the negotiating position of the Scots should the English not deem union in their strategic interest. But, if the union was accorded precedence, it suggested Scottish doubts about the legality of the removal of James II in England and left Scotland open to the imposition of provincialism by the force of English arms. Although the Scottish Estates did nominate twenty-four commissioners to treat for union, there was no reciprocal enthusiasm in the English parliament. Lobbying duly ceased when the Convention became a parliament in July 1689.[18]

Of greater constitutional significance was the unshackling of Court control over the Scottish Estates at the Revolution, which was also marked by a secular addition to the country's burgeoning written constitutions. Without recourse to the religious imperatives of covenanting, the Claim of Right, issued by the Convention in April 1689, stressed the fundamental, contractual nature of the Scottish state by deposing James VII rather than following the English fiction of abdication. Giving teeth to the resurgent role of parliament in this reinvigorated Scottish perspective was a group known as 'the Club', drawn mainly from the gentry and burgesses. Looking back to the radical political agenda of 1640–1, the Club was intent on delaying a final constitutional settlement, to ensure permanent and purposeful consultation between the Court and the Scottish Estates. Although the Claim of Right deemed it 'contrary to the inclinations of the generality of the people', episcopacy was not replaced by a Presbyterian establishment in the Kirk until 1690. The abolition of episcopacy, which rescinded the return of the clerical estate to parliament at the Restoration, facilitated the abolition, rather than the modification, of the committee of articles as a managerial tool of the Court. As in 1640, the loss of the clerical estate led to the enhancement of that of the gentry, with additional commissioners being authorised for the larger shires which were to return three or four, rather than just two, commissioners to parliament from 1693. However, neither the Club nor the Convention Parliament reclaimed the main constitutional gain of 1641, when the Scottish Estates secured control over appointments to the executive and judiciary.[19]

In the immediate aftermath of the Revolution Settlement, incorporating union continued to be promoted by a handful of political careerists associated with the Court, most notably Sir James Dalrymple, Master of

---

[18] *An Account of the Proceedings of the Estates in Scotland, 1689–1690*, ed. E. W. H. Balfour-Melville, 2 vols. (Edinburgh, 1954), I, pp. 42, 50–109; *APS*, IX, pp. 9, 20, 60, 68, 71; Bruce, *REC*, pp. 231–2, 235–6; Jackson, *Restoration Scotland, 1660–1690*, pp. 206–8.

[19] *APS*, IX, c.14 p. 152; J. Halliday, 'The Club and the Revolution in Scotland 1689–90', *SHR*, 45 (1966), pp. 143–59; *A Source Book of Scottish History*, III, pp. 200–10.

Stair, who wished to cast off his former association with the regime of James VII. As a secretary of state, he endeavoured to keep Scotland quiescent in order not to detract from William's continental pre-occupations. Stair's stage-managing of the exemplary massacre of a small Jacobite clan – the MacDonalds of Glencoe – in February 1692 was a by-product of this Unionist careerism.[20]

William of Orange had initially encouraged incorporation and was to recommend it on his deathbed. However, he was not prepared to devote the time and energy required to carry the policy through. Colonial issues re-energised the debate on Union, most notably the Darien scheme, carried out under the auspices of the Company of Scotland, trading to Africa and the Indies. William (as sole ruler following the death of Mary at the outset of 1695) had authorised this Scottish commercial venture in principle. But he had conspicuously failed to back it in practice because of rival English commercial concerns in the East as well as the West Indies, and diplomatic pressure from Spain which claimed overlordship of the Panama Isthmus where the colony was planted (see Chapter 7). The political fall-out from Darien was the mobilisation of public opinion within Scotland, by polemic, petition and pulpit, against the Court, which also replayed Scotland's well-honed grievances against England since the Cromwellian occupation of the 1650s. Also targeted were Scottish secretaries of state who had acquiesced in William's discriminatory treatment of the Company of Scotland, notably James Ogilvie, the future Earl of Seafield, and James Johnston of Warriston, the son of the Covenanting radical and Cromwellian collaborator, Archibald Johnston. Mass mobilisation, on a scale unprecedented since the onset of the Covenanting Movement in 1637–8, supplemented by public rioting and the inflammatory bribing of members of the Scottish Estates, imperilled regal union.[21] The clamour for reparations from England and Spain, which was reinforced by petitions from seventeen (over half) of the Scottish shires, but only ten (less than a sixth) of the royal burghs, led to parliamentary addresses to William seeking such measures 'as may vindicate the rights and privileges' of the Company of Scotland. Beyond extending the

---

[20] Dalrymple, *Memoirs of Great Britain and Ireland*, I, pp. 288–9; Riley, *King William and the Scottish Politicians*, pp. 7–8, 27–33, 48–54, 160–2; A. I. Macinnes, 'Slaughter under Trust: Clan Massacres and British State-Formation' in M. Levene & P. Roberts, eds., *The Massacre in History* (Oxford, 1999), pp. 127–48. Stair and his associates briefly raised the issue of union after his culpability for the Massacre of Glencoe was whitewashed by a royal committee of inquiry but upheld by the Scottish Estates (NAS, Hamilton Papers, GD406/1/4063).

[21] NAS: Leven & Melville MSS, GD 26/13/95, /111; Breadalbane Collection, GD 112/39/182/21; Hamilton Papers, GD 406/1/4362; Campbell of Barcaldine Papers, GD 170/641. GCA, Records of the Maxwells of Pollock, T-PM 113/700–02.

duration of the Company's trading privileges and a promise to consider any reasonable plan for repairing Scottish losses, William was not prepared to take remedial action. However, he was prepared to recommend political incorporation. Simultaneously, he exhorted Scots to concentrate on the improvement of their manufactures and native produce as both the surest foundation of foreign trade and the readiest means of rectifying widespread destitution in Scotland.[22]

Political incorporation, initially floated in the House of Lords to assuage English apprehensions about the Company of Scotland in 1695, was revived as a means of placating the Scots at the outset of 1700. English misgivings about the impact of Scottish competition on woollen manufacturing, fishing and the carrying trade were not abated by the Darien fiasco, however. An implacably hostile Commons, in which Sir Edward Seymour stood out for his vitriol about impecunious Scots, rejected union in March. By this juncture, William was facing more formidable opposition from within Scotland. A Country interest had emerged as a confederated opposition, intent on using Darien as a means not of attacking the king directly but of removing the dominance of the Court and English ministries over Scottish affairs.[23] William, 4th Duke of Hamilton, a sympathiser with the exiled Stuarts, was suspected of involvement, but not directly implicated, in the failed plot to assassinate William of Orange at the outset of 1696. He led this incipient political party, having returned to public life during the Darien crisis. Although Hamilton was ambitious for office he was also financially vulnerable. His mother, the Duchess Anne, a formidable and committed Presbyterian through whom the main ducal line of Hamilton descended, had only resigned the title of duke, and had not made over her extensive Scottish estates to her son. Accordingly, he was dependent on the English estates of his wife Elizabeth, sole heiress of Digby Gerard, Lord Gerard of Bromley. Not an orator of distinction, Hamilton had the presence and the dexterity to draw in and reconcile

---

[22] Company of Scotland Trading to Africa and the Indies, *Scotland's right to Caledonia (formerly called Darien) and the legality of the settlement asserted in three several memorials presented to His Majesty in May 1699* (Edinburgh, 1700); *APS*, x, pp. 126, 132, 134 194, 201, 211, 242–8, 251, 254, 257, 282, 339, and appendix pp. 19, 36–41, 43, 73–86; William R., *His Majesties most gracious letter to the Parliament of Scotland* (Edinburgh, 1700). NAS: Hamilton Papers, GD 406/1/4559, /4594, /4637, /4778, /6595; Campbell of Barcaldine MSS, GD 170/641; Leven & Melville MSS, GD 26/13/119.

[23] BL, Papers Relating to Trade etc., Sloane MS 2902, fols. 2–10; NAS, Hamilton Papers, GD 406/1/4440, /4510, /4581, /4583, /6986, /7278, /7281, /7283, /7285, /7288, /7291, /10341; AUL, Duff of Meldrum Collection, MS 2778/12/2/1/2; Crossrigg, *DPP*, pp. 46–56, 70–2; *SC*, pp. 282–3, 349–52; *JHC*, 13 (1699–1702), pp. 236, 267; *Marchmont*, pp. 150–2; *Lords*, new series, IV (1699–1702), pp. 106–7; Riley, *The Union of England and Scotland*, pp. 23–6. Godolphin chaired the select committee in the House of Lords that considered Union at William's behest.

diverse interests. As well as disappointed placemen and colonial adventurers – such as his kinsman John Hamilton, Lord Belhaven and John Hay, 2nd Marquess of Tweeddale – he engaged occasionally with political gadflies such as John Murray, Earl of Tullibardine and future 1st Duke of Atholl. He also aligned constitutional reformers as the radical heirs of the Club and Jacobites, in the guise of Cavaliers, intent on overturning the Revolution Settlement.[24]

Although prone to disaffections by ambitious politicians in pursuit of office and lacking a cohesive programme in its opposition to Union, the Country party was able to project itself internationally as the party for Scotland (*parti d'Ecosse*) and the Patriot party (*parti de la Patrie*).[25] Its capacity to exploit distinctive Scottish grievances was enhanced when, twelve months after their rejection of union, the English parliament passed an Act of Settlement in 1701, which unilaterally prescribed the succession of the house of Hanover, as the nearest surviving Protestant heirs of the Stuarts through James I's daughter, Elizabeth of Bohemia. Following the death of William's designated successor and sister-in-law, Princess Anne of Denmark, the English throne would pass to Sophia, Electress of Hanover (or her son, the future George I). However, on the death of Anne's father, James II, that same year, Louis XIV had immediately proclaimed the exiled king's son as James III. As was recognised at Court where Union remained on the political agenda for the last two years of his reign, there was a distinct possibility at William's own death in 1702 that his last continental pre-occupation, the War of the Spanish Succession, would turn into the War of the British Succession. At the same time, the succession issue was not just further fuel to Anglo-Scottish antipathies. For a Protestant Succession to all three kingdoms of the Britannic monarchy strengthened the negotiating position of the Scottish Estates, particularly those members persuaded by William Seton of Pitmedden that interests of political economy required closer

---

[24] NLS, Saltoun Papers, MS 17498, fo. 73; HL, Loudoun Scottish Collection, box 18/LO 8600, box 20/LO 9532, box 39/LO 92832, and Huntington Manuscripts, Manuscript Newsletters from London to Tamworth (1690–1704), HM 30,659/57–8, /70, /79; NAS, Hamilton Papers, GD 406/1/4552, /4670–1, /4688, /4790, /6506, /7281, /7283, /7288, and Douglas of Strathendry MSS, GD 446/40/2; *LP*, I, pp. 54–6, 72–4; *MSSM*, pp. 112–16, 135–6; Craufurd, *The Lives and Characters*, pp. 245–6. In April 1705, Hamilton was berated by the formidable dowager Duchess of Argyll, Elizabeth Campbell, from the Tollemache family in Lincolnshire, for his failure to support union with England, which had provided him with a wife, estate and two sons (NAS, Hamilton Papers, GD 406/1/7150). In addition to estates in Kent and in Lancashire where he faced accusations from local Quakers for rack-renting (GD 406/1/7158), Hamilton could also lay claim to estates in Ireland and the American colonies that lay under English jurisdiction.

[25] See BL, Papers of Cardinal F. A. Gualterio; Letters of Queen Mary of Modena and the Princess Louisa Maria, 1701–18, Add.MSS 20,293, fols. 16–17.

association with England. Given their demonstrable lack of mercantilist muscle, the Scots seemed more reliant on access to English domestic and colonial markets with the failure of the Darien scheme. Undoubtedly, the Darien fiasco, like that of Dunbar (see Chapter 3) fifty years earlier, contributed to the national sense of defeatism that facilitated political incorporation.[26]

Union rejected?

Notwithstanding the continuing sniping by Seymour and his Tory associates identified with high-church Anglicanism, both the Commons and the Lords were generally receptive to the queen's initial address to parliament in favour of a union that would close Scotland as a back door to England. The queen was authorised to appoint commissioners to treat with the Scots. At the same time, with a Whig majority in the Lords not replicated in the Commons after the English general election in July–August 1702, the influx of Scottish placemen could expedite the management of both Houses by the Court and, in turn, advance the commitment of Marlborough and Godolphin to winning the War of the Spanish Succession.

Anne had marked her accession by replacing the Whig ministry tainted with the diplomatic manoeuvrings over the partitioning of the Spanish Empire in the last years of William, especially as the failure of these manoeuvres committed her to an expensive and extensive war in transatlantic as well as European theatres. The fiscal–military dominance of Godolphin and Marlborough as the *duumvir* (two men of power) was assured through the support of retained Whigs such as William Cavendish, 1st Duke of Devonshire, and Charles Seymour, 6th Duke of Somerset, and Godolphin's assiduous cultivation of Robert Harley as speaker of the House of Commons. Harley, like Marlborough and Godolphin, had a Tory background but was engaged more by managerial than by ideological objectives. Harley was the most convinced that political incorporation was a necessity, from the final years of William of Orange. Nevertheless, there were underlying tensions within the ministry with David Finch, 2nd Earl of Nottingham, and Lawrence Hyde, 1st Earl of Rochester, more committed to Anglicanism than the Revolution Settlement. Together with Seymour, also brought into the ministry, they

---

[26] Armitage, *The Ideological Origins of the British Empire*, pp. 146–69; Anon., *An essay against the transportation and selling of men to the plantations of foreigners with special regard to the manufactories, and other domestick improvements of the kingdom of Scotland* (Edinburgh, 1699); Sir William Seton of Pitmedden, *The Interest of Scotland in three essays* (London, 1700); NAS, Hamilton Papers, GD 406/1/4651, /4666, /4820, /4907, /5018–19, /7419.

were seemingly intent on questioning Marlborourgh's preference for a European theatre and Godolphin's stewardship of the financial resources at the disposal of the English state. However, the English ministry was then undoubtedly committed to prosecuting to a successful conclusion the war against Louis XIV of France.[27]

But this commitment provoked further political dissent in Scotland, as the English ministry was instrumental in not having the Scottish Estates summoned to confirm the accession of Queen Anne until the far more pliable Scottish Privy Council had agreed to commit to England against France. When the Scottish Estates did meet in June, three months rather than the requisite twenty days after William's death, Hamilton immediately staged a protest before the Duke of Queensberry could read his commission to act for Queen Anne. Appealing to the Claim of Right, Hamilton asserted that any proceedings beyond confirming the accession of the queen, and securing the Protestant religion and the peace of the country, were in breach of 'the Fundamental Laws and Constitutions of the Kingdom'. Hamilton sought to force a general election on the dissolution of parliament, an election not having been held since the outset of the Revolution in Scotland. Queensberry, who had actively colluded with the English ministry in its highly questionable delaying of the Scottish parliament, was understandably reluctant to weaken the Court party through an election. Following a walk out by Hamilton and perhaps as many as 79 members of the Country Party, Queensberry was able to expedite business. Not only was the queen's accession recognised, Protestantism secured and the Presbyterian establishment in the Kirk reaffirmed, but Queensberry was also able to carry a vote of supply for Scottish troops engaged in the War of the Spanish Succession and another vote to authorise Queen Anne's appointment of Scottish commissioners to negotiate political incorporation. When Alexander Bruce of Broomhall (later Earl of Kincardine), burgh commissioner for Sanquhar, occasional placeman and an Episcopalian, maintained that Presbyterianism was incompatible with monarchy, he was expelled from the House. The Dean and the

---

[27] *Marchmont*, p. 154; *MSSM*, pp. 34–5, 40–5; HL, Stowe Papers: Brydges Family Papers, ST 58/vol. 1; NAS, Hamilton Papers, GD 406/1/4666; RC, TKUA England, Akter og Dokumenter nedr Sofart og Handel: Order med Bilag, 1702–7, A.III/208, letter 76; Speck, *The Birth of Britain*, pp. 35–8; Hoppit, *A Land of Liberty?* pp. 287–91. In this context of mobilising finances to advance the war effort, Godolphin's immediate concern with union was not with that of Scotland and England but that of the Old and New East India Companies, which was accomplished in terms of management in 1702, albeit full integration had to wait a further seven years (NAS, Hamilton Papers, GD 406/1/4699; H. Furber, *Rival Empires of Trade in the Orient, 1600–1800* (Oxford, 2004), pp. 99–103; K. N. Chaudhuri, *The Trading World of Asia and the English East India Company, 1660–1760* (Cambridge, 1975), pp. 434–6).

Faculty of Advocates, the elite of the Scottish legal fraternity, were partially censured for endorsing Hamilton's protest. However, the remaining members of the Scottish Estates (from 112 to 119) were not prepared to commit unequivocally to a Protestant Succession. Although only a minority were Cavaliers, the parliamentary rump was not prepared to weaken their position in advance of negotiations with commissioners from the English parliament.[28]

However, while Queensberry was able to ensure that the 27 Scottish commissioners were drawn overwhelmingly from his Court Party, Hamilton had not necessarily committed a serious tactical error by his walk-out.[29] Unrest about political incorporation, though curtailed by a peremptory adjournment of parliament after two weeks, spilled over into large-scale tax avoidance which maintained the momentum of extra-parliamentary protest in the wake of Darien and, in turn, forced Queensberry's hand on dissolution and left the Court Party on the backfoot when electioneering. In the midst of these protests, Hamilton firmed up his contacts with the radical Covenanting remnant, known variously as the Cameronians, the Hebronites or 'the mountain people'. Having rejected the erastian nature of the Revolution Settlement in Scotland, they maintained the Restoration tradition of conventicling and were willing not only to lobby Presbyterian landowners, lawyers and divines opposed to political incorporation, but also to intimidate commissioners named to negotiate Union, such as Sir James Smollett of Bonhill, provost of Dumbarton.[30] At the same time, the Country Party made overtures to sympathetic Whig Lords in England. Their objections to the proposed

---

[28] *APS*, XI, pp. 12–13, 19, 25, 26–7 c.7, 478, and appendix p. 2; Crossrigg, *DPP*, pp. 81–95; *LRS*, pp. 112–13; *Portland*, IV, pp. 42, 44; *LP*, I, pp. 45–9; *MSSM*, p. 143; Wallace, *The History of the Lives and Reigns of the Kings of Scotland*, pp. 186–7; Somerville, *The History of Great Britain*, pp. 154–6, 159–61. According to an anonymous supporter of the confederated opposition, Hamilton's protest won the support of 88 members, 9 of whom remained in the house after the walk-out. Of those 110 remaining, over 80 reputedly had places and pensions from the Court, besides promises and bribes given to others. However, around 30 military officers were not rewarded with new commissions because of the partiality of the Court party (NLS, Wodrow quarto, xxviii, fo. 125). Bishop Gilbert Burnet (*Burnet's HHOT*, pp. 707, 709–11) put these figures respectively at 75 departing and 112 remaining. Patrick Hume, 1st Earl of Marchmont, gave slightly different figures of only 67 joining the protest and 120 remaining in parliament; but his parliamentary calculations were never renowned for their accuracy (*PEM*, III, pp. 238–470).

[29] W. Ferguson, *Scotland's Relations with England*, pp. 200–2; Riley, *The Union of Scotland and England*, pp. 36–9.

[30] NLS, Wodrow folio, xxxv, fols. 64–5; HL, Loudoun Scottish Collection, box 3, LO 7019, and box 20, LO 7018; DH, Loudon Papers, A538/47–8, and A547/413; GCA, Records of the Maxwells of Pollock, T-PM 115/12–14, and Campbell of Succoth MSS, TD 219/3/2; NAS, Hamilton Papers, GD 406/1/5010, /10935, /10937, /10939; PRO, Secretaries of State: State Papers Scotland, series II, SP 54/1/20; *CBJ*, pp. 3–4, 10–11; *Portland*, VIII, pp. 110–11; *PEM*, III, pp. 248–51.

negotiations for Union reiterated the admonition of Sir John Nisbet in 1670 that any fundamental alteration to the constitution without a mandate from the Scottish electorate was potentially treasonable and was being undertaken by politicians with limited sympathy for the Claim of Right and the Revolution Settlement. Campaigning for elections that commenced in September was generally concluded in the burghs by October, but was protracted by unresolved contests and disputes in over a third of the shires throughout the three months of negotiations for political incorporation that actually commenced on 10 November 1702.[31]

The indifference of the English commissioners, which initially delayed proceedings for two weeks, was marked by their persistent failure to constitute a quorum (reduced from thirteen to seven after two months). Nevertheless, the negotiations were not merely an exercise in gesture politics or a collusive ploy that paid lip service to the dying wishes of William that Anne felt obliged to respect.[32] With the status quo of regal union no longer tenable by 1702, the Scots commissioners proved opportune negotiators even if the outcome was inconclusive. It was the Scots, with endorsement from Queen Anne, who resolved initial difficulties arising from the specific lack of parliamentary accountability in the English commission. They maintained that the negotiations at the Cockpit in Whitehall were to draw up proposals for Union, which would subsequently be legislated in both parliaments – a resolve which also exonerated them from charges of treason in Scotland after the general election.

The English opened with a two-point plan for a United Kingdom and the Hanoverian Succession. The Scots responded by agreeing to the initial point but adding two more – the representation of both kingdoms through one parliament with a mutual communication of trade. It was the Scots not the English who pressed for full political incorporation, without committing themselves unequivocally to the Hanoverian Succession or sacrificing their Kirk or civil law. The Scots presented six proposals for commercial integration that ranged far beyond confederation – free trade; same rates of customs; equal access to the plantation trade; removal of discriminatory Navigation Acts in both kingdoms; equality of impositions with the Scots being allowed fiscal rebates, that is equivalents, for

---

[31] NLS, Wodrow quarto, xxviii, fols. 125–8, 'A Letter from a Member of Parliament in Scotland to ane English Lord concerning the Treaty for uniting Both Kingdomes'; NAS, Supplementary Parliamentary Papers, PA 7/25/1/6/2–101. The deaths of some candidates originally returned necessitated fresh elections before the next parliament commenced in May 1703.

[32] Riley, *The Union of Scotland and England*, pp. 177–82; Defoe, *HUGB*, 'Of Affairs in Both Kingdoms', pp. 41–5.

assuming a share of English national debts; manufacturing and other public companies were to remain reserved issues. The first four were secured by mid-December with Queen Anne attending in person to ensure that the English commissioners accepted in principle Scottish access to the colonial trade, which they had been initially reluctant to concede. The Scots also secured equivalents not only for sharing in English national debts but also to develop fisheries and manufactures. It was also agreed that the Scots should pay no more than £48,000 as their proportion of land tax after Union. However, the Scottish claims for £200,000 reparations for Darien and the continued existence of the Scottish Company trading to Africa and the Indies were the stumbling blocks on which negotiations foundered by 3 February 1703.[33]

Reconfiguring Britain

The negotiations of 1702–3 clearly laid the commercial if not the political basis for the subsequent successful treating between the commissioners of both kingdoms in 1706, an outcome undoubtedly facilitated by the continuities in personnel, with fourteen English and twelve Scottish commissioners serving on both occasions. While English ministers were undoubtedly influential in forcing Queensberry to accede to a general election and subsequently in reshaping Queen Anne's Scottish administration on the breakdown of negotiations, the pressure for Union came not from English Tories or Whigs. Nor did the proposed Union occasion a fundamental divide between Whigs and Tories. The Union featured neither in their differences over contractual monarchy and the regulation of trade highlighted by Charles Davenant, the secretary for the English commissioners, nor in the major parliamentary divisions on toleration for Protestant Dissenters or on the conduct and financing of the war.[34]

---

[33] PRO, Secretaries of State, State Papers Scotland, series II, A Journal of the Proceedings upon the Union between the Kingdoms of England and Scotland, 1702–3, SP 54/2/1; NLS, Saltoun Papers, MS 17498, fo. 73, and Wodrow quarto, xxviii, fols. 129–38; HL, Loudoun Scottish Collection, box 18, LO 8600; RC, TKUA England, Akter og Dokumenter nedr Sofart og Handel: Order med Bilag, 1702–7, A.III/207, letters 13, 15; *APS*, XI, p. 101, and appendix, pp. 145–61; Speck, *The Birth of Britain*, pp. 44–5.

[34] Charles Davenant, *The true picture of an ancient Tory in a dialogue between Vassal a Tory and Freeman a Whig* (London, 1702); D. W. Hayton, 'Introductory Survey' in *The House of Commons 1690–1715*, ed. D. W. Hayton, E. Cruickshanks & S. Handley, 5 vols. (Cambridge, 2002), I, pp. 462–99; BL, Hatton-Finch Papers: Letters to the Earl of Nottingham, Secretary of State, vol. I (1694–1703), Add.MSS 29,588, fols. 183–4; HL, Stowe Papers: Brydges Family Papers, ST 58/vol. I; GCA, Records of the Maxwells of Pollock, T-PM 115/15; *A Complete Collection of the Protests made in the House of Lords from 1641 to the dissolution of the last Parliament, June 1747* (London, 1747), pp. 132–7; J. C.

Although parties at this juncture reflected more political tendencies than disciplined membership,[35] the Tories, as led by Nottingham and Rochester, were notably reluctant to make commercial concessions to the Scots that would even have hinted at confederation, far less incorporation. Rochester in 1695 had co-ordinated the address from both Houses of Parliament to William of Orange against the establishment of the Company of Scotland trading to Africa and the Indies as prejudicial to English trading interests. While Nottingham, like Hamilton, had pushed for the dissolution of the Convention Parliament on the death of William of Orange, the Scottish leader of the confederated opposition had regarded the likely parliamentary dominance of the Tories after the English general election of 1702 as advantageous: their leaders, especially those who promoted high-church Anglicanism, were 'ennimies to Scotland'. More visceral, Gothic elements among the Tories deemed a 'Pan-Britannic Union' acceptable only if the Scots restored Episcopalianism and accepted drastically curtailed representation, for nobles no less than gentry and burgesses, in a unified parliament.[36] The Whig position under John Somers, Lord Somers, Thomas Wharton, Lord (later 1st Earl of) Wharton, and Charles Montague, Lord Halifax, was more measured. However, the Scots were clearly given to understand by Blackerby Fairfax, an English naval physician posing as a Scottish polemicist in 1702, that any union and royal succession must conform to that of 'other Gothic constitutions' in terms of parliamentary accountability. A closer union was necessary, not least to combat France, but also to promote greater social as well as commercial and political integration, which in turn ruled out confederation or any other federative arrangement as practised currently in Europe. In turn, the Scots should contemplate greater integration of legal and ecclesiastical institutions while accepting that their nobility should be reduced in power and numbers, not least to facilitate a

---

Sainty & D. Dewar, *Divisions in the House of Lords: an analytical list, 1685-1857* (London, 1976). The invitation from the Lords 'to treat for the weal of both kingdoms' in 1700 was used by the Commons as an excuse to examine past precedents for invitations from the upper house before the offer was cursorily rejected (*JHC*, 13, p. 267).

[35] O'Gorman, *The Long Eighteenth Century*, pp. 43–51; Hoppit, *A Land of Liberty?* pp. 282–7; D. Hayton, 'Traces of Party Politics in Early Eighteenth-century Scottish Elections', *PH*, 15 (1996), pp. 74–99; G. Holmes, *Politics, Religion and Society in England, 1679–1742* (London, 1986), pp. 181–215.

[36] *LRS*, pp. 115–16; *LDN*, pp. 122–3, 135–6, 145, 149, 153; *JHL*, 15 (1691–6), pp. 611–15; *Marchmont*, pp. 150–1; *Portland*, IV, p. 37; BL, Sidney, 1st Earl of Godolphin: Official Correspondence. Home, 1701–10, Add.MSS 28,055, fols. 3–4; NAS, Hamilton Papers, GD 406/1/4699, /4867, /6577; PRO, Secretaries of State: State Papers Scotland, series II, SP 54/1/19; Anon., *A Letter to Sir J. P. Bart., A Member for the ensuing parliament, relating to the Union of England and Scotland* (London, 1702). The MP addressed was almost certainly Sir John Pakington, a Tory.

uniform and centralised administration throughout Britain and the overseas dominions.[37]

Critical to the promotion of Union as a Britannic initiative in 1702 was not only the Court Party in Scotland, but Queen Anne from whom they took their lead. As well as enunciating publicly her firm commitment to Union in her address to both parliaments at the outset of her reign, she let it be known privately at Court that she wished to be served by men who gave precedence to her prerogative, that is ministers and politicians who would uphold the Revolution Settlements but countenance no further encroachments on her monarchical authority.[38] After the influx of Scottish politicians to procure favour at Court at the start of her reign, she manifestly sided with Queensberry over Hamilton who assiduously lobbied Godolphin, Marlborough and his wife, Sarah Churchill, a close confidant of the queen. Queensberry envisaged Union as a bulwark against any further limitations on monarchy. Like others in the Court Party prepared to push for Union – notably Sir John Dalrymple, now 2nd Earl of Stair, and George MacKenzie, 1st Earl of Cromartie (then Viscount Tarbat) – Queensberry had served James II as well as William of Orange, a career pattern not dissimilar to those of Marlborough and Godolphin who were content to let the Scots make the running on political incorporation.[39]

Queensberry's support for the prerogative found ready adherents among such ambitious placemen as James Ogilvie, 1st Earl of Seafield, John Erskine, 6th Earl of Mar, and David Boyle, Lord Boyle of Kelburn (later 1st Earl of Glasgow), who believed that the main issue about Union was not if, but when, it would be accomplished. But the prerogative was not the only element in the pro-Union stance of the Court Party. For other officeholders such as the experienced Patrick Hume, 1st Earl of Marchmont, the Presbyterian establishment in the Kirk, which could not necessarily be guaranteed after the general election, required bolstering as a non-negotiable condition of Union. This position was also taken up by the composed yet underestimated Hugh Campbell, 3rd Earl of

---

[37] [Blackerby Fairfax], *A Discourse upon the Uniting Scotland with England* (London, 1702). Even a united Commonwealth, as that in Poland–Lithuania, was deemed unsatisfactory as being too restrictive in scope and taking too long to bring to perfection.

[38] RC, TKUA England, Akter og Dokumenter nedr Sofart og Handel: Order med Bilag, 1702–3, A.III/207, letters 64, 66; *LQA*, pp. 83–4, 88–91.

[39] *MSSM*, pp. 113–18, 122–3, 126, 128; Craufurd, *The Lives and Characters*, pp. 241–9; NAS, Hamilton Papers, GD 406/1/4940–1, /5010, /5961, /6572–4, /6577–80, /7064, /7500, /7507–8, /8439. Queensberry's leadership of the Court Party and his close links with Tory and Whig politicians in England has been explored thoroughly in C. McKay, 'The Political Life of James Douglas, second Duke of Queensberry, 1662–1711' (University of Strathclyde, Ph.D thesis, 2005).

Loudoun, and the ambitious but erratic William Johnston, 1st Marquess of Annandale, who was more intent on retaining the Presbyterian Kirk than negotiating Union. A reservation exempting the established Kirk (and Scots law) from the negotiations had remained a contentious issue within the Court Party since notice was served to treat for Union. Annandale duly challenged the negotiating stance of Queensberry during the private meetings of the Scottish commissioners in London that commenced on 26 October 1702, albeit his arguments that the Presbyterian establishment of the Kirk should be specified as a reserved issue at the outset of the joint negotiations was rebutted as too confrontational by Tarbat. The predominant stance of the Court Party was that the English parliament was sufficient guarantee of the civil and religious liberties attained at the Revolution. This stance was attractive not only to those established politicians intent on retaining the spoils of office in their hands in Scotland. Union was also becoming the considered position of those such as David Melville, 3rd Earl of Leven, and, from the younger generation, John Campbell, 2nd Duke of Argyll, who sought the wider opportunities for advancement for themselves and their kinsmen opened up by a British fiscal–military state.[40]

Differences in the ordering of priorities in their commitment to the prerogative, the Presbyterian Kirk and the Protestant Succession made the Court Party, no less than the Country, vulnerable to defections by ambitious politicians in pursuit of office. Unlike the Country Party, however, the Court Party was characterised by an uncritical acceptance of the prescriptive right of the English ministry to exercise a controlling influence in appointments to public office, both civil and military, in Scotland. Nevertheless, Queensberry's consistent commitment, as head of the *parti de la Cour*, to the prerogative kept him in relatively good standing with Queen Anne even when he was no longer guaranteed the favour of the English ministry.[41] Behind Queensberry and the Court Party lay the closet influence of William Carstares, Principal of Edinburgh University, meddler par excellence in affairs of Kirk and state and political fixer of Scottish administrations for William of Orange, who firmly favoured political incorporation to uphold the prerogative and Presbyterianism.

---

[40] HL, Loudoun Scottish Collection, box 5 LO 7306, box 30 LO 9283; DH, Loudon Papers, A538/45 and; A547/11–12; ICA, Argyll papers, bundle 144/1. NAS: Clerk of Penicuik Papers, GD 18/3124, /3126; Hamilton Papers, GD 406/1/497; Mar & Kellie Collection, GD 124/15/226. *Mar & Kellie*, p. 227; *LP*, I, pp. 90–2; *LRS*, pp. 123–9, 142–3; *MGC*, I, pp. 50, 101, 131, 152.

[41] RC, TKUA England, Akter og Dokumenter nedr Sofart og Handel: Order med Bilag, 1702–3. A.III/207, letter 55; /208, letter 71; /209, letter 47; /210, letters 13–14, 29, 33. BL, Sidney, 1st Earl of Godolphin: Official Correspondence. Home, 1701–10, Add.MSS 28,055, fols. 27–8, 41, 111–13, 132–3, 140–1, 158–9, 241.

Notwithstanding acerbic party differences between Whigs and Tories in England, he also desired direct rule from Westminster to terminate factionalism within the Scottish Estates. He was sensitive to apprehensions about the current control over parliamentary business in Scotland exercised by the English ministry. But he was convinced that Scottish politicians taking their lead from the English ministry was a natural, not a demeaning, aspect of political life under Queen Anne.[42]

The Court Party, however, were not mere upholders of the political status quo until instructed to change by the English ministry, any more than they were advocates of political incorporation simply for the spoils of office.[43] Support for the prerogative and Union offered Episcopalians the hope of public toleration for their faith, a prospect readily endorsed by leading Anglican bishops in the Lords – notably, Thomas Tenison, archbishop of Canterbury, John Sharp, archbishop of York, and William Nicolson, bishop of Carlisle, as well as the Anglo-Scot, Gilbert Burnet, bishop of Salisbury.[44] But as Tarbat made clear in a polemical broadside during the negotiations of 1702, the potential benefits to his fellow Episcopalians were secondary to issues of political economy, as the Scots as well as the English stood to gain from the merging of both kingdoms into Great Britain. Thus, as a zealous Unionist, Tarbat was even prepared to contemplate the merging of English and Scottish legal systems.

Drawing on contemporary examples of secure, profitable and powerful unions, Tarbat came firmly down on the side of states, such as France and Spain, unified from composite monarchies, over federative arrangements as prevailed in the United Provinces or the Swiss Cantons. Political incorporation would consolidate Britain as an imperial power on an unprecedented global scale. The Kalmar Union of Denmark-Norway and Sweden had sundered (in the early sixteenth century) because regal union had not led to political incorporation. Restricted representation for the Scottish nobility in the Lords was more than compensated by the opening up of colonial trade and by the enhanced capacity of a united kingdom to compete in deep-sea fishing with the Dutch. Above all, political incorporation would end England's discriminatory treatment of Scotland since the regal union as manifest by the Navigation Acts and the neglect of Scottish interests in the making of peace and war. Tarbat also directly addressed English interests that had in the past proved a stumbling block to negotiations for federative as well as incorporating union. The English

---

[42] *Portland*, VIII, pp. 103–7, 114; *SPC*, pp. 714–17; *MSSM*, pp. 125–6; AUL, Duff of Meldrum Collection, MS 2778/12/2/1/1–2.
[43] W. Ferguson, *Scotland's Relations with England*, pp. 186–7; Holmes, *The Making of a Great Power*, pp. 309–10; *LP*, I, pp. 44–5, 52–3.
[44] *MSSM*, pp. 92–4; *LDN*, pp. 145, 157, 191; *Laing*, p. 5; *LP*, I, pp. 74–5.

coal and salt masters would benefit from the equalising of customs which would not affect cheap supplies at home but make these commodities less likely to be undersold by Scots in foreign markets. Competition from the Scottish carrying trade would reduce commercial overheads for English growers and manufactures. With the addition of Scottish manpower, the American plantations would no longer be regarded as a source of English depopulation.[45]

In tying their colours to political incorporation the Court Party were effectively updating the Britannic Engagement of 1648. Simultaneously, the Country Party benefited from a revitalised Scottish perspective as provided by George Ridpath, a sometime Whig polemicist based among the Scottish community in London. A committed Presbyterian, Ridpath was distrustful of any union with Anglicans. Ridpath, however, did not rule out union but, in contrast to Tarbat, he drew on European examples to support a federative arrangement as enjoyed by the Dutch and the Swiss, seeing this as a more equitable means of preserving the honour, religion and liberty of Scotland. He was opposed to any reduced representation in a common parliament, which would lead to the Scottish members being used as Whig pawns against the Tories. Having reviewed all previous attempts at union, he claimed that the terms being negotiated in 1702 were less favourable than those offered to Scotland during the Rough Wooing of the mid sixteenth century. His preferred option was a return to the constitutional arrangement of 1640–1 that secured limited monarchy and English recognition of Scottish sovereignty by the Treaty of London. Confederation would advance the Revolution Settlements in both countries, with the price of closer commercial association with England being a common foreign policy. Confederation would also allow for pragmatic renegotiation, especially on matters of political economy – for he was not convinced that access to the American colonies would compensate for the loss of domestic trade in a free market, Scottish woollen manufactures being particularly vulnerable to English competition.[46]

---

[45] George MacKenzie [Earl of Cromartie], *Parainesis Pacifica, or, A persuasive to the union of Britain* (Edinburgh, 1702). Tarbat also claimed that in return for secure Scottish supplies of cattle, linen and stockings cheaper than could be produced in England, the English would find such a ready market for their cloth that the Scots should not waste their energy on its manufacture. Scottish wool would also be made available to enhance English, rather than Swedish or Dutch, manufacturing. Episcopalians not wholly committed to the return of the exiled house of Stuart genuinely lamented the imminent failure of the union negotiations at the outset of 1703, as evident from A[ndrew] Cant, *A Sermon preached on the XXX Day of January 1702/3 at Edinburgh, by one of the Suffering Clergy in the Kingdom of Scotland* (Edinburgh, 1703).

[46] [George Ridpath], *A Discourse upon the Union of England and Scotland* (Edinburgh, 1702). This tract was written prior to the due commencement of negotiations in October with an addenda to rebut Tarbat's tract in favour of political incorporation. Ridpath interpreted

Balancing interests

Clearly by 1703 there was a realisation on both sides of the party divide and within the wider political nation in Scotland that regal union was no longer sustainable, a realisation that was in advance of political opinion in England on the reconfiguration of the British state. Nevertheless, Scots who favoured political incorporation from a Britannic perspective or a federative arrangement from a Scottish perspective were reliant on some accommodation with the Gothic perspective dominant among Tories and Whigs in England. Moreover, a significant body of opinion within Scotland, no less than in England, had still to be won over for either an incorporative or a federative union. Thus, John Allardyce, burgh commissioner for Aberdeen as well as a Scottish commissioner to negotiate Union, was instructed by the city's magistrates to follow the advice given by the Convention of Royal Burghs: to reserve the Presbyterian Kirk and Scots law, but press for a communication of trade with England, which left the door open to either commercial confederation or commercial union. There was also a realisation that if Scotland was to engage in major commercial projects such as colonial plantations or deep-sea fishing, the country should either enter a closer union with or separate from England. In the latter eventuality, Scotland should be prepared to associate with, as well as emulate, the Dutch, especially as the negotiations in 1702 had reputedly made the States-General of the United Provinces apprehensive about the prospects of British union.[47]

Sir John Maxwell of Nether Pollock, designated Lord Pollock when Justice-Clerk, came from a family with a long history in promoting fishing off the Scottish coasts. In a briefing paper prepared for his consideration when serving as Scottish commissioner in the negotiations of 1702–3, the development of Scottish fishing in association with English capital was seen as the one clear advantage of political incorporation, albeit this development was to be encouraged regardless of the accomplishment of union. The briefing paper was adamant that incorporation was fundamentally to the advantage of England. Scotland, in conforming to a government

---

the conditions for union offered by Edward VI of England during the Rough Wooing as commercial confederation under a single monarchy, with separate laws and customs remaining unaffected by free trade.

[47] *LDN*, pp. 190–1; ACA, Aberdeen Council Letters, vol. 8 (1700–19)/70; J[ohn] B[emde], *A Memorial Briefly pointing out some Advantages of the Union of the Two Kingdoms: Humbly offered to the Consideration of the Commissioners appointed to that end* (London, 1702). The author J. B. would appear to be John Bemde who also commented on the inaccuracies of 'A Treatise of Navigation, Common Sovereignty of the Sea Fishing' by Joseph Gander for the English Council of Trade and Plantations in 1703 (BL, Papers Relating to Trade etc., Sloane MS 2092, fols. 50–1).

in which sovereignty was vested in the Crown in parliament, would be an accession of England. Although both kingdoms would benefit from the strengthening, enrichment and security of a united Britain, the current draining of money from Scotland to the Court would be increased by the more frequent repair of politicians to the British parliament – effectively the English parliament continuing with a Scottish minority presence in the Lords and the Commons. The notion that either the Court or parliament would have a residence in Scotland post-Union was dismissed as 'a vain imagining'.

Political economy was central to the balancing of interests for and against incorporation. The gains to Scottish trade and shipping from free access to English and colonial markets were deemed marginal. In the short term at least, the economic reality was recession. If Scotland lost its capacity to restrict imports and control the value at which coin was circulated, its textile trade would be particularly vulnerable to English competition, superior in quality and cheaper in price. Although coal, salt, linen and cattle could be sold in England without the imposition of customs, any trading surplus that resulted would soon be eroded if profits remained in London to purchase luxuries and other fashionable commodities. If the English paid for these Scottish imports in textiles rather than in specie any notional balance of payments in favour of Scotland would soon evaporate. The plantations were certainly another outlet for the Scottish diaspora long established in Poland and the Baltic States, Ireland, France and the Low Countries. But the opportunities for repatriating capital were outweighed by the disadvantage of diminishing the labour pool for manufactures and fisheries in Scotland. In reality, Scots would be used to strengthen existing English colonies while the more profitable trade in and shipping of colonial commodities would still run through English ports. Profits from the marketing of commodities would continue to accrue to England rather than to Scotland or the plantations. The structural deficiencies of the Scottish economy, notably its lack of depth and diversity, would not be remedied by political incorporation. Nevertheless, the briefing paper favoured union in some form. As it was easier to convince England of the advantages than to dissuade Scotland of the disadvantages of political incorporation, some federative arrangement that would ensure an equitable communication of trade was deemed preferable.[48]

Whereas the House of Commons, no less than that of Lords, was integral to any moves towards federative or incorporative union, the singular

---

[48] GCA, Records of the Maxwells of Pollock, T-PM 109/90; NLS, Wodrow octavo, ix, fols. 109–18.

importance of the nobility as the prime movers among the Scottish Estates should not be overstated. Undoubtedly a cogent case can be made that the shire commissioners were an ancillary rather than a separate political estate from the nobility in so far as kinship, local association and clientage determined political allegiances and opinions.[49] However, Scotland was not a static society locked into a political prism triangulated by Crown, Kirk and nobility. Throughout the seventeenth century, Scotland was not impervious to inflation and price instability, to trading and demographic shifts, and even to climate changes affecting the productivity of marginal uplands in the little Ice Age that culminated in the 1690s. The gentry, more so than the nobility and no less than the burgesses, were distinctive participants in the expansion of landownership, in the commercialisation of estate management, in developing manufactures, in colonial entrepreneurship and in integrating cities and towns with their rural hinterlands. As well as their leadership of religious dissent, they maintained their traditional role as foremost military adventurers. Subsequent ennoblement was an incidental outcome, not necessarily a pre-eminent aspiration.[50] Indeed, two caveats must be observed about the influence of the nobility in the context of Union. Affiliations to the nobility could provide a powerful backbone to the Court and Country, but was not in itself a guarantee of party cohesion. Nor was ennoblement by Queen Anne a guarantee of political commitment to either Court or Country.

The Court Party certainly benefited from the family connections of James Dalrymple, elevated from Viscount to Earl of Stair in 1703. Two of his brothers, Sir Hew Dalrymple of North Berwick, Lord President of the Court of Session, and Sir David Dalrymple of Hailes, Solicitor-General, had served with Stair as Scottish commissioners in the union negotiations of 1702–3, and did so again in the negotiations of 1706. Both distinguished lawyers who had sat throughout the Convention Parliament were returned as burgh commissioners for, respectively, North Berwick and Culross. After the general election, they were joined in the Scottish Estates by two of Stair's sons, William Dalrymple of Glenmure, the diarist and shire commissioner for Ayr, and George Dalrymple of Dalmahoy as burgh commissioner for Stranraer (the seat originally held by his father in the Convention Parliament). In addition to their propensity to secure their

---

[49] K. M. Brown, *Noble Society in Scotland. Wealth, Family and Culture from Reformation to Revolution* (Edinburgh, 2000), pp. 11–22.
[50] Macinnes, *Clanship, Commerce and the House of Stuart*, pp. 142–51; G. Marshall, *Presbyteries and Profits: Calvinism and the Development of Capitalism in Scotland, 1560–1707* (Oxford, 1980), pp. 284–319; I. D. Whyte, 'Poverty or Prosperity? Rural Society in Lowland Scotland in the Late Sixteenth and Early Seventeenth Centuries', *Scottish Economic & Social History*, 18 (1998), pp. 19–31.

return by carpet-bagging in the lesser burghs, the Dalrymples provided a highly partial, occasionally malevolent but always formidable, phalanx for Union. By way of contrast, James, 4th Duke of Hamilton, as leader of the Country Party, could not count on the support of all his ennobled brothers. Charles Douglas-Hamilton, 2nd Earl of Selkirk, though a member of the confederated opposition, was inclined to side with the Cavaliers. John Douglas-Hamilton, 1st Earl of Ruglen, affiliated to the opposition but was absent from the critical votes on Union in 1706–7, as was his brother, George Douglas-Hamilton, 6th Earl of Orkney, who preferred to campaign as a lieutenant-general under Marlborough, albeit he was also inclined to favour rather than oppose Union. Nevertheless, Hamilton was able to detach Sir James Stuart of Ardmaleish, a seeming stalwart of the Court Party who had served as a commissioner for union in 1702–3, in anticipation of his return as shire commissioner for Bute where he was also sheriff. His ennoblement as Earl of Bute in 1703, far from consolidating his affiliations to the Court, led to his renewed association with the Cavaliers and a growing estrangement from political incorporation. But he absented himself rather than vote directly against Union in 1706–7.[51]

For the duration of the Convention Parliament, the additional shire commissioners admitted from 1693 had enhanced rather than enervated the management of the Scottish Estates from the Court. But this situation changed appreciably for the first and last Scottish parliament of Queen Anne that commenced in 1703 and continued until 1707. Notwithstanding Seafield's far-from-adroit managing of the elections in shires and burghs on behalf of the Court, Hamilton's failure to secure a firm electoral rapport with the Cavaliers at the general election of 1702 ensured that the Country and Court Parties were relatively balanced in terms of members returned, a situation that afforded the gentry scope to exercise their initiative as organisers and orators. Party politics were further stimulated by the general election bringing in greater numbers prepared, on the one hand, to stand against direction from the Court and, on the other, to lead debates for and against Union.[52] Into the first category came such political organisers as George Lockhart of Carnwath, shire commissioner for Mid-Lothian, who as a Jacobite in the guise of a Cavalier was energetically

---

[51] *The Parliaments of Scotland: Burgh and Shire Commissioners*, ed. M. D. Young, 2 vols. (Edinburgh, 1993), I, pp. 173–6, and II, pp. 659–60; *LP*, I, pp. 88–90; *Scots Peerage*, ed. Sir J. Balfour-Paul, 9 vols. (Edinburgh, 1904–14), II, pp. 298–9, IV, pp. 383–4, VI, pp. 578–9, VII, pp. 156, 361–3; NAS, Hamilton Papers, GD 406/1/5962, /7142, /7580.

[52] *LP*, I, pp. 53–4; K. M. Brown, 'Party Politics and Parliament: Scotland's Last Election and its Aftermath, 1702–03' in Brown & Mann, eds., *The History of the Scottish Parliament*, pp. 245–86.

committed to maximising national grievances both in and out of parliament to restore the exiled Stuarts. The intellectually accomplished, well-travelled but dogmatically uncompromising Andrew Fletcher of Saltoun, who reinvigorated the constitutional reformers after his election as shire commissioner for East Lothian, came into both categories as an organiser and orator. William Seton of Pitmedden, as shire commissioner for Aberdeen, became a distinctive advocate for an incorporative rather than a federative union. His capacity to influence the Scottish Estates chimed in with the commercial and colonial considerations moving England in favour of political incorporation to secure the balance of trade, no less than the balance of power, in Europe.[53]

While the leadership of the nobility was still generally accepted in the house, this was less certain with respect to extra-parliamentary protests and petitioning. A majority in all three estates were to vote in favour of Anglo-Scottish Union in 1706–7. Whereas the nobility predominantly favoured political incorporation, the commissioners for the shires struck a closer rapport with those for the burghs in more balanced voting for and against. They, to a greater extent than the nobility, held the political fate of Scotland in their hands.[54] For all the political estates, however, an important if understated stimulus to the political reconfiguration of Britain was to come from the experience of Ireland.

---

[53] D. Szechi, 'Constructing a Jacobite: The Social and Intellectual Origins of George Lockhart of Carnwath', *Historical Journal*, 40 (1997), pp. 977–96; Scott, *Andrew Fletcher and the Treaty of Union*, pp. 74–95; *LP*, I, pp. 75–7; *The Parliaments of Scotland: Burgh and Shire Commissioners*, I, p. 243, II, pp. 433, 629. That the shire commissioners in general and Fletcher of Saltoun in particular should agitate in the parliaments of 1704 and 1705 for a new member to be added to their estate for every new noble created by the Court hardly suggests the gentry viewed themselves as an ancillary, rather than as a distinct, political estate (*LP*, I, pp. 106, 122).

[54] A. I. Macinnes, 'The 1707 Union: Support and Opposition' in P. G. B. McNeill & H. L. MacQueen, eds., *Atlas of Scottish History to 1707* (Edinburgh, 1996), pp. 151–3.

5 The Irish dimension

At the same time as the Scots were being courted to enter union with England, Irish overtures for union were rejected, most notably in 1703. Yet dismissive treatment of failed union in 1703 is warranted only from an anglocentric perspective.[1] The failed union of 1703 was the exclusive project of the English interest in Ireland, not an endeavour to engage either Catholics or Protestant dissenters.[2] Conversely, the temptation to view the successful Anglo-Scottish Union as an inclusive British project must bear in mind the contemporary strictures against the Court Party led by the Duke of Queensberry as 'little more than the English interest in Scotland'.[3] The Revolution Settlements in all three kingdoms laid down guidelines for future British state formation, not just the Anglo-Scottish Union of 1707. Indeed, the ambivalent message of William Molyneux's *The Case of Ireland's being bound by Acts of Parliament in England, Stated* (1698) had ramifications for both the Unionist and anti-Unionist camps in Scotland. Molyneux, like Fletcher of Saltoun, has tended to be lionised as a political visionary. Yet both had limited clout in their respective parliaments. Nevertheless, they opened up a fruitful if limited line of engagement between opponents of English hegemony in Ireland and Scotland. Throughout the seventeenth century, Scots had been acutely conscious of Ireland's standing in relation to England and had consistently sought to avoid similar provincial relegation. From 1703, the Scots were patently

---

[1] Speck, *The Birth of Britain*, pp. 49, 98–118; D. Hayton & D. Szechni, 'John Bull's Other Kingdoms: The English Government of Scotland and Ireland' in Jones, ed., *Britain in the First Age of Party*, pp. 241–80; J. G. Simms, 'The Establishment of the Protestant Ascendancy, 1691–1714' in T. W. Moody & W. E. Vaughan, eds., *A New History of Ireland*, vol. IV (Oxford, 1986), pp. 1–30.

[2] J. Kelly, 'The Origins of the Act of Union: An Examination of Unionist Opinion in Britain and Ireland, 1650–1800', *IHS*, 25 (1987), pp. 236–63; J. Smyth, '"Like Amphibious Animals": Irish Protestants, Ancient Britons, 1691–1707', *HJ*, 34 (1993), pp. 785–96. The constitutional subordination of Ireland in the eighteenth century was reaffirmed not just by further rejections of union in 1707 and 1709, but also by the emphatic imposition of the Declaratory Act in 1719, which asserted the right of the English Parliament to Legislate for Ireland.

[3] W. Ferguson, *Scotland's Relations with England*, pp. 186–8.

alluding to Ireland when constitutional issues of dependency, pejoratively described as slavery, were raised in parliamentary and polemical debates. However, proponents of political incorporation argued no less persuasively that, without union, Scotland would effectively become the English satellite that Ireland manifestly was. Ireland became the dog that did not bark, not least because of the spin-doctoring necessary to counteract issues of constitutional subordination.[4] At the same time, the proximity of Ulster to Scotland, the ongoing involvement of Scots in plantations since the regal union, and the particularly strong religious and political affiliations maintained between Scots on both sides of the North Channel were of manifest strategic significance should England have recourse to incorporation by force.

Regal union and plantation

In addition to the Britannic, Scottish and Gothic, a rival perception of British state formation emanated from Ireland and was likewise grounded in myth, humanism and providentialism. This, which can be labelled normatively as 'the Irish perspective', served as a corrective to Scottish antiquarian pretensions as well as to Britannic and Gothic claims to anglocentric hegemony.

The principal text for this Irish formulation was a substantive work of Renaissance scholarship. *Foras Feasa ar Éirinn* by Séathrún Céitinn (Geoffrey Keating) was a history purged of fable but written in Irish around 1634 and subsequently circulated in manuscript only. Keating's refutation of the kingship line fabricated by Boece and Buchanan was part of his wider rejection of the belief that Irish kings were ever dependent on Arthur or any other king of the Britons. Ireland was never part of any foreign dominion prior to the incursion of the Normans from England at the behest of the papacy in the twelfth century. Keating's purpose was to demonstrate that Ireland was not a barbaric backwater that required civilising through conquest, plantation and the imposition of the English common law as argued by Sir John Davis, antiquarian and English attorney-general for Ireland.[5]

In the common classical Gaelic tradition, both the native Irish and the Scots who migrated from Ireland were designated the *Gael* and all other inhabitants and invaders within Britain and Ireland were deemed the *Gall*. The Gael was associated with epic heroism, scholarship and fidelity, and

---

[4] A. I. Macinnes, 'Union for Ireland Failed (1703), Union for Scotland Accomplished (1706–07)' in Keogh & Whelan, eds., *Acts of Union*, pp. 67–94.
[5] H. S. Pawlisch, *Sir John Davies and the Conquest of Ireland: A Study in Legal Imperialism* (Cambridge, 1985), pp. 55–64, 84–100.

the Gall with the foreign and alien cultures that had come initially with Brutus and were perpetuated in Britain by the invasions of the Romans, Saxons, Danes and Normans. William Camden's civilising mission of the Britons against the Irish and Scots was turned on its head. The Irish were comparable to any nation in Europe in valour, learning and religious faith. But Keating, as befitting a descendant of an Old English family, was also concerned to ensure that due place was given to the contribution of the *Sean-Gallaibh* (Old English) as well as the Irish Gael in sustaining Roman Catholicism. Both groups should be designated *Éireannaigh*, that is the Catholic Irish, in contrast to the *Nua-Gallaibh*, effectively the Protestant settlers who arrived as New English under the Tudors and as New British under the Stuarts. Nonetheless, Keating's perspective on constitutional relations was not so much imperial or even federative but associative. Keating was primarily concerned to validate the acceptability of the Stuart dynasty in Ireland through such traditional mechanisms as providence, prophecy and legitimacy. Charles I, like his father James I, should be recognised as the true king of Ireland. In turn, Ireland should be accorded equality with England and Scotland in her constitutional association with the Stuart dynasty as a free, not a dependent, kingdom.[6]

The shift from a Tudor to a Stuart dynasty in 1603 was particularly welcomed in Ireland. James I could claim direct descent not only from Fergus MacEarc who had gone from Ulster as first king of the Scottish Gaels, but also from the kings of the other provinces of Munster, Leinster and Connacht. His right to the high kingship of Ireland was endorsed theologically. The Roman Catholic Church in Ireland taught that James, despite his Protestantism, was *de iure* king of Ireland and entitled to temporal allegiance. This allegiance was eagerly affirmed by the Irish parliament in 1613, notwithstanding the writings of continental Jesuits claiming that a heretical monarch could be deposed at papal instigation – writings which moved James to a vigorous defence of his independent empire, to which unequivocal allegiance was owed by all subjects, whether Catholic or Protestant.[7] Plantations in Munster, Ulster and Connacht

---

[6] B. Ó Buachalla, *Foras Feasa ar Éirinn, History of Ireland: Foreword* (Dublin, 1987), pp. 1–8; B. Cunningham, *The World of Geoffrey Keating* (Dublin, 2000), pp. 31–40, 83–101. These same mechanisms ensured that the Catholic Confederation sought rapprochement with Charles I as the rightful king of Ireland throughout the civil wars of the 1640s (T. Ó hAnnracháin, 'Rebels and Confederates: The Stance of the Irish Clergy in the 1640s' in Young, ed., *Celtic Dimensions*, pp. 96–115; A. Clarke, 'Patrick Darcy and the Constitutional Relationship Between Ireland and Britain' in Ohlmeyer, ed., *Political Thought in Seventeenth-century Ireland*, pp. 35–55).

[7] B. Ó Buachalla, *Aisling Ghearr: Na Stiobhartaigh Agus an tAos Leinn, 1603–1788* (Dubin, 1996), pp. 148–94; J. P. Somerville, *Politics and Ideology in England, 1603–1640* (London, 1986), pp. 117–20.

soon dashed Irish Catholics' hopes that allegiance to the Stuart dynasty would be reciprocated by the granting of liberty of conscience. Nonetheless, Keating and other clerical agents of the Counter-Reformation endorsed the aim of the Catholic political elite for an accommodation with the Crown that would associate Ireland as an equal partner – not as a confessionally disadvantaged satellite – within a composite Britannic Empire.[8]

Ireland's status as a political dependency was enshrined in Poynings' Law (of 1494). This Tudor enactment had stipulated that no bill could be introduced into the Houses, either of Lords or of Commons, in the bi-cameral Irish parliament without prior approval from the king and Privy Council in England. From 1557, the Irish parliament was able to exclude bills drafted in England and amend proposed legislation. Irish subjects were also allowed to make judicial appeals from parliament to the Crown. Initially, Poynings' Law ensured that lord-deputies did not act independently from the king. However, even if the Irish parliament could delay legislation by multiple amendments, it remained firmly reactive rather than proactive under the executive control of the lord-deputy and the Irish Privy Council, a situation unchanged by regal union.[9] In addition to the English backlash provoked by the initial endeavours of James I to accomplish the full integration of his British dominions, Ireland's standing as a political satellite raised serious concerns in Scotland. In his celebrated speech on union to the English parliament in March 1607, James had ridiculed any suggestion that Scotland should be garrisoned like a Spanish province. But his tactless comparisons with Sicily and Naples provoked the Scottish Estates to temper their support for a unified Britannic Empire if it resulted in their governance by a viceroy or lord-deputy. The implicit exemplar was not Spain's Italian provinces but the English dependency of Ireland.[10]

Nevertheless, Scots did become enthusiastic participants in the king's Britannic agenda through plantation in Ireland, a process begun by the Tudors with the plantation of Munster in the 1580s and continued by the early Stuarts with that of Ulster from the 1600s and Connacht from the 1630s. The resultant expropriation and displacement of the Irish can

---

[8] A. Clarke, 'Colonial Identity in Early Seventeenth-Century Ireland' in T. W. Moody, ed., *Nationality and the Pursuit of National Independence* (Belfast, 1978), pp. 57–72; Cunningham, *The World of Geoffrey Keating*, pp. 105–12.

[9] M. Perceval-Maxwell, 'Ireland and the Monarchy in the Early Stuart Multiple Kingdom', *HJ*, 34 (1991), pp. 279–95; A. Clarke, 'The History of Poynings' Law, 1615–1641', *IHS*, 18 (1972), pp. 207–22.

[10] *RPCS*, first series, VII, pp. 534–8; J. Wormald, 'The Union of 1603' in Mason, ed., *Scots and Britons*, pp. 17–40.

undoubtedly appear as colonial victimisation.[11] However, colonialism as a feature of governance must be disengaged from plantations as a form of settlement.[12] Ireland, moreover, enjoyed a process of colonial legitimisation not available to governors or proprietors of the Stuarts' American colonies. Warranted by patent under the Irish Crown from Lord-Deputy Thomas Wentworth in 1632, a colony designated New Albion and located in the Delaware Basin was launched by planters from Ireland with prior knowledge of Virginia. This colony, which was serviced from Ireland, was still recruiting settlers in 1650. The continued existence of New Albion, no less than its authorisation, underlined Ireland's status as a dependent kingdom rather than an English colony. Longer-lived than the Scottish colony of Nova Scotia (see Chapter 6), this Irish colony was no less British in conception or in exploitative intent.[13]

The showpiece British endeavour of the Stuarts' frontier policy, the plantation of Ulster, was launched formally in 1610, when the forfeited estates of exiled Gaelic lords were contracted to undertakers and planters drawn from both England and Scotland. Although this was propagated as a British endeavour, the satellite relationship of Ireland was affirmed by the contractual emphasis on English common law as the determining influence in local government, estate management and conveyancing. The paramount need to promote economic recovery after decades of continuous warfare ensured that there was limited displacement of the native Irish other than in the ranks of the landed classes. That plantations made Ireland integral rather then marginal to the Stuarts' fashioning of

---

[11] See N. Canny, 'The Marginal Kingdom: Ireland as a Problem in the First British Empire' in B. Bailyn & P. D. Morgan, eds., *Strangers Within the Realm: Cultural Margins of the First British Empire* (Chapel Hill, 1991), pp. 35–66; J. H. Ohlmeyer, 'Seventeenth-Century Ireland and the New British and Atlantic Histories', *AHR*, 104 (1999), pp. 446–62.
[12] A. I. Macinnes, 'Making the Plantations British, 1603–38' in S. G. Ellis & R. Esser, eds., *Frontiers and the Writing of History, 1500–1850* (Hannover-Laatzen, 2006), pp. 95–125.
[13] *The Earl of Strafforde's Letters and Dispatches*, ed. W. Knowler, 2 vols. (London, 1739), I, pp. 72–3; Beauchamp Plantagenet, *A description of the province of New Albion and a direction for adventurers with small stock to get two for one, and good land freely and for gentlemen and all servants, labourers and artificers to live plentifully* (London, 1641, 1648 and 1650); 'Plowden's New Albion' in *Collections of the New York Historical Society for 1869*, pp. 213–22; C. Lewis, 'Some Extracts relating to Sir Edmund Plowden and some others from the lost minutes of the Virginia Council and General Court, 1642–45', *William & Mary Quarterly*, second series, 20 (1940), pp. 62–78. New Albion was located on Plowden's Island, named after the founder of the venture, Sir Edmund Plowden. This settlement was bedevilled with misfortune in shipping out planters in 1639, 1649 and 1650. Faced by more attractive prospects for settlement in Virginia, as opposed to contesting an area of Delaware where a Swedish colony was established from 1638, the Irish colonists mutinied against Plowden's leadership in 1643. The civil wars in all three kingdoms further discouraged recruitment.

their Britannic Empire is indicated by the active participation of Catholic landowners as planters and tenants.[14]

Enthusiasm for British plantation as a civilising venture required differentiation between English and Scottish interests. The City of London had to be continuously reminded of their obligations as undertakers for the planting of County Derry and developing the town of Londonderry. Scottish undertakers and planters were able to capitalise on growing domestic prosperity. It was only by the prior acquisition of funds in Scotland that settlers were provided with the necessary stake to develop devastated tracts of Ulster. While the need for venture capital gave an undoubted advantage to migrants from commercially developed areas, planting by Scots in Ulster should not be regarded as the preserve of Lowlanders. As borne out by the muster-rolls for the 1630s, Gaelic-speaking tenants in Ulster were not exclusively Irish. Scottish shipping came to dominate the carrying trade to and from Ulster. Tools and provisions were exported from Scotland along with luxuries from the continent, while agricultural produce from Ulster found a ready market in Scotland. The imposition of punitive tariffs on grain imports by the Scottish Privy Council during the 1620s adversely affected the profitability of farming in Ulster and tangibly reduced immigration. But two bad harvests in successive years in 1635–6 brought a renewed flood of immigrants from Scotland. By the outbreak of the Covenanting Movement, Scottish settlers in the province constituted no less than a third and probably nearer half of the 100,000 reputed immigrants.[15]

However, the Scots were not accorded the same rights as English settlers who became denizens in Ulster until 1630. Even then this was viewed at Court not as a delayed right in the wake of Colvin's Case of 1608, but more as a necessary concession to secure Scottish support for the common fishing of Charles I. Again the common fishing raised fears of Scotland being relegated to the dependent status of Ireland. Irish interests were not represented directly over the two years that the negotiations were

---

[14] B. MacCuarta, 'The Plantation of Leitrim, 1620–41', *IHS*, 32 (2001), pp. 297–320; J. Ohlmeyer, '"Civilizing of those Rude Partes": Colonization within Britain and Ireland, 1580s–1640s' in N. Canny, ed., *The Oxford History of the British Empire*, vol. I: *The Origins of Empire: British Overseas Empire to the Close of the Seventeenth Century* (Oxford, 1998), pp. 124–46.

[15] HL, Bridgewater & Ellesmere MSS, EL 7048–9, 7051, 7058; M. Perceval-Maxwell, *The Scottish Migration to Ulster in the Reign of James I* (London, 1973), pp. 8–10, 29–67, 154–6; R. Gillespie, 'Explorers, Exploiters and Entrepreneurs: Early Modern Ireland and its Context 1500–1700' in B. J. Graham & L. J. Proudfoot, eds., *An Historical Geography of Ireland* (London, 1993), pp. 123–57; P. Robinson, *The Plantation of Ulster* (Belfast, 2000), pp. 108–28.

conducted at Court between the commissioners drawn from the Scottish and English Privy Councils. Instead they were encompassed within the remit of English commissioners who exhibited little concern for their advancement.[16]

Well before the common fishing foundered as a British enterprise, Lord-Deputy Thomas Wentworth had undermined the settlement of Scottish and English planters throughout Ireland. Wentworth was intent on moving beyond the Tudor conquest of Ireland as a dependent kingdom under the common law and parliamentary statute. His governing remit was to expand the resources available to Britannic monarchy through prerogative rule with or without constitutional consensus. Ireland was to become a net contributor rather than a perennial drain on the royal coffers. During his seven-year stint as lord-deputy, his principal objective, which was endorsed by Archbishop Laud of Canterbury, was to reclaim Crown lands and reverse the secularisation of Church lands. Exemplary and remunerative plantations were to be promoted at the same time as the establishment of Episcopalianism was secured. Ireland would thus become a laboratory for British improvement.[17]

The incongruities in this policy were soon evident. Wentworth's reliance on prerogative rather than statutory courts to augment royal revenues and to effect a revocation of land for the benefit of Crown and Church destabilised the plantations. Wentworth interpreted Poynings' Law as vesting the initiative for framing legislation with the lord-deputy and the Irish Privy Council. His vindictiveness towards political opponents and his venality as a land grabber in Munster, Connacht and Ulster alienated the Protestant planters as well as the Catholic Irish. His willingness to restore three-quarters of confiscated land on the payment of compositions was further compounded by his intent to require subscription to the Anglican oath of supremacy not just an oath of allegiance to Britannic monarchy. This requirement was anathema not only to Irish Catholics but also to Scottish Presbyterians and other nonconforming planters. Thus, his promotion of religious uniformity in Ireland served as an exemplary warning for Scots opposed to the liturgical innovations of Charles I, which proved instrumental in the making of the Covenanting Movement.[18] Its formulation of a national consensus in opposition to the

[16] Macinnes, *Charles I and the Making of the Covenanting Movement*, pp. 110–12.
[17] N. Canny, 'The Attempted Anglicisation of Ireland in the Seventeenth Century: An Exemplar of "British History"' in J. F. Merritt, ed., *The Political World of Thomas Wentworth, Earl of Strafford 1621–1641* (Cambridge, 1996), pp. 157–86.
[18] H. Kearney, *Strafford in Ireland, 1633–41: A Study in Absolutism* (Manchester, 1959, 2nd edition Cambridge, 1989), pp. 42–68; J. McCafferty, '"God bless your free Church of Ireland": Wentworth, Laud, Bramhall and the Irish Convocation of 1634' in Merritt, ed., *The Political World of Thomas Wentworth, Earl of Strafford*, pp. 187–208.

authoritarian promotion of uniformity in Kirk and State was reinforced by the potent message from Ulster that leading agents of Britannic monarchy no longer trusted the Scots. In turn, during the negotiations for the Treaty of London, the Scottish Covenanters demonised Wentworth (now Earl of Strafford) for his imposition of the notorious 'black oath' on Scottish settlers during the Bishops' Wars.[19]

The proclamation warranting this oath in May 1639 had actually been welcomed by leading Scottish planters in Ulster who were keen to rid themselves of aspersions of being disloyal subjects. However, the oath was effectively a loyalty test that demonstrated that the Ulster Scots, regardless of their Covenanting affiliations, did not have the confidence of the Court and were not regarded as equal partners in the Britannic projects of the Stuart monarchy. Strafford was unconcerned that the 'black oath' served to drive some settlers back to Scotland. Conversely, his recruitment of Irish Catholics into the army he was building up for Charles to oppose the Scottish Covenanters had forced those settlers who remained to align with the Covenanting Movement in order to preserve their plantations. Presbyterian solidarity across the North Channel enhanced their prospects for preservation. Strafford's persistent advocacy of war caused him to be identified as 'chief incendiary' in the eyes of the Covenanting leadership, which was intent on judicial redress from the English parliament.[20]

Although commissioners from the Irish parliament of 1640–1 were on hand in England to assist in the prosecution of Strafford, his trial reversed the convention under Poynings' Law that the English parliament did not interfere in Irish affairs. By prosecuting Strafford, first by impeachment and then by attainder, primarily for his treasonable conduct, initially as lord-deputy and later as lord-lieutenant, the English parliament claimed supremacy over Irish affairs. Internationally, the judicial proceedings that culminated in Strafford's execution in May 1641 demonstrated that Ireland was a subordinate kingdom. Strafford's trial set a precedent for parliamentary appropriation of areas hitherto regarded as the preserve of the English Crown and was soon followed up by the assertion of control over the Stuarts' American colonies. In turn, this Gothic assertiveness ruled out any recognition of Irish independence or even legislative autonomy as claimed by the Confederation of Irish Catholics during the

---

[19] M. Perceval-Maxwell, *The Outbreak of the Irish Rebellion of 1641* (Montreal, 1994), pp. 82–91.
[20] BL: Original Documents relating to Scotland, the Borders & Ireland, 16th and 17th centuries, Add.MSS 5754, fo. 40; Nicholas Papers, Egerton MS 2533, fols. 89–92. DH, Loudoun Papers, bundle 1/5; HL, Bridgewater & Ellesmere MSS, 7430; *The Earl of Strafforde's Letters and Dispatches*, II, pp. 324, 328, 382–5.

1640s. More immediately, the right of the Irish parliament to wage war was subsumed within the remit of the English parliament when the Treaty of London was ratified with the Scottish Covenanters in August 1641: a situation that stood in stark contrast to the Treaty's formal recognition of the sovereign and independent power of the Scottish Estates.[21]

Confederation and conquest

The Treaty of London did not ameliorate Irish fears of becoming further dependent on England. The Scottish commissioners not only insisted that the English parliament sanction any future raising of forces in England and Ireland by the king, but also wanted the Irish parliament to ratify their acceptance of this dependency. This standpoint was supported by Parliamentarians intent on enforcing dependency on Westminster in order to limit monarchical power in England. The mood in the Irish parliament changed markedly from their support of the pre-trial proceedings against Strafford. Taking their lead from Patrick Darcy, an Old English lawyer, the Irish parliament was now intent on asserting its legislative privileges to impose permanent checks on England's exercise of executive power through Dublin and to secure direct access to monarchy at Court. Although Ireland was to be governed by the common law and general customs of England, all statutes were to be made and approved by the Irish parliament. The annexation of Ireland to the English Crown was accepted. The subordination of the Irish parliament to the English one was not. This doctrine commanded majority support in the Irish Commons and was subsequently endorsed by the Confederation of Irish Catholics. Nevertheless, Irish constitutional opposition should not be overstated – it was a principled parliamentary critique of arbitrary rule.[22] Recourse to a military option was more potent.

Five months after Strafford's execution, the outbreak of rebellion in October 1641 forcibly brought the Irish perspective to the centre stage of British politics. Charles I conveyed news of the Irish rebellion to the Scottish Estates, along with an invitation for armed intervention by the Covenanters to protect the plantations. However, the Covenanting leadership was not prepared to intervene without the consent of the

---

[21] Macinnes, *The British Revolution*, pp. 135, 138, 161; M. Ó Siochrú, 'Catholic Confederates and the Constitutional Relationship Between Ireland and England, 1641–1649' in C. Brady & J. Ohlmeyer, eds., *British Interventions in Early Modern Ireland* (Cambridge, 2005), pp. 207–29.

[22] M. Perceval-Maxwell, 'Ireland and the Monarchy in the Early Stuart Multiple Kingdom'; M. Ó Siochrú, *Confederate Ireland, 1642–9: A Constitutional and Political Analysis* (Dublin, 1999), pp. 21–6, 237–40.

English parliament. The Scottish Estates duly offered their services to the Long Parliament as indiscriminate reports circulated of the 'cruel outrages of the Irish rebels' and the 'pitiful estate of the British in Ireland'. The endeavours of Charles to commit Covenanting forces without waiting for the consent of the English parliament and in blatant disregard of the Treaty of London used up his last reserves of political goodwill in Scotland. His demonstrable untrustworthiness on the Irish issue accelerated the descent to civil war in England. Simultaneously, the blatant Gothic insensitivity of the Long Parliament fuelled the Irish revolt.[23]

Despite appealing to Covenanting precedents for their recourse to arms, the rebels had no coherent constitutional programme to implement prior to the landed elite and the clergy imposing a confederal governmental structure in May 1642. The resultant Catholic Confederation was designed to legitimise rebellion, restrain the excesses of reprisals against Protestant settlers and bring about a measure of political stability among the factions constituting the Irish interest. On the Protestant side, there was no clear British solidarity. The English clergy in Dublin, who compiled the grossly exaggerated depositions on the extent of atrocities against the Protestant plantations, tended to appropriate the designation 'British' for settlers born in England. 'British' became a synonym for the English interest in Ireland.[24]

Nevertheless, confederal unity with Scotland offered the prospect of reducing Ireland to the profession of Protestantism as the true religion, towards which the abolition of episcopacy, as advocated vociferously by Sir John Clotworthy, was but the first step. Clotworthy (later 1st Viscount Masserene) was also to the fore in promoting through the Long Parliament the Adventurers' Act of March 1642, which duly tied the recovery of Ireland to thorough plantation. This combination of religious and speculative interests attracted considerable support from the Protestant elite in Ireland, as well as from London merchants and English Parliamentarians. Scottish subscribers were neither excluded nor encouraged.[25]

---

[23] *The Nicholas Papers, Correspondence of Sir Edward Nicholas, Secretary of State*, ed. G. F. Warner, 2 vols. (London, 1886), I, pp. 25, 33–4, 58–9; D. Stevenson, *Scottish Covenanters and Irish Confederates* (Belfast, 1981), pp. 43–50.

[24] R. Gillespie, 'Destabilizing Ulster' in B. MacCuarta, ed., *Ulster 1641: Aspects of the Rising* (Belfast, 1997), pp. 107–22; N. Canny, *Making Ireland British, 1580–1650* (Oxford, 2003), pp. 461–534.

[25] A. Clarke, 'The 1641 Rebellion and Anti-Popery in England' in MacCuarta, ed., *Ulster 1641*, pp. 139–57; Canny, *Making Ireland British*, pp. 404–8, 553–6, 561. Clotworthy was an English Presbyterian planter in County Antrim and MP for the burgh of Maldon in Essex.

Notwithstanding the hostility of English Parliamentarians and Scottish Covenanters, the Irish Catholics were reluctant rebels. Their ideological standpoint of autonomy under the Stuarts made them anxious for reconciliation with Charles I. When their Confederation was established at Kilkenny in May 1642, Ireland was proclaimed to have the same freedom as that enjoyed by the subjects of the Stuart monarchy in both England and Scotland. Like the Scottish Covenanters with the Treaty of London, the Irish Confederates attempted to negotiate from a position of strength. Despite a similar rhetoric of resistance, the Confederate perspective differed markedly. Their oath of association pledged allegiance to Charles I. But their promise to act in his defence made no distinction between his person and his office. When the Confederates held their first general assembly at Kilkenny, five months later, they elected a supreme council (six members from each of the four provinces). However, this unicameral assembly increasingly circumscribed the executive's scope for independent action. The cause of the Irish Catholics remained a confederation of provincial associations riven by faction, underfinanced yet militarily capable by land and sea.[26]

Apart from these structural weaknesses, the Confederation's objective of negotiating a treaty with Charles I was undermined by prolonged civil war in Ireland for over a decade. Other factors complicated this objective. At the insistence of Clotworthy and the other commissioners from the English parliament, Ireland had been included within the remit of the Solemn League and Covenant concluded at Edinburgh in August 1643. However, the Scots remained reluctant to accord equal standing to a satellite kingdom whose dominant confession was Roman Catholic. Political incompatibilities between the Gothic and Scottish perspectives, no less than the uncompromising commitment of the Solemn League to 'endeavour the Extirpation of Popery', inhibited any negotiated peace for all three kingdoms.[27] On the one hand, the Confederates never secured an all-Ireland government. On the other hand, a military appraisal of the state of Ireland, seemingly commissioned for the English Parliamentarians following a cessation of hostilities between the Royalists and the Confederates in September 1643, was far from pessimistic about Protestant prospects. The Confederation had a controlling interest in twenty out of the thirty-two Irish counties. Accordingly, any calls for Ireland to be a

---

[26] M. Ó Siochrú, *Confederate Ireland, 1642–9*, pp. 205–15; J. H. Ohlmeyer, 'The Civil Wars in Ireland' in J. Kenyon & J. H. Ohlmeyer, eds., *The Civil Wars: A Military History of England, Scotland and Ireland 1638–1660* (Oxford, 1998), pp. 73–102.

[27] *A Source Book of Scottish History*, III, pp. 122–5; R. Armstrong, 'Protestant Churchmen and the Confederate Wars' in Brady & Ohlmeyer, eds., *British Interventions*, pp. 230–51; Macinnes, *The British Revolution*, pp. 150, 162, 169.

'free state' must take account of the fact that the Confederate writ was neither accepted nor unchallenged in over a third of counties and never extended to the whole island prior to the dissolution of the Confederation in 1649.[28]

Certainly, the Confederate forces could more than hold their own against Scottish and English troops in Ireland. However, their military capacity to sustain a standing army cannot be isolated from the state apparatus necessary for its support. Only in Ulster and Leinster was there a possibility of meaningfully servicing a standing army prior to the cessation of 1643. Thereafter, the fiscal basis for sustained support was lacking except in Munster and south Leinster. By its nature, the Confederation was not given to a centralised structure, unlike the Scottish Covenanters from the outset of the Bishops' Wars and the English Parliamentarians from the creation of the New Model Army in 1645. Its provincial forces never controlled or secured supplies from the whole island, and potentially remunerative areas, such as Galway and Mayo in Connacht, lay largely untapped because of the intense factionalism occasioned by the peace process with the Royalists.[29]

The insular Irish perspective required the pursuit of total victory before seeking an accommodation with the king to secure the Catholic recovery of all of Ireland. The alternative Royalist or Britannic perspective encouraged the Confederation to seek an expeditious settlement with the king and the release of Irish forces to counter the threat posed by the English Parliamentarians.[30] On the one hand, the Confederates could draw on the long-established military, commercial and ecclesiastical networks maintained by the Irish diaspora to appeal primarily for financial assistance throughout the 1640s. The Confederates also gained militarily from the return of committed Catholic troops, especially from Spanish service, and confessionally from the disciplined inculcation of the Counter-Reformation by a clergy trained predominantly in continental seminaries. On the other hand, although the Confederation sent envoys to several European capitals and received diplomats in Kilkenny, these were rarely accredited, as Ireland still ranked at best as 'a third rate power'. Diplomatic missions from France and Spain, particularly

---

[28] HL, Hastings Irish Papers, box 8/HA 14987, and box 9/HA 15009; J. S. Wheeler, 'Four Armies in Ireland' in J. H. Ohlmeyer, ed., *Ireland from Independence to Occupation* (Cambridge, 1995), pp. 43–65.

[29] P. Lenihan, *Confederate Catholics at War, 1641–49* (Cork, 2001), pp. 22–72, 117–45; P. Edwards, 'Logistical Supply' in Kenyon & Ohlmeyer, eds., *The Civil Wars*, pp. 234–71.

[30] P. Lenihan, 'Confederate Military Strategy, 1643–7' in M. Ó Siochrú, ed., *Kingdoms in Crisis: Ireland in the 1640s* (Dublin, 2000), pp. 158–75; J. S. Wheeler, *The Irish and British Wars, 1637–1654* (London, 2002), pp. 99–102, 121–3; Stevenson, *Scottish Covenanters and Irish Confederates*, pp. 139–63.

after the arrival of the papal agent Giovanni Battista Rinuccini, Bishop of Fermo, in October 1645, served to destabilise Confederate politics and negate prospects of a secure peace with the Royalists. Only the papacy was committed unconditionally to no accommodation with Charles I without religious concessions. At the same time, the general willingness in Rome to see the war in Ireland purely as a religious struggle led Catholic Confederates to be viewed as more ardent crusaders than they actually were. But the Vatican did not provide remotely adequate funding to match the personal zeal of Rinuccini. Prior to his departure in February 1649, the Catholic Confederation was effectively torn apart by French and papal factions.[31]

The Irish phase of British revolutionary politics had already imploded by 1648. In an attempted patriotic accommodation, Royalists under James Butler, Marquis (later 1st Duke) of Ormond, made common cause with Confederates prepared to espouse a Britannic perspective, with Presbyterian-inclined Parliamentary forces in Munster and with the British forces in Ulster from where the Scots were withdrawing gradually and gracelessly. At the same time, Rinuccini had sought an accommodation with the Independent-inclined Parliamentary forces in Leinster. Internal rivalries within the Confederation served instead to allow the Parliamentarians to push on into Ulster and set the scene for the Cromwellian conquest.[32]

In embarking for Ireland after the regicide in 1649, Oliver Cromwell's immediate priority was civilisation through conquest of a territory now regarded as a dependent state rather than a dependent kingdom. Cromwell did not view conquest as an opportunity either to eradicate the native Irish or to effect their wholesale confiscation. Cromwellian forces had secured Ulster by the end of the year. In Munster, the Presbyterian-inclined forces steadily mutinied and crossed over to join the Independent troops. By Cromwell's departure in May 1650, only the province of Connacht was offering substantial resistance, which took another three years to mop up.[33] Former Confederates were no less conscious than Royalists of the need to make pragmatic arrangements to safeguard their

---

[31] J. H. Ohlmeyer, 'Ireland Independent: Confederate Foreign Policy and International Relations During the Mid-Seventeenth Century' in Ohlmeyer, ed., *Ireland from Independence to Occupation*, pp. 89–111; T. Ó hAnnráchain, 'Disrupted and Disruptive: Continental Influences on the Confederate Catholics of Ireland' in Macinnes & Ohlmeyer, eds., *The Stuart Kingdoms*, pp. 135–50.

[32] Wheeler, *The Irish and British Wars*, pp. 175–8, 195–8; T. Ó hAnnráchain, 'The Strategic Involvement of Confederate Powers in Ireland 1596–1691' in P. Lenihan, ed., *Conquest and Resistance: War in Seventeenth Century Ireland* (Leiden, 2001), pp. 25–52.

[33] I. Gentles, *The New Model Army in England, Ireland and Scotland, 1645–1653* (Oxford, 1992), pp. 350–84; Wheeler, *The Irish and British Wars*, pp. 209–20.

estates. At the same time, the threat of civil sanctions, especially sequestration, was particularly vexing to the English in Ireland.[34]

Whereas the Scots were able to negotiate for a junior partnership, the Irish were summarily incorporated into the Cromwellian union. Issues of political economy also sharply demarcated Ireland from Scotland as a satellite state. The Protectorate was especially supportive of landowners attempting internal plantations on their Scottish estates.[35] However, the Act for the settling of Ireland in August 1652 laid the basis for a punitive policy of land confiscation targeted against the Irish Confederates, Royalists and those who had not actively assisted the Cromwellian conquest. Effectively this Act and the supplementary legislation in June 1653 sought to compensate those who had subscribed to the adventurers' scheme of 1642, which had remained largely unfulfilled. Up to 35,000 officers and men engaged with the New Model Army in the conquest of Ireland were also due to be paid off. Active encouragement for another round of plantations through a series of ordinances from the Lord Protector in 1654 clearly indicated that confiscation was directed against former Catholic Confederates.[36] Public policy favoured the transplantation of the native Irish out of Ulster, Leinster and Munster into Connacht, where their settlements were to be corralled by colonies of soldiers along the Atlantic coast and the banks of the River Shannon to close the door on foreign intervention from Spain or France. In the event, there was only a limited transfer of the native Irish, landed elite and their families to Connacht.[37] The principal beneficiaries of the new round of plantations were not the adventurers or the soldiers who were disinclined to settle permanently in Ireland. Existing planters were able to procure the allotments of the former and purchase the promissory notes or debentures of the latter. The Scottish planters, Catholic as well as Protestant, largely managed to stay their ground.[38] Nevertheless, the renewed round

---

[34] T. C. Barnard, *Cromwellian Ireland: English Government and Reform in Ireland, 1649–1660* (Oxford, 1975), pp. 67–8, 95–8, 148; BL, Petitions, 1648–54, Add.MSS 34,326, fo. 3; Patrick Adair, *A True Narrative of the Rise and Progress of the Presbyterian Church in Ireland (1623–1670)*, ed. W. D. Killen (Belfast, 1866), pp. 135–237; *The Declaration of the British in the North of Ireland, With some queries of Colonel Moncke, and the answers of the British to the queries* (London, 1649).

[35] *APS*, VI ii, p. 745; Williamson, 'Union with England Traditional', pp. 311–12, 320.

[36] Woolrych, *Britain in Revolution, 1625–1660*, pp. 573–9; A. Clarke, *Prelude to Restoration in Ireland: The End of the Commonwealth, 1659–1660* (Cambridge, 1999), pp. 4–17.

[37] Canny, *Making Ireland British*, pp. 556–9; S. Barber, 'Settlement, Transplantation and Expulsion: A Comparative Study of the Placement of Peoples' in Brady & Ohlmeyer, eds., *British Interventions*, pp. 280–98.

[38] Barnard, *Cromwellian Ireland*, pp. 10–15, 20–3, 297–305; K. McKenny, 'The Seventeenth-Century Land Settlement in Ireland: Towards a Statistical Interpretation' in Ohlmeyer, ed., *Ireland from Independence to Occupation*, pp. 181–200.

of planting represented a Gothic consolidation of the English, not the British, interest in Ireland, an interest that was gearing up to defend its political and commercial ascendancy as the Restoration of the Stuart monarchy became a distinct possibility.[39]

Restoration and discrimination

The Ulster Scots were soon made aware that the constitutional settlement in Ireland was primarily directed at the entrenchment of the English interest that had benefited from the Cromwellian regime. Roger Boyle, the newly created Earl of Orrery and former Cromwellian administrator who had instigated military action in Ireland to expedite the Restoration of Charles II, made clear to Ormond on 9 September 1661 that 'a true English Protestant Interest is ye Immoveable foundation' upon which the king intended to build the security of Ireland as well as England.[40] Accordingly, the land issue took clear precedence over the political and religious concerns that had dominated the agenda in England and Scotland. The Acts of Settlement (1662) and of Explanation (1665) and, in the interim, the Irish Court of Claims established in 1663 were certainly concerned to ensure that former Royalists who had fought against the Catholic Confederates as well as the Cromwellian occupation were now recompensed for their past services. The Cromwellian confiscations of the 1650s were further adjusted to take account of 'innocent papists'. However, as Charles II also granted a substantial estate to his brother James, Duke of York (the future James II & VII), from the holdings of former regicides in Ireland, this diminished the stock of land available for restoration to Catholics. Moreover, the Protestant establishment was not averse to resurrecting past approaches by the Catholic Confederates to Spain, France and the papacy in order to question the loyalty of Irish Catholics and their suitability to hold political office, attain royal favour and inherit or acquire estates. Catholic landowners retained merely a third of the estates they held in 1641. The holding and management of estates continued to be monitored more closely in Ireland than in the other two Stuart kingdoms.[41]

---

[39] T. C. Barnard, 'The Protestant Interest, 1641–1660', & A. Clarke, '1659 and the Road to Restoration' in Ohlmeyer, ed., *Ireland from Independence to Occupation*, pp. 218–40, 241–64.

[40] HL, Hastings Irish Papers, box 11/HA 14126, 14368, 14372–5, 15026–8, 15037, 15177; Clarke, *Prelude to Restoration in Ireland*, pp. 92–168; Harris, *Restoration*, pp. 86–104.

[41] BL, Abstract of Decrees of the Court of Claims, 1662, Egerton MS 789, fols. 2–69, and An Abstract of Every Rent per annum in every Barony in Each County in the Kingdom of Ireland, 1678, Add.MSS 15,899; K. McKenny, 'Charles II's Irish Cavaliers: The 1649 Officers and the Restoration Land Settlement', *IHS*, 28 (1993), pp. 409–25; L. J. Arnold, 'The Irish Court of Claims of 1663', *IHS*, 24 (1985), pp. 417–30.

The Restoration era in Ireland, as elsewhere in the British Isles, was marked by successive outings of Protestant nonconformists, by prescription of covenanting and by the public immolation of the Solemn League and Covenant in towns and cities. Ulster Presbyterians, like their Scottish brethren, were disadvantaged by the restoration of erastian Episcopacy. Despite Ulster featuring occasionally in the preaching circuit of Scottish field conventiclers, Presbyterians in the province preferred to maintain a passive rather than a militant profile, in which influential English planters such as Clotworthy, now Viscount Masserene, supported them. This profile, characterised by house conventicles and praying societies, enabled Presbyterianism in Ulster to remain a distinctive layer of association within the Church of Ireland. But the association of Presbyterianism and erastian Episcopacy was not necessarily irenicist or indulged by the English interest, notwithstanding the occasional accommodation offered to Presbyterian ministers removed from the Scottish Lowlands. The resurgence of immigration and the association of covenanting with violence and social disorder made English commanders reluctant to admit Scottish troops into the standing forces in Ulster. The Irish Privy Council was prepared to send troops over to Scotland during peak periods of covenanting dissent in 1674, 1678 and 1684. The persistence of this dissent and the tarnishing of all Presbyterians by association with conventicling had provided the excuse for the Society of London to deny Scottish settlers security of tenure around Derry in 1670. The irony of this situation was compounded when prominent Scottish planters, led by Sir Arthur Forbes of Corse (later Viscount and 1st Earl of Granard), actually sounded out the Duke of Lauderdale on the prospect of military redress for migrants he had hounded out of Scotland.[42]

Notwithstanding their palpably more favourable treatment than Irish Catholics or Scottish Presbyterians, the English interest in Ireland was vociferously aggrieved by the distinctively Gothic mercantilism of the English Navigation Acts of 1660 to 1671, especially the ban on importing cattle into England that came into effect in 1667. Edward Conway, 1st Earl of Conway, and other Anglo-Irish landowners were to the fore in protesting against this discriminatory measure, which they held to undermine the distinctly Anglican, Protestant ascendancy established at the Restoration. Although Conway attempted smuggling through Wales as an expression of civil disobedience, he concentrated on securing alternative markets for salted carcasses, of which the royal navy was the most

---

[42] Anon., *The Funeral of the Good Old Cause, or A Covenant of Both Houses of parliament against the Solemn League and Covenant* (London, 1661); Adair, *A True Narrative*, pp. 238–304. HL, Hastings Irish Papers: box 22/HA 14491; box23/HA 14514, 14517; box 23/HA 14528, 14533; box 25/HA 14512, 14562, 15002, 15109, 15022, 15672, 15674; box 30/HA 14593; box 31/HA 14735. BL, Lauderdale Papers, Add.MSS 23,234, fo. 23.

prominent and the Canaries the most exotic. At the same time, he diversified his estate management in Antrim through the intensive working of potash to facilitate the bleaching of cloth, and the introduction of Walloons skilled in spinning and weaving to promote the manufacture of linen and wool. He also engaged with other English entrepreneurs to export timber to England from as far afield as County Wicklow and promoted shipbuilding to facilitate his trading ventures to France and Spain and lessen his dependence on the Scottish carrying trade. The complaints of Conway and the English interest were partially assuaged when Charles II issued a proclamation in February 1667 suspending the Navigation Acts in so far as they discouraged Irish trade with allied powers in continental Europe and, to a lesser extent, with the plantations, albeit trade to the Americas was boosted by a further suspension of the Acts in 1672.[43]

Undoubtedly the English interest in Ireland was able to profit from an expanding provisioning trade to the colonies, with a ready market for salt beef being established in the Stuart colonies of Newfoundland and the West Indies, as well as French colonies in the Caribbean. However, direct trade in enumerated commodities from the colonies – tobacco, sugar, indigo, cotton, ginger and dye-woods – remained problematic. English customs officers, colonial administrators and merchant adventurers intent on preserving England's monopoly over these commodities secured a lasting restriction on direct Irish trade to the colonies in 1685 that was reaffirmed in 1696. Despite these restrictions, there was a level of commercial integration, involving the repatriation of capital and favourable interest rates between Ireland and England, attainable for English planters such as Conway. This was not possible for the Scottish noble houses of Hamilton and Annandale, also with estates in Ireland, so long as Scotland and England were not united commercially or politically.[44]

There was considerable integration among landed elites through intermarriage and succession to land in Scotland and Ireland, which can

---

[43] HL, Bridgewater & Ellesmere MSS, EL 8558, and Hastings Irish Papers: box 19/HA 14432; box 20/HA 14175, 14445–8, 14450, 14452, 14455–60; box 21/HA 14455–7, 14459–60, 14462, 14467–8; box 23/HA 14522, 14562, 14990.

[44] HL, Hastings Irish Papers, box 22/HA 14469–70, box 25/HA 14555, box 26/HA 14570, box 32/HA 14663, and Huntington Manuscripts, HM 82; NAS, Hamilton Papers, GD 406/1/3265, /3409, /7532, /11559; ACA, Aberdeen Council Letters, vol. 8 (1700–19)/89, and Aberdeen Council Register vol. 58 (1705–21), p. 4; C. M. Andrews, *The Colonial Period of American History: England's Commercial and Colonial Policy* (New Haven, 1943), pp. 109–10, 126–31. A significant stumbling block to closer integration was the reluctance of the English judiciary to accept judgements and decrees of Scottish courts in matters of disputed succession, concerning Scottish heirs and claimants in Ireland, that were to be determined ultimately under English law (*Lords*, original series (1690–1), pp. 488–91).

ostensibly suggest the creation of a British identity well in advance of political incorporation. However, Scottish planters seeking to be embedded within the Anglican ascendancy in Ireland had effectively to concentrate on their Irish rather than their Scottish estates. Thus, Arthur Forbes, Earl Granard, secured his family's continued prominence among the English interest by moving his principal seat from Aberdeenshire to County Leitrim. From his base in Castle Forbes, he expanded his territorial influence in Leinster as well as Ulster while simultaneously advancing through the civil and military establishment during the later seventeenth century. Political and economic advancement clearly required acceptance of English dependency in a British context.[45]

The Scots had certainly benefited from the prohibition on importing Irish cattle into England in 1667, which they had consolidated with their own simultaneous ban on Irish imports. Thus, the droving of cattle and sheep from Scotland under licence had a clear run into English markets. Irish ships trading to the continent but blown off-course into the Firth of Clyde were not allowed to offload their cargoes for sale unless they supported the endeavours of the merchant adventurers of Glasgow to rescind the differential tariffs that discriminated against the Scottish carrying trade to Ireland. Nevertheless, the Scots lacked the political muscle to make other mercantilist measures effective in the Restoration era when overtures for union with England from both Ireland and Scotland featured as central issues of political economy. Scotland had no contemporary equivalent to Sir William Petty, who had cut his polemical teeth while a land surveyor during the Cromwellian confiscations in Ireland. Although an advocate of a free market with England and the colonies, Petty promoted Anglo-Irish union in order to facilitate social engineering, if not ethnic and cultural assimilation, through the transplantation of peoples. While he recognised that Scotland had separate fiscal powers, Petty viewed English leadership, and the prodigious use of public duties to increase wealth from trade and shipping, as the keys to accumulating wealth in all three kingdoms.[46]

---

[45] HL, Hastings Irish Papers: box 24/HA 14153–4, 14530, 14541; box 25/HA 14150–1, 14907, 14909; box 26/HA 14568, 14874, 14912, 14914, 14916–17, 15220, 15237; box 27/HA 14280; box 29/HA 14828, 14919–20; box 32/HA 14922–4; box 33/HA 14925, 15635–6; NAS, Hamilton Papers, GD 406/1/4871.

[46] *RPCS*, third series, I (1661–4), pp. 315–16, 445–6, 479–80, 487–8, 563; VII (1681–2), pp. 651–73; Sir William Petty, *Britannia Languens, or a Discourse of Trade* (London, 1680); Petty, *Political Arithmetick* (London, 1690); Petty *The Political Anatomy of Ireland, 1672* (Dublin, 1691); D. Woodward, 'A Comparative Study of the Irish and Scottish Livestock Trades in the Seventeenth Century' in L. M. Cullen & T. C. Smout, eds., *Comparative Aspects of Scottish and Irish Economic and Social History, 1600–1900* (Edinburgh, 1977), pp. 147–64. Petty also argued in 1672 for union all round, in which the respective

Negotiations for commercial confederation were mooted in 1668 but not resolved as the English House of Commons would not include Ireland as well as Scotland. During these negotiations, the Scottish commissioners were prepared to contemplate indirect access to the Stuart colonies in America along Irish lines in order to sustain the carrying trade. But this should be viewed as a ploy rather than a firm proposal. The significant upturn in Scottish commerce led by the carrying trade in the 1670s not only put discussions on union on hold, but encouraged a more determined – if usually illicit – engagement in trading directly in enumerated commodities from the colonies, to complement legitimate exports of provisions, horses and servants from Scotland. This situation continued largely unchecked until the Revolution, notwithstanding the ire of customs officials, colonial administrators and merchant adventurers whose calls for the enforcement of the English Navigation Acts could not be answered as compliantly in Scotland as in the dependent kingdom of Ireland.[47]

The Whig Party, which had emerged under the leadership of Anthony Ashley Cooper, 1st Earl of Shaftesbury, to promote the exclusion of James, Duke of York, from succeeding his brother, Charles II, regarded the kingdoms of Scotland and Ireland, like the Protestant Churches in France and other parts of the continent, as little sisters 'without breasts' in relation to England. While they were all deserving of protection in relation to Protestantism, vigilance had to be exercised with regard to Scotland and Ireland. The former, under Lauderdale, threatened a backdoor for absolutism and the imposition of slavery on England. The latter threatened a backdoor for France and the imposition of popery, especially as the spurious 'Popish Plot', fabricated to exclude the succession of the Duke of York as an avowed Catholic, had a particular resonance in Ireland, where rapparees in the guise of Tories were preying on the plantations. The predatory activities of the rapparees, which predated the revelation of the plot in 1678 and continued well after the Revolution of 1688–91, tarnished Irish Catholics in the same way that conventicling

---

representation based on population and wealth would relegate Scotland behind England and Ireland, with 450 English, 90 Irish, but only 60 Scottish members of the House of Commons. In 1687, he went on to argue that the policy of transplantation to enhance union should now include the movement of 300,000 Highlanders into the Lowlands of Scotland, as well as 1,000,000 Irish into England (*The Petty Papers*, ed. Marquis of Landsdowne, 2 vols. (New York, 1967), I, pp. 14–6, and II, pp. 264–6).

[47] [Fairfax], *A Discourse upon the Uniting Scotland*, appendix, 'Some Brief Heads of the Papers deliver'd by the Commissioners of Scotland to the Commissioners of England', pp. 73–80; HL, Hastings Irish Papers, box 21/HA 14465; Smout, *Scottish Trade on the Eve of Union*, pp. 175–8, 240–2; Keith, *Commercial Relations of Scotland and England, 1603–1707*, pp. 71–2, 111–28.

tarnished Scottish Presbyterians, and were used to justify their exclusion from positions of public trust, civil or military, under Charles II.[48]

However, the Exclusion Crisis and the subsequent reign of James II had also stirred Irish political aspirations. Gaelic poets, led by David O'Bruadair, commended James for his commitment to Catholicism, for his admission of Irish Catholics into the civil and military establishment and for his galvanising of support from all in Ireland who had not collaborated with the Cromwellian regime. James was the protector of the Irish, who offered redress from Cromwellian expropriations, Protestant triumphalism and the scattering of Irish manpower, whether as continental mercenaries or into colonial servitude in the West Indies. Having rebutted the Scottish interpretation of classical Irish sources, which sustained the mythical progenitors of Fergus MacEarc as kings of Scots, Roderic O'Flaherty, a dispossessed landowner, argued that Ireland, no less than Scotland, should be an independent kingdom in the Stuarts' empire of the British Isles. Writing from Galway to James, as Duke of York, in June 1684, he was adamant that the later Stuarts could claim as their natural, undoubted and hereditary right, 'the regal jurisdiction over all the Britannic dominions'. Accordingly, they were obliged to defend the honour and virtue of Ireland, 'the most ancient nursery of your ancestors', now engendered as a supplicating but fully developed female. Unlike the Scots, the Irish had no first-hand experience of James as a politician until his despatch by Louis XIV to Ireland in March 1689 to tie up British forces that could otherwise have assisted William of Orange's Dutch army. Apart from his military ineptitude during his sixteen-month stay, James, who continued to view Ireland as a political dependency, had a limited grasp of Irish Catholic aspirations despite his wholesale reliance on Irish support in his struggle against William from 1688 to 1691. The thirty-month Jacobite campaign in Ireland ended with the Treaty of Limerick in October 1691, which entrenched the political, social and commercial supremacy of the English interest in Ireland. Simultaneously, Ireland's political standing as an English satellite state was cemented by legislative and judicial discrimination.[49]

---

[48] HL, Bridgewater & Ellesmere MSS, EL 8422, and Hastings Irish Papers: box 21/HA 14131, 14453, 15431; box 25/HA 14176, 14561, 14564, box 26/HA 14567, 15010, 15986; box 31/HA 14660, 15864, 15869; box 33/HA 15704. GCA, Records of the Maxwells of Pollock, T-PM 113/624.

[49] Roderic O'Flaherty, *Ogygia; or, a Chronological Account of Irish Events Collected from very Ancient Documents faithfully compared with each other, and supported by the Genealogical and Chronological Aid of the Sacred and Prophane Writings of the First Nations of the Globe*, 2 vols. (Dublin, 1793), I, pp. xiii–xxii; HL, Hastings Irish Papers, box 31/HA 14304, and box 32/HA 14463-4, 15239, 15788, 15894; A. I. Macinnes, 'Gaelic Culture in the Seventeenth Century: Polarization and Assimilation' in Ellis & Barber, eds., *Conquest*

Spinning union

Notwithstanding the Anglican ascendancy in Ireland, overt English parliamentary interference post-Revolution damaged the wool trade, asserted the jurisdictional superiority of the Lords at Westminster and threatened the redistribution of forfeited Jacobite estates. At the same time, a more stridently Gothic press proclaimed Ireland not so much as a distinctive kingdom like Scotland, but as a distinctive dependency.[50] Complaints from within the English interest in Ireland about the highly partial character of those holding public office made direct rule from London an increasingly attractive prospect. By 1697, the Whig ministry in England was becoming more enamoured of direct rule through Anglo-Irish union, a notion that overrated the common political affiliations of the landed elites in both countries and underestimated the antipathy of the Anglican ascendancy in Ireland to discriminatory treatment by the English ministry.[51] While he regarded union with England as a constitutional ideal, William Molyneux preferred to reassert the primacy of the Irish parliament in the conduct of Irish affairs. Drawing heavily on the contractual theories of John Locke, who had rationalised the Revolution Settlement in England, Molyneux shifted the defence of the English interest in Ireland away from their rights as conquerors, as upheld under Cromwell and reinforced by the Revolution. The English interest were the true heirs of the loyal and freeborn Englishmen who, since the twelfth century, had suppressed rebellion whereby the Irish Gael and the Old English who had not accepted Protestantism had forfeited their rights under common law to participate in the affairs of state. The treasonable conduct of the Catholic Irish justified the land redistribution

---

and Union, pp. 162–94; É. Ó Ciardha, *Ireland and the Jacobite Cause, 1685–1766: A Fatal Attachment* (Dublin, 2002), pp. 52–86; D. W. Hayton, *Ruling Ireland, 1685–1742: Politics, Politicians and Parties* (Woodbridge, 2004), pp. 8–34.

[50] See H. Curson, *A Companion of the Laws and Government Ecclesiastical, Civil and Military of England, Scotland and Ireland, and Dominions, Plantations and Territories thereunto belonging* (London, 1699), pp. 443–86; *Lords*, original series, (1692–3), p. 71; NAS, Hamilton Papers, GD 406/1/7825; BL, Papers Relating to Trade etc., Sloane MS 2902, fols. 137–8. HL: Hastings Irish Papers, box 22/HA 15352, and box 32/HA 15085; Huntington Manuscripts, Manuscript Newsletters from London to Tamworth (1690–1704), HM 30,659/27, /40–1, /50, /69, /74, /77, /82; Stow Papers: Brydges Family Papers, ST 26/ vol.1, James Brydges, 'A Journal of My Daily Actions', 6 February 1697. The full value of Irish estates forfeited after the Revolution amounted to £2,685,130, of which a substantive proportion was restored by favour or legal process, leaving estates in excess of £1,699,343 unrestored. The Crown retained the estates worth £337,942 that had been given to James, Duke of York, in the wake of the Restoration Settlement (BL, Fees, Crown Grants Etc, Stowe MS 597, fo. 44).

[51] BL, Papers Relating to Ireland, vol. II (1691–1700), fo. 13; Hayton, *Ruling Ireland, 1685–1742*, pp. 66–7.

that now overwhelmingly favoured the Anglican ascendancy. *The Case of Ireland* (1698) also asserted that Ireland was as separate and distinct a kingdom as Scotland. Its parliament should be autonomous under the Crown, not subordinated to the English parliament. Though making no more than a passing reference to Scotland, Molyneux instigated a polemical debate that initially differentiated the independence of Scotland from that of Ireland, but then challenged the sovereignty of Scotland in relation to England as an imperial monarchy.[52]

Such were Scottish antipathies to covert English interference post-Revolution that pamphlets advocating English claims of overlordship were publicly burned by the hangman in Edinburgh, while published rebuttals were remunerated by the Scottish Estates.[53] The controversy was further fuelled by Fletcher of Saltoun's publication of his animated conversations with critics of Molyneux, notably with the Earl of Cromartie and Sir Edward Seymour, an unapologetic saboteur of the Irish wool trade and a noted Scotophobe. Fletcher's published account made much of the constitutional and economic slavery of Ireland. Having been from 1703 in the vanguard of those parliamentarians adamant that the Scottish Estates should assert themselves over an intrusive English ministry and a subservient Court Party, his particular design was to solidify the support of young nobles led by John Ker, 5th Earl (later 1st Duke) of Roxburghe, who were loosely attached to the confederated opposition.[54]

The English Tory Sir Christopher Musgrave was also party to these conversations. In polemical terms, their publication influenced further

---

[52] P. Kelly, 'Conquest *versus* Consent as the Basis of the English Title to Ireland in William Molyneux's *Case of Ireland . . . Stated*' in Brady & Ohlmeyer, eds., *British Interventions*, pp. 334–56; J. R. Hill, 'Ireland without Union: Molyneux and his Legacy' in Robertson, ed., *A Union for Empire*, pp. 271–96; J. Robertson, 'Union, State and Empire: The Britain of 1707 in its European Setting' in Stone, ed., *An Imperial State at War*, pp. 224–52; Smyth, *The Making of the United Kingdom*, pp. 95–102.

[53] *APS*, XI, pp. 66, 221, 224, 297, and appendix, p. 81; Ridpath, *PPS*, p. 22. On 30 June 1703, the Estates ordered that John Drake's *Historia Anglo-Scotica* (London, 1703) should be burned for 'several injurious and false reflections on the Sovereignty and Independence of the Crown of Scotland' (Crossrigg, *DPP*, p. 112). On 18 November 1705, James Anderson was awarded £400 for *An Historical Essay shewing that the Crown and Kingdom of Scotland, is Imperial and Independent* (Edinburgh, 1705). A like sum was given to Robert Hodges for supporting, by his writings, 'the sovereign honours of the kingdom'. But two pamphlets written by William Atwood, an English lawyer and disgraced colonial judge as well as a prominent opponent of Molyneux, were ordered to be burnt by the hangman. Offence given by *The Superiority and Direct Dominion of the Imperial Crown of England over the Crown and Kingdom of Scotland, the True Foundation of a Compleat Union, reasserted* (London, 1705) was compounded by *The Scotch Patriot Unmask'd* (London, 1705), which reflected adversely on the honour and independence of the Scottish nation.

[54] Ferguson, 'Imperial Crowns', Kidd, *Subverting Scotland's Past*, pp. 33–50; J. Robertson, 'An Elusive Sovereignty. The Course of the Union Debate in Scotland 1698–1707' in Robertson, ed., *A Union for Empire*, pp. 198–227.

Irish involvement when Henry Maxwell, an Ulster parliamentarian, joined the debate, proposing that Ireland be incorporated into England on the same footing as Wales. Although Maxwell of Finaboge in County Down had a Scottish pedigree, he argued that full integration was necessary not just to correct discrimination against Irish commercial and landed interests, but also to promote and secure prosperity through complementary textile manufacturing, which was currently suffering from French and Dutch competition and from the deleterious impact of the Scottish carrying trade in removing wool from Ireland.[55] Warning against incorporation that concentrated political and economic power, Fletcher was less than convinced that the political economy of Wales had benefited from its incorporation with England. Fletcher's standpoint, that Scotland should only engage in union along federative lines, was duly endorsed by Robert Molesworth, Viscount Molesworth, who chaired the committee of the Irish Commons which had instigated the attempt at political union with England that failed in 1703. Notwithstanding commendations at Court for conducting itself more amenably than the Scottish Estates, the Irish parliament had thrown away their negotiating position over the British Succession. Not only did it fail to challenge the Act of Settlement which the English parliament had imposed unilaterally in favour of the house of Hanover in 1701; it also declared any endeavour to impeach the Act as treasonable, prior to its rejected overture for union in 1703.[56] Indeed, the Irish parliament only demonstrated its political bite towards the English ministry after union was rejected, by passing legislation hostile to beneficial drawbacks for the East India Companies who faced impositions on calicos imported into Ireland from the outset of 1704. The Irish stance in this instance was more robust than that of the Scottish Estates, which remained antipathetic to the Old East India Company for mobilising English parliamentary opinion against Darien. Until the accomplishment of political incorporation, the Scots continued

---

[55] [Henry Maxwell], *An Essay upon an Union of Ireland with England* (London, 1703, and Dublin, 1704). Sir Francis Brewster, *New Essays on Trade* (London, 1702), had also argued for full integration to consolidate the English interest in Ireland, if necessary by encouraging a further round of planting in which migrants from England would be replaced by encouraging French Protestants to migrate to England. Anticipating the debate for Anglo-Scottish Union, Brewster, the MP for Tuam, argued for political incorporation as being in the English interest on the grounds of security and trade – that is, as a counter to Jacobitism and as a means of enforcing commercial regulation to prevent wool exports.

[56] J. Smyth, '"No remedy more proper": Anglo-Irish Unionism Before 1707' in B. Bradshaw & P. Roberts, eds., *British Consciousness and Identity: The Making of Britain, 1533–1707* (Cambridge, 1998), pp. 301–20; Kelly, *Prelude to Union*, pp. 13, 20; RC, TKUA England, Akter og Dokumenter nedr Sofart og Handel: Order med Bilag, 1702–7, A.III/207, letters 67, 69, and /208, letter 71.

only to fulminate, not legislate, against the drawbacks on customs that the Old and New Companies continued to enjoy from all goods re-exported to Scotland. The Companies' respective guarantees to lend £2 million to further William's war effort had been consolidated by their merged management in 1702.[57]

Notwithstanding this instance of more affirmative action, the slavish dependency of the Irish parliament was reiterated specifically or, more usually, in coded references to Scotland being open to 'the influence of foreign councils' by not just Fletcher, but diverse members of the Scottish Estates throughout the legislative war with the English parliament. Hamilton had welcomed Queen Anne on her accession to the independent, imperial Crown of Scotland, at the outset of the parliament in 1703 that passed the Act Anent Peace and War and the Act of Security in retaliation to the English Act of Settlement. Three years earlier, his kinsman, Charles Hamilton, 5th Earl of Abercorn, who sat in the Irish House of Lords as Viscount Strabane, had admonished Hamilton that, if the English parliament secured the same ascendancy over Scotland as they were currently exercising in Ireland, 'they will not practice less tyranny'. Hamilton duly warned the Estates in August 1704 that, unless they insisted upon the royal assent, which was still being withheld from the Act of Security, they 'were like an Irish Parliament who could act nothing but what was concerted in England'. This analogy was resisted vigorously by Stair and Marchmont, who sympathised with recent concerns expressed in the House of Lords about clandestine French influence in Scotland. However, they and their associates within the Court Party who were covertly lobbying the English ministry to support Union were told peremptorily to desist until the English were prepared to share 'the imperium Britannicum that they had usurped'.[58]

Determined to avoid the fate of Ireland as an English dependency, the Scottish Estates were not averse to asserting their distinctive liberties by imposing mercantilist restrictions on the importation of salt, livestock,

---

[57] HL, Loudoun Scottish Collection, box 3/LO 7171, box 48/Lo 10102; H. Horwitz, 'The East India Trade, the Politicians and the Constitution: 1689–1702', *Journal of British Studies*, 17 (1978), pp. 1–18. As this loan was partially to be reimbursed through taxes on salt, it is apposite to note that Scottish MPs in the new British parliament successfully argued that the drawback on goods exported to Scotland by the Company should be struck off from December 1707 as inconsistent with Union (DH, Parliamentary Notes of Colonel William Dalrymple, 1707–8, A 817/3, pp. 59–60; BL, India Office Records, Court Minutes, 22 July 1702 – 19 April 1705, B/47, p. 238).

[58] NAS, Hamilton Papers, GD 406/1/4510; Ridpath, *PPS*, pp. 5, 8–9, 11, 13, 31, 36, 48–9, 57, 59, 68–70; DH, Parliamentary Notebook of Colonel William Dalrymple, 1704–5, A 817/1, pp. 16–17; Penicuik, *HUSE*, pp. 81–5; NLS, Wodrow folio xxv, fo. 124; Crossrigg, *DPP*, pp. 151–3.

dairy produce and grain from Ireland, as well as on the re-export of Irish wool – restrictions which were usually more honoured by their breach than their application in the past, especially in the west of Scotland. The mobilising of troops on the Borders and in Northern Ireland, as well as the naval blockade imposed on the North Channel, trumped Scottish retaliation to the Alien Act of 1705. Along with the threat of subjecting the Scots to the same punitive tariffs as foreigners, however, was an invitation in the Alien Act to treat for incorporating Union.[59] The parliamentary rhetoric of independence and prosperity was now to be spun in favour of Union just as a new Scottish publication of the *Case of Ireland* was being sold in Edinburgh. Indeed, primarily because of the spin-doctoring of William Paterson, founder of the Bank of England and principal promoter of the Darien scheme, Molyneux's writing was to play a part in the making of the Anglo-Scottish Union that was as significant, if less celebrated, than its role in the American Revolution.[60]

Notwithstanding the failure of Darien, Paterson had remained a leading figure among London Scots and an occasional political informant and adviser on trade and plantations to Robert Harley, first as speaker of the House of Commons and subsequently as secretary of state. Paterson had duly moved his polemical standpoint from advocating colonial endeavours in the Americas as the alternative to Union. In 1700, he had recanted his involvement in Darien as a separate Scottish venture by calling for a communication of trade with England to guarantee access to domestic and colonial markets. By 1705, he had become a committed proponent of political incorporation, opposed to differing and interfering jurisdictions in Scotland and Ireland. These 'ridiculous contradictions both in theory and practice' required remodelling and annexing to secure the happiness of England. In this latter capacity as an apologist for English hegemony within the British Isles, Harley, on the promptings of Lord Somers and the Whigs, despatched him north despite the hesitation of Godolphin and the misgivings of the Court Party in Scotland. After his arrival in Edinburgh, prior to the critical session of the Scottish Estates summoned to discuss the Treaty of Union in October 1706, he asserted that his intention in promoting Darien was always to effect British

---

[59] Ridpath, *PPS*, pp. 26, 28–9, 46; DH, Parliamentary Notebook of Colonel William Dalrymple, 1704–5, A 817/1, pp. 62, 75–6, 91, 137–41; GCA, Records of the Maxwells of Pollock, T-PM 113/689 and 115/11; *Ormonde*, pp. 164, 210, 262–4, 281. The increasingly irascible Fletcher of Saltoun, who was currently touting the King of Prussia as a monarch more sympathetic to Scottish Calvinists than was the Lutheran Elector of Hanover, was the sponsor of this mercantilist discrimination against the Irish.

[60] P. Kelly, 'Recasting a Tradition: William Molyneux and the Sources of *The Case of Ireland... stated*' in Ohlmeyer, ed., *Political Thought in Seventeenth-century Ireland*, pp. 83–106; Kelly, *Prelude to Union*, pp. 13–15.

political incorporation. His flirtation with the confederated opposition during the legislative war, he affirmed, was only to flush out their antipathy to Union.[61]

Paterson's spin-doctoring is recorded in five letters written between 7 September and 15 October 1706, which were immediately published to rebut putative arguments of the confederated opposition. He began with a denunciation of any leagues and confederacies, other than incorporation, proposed between Scotland and England; a secondary theme was his dismissal of any continental constitutional analogy. Federative union was not an acceptable middle way between confederation and complete union. Nor could the Claim of Right of 1689 be seen as a safeguard against incorporation, as this fundamental law was passed by a Convention of Estates which sought a united British parliament. Paterson's arguments were virtually repeated on 29 October by the Lord Chancellor Seafield, who presided over the Scottish Estates as a far from impartial speaker. In rebutting the claims of Annandale that an incorporating union was contrary to the Claim of Right, Seafield made much of Annandale as a disappointed placeman who had switched his support from incorporation in 1702 to federal union by 1706. Paterson had been no less vituperative in concluding his first letter with an admonition to the confederated opposition that their reprinting and promotion of Molyneux was misguided. Thus, Molyneux's passing aspiration in favour of union became the essence of his *Case of Ireland*. The real desire of Molyneux and 'all the Protestants in Ireland' was not further to separate, but to have nearer union with England. There was a vast difference between the Protestant interest in Ireland and 'the present scribblers against the Union' in Scotland. The former believed that a more complete communication of government, trade and privileges would increase their people, their commerce and their prosperity. The latter contended that complete union would carry away people, trade and wealth from Scotland. Accordingly, 'nothing in the world can be a greater argument for the Union of this Kingdom, than the present practise, sense and disposition of Ireland'.[62]

---

[61] *Portland*, IV, pp. 44, 60–2, 67–8, 71–2, 74, 330–1, and *Portland*, VIII, pp. 109, 178–80, 243–4; NAS, Mar & Kellie Collection, GD 124/15/449/19. Because of his controversial involvement in Darien, Paterson usually used pseudonyms, or the guise of an anonymous spokesman for the spurious Wednesday Club concerned with public affairs, when propagating his shifting polemical stance. Paterson even claimed to have formulated the articles of the Treaty negotiated earlier in 1706 (DH, Loudoun Papers, unmarked green deed box, bundle 1706/September; [William Paterson alias Lewis Midway], *An Inquiry into the Reasonableness and consequences of an Union with Scotland* (London, 1706); Armitage, 'The Scottish Vision of Empire' in Robertson, ed., *A Union for Empire*, pp. 113–14).

[62] BL, W. Paterson, Treatises on the Union (transcribed London, 1708), Add. MS. 10403, first letter, pp. 1–3, 9–11, second letter, pp. 13–17, third letter, pp. 19–20; printed in

Again, Paterson's spinning brought a parliamentary dividend when Roxburghe, notwithstanding his tutoring by Fletcher of Saltoun on the constitutional and economic slavery of Ireland, spoke in favour of incorporation on 2 November. Roxburghe was an accomplished politician whose ambition and mercurial character had led him from outright opposition to the Court Party to assiduous pursuit of office through the new grouping, the Squadrone Volante, that had emerged in the parliamentary session of 1704 (see Chapter 9). As long as Scotland continued as a separate state from England, the Scots would be but 'absolute slaves' and their government in thrall to English ministries. Scottish divisions and animosities in government could only be overcome, and the happiness of the nation through riches and liberty could only be secured 'be an incorporating Union'. In effect, Roxburghe, like members of the English interest in Ireland in the wake of the Revolution Settlement, was arguing for direct rule from London to correct the partial character of those holding public office through the Court Party.[63] But, as Roxburghe's speech confirmed, the decisive support of the Squadrone for the Court Party was now being delivered at the right time to secure the passage of the Treaty of Union (see Chapter 10).

However, when the Anglo-Scottish Treaty of Union came into force on 1 May 1707, its reception among the English interest in Ireland was distinctly mixed. Longstanding fears that Union would advantage the Scottish linen trade to Irish detriment in England were compounded by the removal of restrictions on Scottish participation in the colonial trade, restrictions that remained in place for Ireland. At the same time, the proficiency of the Scottish carrying trade and the profusion of Scottish migrants, reputedly as many as 50,000 having arrived in the 1690s, was compounded by the commercial networking of their landed and mercantile elites, not only in Ulster but throughout Ireland. Among the English interest there were genuine fears that their ascendancy could be undermined by a Scottish interest in Ireland.[64] Certainly, Francis Hutchison, the future Anglican bishop of Down and Connor, welcomed from the

---

The Writings of William Paterson, ed. S. Bannister, 3 vols. (London, 1859), III, pp. 5–25. Paterson's third letter pointed out how well Wales had thrived since incorporation with England, claiming that the principality's foreign trade was greater than that of Scotland and it was to pay more in land tax than Scotland would be obliged to under the Treaty. At the same time, the parallel economic decline of Cornwall was attributable not to incorporation but to the falling demand for tin!

[63] DH, Parliamentary Memorandums of Colonel William Dalrymple, 1706–7, A 817/2, pp. 27–8, 34–6, 125–6, 142–4; *LP*, I, p. 95; *MSSM*, p. 118; BL, Papers Relating to Ireland, vol. II (1691–1700), Add.MSS 21,136, fo. 13.

[64] *Portland*, VIII, pp. 121–2, 257; *Ormonde*, pp. 125–6, 131; HL, Bridgewater & Ellesmere MSS, EL 9874; BL, Papers Relating to Trade etc., Sloane MS 2902, fo. 218.

pulpit the accomplishment of a perpetual incorporation rather than that of a federative union from 1 May 1707. However, a fellow Anglican cleric was less fulsome and, indeed, more in tune with the continuing distrust of Scottish Presbyterians among the English interest in Ireland, who had feared that any civil unrest provoked by the making of the Union in Scotland could easily spill over the North Channel. Having first served as a priest in Kilroot, County Antrim, a parish dominated by Scottish settlers, Jonathan Swift, dean of St Patrick's Cathedral in Dublin, was especially aggrieved that England in 1703 had spurned the loyal Protestants in Ireland, but from 1705 had courted successfully a country which could not be trusted for its Presbyterianism and its Jacobitism.[65] The key to this courtship was not just political security during the War of the Spanish Succession but also colonial security, particularly in the Americas, where Scottish commercial networks, no less than plantations, had proved a more disruptive and predatory influence than the Irish. Union sought to channel such Scottish entrepreneurship into imperial service.

[65] Francis Hutchison, *Sermon preached at St. Edmund's-Bury on the First of May 1707 being the day of Thanksgiving for the Union of Scotland and England* (London, 1707); *Ormonde*, pp. 62, 78, 85–8, 98, 100–1, 121, 125, 132, 173, 184, 203–4, 274–6; C. Fox, 'Swift's Scotophobia', *Bullán: An Irish Studies Journal*, 6 (2002), pp. 43–65; Smyth, *The Making of the United Kingdom*, p. 99. The legislative war of 1703–5 had been reported in *Impartial Occurrences* and the making of the Treaty from 1706 in the *Dublin Gazette*. James Butler, 2nd Duke of Ormonde, in his capacity as lord lieutenant, had despatched a Scottish settler called Miller back to Scotland in 1704 to report on the largely unfounded fears that Scottish Presbyterians were planning civil disobedience and intended to spread the armed struggle to Ireland.

Part III

The Primacy of Political Economy, 1625–1707

6   The transatlantic dimension

The contemporaneous involvement of Scots in the American colonies prior to the creation of the United Kingdom remains a peripheral aspect of regional diversity within transatlantic historiography. This situation can be attributed in part to Anglo-American imperiousness in viewing related developments in Britain and America from a Whiggish, progressive perspective, and in part to the manifest failure of ill-fated and expendable Scottish colonies in the seventeenth century.[1] Notwithstanding welcome evidence of ongoing transatlantic reappraisal of the British nature of the American colonies, the continuity of commercial links between Scotland and the Americas from the 1620s has been underplayed.[2] For colonial endeavours in the seventeenth century offered Scots the opportunity not just to break out from the mercantilist dominance of the great European powers, but also to sustain regal union without recourse to political incorporation with England. At the same time, the struggle for Scottish footholds in the Americas had important political resonance in raising British consciousness about the colonial dimension to state formation. Indeed, Scotland was dependent on overseas trade, commercial networks and an entrepreneurial willingness to circumvent international regulations for its very survival as a distinctive European nation in the later seventeenth century. Scotland was manifestly not a major European power, nor a significant imperial presence in the Americas, and far less

---

[1] See S. E. Morison, *The Oxford History of the American People*, vol. 1: *Prehistory to 1789* (New York, 1994); N. Canny, 'Writing Atlantic History; or, Reconfiguring the History of Colonial British America', *Journal of American History*, 86 (1999), pp. 1093–114; G. P. Insh, *Scottish Colonial Schemes, 1620–1686* (Glasgow, 1922); I. C. C. Graham, *Colonists from Scotland: Emigration to North America, 1707–1783* (Ithaca, NY, 1956); N. Landsman, *Scotland and its First American Colony, 1683–1760* (Princeton, 1985): I. Adams & M. Somerville, *Cargoes of Despair and Hope: Scottish Emigration to North America 1603–1803* (Edinburgh, 1993).
[2] See J. P. Greene & J. R. Pole, eds., *Colonial British America: Essays in the New History of the Early Modern Era* (Baltimore, 1984); Bailyn & Morgan, eds., *Strangers Within the Realm*; K. O. Kupperman, ed., *America in European Consciousness, 1493–1750* (Chapel Hill, 1995); Canny, ed., *The Origins of Empire*; D. Armitage & M. J. Braddick, eds., *The British Atlantic World, 1500–1800* (Basingstoke, 2002).

in the East Indies. Yet Scottish overseas connections and mercantile activities offer a corrective to the narrow focus on Empire that results from a preoccupation with conflicts for colonial hegemony, such as the territorial aggressiveness of England in competition with Spain (and Portugal), France and the Netherlands, or even Denmark and Sweden. In the case of the Scots, their association with the English in the Americas did contribute to the British character of the Stuarts' overseas dominions, but did not preclude their association with the Swedes, the Dutch and the Danes.[3]

Britannic Empire

Not only have the origins of and impetus for the British Empire been persuasively demonstrated to predate the Anglo-Scottish Union of 1707, but the imperial dynamic can be palpably rooted within Scotland no less than England and Ireland in the course of the seventeenth century (see Chapter 3). The endeavours of James I to instigate a composite monarchy through the accomplishment of a 'complete and perfect union' between England and Scotland had to be abandoned by 1607 in the face of outright opposition from the English parliament and passive resistance from the Scottish Estates. Nonetheless, successive Stuart monarchs ruled their dominions from their British Court and consistently projected an imperial British identity in international affairs, whether co-operating or competing with other colonial powers.[4] The Britannic perception of Empire was particularly suited to colonial endeavours to challenge, by acquisition and settlement, Spanish dominion in the New World, as the Americas were 'beyond the line' of international regulation in the first half of the seventeenth century. As evidenced by the plantation of Ulster, this imperial concept was readily exportable and notably geared to entrepreneurship and exploitation of native peoples. However, the foundations of the Stuarts' dominions in the Americas were not necessarily modelled on Ulster nor were they sustained as an exclusive English endeavour.[5]

---

[3] A. I. Macinnes, 'Introduction. Connecting and Disconnecting with America' in Macinnes & Williamson, eds., *Shaping the Stuart World*, pp. 1–30; D. Dobson, 'Seventeenth-Century Scottish Communities in the Americas' in A. Grosjean & S. Murdoch, eds., *Scottish Communities Abroad in the Early Modern Period* (Leiden, 2005), pp. 105–32.

[4] A. H. Williamson, 'Scots, Indians and Empire; J. Robertson, 'Empire and Union: Two Concepts of the Early Modern European Political Order' in Robertson, ed., *A Union for Empire*, pp. 3–37; Armitage, *The Ideological Origins of the British Empire*, pp. 6–10; A. Calder, *Revolutionary Empire: The Rise of the English-Speaking Empires from the Fifteenth Century to the 1780s* (London, revised 1998), pp. 79–288.

[5] Canny, *Making Ireland British*, pp. 214–15, 297, 312; M. Netzloff, 'Forgetting the Ulster Plantation: John Speed's The Theatre of the Empire of Great Britain (1611) and the

Indeed, the Jacobean re-establishment of colonial Virginia was launched in 1609, slightly in advance of the plantation of Ulster, as the planting of New Britain or Nova Brittania in the Americas. The first code of laws for the colony of Virginia Britannia was promulgated in 1612, when the English common law was still being established in Ulster.[6] Unlike Ulster, Virginia was viewed by Spain as an unwarranted colonial intrusion and its viability remained uncertain until the 1620s. Virginia's survival was due primarily to policy initiatives taken in England (primarily in the City of London rather than the Court) and the movement of settlers directly from the shires of Devon, Warwick, Stafford and Sussex who clearly stamped the colony as English.[7] Nevertheless, it was the peripatetic Scottish educationalist Patrick Copland who offered practical climatic advice on plantations that was more appropriate for semi-tropical colonies in the Americas than reliance on any prior experience of temperate Ireland. Copland commended the use of Armenians, naturalised in England, to lay the basis for the future prosperity of that American colony. At the same time, he became the foremost advocate of colleges in Virginia for Native Americans as well as colonial settlers in the 1620s.[8] Notwithstanding the visionary endeavours of Copland, the imperial impetus for Britannic civilisation was founded not on religious revelation or providential mission, but on commercial opportunity and opportunism in the Americas.[9]

Certainly, the ministers and entrepreneurial gentry who established the Massachusetts Bay Company in 1629 hoped to create a godly as well as an economically stable commonwealth, an aspiration furthered by the

---

Colonial Archive', *Journal of Medieval and Early Modern Studies*, 31 (2001), pp. 313–48; BL, Leeds Papers, vol. XVII, Egerton MS 3340, fols. 171–2.

[6] Anon., *Nova Britannia: offering most excellent fruits by planting in Virginia. Exciting all such as be well affected to further the same* (London, 1609); [Robert Johnson], *The New Life of Virginia: Declaring the former successe and present estate of that plantation, being the second part of Nova Britannia* (London, 1612); *For the Colony in Virginia Britannia. Lawes Divine, Morall and Martiall &c.* (London, 1612).

[7] *A declaration of the state of the colony and affaires in Virginia. With the names of the adventurors, and sums adventured in that action* (London, 1620); *Minutes of the Council and General Court of Colonial Virginia (1622–76)*, ed. H. R. McIlwaine (Richmond, VA, 1979), p. 52; HL, Robert Alonzo Brock Collection, BR 657 and 770.

[8] BL, Edmondes Papers, Stowe MS 172, fols. 307–18, and 174, fols. 170–1; Patrick Copland, *Virginia's God be Thanked* (London, 1622), and *A Declaration of Monies* (London, 1622); S. Vance, 'A Man for all Regions – Patrick Copland and Education in the Stuart World' in Macinnes & Williamson, eds., *Shaping the Stuart World*, pp. 55–78.

[9] D. Armitage, 'Making the Empire British; Scotland in the Atlantic World 1542–1717', *Past & Present*, 155 (1997), pp. 34–63; R. S. Dunn, *Sugar and Slaves: The Rise of the Planter Class in the English West Indies, 1624–1713* (Chapel Hill, 1992), pp. 3–45; A. Pagden, *Lords of all the World: Ideologies of Empire in Spain, Britain and France c. 1500 – c. 1800* (New Haven, 1995), pp. 29–125; C. G. Prestana, 'Religion' in Armitage & Braddick, eds., *The British Atlantic World*, pp. 69–89.

spread of Puritan settlements into Connecticut, Rhode Island and New Haven and the consolidation of Bermuda, over the next decade. However, price instability in the manufacturing districts of England, no less than Puritanism, fuelled migration from East Anglia to New England. Godliness did not rule out the pursuit of profit, or the civilising of Native Americans by encumbering them with debt. Prospects of religious toleration tied to commerce proved as attractive to Roman Catholics as to Puritans, as is evident from the foundation of Maryland in 1634 by Cecil Calvert, Lord Baltimore, who had moved his family's colonial activities from the less congenial climes of Newfoundland. Moreover, Puritanism was no guarantee of godly colonies as was particularly evident from the fate of the Providence Island Company, founded in 1630 but dissolved after little more than a decade. The settlers' predilection for privateering in the Caribbean provoked the Spanish to reassert their claims to sovereignty.[10] The pattern of settlement and governance in New England, any more than that in Ulster, cannot be regarded as typical for the Stuarts' American dominions. The bulk of British migration to the colonies was not to New England, but to Virginia around the Chesapeake, and to Barbados and the Leeward Islands. Colonial endeavours were not strictly demarcated in terms of the movement of people and capital. The landless migrated between Caribbean and mainland colonies in search of better prospects and less hostile environments for family settlement. Conversely, the settler elite invested in diverse colonial companies in Virginia and Bermuda as well as New England, and dispersed their families from mainland colonies to more lucrative plantations in the Caribbean.[11]

At the same time, the ubiquitous concept of the plantation was transportable. The temporary renaming of Newfoundland as New Britaniola in 1628 reflected sustained British endeavours to colonise the island through fishing plantations. As well as the permanent settlement at St John's, established by the original London Company with which Scottish entrepreneurs were associated from 1620, and more seasonal settlements established by Bristol merchants and West Country interests, George Calvert, Lord Baltimore, founded a substantial English plantation at

---

[10] William Wood, *New England Prospects* (London, 1634); Thomas Morton, *New English Canaan or New Canaan* (Amsterdam, 1637); K. O. Kupperman, *Providence Island 1630–1641: The Other Puritan Colony* (Cambridge, 1993), pp. 267–94.

[11] J. P. Greene, *Pursuits of Happiness: The Social Development of Early Modern British Colonies and the Formation of American Culture* (Chapel Hill, 1988), pp. 28–54; G. B. Nash, 'Social Development' in Greene & Pole, eds., *Colonial British America*, pp. 233–61; A. Kulikoff, *From British Peasants to Colonial American Farmers* (Chapel Hill, 2000), pp. 39–72; R. Brenner, *Merchants and Revolution: Commercial Change, Political Conflict, and London's Overseas Traders, 1550–1653* (Princeton, 1993), pp. 93–102.

Ferryland (also known as Avelon). Henry Carey, Viscount Falkland, the English courtier with a Scottish title who served briefly as lord-deputy for Ireland, created an Anglo-Irish plantation at Rivage, while Dr William Vaughan, from Carmarthen, planted a Welsh settlement at Cambriol. Newfoundland not only served as the model for cod fishing plantations from New England to Virginia, but also inspired Charles I to create a company to monopolise the common fishing around the British Isles in 1632.[12]

By the accession of Charles I, less than 10,000 people had left the British Isles for the American colonies, around a third of the British population then settled in Ulster. However, emigration to America increased exponentially with at least 80,000 leaving in the next decade. The vast majority of these came from England, principally from East Anglia and the Home Counties through London, from the West Country through Bristol and from the North-West through Liverpool. However, departing ships also called into ports such as Cork and Galway on the west coast of Ireland to take on additional settlers as well as supplies. London, the largest city in Europe with a population then well in excess of 300,000, was the principal port of departure for colonial migrants from all over the British Isles. Indeed, London was becoming the British, not just the English, metropolis, with an established expertise for mercantile adventuring throughout Europe, Asia, Africa and the Americas.[13]

---

[12] Robert Hayman, *Quodlibets, lately come over from New Britaniola, old Newfoundland. Epigrams and other small parcels, both morall and divine* (London, 1628); E. F. Slafter, *Sir William Alexander and American Colonization* (Boston, 1873), pp. 55–8; *CSP, Colonial* (1574–1660), pp. 25–6; BL, Papers Relating to English Colonies in America and the West Indies, 1627–99, Egerton MS 2395, fols. 256–61. Captain John Mason, the adventurer who brought in Scottish merchants to assist the endeavours of the London Company, Captain John Smith, a founder governor of Virginia and admiral of New England, and Sir William Alexander, the proprietor of Nova Scotia, were leading promoters of the common fishing. However, this British endeavour dominated by English courtiers was deemed particularly unacceptable in Scotland, off whose coasts the major fishing grounds were located. The manifest failure of the common fishing by 1638 did not deter courtiers from establishing the North Atlantic Fishing Monopoly, which featured among its founders two prominent Scottish adventurers, Sir David Kirk and James Hamilton, 3rd Marquess of Hamilton (R. G. Lounsbury, *The British Fishery at Newfoundland, 1634–1763* (New Haven, 1934), pp. 44–5, 77–91; D. W. Prowse, *A History of Newfoundland from the English, colonial, and foreign records* (New York, 1895), pp. 104–5, 119, 143–4; P. W. Coldham, *The Complete Book of Emigrants 1607–1660* (Baltimore, 1987), p. 191).

[13] A. Games, *Migration and the Origins of the English Atlantic World* (Cambridge, MA, 1999), pp. 13–41; W. R. Scott, *The Constitution and Finance of English, Scottish and Irish Joint-Stock Companies*, I, pp. 129–49. The initial endeavours of James to support a supplementary Scottish Company trading through Muscovy to the East Indies in 1617 related more to the unfulfilled quest for a north-west passage than any serious endeavour to challenge the monopoly of the London merchant houses. Indeed, when reaffirming the monopoly of the East India Company in 1632, Charles I specified that, although the

While the American colonies were very much a secondary focus of London merchant adventurers, the changing economic climate in the aftermath of the regal union made them an increasingly attractive option for new joint-stock investments that attracted courtiers and the landed classes. Notwithstanding the establishment of the East India Company in 1600, its trading ventures to the East Indies, far from producing new outlets for English textiles and other manufactured products, had led to an influx of more sophisticated Asian manufactures, along with peppers and spices. Although Asian goods were re-exported through London companies trading to the continent, Muscovy, Turkey and the Levant, their importation became a drain on bullion that was no more than partially relieved by the search for gold and silver in Africa. The creation of American colonies, initially through companies for the plantation of Virginia (1606), Newfoundland (1610), Bermuda (the Summer Isles, 1611) and New England (1620), was vital to the process of import substitution, that is, finding alternative supplies in the Americas for fish, furs, timber, tar and pitch usually imported from Scandinavia and the continent. However, the prospects of new sources for such minerals as copper and iron, as for tobacco and later sugar, were realised belatedly and only when the initial plantation companies were close to dissolution. As was especially evident in the re-founding of the Virginia Company in 1624, joint-stock ventures were moderated to encourage relatively small-scale investors as well as the mercantile and political elite. Again there was no restriction to English investors only as the Stuart dominions in the Americas expanded in the Caribbean to include Barbados and other Leeward Islands.[14]

Scotto-Britannic ventures

The Scottish, like the Irish, engagement with Britannic Empire has been associated with servitor colonialism – that is, the provision of indentured servants, professionals like doctors and clergymen, soldiers and militiamen and, ultimately, colonial governors. However, both kingdoms

---

Company operated under English law, its trade was to be conducted exclusively through London. Its merchant adventurers had the sole right to license ships and crews, factors and soldiers, with no reservation that they must be English. Scots adventurers in the service of the East India Company since the reign of James I continued to be in receipt of pensions paid through an agent in Scotland well into the 1630s ([Charles I], *By the King a proclamation for the better encouragement, and advancement of the trade of the East-Indie Companie, and for the prevention of excesse of private trade* (London, 1632); *The Earl of Stirling's Register of Royal Letters, Relative to the Affairs of Scotland and Nova Scotia from 1615 to 1635*, ed. C. Rogers, 2 vols. (Edinburgh, 1873), I, pp. 150–1; II, p. 608).

[14] R. Davis, *The Rise of Atlantic Economies* (London, 1973), pp. 96–8; N. Canny, 'Asia, the Atlantic and the Subjects of the British Monarchy' in Coward, ed., *The Blackwell Companion*, pp. 45–66.

produced colonial planters as well as mercantile adventurers and privateers who utilised the Americas as a theatre for their entrepreneurship.[15] Certainly, the Irish were notably involved with English adventurers in the forlorn search for suitable places to colonise in the Amazon and they dominated settlement in Montserrat in the Leeward Islands. But apart from the ill-fated colony of New Albion on the Delaware (see Chapter 5), the Irish were not separately engaged in colonial undertakings. The Scots regarded themselves as independent but collaborative players in the Britannic Empire and usually did so with the blessing of the Scottish government who wanted to give depth and diversity to the country's economy. Colvin's Case of 1608 had accorded common nationality to all born within Scotland and England since the accomplishment of regal union. Nonetheless, the abandonment of political and commercial integration had meant that no access to English markets or colonial ventures was freely afforded or guaranteed to Scottish residents. Although Scottish merchants were no longer considered aliens from Christmas 1604, English customs officials remained reluctant to admit their exemption from the discriminatory tariffs on imported merchandise. However, domicile restrictions on colonial engagement were difficult to police given that Scottish courtiers had bases in both countries, Scottish merchant houses opened up in London and migrants from Scotland to the colonies frequently passed through English ports.[16]

Pioneering endeavours in the Americas were as liable to fail as succeed given the often inhospitable nature of the tropical and sub-tropical environments in which plantations were located, the antipathy of native peoples to acquisitive settlers and the vulnerability of traders to privateering and piracy.[17] Scottish entrepreneurs had one further disadvantage. Their interests were deemed expendable when their commercial aspirations conflicted with the international diplomacy of Britannic monarchy. The discriminatory precedent for the Darien fiasco in the 1690s (see Chapter 7) was actually set over the plantation of Nova Scotia in the 1620s.

---

[15] E. Richards, 'Scotland and the Uses of the Atlantic Empire' in Bailyn & Morgan, eds., *Strangers Within the Realm*, pp. 67–114; R. S. Dunn, 'Servants and Slaves: The Recruitment and Employment of Labor' in Greene & Pole, eds., *Colonial British America*, pp. 157–94.
[16] T. K. Rabb, *Enterprise & Empire: Merchants and Gentry Investment in the Expansion of England, 1575–1630* (Cambridge, MA, 1967), pp. 1–101; N. Canny, *Kingdom and Colony: Ireland in the Atlantic World* (Baltimore and London, 1988), pp. 44–59; B. Lenman, *England's Colonial Wars 1550–1688: Conflicts, Empire and National Identity* (Harlow, 2001), pp. 173–5.
[17] R. B. Sheridan, *Sugar and Slavery: An Economic History of the British West Indies, 1623–1775* (Barbados, 1974), pp. 75–96; Kulikoff, *From British Peasants to Colonial American Farmers*, pp. 73–123.

Sir William Alexander of Menstrie, a noted poet, polemicist and courtier who originally planned to develop a plantation he had secured from the Newfoundland Company, proposed a scheme for a New Scotland in the Canadian Maritimes in 1621. English colonies in Virginia and New England were still pioneering ventures and no meaningful English presence had yet been established in the Caribbean. Hence, Scottish ambitions were portrayed as no less legitimate than the presence of New Spain, New France or the New Netherlands.[18]

Indeed, in Alexander of Menstrie's proposal, New England was to be complemented by New Scotland to bolster the British cause against the French settlement in North America designated 'Acadia'. A Canadian colony offered the remunerative prospect of channelling Scottish migration away from Northern Europe, especially Poland-Lithuania, to exploit the reputedly abundant sources of timber, fish and furs – the latter commodity offering lucrative prospects from the sale of beaver pelts in continental markets. At the same time, New Scotland offered a distinctive British alternative to Ulster, in which Scots law would be utilised to implement and direct plantations. The British undertaking in Ulster had offered the inducement of baronetcies under English patent, so Canadian undertakers were invited to purchase the title of baronet under Scottish patent. Sales of titles, which were initially intended to realise a limited income (around £16,667) to the Crown from Scottish gentry, were never fully subscribed notwithstanding the admission of English, Irish and even French gentry as baronets of Nova Scotia from 1629. Sales of titles did demonstrate the commitment of Britannic monarchy to the capitalising of colonial projects, albeit the Nova Scotia venture remained chronically underfunded. No less vital, and in marked contrast to Ulster, were the logistical difficulties of elongated supply lines in supporting initial settlement.[19]

The first exploratory venture sent out by Alexander of Menstrie in 1622 had to take refuge with the Newfoundland fisheries. A second in the following year was able to reconnoitre the coastline of Nova Scotia. Obliged to subcontract the settlement of Cape Breton Island, under the guise of New Galloway, to his fellow Scot, Sir John Gordon of Lochinvar, Sir William was able to tap into colonial expertise from Ulster when the

---

[18] *RPCS*, first series, XI, pp. 288–9, 313–17, 353–4, 358–9; XII, 510, 774–5; *CSP, Colonial* (1574–1660), pp. 25–6; Insh, *Scottish Colonial Schemes*, pp. 27–39; J. G. Reid, *Acadia, Maine and New England: Marginal Colonies in the Seventeenth Century* (Toronto, 1981), pp. 20–8.

[19] *RPCS*: first series, XII, pp. 14–15, 616–17, 633–4, 649–51, 720–2; second series, I, pp. 80, 122–4, 355–6, 365. Reid, *Acadia, Maine and New England*, pp. 29–42, 81–2, 88–90; Sir William Alexander, *An Encouragement to Colonies* (London, 1624).

first cohort of settlers set sail under the command of his son William in the spring of 1628. By the following year, this son had brought out a new cohort from the Kentish Downs in a venture effectively more British than Scottish in terms of personnel and pioneering intent. Fortified settlements were established at the former French mainland base of Port Royal and at Port aux Balemes in Cape Breton. However, the viability of the Scottish venture was undermined by a rival English project, led by two London-based Scottish entrepreneurs, David and Lewis Kirk, who were intent on capturing Quebec from the French as well as exploiting the commercial potential of the Maritimes. Displaced French were also determined to retain their foothold in Acadia. While internal British rivalries were partially resolved by the formation of the English and Scottish Company to pursue the fur trade on the St Lawrence, Nova Scotia remained vulnerable to French military and diplomatic pressure. The French soon overran the Cape Breton settlement, while the continuance of that at Port Royal was jeopardised by the commencement of peace negotiations to resolve Charles I's martial differences with Louis XIII in 1629. The French were insistent not only that they should reclaim Quebec, but that the Scots should vacate Port Royal, which they viewed as having been settled by conquest in time of war. The necessity of the Scots to vacate was a non-negotiable point of honour to which Charles, against the advice of his Scottish Privy Council, eventually assented in 1632.[20]

Charles I had offered ostensible pledges of support for Nova Scotia, signalled by Alexander of Menstrie becoming first Viscount, then Earl, of Stirling by 1632, when he was compensated with the right to mint copper coinage to the value of £10,000. However, the enforced vacation of Port Royal served as a disincentive to further plantation. Stirling was intimately associated with the Court's imposition of administrative and economic uniformity throughout the British Isles. His issue of copper coinage caused currency debasement. As a result, there was no political will within Scotland to sustain his Canadian undertaking. Stirling received further colonial recognition in 1635, when he was accorded a compensatory interest in New England, where Maine bordered the Maritimes, with Long Island as a somewhat distant appendage. More importantly, Stirling's personal involvement in both New England and Nova Scotia continued to promote British association in colonial councils. Stirling was regarded as

[20] N. E. S. Griffiths & J. G. Reid, 'New Evidence on New Scotland, 1629', *William and Mary Quarterly*, third series, 39 (1992), pp. 492–508. *RPCS*: second series, II, pp. 271–2, 313–14, 489; III, pp. 392–5, 543, 614–15. *Stirling's Register of Royal Letters*, II, pp. 463, 544–8, 599; *CSP, Colonial* (1574–1660), pp. 119–20; *APC, Colonial* (1613–80), pp. 181–3, 253; Coldham, *The Complete Book of Emigrants*, p. 86; BL, Papers Relating to English Colonies in America and the West Indies, 1627–99, Egerton MS 2395, fo. 25.

a key player in facilitating inter-colonial trade with Virginia and the Native Americans, albeit the Virginians tended to view this trade as a means of drawing settlers from other British plantations in the Americas, especially to Kent Island in Chesapeake Bay.[21] Stirling also became an active participant in the essentially English debate then raging over the viability, suitability and legality of overseas plantations. Nevertheless, neither he nor his immediate family sought direct involvement in further colonial ventures in the Americas.[22]

Despite its effective abandonment by 1634, the proprietorial model under which Alexander of Menstrie colonised Nova Scotia became the favoured means for promoting colonies other than Virginia and Massachusetts. Menstrie had been awarded regalian powers under Scots law, the English equivalent being a palatinate. Effectively, he and his fellow American proprietors received heritable jurisdictions that privatised colonial government and the levying of customs on commodities exported from the colonies. Thus, Barbados and the Leeward Islands were assigned from 1629 to the proprietary control of James Hay, 1st Earl of Carlisle, the former head of the British espionage service under James I, an investor in Virginia and a member of the Council for New England. Although these

---

[21] *RPCS*: second series, IV, pp. 46–7, 269; V, 219–21. *CSP, Colonial* (1574–1660), pp. 115, 195, 204; Macinnes, *Charles I and the Making of the Covenanting Movement*, pp. 49, 120–1; Reid, *Acadia, Maine and New England*, pp. 49–51, 186–7, 246–9; Coldham, *The Complete Book of Emigrants*, pp. 139, 208; *Minutes of the Council and General Court of Colonial Virginia (1622–76)*, p. 484. The Virginian trading venture was licensed to William Clayborne who bloodily contested Kent Island with rival settlers from Maryland in the 1630s. The English Privy Council arbitrated on the side of the latter in 1638, especially as they discovered that Clayborne's licence was issued as a Scottish patent (www.mdarchives.state.md.us/ Proceedings of the Council of Maryland, vol. 3 (1636–67), pp. 20, 71–3, 243).

[22] Sir William Alexander, *The mapp and description of New England, together with a discourse of plantation and colonies; also a relation of the nature of the climate, and how it agrees with our owne-countrey England* (London, 1630); Richard Eburne, *A plaine pathway to plantations* (London, 1624); John Smith, *Advertisements for the inexperienced planters of New England or anywhere* (London, 1631); J. Day, *A publication of Guiana's plantation newly undertaken* (London, 1630). Stirling was an associate of courtiers promoting plantations along the Piscataqua River in New England to secure that initially established by the Scottish adventurer David Thomas, as undertaker for settlers from the English West Country in the mid-1620s. Stirling's Scottish sales agent, James Farrett, also initiated English settlement on Shelter Island adjacent to the colony of New Haven, and on Long Island, by 1640. However, the former settlement struggled to remain independent of New Haven and the latter, at Oyster Bay, was harried out of existence by the Dutch, who also saw off the efforts of Captain Andrew Forrester, a veteran of the Nova Scotian plantation, who acted on behalf of Mary, widow of Henry, 3rd Earl of Stirling, in 1649 (BOU, Memorandum of Meetings relating to land in New England 1635–8, Bodl. MS. Bankes 23, fo. 13; Slafter, *Sir William Alexander and American Colonization*, pp. 84–91; *CSP, Colonial* (1574–1660), pp. 298, 302, 497; *Narratives of New Netherlands*, ed. J. F. Jameson (New York, 1909), pp. 307–8).

Caribbean colonies were certainly English in terms of government, the character of their settlement can be viewed as British. Carlisle's principal factor was his Scottish kinsman, Peter Hay of Haystoun. Scots also featured in the London merchant syndicate favoured with leases for the best land in Barbados. The designation of a 'Scotland' district on that island suggests that place names related as much to settlers' backgrounds as to geographic features.[23]

The ill-fated Canadian venture also stimulated trade from the Scottish western seaboard to the American colonies. From the 1630s, ships from Ayr and Glasgow directly re-exported tobacco through the Øresund (Baltic Sound). East coast ports, such as Aberdeen and Dundee, also became involved in the Chesapeake two decades before the official opening-up of English colonial trade to the Scots in the 1650s. John Burnett from Aberdeen was licensed in 1638 as the sole merchant from Scotland to supply the plantations in Virginia, where he also served as a factor. Nova Scotia redirected Scottish entrepreneurial endeavours westward, to diversify from, but not replace, trade to continental Europe and Scandinavia.[24]

Gothic appropriation

The emergence of the Covenanting Movement and the subsequent Wars for the Three Kingdoms terminated the first phase of Britannic Empire. Colonial endeavours were not set aside, however. The Americas became a haven for Royalists and Parliamentarians ousted by the civil wars. Although the ousted eventually established themselves as the ruling elite in colonies such as Virginia, they brought disruption to some colonies and aggravated tensions occasioned by disputed proprietary control in others – a situation compounded by Charles I and his Parliamentary opponents granting rival titles to colonial plantations and governorships.[25] The Scots, for their part, did not become so embroiled in military

---

[23] Dunn, *Sugar and Slaves*, pp. 49–53; NAS, Hay of Haystoun Papers, GD 34/920-33, /924; www.mdarchives.state.md.us/ Proceedings of the Council of Maryland, vol. 3 (1636–67), pp. 13–19. Carlisle's title to Barbados and the Leeward Islands was disputed by a syndicate associated with their discoverer and first planter, the Anglo-Dutch entrepreneur Sir William Courten (HL, Bridgewater & Ellesmere MSS, EL 3445; *CSP, Colonial* (1574–1660), pp. 282–3).

[24] *Tabeller over Skibsfart og Varetransport gennem Oresund, 1492–1660*, ed. N. E. Bang & K. Korst, 3 vols. (Copenhagen, 1906–22), I, pp. 266–389, II, pp. 352–607; DCA, Dundee Register of Ships, 1612–81, entries for August and October 1637, and Dundee Council Book, IV (1613–53), fo. 126; Calder, *Revolutionary Empire*, p. 111; Reid, *Acadia, Maine and New England*, p. 30; *CSP, Colonial* (1574–1660), p. 277; Coldham, *The Complete Book of Emigrants*, pp. 78, 199.

[25] B. Bailyn, 'Politics and Social Structure in Virginia' in S. N. Katz, J. M. Murrin & D. Greenberg, eds., *Colonial America: Essays in Politics and Social Development* (New York,

engagements in all three kingdoms that they lost sight of the need to maintain their competitive position in the American colonies. Thus, in the course of the negotiations for the Treaty of London, the Scottish commissioners felt sufficiently emboldened, by 25 May 1641, to demand equality of treatment with the English and Irish in conducting free trade throughout the Stuart dominions, securing access to colonial commerce and gaining admission to mercantile companies.[26]

The claims for reciprocity and parity in commercial benefits were directed more against Gothic, rather than Irish, interests, however. For the Gothic predilection for an exclusively English rather than an inclusively Britannic agenda had already been evident in appeals to the Long Parliament to enforce English jurisdiction over the Stuart colonies. The only concession to Scottish interests during the Treaty of London was a clerical petition, supported by seventy English divines – mainly Puritans from London and East Anglia – asking that Alexander Henderson 'and some other worthy ministers of Scotland' should be associated with any scheme to promote Reformation as well as plantations in the West Indies. This was to be viewed as a British endeavour as there was a reported shortage of people from England willing to engage in plantation, yet both England and Scotland were overstocked with people. Notwithstanding that Henderson was joint author of both the National Covenant of 1638 and the Solemn League and Covenant of 1643, the resubmission of the scheme for Reformation in 1644 was not welcomed by the Parliamentarians. Indeed, prior to the formalisation of confessional confederation through the Solemn League, the Parliamentary naval commander – with a rather chequered colonial past as an adventurer and privateer – Robert Rich, 1st Earl of Warwick, was appointed governor in chief of all the English colonies in North America and the West Indies. An exclusively English parliamentary committee for trade and plantations shaped policy for the Americas. Simultaneously, an invitation was extended to the well-affected in straitened circumstances, and to the public-spirited, to transport themselves, their servants or agents to the Caribbean, 'for propagating the Gospell, and increase of trade' for the benefit of England, not Britain.[27] Notwithstanding continuing calls from New England to attract ministers and church-government according to the best Reformed

---

1993), pp. 17–41; *APC, Colonial* (1613–80), pp. 255, 280–1; NAS, Hay of Haystoun Papers, GD 34/939–40, /943, /945; *Order of Charles I empowering Company of Adventurers for the Plantation of the Island of Eleuthera* (London, 1647).

[26] Macinnes, *The British Revolution*, pp. 138–9.

[27] [William Castell], *A Petition of W. C. exhibited to the High Court of Parliament now assembled, for the propagating of the Gospel in America and the West Indies* (London, 1641), and William Castell, *A Short Discoverie of the Coasts and Continent of America, from the equinoctiall northward and the adjacent isles* (London, 1644); Anon., *Certaine Inducements to Well Minded People* (London, 1643).

tradition in Scotland and England, leading Covenanters were not enamoured by the separatist tendencies of the Puritans. Although they sympathised with the Puritans' desire to escape 'from the yoke of Episcopal persecution', they were concerned that their disregard for a structured church polity could be re-exported back across the Atlantic 'to be dangerous to the rest of the world'.[28]

Of more immediate concern was the impact of Warwick's appointment in Barbados, where Scottish estate management waned as the heavily indebted James, 2nd Earl of Carlisle, was obliged to cede control over the Leeward Islands to William Willoughby, Lord Willoughby of Parham. This was part of a wider assault on proprietary control as parliament attempted to enforce its jurisdiction and secure control over customs on commodities exported from the colonies. Indeed, the proprietary control exercised by Carlisle over the Leeward Islands came under attack in the House of Commons in March 1646. The Islands were 'not fit for any subject to have the regality of them', especially as their governance hitherto was characterised by an arbitrary power that threatened to reduce the English to 'slavery absolute'.[29] Although Scottish managerial influence in Barbados had been eclipsed by 1649, Scottish ships from such ports as Leith and Bo'ness on the east coast, as well as Ayr and Glasgow on the west coast, still made occasional and remunerative trips to the Caribbean, where provisions and indentured servants were traded for tobacco. Sometimes, but not invariably, these ventures were undertaken in association with London merchants.[30]

---

[28] Robert Baillie, *A Dissuasive from the Errours of the Times* (London, 1645); John Child, *New England's Jonas cast up in London* (London, 1647).

[29] NAS, Hay of Haystoun Papers, GD 34/835–6, /889, /899, /941, /950; Coldham, *The Complete Book of Emigrants*, pp. 207, 211; *An Abstract of the Laws of New England as they are now established* (London, 1641); *Virginia and Maryland. Or, the Lord Baltimore's printed Case, uncased and answered. Shewing the illegality of his Patent and usurpation of Royal Jurisdiction and Dominion there* (London, 1848).

[30] NAS, Hay of Haystoun Papers, GD 34/833, /836, /924, /937, /947, and Supplementary Parliamentary Papers, 1644, PA 2/23, fols. 110–11; DCA, Dundee Register of Ships, 1612–81, entries for June 1642, November 1643, October 1645, February and August 1651, and Dundee Council Book, IV (1613–53), fo. 198; *CSP, Colonial* (1574–1660), p. 343; Coldham, *The Complete Book of Emigrants*, p. 229; T. Barclay & E. J. Graham, *The Early Transatlantic Trade of Ayr, 1640–1730* (Ayr, 2005), pp. 12–14. The leading Scottish entrepreneur of this period in the Caribbean was James Hamilton of Boghall, who, as a commissioner for excise in Scotland, was not averse to securing reduced terms for tobacco imports that undercut indirect shipments from London or the Netherlands. By this juncture Scottish colonial aspirations were also shifting from the West to the East Indies, with two trading schemes, one inspired by Danish practice, the other by French enterprise, under active consideration, but not implemented by the Scottish Estates (*APS*, VI (i), c.118, p. 344; c.164 6, pp. 372 5). Charles II, during his brief sojourn in Scotland for the patriotic accommodation between Covenanters and Royalists, seems to have licensed trade with Virginia in September 1650 (*Minutes of the Council and General Court of Colonial Virginia (1622–76)*, p. 503).

Notwithstanding this limited entrepreneurial engagement with the colonies appropriated by the English parliament, the Scots were as likely to trade with the Dutch and, to a lesser extent, the Swedes in the Americas. Not only were the Dutch Scotland's major trading associates for much of the seventeenth century, but Scottish ships were used as flags of convenience for the Dutch whose ships were expediently crewed by Scots after the resumption of hostilities between the United Provinces and Spain in 1621. Such trading associations extended from the Baltic to the East Indies, with Scots in Batavia even engaged in the financing of the silk trade from Japan.[31] That same year, the creation of the West Indian Company (WIC), largely as an endeavour of the province of Zeeland, served to channel informal Scottish links with the Dutch on the 'Wild Coast' (Guyana and Venezuela) into the establishment of sugar works in Brazil during the 1630s. This association continued with the introduction of sugar and slavery into Barbados in the early 1640s. Scots were also associated with the Dutch endeavours to secure Tobago, which endured into the 1650s, by which time Scottish commercial and planting networks had become embedded within the WIC's main base in North America, the colony of New Netherlands centred on New Amsterdam (later New York). In turn, Scottish merchants and settlers were well placed to take advantage of the Dutch conquest of the Swedish colony on the Delaware in 1655.[32]

The short-lived colony of New Sweden along the Delaware was established in 1638 and supplied primarily from Gothenburg. As Sweden's main Atlantic outlet, Gothenberg had been founded in 1621 according to a town plan identical to that of Batavia. The Scots, after the Dutch, formed a significant mercantile presence in Gothenburg. Indeed, as New Sweden had primarily been encouraged by Amsterdam commercial interests discontented with Zeeland's dominance of the WIC, Scots and Dutch were also engaged to establish the colony through negotiations with the Native Americans, and to supply annual shipments of colonists.

[31] J. L. Israel, 'A Conflict of Empires: Spain and the Netherlands 1618–1648', *Past & Present*, 76 (1977), pp. 34–74; S. Murdoch, 'The Good, the Bad and the Anonymous: A Preliminary Survey of the Scots in the Dutch East Indies 1612–1707'. *Northern Scotland*, 22 (2002), pp. 63–76; NAS, Trinity House Leith, GD 226/18/21.

[32] E. Mijers, 'A Natural Partnership? Scotland and Zeeland in the Early Seventeenth Century' in Macinnes & Williamson, eds., *Shaping the Stuart World*, pp. 233–60; Sheridan, *Sugar and Slavery*, pp. 128–34; Dunn, *Sugar and Slaves*, pp. 15–21, 59–67; *Narratives of New Netherlands*, pp. 66–96; *Calendar of Records in the Office of the Secretary of State, 1664–1703*, ed. W. Nelson (Paterson, NJ, 1899), pp. 9–11, 13–16. Ongoing territorial disputes between Maryland and Virginia allowed the Dutch and the Swedes to insinuate themselves successfully in the Indian trade for furs, especially beaver skins in the Delaware (www.mdarchives.state.md.us/ Proceedings of the Council of Maryland, vol. 5 (1667–88), pp. 175–239, 411–17).

The Gothenburg-based Scottish merchant, Hans Mackleir (alias John Maclean), became the principal agent for the equipping and provision of ships for New Sweden, and the marketing of its tobacco crops, in the decade before the colony's acquisition by the WIC.[33]

Mackleir had earlier come to prominence when Gothenburg became the main port of supply for the Covenanting Army that defeated Charles I in the Bishops' Wars of 1639–40. Hence, when the Covenanters in the course of their negotiations with the English parliament in 1641 sought to broaden confessional confederation to include the Dutch and the Swedes, there was also a hinterland of commercial and colonial affiliations to promote expanded British Union through the Treaty of London.[34] Although the Solemn League and Covenants reinforced such confederation between England and Scotland in August 1643, the colonial equivalent, drawn up three months earlier, not only drew on the separate English tradition of Covenanting, but also was targeted against Scottish engagement with the Dutch and the Swedes in the American colonies. For the Confederation of New England, effected by the four colonies of Massachusetts, Plymouth, Connecticut and New Haven, engaged in a defensive and offensive alliance ostensibly against the French, the Dutch and the Indians, but also carried an implicit warning to Scots, Swedes and other colonial interlopers.[35]

Continuing Covenanting endeavours to effect British confederation, which were on the defensive after the emergence of the New Model Army launched Oliver Cromwell to political prominence, were shattered by the unilateral English execution of Charles I in 1649. Nevertheless, the Covenanters' immediate recognition of Charles II as king of Great Britain and Ireland carried an American resonance. Charles II was proclaimed as the rightful heir to all three kingdoms in Maryland, Virginia, the Summer Isles (Bermuda), Antigua and Barbados. A power struggle

---

[33] *Narratives of New Netherlands*, pp. 257–63; A. Johnson, *The Swedish settlements on the Delaware: the history and relation to the Indians, Dutch and English, 1638–1664*, 2 vols. (New York, 1911), I, pp. 182–4, 232, 255, 258, 266, 283, 291–2, 327, and II, pp. 483, 631, 683; A. Grosjean & S. Murdoch, 'The Scottish Community in Seventeenth-century Gothenburg' in Grosjean & Murdoch, eds., *Scottish Communities Abroad*, pp. 191–223. John Maclean was descended from the chiefs of the Macleans of Duart on the Isle of Mull in the Inner Hebrides. Jacob Evertsen Sandelin (James Sandilands), a Scot, who assisted the first governor of New Sweden, Peter Minuit, a Dutchman, to negotiate territory in 1638, returned with provisions in a ship called the *Scotch Dutchman* in 1646.

[34] G. Behre, 'Gothenburg in Stuart War Strategy 1649–1766' in G. G. Simpson, ed., *Scotland and Scandinavia 800–1800* (Edinburgh, 1990), pp. 107–18; Grosjean, *An Unofficial Alliance*, pp. 165–90.

[35] *The Journal of John Winthrop, 1630–1649*, pp. 429–40; H. M. Ward, *The United Colonies of New England, 1634–90* (New York, 1961), pp. 49–59; Valance, *Revolutionary England and the National Covenant*, pp. 61–81.

in the latter between Royalists and Parliamentarians led to the governor of the Leeward Islands, Lord Willoughby of Parham, expediently recognising Charles II until a Commonwealth fleet retook Barbados in January 1652. This recovery paved the way for the Commonwealth's assertion of control over Virginia and Maryland. Transatlantic naval operations coincided with the reclamation of the Scillies, the Isle of Man, and the Channel Islands where 340 troops, consisting of 'French, German, Danes, Switzers, Scots, Dutch, Irish, English and islanders', were allowed free passage to Virginia 'or any other plantation in America'. The decanting of dissidents, which Cromwell had instigated in Wales in 1648 then extended to Ireland and Scotland in 1649–51, demonstrated the exclusive nature of the Gothic supremacy that had inspired the regicides, when proclaiming the Commonwealth in May 1649, to claim that the English parliament had supreme authority over the American colonies and all Stuart dominions overseas. The American colonies, whose governance came under the remit of the Council of State from 1650, were not written off as a dumping ground, however. They were to be made more productive by the supply, both voluntary and enforced, of indentured labour from the British Isles.[36]

In turn, Scottish engagement with the American colonies was altered significantly in the 1650s. Servitor colonialism was imposed through the indenture of around 2,000 military prisoners into service for 7 years in plantations in the Caribbean, Virginia and New England. This precedent, once initiated in 1650, led to the regular transportation of political prisoners and social undesirables such as vagrants, thieves and prostitutes prior to the Restoration. At the same time, contemporaneous evidence from Boston would suggest that indentured servants, who were mainly employed in the iron works at Saugus, found a welcoming network among an established Scottish community. The foundation of the Scottish Charitable Society in 1657, the first identifiable ethnic anchor for Scots in the American colonies, which anticipated a similar society in London (the Royal Scottish Corporation) by eight years, coincided with the ending of the initial period of enforced indentures. Included among the Boston society's founders were migrants who had arrived in the Caribbean from 1634 and who had subsequently progressed to New England and prospered as

---

[36] *The Perfect Diurnall*: (London, 1650), no. 31 (8–15 July), pp. 359–60, and no. 34 (29 July – 5 August), pp. 402–3; (London, 1652), no. 108 (29 December 1651 – 5 January 1652), pp. 1560–2, 1567–8, 1570. *CSP, Colonial* (1574–1660), pp. 360, 368–9; Graham, *Colonists from Scotland*, pp. 10–11; www.mdarchives.state.md.us/ Proceedings of the Council of Maryland, vol. 3 (1636–67), pp. 243, 304, 311–12, and Proceedings of the Provincial Court, 1658–62, vol. 41, p. 277, vol. 42, p. 103; Coldham, *The Complete Book of Emigrants*, pp. 284, 354, 393; Andrews, *The Colonial Period of American History*, pp. 33, 35, 55.

merchants, shipmasters, planters, surgeons, craftsmen and shopkeepers. This Caribbean connection was retained and fructified through trade, ensuring that Boston became an American hub for Scottish commercial networks in the later seventeenth century.[37]

Despite the forcible incorporation of Scotland into the Cromwellian Commonwealth and Protectorate, entrepreneurial opportunities for Scots in the Americas were seemingly enhanced by the concession of free trade. This concession was particularly advantageous to Glasgow, where an elite group of merchant adventurers, whose trading activities ranged from the Levant to the American colonies (sugar now being imported as well as tobacco), had emerged by the Restoration in 1660. Following the seizure of Jamaica in 1655, in compensation for the palpable failure of Cromwell's Western Design to secure Hispaniola, Scots were among the migrants who settled there from other Caribbean islands, as well as directly from Scotland or indirectly through England. Indeed, by the Restoration, the Scottish Privy Council was receptive to mercantile schemes for the compulsory transportation of social undesirables to encourage both Scots and English entrepreneurs planting in Jamaica and Barbados. There was also a continuous demand for Scots as planters and servants in established colonies such as Antigua and in new English ventures such as Surinam.[38]

However, while the transatlantic dimension can appear as an advantageous aspect of Cromwellian Union, there was a more substantial downside. The standardisation of customs and excise undermined the cutting edge of the Scottish carrying trade in taking commodities to and from the colonies. As was particularly evident in the Cromwellian conquest of Barbados, the formative English fiscal–military state placed emphasis on the more effective and remunerative collection of customs and excise from colonial commodities rather than encouraging trade between the colonies

---

[37] *Passengers to America*, ed. M. Tepping (Baltimore, 1978), pp. 147–9; Coldham, *The Complete Book of Emigrants*, pp. 256, 276, 285–6, 316, 319–20, 322; New England Historic Genealogical Society, Boston, Biographical Sketches of the Founders of the Scots Charitable Society, MSS B 536/V.12; J. Taylor, *A Cup of Kindness: The History of the Royal Scottish Corporation, a London Charity, 1603–2003* (East Linton, 2003), pp. 28–46. Leading members of the Scottish émigré community in London had effectively operated as a philanthropic association since the regal union, with a poor box in existence since 1613 to help their impoverished countrymen. A second charter of 1676 confirmed the Corporation as the premier ethnic anchor for Scots in the city of London.

[38] *RPCS*, third series, I, pp. 154, 181, 266, 479–80, 497–8; II, p. 101; VII, pp. 664–5. *CSP, Colonial* (1574–1660), pp. 343, 360, 368–9, 446, and (1660–68), pp. 319–20; Dunn, *Sugar and Slaves*, pp. 151–5; Barclay & Graham, *The Early Transatlantic Trade of Ayr*, pp. 14–16; BL, Papers Relating to English Colonies in America and the West Indies, 1627–99, Egerton MS 2395, fols. 123, 277–8, 291; DCA, Dundee Register of Ships, 1612–81, entry for June 1658; *CSP, Colonial* (1574–1660), p. 446.

through fiscal incentive and rebates.[39] Navigation Acts further hampered Scottish commerce with the Dutch in the Caribbean. Conceived essentially as a reaction to foreign trade embargoes and continued expressions of loyalty to the Stuarts in the American colonies, the first Navigation Act in August 1650 was designed to ring-fence, rather than liberalise, English overseas trade. The second Navigation Act, in October 1651, freed up trade without threatening the dominance of the English merchant companies. This Act primarily asserted English independence of the Dutch carrying trade, which had benefited from the domestic and colonial disruption occasioned by the civil wars of the 1640s. It sought to ensure the more systematic deployment of English convoys. Foreign access to the English colonies in North America and the Caribbean was strictly licensed, not prohibited.[40]

Despite its maladroit operation, the Western Design stimulated the revival of schemes for a West Indian association, first mooted in the 1620s and again at the outset of the Long Parliament, to mount a sustained military and commercial assault on Spanish imperial power in the Caribbean. Duly formulated as a complement to the East India Company, the West India Company for the 'improvement of English interests' in the Caribbean was intended to operate like its immediate rival, the Dutch WIC, as a commercial monopoly, led by Lord Willoughby of Parham and mercantile adventurers from the city of London. Although this scheme was laid aside at the Restoration, its implementation would have reduced Scottish-based entrepreneurs to the status of interlopers in the Caribbean. Gothic appropriation remained the watchwords for the Cromwellian Union under the Protectorate. Nova Scotia was in part at least assumed to be under English jurisdiction, an assumption which ignored Scottish as well as French patents for the colony. Although membership on the committees dealing with trade and plantations was broadened from parliamentarians to include merchants from the city of London, Scotland, as a junior partner in Union, was conceded no place.[41]

---

[39] NLC, George Martin, An Essay on Barbados (1651), Ayer MS 276; [A.B. a diligent observer of the Times], *A Brief Relation of the beginning and ending of the Troubles in the Barbados; with the True Causes thereof* (London, 1653); Keith, *Commercial Relations of England and Scotland, 1603–1707*, pp. 55–70.

[40] Brenner, *Merchants and Revolution*, pp. 577, 622, 625, 663–7; Pincus, *Protestantism and Patriotism*, pp. 40–50; W. Klooster, 'Anglo-Dutch Trade in the Seventeenth Century: An Atlantic Partnership?' in Macinnes & Williamson, eds., *Shaping the Stuart World*, pp. 261–82; BL, Papers Relating to English Colonies in America and the West Indies, 1627–99, Egerton MS 2395, fols. 256–61.

[41] *CSP, Colonial* (1574–1660), pp. 453, 496–8; BL, Papers Relating to English Colonies in America and the West Indies, 1627–99, Egerton MS 2395, fols. 23, 87–90, 99–100,

Acquisitive associations

Bolstered by the restoration of aristocracy and episcopacy and with the king in parliament firmly anchored as the basis of sovereign power in England, the question remained whether Charles II would act in an inclusive Britannic or an exclusive Gothic manner from 1660. In terms of a colonial perspective, the dice seemed loaded firmly in favour of the latter. The English Privy Council was restored as the king's executive agency for the government of the dominions as well as England. Reporting to this Council were permanent commissions for trade and the plantations, which followed Cromwellian precedent by involving merchants, mainly from the city of London, planters and sea-captains as well as royal advisers, and by according no place for Scots, other than the less than benign influence of Lauderdale as the manager for Scottish affairs. Residual proprietorial claims of Scottish families in the colonies were set aside, most notably that of the house of Stirling in Nova Scotia, New England and Long Island, and that of the house of Carlisle in Barbados and the Leeward Islands, the latter claim having devolved on the Perthshire-based William Hay, 4th Earl of Kinnoull. While English interests also lost out through the king's exercise of his prerogative powers to realign control over the colonies, Scottish interests were completely wiped out.[42] Scots in

---

108, 138, 202–37, 311–28. The English claim to Nova Scotia rested on the voyages of discovery by Sebastian Cabot at the behest of Henry VII in the late fifteenth century, and subsequent engagements won over the French until the outset of the seventeenth century. Sir William Alexander recognised these precedents, but his patent was issued under Scots not English law. He subsequently devolved, under Scots law, part of his proprietary interest to a French planter, Claud St Stephen, Seigneur de la Tour, who had actually settled in Acadia with his father around 1605. Claud de la Tour further secured his plantation (at St John's Fort) with a French patent. But running into conflict with the French authorities, he had first taken English partners to help relieve his debts and finally sold out his interest to them in the 1650s. On these tenuous grounds, the Protectorate reclaimed Nova Scotia for England. The French were to establish their own West Indian Company in 1664 (*Edit du roy pour l'establisement de la Compagne des Indes occidentals. Verifié en Parlement le unziéme jour de iullet 1664* (Paris, 1664)).

[42] HL, Blathwayt Papers, BL 370, 375, 379, 382–3, 389, 396; *APC, Colonial* (1613–1680), pp. 301, 304–5, 324, 362–5, 484–5, 490, 493, 497, 539–4, and (1660–8), pp. 39–40, 502–06, 541–2; Coldham, *The Complete Book of Emigrants*, pp. 320, 460; *Province and Court Records of Maine*, ed. C. T. Libby, R. E. Moody & N. W. Allan, 6 vols. (Portland, ME, 1928–75), III, pp. vii–xi. Kinnoull was at least accorded a pension after he surrendered his patent in 1663, albeit this differential award, of £500 p.a. for five years and thereafter £1,000 p.a. for life, was subject to adjustment and no more than partial payment and all but ignored by 1682 (*CSP, Colonial* (1681–5), pp. 363–4, 435). The Earls of Stirling, having been compensated on paper for the loss of Nova Scotia in the 1630s, received no further reimbursement except an acknowledgment of arrears even when they offered to sell all their patents for Nova Scotia, New Hampshire and Maine to the Crown in 1674. Although the house of Stirling was seemingly promised compensation of £3,500

England and in the colonies were accorded the same rights as Englishmen so long as they lived under English jurisdiction. But Scots based in Scotland were treated as foreigners and aliens by the Navigation Acts promulgated in 1660 and 1663 and subsequently modified and explained, but never basically altered, by further enactments in 1662, 1670, 1671 and 1673.

The purpose of these Acts was distinctly mercantilist with a Gothic flavour: to advance foreign commerce, increase royal revenue and regulate the colonies on the one hand, and promote shipping, manufacturing and a favourable balance of trade on the other. The Act of 1660 specified that no goods or commodities, regardless of where they were produced, could be imported into or exported out of any English plantation except in a ship built in England, or the plantations, whose master and three-quarters of the crew were English. The same Act enumerated colonial commodities, basically raw materials and produce, that were to be exclusively traded through English markets. No direct trade was to be permitted between continental Europe and the American colonies. The Act of 1663 stated that England was to be the staple for all European goods imported into the colonies, and all masters of ships sailing for the colonies were obliged to provide a detailed manifest of their ships and cargos on arrival in England and to lodge a bond for payment of customs prior to their departure.[43]

These Acts, which proclaimed English hegemony within the British Atlantic, were complemented by the continuance of the fiscal–military state from the Cromwellian regime in every Stuart dominion except England. Thus Scotland's constitutional standing at the Restoration was not so much approximate to that of England as realigned to that of Ireland

---

when Long Island and adjacent islands bordering New England were subsumed in the proprietary grant of New York to James, Duke of York, in 1664, no payments were evidently made, even when the capital sum was commuted into a life pension, with at least £9,000 in arrears having accumulated by 1713 (HL, Huntington Manuscripts, HM 1356; Slafter, *Sir William Alexander and American Colonization*, pp. 70–1). The house of Hamilton was also stripped of its patents to Newfoundland as well as, later, for estates claimed but never settled in Connecticut (HL, Bridgewater & Ellesmere MSS, EL 9604; BL, Papers Relating to English Colonies in America and the West Indies, 1627–99, fols. 340–2).

[43] Andrews, *The Colonial Period of American History*, pp. 50–143; M. Kamen, *Empire and Interest: The American Colonies and the Politics of Mercantilism* (New York, 1970), pp. 20–9; J. M. Soisin, *English America and the Restoration Monarchy of Charles II: Transatlantic Politics, Commerce and Kinship* (London, 1980), pp. 39–73. The Navigation Acts were certainly not theoretical mercantilist constructs and were the process of pragmatic negotiation and accommodation between courtiers and other colonial projectors, planting and mercantile interests (J. Appleby, *Economic Thought and Ideology in Seventeenth-Century England* (Princeton, 1978), pp. 37–41). Nevertheless, they enunciated protectionist measures that were classically mercantilist and were perceived as such outside England, especially in Scotland.

where a dependent parliament was restored. Like the Irish parliaments and constitutional assemblies in Caribbean colonies, the Scottish Estates in 1661 awarded Charles a substantive annuity (£40,000 sterling) for life – raised more through the excise than on customs in the case of Scotland. Such awards obviated the need for regular parliaments to vote supply. Scotland also became a training ground for the oppressive use of the armed forces, albeit the continuity of governors-general and in colonial administration has focused more attention on Ireland and the Stuarts' American dominions as fiscal–military dependencies.[44]

However the Britannic perspective was not entirely lost under Charles II. After the first imposition of the Navigation Acts, Charles II had used his prerogative powers to grant an individual dispensation to a seafaring entrepreneur, John Browne, who had secured a patent to establish a sugar works in Glasgow. This licence, for four ships to trade anywhere in America, Africa and Asia was awarded first in 1663 and was renewed in 1664. Brown used this dispensation to trade initially in Virginia and subsequently in Barbados.[45] This dispensation was also extended to other entrepreneurs wishing to sustain sugar works in Glasgow and later in Edinburgh. The development of these manufactures demonstrates the active involvement of Scotland, notwithstanding the Navigation Acts, in the transatlantic trade to the West Indies, as well as to the Chesapeake and the Delaware for tobacco. As the Stuarts' overseas dominions in the Americas expanded in the Restoration era, so did assiduous commercial networking by Scottish entrepreneurs, from Boston to New York and on to Philadelphia by the 1680s. Glasgow, which had developed Port Glasgow further down the Clyde as its Atlantic gateway in 1667, maintained a position of leadership in transatlantic trade, which stimulated engagement not only by Ayr but also by lesser ports, such as Dumfries in the south and Irvine, Greenock and Dumbarton in the west. Indeed, by 1684, the Glasgow merchant, Walter Gibson, who regularly sailed to Virginia and Maryland, was openly advertising to take settlers to the plantations. Consortia from Edinburgh soon followed through the port of Leith in regular commerce with the Americas, which, in turn, stimulated the engagement of such neighbouring east coast towns as Prestonpans and Burntisland, and Kirkcaldy as well as Bo'ness on the Firth of Forth. In terms of further engagement with the Atlantic economy, Perth joined Dundee from Tayside, while Montrose and Peterhead supplemented the

---

[44] HL, Blathwayt Papers, BL 389, 396; Webb, *The Governors-General*, pp. 329–466; Smyth, *The Making of the United Kingdom*, pp. 77–87.
[45] BL, Maitland & Lauderdale Papers, 1532–1688, Add.MSS 35,125, fo. 74; NAS, Society of Antiquaries Papers, GD103/2/4/42; *Minutes of the Council and General Court of Colonial Virginia (1622–76)*, pp. 493, 507, 511; *CSP, Colonial* (1660–1668), nos. 543, 849, 867.

endeavours of Aberdeen in the north-east, as did Inverness in the Highlands and even Stromness in the Orkney Isles by the 1680s.[46]

As Duke of York, the future James II had played a key public role in upholding a Britannic perspective for imperial monarchy which sought to be inclusive of Scottish, Irish and Welsh as well as English interests. James, who believed more in the promotion of trade and plantations through monopolistic commercial companies and proprietary government than in regulation through the Navigation Acts, was instrumental in using the Crown's prerogative powers to suspend laws restricting Scottish participation in English overseas ventures. The issuing of letters of marque to Scottish privateers, the pressing of Scots into service in the Royal Navy and the less than welcome conscription of Scots seamen to serve in the Second (1666–7) and Third (1672–4) Dutch Wars against their main commercial partner further encouraged a laxity in applying trading prohibitions.[47] Having been awarded New York as a proprietary colony on its wresting from the Dutch in 1664, James had been an assiduous and tolerant promoter of a durable Scottish and Dutch commercial network that was based in Albany – named after his Scottish ducal title – where the Scot, Robert Livingstone, served as a frontier colonial administrator throughout the Restoration era. James also took the initiative in encouraging the extensive settlement of Scots on the lower Delaware, a district hitherto settled mainly by Danes, Swedes and Finns that had not been included in his original proprietary grant of New York, but was acquired by conquest in 1664.[48] He subsequently opened up participation

---

[46] *RPCS*, third series: I (1661–4), p. 154; II (1665–9), pp. 101, 128–9, 201–2, 358, 446, 502–3, 642; III, pp. 20–2, 98, 173, 259, 299–300, 331, 407, 650, 658, 679; IV (1673–6), pp. 83–4, 144; V (1676–8), pp. 125, 227, 231; VI (1678–80), pp. 285, 330–1, 537; VII (1681–2), pp. 178, 534; VIII (1683–4), pp. 193, 253, 377, 379, 519–22, 526–7, 682, 709–11; IX (1684), pp. 12–13, 28–9, 69–70, 102, 208; X (1684–5), pp. 19–20, 90–1; XI (1685–6), pp. 94, 145, 208–9, 251–2; XII (1686), pp. 36–7; XIII (1686–9), p. 358; XIV (1689), p. 522; XV (1690), pp. 179, 185, 307, 384–5, 444. GCA, Records of the Maxwells of Pollock, T-PM 113/565, /572, /574, and Research Papers and Notes compiled by R. F. Dell, TD 1022/11: Register of Deeds, B.10.15, no. 1811; NAS, Biel MSS, GD 6/1249, and Scarth of Breckness MSS, GD 217/586; 'Proposals by Walter Gibson, merchant in Glasgow, to persons who wish to transport themselves to America, 1684' in *The Bannatyne Miscellany*, vol. III, ed. D. Laing (Edinburgh, 1855), pp. 383–4; Smout, *Scottish Trade on the Eve of Union*, pp. 175–8, 242; Barclay & Graham, *The Early Transatlantic Trade of Ayr*, pp. 21–38.

[47] *RPCS*: third series, I, pp. 600–1, 606–7, 641–3; II, pp. 512–13; III, pp. 463, 499–505; IV, p. 42. NAS, Trinity House Leith, GD 226/115; DCA, Dundee Council Books, V (1663–9), fols. 10–13, 15, and VI (1669–99), fo. 35; *APC, Colonial (1613–1680)*, pp. 457–8; *CSP, Colonial* (1669–74), pp. 59–60.

[48] NAS, Letters and Papers of Thomas Bannatyne, RH15/14/41; *APC, Colonial* (1613–80), pp. 512, 516–17; *CSP, Colonial* (1669–74), pp. 13–14, 16–17; *The Dongan Papers, 1683–1688*, ed. P. R. Christoph, 2 vols. (Syracuse, NY, 1993–6), I, pp. 14, 44, 57, and II, p. 370; Walter Wharton, *Land Survey Register, 1675–1679, West Side Delaware River*, ed. A. C. Myers (Wilmington, DE, 1955), pp. 10, 13–18, 31, 43–5, 48–50, 59–62, 65–6, 82–4,

to all three kingdoms in the Royal Africa Company from the 1670s and the Hudson's Bay Company during the 1680s.[49]

Royal patronage notwithstanding, this enhanced activity can be attributed primarily to accumulating Scottish expertise and sophistication in circumventing the Navigation Acts.[50] Scottish endeavours to have the Acts suspended were peremptorily rejected in 1661 because of perennial English fears about the competitive edge enjoyed by the Scottish carrying trade. Nevertheless, the Acts themselves contained significant loopholes and exemptions that could be exploited by Scottish entrepreneurs.[51] Flexibility in the loading and unloading of colonial commodities off-shore rather than just at the port of Berwick-upon-Tweed was stretched as far as direct shipments to and from the Firth of Forth that nominally cleared customs in the Holy Isles. As long as ships were allowed to land colonial goods in Ireland, the North Channel served the same purpose for ports in the west of Scotland. There were three areas exempt from the Navigation Acts – Newfoundland, where there was a lucrative trade in fish to Spain, Portugal and the Italian states; Guinea, the centre of the African slave trade; and Delaware, the district contested by Maryland, the Dutch and Swedes which remained contested and exempt when incorporated into New York in 1664. This latter area was of greatest significance to Scottish commercial ambitions through the tobacco trade.

No less pertinently, there were three key exceptions to the staple provision that all goods had to be exported from England – salt for the fisheries of Newfoundland and New England; servants, horses and provisions from Scotland as well as Ireland; and, in keeping with Charles II's marriage treaty with Catherine of Braganza in 1662, wines from the Portuguese islands of Madeira and the Azores. A steady supply of political prisoners, from the later Covenanting Movement as a militant party of protest,

---

88–90; *Records of the Court of New Castle on Delaware*, 2 vols. (Lancaster, PA, 1904–35), II, 100–1, 123–5, 167, 170–4; William Penn, *A letter . . . to the Committee of the Free Society of Traders of that province [Pennsylvania], residing in London* (London, 1683); N. C. Landsman, 'The Middle Colonies: New Opportunities for Settlement, 1660–1700' in Canny, ed., *The Origins of Empire*, pp. 351–74.

[49] R[ichard] B[urton], *A View of the English Acquisitions in Guinea, and the East-Indies* (London, 1686); *The Dongan Papers*, I, pp. 171–2, 268–73; R. Robert, *Chartered Companies: Their Role in the Development of Overseas Trade* (London, 1969), pp. 103–8, 133–40; *Scotland and the Americas, c. 1650 – c. 1939: A Documentary Source Book*, ed. A. I. Macinnes, M. D. Harper & L. G. Fryer (Edinburgh, 2002), pp. 135–6.

[50] A. I. Macinnes, 'Circumventing State Power – Scottish Mercantile Networks and the English Navigation Laws, 1660–1707' in Borschberg & Krieger, eds., *Water and State in Europe and Asia*, forthcoming; Keith, *Commercial Relations of England and Scotland, 1603–1707*, pp. 111–21.

[51] Andrews, *The Colonial Period of American History*, pp. 85–107, 145–77; Soisin, *English America and the Restoration Monarchy*, pp. 59–66.

featured on the individual dispensations given to Scottish consortia to trade with the Americas. However, the other two exemptions encouraged tramp trading; that is, the conveying of goods to and from several ports rather than directly across the Atlantic. Tramping, which was the prevailing form of Scottish commerce in the Baltic (see Chapter 8), was now transferred to the Caribbean and the North Atlantic. Tramping was further encouraged by the concession that ships could trade freely between the colonies, a trading practice not checked by the imposition of intercolonial duties from 1673, not least because of the limited number of colonial officials in place or willing to collect these impositions. The need to provide bonds specifying ships and cargoes to and from the Americas was circumvented by transferring bonds from legitimate English to illicit Scottish shipping, by outright forgery, by disguised ownership, by smuggling and by collusion with colonial officials[52] – practices which became the stock in trade of Scottish commercial networks operating in the Americas, whose vitality has tended to be downplayed by disparate patterns of Scottish immigration and settlement in the Stuarts' dominions.[53]

Networks headed by London Scots that traded legitimately with the colonies had the added bonus of enrolling their ships in convoys protected

---

[52] RC, Danske Kancelli, divers breve, documenter og akter, C.63-III, Den af Isack Holmes Fuldmaglig, Seneca Torsen holde Journal paa alle engelske og skotske Skippere saavel fra Vestersoen som fra Østersøen, der har passeret Øresund, 1681–4; HL, Huntington Manuscripts, HM 32,266; NLC, Sir Richard Dutton, The State of Barbados (1684), Ayer MS 827; *APC, Colonial* (1613–89), pp. 318–19, 407; *CSP, Colonial* (1681–5), pp. 254–6, 361–3; *Minutes of the Provincial Council of Pennsylvania, 1683–1775*, ed. S. Hazard, 10 vols. (1851–2), I, pp. 26–9, 90–1; www.mdarchives.state.md.us/ Proceedings of the Council of Maryland, vol. 3 (1636–67), pp. 366–79, and vol. 17 (1681–8), pp. 392–8; Messrs Wingate & Washington, *An Abridgement of the laws in force and use in Her Majesty's plantations* (London, 1704), pp. 54–7, 64–5, 69–77, 90–1, 140–3,153–7, 211–12; Barclay & Graham, *The Early Transatlantic Trade of Ayr*, pp. 17–21.

[53] N. C. Landsman, 'Nation, Migration, and the Province in the First British Empire: Scotland and the Americas, 1600–1800', *AHR*, 104 (1999), pp. 463–75; D. Dobson, *Scottish Emigration to Colonial America, 1607–1785* (Athens, GA, 1994). Although no more than 7,000 Scots probably migrated to the American colonies, as against the 70,000 to Scandinavia and the Baltic and at least 100,000 to Ulster during the seventeenth century, there was a distinct shift later in the century in favour of transatlantic migration – albeit Ulster clearly remained the preferred British domain for the migrant Scot (T. C. Smout, N. C. Landsman & T. M. Devine, 'Scottish Emigration in the Seventeenth and Eighteenth Centuries' in N. Canny, ed., *Europeans on the Move: Studies on Migration, 1500–1800* (Oxford, 1994), pp. 70–112). Moreover, this transatlantic migration, which usually departed from English ports in conformity with the Navigation Acts, was not static but ongoing, as Scots removed and relocated continuously from the Caribbean to mainland plantations. In some instances, indentured servants were transferred from Barbados to New York through Scottish commercial networks (M. Ghirelli, *List of Emigrants from England to America, 1682–92* (Baltimore, 1968); *Bristol and America: A Record of the First Settlers in the Colonies of North America, 1654–1865*, ed. W. D. Bowan (London, 1929); *Minutes of the Court of Albany, Rensselaerswyck and Schenectady (1668–1680)*, ed. A. J. F. Canhaer, 3 vols. (Albany, 1926–32), II, pp. 483–4, and III, p. 70).

by the Royal Navy. However, Scottish entrepreneurs and their colonial associates were no less willing to use Rotterdam, Amsterdam and even Hamburg as commercial hubs. The Atlantic connection certainly contributed to the reinvigoration of Scottish networks in Bordeaux and their installation in Lisbon and Cadiz/Seville by the 1680s. The Irish ports of Belfast and Londonderry were locked into the Scottish transatlantic as well as the Baltic carrying trade. Whereas established Bristol merchants found themselves on the defensive by the 1650s against interlopers intent on the free trade in indentured servants, Scottish engagement with the Atlantic trade raised interloping from an urban to a national endeavour in the Restoration era.[54] At the same time, there was steady pressure from the colonies for Scots to serve in the Caribbean as servants and in the Chesapeake and Delaware as frontiersmen. Scots, especially Highlanders, were viewed as excelling in the latter role, but able-bodied men from all districts were welcome to rebuild societies devastated by hurricanes and increasingly fearing internal upheaval from revolts as slavery increased exponentially with the profitability of sugar and rum. External threats from the French, the Spanish and the Dutch also had to be faced. Indeed, the failure of the English endeavour to take St Lucia in 1669 was largely attributed to the lack of Scottish auxiliary troops. Barbados, which was to the fore in providing settlers to consolidate Jamaica and extend the Stuarts' dominions in North and South Carolina, was the main promoter of Scottish immigration and open trade through Scottish commercial networks.[55]

[54] D. Harris-Sax, *The Widening Gate: Bristol and the Atlantic Economy, 1450–1700* (Berkeley, 1991), pp. 14–15, 251–77; *Record of the Court of Assistants of the Colony of Massachusetts Bay, 1630–1692*, ed. J. Noble, 3 vols. (Boston, 1901–28), III, pp. 41–2, 93–4; *Minutes of the Provincial Council of Pennsylvania*, I (1683–1700), pp. 90–1, 527, 550–1; *The Dongan Papers*, II, pp. 117–18; *CSP, Colonial* (1675–6), p. 377, and *(1681–1685)*, p. 667; NAS, Letter book of John Swinton of that Ilk, merchant, London, 1673–7, CS 96/3264, and Andrew Russell Papers, GD 1/885/2/1–2 and /801; NLS, Dunlop Papers, MS 9250, fo. 13; GCA, Dunlop of Garnkirk Papers, D 12/1–44; Records of the Maxwells of Pollock, T-PM 113/26–7, /32, /439, /562, /795; DCA, Dundee Register of Ships, entries for January 1675 and June 1678.
[55] *APC, Colonial* (1613–80), pp. 479–80, 788; *CSP, Colonial:* (1660–8), pp. 429–30, 486–7, 525–6; (1669–74), pp. 96, 115–17, 165–6, 199–200, 230–1, 475, 506–7; (1675–6), pp. 288–9, 304, 497–502; (1677–80), pp. 352, 528–30, 571–4. BL, Papers Relating to English Colonies in America and the West Indies 1627–99, Egerton MS 2395, fols. 291, 531–2, 625–6, 629–35; www.mdarchives.state.md.us/ Proceedings of the Council of Maryland, vol. 5 (1667–88), pp. 148–9; Insh, *Scottish Colonial Schemes*, pp. 229–32; William Hilton, *A Relation of a Discovery lately made on the Coast of Florida* (London, 1664); Anon., *A Brief Description of the Province of Carolina on the coasts of Floreda* (London, 1666); J. P. Greene, 'Colonial South Carolina and the Caribbean Connection' in Katz, Murrin & Greenberg, eds., *Colonial America*, pp. 179–98. The governor of the first settlement in Carolina, in the northern county of Albemarle, was a Scot, William Drummond, who arrived from Virginia in 1664. However, he returned to Virginia three years later to pursue a rather

Scottish networks did not confine their commercial activities in the Caribbean to the Stuart dominions. In ventures to the Lesser Antilles throughout the Restoration era they traded sporadically with the Dutch, the French and the Danes. Moreover, Scottish entrepreneurs were considerably more flexible than the English in switching political allegiance. While the Scots readily transferred over from the Dutch to the English in New York in 1664 and again after a brief period of Dutch reconquest in 1673, the Scottish planting elite in Surinam not only accepted Dutch control from 1667, but actively connived with the Dutch authorities to expropriate disaffected English planters.[56]

Networks based on ties of kinship and local association were no more exclusively Scottish in North America than in Northern Europe.[57] Indeed, even where networks were predominantly Scottish, they were not always complementary and were occasionally involved in antagonistic sharp practices.[58] However, colonial officials from New Hampshire to

chequered career as colonial trader, lawyer and politician, eventually being executed for his complicity in the Nathaniel Bacon rebellion of 1676 (*North Carolina Higher Court Records 1670–1696*, ed. M. E. E. Parker (Raleigh, NC, 1968), pp. xvii–xx, xxxiii–xxxiv; *Minutes of the Council and General Court of Colonial Virginia (1622–76)*, pp. 315, 334, 342, 362, 432, 456, 512; www.mdarchives.state.md.us/ Proceedings and Acts of the General Assembly of Maryland, vol. 2 (1666–76), pp. 143–4).

[56] HL, Blathwayt Papers, BL 368; *CSP, Colonial* (1660–8), p. 320; Daniel Denton, *A Brief Description of New York formerly called New Netherlands* (London, 1670); Anon., *The Conduct of the Dutch relating to the Breach of Treaties with England* (London, 1760), pp. 4–51. By the Treaty of Breda which concluded the Second Dutch War in 1667, New York was recognised as being part of the Stuarts' American dominions while Surinam was ceded to the Dutch. The principal English planter expropriated by the Dutch was Jeronimy Clifford, with a Scottish planter, Henry Mackintosh from Glasgow, taking a prominent part in the legal process against him that lasted from 1684 to 1691.

[57] Murdoch, *Network North*, pp. 13–83; C. Dalhede, *Handelsfamiljer p Stormakstidens Europamarknad*, 2 vols. (Stockholm, 2001), I, pp. 13–46; Soisin, *English America and the Restoration Monarchy*, pp. 5–23.

[58] *The Dongan Papers*, II, pp. 25–6, 368; *Minutes of the Council and General Court of Colonial Virginia (1622–76)*, pp. 210, 223, 367; www.mdarchives.state.md.us/ Proceedings of the Provincial Court of Maryland, vol. 69 (1679–80), pp. 240–1. Antagonisms between rival networks were most flagrantly illustrated by the case of George Lockhart and English Smith against Walsall Cobbe, which was decided in favour of the latter after protracted litigation in Scotland and New York. Lockhart, who was also a surgeon, and Smith were based as merchants in New York, seeking to break into the transatlantic trade by chartering a ship of dubious provenance known as the *Seaflower*, of which Walsall Cobbe was master in June 1683, when laid up on the River Thames. Lockhart and Smith intended to use their contacts among Scots at London and Edinburgh to run contraband goods into New York under the guise of a dispensation to bring Covenanting prisoners to the colonies. Cobbe, however, was also part of a network of illicit traders with established contacts in London, the port of Leith and the city of New York. The chartered ship turned out to be French-built and therefore ineligible for the colonial trade. Lockhart and Smith obtained judgement in their favour at the Scottish High Court of Admiralty in May 1684, when the blame for duplicity over the charter contract was laid firmly to the account of Cobbe. However, Cobbe, with assistance from associates in

The transatlantic dimension 163

South Carolina noted the clannish cohesion, as well as the acquisitiveness, of Scottish entrepreneurs who consistently outsold English competitors by focusing on quantity rather than quality in marketing goods for servants and slaves.[59] In Delaware especially, Scottish networks came to dominate the three southern counties of New Castle, Kent and Sussex. The Scots took advantage of these counties being regularly contested between Maryland and, initially, New York, then Pennsylvania. The issue was decided in favour of William Penn's colony in 1685. By then, the Scots were viewed as a greater threat to the operation of the Navigation Acts than either the Dutch or even the Caribbean buccaneers. Local initiatives by English colonial officials to have the Scots declared foreigners and aliens incapable of wholesale trading or holding public office were summarily thrown out by court officials and juries.[60]

Leith, absconded with the ship from the Firth of Forth and had the Scottish judgement reversed in the Admiralty Court of New York in December 1684, where he was able to bring into play corroborating evidence from his associates who colluded in declaring the ship and its cargo in breach of the Navigation Acts in return for a share of the profits arising from this discovery (*The Dongan Papers*, I, pp. 81–156, and II, pp. 22, 345, 363, 368, 404, 408, 433–5; *RPCS*, third series, VIII, pp. 253, 377, 709–10).

[59] *CSP, Colonial* (1681–5), pp. 368–9, and (1685–8), pp. 92, 353–4. Only in Maine, a precariously independent province of New England from 1665 to 1685, were Scottish networks not actively operative in colonial trade. The Scottish presence, which was first evident in the 1650s among indentured prisoners dispatched by the Cromwellian regime, was on record primarily as settlers and retailers in the County of York (*Province and Court Records of Maine*, II, pp. 28, 104, 307, 345, and III, p. 5).

[60] See www.mdarchives.state.md.us/ Proceedings of the Council of Maryland, vol. 5 (1667–88), pp. 418–21, 446, 452–60, and vol. 17 (1681–6), pp. 78, 471–5; and Proceedings of the Provincial Court of Maryland, vol. 69 (1679–81), p. 308; and Proceedings of the County Court of Charles County, vol. 60 (1666–74), pp. 110, 485; and Somerset County Judicial Records, vol. 89 (1675–7), pp. 106–9. *Records of the Courts of Sussex County, Delaware, 1677–1710*, ed. C. W. Horle, 2 vols. (Philadelphia, 1991), I, pp. 6–11, 458, 466–7, 472–4, 479–80, 484, 491, 505, 510–14, 540–1, 584, 658. In July 1687, a local customs officer, Norton Claypoole, sought to bring Adam Johnston, an established tobacco dealer and serial litigant, to account by claiming that he was not entitled to trade as a merchant or factor as he was a Scotsman lacking a testimonial that he was naturalised as a denizen of the county. Johnston's claim to be a legitimate trader was upheld by the court. Claypoole again pressed charges in October to debar Johnston as an alien, as evident from his speech. But the court asserted 'that Scotchmen are as free as Englishmen' and the jury duly found Johnston, who admitted to having been born in Scotland, not guilty of rum smuggling. Johnston had actually come to the Delaware with his parents when still a child. The use of patents of denisation by Scots in the colonies was seemingly rare and usually at their own instigation to ensure that they could bring over their family and servants from Scotland. Usually, Scots were comprehended within the broad definition of freemen entitled to hold lands as persons of British or Irish descent – a status to which Dutch, Swedes, Germans, French or Spaniards seeking to settle in the Stuarts' dominions as freemen aspired through the acquisition of patents and testimonials (www.mdarchives.state.md.us/ Proceedings and Acts of the General Assembly of Maryland, vol. 2 (1666–76), pp. 89–90, 144–5, 205–6, 270–2, 282–3, 400–2, 403–4, 460–1, and Proceedings of the Council of Maryland, vol. 3 (1636–67), pp. 435–6,

Usually dominated by literate laymen not averse to litigation and willing to represent each other in a diversity of jurisdictions covering commerce by land and sea, Scottish networks were also able to take advantage of differing traditions of jurisprudence and legal practice in the colonies. In the middle colonies of New York, New Jersey, Pennsylvania and, to a lesser extent, Maryland, the normal practice of conforming to English statute and common law had to take account of Dutch and Scottish affinities for and grounding in civil law. Moreover, in all colonies from New England to the Carolinas, juries became notorious in the eyes of English officials for their disregard of the alleged facts in returning, even with repeated redirection, not guilty verdicts against practised evaders of the Navigation Acts. This complaint became repeatedly targeted against the proprietary colonies. In Pennsylvania, the presence of a large Quaker community from the founding of the colony in 1683 certainly softened the formal nature of due process. However, all proprietary colonies were deemed to be lacking in rigour in their prosecution of illicit traders and in their enforcement of the Acts.[61] In the interim, however, concerns about the autonomy of Scottish commercial networks were heightened by their endeavours to establish Scottish colonies with full backing from the Scottish Privy Council and the future James II.

Federative colonies?

In the wake of the failed negotiations for union in 1670 (see Chapter 4), the Duke of Lauderdale had procured the Scots licence to colonise in either Florida or the island of Dominica. The first option potentially clashed with the Treaty of Madrid concluded between Charles II and Spain in 1670, whereby the Spanish monarchy recognised the existing Stuart dominions in the Americas in return for a guarantee that there would be no further plantations in areas already settled from Spain. Dominica, the main base of the Carib Indians who had a reputed

---

490; *Acts of Assembly passed in the Colony of Virginia from 1662 to 1715* (London, 1727), pp. 106, 132–3; Wingate & Washington, *An Abridgement of the laws in force and use in Her Majesty's plantations*, pp. 37, 42–3, 96, 121, 288).

[61] *Record of the Court of Assistants of the Colony of Massachusetts Bay*, III, pp. 175, 209–10, 241–2, 251, 345; *Journal of the Courts of Common Right and Chancery of East New Jersey, 1683–1702*, ed. P. W. Edsall (Philadelphia, 1937), pp. 4–5, 54–5, 134–7, 192–4, 221, 238; *Minutes of the Provincial Council of Pennsylvania*, vol. V (1667–88), pp. 125–30; *Acts of Assembly passed in the Colony of Virginia*, pp. 1–2, 13–14, 96–7, 152; *Records of the Court of Chancery of South Carolina, 1671–1779*, ed. A. K. Gregorie (Washington, DC, 1950), pp. 3, 20; *CSP, Colonial* (1681–5), pp. 361–3.

penchant for cannibalism, was not a particularly attractive alternative.[62] Accordingly, Scottish endeavours switched to the neighbouring but less hostile, and hitherto sparsely settled, island of St Vincent, which had first been identified by the sugar adventurer, John Browne, from his extensive Caribbean sojourns. Basically this was another project to be launched from Barbados, and was British in its intent to pre-empt French control over an island that was to be settled and governed under a Scottish patent in conformity to Scots law. Although this project never got off the ground, it remained on the drawing board when a Committee of Trade, especially commissioned by James, Duke of York, in 1681, was encouraged to establish a colony in the Americas after consulting with a Glasgow adventurer, William Colquhoun, who had been a planter on the Dutch island of Aruba for twenty years. With a colony seen as essential if Scotland was to break out of the constrictions of European mercantilism and avoid recourse to a negotiated union with England, James opted to authorise Scottish colonies in South Carolina from 1682 and in East New Jersey from 1685.[63]

Leading undertakers for the Scottish venture to South Carolina were associated with the Earl of Shaftesbury, serial plotter and one of the original proprietors of Carolina. However, South Carolina was not a dissident Whig venture that served as a front for Scottish and English engagement in the failed Rye House Plot to assassinate Charles II and James, Duke of York, in 1683; nor was it conceived as a religious refuge.[64] Rather it was a considered Scottish response by experienced transatlantic traders, such as Walter Gibson from Glasgow, in concert with entrepreneurial nobles and gentry primarily from west and central Scotland, to overtures issued by the proprietors to attract settlers from England, Scotland and Ireland. The Scottish undertakers actually commissioned Gibson to oversee a pilot reconnaissance of the proposed site on the Ashley River a year before the initial settlement was established in the county of Port Royal at Stuart's Town, named in honour rather than in defiance of their royal

---

[62] NAS, Ogilvie of Inverquharity Papers, GD 205/40/13/3–4; *A Treaty for the Composing of Differences and Establishing of Peace in America between the Crowns of Great Britain and Spain* (London, 1670); B[urton], *The English Empire in America*, pp. 171–81.

[63] NAS, Society of Antiquaries Papers, GD103/2/4/42; *RPCS*, third series, VII, pp. 599–600, 651–5, 664–5. The colonising of St Vincent was costed at between £40,000 and £50,000 and was deemed to require 1,000 able-bodied men if the island was to be acquired by conquest; 500 would still be needed even if a sale could be negotiated as the Carib Indians were not deemed trustworthy.

[64] P. Karsten, 'Plotters and Proprietaries, 1682–83: The "Council of Six" and the Colonies', *Historian*, 38 (1976), pp. 474–84; Insh, *Scottish Colonial Schemes*, pp. 143, 186–211; Graham, *Colonists from Scotland*, p. 11. Covenanters had considered, but never established, refuges in Carolina in 1672 and in New York in 1682.

patrons, in 1683.⁶⁵ The proprietors of Carolina welcomed the Scottish colonists as a counterweight to settlers from Barbados who were undermining their governance, engaging in an illicit Indian slave trade and consorting with pirates. The proprietors, primarily Shaftesbury in association with the future Whig ideologue, John Locke, had prescribed the fundamental constitution for contracting into and governing civic society which, in turn, offered the Scots the prospective of a federative association within the essentially English colony. This prospect was further enhanced by the proprietors' acceptance that colonial financing could accord with either English or Scots law, by their requirement that the Scots should settle Port Royal as contiguous but not too close to existing counties or Charleston, and by their inducement that the Scots could expand their settlements north into a second county.⁶⁶

However, the two Scottish undertakers in charge of the colonial venture in South Carolina, the irascible Henry Erskine, Lord Cardross, and the more amenable William Dunlop (a future principal of Glasgow University) were intent on breaking into the legitimate Indian trade in furs and extending their commercial contacts with Native Americans into Spanish New Mexico. This policy, which was to be enforced by a trading monopoly within the precincts of the Scottish settlement, ran into jurisdictional disputes with the existing colonial government as well as English trading rivals. More seriously, it provoked a Spanish backlash, particularly after the Scots had fomented Indian assaults on Spanish settlements at St Augustine in Florida. Two Spanish raids mounted from Florida and Cuba in the course of 1686 effectively wiped out the Scottish settlement.⁶⁷ However, there were also structural difficulties threatening the viability of the Scottish endeavour.

Only one of the three vessels carrying settlers from both sides of the North Channel initially made it to South Carolina in 1683; one was lost at

---

⁶⁵ L. G. Fryer, 'Documents Relating to the Formation of the Carolina Company in Scotland, 1682', *South Carolina Historical Magazine*, 99 (1998), pp. 110–34; DH, Loudoun Papers, A20/1–5, /7–10, /12, /14, /16–20, /24–5; Thomas Amy, *Carolina: or, A brief description of the present state of that country, and the natural excellencies thereof* (London, 1682); Samuel Wilson, *An Account of the Province of Carolina in America* (London, 1682); [R. F.], *The Present State of Carolina with Advice to the Settlers* (London, 1682); Anon., *Carolina described more fully than heretofore* (Dublin, 1684).

⁶⁶ M. E. Sirmans, *Colonial South Carolina: A Political History, 1663–1763* (Williamsburg, VA, 1966), pp. 36–7, 40–1, 44; R. M. Bliss, *Revolution and Empire: English Politics and the American Colonies in the Seventeenth Century* (Manchester, 1990), pp. 209–18; *CSP, Colonial* (1681–5), pp. 338–9, 509–10, 661–3, and (1685–8), pp. 118, 178–9, 452, 623–6; DH, Loudoun Papers, A20/6, /11; NLS, Wodrow quarto, xxxiv, fo. 35; NAS, Home of Marchmont MSS, GD 258/847–8.

⁶⁷ *CSP, Colonial* (1681–5), p. 760, and (1685–8), pp. 5–6, 19, 22–3, 40, 46–7, 337–8, 451–2; NAS, Eglinton MSS, GD 3/5/775–7.

The transatlantic dimension 167

sea, and when the other arrived belatedly the passengers refused to settle in the designated Scottish colony. Because of a debilitating sickness that struck on arrival, women and children were left at Charleston and never actually moved out over the next three years. Cardross and Dunlop were the only two of the original undertakers who came to South Carolina. A ship carrying another two undertakers in 1686 preferred to concentrate on trade in Antigua rather than reinforce the Scottish settlement that never numbered more than 200 able-bodied men. Although it had been intended that 72 undertakers would finance the venture, no more than 42 subscribed. With leading London Scots, such as James Foulis, actively discouraging involvement in the colony, credit as well as venture capital dried up, a situation hastened by several undertakers being compromised for their involvement in the abortive rebellion of Archibald Campbell, 9th Earl of Argyll, in 1685. Nevertheless, the Scottish presence in South Carolina did not terminate with the razing of Stuart's Town and the acrimonious departure of Cardross in 1687. The surviving Scots regrouped in Charleston and formed the nucleus of a commercial network that not only survived Dunlop's departure after the Revolution, but went on to establish itself, after Boston, New York and Philadelphia, as a hub for Scottish engagement in the Caribbean.[68]

In the interim, the Scottish colony established in East New Jersey in 1685 had drawn off undertakers and settlers from South Carolina. But this undertaking served both to deepen and to diversify the colonial expertise within a commercial network that drew support from the Highlands as well as from Scotland north of the Forth.[69] No less significant was the proactive role adopted by the leading Scottish promoters who used a variety of confessional contacts to promote the viability of the undertaking. Robert Barclay of Urie was instrumental in persuading his fellow Quaker, William Penn, to allow twenty-three Scottish associates to buy out around half the existing English and Irish proprietors. George

---

[68] NLS, Dunlop Papers, MS 9250, fols. 16–17; DH, Loudoun Papers, A20/13, /15, /21–3; GCA, Dunlop of Garnkirk Papers, D 12/25–7, /33, /38, /41; NAS, Eglinton MSS, GD 3/5/773, /5/778, and Society of Antiquaries Papers, GD103/2/222; NLS, Wodrow quarto xxxvi, fols. 223–4; *CSP, Colonial* (1685–8), pp. 22–3, 353–4; *RPCS*, third series, x, pp. 206, 256; Barclay & Graham, *The Early Transatlantic Trade of Ayr*, pp. 34–6; Robert Wodrow, *The History of the Sufferings of the Church of Scotland from the Restoration to the Revolution*, ed. R. Burns, 4 vols. (Glasgow, 1829–30), IV, p. 519. Dunlop, who was the brother-in-law of William Carstares, the political fixer for William of Orange and future principal of Edinburgh University, returned to Scotland after the Revolution to attempt to persuade William of Orange to seek reparations from Spain (NAS, Leven & Melville MSS, GD 26/7/277).

[69] Insh, *Scottish Colonial Schemes*, pp. 67–94; Landsman, *Scotland and its first American Colony, 1683–1760*, pp. 99–130; L. G. Fryer, 'Robert Barclay of Urie and East New Jersey', *Northern Scotland*, 15 (1995), pp. 1–17.

Scot of Pitlochy, an entrepreneur of noted Presbyterian sympathies, who had initially been involved in the South Carolina venture, was particularly prominent not only in promoting the colony but in rebutting any claimed dissatisfaction among early migrants. Through the publishing of letters from satisfied settlers he encouraged the chain migration of families from Ireland and the north of England as well as Scotland, from the Hebridean isle of Lewis to the Border town of Kelso.[70] In further contrast to the earlier undertaking, the principal Scottish patrons were well connected at Court – namely, the Drummond brothers, James, 4th Earl of Perth, and William, 1st Earl of Melfort, who were Catholic converts. In their honour, the principal town where the Scots settled was named Perth Amboy. Although nonconformists were shipped out in bulk to East New Jersey as political prisoners, religious toleration became a feature of the colony before it was fully implemented, albeit briefly, by James II in Scotland.[71]

Essentially, the Scottish proprietors promoted East New Jersey within the context of added security gained from association with the English plantations. In a call that presaged future debates on Anglo-Scottish Union, the proprietors claimed that if they were disjoined from the English dominions the Navigation Acts would debar them from colonial trade. The advantages of the colony being under the protection of the Crown of England were further cited as the common monarchy; the lack

[70] NLS, Wodrow octavo ix, fo. 142; NAS, Advertisement: Emigration to New Jersey 1688, RH 18/1/93; 'Advertisement to all Tradesmen and others, who are willing to transport themselves into the Province of East New Jersey in America, 1684' in *The Bannatyne Miscellany*, III, pp. 385-8; George Scot of Pitlochy, *A Brief Advertisement Concerning East-New-Jersey in America* (Edinburgh, 1685); [David Barclay & Arthur Forbes], *An Advertisement concerning the Province of East-New-Jersey in America* (Edinburgh, 1685); Insh, *Scottish Colonial Schemes*, pp. 237-77; *A Brief Account of the Province of East-Jersey in America Published by the present proprietors thereof* (London, 1682); Thomas Budd, *Good Order established in Pennsylvania & East New Jersey in America, being a true account of the country* (Philadelphia, 1685). Pitlochy had reputedly been preparing himself for this venture since a visit to London to consult colonial entrepreneurs with experience of America. He even claimed that Ulster could spare 40,000 Scots men and women to be transported to America (*The Model of Government of the Province of East-New-Jersey in America* (1685) – which incorporates all other adverts and schemes for the colony). His father was Sir John Scot of Scotstarvit, an associate of William Alexander, Earl of Stirling, in his ventures to Newfoundland and Nova Scotia. Having become embroiled in a dispute with the Scottish Privy Council over the colonial records retained by his father, a former government official, and having also admitted attending Covenanting conventicles, Pitlochy occasionally found his recruiting endeavours for East New Jersey disparaged as the transporting of 'criminals, wastrels and malcontents' (*RPCS*, third series, XI, pp. 89, 137, 148, 154-6, 159, 162-3, 165-7; Fountainhall, *HNS*, II, pp. 532, 586, 627, 641-2, 658, 664).

[71] NAS, Titles to Lands in East New Jersey, RH 15/131/1; *CSP, Colonial* (1681-5), pp. 360, 367, 554; *Proposals by the Proprietors of East-Jersey in America, for the building of a town on Ambo-point* (London, 1682); Fountainhall, *HNS*, II, pp. 550, 869.

of a Scottish navy paid out of the public purse; and the latitude in their patent which meant the Scottish plantation was not necessarily tied to the laws of England. Indeed, the fundamental constitutions of the colony reputedly afforded scope for the colonists to take on Scots law where more advantageous to their interests. The Scottish proprietors certainly sought to build up Perth Amboy as a colonial port of entry independent of New York, a brief accomplishment that also benefited the predominantly English colony of West New Jersey and the entrenched Scottish community in the southern counties of Delaware for three years from 1685. Moreover, as the proprietors increasingly assumed the governorship and other official positions of leadership within East New Jersey, they began to move the governance of the colony in the direction of Scottish legal practice and procedure, with more than a hint of a distinctly federative arrangement to promote Scottish interests both within the colony and in relation to New York. Although Scot of Pitlochy had died en route to East New Jersey in 1685, prospects of making a secure livelihood from corn and cattle, in a colony which could claim to be not only self-sufficient but also (with New York) the store house and granary for the West Indies, ensured a substantial movement of people that sustained and entrenched the Scottish presence.[72]

Taking stock

Notwithstanding the prominence of Scots as governors and settlers, hopes of a distinctive federative arrangement within the Stuart dominions were dashed by a major switch in colonial policy that commenced in 1686 with the foundation of the Dominion of New England to replace the existing colonial confederation operative since 1643. This dominion was subsequently expanded to include New York, then East and West New Jersey, and even the contested counties on the Delaware by 1688. During the Restoration era, both Charles II and James, Duke of York, viewed the expansion of proprietary colonies such as Philadelphia and the Jerseys as strengthening the royal prerogative.[73] However, once James

---

[72] NLS, Wodrow quarto xxxvi, fols. 255–8, and Wodrow folio xxxiii, fols. 201–2; NAS, John McGregor Collection, GD 50/186/65/1–2; HL, Huntington Manuscripts, HM 1348; *A Brief Account of the Province of East-New-Jersey in America: published by the Scottish Proprietors having interest there* (Edinburgh, 1683); *Journal of the Courts of Common Right and Chancery of East New Jersey, 1683–1702*, pp. 38–9; *CSP, Colonial* (1685–8), pp. 42, 289, 396, 419.

[73] *Commission of King James The Second to Sir Edmund Andros June 3, 1686* (London, 1686); *CSP, Colonial* (1685–8), pp. 525–6; M. K. Geiter, 'The Restoration Crisis and the Launching of Pennsylvania, 1679–81', *EHR*, 112 (1997), pp. 300–18; Soisin, *English America and the Restoration Monarchy*, pp. 297–312.

became monarch in 1685, his proprietary colony of New York came under the direct rule of colonial officials in London who (since 1675) reported to the English Privy Council's standing committee for Trade and Plantations, of which William Blathwayt was secretary. Blathwayt was particularly supportive of the attacks on proprietary colonies, for their laxity in applying the Navigation Acts, that emanated mainly from Edward Randolph, the Crown's chief customs official in North America. Mounting official pressure for direct rule was supported by politicians of stature, such as Godolphin, and across the political spectrum from Tories such as Rochester to Whigs such as Halifax. The merging of proprietary colonies within the Dominion of New England on the eve of the Revolution clearly signalled a limited tolerance for the continuance of the clannish acquisitiveness of Scottish commercial networks. Also ruled out was any distinctive accommodation, federative or otherwise, with Scottish colonies in the Americas. Moreover, proprietary colonies were the least remunerative to the Crown, an issue of paramount importance to the expanding fiscal–military state in the wake of the Revolution.[74]

However, there was also a significant rethinking among commentators on political economy about the relative importance of the colonies and the operation of the Navigation Acts. Criticisms of the Acts in the Restoration era ranged from relatively mild qualifications by the likes of Sir Josiah Child to the swingeing attacks from free traders such as Carew Reynell and Roger Coke. In keeping with his belief that wealth was primarily generated through landed enterprise, Childs, though primarily concerned with the East Indies rather than the Americas, favoured an imperial policy weighted towards a balance of temperate and tropical colonies that would allow a complementary commodity exchange from different climatic zones. Reynell, by way of contrast, promoted a policy loaded in favour of the tobacco and sugar plantations on the grounds that wealth was based first and foremost on trade, while Coke argued on similar premises against concentration on the colonies at the expense of trade with Northern Europe, the Mediterranean and Africa.[75] Where

---

[74] HL, Blathwayt Papers, BL 230, and Huntington Manuscripts, HM 32,265; *CSP, Colonial* (1681–5), pp. 666–7, and (1685–8), pp. 62, 67, 73, 650.

[75] Sir Josiah Child, *A treatise wherein it is demonstrated . . . That the East-India trade is more profitable and necessary to the kingdom of England, than to any other kingdom or nation in Europe* (London, 1681), and *A Discourse about Trade* (London, 1690); Carew Reynell, *The True English Interest, or an Account of the Chief National Improvement* (London, 1674); Roger Coke, *A Discourse of Trade in two parts* (London, 1670), and *England's improvements in two parts: in the former is discoursed how the kingdom of England may be improved; in the latter is discoursed how the navigation of England may be increased and the sovereignty of the British Seas more secured to the crown of England* (London, 1675); Andrews, *The Colonial Period of American History*, pp. 131–4; Sheridan, *Sugar and Slavery*, pp. 7–16.

there was common ground among commentators and colonial officials was in the preference for imperial consolidation. Faced with aggressive French competition in the Americas, there was a growing realisation that England did not have the demographic capacity for overseas expansion without draining its domestic manufactures of labour.[76] Indeed, there was no immediate prospect of expanding Empire unless migrants were attracted to England and the colonies or England re-engaged in state formation. In either case, Scotland was in pole position to benefit should Britannic pragmatism temper Gothic policymaking.

[76] HL, Blathwayt Papers, BL 33–4, 416, and Bridgewater & Ellesmere MSS, EL 9611; BL, Papers Relating to English Colonies in America and the West Indies, 1627–99, Egerton MS 2395, fols. 574–8.

7 The Scottish question

In addition to the short-lived federative arrangements that were attempted in South Carolina and truncated in East New Jersey during the 1680s, there were effectively three other models for Scottish colonial engagement prior to the Revolution. Firstly, there were the distinctive Scottish commercial networks in New England, the middle colonies, and the tobacco and sugar plantations in the southern colonies and the Caribbean that were sustained as British enterprises. However, these Scottish networks were subject to sustained criticism from the English colonial administration for their clannishness, their diligence in securing positions of influence and their circumventing of the Navigation Acts. Secondly, there were Scottish networks associated with Dutch colonies, albeit mercantilist competition was constricting the close commercial association that Scotland had long enjoyed with the United Provinces. Thirdly, there was the lingering desire that Scotland should pursue a separate colony that would still be under the protection of the common monarchy but no more dependent on England than on Spain, a desire that culminated in the endeavour to colonise Darien on the Panama Isthmus between 1697 and 1700. If the Scots had created an international entrepôt for the Pacific as well as the Atlantic at Darien, there seemed a real prospect that their domestic market would grow to include Ireland and that their entrepreneurial endeavours in the Delaware would lead to the secession of up to three counties to form a Scottish colony of interlopers. As Darien turned from a scheme into a fiasco, the call for reparations contributed to a marked deterioration in Anglo-Scottish relations on the outbreak of the War of the Spanish Succession. For the Scots, the Darien fiasco was an expensive demonstration of the need for purposeful British collaboration. Darien also hastened a major restructuring of English colonial policy to meet the expansive needs of the fiscal–military state. Political incorporation, through the Treaty of Union in 1707, not only put an end to Scottish flouting of English state power, but also became the means to harness the Scots into imperial service. The Scottish carrying trade and commercial networking were to become productive rather than disruptive influences on English global outreach. As a bonus, Scottish military expertise as frontier governors – formerly more at the disposal of the French, the Dutch, the Danes and the Swedes than of the English[1] – was turned to the service of the new British Empire.

The Darien scheme

The Revolution effectively transformed a Britannic Empire based on the Stuarts' royal prerogative into an English Empire subject to constitutional oversight by parliament. However, the Gothic nature of the Revolution Settlement in England stimulated a lively public debate on domestic and imperial issues of political economy. Sir Dalby Thomas questioned the efficacy and sustainability of the English Navigation Acts. Hugh Chamberlen argued that indigenous enterprise could be galvanised by the establishment of land banks in England and Scotland. At the same time, Scots were markedly, but not irrevocably, disadvantaged in both the British Isles and the colonies by reinforced Navigation Acts, which instigated a tariff battle with England from 1693.[2] Indeed, the debate on political economy, which was accompanied by polemical rebuttals of the idea that Scotland was in any way subordinate to England, belied the notion that Scottish commercial aspirations were enshrouded in gloom or that trade and manufactures were in terminal decline. Growth was obtainable through flexible credit arrangements and by the revival of Scottish colonial aspirations, with overtures for a plantation in the West Indies resurfacing by 1693. This proposal was to be carried out in a conscious spirit of emulation of England, but the anonymous Scottish adventurers were also adamant that it was 'in the interest of England that Scotland have plantations in the West Indies' which would together serve as a bulwark against other European competition.[3]

---

[1] See A. Mackillop & S. Murdoch, eds., *Military Governors and Imperial Frontiers c. 1600–1800: A Study of Scotland and Empires* (Leiden, 2003).

[2] Sir Dalby Thomas, *An Historical Account of the Rise and Growth of the West-India Colonies and of the great advantage they are to England in respect of Trade* (London, 1690); [Hugh Chamberlen], *Dr Chamberlen's Petitions and Proposals for a Land Bank to Increase Trade, humbly offered to the House of Commons* (London, 1693), and Chamberlen, *Papers relating to a Bank of Credit upon Land Security proposed to the Parliament of Scotland* (Edinburgh, 1693); *Lords*, new series, III (1697–9), pp. 259–60; Armitage, *The Ideological Origins of the British Empire*, pp. 146–69; Smout, *Scottish Trade on the Eve of Union*, pp. 205, 244–51; Whatley, *Scottish Society*, pp. 31–9.

[3] Edinburgh City Archives, Convention of Royal Burghs, Moses Collection, SL 30/215; Sir Thomas Craig, *Scotland's Sovereignty Asserted*, translated from Latin by George Ridpath (London, 1695); Robert Murray, *A proposal for a national bank consisting of land, or any other valuable securities or depositions, with a grand cash for returns of money* (London, 1695); [Philanax Verax], *A letter from a member of the parliament of Scotland to his friend at London*

William of Orange was now caught in the horns of a British commercial dilemma. Government ministers and officials, merchants and commercial commentators were determined to ensure that English, not British, interests prevailed in the colonies. William's Scottish government, however, was by no means averse to the promotion of schemes for economic growth, especially those that took the political heat out of the Massacre of Glencoe (see Chapter 4). Building upon an Act of 1693 for the encouragement of foreign trade through the creation of commercial companies as co-partneries based on joint-stock investments, the Scottish Estates licensed two flagship endeavours in 1695 – the Bank of Scotland and the Company of Scotland trading to Africa and the Indies. When subscription lists were opened in 1696, the Bank and the Company of Scotland attracted, respectively, individual and corporate pledges for £60,000 and £400,000, and sums in hard currency amounting to £6,000 and £34,000. As an intense and debilitating famine was beginning to grip Scotland, these levels of investment could be taken as indicators of a blind optimism that would destabilise a fragile domestic economy. Yet these subscriptions were not unrealistic in terms of inward investment that reflected the close integration of Scottish mercantile communities at home and abroad. A key group in the promotion of both ventures were London Scots associated with the Royal Scottish Corporation. This entrepreneurial group had already taken the lead in developing textiles, notably the manufacturing of coarse cloth and linen in and around Edinburgh using English pattern books (see Chapter 8). Initially they mobilised subscriptions in London to the value of £300,000 until ordered to refrain on the threat of impeachment by the English parliament in December 1695.[4]

One of these London Scots, William Paterson, polemicist, colonial adventurer and founder of the Bank of England, used his far-from-benign influence to shape the Company of Scotland into doing his bidding. Between February and October 1696, the Company was structured with an executive Court of Directors elected by and reporting to a General Committee of stockholders. Paterson and, at his suggestion, four

---

concerning their late act for establishing a company of that kingdom tradeing to Africa and the Indies (London, 1695).

[4] *APS*, IX: c.49–53, pp. 313–19; c.10, pp. 377–81; c.34, pp. 420–1; c.41, p. 429; c.43, pp. 430–1; c.73, p. 463; c.83, pp. 490–1; c.88, pp. 494–7. HL, Huntington Manuscripts, Manuscript Newsletters from London to Tamworth (1690–1704), HM 30,659/48, /54, /59, /62, /64; NAS, Hamilton Papers, GD 406/1/6784; W. D. Jones, '"The Bold Adventurers": A Quantitative Analysis of the Darien Subscription Lists (1696)', *Scottish Economic & Social History*, 21 (2001), pp. 22–42; Taylor, *A Cup of Kindness*, pp. 248–9. Five of the twelve London Scots who established the Company of Scotland held office in the Royal Scottish Corporation between 1679 and 1705. Of this group of the London Scots, six were also involved in establishing the Bank of Scotland.

other London Scots were appointed as supernumerary to the twenty-five resident Scottish directors. They duly reaffirmed their own investment of £3,000 each in the Company and clandestinely raised English subscriptions. Paterson persuaded the Court to constitute three committees. The first was the Treasury charged with the running of financial affairs. The second was for Foreign Trade, under whose auspices Scottish commercial networks in Sweden, as well as in the commercial hubs of Amsterdam, Rotterdam and Hamburg, were belatedly tapped into once it became clear that the English parliament would not tolerate a 'Scotch East India Company'. The third was designated for Improvements, charged with placing domestic contracts necessary to sustain any venture overseas. Paterson also secured reimbursement of £20,000 for his prior endeavours in researching areas that would serve best for a Scottish colony – a sum almost seven times his own investment – even though he had been attempting to attract Dutch as well as English investors to his project for an international free port since the 1680s. In the course of 1696, the Scottish Court of Directors appeared more concerned with running a banking operation to rival the Bank of Scotland, developing a fishery and a salt works, acquiring a prestigious Edinburgh premises and securing a suitable heraldic letterhead. Management was increasingly left to Paterson and a small core of directors who prioritised bureaucracy over enterprise. Paterson was duly instrumental in persuading the Company of Scotland to concentrate its endeavours on an American settlement that would serve an entrepôt capable of attracting trade from the East and West Indies through its location at Darien on the Panama Isthmus. Paterson's insistence on secrecy in all matters relating to the choice of Darien served to wrong-foot hostile English colonial interests, who did not gain intelligence of the proposed Scottish settlement until the first venture sailed in 1698.[5]

The investors included a substantial number of past colonial adventurers to South Carolina and East New Jersey, albeit only five of the twenty-five elected, and one of the seven eventually co-opted, directors in 1696 had colonial experience, primarily in South Carolina.[6] Whereas East New

---

[5] NAS, Society of Antiquaries Papers, GD103/2/4/41, and Hamilton Papers GD 406/1/9078; HL, Huntington Manuscripts, Manuscript Newsletters from London to Tamworth (1690–1704), HM 30,659/77, /81; AUL, Duff House (Montcoffer Papers), MS 3175/A/2348; *CSP, Colonial* (1699), pp. 240, 464; Scott, *The Constitution and Finance of English, Scottish and Irish Joint-Stock Companies*, II, pp. 207–27; G. P. Insh, *The Company of Scotland trading to Africa and the Indies* (London, 1932), pp. 39–105; Marshall, *Presbyteries and Profits*, pp. 198–209.

[6] Those who can be identified as promoters, whether as proprietors, projected investors, subscribers, recruiting agents or shippers, constitute 100 for South Carolina and 64 for East New Jersey with only 5 involved in both ventures. Of this group of 159, just under

Jersey was a colony specialising in agricultural produce, South Carolina, and even more so Darien, seemingly were modelled along Dutch lines, essentially as trading ventures. However, the Court of Directors did not commission engineers to plan and construct the proposed settlement or take along artists to create visual impressions that would attract further investment, as practised by the Dutch from Brazil to Batavia in the seventeenth century.[7] Funded eventually as a national enterprise, as a commercial compact between God and the Scottish people, surveying, provisioning and leadership were deficient even though Scottish commercial networks in Boston, New York and Philadelphia provided logistical support. The Scottish directors can certainly stand accused of incompetence and even of swindling and profiteering at the expense of their over-optimistic investors and colonists. They were obliged to proceed unilaterally, however, without substantive support from Amsterdam, Rotterdam and Hamburg as well as London. This deficiency, which turned Darien from a visionary enterprise into a fiasco, was attributable primarily to William of Orange.[8]

Notwithstanding his sanctioning of both the Bank and the Company of Scotland in 1695, William could not endorse the Darien venture without the support of the English parliament, which preferred to tighten

---

30 per cent (47) invested in Darien, a proportion which rises to just over 44 per cent if one-third of the original promoters can be discounted due to death, settlement overseas or political exile from Scotland (as Jacobites). Around 37 per cent of the South Carolina promoters invested in Darien as compared with just over 17 per cent of the promoters of East New Jersey (*List of the several persons Residenters in Scotland who have subscribed as Adventurers in the Joynt-Stock of the Company of Scotland Trading to Africa and the Indies* (Edinburgh, 1696); DH, Loudoun Papers, A20/1–25; Barclay & Forbes, *An Advertisement concerning the Province of East-New-Jersey in America*; Scot, *The Model of Government of the Province of East-New-Jersey in America*; *A Brief Account of the Province of East-New-Jersey in America*; Insh, *Scottish Colonial Schemes*, pp. 233–277). Four of the directors were associated with South Carolina and two with East New Jersey. However, of the 20 original members of the Company nominated by the Scottish Estates in 1695 and the 20 added by elections from subscribers to formulate the Scottish Court of Directors in 1696, 10 had past colonial experience and six became directors (*General Meeting of the Company of Scotland, Trading to Africa and the Indies, Edinburgh, April 3 1696* (Edinburgh, 1696); *General Meeting of the Company of Scotland trading to Africa and the Indies, Edinburgh, 12 May 1696* (Edinburgh, 1696)).

[7] Armitage, 'Making the Empire British', E. Pijning, 'Idealism and Power. The Dutch West India Company in the Brazil Trade (1630–1654)' in Macinnes & Williamson, eds., *Shaping the Stuart World*, pp. 233–60.

[8] NAS, Leven & Melville MSS, GD 26/13/101, /105, and Hamilton Papers, GD 406/1/4382–3, /4392–3, /4404, /4462–4, /4485, /4541, /4572, /4749, /6484, /6553, /6983, /9078,/9086, /9115; GCA, Records of the Maxwells of Pollock, T-PM 113/649, /652, /662, /688, /696, and Hamilton of Barns Papers, TD 589/1005; Orkney Archives, Kirkwall, Papers relating to the family of Moodie of Milsetter, SC 11/86/17/7/2; *CSP, Colonial* (1700), p. 195; E. M. Graham, *The Oliphants of Gask: Records of a Jacobite Family* (London, 1910), pp. 471–6; Devine, *Scotland's Empire*, pp. 40–8.

up its Navigation Acts to the detriment of Scottish commerce. Although the proposed colony did fit the legislative requirement that commercial activity was only to be conducted in those parts of the world not then at war with William, the Company of Scotland was conceived and received as a rival to the English East India Company, whose established block of members in the English parliament were more than capable of impeding William's need for financial supply during his Nine Years' War against Louis XIV. As the legality of English residents investing in the Company of Scotland was ambiguous, the East India Company, with royal approval, successfully pushed a series of hostile measures through the English parliament in December 1695. Frustrated English-based investors formed a New Company trading to the East Indies in 1698 to challenge the monopoly of the Old East India Company. William turned this situation to his advantage by securing a loan of £2 million from the latter to further his war effort. Scottish antipathies were not abated by the Old East India Company continuing to earn a drawback on customs from all goods exported to Scotland. At the same time, William desired to appease Spain who claimed sovereignty over the Panama Isthmus. As he brokered a military alliance against Louis XIV, Scottish interests became expendable. Darien was thus reduced from a confederation of Scottish, English, Dutch and German commercial interests to a separatist endeavour. William clearly prioritised the balance of power in Europe over the balance of trade in Scotland.[9]

William's pragmatic hostility, however, does not fully explain why the Scots, with their longstanding commercial associations in the East and West Indies, did not press the Dutch to assist the Darien scheme. For the mercantile houses of Amsterdam, supplemented by those of Hamburg, effectively ran the Danish West Indian and Guinea Company, which used St Thomas in the Virgin Islands less as a base for slave trading than as an entrepôt for the exchange of Brazilian timber for Norwegian stockfish. The Danish Company also offered a model of sorts for a colonial partnership. The African Company of Brandenburg had its Caribbean base on St Thomas. That William of Orange was aware of

---

[9] HL, Loudoun Scottish Collection, box 3/LO 7171, box 48/Lo 10102, and Blathwayt Papers, BL 10; Scott, *The Constitutions and Finance of English, Scottish and Irish Joint-Stock Companies*, II, pp. 207–27; Anon., *Some considerations upon the late act of the Parliament of Scotland, for constituting an Indian company in a letter to a friend* (London, 1695); Anon., *Some considerations concerning the prejudice which the Scotch act establishing a company to trade to the East and West-Indies (with large priviledges, and on easie terms) may bring to the English sugar plantations, and the manufactury of refining sugar in England, and some means to prevent the same from Scotland and other nations* (London, 1696); *JHL*, 15 (1691–6), pp. 510, 603, 605, 607–8, 610–16, 618–19; *Lords*, new series, II (1695–7), pp. 3–7, 13–24, 29–55.

these alternative paths to colonialism can be no more than mooted. However, William Blathwayt, then William's resident agent at The Hague, from where Dutch assistance was discouraged, was fully informed from his diplomatic sources that there were longstanding tensions between the Danish and Brandenburg Companies, with the latter attempting to secure its own independent entrepôt elsewhere in the Virgin Islands (on Tortola or St Croix). Blathwayt undertook co-ordination between diplomatic and colonial officials opposed to the Scottish venture. The English resident in Hamburg, Sir Paul Rycaut, duly admonished the city's senate that William of Orange would regard licensing of subscriptions to the Company of Scotland as a hostile act. Notwithstanding aggressive English lobbying, Dutch reluctance to support a working accommodation with the Scots can be attributed partly to the diversity of commercial and provincial interests between Zeeland and Holland. Clear concerns were also expressed from Surinam and Curaçao, key centres for the colonial tramping trade, that the Scots should now be viewed more as rivals than, as hitherto, as partners – concerns that were not abated by Scottish trading ventures in the Caribbean from their first settling at Darien.[10]

English diplomats and colonial officials sowed doubts at home and abroad about the legality of the Scottish enterprise in relation to the Treaty of Madrid concluded in 1670 by Charles II and the Spanish monarchy. However, their purported concern for the sovereign rights of Spain over the Panama Isthmus were tempered by the absence of sustained Spanish settlement in the area since the early sixteenth century, and by its potential as an English entrepôt. Indeed, private ventures there by English entrepreneurs had come to grief before the Scots embarked for Darien. The area was notably attractive for entrepreneurial exploitation. The Isthmus carried the overland route for the silver mined in Peru then shipped to Spain from Portobello and Cartagena in the Caribbean. Detailed hydrographic maps, captured from the Spaniards, which give illustrated cross-sections of the mountains and seas as well as the coastal indentations of the Panama Isthmus, had been circulating in the British Isles since the 1680s. English concerns for Spanish interests were thus far from altruistic. A naval squadron, under the command of Admiral John Benbow, operated in the vicinity when the Scots mounted their ill-fated endeavours to settle Darien, which foundered in 1700, after successive

[10] RC, TKUA, England, A II, 36, Politiske Forhold, 1679–1701: Greg's Diplomatic Papers (1694–9), and Vestindisk-guineisk Kampagne, 1671–1755, A 4/465–7, Direktionens correspondence – Supplikationskopibøger (1690–1712); *CSP, Colonial* (1693–1696), p. 520; Anon., *The Conduct of the Dutch*, pp. 88–9; NAS, Douglas of Strathendry MSS, GD 446/39/15–16.

expeditionary fleets that sailed in 1698 and 1699 failed to establish a permanent colony.[11]

The defeat of Spanish forces at Tubuganti on 15 February 1700, by a combined force of Scots and Cuna Indians under the command of Colonel Alexander Campbell of Fonab, offered only a brief respite. English polemicists declared open season in ridiculing the audacity of Scottish enterprise. James Vernon, the English secretary of state with a watching brief over the Darien venture, sponsored belittling accounts by Walter Herries, a Scottish surgeon who apparently absconded from the first expedition in 1698. His purported exposé and his use of the pseudonym 'Philo-Britain' to differentiate Scottish from British interests provoked the Scottish Estates to offer a bounty for his capture and to order the Edinburgh hangman to publicly burn his works.[12] Duly glossed over in these exchanges was William of Orange's instruction to the governors of Jamaica and the other Caribbean colonies to offer no assistance to the Scots, admittedly issued at a time when Darien was reportedly thriving in December 1699. Spanish tenacity on the issue of the Panama Isthmus was wholly underestimated. The fiasco was in no small measure due to misplaced British – not just Scottish – disrespect for Spain as 'the sick man of Europe'.[13]

In the course of the Darien venture, Scottish polemicists moved from demonstrating that the Company of Scotland was a calculated

---

[11] HL: Bridgewater & Ellesmere MSS, EL 9740; Blathwayt Papers, BL 6–9, Huntington Manuscripts, HM 265; *CSP, Colonial* (1699), pp. 476–8, and (1700), pp. 597–8; C. Storrs, 'Foreign Penetration of the Spanish Empire 1660–1714: Sweden, Scotland and England' in Macinnes & Williamson, eds., *Shaping the Stuart World*, pp. 337–65; H. Kamen, *Empire: How Spain Became a World Power 1492–1763* (New York, 2003), pp. 84–6, 377, 428.

[12] Walter Herries, *The Defence of the Scots Settlement at Darien answer'd paragraph by paragraph* (London, 1699), and *An Enquiry into the Caledonian Project, with a defence of England's procedure (in point of equity) in relation thereunto* (London, 1701), and *A New Darien Artifice Laid Open* (London, 1701); Anon., *Caledonia; or, the Pedlar turn'd Merchant. A Tragi-Comedy, as it was acted by His Majesty's Subjects of Scotland in the King of Spain's Provinces of Darien* (London, 1700); Crossrigg, *DPP*, pp. 16–18; *APC, Colonial* (1680–1720), p. 296.

[13] HL, Bridgewater & Ellesmere MSS, EL 9803, and Huntington Manuscripts: West Indies, HM 32282–3; *CSP, Colonial* (1693–1696), p. 431, and (1699), p. 239; *Legislative Journals of the Council of Virginia* (1680–1721), ed. H. R. McIlwaine, 3 vols. (Richmond, VA, 1925–8), I (1680–99), pp. 350, 428, 437, 455; *The Colonial Records of North Carolina*, vol. I (1662–1712), ed. W. L. Saunders (Raleigh, NC, 1886; reprinted Wilmington, NC, 1993), pp. 458–9; *Lords*, new series, IV (1699–1702), pp. 68–73; C. Storrs, 'Disaster at Darien (1698–1700)? The Persistence of Spanish Imperial Power on the Eve of the Demise of the Spanish Habsburgs', *European History Quarterly*, 29 (1999), pp. 5–38. Not all English colonial governors were hostile to the Darien venture. Governor Isaac Richier in the Bermudas regretted that the Scots had not had the foresight to use the islands as a source of fresh provisions and for recuperation from the debilitating diseases associated with the Panama Isthmus (HL, Bridgewater & Ellesmere MSS, EL 9608).

investment, to bolstering the country's commercial confidence in the face of English hostility, and on to a strident defence of a Caledonian right of presence in the Caribbean.[14] Darien provoked the formation of the Country Party, under the leadership of the Duke of Hamilton, that mobilised public opinion within Scotland against the Court, the English ministry and their Scottish collaborators (see Chapter 4). Although demonstrative addresses ran out of momentum by 1701, reparations for Darien continued to be a rallying cry for the Party in the run-up to Union, albeit Hamilton himself, unlike his mother, the Duchess Anne, had refrained from making any substantial investment. However, the prospect of securing reparations through office made the Country Party vulnerable to desertions – as in 1704 by Lord Belhaven, temporarily, and the Marquess of Tweeddale, permanently – with the formation of the New Party.[15] The Church of Scotland, which had commended Darien as a patriotic endeavour, refrained from recriminations that could be used to party advantage. Sympathising with the tribulations of the failed first expedition, the Kirk remained concerned that the adventurers should maintain righteous conduct, especially towards the Cuna Indians. Before news arrived of the failed second expedition, the Kirk had set an apolitical precedent for its institutional positioning that it sustained on the issue of political incorporation, being duly rewarded with confirmation of its establishment status and Presbyterian governance.[16]

[14] Cf. Anon., *A letter from a gentleman in the country to his friend in Edinburgh wherein it is clearly proved, that the Scottish African and Indian Company is exactly calculated for the interest of Scotland* (Edinburgh, 1696); [John Holland], *A short discourse on the present temper of the nation with respect to the Indian and African Company, and of the Bank of Scotland also, of Mr Paterson's pretended fund of credit* (Edinburgh, 1696); Anon., *In the act for raising two million, and for settling the trade to the East-Indies are the following clauses* (Edinburgh, 1698); Anon., *A proper project for Scotland to startle fools, and frighten knaves, but to make wise-men happy* (Edinburgh, 1699); [Philo-Caledon], *A defence of the Scots settlement at Darien. With an answer to the Spanish memorial against it. And arguments to prove that it is in the interest of England to join with the Scots and protect it* (Edinburgh, 1699).

[15] [Roderick MacKenzie], *A Full and Exact Account of the Proceedings of the Court of Directors and Council-General of the Company of Scotland Trading to Africa and the Indies, with relation to the Treaty of Union now under the Parliament's Consideration* (Edinburgh, 1706); NAS, Leven & Melville MSS, GD 26/13/133; Crossrigg, *DPP*, pp. 44–52, 58–62, 76–9; NLS, Wodrow folio xxviii, fo. 183; ACA, Aberdeen Council Letters (1700–19), 8/12, and Aberdeen Council Registers, 57 (1681–1704), p. 767; W. Ferguson, *Scotland's Relations with England*, pp. 185–8; Riley, *The Union of Scotland and England*, pp. 213–15; P. H. Scott, *Andrew Fletcher and The Treaty of Union*, pp. 54–6; C. A. Whatley, *Bought and Sold for English Gold? Explaining the Union of 1707* (East Linton, 1994; 2nd edition, 2001), pp. 48–9. As the Darien venture was being launched, Hamilton and his mother had attempted unsuccessfully to revive family claims to territories in the south of New England that had been abrogated in 1662 (HL, Bridgewater & Ellesmere MSS, EL 9710).

[16] *A Letter from the Commission of the General Assembly of the Church of Scotland met at Glasgow, July 21, 1699* (Edinburgh, 1699); *APS*, x, p. 215 c. 2; NLS, Wodrow folio xxviii,

The commercial impact of Darien was a critical but not a crippling loss of venture capital, probably just over £153,000 from the £434,000 pledged or offered in cash. The Company of Scotland continued to operate and license ships to Africa and the East Indies, which also served to recompense losses incurred at competitors. Scottish commercial networks continued to operate illicitly in the Americas.[17] Although William of Orange had not been prepared to offer any specific remedial action, Queen Anne at her accession stated she would concur with any reasonable proposal for reparations. This stance aided the Duke of Queensberry and his associates, who preferred discreet lobbying at Court rather than the public demonstrations against the English ministry and their Scottish collaborators mounted by the Country Party. While Queensberry had been a substantial investor in Darien, his family had long been sceptical about the viability of Scottish engagement in colonial ventures.[18] In addition to causing the defeatism and recriminations that characterised the public reaction to the fiasco, Darien had also demonstrated the pressing need for some form of British collaboration. In this context, the fiasco in Panama was not necessarily a factor that favoured the Country over the Court Party. No less pertinently, the Darien venture did lead to a decisive shift in English perceptions and policy with respect to the questionable involvement of Scots in Empire.

Reappraising policy

In denying funding, expertise and assistance to the Company of Scotland, William had undoubtedly responded not just to the East Indian

---

fols.177–8. While the Kirk accepted that the Darien enterprise might involve slavery, the Cuna Indians of Darien were to be treated as confederates and allies in the hope that equity, justice and kindness would secure their conversion to Christianity.

[17] D. Watt, 'The Management of Capital by the Company of Scotland 1696–1707', *Journal of Scottish Historical Studies*, 25 (2006), pp. 97–118; Insh, *The Company of Scotland Trading to Africa and the Indies*, pp. 245–77; Fry, *The Scottish Empire*, pp. 29–30. NAS: Leven & Melville MSS, GD 26/13/118; and Hamilton Papers, GD 406/1/4688, /4697, /4711, /5640; and Scott of Ancrum MSS GD 259/4/29. Only the first of four subscriptions was called up with any meaningful return, and subscribers spread risks by taking on other associates in their shareholdings. It became more profitable to lend to, rather than invest in, the Company of Scotland (ACA, Aberdeen Council Letters, (1700–19), 8/82; AUL, Duff House (Montcoffer Papers) MS 3175/A/2348; GCA, Records of the Maxwells of Pollock, T-PM 113/691, and Research Papers and Notes compiled by R. F. Dell, TD 1022/11: Register of Deeds, B.10.15 no. 2448; NAS, Biel MSS, GD 6). Of the four vessels sent out to Africa and the Indies in the wake of Darien, one was lost at Malacca when returning from Java and China, but her cargo was salvaged. Two were seized for redeployment in piracy at Madagascar, and the fourth successfully returned from Guinea with a cargo of gold and ivory which realised a profit of less than £4,000 (Insh, *The Company of Scotland Trading to Africa and the Indies*, pp. 245–77).

[18] *APS*, XI, pp. 13, 159; Fountainhall, *HNS*, II, p. 586.

lobby, but also to the real determination within governmental as well as mercantile circles in England that the Darien enterprise should not succeed. Indeed, English attitudes to Darien were largely shaped by colonial policy in the wake of the Revolution, and the servicing of the fiscal–military state in the course of the Nine Years' War with France that was concluded by the Peace of Ryswick in 1697. The Revolution created a more prolonged period of uncertainty in the North American colonies than in Ireland and Scotland, the main theatres of William of Orange's campaigns against the Jacobites. The dominion of New England imploded leaving Boston and a revived Massachusetts Bay colony acting as if they were autonomous, a status for which New York appeared to be striving, with considerable unrest being expressed against colonial government throughout the 1690s.[19] Proprietary control was reasserted in East and West New Jersey, but only by their effective amalgamation from 1692 to fend off pressures from freeholders to have a greater say in their governance. Maryland accepted the appointment of a royal governor but the colony still remained under the proprietary control of the Lords Baltimore. North and South Carolina, though still under the same proprietors, acted quite separately in terms of their legislative and judicial affairs, with freeholders in the latter province being notably resistant to the financial direction of the proprietors. Although proprietary government in Pennsylvania continued throughout the Revolution, Welsh settlers were agitating for autonomy in Clare County, and Scottish dominance of judicial, fiscal and political offices in the Lower Counties on the Delaware became entrenched.[20]

---

[19] J. P. Greene, *Peripheries and Center: Constitutional Developments in the Extended Politics of the British Empire and the United States, 1607–1688* (Atlanta, 1986), pp. 7–42; J. M. Murrin, 'Political Development' in Greene & Pole, eds., *Colonial British America*, pp. 408–56; *CSP, Colonial* (1689–1692), pp. 156–7, 520–1. HL: Bridgewater & Ellesmere MSS, EL 9765, 9775–7; Blathwayt Papers, BL 418; Huntington Manuscripts, HM 67,584.

[20] Landsman, *Scotland and its first American Colony, 1683–1760*, pp. 163–91; *Minutes of the Provincial Council of Pennsylvania*, I (1683–1700), p. 266; *Records of the Courts of Sussex, Delaware, 1677–1710*, I, pp. 20–1, and II, pp. 675–6, 730, 736, 797, 805, 832, 836, 845–6, 869–70, 875, 888, 908, 910, 954; www.mdarchives.state.md.us/ Proceedings of the Council of Maryland, vol. 8 (1688–93), p. 185. *Journal of the Commons House of Assembly of South Carolina (1692–1708)*, ed. A. S. Salley, 16 vols. (1907–34): II (1693), pp. 16–18, 22–3, 35–6; IV (1695), p. 6; V (1696), pp. 16–17, 40–1. In the twenty months between April 1695 and December 1696, Valentine Prowse, the English agent in Scotland for the commissioners of customs, noted that twenty-nine ships, from 40 to 170 tons, had traded to and from Scotland and the tobacco plantations (*Lords*, new series, II (1695–7), p. 464). Litigious members of Scottish commercial networks were also able to take advantage of the limited literacy in the American colonies, other than New England (*Colonial Records of North Carolina, second series X. The Church of England in North Carolina: Documents 1699–1741*, ed. R. J. Cain (Raleigh NC, 1999), pp. 10–11).

As well as taking advantage of the temporary relaxation of the Navigation Acts in relation to trade with the West Indies, Scottish commercial networks from New England to the Carolinas notably exploited the unsettled political situation in North America. Despite the covert placing of English customs agents to monitor Scottish shipping, Glasgow merchants were to the fore in expanding their operations into Norfolk County in North Carolina, from where tobacco was shipped either directly to Scotland or to the stores controlled by Scots on the Lower Delaware. Glasgow also took the lead in forging ready supplies of documentation to pass off their shipping and their commodity trading as English. Much to the ire of merchants in London, Bristol and Liverpool, the port of Whitehaven in the north-western county of Cumberland came to complement Berwick upon Tweed on the east coast, as an English port of convenience for Scottish colonial traders. Even on the rare occasions when colonial officials attempted the strict enforcement of the Navigation Acts, Scottish merchants could still charter ships from London and other English ports and travel to the colonies as supercargoes responsible for the actual trading of commodities. In cases of doubt, colonial juries still continued to side with the commercial networks over Crown officials, much to the chagrin of Edward Randolph who continued as chief collector of customs in the colonies.[21]

Randolph was especially vociferous in his critique of the act of the Scottish Estates creating the Company of Scotland in 1695. The inducement of a tax break for twenty-one years for Scottish adventurers trading to and from the yet-to-be-established colonial entrepôt raised his pulse. The accompanying encouragement for all Scottish entrepreneurs not directly engaged with the Company to trade with all other American colonies of the European powers was viewed apoplectically as a blatant invitation not just to circumvent but to breach the English Navigation Acts. Indeed, Randolph expressed to the commissioners of the customs in England his concern that, if Darien became a success, the Scots would lay claim to a settlement in New Castle, Kent or Sussex, the Lower Counties of Delaware located uneasily between the colonies of Philadelphia and Maryland. A persistent presence since the 1630s was

---

[21] *CSP, Colonial* (1689–1692), pp. 656–60, 752, and (1693–1696), pp. 279–80, 518–20, 643–4, 654–5; *Lords*, original series, (1692–3), pp. 72–4; NAS, Andrew Russell Papers, GD 1/885/23, /801; *Records of the Court of Assistants of the Colony of Massachusetts Bay, 1630–1692*, pp. 342–4; *North Carolina Higher Court Records 1670–1696*, pp. 103, 177, 237, 263, 282; *Legislative Journals of the Council of Virginia*, I (1680–99), pp. 138, 205, 217, 221–2, 241–2, 299–301; Keith, *Commercial Relations of England and Scotland, 1603–1707*, pp. 124–6.

now deemed particularly disruptive, with the emergence of Gustavus Hamilton as resident conservator, based in Delaware, for Scottish commercial networks that stretched from New England to the southern colonies. Their indigenous mercantile community was not only shipping enumerated commodities from the Delaware, but also developing overland routes to Maryland. Tobacco freighted in small ships was conveyed in sleighs or great carts eight miles across the narrow isthmus between the Bohemia and Delaware Rivers. As practised masters in the evasion of the Navigation Acts, the Scots were deemed capable of establishing an independent staple for European manufactures within the territorial bounds of the English colonies. Such a free port would be considerably more menacing to English interests than that operated by the Dutch on the island of Curaçao.[22]

Randolph's apprehensions about the Company of Scotland struck a sympathetic chord not only with the commissioners for the customs, but also with those for the Royal Navy, which had actually been deployed at the Revolution to blockade the Firth of Clyde in order to embargo colonial trading between Boston and Glasgow, as well as to prevent Jacobite interaction across the North Channel. More generally, Randolph tapped into the concerns of English councillors overseeing trade and plantations about their lack of direct control over the proprietary colonies, which were deemed notably resistant to the appointment of Admiralty Courts and attorney-generals by the Crown to enforce the Navigation Acts. A further consideration in this respect was their rather limited fiscal and military contribution towards the furtherance of the war effort against France in the American theatre of the Nine Years' War.[23] The launch of the Scottish Company for Africa and India in 1695 had certainly hastened, but not instigated, the formation of the Council for Trade and Plantations

---

[22] HL, Bridgewater & Ellesmere MSS, EL 9776–7, 9802–3, 9880; *CSP, Colonial* (1693–1696), pp. 625–6, 638–9, and (1696–1697), pp. 71–5; *Lords*, new series, II (1695–7), pp. 446–67; *The Colonial Records of North Carolina*, I (1662–1712), pp. 440–2. www.mdarchives.state.md.us/: Proceedings and Acts of the General Assembly, vol. 19 (1693–7), pp. 545, 582, and vol. 20, p. 175; and Proceedings of the Council of Maryland, vol. 20 (1693–7), pp. 345–55, 569, and vol. 23 (1697–8), pp. 84–8. Hamilton was a business associate of James Foulis, the acknowledged leader of the London Scottish merchant community. Randolph was also concerned that the Scots would attempt to plant a colony in the offshore Carolina islands or even in the Bahamas.

[23] J. M. Soisin, *English America and the Revolution of 1688* (London, 1982), pp. 231–44; *RPCS*, third series, XIV (1690), pp. 92–3, 153–5, 307, 384–5, 444, 590, 607, and XV (1691), pp. 329–30, 335–6, 366–7, 320–1; *APC, Colonial* (1680–1720), pp. 219, 272–3; *CSP, Colonial* (1693–1696), pp. 639–40, 644–5; *Lords*, new series, II (1695–7), pp. 419, 440–5; *The Colonial Records of North Carolina*, I (1662–1712), pp. 461–3. HL: Bridgewater & Ellesmere MSS, EL 9880; Blathwayt Papers, BL 420; Huntington Manuscripts, HM 32,265.

in the following year. The creation of this permanent board, like the passage of the Navigation Acts in the Restoration era, was the outcome of widespread discussion involving pragmatic accommodation between parliamentarians, planters, merchants and commentators on political economy. The Council – or, more commonly, the Board – of Trade and Plantations was instituted finally as an advisory rather than an executive body, answerable to the English Privy Council but also licensed to report on colonial issues to parliament, with or without a specific commission from either the Lords or the Commons. In essence, the Board professionalised the oversight of the acclaimed English colonies in America and promoted uniformity in their governance. Thus, the inclusive Britannic formula that the colonies should be governed by laws 'not repugnant' to those of England was supplanted by the exclusive Gothic mantra that their laws should 'be agreeable' to those of England. In keeping with this exclusivity, the Navigation Acts were reinvigorated with a particular emphasis on curtailing documentary fraud, promoting probity among offices, and appointing to places of trust in the plantations only natives of England, or Ireland, which was particularly interpreted as a licence to treat Scots as aliens and ineligible for public employment, be that civil or military.[24]

In this rigorous revamping of the Navigation Acts, Scottish residents in the colonies were not only to be stripped of public office, but were also the only residential group denied the prospect of naturalisation. Among the high-profile casualties of this policy were Andrew Hamilton, the proprietary governor of East and West New Jersey and postmaster general for the American colonies; James Blair, founder of the College of William and Mary and member of the governing Council of Virginia; and Alexander Skene, secretary for the governing Council of Barbados. The London Scots led the outcry against this discriminatory treatment, which served as a precedent for the Alien Act of 1705 that prejudiced Scottish access to English markets (see Chapter 9). Notwithstanding discreet lobbying at Court by Queensberry, the gradual relaxation of this stricture was attributable primarily to the attorney-general in England, Thomas Trevor. In 1699, he revisited the precedent of Colvin's Case of

---

[24] Andrews, *The Colonial Period of American History*, pp. 157–68, 272–317; Speck, 'The International and Imperial Context' in Greene & Pole, eds., *Colonial British America*, pp. 384–407; Curson, *A Companion of the Laws and Government*, pp. 497–9, 510–12, 527–32; *Lords*, new series, II (1695–7), pp. 410, 414–15, 475–91; *The Colonial Records of North Carolina*, I (1662–1712), pp. 463–71; *Records of the Court of Chancery of South Carolina, 1671–1779*, pp. 25, 64; HL, Blathwayt Papers, BL 290; NLC, Edward E. Ayer Collection, Box Ayer MS 464; *CSP, Colonial* (1702–1703), p. 259, and (1706 1708), pp. 3–6. Proprietors were also prohibited from selling lands to facilitate the establishment of a Scottish colony in North America or the Caribbean.

1608, to declare that even though the jurisdiction of Scotland was separate from that of England, Scots born under the personal protection of the common monarchy should be treated as having the same rights as the freeborn English in the plantations and as Scots resident in England or Ireland. Hamilton even went on to become the lieutenant-governor in Pennsylvania on behalf of the proprietor, William Penn, where he was instrumental in preserving the unity of the colony against any attempts to have the tobacco-producing Lower Counties of the Delaware secede and thereby pave the way for direct rule by the Crown.[25]

The restructuring of colonial governance in 1696 was actually more impressive on paper than in performance. Proprietary colonies did not immediately become amenable to Admiralty Courts or attorney-generals appointed by the Crown. Proprietors generally showed no inclination to follow the precedent of Maryland and allow their governors to become royal appointees. Indeed, only New Jersey in 1702 ceased to be a proprietary colony. Illegal trading by Scots and Dutch, as well as piracy, continued to be features of colonial life – a situation not checked by the failure of colonies under direct rule, no less than proprietary colonies, to recruit and retain sufficient customs officials to man ports of entry. Indeed, designated ports of entry for the collection of customs and authentication of trading documents remained inadequate to deal with the volume of trade. Policing by frigates cruising in Chesapeake and Delaware Bays proved more expensive than remunerative. Scottish commercial networks became particularly adept at using their London contacts to attach their ships to Royal Navy convoys across the Atlantic, and then slipping away under cover of darkness before the ships entered the English Channel. Particularly galling for English officials determined to curtail Scottish

---

[25] *CSP, Colonial*: (1696–1697), p. 69; (1697–1698), pp. 329–30; (1699), pp. 20, 37, 311, 316, 421–2; (1700), pp. 31, 87–8, 133–4, 247–8, 255–6, 306, 351, 443–4, 525–6, 536–7, 567, 609–10, 639–40, 726–8; (1701), pp. 95, 202, 279, 679–81, 725–8; (1702), pp. 143–4, 320–1, 395, 424–5, 498. *APC, Colonial* (1680–1720), pp. 419–20; J. H. Kettner, *The Development of American Citizenship 1608–1870* (Chapel Hill, NC, 1978), pp. 22–7, 45–6; [George Ridpath], *The Case of Scots-men residing in England and in the English Plantations* (Edinburgh, 1703); HL, Bridgewater & Ellesmere MSS, EL 9724; *Journal of the Courts of Common Right and Chancery of East New Jersey, 1683–1702*, pp. 25–6, 29, 31, 34; *Minutes of the Provincial Council of Pennsylvania*, II (1700–17), pp. 56–9, 62–3, 66–70, 71–4, 83–6, 119, 125–9; www.mdarchives.state.md.us/ Proceedings of the Council of Maryland, vol. 20 (1693–7), p. 569, and Proceedings and Acts of the General Assembly, vol. 19 (1693–7), pp. 281, 545; *Legislative Journals of the Council of Virginia*, I (1680–99), pp. 272–3, 294–5, and II (1699–1705), pp. 146, 226; *North Carolina Higher Court Records, 1697–1701*, ed. M. E. E. Parker (Raleigh, NC, 1971), pp. 176–7; *Journal of the Commons House of Assembly of South Carolina*, VII (1697), pp. 6–7, 11, 13–14, and XIII (1703), pp. 42, 49–50. The treating of Scots as aliens was invariably used to settle old scores in colonies where governance was disputed, and to curtail the dissent occasioned by Darien among Scottish networks in the colonies.

engagement in the Americas was the competitive edge enjoyed by their networks, which were also diversifying into textile and other manufactures that were prohibited colonial endeavours.[26]

For the Scots, circumvention of the Navigation Acts went hand in glove with commercial innovation. Glasgow merchants used both consignment and store systems, first to break into the staple Atlantic trade in tobacco and then to secure a position of dominance. Under the consignment system the planter bore the risk of marketing, which was borne by the merchant under the store system that tied advances of credit against tobacco sales in Europe to the purchase of merchandise from the colonial store. The consignment system continued to be used by Scots trading through London, but this practice was increasingly challenged, in terms of both price and quality, by tobacco brought in through the stores. This latter system was particularly suited to the expansion of small plantations along the Chesapeake and the Delaware into the hinterlands of Maryland, Virginia and the Carolinas. It carried higher risks but greater profits. In addition to using Whitehaven as an outstation of Glasgow, the Isle of Man was developed as the major centre of Scottish smuggling operations in the North Channel. Colonial commodities brought into Whitehaven were reexported to Man, giving the Scots the benefit of a drawback on customs, and then smuggled into Scotland via the Firths of Clyde and Solway or into Belfast, Londonderry and Dublin by Irish associates. Newcastle

---

[26] *CSP, Colonial*: *(1697–1698)*, pp. 233, 239–40, 330, 349, 380–4, 402–3, 414–15; (1699), pp. 13, 382–4; (1700), pp. 106–9, 121–2, 348, 634–8, 650–5; (1701), pp. 89–92, 132–4; (1702), pp. 328–30, 395–6, 696; (1702–1703), p. 424; (1704–1705), pp. 161–3. *APC, Colonial* (1680–1720), pp. 318, 358–9; *Lords*, new series, IV (1699–1702), pp. 314–55, and V (1702–4), pp. 66–100; *Journal of the Courts of Common Right and Chancery of East New Jersey, 1683–1702*, pp. 136–7; *Minutes of the Provincial Council of Pennsylvania*, I (1683–1700), pp. 527, 550–1, and II (1700–17), pp. 174–6, 262–6, 328–36. www.mdarchives.state.md.us/: Proceedings of the Council of Maryland, vol. 20 (1693–7), pp. 496–9, 546–7, 578–9, and vol. 23 (1697–8), pp. 311–16, 402, 551; Proceedings and Acts of the General Assembly, vol. 22 (1698–9), pp. 21–2. *Legislative Journals of the Council of Virginia*, I (1680–99), pp. 354, 364, and II (1699–1705), pp. 25–6, 171–2; *North Carolina Higher Court Records, 1697–1701*, pp. 517–21; *Journal of the Commons House of Assembly of South Carolina*, VIII (1698), pp. 15, 34–5, and XI (1701), pp. 10, 18, 21. HL: Bridgewater & Ellesmere MSS, EL 9171, 9714, 9741, 9755; Blathwayt Papers, BL 172, 216; Huntington Manuscripts, HM 7096. NLC, Edward E. Ayer Collection, Box Ayer MS 337; W. R. Brock, *Scotus Americanus: A Survey of the Sources for Links Between Scotland and America in the Eighteenth Century* (Edinburgh, 1982), pp. 11–12; J. M. Soisin, *English America and Imperial Inconstancy: The Rise of Provincial Autonomy 1696–1715* (London, 1985), pp. 23–36. As the timing of transatlantic convoys became more unreliable during the Nine Years' War, and later the War of the Spanish Succession, Scottish as well as English ships preferred to rely on Mediterranean passes issued by their respective Admiralties: that is, the Crown negotiated protection against Barbary pirates based in Algeria, to which all British shipping had been entitled since the Restoration era (Andrews, *The Colonial Period of American History*, pp. 208, 276).

was also brought into play on the east coast, as well as Berwick upon Tweed. Scottish entrepreneurs covertly procured shares in the ownership of transatlantic vessels. Networks immersed in the colonial tramping trade established branches of Edinburgh merchant houses on the Tyne. Bilbao and San Sebastian in northern Spain also became tramping destinations for Scottish ships engaged in the Newfoundland fisheries, where the Scots also encountered New England traders carrying enumerated commodities for European markets.[27]

Illicit Scottish enterprise notwithstanding, the legislative measures and colonial restructuring of 1696 demonstrated in advance of the Darien scheme that co-operation with Scotland was not a pressing concern of political economy in England. The measures of 1696 were implemented against a backdrop of unsound money, debased coinage and downwardly spiralling exchange rates. The substantial expansion of the military and naval establishments in the course of the Nine Years' War, compounded by the predatory operations of French privateers, had largely occasioned such financial instability. The National Debt was still an insecure strategy for deficit financing.[28] The creation of the Board of Trade and Plantations, and the revamping of the Navigation Acts, marked a greater

---

[27] GCA, Records of the Maxwells of Pollock, T-PM 109/101, and Research Papers and Notes compiled by R. F. Dell, TD 1022/11: Register of Deeds, B.10.15 nos. 2135, 2153, 2179. NAS: Journal of William Fraser, merchant, London, 1699–1711, CS 96/524, pp. 1–189; Letter and account book of John Watson, younger, merchant, Edinburgh, 1696–1713, CS 96/3309, pp. 1–144; Hamilton Papers, GD 406/1/5107, /5144, /5158. HL, Blathwayt Papers, BL 66. *CSP, Colonial*: (1702), p. 724 (1704–1705), pp. 297–8, 639; (1706–1708), pp. 122–3. See www.mdarchives.state.md.us/ for Proceedings of the Council of Maryland, vol. 23 (1697–8), pp. 11–12; Proceedings and Acts of the General Assembly, vol. 27 (1707–10), pp. 248–9, 311–12; Proceedings of Maryland Court of Appeals, vol. 77 (1695–1729), pp. 102–3; *North Carolina Higher Court Records, 1702–1708*, ed. W. S. Price (Raleigh, NC, 1974), pp. 21, 457–9. Greater Spanish engagement in turn led the Scots to take advantage of the rather grey area in the Navigation Acts concerning the Canary Islands, whose wine was used as a transatlantic alternative to that permitted to be exported from Madeira. As the Canaries were under Spanish control, their wine could be classed as European and therefore direct shipments to the colonies were prohibited. However, Scots made use of the argument that the location of the Canaries was African, therefore their wines were exempt from the proscriptions in the Navigation Acts (Andrews, *The Colonial Period of American History*, pp. 67, 110–13).

[28] D. W. Jones, *War and Economy in the Age of William III and Marlborough* (Oxford, 1988), pp. 127–68; HL, Bridgewater & Ellesmere MSS, EL 9862, and Huntington Manuscripts, Manuscript Newsletters from London to Tamworth (1690–1704), HM 30,659/37, /39, /43, /45–8, /50–3, /55, /58, /60–3, /65, /69–73. As part of the legislation on trade and navigation in 1696, greater bounties were offered to English privateers by the Crown effectively waiving its right to share in prizes. Rather than act as a counter to the French privateers, this measure only served to intensify collusion – between privateers and the Royal Navy on the one hand, and with French privateers on the other; again the Scots were past masters of collusive practices (HL, Bridgewater & Ellesmere MSS, EL 9181, 9183, 9187, 9189).

emphasis on bullion retention as an aspect of public policy. Indeed, landed enterprise and manufacturing was preferred to overseas trade and commerce. In turn, greater revenue was to be generated from indirect taxation, such as customs, and more especially excise, on consumable commodities, rather than directly from the land tax, which required annual parliamentary votes of supply.[29]

A demographic deficit?

Between December 1697 and January 1698, the Board of Trade and Plantations completed a review of English trade from 1670 until the recent Peace of Ryswick whose broad conclusions were endorsed by the commissioners for customs. Focusing on commercial exchange, the balance of payments and the competitive impact of mercantilist regulation, the Board noted that expansion of English trade in the Restoration era had gone into a measurable decline since the Revolution. Global threats to English trade were more pressing than transatlantic opportunities for colonial expansion. Exports to the colonies were vital to a marginal balance of trade, with a surplus of £74,000 from a turnover of £6,174,000. The re-export of colonial commodities, no less than those from the Far East, was a vital counterbalance to the outflow of bullion, primarily through the East India Company. Expanding the manufacturing base, particularly in relation to the export of textiles, was no less integral to a healthy balance of payments. However, English trade was in general decline in Scandinavia, France, Russia and the East Indies, where the pepper trade had been effectively ceded to the Dutch. While continuous war with France certainly diverted national resources by land and sea, war had helped reverse the decline in the English trade with Holland and Flanders. English trade was only vibrant through Hamburg and in Iberia, the Mediterranean and Africa. Serious misgivings were expressed about woollen manufacturing, fishing and the carrying trade, particularly that from the plantations. The uncooperative presence of Scottish commercial networks loomed large. Not only was wool necessary for English manufacturing being exported out of England, Ireland and Scotland, but Scottish carriers were dominating this trade from the three kingdoms, with their networks becoming entrenched in Norwich, the main exchange for English wool. There was no evidence that the Scots were inclined to collaborate in a British fisheries project. In the colonies, the activities of Scottish entrepreneurs in the rivers and creeks 'far removed

---

[29] Appleby, *Economic Thought and Ideology*, pp. 248–50; Brewer, *The Sinews of Power: War, Money and the English State, 1688–1783*, pp. 138–61.

from the places where the Collectors and other Officers of the Customs are directed to keep their offices', were deemed as competitive as those of the Dutch and no less damaging than those of the pirates.[30]

An opponent of Irish claims for parliamentary independence from England, John Cary, a Bristol merchant and commercial commentator, was particularly concerned by 1695 that Scotland should not be encouraged to develop companies for textiles, fishing and colonies. Since the Scottish domestic market was limited, these putative companies could only be successful if Scotland attained dominance in Irish markets at English expense. As a rebuttal to William Molyneux, Ireland should be reduced to an English colony and every effort made to contest Scottish commercial expansion by ensuring that it was not attractive to English investment. Cary was stating in public what English diplomatic and colonial officials were expressing in private. Indeed, the Board of Trade and Plantations had become particularly apprehensive about the purported dominance of Scottish commercial networks in Ireland since the Revolution. Not only did Scottish merchants in the trading towns and the Scottish gentry in plantation districts actively collude, but they 'are generally Frugall, Industrious, very nationall, and very helpful to each other agst any Third [party]'. Associated claims that an additional 50,000 Scots emigrated to Ireland in the 1690s should be viewed as guesstimates rather than estimates.[31] Nevertheless, Scottish dominance of the Irish carrying trade was recognised in reports from America. Dublin, no less than Belfast and Londonderry, was locked into Scottish commercial networks during that decade.[32]

Yet, in the wake of Darien, Scots moved from significant obstructions to trade to potential pillars of Empire among shapers of English

---

[30] BL, Papers relating to Trade etc., Sloane MS 2902, fols.115–16, 171–80, 244; HL, Bridgewater & Ellesmere MSS, EL9735, 9807, 9874; *CSP, Colonial* (1699), pp. 3, 17; *Lords*, new series, III (1697–9), pp. 102–11.

[31] John Cary, *A Discourse concerning the Trade of Ireland and Scotland as they stand in Competition with the Trade of England* (Bristol, 1695, and London, 1696); BL, Papers relating to Trade etc., Sloane MS 2902, fols. 137–8, 218. The Board was particularly concerned to establish the reliability of reports that the Scots controlled two-thirds of Irish trade, as 30,000 were said to have migrated to Ireland to take advantage of the reconstruction necessary after the Jacobite rising, and another 20,000 allegedly had gone over following the outbreak of the famine in 1695. The associated assertion that the Scots had infiltrated 10,000 seamen into English service and similar numbers into the service of the Dutch and the French was no less hyperbolic but did serve to notify the threat to English interests that came from disguised ownership and flexible crewing of ships. Not only were the Scots continuing their commercial collaboration with the Dutch, but any whiff of the 'auld alliance' with England's main imperial rival could only be viewed as politically and economically inimical.

[32] *CSP, Colonial* (1699), p. 125; NAS, Journal of William Fraser, merchant, London, 1699–1711, CS 96/524, pp. 18–73; *RPCS*, third series, XIII (1686–9), pp. 387–90, 397, 538.

colonial policy. This change in official thinking was primarily brought about by the altering perspectives on how to service the fiscal–military state with the renewal of war with France in the shape of the War of the Spanish Succession in 1702. The acquisition of the Spanish Crown by Philip of Anjou, a grandson of Louis XIV, not only threatened to create a Bourbon hegemony in Europe, but also made the fate of the Spanish Empire a key issue of the war. The Spanish colonial administration opted for the French candidate, rather than the leading Habsburg candidate, the Austrian Emperor, Leopold I, who was favoured by the English and the Dutch. The English colonies in America were threatened by an arc of menace that stretched from the North Atlantic through to the Gulf of Mexico and into the Caribbean. The longstanding French threat to English ventures, from Hudson's Bay and Newfoundland through to New England and New York, now gained a southern dimension which bolstered the well-worn Spanish antipathy to Virginia and the Carolinas. The Nine Years' War had severely debilitated the English colonial alliance with the League of Iroquois Nations, and Louisiana had been established in 1699 as a French colonial intrusion in the Gulf of Mexico. The Caribbean remained particularly vulnerable due to reluctance of Marlborough and Godolphin to commit troops and naval resources away from the main European theatres of war.[33] At the same time, the need to harmonise the plantation trade with English manufacturing, as soldiers and sailors were being mobilised on an unprecedented scale for war, created a demographic deficit that was no less threatening to English interests in the long as well as the short term. Did England have the capacity to sustain a colonial presence in the Americas, develop manufacturing at home and recruit extensively for the army and the navy without recourse to external assistance?

Although London had grown in the Restoration era to become Europe's largest city, its population, estimated at 530,000, was purportedly stagnating, as was that of England as a whole at no more than 5.5 million souls. These relatively accurate estimates were made by Gregory King in 1696 in an endeavour to demonstrate to the English ministry that England did not have the resources in population and national income to prolong the war beyond 1698. King was not arguing that the respective figures for London and England represented a static population. Population had

---

[33] B. Lenman, *Britain's Colonial Wars 1688–1783* (Harlow, 2001), pp. 13–46. HL, Blathwayt Papers, BL 14, 26–7, 361, 415; Robert Alonzo Brock Collection, BR 744; Huntington Manuscripts, Manuscript Newsletters from London to Tamworth (1690–1704), HM 30,659/87; *CSP, Colonial* (1702), p. 595; *Lords*, new series, IV (1699–1702), pp. 437–63, and V (1702–4), pp. 311–35; *Journal of the Commons House of Assembly of South Carolina*, XIII (1703), pp. 47–8, 64, 76–8.

shifted through the intensification of commercialised agriculture and the diversification into manufacturing, particularly of woollens, which had led to gradual urbanisation. However, the natural increase in population, which was seen as the basis of sustainable national prosperity, had been channelled mainly towards emigration to Ireland and the American colonies.[34] King's figures and his use of political arithmetic were taken up by Charles Davenant, whose concerns over the ways and means to finance the war effort led him to take a wider, multilateral approach to the balancing of trade.

In contrast to the London merchant, John Pollexfen, an influential member of the Board of Trade who questioned the value of the oligopolistic trade to the East Indies for its drawing-off of bullion to the advantage of a limited number of stockholders, Davenant emphasised the importance of manufacturing and of re-exporting goods from the plantations, as from the East Indies and the Levant. Initially the perspective of Pollexfen, who agreed with Cary that Ireland should be reduced to an English colony and Scotland treated warily as an economic competitor, held sway in the years of peace between 1698 and 1701. Accordingly, the Board of Trade reported to the House of Lords in February 1702 that there was a favourable balance of trade with Africa, Flanders, France, Holland, Portugal and Madeira. Other than with Spain, trade with the Mediterranean was not pronouncedly favourable to England, likewise the American colonies apart from Newfoundland. The growing rapport between the Old and New East India Companies, itself stimulated by the potential Scottish challenge through Darien, had opened up trading participation in the Far East and simultaneously cut back on superfluous exports of bullion. Despite a favourable balance now being recorded for the East Indies, the continuing bulk exports of bullion there, along with the need to make specie payments in recently milled coin to Scandinavia, Russia, Germany and Eastern Europe, were deemed the principal causes of an overall trading imbalance to England's disadvantage.[35]

However, the renewal of war in 1702 led to important shifts in fiscal policy. In the first place, the balance between direct and indirect taxes in underwriting the costs of the national debt moved away from the direct land tax, which had primarily sustained deficit financing during the Nine

---

[34] *Two Tracts by Gregory King*, ed. G. E. Barnett (Baltimore, 1936); E. A. Wrigley & R. S. Schofield, *The Population History of England, 1541–1871: A Reconstruction* (London, 1981), pp. 174–9, 207–15; Hoppit, *A Land of Liberty?* pp. 52–5.

[35] Charles Davenant, *Discourses on the Publick Revenues, and on the Trade of England: Part I – Of the Use of Political Arithmetick, in all Considerations about the Revenues and Trade* (London, 1698); J[ohn] P[ollexfen], *Of Trade* (London, 1700); *Lords*, IV (1699–1702), pp. 430–6.

Years' War, towards indirect taxes raised through customs and excise. This shift reflected not only the dominance of the landed influence in the English parliament, but also the tilting of the balance in favour of the advocates of national prosperity through landed enterprise and manufacturing rather than through overseas trade. In the second place, there was a shift in the nature of recruitment to the army, if not the navy. While the Royal Navy was voted supplies for 40,000–42,000 men in both the Nine Years' War and the War of the Spanish Succession, ships of the line increased from 173 in 1688 to 224 by 1702. The size of the army was raised from around 76,000 to 92,000 men. Masked by this growth in military manpower was an increased reliance on foreign auxiliaries – that is, England was becoming more dependent on recruiting continental troops than those raised within the British Isles. Whereas 26 per cent of the troops raised in the Nine Years' War were foreign auxiliaries, this fluctuated between 54 and 67 per cent during the War of the Spanish Succession when the bulk of the English troops were committed to Marlborough in the Low Countries and Germany. The Peninsular campaign in support of Portugal and Catalonia was predominantly fought by Irish and Scottish troops. The Italian front was left entirely to the allies.[36]

The reliance on foreign auxiliaries secured by generous subsidies to the allied powers undoubtedly reflected concerns from the Nine Years' War that the maintenance of a standing army – duly scaled back to 8,000 in 1697 – was a threat to civil liberties. Even though forces raised in Scotland came to be supported from English expenditure, there was widespread resistance to pressed recruitment by land and sea that was shared throughout the British Isles.[37] At the same time, the shift towards foreign auxiliaries demonstrated England's finite demographic resources. Indeed, around 15 per cent of men of serviceable age were either in the armed forces or in the supply services for the war effort. As the prevailing

---

[36] Jones, *War and Economy*, pp. 1–65; HL, Stowe Papers: Brydges Family Papers, ST 8/vol. 1, 'The Account of James Brydges, Esq., Paymaster General of her Majesties Forces acting in Conjunction with those of her Allies', and /vol. 2, 'Three Year Accounts of ye Payments made to the Forces in Flanders by the Rt. Hon. James, Earl of Carnarvon from 1706 to 1709'.

[37] Smith, *A History of the Modern British Isles*, pp. 306–17; J. G. A. Pocock, *The Machiavellian Moment: Florentine Political Thought and the Atlantic Republican Tradition* (Princeton, 1975), pp. 423–61; HL, Stowe Papers: Brydges Family Papers, ST 64, 'Charles Cornwallis, 4th Baron of Cornwallis, Proposals for Her Majesties and the Nations Glory, 1706'; *RPCS*, third series, xv (1690), pp. 14–15, 77, 197–8; *Lords*, original series (1690–1), p. 404, and new series, I (1693–5), p. 147. ACA: Aberdeen Council Letters (1682–99), 7/137, /149, /184, /205, and (1700–19), 8/12; Aberdeen Council Registers, 57 (1682–1704), pp. 329; Orkney Archives, Kirkwall, Town Council Minute Book, 1691–1732, fols.20–1, 95. Scottish merchant ships were also liable to be pressed into service with the Royal Navy (*Lords*, original series (1692–3), p. 200).

strategy in both wars required the offensive commitment of both the army and the navy, costs rose significantly from an annual average of around 2.5 million in the Nine Years' War to over £4 million during the War of the Spanish Succession. Merchant shipping remained notoriously vulnerable to French privateers. The Bank of England, funded on the basis of a public loan of £1.2 million towards the war effort in 1694, with interest at 8 per cent and repayment guaranteed by taxation, was overstretched in 1696–7 and again in 1705. The prospect of renewed war had led to a temporary stop on the circulation of paper credit through the Bank in 1701. The associated market in government stocks integral to the National Debt remained highly volatile throughout. The Royal Navy continued to be supplied mainly by direct requisitioning of supplies bought by taxes or through loans. But the army was provisioned through subventions paid through the paymasters to designated domestic and continental agents. Notwithstanding parliamentary scrutiny, which certainly held embezzlement and other frauds in check, this system created significant opportunities for inflating expenses and manipulating exchange rates to the benefit of Scottish as well as English commercial networks.[38]

Demographic and fiscal pressures led to a renewed debate on the value of the plantation trade. Davenant, who was brought onto the government payroll by Godolphin at the outbreak of the War of the Spanish Succession, argued for selective support through continuing migration, notably of foreigners as well as slaves, to promote colonies whose economies were dominated by tobacco and sugar plantations, which were, in turn, to be provisioned with fish, grain and livestock from the more agriculturally diverse northern colonies. In order to avoid possible confrontation with English interests, the northern colonies were not to be encouraged to build up their naval capacity, notwithstanding the French threat. However, Davenant favoured a more relaxed and supportive attitude towards proprietary colonies. His views were challenged from America. Davenant had little awareness of the expansion of tobacco cultivation from the Chesapeake and the Delaware. He had no knowledge of the extension of the plantation economy for rice growing in South Carolina, which became a highly profitable activity from the 1690s. Above all, his determination to have the southern colonies provisioned

---

[38] Jones, *War and Economy*, pp. 131–68; Hoppit, *A Land of Liberty?* pp. 123–31; K. Wrightson, *Earthly Necessities: Economic Lives in Early Modern Britain* (New Haven, 2000), pp. 255–60; NAS, Hamilton Papers, GD 406/1/4808, /6506. HL: Stowe Papers: Brydges Family Papers, ST 57/vol. 1, pp. 5–7, 47–9, 51, 55, 58–9, 62–6, 69, 75–6, 80–1, 101, 112, 115–16, and ST 58/vol. 1, pp. 41, 43–7, 49–54, 56–7, 94–5, 103–6, 114–6, 144, 150–2; Huntington Manuscripts, Manuscript Newsletters from London to Tamworth (1690–1704), HM 30,659/92.

by the northern ignored the prospects of real commercial growth through trade with the Native Americans that could otherwise fall to the French.[39]

However, Davenant did strike a receptive chord with the Board of Trade and Plantations through his concern that American colonies should not replicate English goods and manufactures, and that continuing migration should concentrate on the planned consolidation rather than the haphazard expansion of existing settlements. No more tolerant of rival woollen manufactures in the colonies than in Ireland, the Board was especially concerned that the attraction of migrants, particularly to the proprietary colonies, was not only depriving English manufactures of skilled labour, but mounting effective competition that undercut English products with respect to price, quality and fashion. Colonial manufactures not only impaired the balance of trade with the Americas, but also diminished the prospect of earning revenue from the re-export of colonial raw materials once manufactured in England. These concerns, which were first raised vociferously by the Board in November 1702, became as regular a feature of their parliamentary reports as bullion supplies, through to the Union of 1707. Over the same period, English agriculture and manufacturing experienced a war boom with increased demand for grain and textiles in Russia, the Low Countries and Germany, particularly as the Great Northern War dislocated grain supplies from the Baltic and textile production in Saxony and Silesia, while the discovery of gold in Brazil fuelled increased sales of goods to Portugal. But this boom also put a premium on retaining population rather than encouraging migration to the American colonies.[40]

If emigration was not to damage the basis for English national prosperity or weaken its military commitments by land and sea, some alternative source of productive and reliable manpower needed to be found. French Protestant émigrés fitted both requirements, but in insufficient numbers. Ireland, whose population had reputedly increased in excess of 2 million, largely through migration within the British Isles, was still predominantly Roman Catholic (at least 80 per cent of the populace) and therefore deemed unsuitable on both accounts. Although its population

---

[39] *The Political and Commercial Works of Charles D'Avenant*, ed. C. Whitworth, 5 vols. (London, 1771; reprinted 1968), II, 1–77; [An American], *An Essay upon the Government of the English Plantations on the Continent of America* (London, 1701).

[40] *Lords*, new series: V (1702–4), pp. 66–100, 311–35; VI (1704–6), pp. 87–109; VII (1706–8), pp. 226–324. Centre historique des Archives Nationales, Paris, Affaires Estrangers (consulats) Etates Unis: Etats de commerce et de navigation des ports 1697–1830, B/111/444; HL, Huntington Manuscripts, HM 821; Jones, *War and Economy*, pp. 169–210. The Great Northern War of 1700 to 1721 ranged Sweden against Denmark, Poland-Lithuania and Russia.

had in all probability fallen to below a million, Scotland came into the position of favoured nation and was indeed identified as such by the botanist Nehemiah Grew in a private memorandum to Queen Anne in 1706 on the importance of human propagation to ensure 'a most Ample Encrease of the Wealth and Stock of England in a few years'. Concerned that England had been outperformed commercially on a global scale by the Dutch and was under-resourced in relation to France, Grew viewed impending Union with Scotland as integral to the expansion of the population base vital for the wealth and strength of any state. Although he grossly overestimated the current English population as between 11 and 12 million, he sought to double this figure within twenty-four years through greater procreation from earlier marriage. Every couple between the ages of sixteen and forty was deemed capable of producing four children. To further multiply the population he advocated wholesale immigration, with Scots to the fore. If the reputed 12,000 migrants who annually left Scotland were encouraged to come to England, they would form the core of the 25,000 couples necessary to add a further 3 million to the population base in the time prescribed.[41]

While there is no evidence to substantiate that Grew had any direct input to policy making, his call for Scots to be used in the wider service of England won endorsement from the colonies. In advance of the War of the Spanish Succession, and no doubt with a measure of discreet lobbying by Scottish commercial networks, planters in Barbados and the Leeward Islands were calling for free trade with Scotland as a means of securing supplies of servants and militiamen. Colonial governors also expressed their frustration that, with English forces stretched to the limits, they were disadvantaged by a continuing reluctance to give Scottish officers leading positions of command when confronting the French in the Caribbean. However, as well as complaints from Newfoundland that the Scots as well as the French were encroaching on English fisheries, there were also resurgent fears that clannish Scottish networks, in Virginia, East New Jersey and Barbados especially, were subverting English governance.[42] Notwithstanding his stated aversion to Scottish collusive practices in

---

[41] HL, Huntington Manuscripts, HM 1264, [Nehemiah] Grew, 'The Meanes of a most Ample Encrease of the Wealth and Strength of England in a few years humbly presented to Her Majesty in the 5th Year of Her Reign'; M. Flinn, *Scottish Population History from the 17th Century to the 1930s* (Cambridge, 1977), pp. 7–8, 187–200. Similar sentiments on the Scots providing manpower for Empire and giving a potential competitive edge to English competition with the Dutch, especially in the fishing trade, were expressed by a [Person of Quality], *Great Britain's Union and the Security of the Hanoverian Succession Considered* (London, 1705).

[42] *CSP, Colonial*: (1699), pp. 590–1; (1700), p. 524; (1701), pp. 207–8; (1702–3), pp. 259, 644–6, 884–8; (1704–5), pp. 258, 297–8, 407–10, 426–7, 638–40. *Lords*, new series, VI (1704–6), 363–82. Indeed, in Barbados, complaints about subversive influence drew on civil war tropes of the 1640s, revived by the tensions over Darien, depicting the Jews and

circumventing the Navigation Acts in Massachusetts and New Hampshire, Governor Joseph Dudley wanted a Scottish colony of frontiersmen to be established in Maine from 1703 to settle lands actually granted to the Earl of Stirling in 1635 in recompense for the loss of Nova Scotia (see Chapter 6). Around the same time, calls for 2,000–3,000 Scotsmen to be given free passage to Jamaica to facilitate the defence of the island complemented the plea from Governor Thomas Handasyd that existing Scottish settlers, along with other foreigners of proven substance, should not be denied the opportunity to serve in civil and military office.

As the Treaty of Union was passing through the Scottish Estates in late 1706 and early 1707, Daniel Parks, governor-general of the Leeward Islands made vituperative but not entirely facetious overtures to the effect that the French threat to the island could be averted by the dispatch of an expendable Scottish force to attack Martinique or even Puerto Rico. While this was rebuffed by the English ministry as both inopportune and insensitive, there was no outright rejection of using Scots in the frontline of imperial policy. Indeed, a proposal from within the Scottish community in Boston, supported by Governor Joseph Dudley, that an expeditionary force of up to 5,000 men should be recruited from Scotland to retake Nova Scotia and threaten Quebec was under active consideration as the Union progressed through the English parliament.[43] The key difference from the Britannic situation under the early Stuarts was that Scottish ventures were no longer viewed as complementary, but as initiatives only acceptable if firmly under English control. Thus, once Union was formally accomplished on 1 May 1707, the governors in all the North American and Caribbean colonies were sent strict instructions that the Treaty was to be observed to the letter. The Gothic spirit in which 'a perfect and entire union' was to operate was spelled out to Governor Handasyd by the Board of Trade and Plantations on 9 May: 'Scotchmen are thereby to be looked upon for the future as Englishmen to all intents and purposes whatsoever.'[44]

Harnessing Scotland

That English control over Scottish participation in Empire was negotiated rather than imposed is borne out by a draft scheme for union drawn up at

---

Scots as 'nations epidemical' (John Cleveland, *The Character of a London-diurnall with severall poems* (London, 1647), pp. 33–40; Edward Ward, *A Journey to Scotland giving a character of that country, the people and their manners* (London, 1699)).
[43] *CSP, Colonial (1702–3)*, pp. 424, 692, 700–1, 921, and (1706–8), pp. 357–8, 378–9, 379–82, 392–3, 411; HL, Huntington Manuscripts: Sunderland Collection, HM 9916 and 22,281; Lenman, *Britain's Colonial Wars*, pp. 35–8.
[44] *CSP, Colonial* (1706–8), pp. 426–7, 431; www.mdarchives.state.md.us/ Proceedings of the Council of Maryland, vol. 25 (1698–1731), pp. 244, 248–9.

the behest of the English ministry in 1705, not only as a resolution to the legislative war with Scotland, but in the midst of a drive to restore financial stability as the Bank of England underwent its most pronounced crisis since 1696–7. The heads of proposals for a union built upon the negotiations of 1702–3, with one significant difference. No access to the English colonies was conceded to Scottish entrepreneurs. A communication of trade extended only the creation of a common market in a united kingdom. An accompanying Act sought to prohibit the export of wool from England and Ireland to Scotland. However, the Scots were to be granted equivalents, not only for sharing in English national debts and to develop fisheries and manufactures, but also to cover reparations for Darien, the stumbling block in the negotiations of 1702–3 (see Chapter 4). Moreover, these reparations were set at a generous £600,000, of which £230,000 was to be apportioned to investors in the Company of Scotland: twice as much as was actually to be offered in 1706–7.[45] That guaranteed access to the English colonies would appear to have been traded off for lower equivalents suggests that the treating for Union between the English and Scottish commissioners in 1706 was the culmination of a process of negotiation. Far from the Scots accepting a predetermined English script, the English ministry responded positively to clear overtures from the Scottish Estates, in the wake of the Alien Act of 1705, that free trade with the plantations was fundamental to any lasting political settlement.[46]

While detailed analysis of the actual articles of Union will be covered later (see Chapter 11), the Treaty undoubtedly secured meaningful English control in several key areas of political economy. The Scottish carrying trade was curtailed by the banning of wool exports from the United Kingdom and by the English Admiralty taking over the issuing of Mediterranean passes, which also covered transatlantic trading. The Scottish Admiralty could no longer issue independent licences to privateers. Scottish access to the American colonies was guaranteed but only by accepting English fiscal rates for customs and excise, as well as for land tax. The Navigation Acts were not repealed, merely adjusted

---

[45] BL, Hanover State Papers, vol. I, 1692–1706, Stowe MS 222, fols. 343–4; *Lords*, new series, VI (1704–6), pp. 233–8; Scott, *The Constitution and Finance of English, Scottish and Irish Joint-Stock Companies*, I, pp. 352–74.

[46] W. Ferguson, *Scotland's Relations with England*, p. 235; Riley, *The Union of England and Scotland*, pp. 182–9; P. H. Scott, *Andrew Fletcher and the Treaty of Union*, pp. 151–61; NAS, Leven & Melville MSS, GD 26/7/245, and Montrose MSS, GD 220/5/53/2; DH, Parliamentary Notebook of Colonel William Dalrymple, 1704–5, A 817/1, pp. 92–6, 114–21, 129–34. The shift in the English position can probably be attributed less to Godolphin than to Harley who had stated privately to Hamilton in the wake of Darien that he hoped that eventually Scotland would be allowed to trade with the colonies (NAS, Hamilton Papers, GD 406/1/4668).

to incorporate Scotland. Moreover, the winding up of the Company for Scotland trading to Africa and India effectively excluded Scottish-based entrepreneurs from the East Indies. In the process, interloping under licence from the Company of Scotland was terminated. India remained the monopoly of the merging Old and New East India Companies.

Darien had certainly discouraged investors from advancing money for trade. In turn, the failure of the Scots to break free from the mercantilist dominance of the European powers made them more reliant on access to English domestic and colonial markets. Nevertheless, Scotland continued to enjoy a positive balance of trade with England and, unlike Ireland, was still in a position to threaten English interests politically and economically. Thus the English ministry had rejected union with Ireland in 1703 and actively pursued union with Scotland over the next four years. England already controlled the levers of Irish economic policy. The Anglican ascendancy in Ireland was underwritten by the English fiscal–military state. The ongoing Catholic diaspora into the Irish brigades in French and Spanish service was still viewed as a latent rather than as an actual threat, especially as this recruitment was more than countered by heavy Irish engagement under Marlborough. Irish commercial networks were certainly well established in continental Europe and, like the Scots, were more than capable of trading covertly with France despite the renewal of war in 1702. However, the Irish networks were not viewed as being as disruptive as the Scottish in a transatlantic context. Until harnessed by Union, the disruptive influence of Scottish commercial networks was particularly evident on the colonial trade, which at 14 per cent of gross turnover in 1701 was the largest single component in English overseas commerce and, along with the Mediterranean and East Indies, formed the major growth point for English trade in the seventeenth century. By way of contrast, recorded trade with Scotland represented no more than 0.53 per cent of gross English turnover. Yet Scottish commercial networks were so pervasive from the Baltic to the Caribbean that any concessions to the Irish linen trade prior to 1707 were seen as keeping a back door open for Scottish access to colonial markets.[47]

---

[47] Wrightson, *Earthly Necessities*, pp. 260–8; HL, Stowe Papers: Brydges Family Papers, ST 8/vols. 1–2; *Lords*, new series, V (1701–4), pp. 343–51, and VI (1704–6), pp. 111–15, 189–210; *Legislative Journals of the Council of Virginia*, III (1705–21), pp. 157, 193–4; L. M. Cullen, 'Merchant Communities, the Navigation Acts and Irish and Scottish Responses' in Cullen & Smout, eds., *Comparative Aspects of Scottish and Irish Economic and Social History*, pp. 165–76. According to the Board of Trade in 1701, English turnover in imports and exports amounted to £33,073,992, of which trade to and from Scotland constituted £175,494; the Scots enjoyed a favourable balance of imports over exports of £29,088 with England. The comparative turnover for English trade with the American colonies (including Newfoundland) was £4,589,884, with the Mediterranean from the Straits of

Not only had the Scots retained strong commercial links to the Dutch and the French, but their American experience had given them the confidence to look for alternative federative arrangements – not necessarily with England – rather than meekly accepting political incorporation. The accomplishment of Union signposted a collective crisis of political will among the Scots to pursue a separate commercial agenda, not an entrepreneurial lack of ambition. In the process, the Scottish debates on Union and Empire were not based solely on theoretical concepts and empirical considerations,[48] but also on pragmatic ventures and practical endeavours at home and abroad.

>Gibraltar to the Levant (itemised as Spain, Italy, Venice and Turkey) was £5,162,350 or 17 per cent of gross turnover, and with the East Indies, £3,316,570 or 10 per cent of turnover (*Lords*, new series, IV (1699–1702), pp. 430–6).
>
>[48] J. Robertson, 'An Elusive Sovereignty. The Course of the Union Debate in Scotland 1698–1707' in Robertson, ed., *A Union for Empire*, pp. 198–227, and 'Union State and Empire: The Britain of 1707 in its European setting' in Stone, ed., *An Imperial State at War*, pp. 224–57.

8 Going Dutch?

Political economy was born out of emulation of the Dutch. While the Dutch preferred the visual to the literate commemoration of their 'golden age' in the seventeenth century,[1] English commentators, stirred initially by rivalries in the East India trade, drew attention to several key features of Dutch commercial leadership. Superior corporate organisation had led not only to their dominance of the herring industry in the North Sea but also to their command over the products of other nations in Asia, Africa and the Americas as well as Europe. Although they lacked their own timber resources, the Dutch became leading shipbuilders, customising ships for the different trades from the Baltic and Mediterranean as well as from the West and the East Indies. As well as maintaining low interest rates, they also stimulated commerce by taxing consumption through the excise, rather than trade through customs or agrarian enterprise through a land tax. Revolt against Spain in the late sixteenth and early seventeenth century led them to pioneer deficit financing tied to a central bank in the services of the state.[2] Despite their admiration of Dutch commercial acumen, the English viewed them as global rivals with whom they fought three wars in the course of the seventeenth century, a situation not changed by the Revolution in which William of Orange replaced James II and subsequent military alliances throughout the Nine Years' War and the War of the Spanish Succession.[3]

---

[1] See. J. I. Israel, *The Dutch Republic: Its Rise, Greatness and Fall, 1477–1806* (Oxford, 1995), pp. 547–64, 863–8; S. Schama, *The Embarrassment of Riches: An Interpretation of Dutch Culture in the Golden Age* (London, 1991), pp. 290–323.

[2] Appleby, *Economic Thought and Ideology*, pp. 73–98; N. Ferguson, *Empire: How Britain Made the Modern World* (London, 2004), pp. 17–30; HL, Bridgewater & Ellesmere MSS, EL 8448, 'Anon., The Politia of the United Provinces, c.1621'; Tobias Gentleman, *England's Way to Win Wealth and to Employ Ships and Mariners* (London, 1614); Sir Thomas Smith, *The Defence of Trade* (London, 1615); [Thomas Scott], *A Relation of Some Points concerning the State of Holland* (London, 1621); Anon., *More Excellent Observations of the Estate and Affairs of Holland* (London, 1622).

[3] See HL, Bridgewater & Ellesmere MSS, EL 8818, 8917, and Stowe Papers: Brydges Family Papers, ST 58/1, pp. 51–4; Anon., *The Dutch Drawn to Life* (London, 1660);

The Scots, however, viewed the Dutch as their principal trading partners with only the pressures from mercantilism undermining this position from the 1690s. In shaping Scottish attitudes to union, colonial association with the Dutch was no less significant than that with the English. The decision of the English ministry to push for political incorporation from 1705 led Scots to question whether they would not be better served by becoming the eighth member of the United Provinces rather than the junior partner in the United Kingdom. Among Scottish and English debaters, the key issue was whether sustainable prosperity could be achieved through manufacturing supported principally by overseas trade or by landed enterprise. The Dutch connection raises two important, if contradictory, features of this debate. Firstly, before determining that the economic case made union inevitable and realistic, Scottish constitutional options must be explored.[4] Secondly, the dismissive attitudes of a commentator such as Lockhart of Carnwath for whom issues of political economy were a diversion from, not integral to, the passage of Union should not be accepted uncritically.[5]

Defining national interests

Under the early Stuarts, issues of political economy tended to be project-based, notably with respect to such topics as colonies, fishing, coal and

---

William Aglionby, *The Present State of the United Provinces of the Low Countries* (London, 1667); Roger Coke, *A Discourse of Trade: in two parts . . . The latter of the growth and increase of the Dutch trade above the English* (London, 1670); Anon., *A Familiar Discourse between George, a true-hearted English gentleman and Hans a Dutch merchant: concerning the present state of England* (London, 1672); William de Britaine, *The Dutch Usurpation or, a brief view of the behaviour of the States General of the United Provinces, towards the Kings of Great Britain: with some of their cruelties and injustices exercised upon the subjects of the English nation* (London, 1672); Sir William Temple, *Observations upon the United Provinces of the Netherlands* (London, 1673); William Carr, *Travels through Flanders, Holland, Germany, Sweden and Denmark* (London, 1691); Robert Ferguson, *A Brief Account of some of the late incroachments and depredations of the Dutch upon the English* (London, 1695).

[4] See Smout, 'The Road to Union' in Holmes, ed., *Britain After the Glorious Revolution*, pp. 455–67; Whatley, 'Taking Stock: Scotland at the End of the Seventeenth Century' in Smout, ed., *Anglo-Scottish Relations*, pp. 103–25.

[5] Riley, *The Union of England and Scotland*, pp. 196–253; *LP*, pp. 115–19. Colonel William Dalrymple regarded debates on trade and commerce as no less integral to the parliamentary process than party manoeuvering and political procedures during the legislative wars (DH, Parliamentary Notebook, 1704–5, A 817/1, pp. 25–7, 45–9, 59–92), a standpoint supported by another parliamentary diarist, Sir David Hume (Crossrigg, *DPP*, pp. 162–72). The Danish envoy extraordinary at Court, Iver Rosenkrantz, reported that commercial considerations were to the fore in Scottish negotiations for Union as well as in the parliamentary proceedings of the Scottish Estates during the legislative war with the English parliament from 1703 to 1705 (RC, TKUA, England, Akter og Dokumenter nedr Sofart og Handel: Order med Bilag, 1702–7, A.III/ 207/57, /59, /63, and 209/45, and 210/26, /41–2, /46/48).

salt, monopolies and currency. In the 1630s however, a pathbreaking work by Gervaise Markham, based on empirical evidence from Kent, promoted wealth accumulation through landed enterprise and, like the contemporaneous writings of William Lithgow on the regeneration of Scotland, saw plantations as the key to the productive working of land and to rural diversification. On the side of trade, the Calvinist emphasis on the productive use of worldly wealth in secular callings and a vocational desire among the mercantile community to emulate the Dutch led to the publication of commercial information packs.[6] During the 1640s, the Long Parliament held debates on how to promote the revival of English trade, abate interest rates and sustain a sound currency, with Sir Ralph Maddison making an incisive exposition on the balance of trade. London merchants became notably adept at remonstrating against the decline in trade and manufactures with calls to open up overseas trade, particularly to the East Indies. Although the Scottish Covenanters remained keen to secure a commercial presence in the East and West Indies, their primary policy focus was on landed enterprise, to develop and preserve indigenous plantations characterised by parks, dykes and enclosures.[7]

Prior to the creation of the Commonwealth as a free state, Henry Parker issued a seminal work which tied judicial freedom to commercial freedom and, in the process, signposted the shift away from confessional to commercial confederation among Northern European powers. Freedom and patriotism became synonymous with the advancement of overseas trade and navigation under the Commonwealth. William Potter, who promoted the expeditious working of money through bills of exchange, sought a proactive role for parliament in the promotion of mercantile enterprise as a national endeavour and the creation of a land bank to extend the credit basis for agricultural improvements and industrial diversity.[8] Thomas Violet, a London goldsmith, endorsed the public expansion

---

[6] Gervaise Markham, *A Way to Get Wealth: containing the Sixe Principal Vocations or Callings, in which everie good Husband or House-wife may lawfully employ themselves* (London, 1631 and 1648); William Lithgow, *Scotlands welcome to her native sonne, and sovereign lord, King Charles* (Edinburgh, 1633); Robert Lewes, *The Merchants Mappe of Commerce wherein, the universall maner and matter of trade is compendiously handled* (London, 1638).

[7] Sir Ralph Maddison, *Englands looking in and out presented to the High Court of Parliament now assembled* (London, 1640) – this work was to be republished as *Great Britain's remembrancer* (London, 1655); John Battie, *The Merchants Remonstrance. Wherein is set forth the inevitable miseries which may suddenly befall this kingdome by want of trade, and decay of manufacture* (London, 1644 and 1648); Thomas Johnson, *A Discourse Consisting of Motives for the Enlargement and Freedom of Trade, Especially that of cloth, and other woollen manufactures, engrossed at present contrary to the law of nature, the law of nations and the lawes of this kingdom* (London, 1645); *APS*, v, pp. 240, 654, c.128.

[8] Henry Parker, *Of a Free Trade. A discourse seriously recommending to our nation the wonderful benefits of trade, especially of a rightly governed and ordered trade* (London, 1648); Henry

of credit facilities beyond that which the Dutch enjoyed through the Bank of Amsterdam, where loans were tied to monetary deposits. A proactive discourse on wealth creation certainly contributed to the political conditioning in favour of the Navigation Acts of 1650-1 and the First Dutch War of 1652-4. Similar conditioning was evident during the Protectorate, when supporters of the Western Design (a pre-emptive strike against the Spanish Empire) insisted the Spaniards accept free trade in the West Indies.[9]

Lobbying for a proactive approach to political economy through land reclamation, fen drainage and plantations on the one hand, and through an increased volume of overseas trade and shipping on the other, had an ulterior motive. Enhanced national prosperity, channelled through London as the British imperial entrepôt, would generate a greater revenue base for government and lessen the current fiscal burden of sustaining the army and navy.[10] Within this context, enterprising Scottish landowners attempting internal plantations and developing extractive industries were supported under the Protectorate. Sir James Hope of Hopetoun, a Cromwellian collaborator with a proven track record as a metallurgist and mining entrepreneur, was committed to the exploitation of indigenous silver resources that would lessen dependence on imports from the Americas.[11]

Robinson, *Brief Considerations, concerning the advancement of trade and navigation is humbly tendered unto all ingenious patriots* (London, 1649), and *Certain proposals in order to the peoples freedome and accommodation in some particulars with the advancement of trade and navigation in this commonwealth in general* (London, 1652); William Potter, *The Key of Wealth: or, A new way, for improving trade* (London, 1650), and *The Trades-man's jewel: or a safe, easie, speedy and effectual means for the incredible advancement of trade, and multiplication of riches* (London, 1650), and *Humble proposalls to the honourable Councell for Trade and all merchants and others who desire to improve their estates* (London, 1651).

[9] Thomas Violet, *The Advancement of Merchandize: or, Certain propositions for the improvement of trade of this Common-wealth, humbly presented to the right honourable the Council of State* (London, 1651); Thomas Scott, *The Spaniards Cruelty and Treachery to the English in the time of peace and war* (London, 1654); Richard Baker, *The Marchants Humble Petition and Remonstrance to his late Highenesse, with an accompt of the losses of their shipping, and estates, since the war with Spain* (London, 1659).

[10] W. Blith, *The English improver improved or the survey of husbandry surveyed discovering the improveableness of all lands* (London, 1652); John Marius, *Advice Concerning Bills of Exchange* (London, 1655); James Howell, *Londinopolis, an historical discourse or perlustration of the city of London, the imperial chamber, and chief emporium of Great Britain* (London, 1657); Zachary Crofton, *Excise Anatomiz'd, and Trade Epitomiz'd: declaring, that the unequall imposition of excise, to be the only cause of the ruine of trade, and universall impoverishment of this whole nation* (London, 1659); John Bland, *Trade Revived, or, A way proposed to restore, increase, inrich, strengthen and preserve the decayed and even dying trade of this our English nation* (London, 1659 and 1660); Thomas Willsford, *The Scales of Commerce and Trade* (London, 1660).

[11] *APS*, VI ii, p. 745; Williamson, 'Union with England Traditional', pp. 311-12, 320.

Scottish trade to the Baltic had come to a standstill in the midst of the First Dutch War, however. In its aftermath, Thomas Tucker, the English fiscal official despatched to Scotland to regularise payments of customs and excise to support the army of occupation, reported that there were only between seventy and eighty ships of significant burden (above 25 tons) registered in Scottish ports. There was little innovative trade of significance apart from occasional forays by ships from Glasgow to Barbados. But he did discover that the Scots were seasoned evaders of customs, especially on imported wine and exported salt, as well as of the excise levied on salt and other consumables. They were also accomplished practitioners in forging passes to allow their ships to trade internationally as Dutch but to revert to Scottish ownership when they returned laden to their home ports. The ground was thus well prepared for their transatlantic circumvention of the English Navigation Acts in the Restoration era.[12]

Defending the national interest

Faced with the unrelenting Gothic mercantilism of the Navigation Acts, the Scottish Privy Council at the Restoration revived a practice used under Charles I in the 1630s to discuss currency devaluation and tariff reform.[13] A plenary meeting of the landed and mercantile elites was summoned to defend the national interest in 1661. With their backing, the Privy Council sought to encourage overseas trade through the establishment of companies for manufactures, shipping and fishing. Whereas the equivalent initiatives in England were part of the debate on national improvement through commerce, these moves in Scotland were integral to the debate on national survival through entrepreneurship. The Scots certainly benefited from the prohibition on importing Irish cattle into England in 1667, which they had consolidated with their own simultaneous ban on Irish imports. The droving of cattle and sheep from Scotland under licence had a clear run into English markets over the next three decades. Notwithstanding niggling English restrictions on seasonal access to droves and exploitative customs officials on the English Borders, the expansion of London into Europe's largest city and the steady provisioning of salted beef for the Royal Navy created an increasing demand for Scottish livestock driven on the hoof and fattened on the green fields of

---

[12] 'Report by Thomas Tucker upon the Settlement of the Revenues of Excise and Customs in Scotland, A.D. MDCLVI' in *Miscellany of the Scottish Burghs Record Society*, ed. J. D. Marwick (Glasgow, 1880), pp. 8–31; Macinnes, *The British Revolution*, p. 208; Smout, *Scottish Trade on the Eve of Union*, p. 53.
[13] Macinnes, *Charles I and the Making of the Covenanting Movement*, pp. 116–22.

southern England. Suppliers from the Highlands (an area Tucker considered of no commercial potential in 1656) were moving towards a position of dominance in the droving trade in cattle by the 1680s.[14] Nevertheless, when the Privy Council established a new committee of inquiry into trade in 1681, calls for another round of protection were made even though the Scots recognised they lacked the political muscle to take effective reprisals against the major European powers. This Committee of Trade duly reported that the only realistic way for the country to cope with mercantilism was not just to reinvigorate the commercial companies or co-partneries proposed in 1661, but also to develop overseas colonies as alternatives to closer union with England.[15]

James, Duke of York, welcomed in Scotland as Duke of Albany, had endeavoured persistently to moderate Gothic mercantilism from a Britannic perspective. He duly authorised Scottish ventures to South Carolina in 1682 and East New Jersey from 1685 (see Chapter 6). At his instigation, the Committee of Trade was intent on a broad-brush approach to political economy. Having engaged in a series of policy discussions with merchants, as well as nobles and gentry intimately engaged in commerce, the Committee offered a forensic analysis of the Scottish economy since the 1650s and a considered prospectus for growth. Meeting in the last two weeks of February 1681, the Committee identified an unfavourable, and purportedly critical, balance of trade with England and France, respectively Scotland's third and second most important trading partners, and a worrying tilting of this balance with the United Provinces, Scotland's most important commercial associates.[16]

The French, under the fiscal direction of Jean-Baptiste Colbert, were the principal exponents of mercantilism, which had all but ended Scotland's favoured-nation status in the wine trade. Although Colbert was not personally to blame for an additional imposition on every shipment of wine from 1659, he was instrumental in ensuring that this imposition remained an unrequited grievance.[17] However, the threat from England, with whom Scotland shared a common monarchy, was more insidious. Although targeted principally against the Dutch, the Navigation

---

[14] *Lords*, original series (1678–88), pp. 266–7, and new series, I (1693–5), pp. 351–3; *RPCS*, third series, III (1669–72), pp. 16–17; NROB, Berwick Guild Book (1659–81), B 1/12, fols. 43, 248; Macinnes, *Clanship, Commerce and the House of Stuart*, pp. 142–3.

[15] *Aberdeen Council Letters*, IV (1660–9), pp. 152–7; *RPCS*, third series, I, pp. 89, 97–8, 114, 127, 158–9, 173, 182, 271, 315–16.

[16] *RPCS*, third series, VII (1681–2), pp. 652–73; *Aberdeen Council Letters*, VI (1678–81), pp. 288–9, 296–7.

[17] M. Vergé-Franceschi, *Colbert: La politique du bon sens* (Paris, 2003), pp. 231–8, 337–65; *Extracts from the Records of the Convention of the Royal Burghs of Scotland, 1677–1711*, ed. J. D. Marwick (Edinburgh, 1880), pp. 31, 39–40; DCA, Dundee Council Book, vol. VI (1669–99), fols. 29, 235–6. This additional imposition was for 50 sous.

Acts inflicted collateral damage on Scottish shipping and commerce. The continuing confusion of Scottish, English and British appellations had led Scottish skippers to face double consulate fees for coal shipments to Flanders. Payments were required from English as well as Scottish consuls, even though Veere in Zeeland was reaffirmed in 1676 as the staple port with a resident Scottish conservator charged with the legal and commercial oversight of Scottish commodities shipped to and from the Low Countries. At the same time, the vested commercial interests of the English Eastland Company in the Baltic and Eastern Europe made it extremely difficult for Scottish merchants to trade directly through Hamburg.[18]

Notwithstanding international complications and a pessimistic mood among the merchants attending the Committee of Trade, the commercial situation of Scotland was far from gloomy. Scottish trade had undergone a remarkable recovery from the civil wars of the 1640s and the Cromwellian occupation of Scotland in the 1650s. Scottish merchants and mariners had taken full advantage of the Second (1664–7) and, especially, the Third (1672–4) Dutch Wars to develop a lucrative privateering trade, which they preferred to service with the English in the Royal Navy.[19] As a result, the Committee of Trade was able to report a virtual tripling of Scottish ships of burden to 215 by 1668 and a subsequent doubling by 1681: in all, a six-fold increase in shipping despite reported trading difficulties in the war years of 1667, 1672, 1673 and 1674. The accompanying comment that these newly acquired ships were too numerous, and some of them were too large, for trade to and from Scottish ports needs to be treated with caution. Certainly Scots were concerned to ensure that ships were fit for purpose and that vessels should be built and procured accordingly, with a preference for frigates which could also serve as privateers should Scotland continue to be dragged into England's wars.[20] No less pertinent, the Scottish mercantile networks were operating a successful carrying trade through the principal international hubs of London, Rotterdam, Amsterdam and Hamburg where, in an expansion of the practice of the 1650s, ships' passes did not always correlate with the ships' ownership and where flags of convenience disguised the Scottish connection.[21]

---

[18] *Extracts from the Records of the Convention of Royal Burghs, 1677–1711*, pp. 41, 43.
[19] S. Murdoch, A. Little & A. D. M. Forte, 'Scottish Privateering, Swedish Neutrality and Prize Law in the Third Anglo-Dutch War, 1672–1674', *Forum Navale*, 59 (2003), pp. 37–65; E. J. Graham, *Maritime History of Scotland, 1650–1790* (East Linton, 2002), pp. 19–25, 27, 75.
[20] *RPCS*, third series, VII, pp. 654, 659, 666, 671; Smout, *Scottish Trade on the Eve of Union*, pp. 52–3.
[21] S. Murdoch, *Network North*, pp. 240–8; NAS: Waste book, Leith, 1675–8, CS 96/157; Letter book of John Swinton of that Ilk, merchant, London, 1673–7, CS 96/3264; Andrew Russell Papers; GD 1/885/1; Clerk of Penicuik Papers, 1676–7, GD 18/2567; Kinross

Furthermore, and this does much to account for the pessimism of merchants attending the Committee, Scottish overseas trade had been opened up since 1672. Hitherto, this trade had been restricted to the merchant guilds in the royal burghs – that is, towns and cities holding their privileges directly from the Crown. But in the intervening nine years, ships and cargoes from the 'unfree' or dependent burghs – that is, towns holding their privileges within the heritable jurisdictions of lords of barony and of regality – were permitted to participate. Effectively this licensed a practice already prevalent throughout the seventeenth century. But open trading had made reliance on Veere as the sole Scottish gateway to the Low Countries an anachronism. Notwithstanding their reluctance to give up restrictive practices, the merchants from the royal burghs were not totally averse to open trading or direct trading to Rotterdam, Amsterdam and Antwerp, so long as the dependent burghs took an equitable share of the national taxation. How this was to be implemented remained a sticking point between the royal and the dependent burghs, a situation aggravated by ships from dependent burghs on the Firths of Clyde and Forth becoming irregular participants in the transatlantic trade.[22]

Whereas the expansion of shipping through privateering was a concerted endeavour by the commercial interest, fishing developed on a more piecemeal basis. Its promotion through joint-stock companies or co-partneries was complicated by national rivalries within the British Isles and provoked voluble complaints from the royal burghs that were intent on maintaining restricted access to Scottish inshore waters. The Company of the Royal Fishery of Great Britain and Ireland, as established in 1661, which drew upon the expertise of agents involved in the abortive common fishing of Charles I during the 1630s, was regulated by English common law and initiated from the Thames estuary in an endeavour to secure the fishing resources around the British Isles solely for English benefit.[23] Despite remodelling in 1664, and its reincarnation

House Papers, 1668-85, GD29/1471, /1906, /1959, /2048; Miscellaneous Foreign Papers RH 9/5/23; Andrew Russell Papers, RH 15/106/178-80, /199, /236. GCA, Records of the Maxwells of Pollock, T-PM 113/439, /1012.

[22] *RPCS*, third series, VII, pp. 43, 345, 351, 483-4, 666-8, and XV (1690), pp. 300-2, 368; *Extracts from the Records of the Convention of Royal Burghs, 1677-1711*, p. 28; Fountainhall, *HNS*, II, p. 854; *Aberdeen Council Letters*, VI, pp. 306-9, 323-4, 331, 335-6, 339-40, 343-8; DCA, Dundee Council Book, VI, fols. 200, 235-6. Nevertheless, the Convention of Royal Burghs sponsored, both on its own initiative and in conjunction with the Privy Council, the levying of voluntary contributions regionally and nationally for the creation of harbours for all coastal burghs.

[23] Captain John Smith, *The Trade & Fishing of Great-Britain displayed with a description of the islands of Orkney and Shetland* (London, 1662); [Robert Codrington], *His Majesties Propriety, and dominion on the British Seas asserted: together with a true account of the Neatherlanders insupportable insolencies, and injuries, they have committed; and the inestimable*

Going Dutch? 209

as the Company of the Royal Fishery of England under the leadership of the Duke of York in 1677, its continuing operation was compromised by the existence of a separate Scottish initiative, operating from 1661 through provincial associations that were refashioned in 1670 as the Royal Company of Fishery in Scotland. This venture, which stuttered on for the next two decades, remained distinct from, and detrimental to the viability of, the complementary Company of the Royal Fishery of England. Regardless of any resolution on respective territorial waters claimed for Scotland and England, neither company could operate independently of Dutch fishing expertise around the British Isles. The Scots, like the English, lacked the technical expertise as well as the capital necessary to compete effectively with the Dutch fleets in deep seas.[24] Nevertheless, the response of the royal burghs to the corporate challenge was not wholly negative. The city of Glasgow, where the Greenland Fishing and Soap Works Company had been established successfully in 1667, adapted by buying-out competing fishing interests in the River Clyde. Aberdeen began to expand its fish-procuring activities in both the Western and the Northern Isles, in the process actively competing with the Hanse and Dutch merchants who had hitherto dominated the trade in the Orkneys and Shetlands.[25]

Undoubtedly, the Committee of Trade's selection of data, based on the customs returns of 1668, was outdated, set a tone of exaggerated gloom and painted a misleading picture of decay. However, the temptation to view the proposed legislative action as conventionally mercantilist – to restrict imports and maximise protection for native manufactures – should be resisted.[26] In seeking to promote co-partneries, the Committee was attempting to provide a more attractive and focused portfolio for investment from the mercantile and landed elites, as well as for Scottish commercial networks overseas, which would encourage the growth not only of textiles, deep-sea fishing (including whaling) and shipbuilding, but also of colonial endeavours in the Americas. Devaluation of the coinage to improve international rates of exchange was resisted as

---

benefits they have gained in their fishing on the English Seas (London, 1665 and 1672); Coke, *England's improvements in two parts*.

[24] NLS, Wodrow MSS, quarto ix, fols. 109–18, 'Sir George Maxwell of Nether Pollock, Information for the Herring Fishing and others Relating unto'; Shetland Archives, Bruce of Sunburgh Papers, D8/31; W. R. Scott, *The Constitutions and Finance of English, Scottish and Irish Joint-Stock Companies*, II, pp. 361–82; T. W. Fulton, *The Sovereignty of the Sea: An Historical Account of the Claims for Dominion of the British Seas* (Edinburgh, 1911), pp. 441–9, 461, 465, 494, 515–16.

[25] *Extracts from the Records of the Burgh of Glasgow, 1666–1690*, ed. J. D. Marwick (Glasgow, 1905), pp. 327–8, 331–4, 343–5; *Aberdeen Council Letters*, VI, pp. 257–60.

[26] Smout, *Scottish Trade on the Eve of the Union*, pp. 242–3.

damaging to commercial confidence in Scottish goods abroad. Strangers, provided they were Protestants, were encouraged to migrate to Scotland. In return for applying their expertise to developing new manufactures, they were to be offered naturalisation and an exemption from all taxes for nineteen years.[27]

Much of the commercial programme that emanated from the Committee of Trade's discussions proved difficult to implement. Co-partneries for the manufacture of textiles in Glasgow and Edinburgh were stimulated. The woollen manufactory at Newmills, East Lothian, supported by investment and industrial espionage on the part of the London Scottish community, proved the most durable. No less significant for traditional manufacturing outlets than restrictions on exports of wool, and of woollen and linen yarn, was the Committee's insistence on the standardisation of the quality as well as the breadth of Scottish cloth exported – measures that laid the groundwork for the expansion of linen exports, primarily but not exclusively to England, in the next decade. If deep-sea fishing was not developed, the Arctic whaling ventures of the Greenland Fishing and Soap Works Company were certainly boosted.[28] Official thinking remained dominated by the balance of payments between exports and imports. Six months after the programme's launch, renewed stress was laid on the increased duties that were to be imposed on imports of French, Spanish and 'Rhenish' wine, and on American tobacco, to pay for the bounties and tax breaks offered in April 1681 to encourage herring fishing and shipbuilding. This decision reversed a former recommendation that discriminatory tariffs on French wine would facilitate the revival of Scottish trade to Spain, formerly a significant currency earner. The increase on duty from tobacco coming from the plantations, which continued to discriminate in favour of that shipped directly – over that shipped indirectly from London, Rotterdam and Amsterdam – demonstrated an unswerving conviction in the Scottish capacity to continue circumventing the English Navigation Acts.[29]

---

[27] *RPCS*, third series, VII, pp. 666–72; GCA, Records of the Maxwells of Pollock, T-PM 113/575, /613; Fountainhall, *HNS*, I, pp. 318–19. This tax break was to apply to all co-partneries engaged in manufactures and was also extended to existing manufactures to facilitate their consolidation, if not expansion.
[28] W. R. Scott, *The Constitutions and Finance of English, Scottish and Irish Joint-Stock Companies*, III, pp. 138–59; *RPCS*, third series, XIII, pp. 61–5, 80–3; NAS, Supplementary Parliamentary Papers, PA 2/32, fo. 175; Smout, *Scottish Trade on the Eve of the Union*, pp. 233–4.
[29] *RPCS*, third series, VII, pp. 210–12. Edinburgh merchants circumvented the restrictions on wine imports by forming themselves into a joint-stock company to monopolise the trade, with official approval being accorded in August 1684 (Fountainhall, *HNS*, II, p. 554).

A Baltic snapshot

The Committee of Trade's impact on Scottish economic development cannot be definitively quantified. However, a consular official's record of Scottish and English shipping passing through the Øresund at Elsinore between 1681 and 1683 has provided a unique snapshot of Scottish commerce.[30] Trade between Scotland and the Baltic was reportedly 'carried on with a tolerable equality'. The Baltic ports were major importers of herring and the major suppliers of 'all materials necessary for building and rigging of ships' which were to enjoy free importation into Scotland.[31] In terms of Scottish trade to the Baltic between the regal union in 1603 and the parliamentary Union in 1707, this three-year snapshot features in the highest plateau, which lasted from 1675 until the Revolution in 1688. With from forty-three to sixty ships trading annually through the Øresund, Scottish skippers were as active as those from Hull and Newcastle, the two principal trading zones outside London.[32]

Within Scotland, the Baltic trade was dominated by the leading royal burghs, with the striking exception of Bo'ness, a dependent but enterprising burgh on the Firth of Forth. This trading pattern broadly justifies the realignment of tax burdens which the royal burghs carried out at their Convention in the summer of 1681, when Glasgow, Kirkcaldy and Montrose were expected to make additional contributions because of their expanding trade. Glasgow was now clearly established as the second Scottish entrepôt after Edinburgh and, despite its western location, the main growth point in Scottish commerce to the Baltic, hitherto regarded

---

[30] RC, Dansk Kancelli, diverse breve, documenter og akter, C. 63-III, 'Den af Isack Holmes Fuldmaglig, Seneca Torsen holdte Journal paa alle engleske og skotske Skippere saavel fra Vestersøen som fra Østersøen, der har passeret Øresund, 23 April 1681 – January 15, 1684'. This snapshot of Scottish and English shipping compiled by an English consular official deals only with the volume, not the quantity or value, of trade passing through the Øresund, in marked contrast to the detailed tabulation of cargoes in the Sound Toll registers (*Tabeller over Skibsfart og Varetransport gennem Oresund, 1661–1783 og gennem Storebaelt, 1701–1748*, ed. N. E. Bang & K. Korst, 4 vols. (Copenhagen, 1930–53), I, pp. 22–5, 136–7, 217–18, 362–3, and II, pp. 226–70). The shipping journal, though the record for 1681 breaks off peremptorily in August, deals with the passage of 195 ships from registered Scottish ports, out of a total of 873 that sailed from the British Isles, between 23 April 1681 and 15 January 1684. For a fuller discussion of the provenance of the journal, its comparative value in relation to the registers, for the tabulation of trading statistics, and for the technicalities involved in estimating days at sea, see A. I. Macinnes, 'Scottish Commerce: An Øresund Snapshot, 1681–83' in G. Fouquet, M. Hansen, C. Jahnke & J. Schlürmann, eds. *Von Menschen, Ländern, Meeren: Festschrift für Thomas Riiss* (Töming 2006), pp. 341–64.

[31] *RPCS*, third series, VII, pp. 103, 670; *Aberdeen Council Records*, VI, p. 308.

[32] *Tabeller over Skibsfart og Varetransport gennem Oresund, 1492–1660*, I, 165–389; II A, 352–607; II B, 115–23, 165–9, 173–5.

as the preserve of the eastern Scottish ports.[33] There was apparently little change in the principal commodities transported directly from Scotland through the Øresund, with textiles, herring, salt, skins and hides continuing to predominate. Nevertheless, there were certain distinctive changes in trading patterns during the Restoration era. Shipments of unprocessed wool were rare rather than routine, with little more than an annual shipment to Norrköping where Scottish commercial networks were intimately involved in Sweden's developing textile trade.[34] The range of manufactured textiles was not particularly sophisticated, but there were clear specialisms in relation to stockings, gloves (mitts) and headwear (bonnets) targeted towards the quantitative rather than the qualitative market, with the exception of a few shipments of tablecloths. While exports of skins and hides remained buoyant, as in textiles there was a discernible move in favour of manufactured leather gloves, hats and shoes.

In keeping with the growing prominence of Glasgow and the determination of the city's magistrates to buy out rival fishing interests, there was a marked shift in the herring trade in favour of the west of Scotland with ships registered in ports on the east coast leaving from the River Clyde. Again, however, there is no clear evidence that the alteration in salt bounties in 1681 gave any meaningful boost to the herring trade. Trade in fish other than herrings had lost its market position since the political disruption of the 1640s. However, a significant trade in oysters, presumably packed in either brine or seaweed to keep them alive, had emerged in the Restoration era from Dunbar to Montrose, and compensated the relative decline in the herring trade from the east coast. As evident from the growing participation of dependent burghs along the Firth of Forth, domestic salt, produced from pans filled with seawater and fired by coal, was a consolidated export, albeit Scottish exporters of cured herrings preferred the solar evaporated salt from the Bay of Biscay and Iberia.

As was the case with exports, the principal imports to Scotland from the Baltic appear deceptively unchanging – iron, copper, timber, tar, pitch, ashes, flax and hemp. But the shifting balance of imports from Sweden over those from Danzig and the southern Baltic had implications for Scottish manufacturing, land use and urbanisation. Scottish commercial networks were as integral to the development of the Swedish iron and steel industry as to textile manufacturing.[35] Mercantilist desires to embargo block exports to Scotland of pig-iron from Sweden did not restrict large-scale imports to Scotland of malleable bar-iron. Albeit some of this

---

[33] *Extracts from the Records of the Convention of Royal Burghs, 1677–1711*, p. 40; Smout, *Scottish Trade on the Eve of Union*, p. 161.
[34] Murdoch, *Network North*, pp. 144–7, 174–7, 244–7.   [35] *Ibid.*, pp. 184–294.

iron may have been re-exported, Scots were as capable of a degree of secondary processing in their own country as in Sweden. Such production was concerned not only with such everyday utensils as pots, nails, spades and horseshoes, but also with pans for the manufacture of salt and sugar. Likewise copper, which was imported already worked into pots and kettles for domestic usage, was also supplied in sheets for fashioning into vats for brewers and dyers. The agricultural use of iron was limited. Yet, among the regular uses noted for Swedish imports prior to Union, was the replacement of wooden by iron blades for ploughing.[36]

Imports of flax and hemp had clear manufacturing implications not only for linen but also for coarse cloth, sacking and rope making. Imported potash and wood-ash were vital to the bleaching and finishing of cloth and, like the frequent shipments of spinning wheels, testify to a consolidating textile industry. Imports of timber, along with tar and pitch, were integral to the development of a native shipbuilding industry, as desired by the Committee of Trade. Notwithstanding the clear specification of masts, wax and merchandise for the use of ships, trade to Riga and other northern ports specialising in shipping stores remained limited. From 1685, the Privy Council attempted to promote shipbuilding by restrictive licences. Skippers and mercantile consortia were only allowed to purchase Dutch or other foreign ships to replace Scottish ships lost at sea, a restriction that had to be relaxed in the following year because of a shortage of skilled labour and inadequate supplies of Scottish timber.[37] Nonetheless, imported timber, particularly 'claphout' – boards for framing – as well as planks, had a ready application in house building, which was also stimulating indigenous lead-mining and slate quarrying. There was a sustained demand, not just for mansion houses and town houses for the landed and mercantile elites. Settlement in coastal villages also increased, as indicated by the expansion of salt panning, particularly along the Firth of Forth.[38]

The engagement of Scottish commercial networks in the manufacture of textiles and iron in Sweden indicates a clear outflow of venture capital.

---

[36] NAS, Letter and Account Book of John Watson, younger, merchant, Edinburgh 1696–1713, CS 96/3309; NROB, Berwick Guild Book (1659–81), B 1/12, fo. 301. A surer indicator of the growing productivity in arable farming was the marked decline in imports of grain, with only rye, rarely grown in Scotland, featuring on a considerably reduced scale from that of the first half of the seventeenth century.

[37] *RPCS*, third series, XI, pp. 140, 219, 250, 449, 532, 561, 615, and XII, pp. 162, 168–9.

[38] Smout, *Scottish Trade on the Eve of Union*, pp. 158–66, 230–2; M. Glendinning, R. MacInnes & A. MacKechnie, *A History of Scottish Architecture, From the Renaissance to the Present Day* (Edinburgh, 1996), pp. 71–102, 131–46; C. A. Whatley, *The Scottish Salt Industry, 1570–1860: An Economic and Social History* (Aberdeen, 1987), pp. 4, 10–12, 98–100.

Table 1. *Scottish ships engaged in tramping and the carrying trade*[39]

Year	1681	1682	1683
Registered ships	43	52	60
Tramping to the Baltic	4	4	11
Tramping from the Baltic	2	3	10
Tramping within the Baltic	5	7	8
Sub-total (% of shipping)	11 (25.6)	14 (26.9)	29 (48.3)
Carrying foreign commodities	3	5	4
Excess time in the Baltic	3	14	13
Total (% of shipping)	17 (39.5)	33 (63.5)	46 (76.6)

Whether this was matched by comparable inward investment awaits further research, though the occasional shipment of chests of gear that easily concealed gems such as pearls suggests some repatriation of capital. The snapshot does reveal a key indicator of economic health, notably involvement in the carrying trade through both tramping and the shipment of foreign commodities. The composite picture of tramping and carrying in table 1 presents a distinctive feature of Scottish commerce that was more akin to Dutch than to English practices.[40]

The volume of Scottish shipping engaged in tramping and the carrying trade, reinforced by skippers making bi-annual, annual and bi-ennial voyages through the Øresund, suggests that the Baltic expertise already identified for Montrose was present in other Scottish ports. Kirkcaldy and Bo'ness were also to the fore in the carrying of goods from continental and Scandinavian ports in and out of the Baltic, notably from the Bay of Biscay, the Low Countries, Norway and the extraneous Swedish port of Gothenburg.[41] Tramping to and from the Øresund was reinforced by ships travelling between specified ports within the Baltic, a practice spread fairly evenly among skippers from the leading Scottish ports. Proportionally, Scottish shipping would appear to be much more

---

[39] Registered ships are only counted once per voyage, priority being accorded to tramping to and from the Baltic, then to those tramping within the Baltic. Ships carrying foreign goods are in addition to those engaged in tramping; likewise those deemed to have spent excess time in the Baltic for a single journey are in addition to those engaged in tramping or carrying foreign commodities.

[40] J. I. Israel, *Dutch Primacy in World Trade, 1585–1740* (Oxford, 1990), pp. 196–224, 269–82, 299–304.

[41] Riis, 'The Baltic Trade of Montrose in the Sixteenth and Seventeenth Centuries' in G. Jackson & S. G. E. Lythe, eds., *The Port of Montrose: A History of its Harbour, Trade and Shipping* (New York and Tayport), pp. 102–14; *RPCS*, third series, VII, pp. 416–18, 443–5.

engaged in tramping than was the English. Never less than 25 per cent and usually just over 48 per cent of skippers were engaged in this version of the carrying trade. Ships engaged in the re-export from Scotland of French and Spanish wines, brandy, vinegar, French salt, wrought silk and Irish cloth intensify this proportional involvement.

Scottish involvement in the carrying trade is further enhanced by the addition of ships that appear to have spent excess time at their specified Baltic port, a trait particularly evident among skippers bound for Stockholm. Undoubtedly, sailing time could be increased through delays in clearing at Elsinore, by days waiting to unload and load, and by skippers not calling in at the ports specified when passing through the Øresund. However, as the time listed as excess is based on a comparison with days spent by ships cited as tramping, there would appear to be strong grounds for considering this factor as another aspect of the carrying trade within the Baltic. Scottish skippers were less likely than the English to pay their consulate dues in advance, signifying that they were not as sure of the commodities they would be transporting back through the Øresund. It is therefore possible that at least 50 per cent, and as much as 75 per cent, of Scottish shipping in this snapshot was engaged in tramping, a practice that was of immense value in being transportable to the Caribbean to become the basis of Scottish commerce with the American plantations in the Restoration era (see Chapter 6).

This snapshot, particularly with respect to tramping and the carrying trade, suggests that there was an underlying strength, flexibility and resilience to Scottish commerce, characteristics that were beginning to permeate official thinking in the 1680s. Certainly, confidence rather than apprehension influenced the decision of the Scottish Privy Council, at the behest of James II, to constitute a Commission of Trade in 1685, in order to negotiate with English commissioners for free trade between both kingdoms. Three years later, a standing Council of Trade was established to protect and develop Scottish manufacturing, particularly of textiles, in the face of English competition.[42] Nevertheless, for the purposes of making peace and war, and of conducting trade and commerce, the interests of England remained manifestly paramount both before and after the Revolution.[43]

---

[42] NAS, Supplementary Parliamentary Papers, PA 2/32, fols. 165–6; *RPCS*, third series, XII, p. 90, and XIII (1686–9), pp. x, xvii, xxiii, 80–3.
[43] RC, TKUA, England, A I, 3–4, Breve, til Vels med Bilag fra Medlemmer af det engelske Kongehus til medlemmer af det danske, 1613–1726, and England, A II, 33–7, Politiske Forhold, 1679–1701: State Papers Denmark – Greg's Diplomatic Papers (1694–9); Penicuik, *HUSE*, pp. 81–3.

Crisis and depression?

The Revolution and the Nine Years' War certainly did impact adversely on trade. However, a report into the state of the royal burghs in 1692 makes clear that the decay in commerce had only a marginal impact on the leading towns and cities engaged in overseas trade. A commission of inquiry established by the Convention of Royal Burghs visited 58 of its 63 constituent towns. Although there were general comments on a trading downturn, all the leading burghs engaged in the snapshot of Baltic trade in 1681–3 were still active in overseas trade, with the exception of Burntisland. The most persistent complainers about the decay of trade were the inland and small coastal burghs that concentrated, respectively, on agrarian markets and fishing, rather than on overseas trade. Where leading burghs complained of a downturn, special pleading must be taken into account, particularly with regard to avoidance of further taxation. Aberdeen did not even admit to having any foreign trade. Glasgow, whose complaints were at odds with its thriving overseas commerce, made no mention of its transatlantic adventuring and instead attacked dependent burghs threatening its trading dominance in the west of Scotland. Indeed, the complaints from 38 royal burghs about decay stood in sharp contrast to their claims that at least 140 dependent burghs were damaging their commerce. Where the leading burghs reported losses in shipping, these were attributable mainly to disaster at sea over a protracted period, rather than the immediate impact of the Revolution.[44]

Undoubtedly, Scottish commerce was markedly disadvantaged by reinforced Navigation Acts, which instigated a tariff battle with England from 1693 and treated Scots as aliens in the American colonies from 1696, as well as by the failure to establish a colonial entrepôt at Darien on the Panama Isthmus between 1698 and 1700 (see Chapter 7). As was particularly evident in the aftermath of Darien, Scottish endeavours to take retaliatory action against English mercantilist regulation lacked political clout. Nevertheless, the tariff battle did facilitate an expansion of Scottish

---

[44] 'Register containing the State and Condition of Every Burgh within the Kingdom of Scotland, in the year 1692' in *Miscellany of the Scottish Burgh Record Society*, pp. 49–157. The demonstrable decline in trade to the Baltic could be traced to the contrary nature of the herring shoals off the east coast as much as to the impact of war. Kirkcaldy had lost thirty ships in the previous decade, but three were sold outside the burgh on the death of their owners, three were captured as naval prizes (albeit one was ransomed back) and the remainder were shipwrecked. Ayr, which lost seven ships in the previous seven years, had lost a total of forty ships over the previous thirty years, all shipwrecked, including one in the West Indies. Perth had lost all three of the ships commissioned by its town-council since 1679 – two were wrecked and the third was purloined by its skipper, George Ferguson, a seasoned tramp trader in the Baltic, who had never returned from Virginia.

manufacturing. Whereas there had been only twenty-nine manufacturing enterprises established in Scotland before 1660, thirty were created in the Restoration era and another forty-seven between the Revolution and the Union. Albeit most of these were relatively short-lived, there was a sustainable concentration on textiles, papermaking, sugar refining, soap production, glass works, lead mining and outfitting of ships. Indeed, English traders in textiles to Scotland had warned the House of Lords in 1698 that the imposition of discriminatory tariffs, particularly on linen, the main commodity traded for fine wools, could rebound to the advantage of Scottish textile manufacturers. In turn, the Scottish balance of trade with England was recorded as over £29,000 by the English Board of Trade in 1702, a noted shift from the purportedly dire position recorded by the Scottish Committee on Trade in 1681.[45]

Chronic famine in Scotland in the later 1690s was also severely debilitating, but not crippling. Presbyterians viewed the famine as a providential judgement on a sinful nation, which required timely repentance from 'the whole island of Britain'. The more enduring legacy, however, was the Jacobite biblical analogy that the famine constituted the seven ill years of William. In substance, the famine can be attributed to a climatic shift, a little Ice Age which made marginal land unproductive not only in Scotland but in Nordic areas during the 1690s.[46] Yet, its judgemental association with William's reign was not entirely a rhetorical exaggeration. Although the shortage of grain was most severe in the aftermath of the successive failed harvests from 1695 to 1698, localised dearth had actually commenced with the harvest of 1694. A mortality crisis, intensified by the spread of typhus and dysentery among the population and compounded by the spread of murrain among cattle, continued in parts of the Highlands and the north-east beyond 1700. From an estimated base of around 1.2 million, the population of Scotland fell by perhaps as much as 15 per cent, albeit this drop cannot be attributed wholly to mortality and falls in births, as Scots migrated in droves, particularly to Ulster.[47]

Contemporary commentators, who ranged from Sir Robert Sibbald, a pioneer of the life sciences, to Patrick Walker, an apologist for the Cameronians, noted that a third or more of the population had died

---

[45] Marshall, *Presbyteries and Profits*, pp. 284–319; W. R. Scott, *The Constitution and Finance of English, Scottish and Irish Joint-Stock Companies*, II, pp. 123–98; Crossrigg, *DPP*, pp. 31–3, 39–40; *Lords*, new series, III, pp. 259–60, and IV, pp. 430–6; *RPCS*, third series, VII, pp. 669–70.
[46] Anon., *A Call to Scotland for threatening famine* (Edinburgh, 1698); RC, TKUA, England, AII, 35, Politiske Forhold, 1679–1701: Greg's Diplomatic Papers (1694).
[47] Flinn, *Scottish Population History*, pp. 164–86; C. Smout, *A History of the Scottish People, 1560–1830* (Glasgow, 1969 and 1979), pp. 143–5, 225.

or fled from some localities. Their testimony was not so much numeric as impressionistic. For the Scots, who had become unused to dearth in the later seventeenth century, were no longer familiar with the coping mechanisms necessary for survival. Yet, by the end of William's reign in 1702, a nationwide recovery was well underway. Landlords no longer felt obliged to rebate rents or accept accumulated arrears in their payment by tenants. Agricultural productivity was restored and demographic stability was returning.[48]

The Privy Council sought to contain famine from 1696 by offering bounties on imported grain. Limited efforts were made by the Scottish Estates to overhaul poor relief beyond giving landlords and the town-councils, in rural and urban parishes respectively, the primary responsibility for policing vagrancy. The scale of destitution exceeded the immediate assistance afforded by stents (local taxes) levied on landlords, who could recover half their costs from their tenants through increased rents. Although the marked drop in agricultural productivity severely limited the capacity of landlords and tenants to pay, this arrangement was implemented in 1696 to guarantee the continuance of schooling, a clear priority being accorded to education over social welfare. Famine was not compounded by a stop in trade. Cities such as Edinburgh – where around £10,759 was raised from its citizens, hospitals and private charities – were able to make a disproportionate contribution to poor relief.[49]

Although the magistrates of Aberdeen subscribed shares to the value of £300 in the Darien venture in 1696, they also laid out £333 to purchase grain to supply starving and destitute citizens and more than doubled this expenditure over the next four years. Having searched as far as Stockton-on-Tees in the north of England for grain supplies in 1696, they were subsequently able to secure sufficient meal and barley by bulk-buying of crops from local suppliers. At the same time, petty customs and other fiscal dues were relaxed to encourage trade. Only in 1698 were the magistrates apprehensive about public disorder, largely because they were also obliged to provide grain for troops quartered in the city, an additional burden that required them to secure forage from their hard-pressed,

---

[48] Sir Robert Sibbald, *Provision for the Poor in Time of Dearth and Scarcity* (Edinburgh, 1699); Patrick Walker, *Six Saints of the Covenant*, ed. D. H. Fleming, 2 vols. (London, 1901), II, pp. 28–33; NAS, Letter and Account Book of John Watson, younger, merchant, Edinburgh, 1696–1713, CS 96/3309.

[49] *APS*, IX (1689–95), c.74 p. 463, and X (1696–1701), c.26–7 pp. 63–4, c.19 p. 64, c.40 pp. 177–8, appendix pp. 99–100; BL, Papers Relating to Trade etc., Sloane MS 2902, fo. 248; GCA, Records of the Maxwells of Pollock, T-PM 109/83; HL, Huntington Manuscripts, Manuscript Newsletters from London to Tamworth (1690–1704), HM 30,659/59. Edinburgh also had to contend with a devastating fire that razed the meal market and much of the property around the Scottish parliament in February 1700 (NAS, Letter and Account Book of John Watson, younger, merchant, Edinburgh, 1696–1713, CS 96/3309, p. 69).

rural hinterland. In both 1696 and 1698, the magistrates imposed stents on citizens who had refused to make voluntary contributions for poor relief. By 1701, they were less concerned with policing vagrancy than with re-establishing a correction house to engage the able-bodied poor in manufacturing.[50]

A public debate on measures to prevent the recurrence of dearth emphasised community self-help as well as state direction through a reinvigorated Council of Trade. Contributions ranged from the call for improved agricultural practices by James Donaldson to a plea for greater commercial diversification supplemented by vocational education to stimulate trade and manufactures by Andrew Fletcher of Saltoun, who was even prepared to contemplate the extension of serfdom, hitherto restricted to the manufacture of coal and salt and to some fishing districts. The famine actually reinvigorated the Scottish carrying trade to the Baltic, which was restored to a high plateau by the early 1700s – albeit not as high as in the 1680s.[51]

Recovery from the famine demonstrates that the Scottish economy, notwithstanding structural weaknesses and vulnerability to mercantilist policies, was neither stagnant nor on an irreversible downward spiral from the Revolution. Official reports, customs records, fiscal returns and deficient military and civil expenditure cannot necessarily be taken as accurate indicators of the Scottish economy; nor do they present a holistic picture of commercial activity, especially in relation to networking, the carrying trade and tramping.[52] Considerable caution must be exercised

---

[50] ACA, Aberdeen Council Letters (1682–1699), 7/217–18, /243, /269, and Aberdeen Council Register, 57 (1681–1704), pp. 524, 535, 544, 552, 556, 617, 622, 626–7, 640, 645–7, 657–8, 686, 690, 698, 700–1, 722, 724, 740, 749, 768, 770, 813. The magistrates during the famine had also imposed compulsory church attendance on the poor to determine those deserving of relief.

[51] James Donaldson, *Husbandry anatomized* (Edinburgh, 1697); Andrew Fletcher of Saltoun, *Selected Political Writings and Speeches*, ed. D. Daiches (Edinburgh, 1979), pp. 27–66, 106–37; *Tabeller over Skibsfart og Varetransport gennem Oresund, 1661–1783*, I, pp. 2–51.

[52] Smout, *Scottish Trade on the Eve of Union*, pp. 205, 244–56; Whatley, *Scottish Society*, pp. 31–9. Thus, port records relate that only Glasgow and Ayr sent ships to and from the American colonies between 1680 and 1686. East coast ports sent ships out but none apparently came back between 1680 and 1685 (Smout, *Scottish Trade on the Eve of Union*, p. 287). Likewise, a general survey of direct trading between Scotland and America prior to the Union reveals that 134 ships went out and only 48 came back (L. D. S. Dobson, 'Scottish Trade with Colonial Charlestown, 1683–1783' (University of Aberdeen, Ph.D. thesis, 2005), p. 101). Discounting enormous losses at sea, for which there is no supporting evidence, these figures mask the nature of Scottish tramp trading. Transatlantic trade accounts for only 1.3 per cent of both Scottish imports and exports according to the customs returns for 1680–6, yet Glasgow, the recognised growth point among the Scottish burghs, demonstrably generated most of its customs returns from the transatlantic trade (M. Lynch, 'Scottish Trade in the Seventeenth Century' in McNeill & MacQueen, eds., *Atlas of Scottish History*, pp. 282–3).

before accepting claims about impoverishment or even bankruptcy when applied to Scotland as a whole, as distinct from its government, central or local. In the case of central government, Treasury accounts were never finalised or audited after 1692.[53]

Its fiscal base, in relation to taxes levied, taxes collected and taxes avoided, was integral to the functioning of central government. In Scotland there was a plethora of taxes levied, notably the land tax and cess, mainly on the estates of the nobles and gentry, with the royal burghs responsible for a sixth of the total apportioned; the customs and excise on trade and consumption, respectively; and the hearth and poll taxes on households. On grounds of technical complexity as well as cost, nobles and gentry were not enthusiastic about regular reviews of valuation rolls on which land taxes were based. As a result, tax returns did not keep pace with the rise in rental income.[54] Royal burghs were particularly vociferous in pleading poverty to prevent proportional readjustments to the burgh quota in line with improved economic performance. After the Revolution, Edinburgh consistently sought adjustments from leading burghs to lessen the fiscal burden of the capital. Yet Glasgow, having been coerced into accepting an upward revaluation in 1681, was not prepared to countenance any further increased liability. Other leading burghs followed suit. At the same time, dependent burghs were not prepared to conclude an internal communication of trade that would have required them to take over a fixed proportion of the burgh quota. Again, burghs such as Bo'ness and Greenock which were involved in the transatlantic trade pleaded incapacity through poverty in the run-up to Union.[55] Moreover, taxes were rarely collected directly by royal officials but were usually farmed out and

---

[53] Mitchison, *A History of Scotland*, pp. 215–16; A. L. Murray, 'Administration and Law' in T. I. Rae, ed., *The Union of 1707: Its Impact on Scotland* (Glasgow, 1974), pp. 30–57. As far back as the 1630s, the Scots claimed to be the most taxed nation in Europe, a perception that had more to do with resistance to the fiscal burdens imposed under the authoritarian rule of Charles I than actual comparative accuracy. Glasgow was second only to Edinburgh in terms of the profitable working of money. However, Glasgow consistently played down its standing as Scotland's second city until its remunerative transatlantic trade obliged it to accept this responsibility in the tax review carried out by the Convention of Royal Burghs in 1681 (A. I. Macinnes, 'Covenanting, Revolution and Municipal Enterprise' in J. Wormald, ed., *Scotland Revisited* (London, 1991), pp. 97–106, and Macinnes, *Charles I and the Making of the Covenanting Movement, 1625–1641*, pp. 133–4).

[54] See ACA: Aberdeenshire Commissioners of Supply – Valuation Book c. 1685, 1/10/19, and Valuation Roll 1701–4, 1/10/20, and Valuation Rolls 1674 and 1741, 1/15/2; Aberdeen Council Letters (1682–99), 7/82.

[55] ACA, Aberdeen Council Letters (1682–99), 7/233; (1700–19), 8/41, /43, /64, /73, /96, 233; (1700–19), 8/41, /43, /64, /72–3, /96. AUL, Duff House (Montcoffer Papers) MS 3175/A/2380; NAS, Hamilton Papers, GD 406/1/4401, /4422, /4757, /4991, /5420, /6486, /10892, /10894–5, /10897, /10899.

regionally sub-contracted to consortia of landowners and merchants who were not averse to discounts for favoured customers and insider dealing to exploit trading opportunities, even though tax farmers were expected to refrain from trading on their own account. Given that the Scots who were engaged in the transatlantic trade had demonstrated considerable expertise in circumventing the English Navigation Acts, the country's fiscal standing as a rogue nation was further compounded by a penchant for tax evasion at home. Smuggling was an endemic coastal pursuit.[56]

Arrears in revenue returns meant in effect that deficit financing in Scotland had to be met from the personal resources of ministers and leading officials. Notwithstanding the opportunities for exercising political power and control over the apparatus of government, officeholding in Scotland was a financial liability belatedly recompensed through pensions. Although officeholders could exact fees and lay first claim on royal revenues to recover their personal outlays, such actions in the absence of public auditing could be viewed as grasping and self-serving, characteristics that were all too easily translated into a willingness among ambitious politicians to accept bribes or receive covert payments from English, French or Dutch sources.[57] Pursuit of office, in turn, can be viewed as corrupt and corrupting. The absence of probity and of principle that featured in satirical poetry and other political lampoons can be seen too easily as the defining features of Scottish politics in the run-up to Union.[58] The financial liabilities of officeholding were compounded by the marked increase in the standing forces under William of Orange. Their cost in Scotland rose from around £29,335 under James, Duke of York, in 1684, to over £65,740 by William's death in 1702. In addition to the increased number of regiments and their complement of companies, there was a switch away from reliance on the militia, who composed

---

[56] *Aberdeen Council Letters*, VI, pp. 257–60; Fountainhall, *HNS*, II, p. 537; *RPCS*, XIII, pp. xxxiii, lii–liii, 135–8, 154–5; Crossrigg, *DPP*, pp. 6–8; *Lords*, new series, VI, pp. 111–15, 189–211; GCA, Records of the Maxwells of Pollock, T-PM /109/101, /113/689, /115/11; HL, Huntington Manuscripts, Manuscript Newsletters from London to Tamworth (1690–1704), HM 30,659/51–2, /55–6; NAS, Seafield Papers, GD 248/57/1/6/11, and Cromartie MSS, GD 305/1/159/130; PRO, Secretaries of State: State Papers Scotland, series II, Abstract of the General Account of the Commissioner and Governors for the Revenue of the Excise for 1 year end 1 May 1708, SP 54/3/18B.

[57] *SPC*, pp. 694, 699–700, 704, 746; *Burnet's HHOT*, p. 738; Cunningham, *The History of Great Britain*, II, pp. 60–1; *LDN*, p. 131; *Mar & Kellie*, p. 239; NAS, Hamilton Papers, GD 406/1/4778.

[58] PRO, Secretaries of State: State Papers Scotland, series II, Lynes upon the Nobility of Scotland 1703, SP 54/1/14; NLS, Wodrow MSS, folio xxv, fols. 125–6, and folio xxviii, fols. 194–5, 197; [Sir Archibald Sinclair], *Some Thoughts on the present State of Affairs* (1703); *Orain Iain Luim*, pp. 222–9; Riley, *The Union of Scotland and England*, pp. 8–22; W. Ferguson, *Scotland's Relations with England*, pp. 180–96.

over half the forces in 1684, to a wholly professional army by 1702. The ongoing Scottish debate on the standing army was as much concerned with the cost of fiscal impositions as with civil liberties.[59]

At the same time, deficit financing through officeholding left limited scope for naval protection for Scottish mercantile shipping. Notwithstanding repeated overtures from the royal burghs for the outfitting of three frigates consequent on the War of the Spanish Succession, Scottish skippers continued to rely on convoy protection from English and Dutch fleets. Despite another confirmation of Veere as the Scottish staple port in the Low Countries in 1697, the province of Zeeland frequently reneged on its biannual provision of convoys between Scotland and Veere. Scottish entrepreneurs generally ignored the staple port and relied on insurance, with or without convoy protection, purchased usually through Amsterdam or London.[60] The lack of an effective Scottish navy was partially countered by the increased licensing of privateers from the Nine Years' War to the War of the Spanish Succession. Indeed, the Scottish Admiralty and Privy Council were prepared to license Irish and eventually English shipping that could demonstrate some Scottish connection in terms of the skipper's ancestry, the ship's ownership or involvement in the Scottish carrying trade. This was not just a remunerative source of additional income. As in the Third Dutch War, the Scottish maritime trade seemingly gained more than it lost by privateering. Indeed, the War of the Spanish Succession reinvigorated Scottish shipping, as English and Dutch trading losses actually increased.[61] However, earnings from

---

[59] 'Establishment for the Pay of H. M.'s Standing Forces in the Kingdom of Scotland, 16 June 1684 & 15 May 1702' in *Miscellany of the Maitland Club*, vol. III, ed. J. Dennistoun & A. Macdonald (Edinburgh, 1843), pp. 73–98; Crossrigg, *DPP*, pp. 43, 63–71; *RPCS*, XIII, pp. xxviii–xxix, li; ACA, Aberdeen Council Letters (1700–19), 8/12; HL, Loudoun Scottish Collection, box 7/ Lo 8163, 8167; Andrew Fletcher, 'A Discourse of Government with relation to Militias' (Edinburgh, 1698) in Fletcher of Saltoun, *Selected Political Writings and Speeches*, pp. 1–27.

[60] *RPCS*, XV, pp. 338–9, and XVI, p. 357. NAS: Leven & Melville Papers, GD 26/13/73; Journal of William Fraser, merchant, London, 1699–1711, CS 96/524, pp. 103–32, 157–81; Letter and Account Book of John Watson, younger, merchant, Edinburgh, 1696–1713, CS 96/3309. ACA: Aberdeen Council Letters (1682–99), 7/207, /212, /239, and (1700–1719), 8/96; Transcript of Propinquity Books, I (1706–22), pp. 1–15. HL, Huntington Manuscripts, Manuscript Newsletters from London to Tamworth (1690–1704), HM 30,659/ 52, and Loudoun Scottish Collection, box 23/ Lo 8831, box 43/ Lo 10045. The confirmation of the staple port was accomplished after pressure from William of Orange in his capacity as Marquess of Veere (AUL, Duff House (Montcoffer Papers), MS 3175/A/2382).

[61] E. J. Graham, 'In Defence of the Scottish Maritime Interest, 1681–1713', *SHR*, 71 (1992), pp. 88–109. *RPCS*: XIII, pp. 387–90, 397; XV, pp. 74–7, 247–8, 311–13; XVI, pp. 276–8. HL, Loudoun Scottish Collection, box 23/ 8806; Orkney Archives, Balfour of Balfour and Trenaky, D2/7/6, /48/1, and 50/34.

the carrying trade, as from tramping, tended to remain as they can be classified – as invisible in terms of returns to central government.

Pleas of impoverishment must be treated with caution in local no less than in central government.[62] Despite being acclaimed as a specially favoured burgh in the 1680s, Aberdeen in the wake of the Revolution became a past master in such pleading. Initially, these pleas were made to recover the disproportionate costs faced by the city in quartering troops during the first Jacobite rising of 1689–91. Although these costs were met in part by tax rebates, government assistance and increased petty customs, the city still claimed to be deeply in debt as a result of the decay in trade. Despite competition from dependent burghs in terms of the marketing of agricultural produce and fishing, Aberdeen faced no meaningful challenge to its regional dominance in overseas trade. The city, nevertheless, remained adamant that it was in no position to accept any increase in its share of the tax quota imposed on the royal burghs.[63] Yet the city's programme of civic improvements from the 1680s continued throughout the 1690s, the ravages of famine notwithstanding. Aberdeen was notably entrepreneurial in the extension of its harbour facilities, bringing in timber from Hamburg and attracting inward investment from overseas commercial networks. A Convention of Royal Burghs held in Aberdeen in 1700 ratified a grant, equivalent to £133, towards the harbour extension. Two years later, the city's provost, George Walker, a goldsmith, toured the United Provinces and raised the equivalent of £665 from his contacts in Veere, The Hague, Rotterdam and Amsterdam for the same purpose. The city also removed petty customs on salmon exported from its harbour in order to preserve the dominance city merchants enjoyed in the

---

[62] Reports of bankruptcy often reflected poor management rather than impoverishment, a situation that was usually retrievable within a relatively short space of time. By 1705, burgesses of Dundee were refusing to accept election to the town council and councillors were declining posts as magistrates because of the city's seemingly insuperable debts. Yet, within two years, Captain George Yeaman, a transatlantic trader, had turned this predicament around. First as bailie, then as provost, he promoted effective policies of financial retrenchment. Peripheral town lands were sold to local gentry. Charters to other town lands were granted to existing tenants prepared to purchase their holdings in perpetuity. Dundee remained the principal port of entry to Scotland for Norwegian timber. By September 1706, Yeaman was instrumental in raising over £35,106 to meet debts assessed at £45,000 Scots (£3,750 sterling). Yeaman, who was also a committed Jacobite, ensured that the town was on a secure financial footing before it voted emphatically, if not always consistently, against political incorporation in the final session of the Scottish Estates in 1706–7 (DCA, Dundee Council Books, VII (1699–1704), pp. 234, 281, and VIII (1704–15), from September 1704 to April 1707, and Dundee Register of Ships, 1612–81; Macpherson, *OP*, II, p. 16).

[63] ACA: Aberdeen Council Letters (1682–99), 7/46, /149–50, /169, /179, /195, and (1700–19), 8/28, /30, /70, /207–8, /452; Aberdeen Council Register, 57 (1681–1704), p. 710. Aberdeen claimed to be in debt to in excess of £100,000 Scots (£8,333 sterling) in 1694.

marketing of catches from all rivers in the north-east from the Dee to the Spey.[64]

Robert Gerrard Sr, who occasionally conducted business while imprisoned for his Quaker beliefs in the 1670s, had traded conventionally from Aberdeen to the Netherlands (usually through Veere), to Bordeaux and Rouen in France, to Hamburg and through London, where he opened up a salmon trade to Italy. However, his trading endeavours appear to have terminated in 1685 with his involvement as an undertaker for, rather than as a colonist in, East New Jersey. His son, Robert Gerrard Jr, concentrated from 1696 on rebuilding commercial links with London, from where he branched more vigorously into salmon trading through Irish contacts in Livorno and Venice. Reflecting the resurgence in Baltic trading, he commenced regular shipments to Danzig from 1699. Aberdeen was the leading Scottish burgh that consistently supported the retention of Veere as the staple port for the Low Countries, principally because of the prominence of factors drawn from the city's commercial community. However, the Gerrards, like other members of this relatively tight community of merchants and local gentry, were increasingly prepared to trade through Rotterdam and Amsterdam, which they used as their main centres of international exchange and shipping insurance prior to the Union. Indeed, the Dutch connection, no less than networking with London Scots, had financed the expansion of Aberdeen's commerce through Spain and Portugal into the Mediterranean, with ships from Aberdeen regularly tramping to and from Livorno and Venice by 1706. Growth in the carrying trade did not necessarily increase the revenues of Aberdeen, however. Based on his reported trading activities in the city, Patrick Gordon, a prominent merchant, was taxed the equivalent of just over £13 in 1698. Yet his actual involvement in the carrying trade through

---

[64] ACA: Aberdeen Council Letters (1682–99), 7/118, /125, /221–2, /245; Aberdeen Council Register, 57 (1681–1704), pp. 24–5, 50, 63, 207–8, 475, 452, 499, 627–8, 631, 639, 692, 698, 733, 736, 747, 770, 799, 813, 822–3, 838, 841, 871, 875, 877, 880, 882, 889, and 58 (1705–21), pp. 3, 23, 38, 40, 43–4, 71. AUL, Duff House (Moncoffer Papers), MS 3175/Z/156. Aberdeen continued to finance external repairs and internal restructuring for churches and the town prison, the (lead) piping of waters from wells, the building of a new market cross and an observatory, the adaptation of hospitals and correction houses for woollen manufactures, and urban expansion through land purchases. By 1705, the city magistrates had also sponsored the establishment of a coffee house, the smooth transition of the town's press to women printers, and the provision of navigation lessons by a teacher from France. Writing schools for basic literacy and numeracy were supplemented with one specialising in teaching Italian. Aberdeen's only serious British competition in the salmon trade came from the town of Berwick-upon-Tweed, which jealously guarded its fishing rights and curing techniques from Scottish interlopers (NROB, Berwick Guild Books (1659–81), B 1/12, fo. 254, and (1681–97), B 1/13, fo. 242, and (1697–1716), B 1/14, fo. 132).

London realised £500 annually, that is almost four times the amount of trade he admitted conducting through Aberdeen for the purposes of assessing his tax liability.[65]

Not only in Aberdeen, but throughout and beyond Scotland, there is clear evidence that Scottish commercial networks were thriving and expansive rather than afflicted by stagnation and decay in the run-up to Union.[66] Two merchants from the town of Inverness and its hinterland in Easter Ross established themselves as lynchpins of a commercial network operating through Edinburgh and London. John Watson had moved to Edinburgh around 1695. Specialising initially in the droving trade, he soon engaged with existing commercial networks in Edinburgh and Glasgow trading from the Baltic to the Caribbean. He actively encouraged William Fraser, an occasional dealer in London, to move permanently to the metropolis to act as his principal agent from 1699. Upon his arrival in London, Fraser had already invested in the stock of the Pennsylvania Company and acquired eight houses in prime city locations from which he earned a rental income of £1,008, which facilitated his ready acceptance in the émigré Scottish community. Initially, Fraser operated as a supplier of colonial produce from the East and West Indies to Watson and their mutual mercantile contacts from Edinburgh to Inverness. Fraser also mobilised London capital to finance Watson's expanding commercial operations from Newfoundland through Spain to the Mediterranean. At the same time, Fraser was co-ordinating payments on bills of exchange passing between Scottish cattle drovers and wool traders in Norwich, transferring money and commodities between Scottish commercial networks in Belfast, Dublin, Berwick and Newcastle, and ensuring that the supplies of raw materials and credit from Amsterdam and London to Newmills, the leading Scottish manufactory at Haddington, were honoured. Fraser developed, as a lucrative sideline, advances on pay and expenses to Scottish army and naval officers in the service of the English

[65] AUL, Duff House (Montcoffer Papers), MS 3175/Z/156, and /Z/175. ACA: Aberdeen Council Letters (1682–99), 7/96, /199, /233, /275, and (1700–19), 8/2–5, /8–11, /29, /41, /43; Transcript of Propinquity Books, 1 (1706–22), pp. 1–12, 16–19, 22–4. AUL, Leith-Ross MS 3346/12/7. Olive oil, parmigiana cheese and silk stockings were among the commodities imported to Aberdeen from Italy in exchange for salmon and woollens.

[66] Entrepreneurial gentry in the Shetland Isles were no longer content to sell fish to traders from Hamburg and Bremen or merely to rent out landing facilities to Dutch fishermen. Using their mercantile contacts in Edinburgh, they began to compete directly with the Dutch in herring fishing and to sell their produce in, not just through, Hamburg, by 1700. Direct trading to Hamburg also facilitated sales of butter and (fish) oil. Ships from the dependent burgh of Fraserburgh were also used to enhance direct marketing of Shetland produce on the Scottish mainland, usually in return for tobacco and other consumer goods (NAS, Miscellaneous Papers of Charles Mitchell of Pitteadie, Writer in Edinburgh, RH 15/19/14–16).

fiscal–military state. He and Watson also built up an impressive clients list of politicians, headed by Queensberry and Mar from the Court Party, who required to borrow extensively to sustain their political position in Edinburgh and London. Although Fraser, like Watson, invested in shipping from Bo'ness to London that plied transatlantic routes, he began to concentrate his business on the global provision of shipping insurance rather than continuing to engage directly in the carrying trade. Watson, for his part, diversified his commercial activities into a fine cloth manufactory in Musselburgh.[67]

Manufacturing prosperity

However, national prosperity through overseas trade faced critical problems in relation to money supply and manufacturing investment. Central government in Scotland exercised no meaningful control over exchange rates for trading commodities, which were essentially determined through Amsterdam and London. Scottish coinage conformed to the best international standards in terms of quality but, in the absence of central controls over exchange, tended to trade below its intrinsic value. Although Scotland, since the regal union of 1603, had a fixed exchange rate of £12 Scots to £1 sterling with England, war distorted these rates internationally as Scottish rates of exchange in overseas markets tended to be tied to, rather than assessed separately from, English economic performance. Moreover, Scottish financial deals in London that were based on bills or other paper transactions were not necessarily accorded the fixed exchange rate of 12:1 and rates were frequently pushed up by financial traders demanding discounts. While this was a customary practice in English as well as in continental markets, Scottish dealers effectively faced a double indemnity of added discounts when converting Scots currency into its sterling equivalent. Accordingly, the Bank of Scotland preferred to issue its notes from the outset in sterling. Most commercial networks operating within Scotland faced a cash flow problem, with scarcity of money becoming a frequent complaint, particularly during years of war. In 1696, Scotland endured a financial crisis in the wake of the English one, but in 1704 the situation was reversed with the Bank of Scotland being obliged to close temporarily that December.[68]

[67] NAS: Journal of William Fraser, merchant, London, 1699–1711, CS 96/524; Letter and Account Book of John Watson, younger, merchant, Edinburgh, 1696–1713, CS 96/3309; Hamilton Papers, GD 406/1/6716.
[68] NAS: Montrose MSS, GD 220/5/798/28; Scott of Ancrum MSS, GD 259/4/29; Hamilton Papers, GD 406/1/5009, /5081, /5187. ACA, Aberdeen Council Letters (1682–99), 7/224; AUL, Leith-Ross MS 3346/12/11, and Duff House (Montcoffer Papers) MS 3175/A/2380;

However, this crisis was not irreversible or only addressed through Union.[69] Private banking through merchant houses at home and abroad, which was no less important than the Bank of Scotland to the operation of the Scottish economy, remained resilient. There was undoubtedly a scarcity of money but not a financial crash, even in 1705 when the Bank of England ran into difficulties. Commercial networks survived by drawing on family resources, extended credit and, ultimately, on the goodwill of their customers and suppliers.[70] However, the tightening of financial constraints did underline the need for a clear and equitable association with a strong international currency; but, in this context, closer political ties with the United Provinces and the Bank of Amsterdam were as appropriate as those with England.

The development of textile manufacturing and fishing and the reprocessing of imported materials for re-export primarily rested on the initiatives taken within the mercantile community. Notwithstanding the undoubted, but largely immeasurable, profitability of the tramping and carrying trades, there was a limited commitment among those engaged in overseas trade to invest in domestic manufacturing. The landed elite was primarily influential in the development of extractive industries such as coal, salt, lead, iron, slate and lime. Their tenantry were also engaged productively in textile manufacturing through the practice of putting-out of wool and flax to be spun into yarn, then of yarn to be woven into cloth. While nobles tended to remain passive investors, entrepreneurial

---

HL., Huntington Manuscripts, Manuscript Newsletters from London to Tamworth (1690–1704), HM 30,659/51–2; GCA, Records of the Maxwells of Pollock, T-PM 113/30, and Research Papers and Notes compiled by R. F. Dell, TD 1022/11: Register of Deeds, B.10.15/2136, /2180; *RPCS*, VII, pp. 651–2, 669–70, and XIII, p. xxxiv; W. R. Scott, *The Constitutions and Finance of English, Scottish and Irish Joint-Stock Companies*, I, pp. 356, 372–4; S. Checkland, *Scottish Banking*, pp. 31–9. Money was less scarce between the ending of the Nine Years' War in 1697 and the outbreak of the War of the Spanish Succession in 1702 because of bullion brought back from the Gold Coast in 1700 by the *African Merchant*, a ship chartered to the Company of Scotland. The gold was duly converted into coin and issued in 1701 as Darien pistoles and half-pistoles, worth respectively the equivalent of £1 and 10s sterling (Insh, *The Company of Scotland Trading to Africa and the Indies*, pp. 246–52). The Bank of Scotland recommenced issuing bank notes in May 1705 following remedial action instigated by the Scottish Privy Council, and dividends to shareholders which had fallen to 6 per cent, were soon restored to the annual average of 20 per cent enjoyed from 1701 to 1705 (Checkland, *Scottish Banking*, pp. 39, 46).

[69] Mitchison, *Lordship to Patronage*, p. 131; Smout, *Scottish Trade on the Eve of Union*, p. 262.
[70] Checkland, *Scottish Banking*, pp. 68–9; NAS, Letter and Account Book of John Watson, younger, merchant, Edinburgh, 1696–1713, CS 96/3309; AUL, Leith-Ross MS 3346/12/8. Berwick-upon-Tweed particularly welcomed political incorporation as the dominance of Scottish commerce in the town meant that its trade was conducted using Scottish, rather than the more favourable English, rates of exchange (NROB, Berwick Guild Book (1681–97), B 1/13, fo. 63, and (1697–1716), B 1/14, fols. 23, 132).

gentry engaged in partnerships with merchants to develop manufactures for glass, leather, soap, whaling and deep-sea fishing in the Restoration era, to which processes can be added textiles, paper, sugar and gunpowder after the Revolution. At the same time, Scotland was also becoming more attractive to inward investment, notably from displaced Huguenots and from English consortia usually led by London merchants, which deepened Scottish investment in textiles, papermaking, leather-processing, mining for minerals and the manufacture of miscellaneous hardware. Manufacturing, however, had a limited impact outside the central belt. Edinburgh and its environs remained the dominant manufacturing centre in the seventeenth century. Glasgow's prominence in the transatlantic trade did diversify Scottish manufacturing during the Restoration era. Co-partneries for sugar refining, rum distilling, soap making and whaling were duly complemented by the manufacturing of textiles, especially linen and fine woollens, to which were added outfitting of ships, porcelain and earthenware after the Revolution. Elsewhere in Scotland, only Aberdeen made a distinctive contribution in terms of woollens, paper and pin making.[71]

As well as limited depth outside the central belt and a lack of diversity outside Edinburgh and Glasgow, there was limited scope for expansion in relation to the Scottish domestic market, factors which again favoured links with a larger political partner. But again, this was not necessarily England. Collaboration as an issue of political economy was central, not incidental, to proceedings in the Scottish Estates in response to passage of the Alien Act through the Scottish parliament. John Spreull, a Glasgow merchant adventurer with a radical Covenanting past, had argued cogently that, if the Scottish Estates would not treat for political incorporation, any embargo on key Scottish commodities exported into England was a bluff that could be called. With the phenomenal growth of

---

[71] Marshall, *Presbyteries and Profits*, pp. 284–319; AUL, Duff House (Montcoffer Papers), MS 3175/A/801; GCA, Records of the Maxwells of Pollock, T-PM 113/439, /575, /613, and Research Papers and Notes compiled by R. F. Dell, TD 1022/11: Register of Deeds, B.10.15/2143–4, /2397, /2490. So intensively was it mined that lead was made a staple export when the Convention of Royal Burghs and the Province of Zeeland amplified and renewed the staple contract for Veere in 1699 (ACA, Aberdeen Council Letters (1682–99), 7/239). Sugar manufacturers were not averse to passing off rum as brandy during the 1680s (Fountainhall, *HNS*, II, pp. 505–6; T. C. Smout, 'The Early Scottish Sugar Houses, 1660–1720', *Economic History Review*, new series, 14 (1961), pp. 240–53). William Dunlop, principal of Glasgow University and the former undertaker for the Scottish colony in South Carolina, led the establishment of Scotland's largest textile manufacturing business in Glasgow in 1699. However, this co-partnery for fine woollens did not survive the standardisation of customs between Scotland and England at the Union (T. C. Smout, 'The Development and Enterprise of Glasgow, 1560–1707', *Scottish Journal of Political Economy*, 7 (1960), pp. 194–212).

London, England had limited alternative sources of supply for livestock, coal and even linen. Moreover, any adverse impact upon the balance of trade could easily be adjusted in Scottish favour by retrenchment in importing luxury goods and other English commodities, by a concerted effort to develop Scottish manufactures from imported raw materials, and by an expansion of Scottish overseas trade on a global scale. Spreull worked in concert with the two Presbyterian émigrés in London, George Ridpath, the champion of the Covenanting constitution of 1640–1, and James Hodges, the foremost protagonist of a federative accommodation. Regularly shipped north for their polemical abilities by the Country Party, they argued forcibly, as did Spreull, that any communication of trade with England should not involve political incorporation.[72]

However, the political dominance of the landed elite made the Scottish Estates more receptive to specific proposals to secure national prosperity through landed enterprise and manufacturing, particularly with a view to determining, in advance of any negotiations for Union, the political nature of a communication of trade with England. This task was entrusted to a Council of Trade, established in August 1705, not as a sub-committee of the Privy Council but now as a session committee with twenty-one members elected equally from each of the three parliamentary estates. Despite concerns within the English ministry at its creation without the approval of Queen Anne, adherents of the Court Party dominated the Council's membership, other than those returned for the gentry. Two published proposals for land banks to secure an adequate money supply and to realise venture funding for manufacturing were initially filtered through this Council. Both were rejected. The first proposal, from Hugh Chamberlen, an inveterate campaigner for land banks in both England

---

[72] John Spreull, *An Account Current betwixt Scotland & England balanced together with An Essay of a Scheme of the Product of Scotland, and a few Remarks on each* (Edinburgh, 1705); Fountainhall, *HNS*, I, p. 226; NLS, Wodrow MSS, quarto xxv, fols. 265–6. Spreull did not acknowledge a complementary proposal to his scheme to enhance national prosperity that was penned by William Paterson, under the patriotic pseudonym 'Philopatris', during a brief flirtation with the Country Party in 1704. First proposed as a British venture in 1700, Paterson now argued that a Council of Trade should be established independent of the Court on a Dutch rather than English model, in order to give Scots free and uninterrupted commerce with the American plantations of all the European powers ('Philopatris', *An Essay Concerning Inland and Foreign, Publick and Private Trade; together with some Overtures, shewing how a Company of National Trade, may be constituted in Scotland, with the Advantages which will result therefrom* (1704)). However, George Ridpath, *Considerations upon the Union of the Two Kingdoms* (London, 1706), did take up the idea of a Council of Trade, as the commercial equivalent to the Committee of Both Kingdoms during the 1640s, charged with managing the joint interests of England and Scotland when their respective parliaments were not sitting. When the parliaments were sitting, the English parliament was to receive deputations from the Scottish Estates to discuss the making of peace and war and the operation of a communication of trade.

and Scotland and an enthusiastic advocate of Union, was deemed too optimistic in assessing amounts that could be lent on the basis of rental values, especially as he made no allowance for the inflationary effects of overvaluation. The second, from John Law, a financial impresario addicted to gambling and suspected of Jacobite leanings, was deemed too adventurous in issuing banknotes as paper credits. Law sought to generate a surplus in exports over imports in the flawed belief that an expanded money supply would lead to greater employment and increased output from manufacturing. However, there were two unpublished papers tabled that had considerably more influence on the Scots agreeing to treat for Union and in shaping the conduct of the Scottish commissioners negotiating with their English counterparts in the spring of 1706, particularly as eight members of the Council also served as commissioners.[73]

The first paper specified a chronic deficit in the balance of payments, a deficit of £171,667 – that was marginally less than the total value of Scottish exports (£184,333) – in relation to imports (£356,000). These figures did not take account of imports processed for re-export or of goods carried to Scotland for re-export to continental or colonial markets. Indeed, ten of the top fifteen imports were capable of some kind of reprocessing. Revenues from manufacturing for domestic consumption taxed as excise were not taken into consideration, and nor were likewise bullion, coin or jewels returned from the profits of the carrying trade. At the same time, money and bullion carried out of the country by politicians and merchants were not factored into this equation which, in conventional mercantilist terms, painted an extremely gloomy picture that did little to stiffen the resolve of the Scottish Estates to call the bluff of the Alien Act, which targeted three of the ten principal exports from Scotland, which were also the three (linen, coal and cattle) in which the landed elite had the prime interest. These statistics, which were also reproduced in committee as the Union was passing through the Scottish Estates in late 1706, served as an immediate counter to Spreull. The global expansion of Scottish trade had not so much stimulated manufacturing as increased imports of luxury and processed commodities.[74]

---

[73] *APS*, XI, pp. 221–2, 243, c.94 pp. 294–5. NAS: Leven & Melville MSS, GD 26/15/19–20; Mar & Kellie Collection, GD 124/10/438, /445; Hamilton Papers, GD 406/1/5435; BL, Sidney, 1st Earl of Godolphin: Official Correspondence, Home, 1701–10, Add.MSS 28,055, fols. 300–2; Checkland, *Scottish Banking*, pp. 39–44; Dicey & Rait, *Thoughts on the Union*, pp. 382–3.

[74] *APS*, XI, pp. 341, 345; AUL, Duff House (Montcoffer Papers), MS 3175/A/2380. This estimate of trade is among the papers of Sir Alexander Cumming of Culter who became the Scottish conservator at Veere in 1705. The principal Scottish exports cited were, in descending order, linen, herring, wool and wool skins, black cattle, stockings, plaiding and serges, coal, lead and lead ore, salmon and salt. The principal imports were, again

The second paper stressed that sustained growth could only be achieved through manufacturing of assured quality, particularly in relation to textiles, hat making and the curing of beef, pork and fish. English trade regulation was particularly commended in this respect. Increased domestic production from a labour pool enhanced by the release of workers from the land through more intensive commercial farming would generate greater foreign trade and promote a more favourable balance of payments. At the same time, increased consumption of arable produce by the manufacturing workforce would expand the domestic grain market and lessen the need to export surplus grain, especially as traditional markets in Norway and the Netherlands were imposing discriminatory tariffs on imports.[75] English and Scottish interests appeared to be coming into line in terms of the Council of Trade in 1705 following the English path taken, in favour of landed enterprise and manufacturing, with the establishment of the Board of Trade in 1696. However, the English priority in seeking Union in terms of political economy was to secure Scottish labour for English wars, colonies and manufactures, not necessarily to promote manufacturing to retain labour within Scotland.

Debatable options

The three-month negotiations between the parliamentary commissioners from Scotland and from England that concluded in July 1706 brought into the public domain the issue of whether national prosperity could be better sustained through manufacturing generated internally through landed enterprise or generated externally through overseas trade. This debate, which continued through the parliamentary passage of Union, has tended to be viewed as the economic case for and against political incorporation.[76] However, the debate was a more complex yet fundamental discussion on political economy – what constitutional arrangement could best secure and sustain national prosperity. Support for landed enterprise tended to be favourable to a Unionist standpoint, but did not automatically correlate with it, any more than investment in the

---

in descending order, muslin and fine cloths, leather, household furnishings, tobacco, iron and copper, flax and hemp, wines, brandy and spirits, timber and tar, woollen manufactures from England, Spanish wool and camel hair, dye stuffs, ships and ships' furniture, sugars and candy.

75 AUL, Crathes Papers (Burnet of Leys), MS 3661/2/81/5, and Duff House (Montcoffer Papers), MS 3175/A/236/20.

76 Mackinnon, *The Union of England and Scotland: A Study of International History*, pp. 240–72; Carstairs, 'Some Economic Aspects of the Union of Parliaments', Smout, *Scottish Trade on the Eve of Union*, pp. 262–70; J. Robertson, 'Union State and Empire: The Britain of 1707 in its European Setting' in Stone, ed., *An Imperial State at War*, pp. 224–57.

Darien scheme can be taken as a key indicator of anti-Unionist, polemical positioning.[77]

Polemicists supportive of landed enterprise tended to advocate Union as negotiated in 1706. Some were disappointed investors in Darien or scarred by other colonial adventures. But there is no direct correlation between landed enterprise, Darien and the Union, even though this was the path recommended by William of Orange in 1700 when calling on the Scots to concentrate on improving their manufactures as both the surest foundation of foreign trade and the most expeditious means of rectifying widespread destitution. In taking up this mantle, William Seton of Pitmedden tied measures for national recovery to another round of British state formation.[78] He and George MacKenzie, Earl of Cromartie, became the foremost propagandists at the disposal of the Court Party in arguing politically not just for collaboration, but incorporation, to improve Scotland's economic prospects at home and abroad. A federative arrangement was deemed less conducive to economic stability and integration. Having acquired a proprietary interest in East New Jersey as Viscount Tarbat, Cromartie appealed to the founding spirit of that colony in promoting the benefits to be gained by Scots from accepting and working within the English Navigation Acts.[79]

Their arguments for the primacy of landed enterprise were also endorsed by two polemicists with strong family links to Scottish commercial networks: namely, the eminent lawyer Francis Grant (later a judge

---

[77] Indeed, of the thirty-four recognised Scottish polemicists who wrote on the issue of Union, fourteen had been investors in Darien. Of the nine former investors who commented on specific or general matters of political economy, the majority, by six to three, opposed political incorporation (McLeod & McLeod, *Anglo-Scottish Tracts, 1701–1714*, pp. 154–209; *List of the several persons Residenters in Scotland who have subscribed as Adventurers in the Joynt–Stock of the Company of Scotland*). Identifiable Scottish-based commentators on political economy who had not invested in Darien were evenly split, three for and three against political incorporation; of the four commentators who were not based in Scotland but in London or Rotterdam, the split was one for (William Paterson) and three against (George Ridpath, James Hodges and David Black).

[78] Sir William Seton of Pitmedden, *Some Thoughts, on ways and means for making this nation a gainer in foreign commerce* (Edinburgh, 1705), and *Scotland's Great Advantages by an Union with England: shewn in a letter from the country to a Member of Parliament* (1706); Armitage, *The Ideological Origins of the British Empire*, pp. 160–3.

[79] NAS, John McGregor Collection, GD 50/186/65/1, and Mar & Kellie Collection, GD 124/15/279/14; DH, Loudon Papers, A20/22–3; George MacKenzie, Earl of Cromartie, *My Lord Chancellor, it was my humble opinion on the beginning of this session of Parliament, that the interest of this kingdom and the posture of publick affairs, did invite upon us on several accounts to have begun with an act and commission for a treaty with England* (Edinburgh, 1703), and *A Speech in Parliament, concerning the exportation of wool* (Edinburgh, 1704), and *A Letter from E[arl of] C[romartie] to E[arl of] W[harton] Concerning the Union* (Edinburgh, 1706), and *A Second Letter, on the British Union* (Edinburgh, 1706). Arguably, Cromartie's experience as an adventurer in East New Jersey was more relevant than Darien, in that the former was based on landed enterprise rather than overseas trade.

as Lord Cullen), who specialised in commercial law, and Sir John Clerk of Penicuik, who was a member of the Council of Trade and a commissioner for negotiating Union. The latter had lamented but not invested in Darien.[80] However, two polemicists who supported the primacy of landed enterprise spoke and wrote vociferously against political incorporation – namely John Hamilton, Lord Belhaven, and Andrew Fletcher of Saltoun, both of the Country Party. Whereas Belhaven argued against Union primarily on apocalyptic rather than commercial grounds, the latter offered an alternative, federative vision of Scotland in Europe conducive to commercial enterprise and political reform.[81] Both had invested in Darien, as had John Spotiswood, a Berwickshire landowner and lawyer, and Andrew Brown, possibly a doctor from Lanarkshire. They also preferred landed enterprise for national regeneration but took differing standpoints on how Scotland should secure the best deal possible from Union. For the latter, a federative accommodation was the most beneficial to Scottish material and spiritual development. Spotiswood took a more contrary line in being willing to support Union, but preferably without a Hanoverian Succession.[82]

The case for Union made by the proponents of landed enterprise and indigenous manufacturing was strongly reinforced by Scottish merchants in the commercial hubs of London and Amsterdam. In part, this can be attributed to their desire to open up the debate to consider benefits of unfettered access to imperial as well as domestic markets accruing from incorporation with England. London Scots with a longstanding preference for colonies supported by landed enterprise no less than trade shared Cromartie's perspective that more was to be gained from working within, rather than against, the English Navigation Acts. The London Scots were also bolstered by the profits accruing to their community from

[80] Francis Grant, *The Patriot Resolved* (1707); Sir John Clerk of Penicuik, *A Letter to a Friend, giving an account how the Treaty of Union has been received here* (Edinburgh, 1706); ACA, Aberdeen Council Letters (1700–19), 8/92–4; NAS, Clerk of Penicuik Papers, GD 18/2572, /5674.
[81] John Hamilton, Lord Belhaven, *The Lord Beilhaven's Speech in Parliament the second day of November 1706. On the subject-matter of an union betwixt the two Kingdoms of Scotland and England* (1706); Andrew Fletcher of Saltoun, *Speeches, by a Member of Parliament, which began at Edinburgh the 6th of May 1703* (Edinburgh, 1703), and *State of the Controversy betwixt United and Separate Parliaments* (1706).
[82] Andrew Brown, *Some Very Weighty and Seasonable Considerations tending to dispose, excite and qualify the nation, for the more effectual treating with England in relation to an union of confederacy* (Edinburgh, 1703), and *An Essay on the Project for a Land-Mint* (1705), and *A Scheme Proposing a True Touch-Stone for the due trial of a proper union betwixt Scotland & England* (Edinburgh, 1706); John Spotiswood, *A Speech of one of the Barons of the Shire of B[erwick] at a meeting of the Barons and Freeholders of that shire, for choosing commissioners to represent them in the ensuing Parliament, summoned to convene at Edinburgh the 12th day of November* (Edinburgh, 1702), and *The Trimmer: or some necessary cautions concerning the union of the kingdoms of Scotland and England* (Edinburgh, 1706).

their servicing of the fiscal–military state as regimental agents and outfitters, as well as financiers. Though no polemicist, William Fraser can be counted among this lobby, as can John Drummond, the Scottish partner in the Amsterdam Company of Vanderheiden and Drummond which specialised in insider dealing in stocks and shares in association with the English government's paymaster general for the forces in Flanders, John Brydges (later 1st Duke of Chandon), who also placed lucrative supply contracts in their direction. Drummond and Vanderheiden were also the principal overseas financiers for the Newmills woollen manufactory at Haddington and prominent inward investors in Aberdeen harbour.[83]

An attack from within the Scottish merchant community mounted by William Black, advocate for the royal burghs and a woollen manufacturer from Aberdeen, vigorously rebutted the case of the London Scots and demonstrated that Darien had not irreparably discouraged Scottish colonial investors nor disabused them of their belief that growth was primarily delivered through overseas trade. The dubious prospect of free trade was not 'a sufficient Equivalency for our Sovereignty, Independency and Laws'. A federative communication of trade would allow the Scots to harmonise their economic regulation with English interests, rather than subordinate it.[84] At the same time, David Black, a commercial contact of John Drummond in Rotterdam, continued this critique that supported a Dutch rather than an English association. Backed by English critics of the East Indian Companies, and endorsed by London Scots not tied to the fiscal–military state, Black persuasively demonstrated that overseas trade as conducted by the Dutch was more cost-effective than the English model. The Dutch emphasis on excise rather than customs was manifestly more favourable to commercial networks. This argument was further supported by reference to Dutch expertise in deep-sea fishing, which offered the prospects of a lucrative collaboration even if the Scots, in the wake of Darien, no longer wished to pursue imperial adventures.

---

[83] *A Letter Concerning Trade from several Scots Gentlemen that are Merchants in England, to their Countrymen that are Merchants in Scotland* (London, 1706); HL, Stowe Papers: Brydges Family Papers, The Accompt of James Brydges , Esq., Paymaster General of His Majesties Forces in conjunction with those of her allies, 1705–6, ST 8/vol. 1, pp. 115–6, 129–88, 269–94, and Three Years Accounts of ye Payments made to the Forces in Flanders by the Rt. Hon. James, Earl of Carnarvon, from 23rd December 1706 to 23rd December 1709, ST 58/vol.2, pp. 25–66, and Correspondence ST 58/1, pp. 49–54, 115–16, 175–7; NAS, Letters of W & R Fraser, London, RH 15/13/30; GCA, Dunlop of Garnkirk Papers, D 12/1/25, /27, /38.

[84] [William Black], *Answer to a Letter concerning Trade sent from several Scots Gentlemen, that are Merchants in England to their Countrymen that are Merchants in Scotland* (Edinburgh, 1706); Anon., *Essay upon the Union* (London, 1706); Crossrigg, *DPP*, p. 130. ACA: Aberdeen Council Letters (1682–99), 7/258, and (1700–19), 8/102; Aberdeen Council Register, 57 (1681–1704), p. 870, and 58 (1704–21), pp. 30, 47.

Black's argument for closer association with the Dutch in terms of commercial practices, trading priorities and even federative politics appealed not only to Scotland's longstanding global association with Dutch commerce but to a familiarity with the constitutional structure of the United Provinces that was deemed more supportive of distinctive Scottish interests, particularly Presbyterianism.[85]

Building upon the example of the United Provinces, James Hodges forcibly made the point that breakaways from incorporating unions, notably Sweden from Denmark in the sixteenth century and Portugal from Spain in the seventeenth, had advanced their wealth as nations rather than consigning themselves to poverty as provinces. The discriminatory and prejudicial treatment of Protestant dissenters, American colonists and, above all, the Irish in the wake of the Revolution reinforced religious as well as commercial and political doubts about incorporation at the dictate of the English ministry. Patrick Abercromby thinly disguised his Jacobitism in taking this argument further. He upheld the independence of Scotland, but did not rule out the possibility of entering a federative arrangement with the Dutch and, if that should fail, with the French, with whom the Scots enjoyed a favourable balance of trade: imports of wines and brandy being more than compensated by exports of salmon and herrings, with the re-export trade in colonial commodities being an added if irregular bonus. The 'auld alliance' recast as a commercial league would rival English trade on a global scale.[86]

Both Hodges and Abercromby were implacable opponents of Daniel Defoe, sent north under the control of Harley in the autumn of 1706 to rebut any discussions on alternatives to political incorporation. The English ministry, which had assiduously insinuated informants into Scotland since 1705, was no longer content to rely on freelance favourers

---

[85] David Black, *An Essay upon Industry & Trade shewing the Necessity of the One, the Conveniency and Usefulness of the Other and the Advantages of Both* (Edinburgh, 1706); HL, Stowe Papers: Brydges Family Papers, Correspondence ST 58/1, pp. 46–7, 94–5, 103–6, 187; Anon., *The Profit and Loss of the East-India-trade, stated, and humbly offer'd to the consideration of the present Parliament* (London, 1700); Anon., *A Letter Concerning the Consequence of an Incorporating Union in Relation to Trade* (Edinburgh, 1706); Anon., *The Smoaking Flax Unquenchable: where the union betwixt the two kingdoms is dissecated, anatomized, confuted and annulled* (1706); Anon., *The History of the Republic of Holland from its First Foundations to the Death of King William*, 2 vols. (London, 1705).

[86] [James Hodges], *The Rights and Interests of the Two British Monarchies with a Special Respect to An United or Separate States. Treatise III* (London, 1706); Patrick Abercromby, *The Advantages of the Act of Security Compared with these of the Intended Union Founded on the Revolution Principles Publish'd by Mr Daniel De Foe* (1706); AUL, Duff House (Montcoffer Papers), MS 3175/A/238. Notwithstanding the expulsion of the Huguenots since the 1680s, France was not deemed inimically hostile to Protestant allies, according to Abercromby.

of incorporation such as Peter Paxton.[87] In terms of political economy, Defoe's principal remit was to propagate the primacy of landed enterprise over overseas trade in the development of manufactures, in the productive use of labour and in the attainment of sound money. William Black, who was particularly concerned about the adverse impact of English tax rates on Scottish trade in the event of incorporation, went round by polemical round with Defoe.

Defoe asserted that Scotland should build upon its favourable balance of trade with England and secure prosperity through the Union, which would facilitate the complementary development of Scottish linen and English woollen manufactures and allow Scots to become a more significant presence in the Baltic trade than were the ports of northeast England. He extolled the advantages for Scottish commerce of free access to English and imperial markets, and claimed only religious scruples and other national prejudices, which he also discounted, stood in the way of the mutually beneficial partnership being ratified.[88] However,

---

[87] [Peter Paxton, *A Scheme of Union Betwixt England and Scotland with Advantages to both Kingdoms* (London, 1705); *Portland*, IV, pp. 61–2, 67–8, 74–6, 83, 87–9, 98, 136–8, 146–9, 159, 181–4, 194–211, 213–15, 217–18, 220–36, 238–48, 269–72, 300–2, 305, 323, 326–8, 330–4, 336, 339–41, 400–1, and VIII, pp. 109, 178–80, 196–7, 202–8, 243–4, 275–6, 285–6. Defoe was an occasional correspondent with William Paterson during the legislative wars when both sought to provide Harley with political intelligence and polemical backing, the former focusing on Scotland, the latter on England. By 1705, Harley had despatched William Greg to Scotland as his principal informant until the arrival of Defoe and Paterson in the autumn of 1706. Greg in his initial reports claimed that such was the epidemical distemper of poverty in the country that the pirate-infested island of Madagascar was to be franchised as a legitimate enterprise by the Company of Scotland! He remained in Scotland in rather impecunious circumstances until April 1707. Harley recruited another Scottish informant, David Fearne, in the course of 1705, who despatched his last report in March 1707. Fearne's principal service appears to have been his initial classification of the nobles and leading gentry of Scotland in relation to their political standpoints, party affiliations and personal following.

[88] K. P. Penovich, 'From "Revolution Principles" to Union: Daniel Defoe's Intervention in the Scottish Debate' in Robertson, ed., *A Union for Empire*, pp. 228–42. [Daniel Defoe]: *The Advantages of Scotland by an Incorporating Union with England, Compar'd with these of a Coalition with the Dutch or League with the French* (1706); *An Essay at Removing National Prejudices against a Union with Scotland. Part I & Part II* (London, 1706), *Part III* (Edinburgh, 1706); *The State of the Excise after the Union, compared with what it is now* (Edinburgh, 1706); *The State of the Excise &c, Vindicated* (Edinburgh, 1706); *Considerations in Relation to Trade Considered, and a short view of our present trade and taxes* (Edinburgh, 1706); *A Fourth Essay at removing national prejudices (Edinburgh* 1706); *A Fifth Essay, at removing national prejudices* (Edinburgh, 1707). William Black. *A Short View of the Trade and Taxes of Scotland* (1706); *Some Considerations in Relation to Trade* (Edinburgh, 1706); *A Letter Concerning the Remarks upon the Consideration of Trade* (1706); *Some Few Remarks Upon the State of the Excise after the Union, compar'd with what it is now* (1706); *Wednesday 18th December 1706. Remarks upon a pamphlet intitul'd*, The Considerations in Relation to Trade Considered, and a short view of our present trade and taxes reviewed (1706); *Some Overtures and Cautions in Relation to Trade and Taxes* (1707); *The Preface to the Fifth Essay, at removing national prejudices* (Edinburgh, 1707).

the powerful Anglo-Irish linen lobby already challenged the prospects for complementary manufacturing and the Scots had been outperforming northern English ports in the carrying trade to the Baltic since the 1680s. Moreover, as Black readily protested, the standardisation of fiscal regulations to accord with English practice would undercut the cost advantage enjoyed by Scottish commodities in overseas trade. The price paid would be recession not prosperity. Nevertheless, Defoe was able to reply that, without a British incorporation, the Scottish economy would lack stable underpinning. In this context, fears for continuing employment in the textile industry, particularly in coarse as well as fine woollens, elicited a purported response from Aberdeen that apparently undercut Black's criticisms. Seemingly the only female intervention in the polemical debate on Union, women workers engaged in woollen manufacturing in Aberdeen favoured incorporation as a means of job protection.[89]

Defoe gained a further polemical advantage as he strove to ensure that the Court Party did not accept any material alterations as the Treaty of Union passed through the Scottish Estates. Advance news that the Bank of England would underwrite the Equivalents to be offered for reparations and the promotion of fishing and manufacturing undoubtedly served to reassure the political as well as the commercial elite about the merits of the Treaty, albeit financial security was not guaranteed. Political sceptics such as James, Earl of Mar, were dismissive about the value of the polemical debate to the Court Party. Yet others in his camp clearly gained confidence from the prospect of restoring financial credibility through the pooling of resources in a common market, to the extent that they wholly discounted the prospect of economic recession should the Union prevail.[90] Defoe also had the wit to share with his sympathisers and detractors among Scottish polemicists the view that the ratification of the Treaty did not entail the absolute surrender of Scottish sovereignty. Should ensuing British parliaments breach fundamental safeguards for the Presbyterian establishment, education, Scots law and local government, Scotland would be reduced from partnership to the satellite status of the Irish, which would, in turn, imperil the continuance of Union.[91]

[89] [Henry Maxwell], *An Essay upon an Union of Ireland with England* (London, 1703, and Dublin, 1704); *To His Grace Her Majesties High Commissioner and the Honourable Estates of Parliament, the humble petition of the peer shank workers and fingren spinners of Aberdeen and places thereabout* (Aberdeen, 1706).
[90] NAS: Mar & Kellie Collection, GD 124/15/496/19–20; Hamilton Papers, GD 406/1/5487; Supplementary Parliamentary Papers, Memorandum in relation to the Union and Trade by Robert Menzies of Culterallers, November 1706, PA 7/20/71. *Mar & Kellie*, p. 310; ACA, Aberdeen Council Register, 58 (1705–21), p. 71.
[91] L. Dickey, 'Power, Commerce and Natural Law in Daniel Defoe's Political Writings' in Robertson, ed., *A Union for Empire*, pp. 63–96; Francis Grant, *The Patriot Resolved*

Defoe's greatest advantage, however, lay in the nebulous nature of alternative associations to alliance with England. Scottish concerns about being informed of Dutch and French standpoints on the Treaty of Union had led the Privy Council to authorise the translation and publication of the *Haarlem Courant* and the *Paris Gazette* from the outset of 1706. However, there would appear to be little evidence that the Scots actually asked the United Provinces if they wished a closer association. Indeed, the only public precedent for a political link was extremely negative, the province of Zeeland having advocated that England jettison Ireland and Scotland in its favour in 1673. Zeeland, the province that exercised principal Dutch oversight of British affairs, was also embroiled in a bitter controversy with the Convention of Royal Burghs about the continuance of the Scottish staple port at Veere. Indeed, the only corroborative evidence that the Dutch were prepared to confederate with the Scots were hints from Prussian diplomats that money was being dispatched from the United Provinces, through Scottish networks, to bolster the resolve of politicians to resist political incorporation.[92] Such financial rendition, however, more likely relates to the intent of Dutch and Scottish consortia to exploit fiscal loopholes operative in the months between the parliamentary ratification and the actual implementation of Union on 1 May 1707 (see Chapter 10).

In the wake of the Peace of Ryswick in 1697, French diplomats, though holding out no meaningful prospect for a revival of the 'auld alliance', did consider the noted Scottish antipathy to the English as potentially beneficial to Louis XIV. Indeed, the French were willing to countenance separate commercial negotiations with the Scottish Convention of Royal Burghs in 1701 and the Scots were accorded favoured-nation status in the ensuing War of the Spanish Succession, to the extent that their ships were readily ransomed when captured by privateers, a concession terminated by Union.[93] Nevertheless, even if the past expulsion of the Huguenots was

(1707); [Daniel Defoe], *An Essay at Removing National Prejudices against a Union with Scotland. Part I & Part II* (London, 1706), *Part III* (Edinburgh, 1706); [Hodge], *The Rights and Interests of the Two British Monarchies*; Spotiswood, *The Trimmer* (Edinburgh, 1706).

[92] HL, Loudoun Scottish Collection, box 43/LO 10045; PRO, Prussia – State Papers, 1706-8, SP 90/4, fols. 171–5, 313–14, 327–33, 337–40; NAS, Mar & Kellie Collection GD 124/15/479, and also *Mar & Kellie*, pp. 353–4; [Joseph Hill], *The Interests of these United Provinces Being a Defence of the Zeelanders Choice* (Middleburgh, 1673); Cunningham, *The History of Great Britain*, II, p. 61; ACA, Aberdeen Council Letters (1682–99), 7/219, /239, and (1700–19), 8/37, /76; AUL, Duff House (Montcoffer Papers), MS 3175/A/2382.

[93] NLC: Edward E. Ayer Manuscript Collection: Memoranda on French colonies in America, including Canada, Louisiana and the Caribbean (1702–50), 4 vols., Ayer MS 293, I, pp. 138–41; NAS, Macpherson of Cluny Papers, GD 80/868; BOU, Carte Papers (1701–19), MS Carte 180/20; ACA, Transcript of Propinquity Books, I (1706–22),

to be discounted, a French alliance raised the spectre of Jacobitism and armed English intervention in Scotland. The French certainly infiltrated money and agents into Scotland during and after the legislative war, but their encouragement of opposition to parliamentary incorporation with England was somewhat abated by their efforts to seek a peaceful resolution after Marlborough's crushing victory at Ramillies in May 1706, efforts which continued throughout the passage of Union through the Scottish Estates.[94]

Union by default?

In the face of no achievable alternatives, it is tempting to consider that the association of Scotland with England largely went by default in 1706–7. However, the later seventeenth century had witnessed a growing but not yet a prevailing trend among the Scottish landed elite for intermarriage and social intercourse with their English counterparts, and for having their children – girls as well as boys – educated in England. By the accession of Queen Anne, there was a growing payroll vote in the Scottish Estates whose careers were increasingly tied to the English fiscal–military state. Serving officers in particular felt accountable to Godolphin for their parliamentary conduct during the legislative war. The English ministry, for their part, were prepared to use the resources of the Treasury to lubricate the politics of influence in Scotland as well as to relieve arrears of salary and pensions.[95] In the attainment of Union, therefore, the national interest was not necessarily equatable to rational self-interest on the part of the political elite who favoured political incorporation.[96]

---

pp. 1–12, 22–4; GCA, Research Papers and Notes compiled by R. F. Dell, TD 1022/11: Register of Deeds B.10.15/2452; *RPCS*, XV, p. 125; *SPC*, pp. 694, 710; Cunningham, *The History of Great Britain*, I, pp. 238, 709–10.

[94] NAS: Papers pertaining to the Argyll Family, GD 1/1158/4; Dalhousie MSS, GD 45/14/335; Mar & Kellie Collection, GD 124/15/449/19. *Mar & Kellie*, pp. 275–6, 280–1, 286; Anon., *A Seasonable Warning or the Pope and King of France Unmasked* (1706); *MGC*, II, pp. 665–6, 706–9, 714–15, 730–2.

[95] AUL, Duff of Meldrum Collection, MS 2778/12/1/6/3–4, and Duff House (Montcoffer Papers), MS 3175/A/236/5, /8, /20; NAS, Kennedy of Dalquharran Papers, GD 27/6/2; BL, Sidney, 1st Earl of Godolphin: Official Correspondence, Home, 1701–10, Add.MSS 28,055, fols. 17–8, 72–5, 82, 98, 111–13, 132–3, 144–5, 241; *MGC*, I, pp. 256–7, 297, 500, 542, 554; K. M. Brown, 'The Origins of a British Aristocracy: Integration and its Limitations Before the treaty of Union' in Ellis & Barber, eds., *Conquest & Union*, pp. 222–49. While Scots continued to seek mercantile adventure, political refuge and higher education in the United Provinces, this Dutch connection primarily served the commercial elite and the professions rather than the landed elite who dominated the Scottish Estates (D. Catterall, 'Scots along the Maas, *c.* 1570–1750' & E. Mijers, 'Scottish Students in the Netherlands, 1680–1730' in Grosjean & Murdoch, eds., *Scottish Communities Abroad*, pp. 169–89 & 301–31).

[96] Whatley, *Bought and Sold for English Gold?*, pp. 66–9, 84–90.

Nor should patriotism be considered more than an optional discourse on Union. During the polemical debate of 1706, proponents of Union could appeal to a nascent British patriotism as well as the Scottish patriotism claimed by their opponents. But there is an alternative discourse, that of political competence which has been developed by the adherents of the belief that the politics was primarily a self-serving process, though only partially in relation to the Country Party.[97] The issue of competence relates not just to their effectiveness in opposing the Court Party, but also to the capabilities of the Scottish commissioners who negotiated Union. This issue, perceptively raised by Alexander Cunningham, James 'Ossian' Macpherson and John Struthers in the late eighteenth and early nineteenth century was subsequently subsumed in a Whig historiography intent on linking statesmanship, patriotism and Union (see Chapter 2). An alternative discourse on political competence brings into play two perspectives vital to the making of the United Kingdom in 1707: the fear of Jacobitism and the commitment of Queen Anne to the defence of the royal prerogative. Endeavours in the Scottish Estates to impose further limitations on the common monarchy as the price of the Hanoverian Succession were pre-empted by the Treaty of Union.

[97] W. Ferguson, *Scotland's Relations with England*, pp. 232–69; Riley, *The Union of England and Scotland*, pp. 254–338.

Part IV

Party Alignments and the Passage of Union

9 Jacobitism and the War of the British Succession, 1701–1705

Issues of political economy were the prime influences on the making of the United Kingdom in 1707. However, other issues, notably those of confessionalism and of sovereignty were important considerations, not least as roadblocks to further British state formation. The principal roadblock as perceived by the English ministry was Jacobitism in Scotland. Jacobitism was certainly counter-revolutionary in wishing to subvert and ultimately overturn the Revolution settlements of 1689–91, but not necessarily the reactionary or regressive influence portrayed in Whig polemics and historiography. As an alternative path to modernity, Jacobitism favoured landed enterprise rather than overseas trade, commercial regulation rather than free marketing and, in a colonial context, proprietary government rather than direct rule by royal officials.[1] Support for the exiled house of Stuart at Saint-Germain was based on more than abstract concepts of order, hierarchy and authority in church and state. Jacobitism represented an organic rather than a contractual view of state formation that stressed inclusion over exclusion. In Scotland, the governance of the future James VII & II as Duke of Albany & York won relatively favourable reviews, especially when contrasted with the far-from-benign reign of his successor, William of Orange. In 1701, the English parliament's unilateral pronouncement in favour of the house of Hanover was matched by Louis XIV of France recognising the Jacobite heir as James VIII & III. Accordingly, the accession of Queen Anne, after the death of all her children and a few months prior to the outbreak of war, threatened to turn the War of the Spanish Succession into the War of the British Succession. The dynastic issue, coupled to the prospect of political incorporation to secure the eventual succession of the Hanoverians, provided a patriotic fillip to Scottish Jacobitism.[2] The enhanced presence of

---

[1] S. Pincus, *England's Glorious Revolution 1688–1689: A Brief History with Documents* (Boston, 2006), pp. 21–33.

[2] A. I. Macinnes, 'Le jacobitisme en Écosse, cause épisodique ou mouvement national?' *L'évolution des mondes modernes, Séminaire de D.E.A. De l'Institut de Recherches sur les Civilisations de l'Occident Moderne*, Université Paris Sorbonne, 2 (2004–5), pp. 1–28.

Jacobites in the Scottish Estates from 1703 and their willingness to act independently from the Country Party made them more a disruptive than a constructive presence during the legislative war that terminated in 1705. Nevertheless, their influence in determining the political agenda tended to be overstated not only by the English ministry, but also by the Court in exile at Saint-Germain. A further complicating factor was Queen Anne. Despite her steadfast pronouncements in favour of political incorporation, her support for the Revolution as for the Hanoverian Succession cannot be taken as unequivocal.[3]

Subversive Jacobitism

Jacobitism in the three kingdoms had little in the way of a common cause other than a wish to restore the Stuarts (initially James VII & II and subsequently his son, James VIII & III) to their rightful thrones.[4] The traditional historiographic focus on the Jacobite Courts in exile has accorded primacy to diplomacy and campaign issues that facilitated the Scottish and Irish risings of 1689–91 in opposition to the spread of the Revolution from England, and to the subsequent plots associated with King James in 1692 and 1695–6, and with his son James in 1703 and 1705. International recognition from France, and more equivocally from the papacy during the reign of Louis XIV, gave continuous credibility to Jacobitism in the run-up to Union. However, this support was expendable, unreliable and manipulative. French agents, such as Captain Nathaniel Hooke, who operated fitfully in Scotland from 1703 to 1707, acted principally for Louis XIV rather than his client at Saint-Germain. At the same time, rivalries among courtiers in exile have derailed considerations about the effectiveness of liaison between the constituent kingdoms of the British Isles.[5] The Court at Saint-Germain, particularly after the death of James VII & II in 1701, gave less weighting to Scottish than to English and Irish influences and personalities. This became a festering grievance within Scottish Jacobite communities at home and abroad, which undermined their trust in the exiled royal

---

[3] RC, TKUA, England, Akter og Dokumenter nedr Sofart og Handel: Order med Bilag, 1702–7, A.III/ 207–10; E. Gregg, 'Was Queen Anne a Jacobite?' *History*, 57 (1972), pp. 358–75.
[4] Smyth, *The Making of the United Kingdom*, pp. 108–34; D. Szechi, *The Jacobites: Britain and Europe, 1688–1714* (Manchester, 1994), pp. 29–72.
[5] Sir C. Petrie, *The Jacobite Movement: The First Phase, 1688–1716*, (London, 1950), pp. 66–124; B. P. Lenman, *The Jacobite Risings in Britain, 1689–1746* (London, 1980), pp. 28–88.

family,⁶ and, in turn, made them over-reliant on agents of extremely doubtful repute.⁷

A further complication for co-ordination through the Court in exile was the comparative standing of Jacobite organisations in Ireland and England. Although Ireland was the primary theatre for Jacobite military operations only in the rising of 1689–91, Irish Jacobites remained consistently well represented overseas – a situation attributable primarily to the international connections of the Catholic clergy, but also supported by the Irish brigades in the military service of France and Spain and by Irish commercial networks throughout Western Europe. At home, Irish Catholics were rigorously excluded from power by the ruling Anglican ascendancy. As a result, Irish Jacobitism was sustained covertly by the Catholic clergy, as by Gaelic poets and sympathetic members of the landed and mercantile elites. A less convincing feature of Irish Jacobitism was the prevalence of rapparees who used the cause as cover for their predatory activities, which were not confined to reprisals against members of the ascendancy.⁸ Notwithstanding the suspected, if contested, Jacobite sympathies of leading English politicians and the presence of English peers in key positions at Saint-Germain, English engagement in extra-parliamentary Jacobite activity was marginal. Jacobitism was an integral part of English political culture, as represented through the plethora of clubs, societies and associations for improvement and learning, welfare and conviviality. Its cultural distinctiveness, however, did not constitute a sustained political threat in England.⁹

---

⁶ *Mémoires Du Comte De Forbin (1656–1733)*, ed. M. Cuénin (Paris, 1993), pp. 459–93; *MSSM*, pp. 16–31; N. Genet-Rouffiac, 'Jacobites in Paris and Saint-Germain-en-Lay' in E. Cruickshanks & E. Corp, eds., *The Stuart Court in Exile and the Jacobites* (Rio Grande, OH, 1995), pp. 15–38; *Correspondence of Colonel N. Hooke, Agent from the Court of France to the Scottish Jacobites in the years 1703–1707*, ed. W. D. MacRay, 2 vols. (London, 1870–1), I, pp. 163–7, 223–30, 269–77, 305–27, 358–61; II, pp. 39–42, 67–9, 191–4, 206–11, 222–37.

⁷ BOU, Carte Papers: Nairn's Papers, vol. II (1689–1706), MS Carte 209/51, /71; HL, Huntington Manuscripts, Manuscript Newsletters from London to Tamworth (1690–1704), HM 30,659/74, /82; [Nathaniel Hooke], *Secret History of Colonel Hooke's Negotiations in Scotland in 1707* (Edinburgh, 1760), pp. 7–65; [Charles Gildon], *The Post-Boy Robb'd of his Mail: or, The Pacquet Broke Open* (London, 1706); [Daniel Defoe], *Memoirs of John, duke of Melfort; being an account of the secret intrigues of the Chevalier de S. George, particularly relating to the present times* (London, 1714).

⁸ Ó Ciardha, *Ireland and the Jacobite Cause*, pp. 89–95, 116–36, 183–218, 335–49; N. G. Rouffiace, 'The Irish Jacobite Exile in France, 1692–1715' in T. Bernard & J. Fenlon, eds., *The Dukes of Ormonde, 1610–1745* (Woodbridge, 2000), pp. 195–210.

⁹ F. McLynn, *The Jacobites* (London, 1985), pp. 142–71; P. Clark, *British Clubs and Societies, 1580–1800: The Origins of an Associational World* (Oxford, 2000), pp. 60–93; P. K. Monod, *Jacobitism and the English People, 1688–1788* (Cambridge, 1995), pp. 95–158, 161–94; A. Hanham, ' "So Few Facts": Jacobites, Tories and the Pretender', *PH*, 19 (2000), pp. 233–57; E. Cruickshanks, 'Jacobites, Tories and "James III"', *PH*, 21 (2002), pp. 247–54.

Jacobitism's main British feature was its polarising impact. On the Whig side, the interchangeable use of 'party', 'faction' and 'interest' were loaded to suggest desperation and disruption rather than legitimate aspirations or patriotic principles. The Jacobites, for their part, vested moral authority in their 'good old cause', which stood out as a bulwark against Whig corruption, partiality and mendacity.[10] Polemicists in Scotland, where the distinction between Tory and Jacobite was less nuanced than in England,[11] carried this debate further by claiming that there was no middle ground, no place for trimming. Monarchical authority reinforced by Episcopacy stood against a parliamentary and Presbyterian consensus. Nevertheless, these attested fundamental differences between Jacobites and Whigs were clouded by subterfuge. Considerable numbers of the political elite disguised their Jacobite sympathies by subscribing to loyal addresses and swearing oaths of allegiance and abjuration in order to hold office in town and country – a practice first evident under William of Orange and reputedly intensified by the prospect of a Hanoverian Succession after 1702.[12] This paradox of clear disagreement on constitutional fundamentals in Kirk and State, yet disguised loyalties in the running of central and local government, suggests that Jacobitism was more sustained and more subversive within Scotland than in either England or Ireland. In England, Jacobitism in parliament was covert, not co-ordinated to extra-parliamentary force. In Ireland, there was a thriving extra-parliamentary underground, but no presence in parliament. In Scotland, there was an identifiable Jacobite presence in parliament that was sustained by extra-parliamentary activism made potentially potent by the embedding of Jacobites in the military, in the customs and other fiscal services, and in commercial networks at home and abroad.[13]

[10] See Anon., *The True Picture of a Modern Tory* (London, 1702); Charles Lawton, *The Jacobite Principles vindicated; in Answer to a Letter sent to the Author* (London, 1693); HL, Bridgewater & Ellesmere MSS, EL 9882 and 10112.
[11] J. C. D. Clark, *Revolution and Rebellion: State and Society in England in the Seventeenth and Eighteenth Centuries* (Cambridge, 1986), pp. 120–63; Hayton, 'Traces of Party Politics in Early Eighteenth-century Scottish Elections'.
[12] ACA, Aberdeen Council Letters (1700–19), 8/40, /45, and Aberdeen Council Register, 57 (1681–1704), pp. 302, 306, 817–18, 875–7; AUL, Duff House (Montcoffer Papers), MS 3175/Z/45/1; GCA, Records of the Maxwells of Pollock, T-PM/113/672; Orkney Archives, Kirkwall, Town Council Minute Book 1691–1732, fols. 85–6, 94, 108.
[13] *Correspondence of Col. N. Hooke*, I, pp. 274–5, 280–2, 288–9, 333–6, 342–3, 372–428, and II, pp. 17–21, 203–4; NAS, Bruce of Kinross Papers, GD 29/115; *RPCS*, xv, pp. 127–9. These networks preferred to minimise customs on goods by making paper transfers through bills of exchange discounted through private banks. Likewise, they tended to use easily disguised, transportable commodities such as pearls or jewellery rather than specie or bullion, which allowed Jacobites to move funds into Scotland without attracting overly close surveillance from customs officials in the ports. Women of some social standing

The personal rule of James, first as Duke of Albany & York, then as monarch in the 1680s, was undoubtedly a defining and distinctive feature of Scottish Jacobitism. Whig historiography has focused on the continuous harassment of Covenanters, especially the infliction of summary justice, known as 'the killing times', during that decade. The Cameronians, the most militant Covenanting activists in the Restoration era, operated as rural guerrillas and claimed the right to wage war on an ungodly government. James, like the Duke of Lauderdale before him, used their conventicling in fields and hills as an excuse to impose fines exacted through military quartering on peaceful Presbyterians.[14] Yet his governance of Scotland deserves rehabilitation. For James was as much an understated success as a qualified failure. His reversal of the policy, operative from the Restoration, of fiscal repression, in favour of judicial conciliation, was particularly appealing to the clans.[15] Indeed, James was the only Stuart to work proactively with chiefs and leading gentry to eradicate banditry and social disorder in the Highlands. During his retreat from the Exclusion Crisis in England, he established his Court in Edinburgh. Attendance at Holyrood Palace and celebration of royal birthdays were manifestations of Britishness that demonstrated Scottish solidarity with the Stuart dynasty.[16] His Britannic inclusiveness also made him sensitive to Scottish commercial aspirations in seeking economic development through colonialism rather than unionism (see Chapter 6). For William of Orange, however, the interests of England were paramount.[17]

William of Orange earned contemporaneous plaudits from Protestants throughout the British Isles for delivering them from the perceived threat of popery associated with James II's religious toleration and political preferment for Roman Catholics. Presbyterians in Scotland were notably supportive of the Revolution of 1688–91, which had terminated the Episcopalian religious establishment. Although William continued to be

---

were notably deployed as couriers between the Court in exile and commercial networks inclined towards Jacobitism.

[14] Donaldson, *Scotland: James V – James VII*, pp. 358–84; I. B. Cowan, *The Scottish Covenanters, 1660–88* (London, 1976), pp. 64–133.
[15] K. F. McAlister, 'James VII and the Conduct of Scottish Politics, c. 1679 – c. 1686' (University of Strathclyde, Ph.D. thesis, 2003); A. J. Mann, '"James VII, King of the Articles": Political Management and Parliamentary Failure' in Brown & Mann, eds., *The History of the Scottish Parliament*, vol. II, pp. 184–207; Macinnes, 'Repression and Conciliation'.
[16] K. M. Brown, 'The Vanishing Emperor; British Kingship in Decline' in Mason, ed., *Scots and Britons*, pp. 58–87; Penicuik, *HUSE*, pp. 78–83.
[17] RC, TKUA, England, A I, 3–4, Breve, til Vels med Bilag fra Medlemmer af det engelske Kongehus til medlemmer af det danske, 1613–1726, and England, A II, 33–7, Politiske Forhold, 1679–1701: State Papers Denmark – Greg's Diplomatic Papers (1694–9); Penicuik, *HUSE*, pp. 81–3.

eulogised in both Scotland and England for standing up to the expansive ambitions of Louis XIV of France, these eulogies – even among Scottish Presbyterians – became increasingly formulaic.[18] Simultaneously, the contemporaneous Scottish supporters of the Stuart monarch exiled at the Revolution had well-worked antipathies to William for his leading role in the removal of his father-in-law. Jacobite antipathies were further fuelled by William's reputed complicity in the Massacre of Glencoe (1692), in the causes of the famine of 1695–1700 ('the seven [sic] ill years of William') and in the Darien colonial fiasco (1697–1700). In relation to these lamentable events, William's culpability was, respectively, not proven, not guilty and guilty. James himself was not averse to exploiting the Massacre of Glencoe to call upon Scottish assistance for his restoration in 1692, which he intended to accomplish by returning to England with French backing. On the Whig side, this published call to arms was interpreted as endorsement from Saint-Germain for French-instigated endeavours to assassinate William, first in the spring of 1692 and subsequently in the winter of 1695.[19] Jacobite polemics remained focused on the disastrous events of William's reign and glossed over the failed assassination plots.[20]

---

[18] See 'The address of the provost, baillies, town council and citizens of Glasgow to King William and Queen Mary upon their majesty's accession to the throne, 1 Feb. 1690' in *Miscellany of the Maitland Club*, vol. III, pp. 59–61; John Whittel, *Constantinus Redivivus, or, A full account of the wonderful providences and unparallell'd successes that have all along attended the glorious enterprises of the heroical prince, William the 3rd, now King of Great Britain* (London, 1693); George Ridpath, *The Scots Episcopal Innocence* (London, 1694); Anon., *Britannia's Triumph* (London, 1697); [M]. Emeris, *A Panegyrick upon William II* (Edinburgh, 1699); Anon., *Advice to Great Britain &c. A Poem by a hearty Lover of his Country* (London, 1701).

[19] [James VII], *His Majesties most gracious declaration to his good people of his ancient kingdom of Scotland commanding their assistance against the Prince and Princess of Orange, and their adherents* (Edinburgh, 1692); Anon., *A True Account of the Horrid Conspiracy against the Life of His Sacred Majesty William III* (Edinburgh, 1692); Anon., *The art of assassinating kings taught Louis XIV and James II by the Jesuits* (London, 1696); Anon., *Impartial history of the plots and conspiracies against the life of King William III contrived by the devices of our enemies at the Court of France* (London, 1696); E. Howard, *A pastoral poem upon the discovery of a late horrid conspiracy against the sacred person of William III, King of England* (London, 1696); Richard Burton, *The history of the Kingdom of Scotland, containing an account of the original of that nation, and of the most remarkable transactions and revolutions during the reigns of seventy two kings and queens to the seventh year of William III* (London, 1696); Thomas Percival, *The Rye-house travestie, or, A true account and declaration of the horrid and execrable conspiracy against His Majesty King William III* (London, 1696); Sir Richard Blackmore, *A true and impartial history of the conspiracy against the person and government of King William III of glorious memory, in the year 1695* (London, 1723).

[20] A. I. Macinnes, 'William of Orange: Disaster for Scotland?' in E. Mijers & D. Onnekink, eds., *Redefining William III: The Impact of the King-Stadholder in its International Context* (Aldershot, 2007), pp. 201–23; P. Hopkins, *Glencoe and the End of the Highland War* (Edinburgh, 1986), pp. 38–50; W. Troost, *William III, the Stadholder-King: A Political*

In the course of these plots during the Nine Years' War and subsequently during the War of the Spanish Succession, Jacobites in Scotland seem to have adopted the cellular structure associated with resistance movements. Such a structure was rooted in the federative associations constructed according to the teachings of the early seventeenth-century German philosopher Johannes Althusius. This was actually put into practice by Covenanting activists engaged in a protest movement that depended on atomised rather than nationwide organisation in the Restoration era. Sustained by covert praying societies and open-field conventicles, the Covenanters staged episodic uprisings that involved the mobilisation of numbers between 4,000 and 14,000 – figures similar to the numbers that were to be mobilised through clandestine Jacobite plotting by nobles and gentry in support of French invasions.[21]

By the accession of Queen Anne, Jacobite plotting had an increasingly Scottish focus, partly on account of the claimed facility of Scottish Jacobites to raise the Highland clans and partly as a reflection on the increasing unpopularity of William of Orange in Scotland. Plots consistently featured Hamilton, and other politicians, deemed not amenable to direction from the English ministry, who came to be associated with the Duke in the Country Party from 1698.[22] In turn, their purported clandestine association with the French during the War of the Spanish Succession served as justification for the English ministry to countenance armed intervention in Scotland from 1703, as the latter struggled to come to terms with the legislative war instigated by the Scottish Estates' refusal to accept

---

Biography (Aldershot, 2005), pp. 273–6. William was not directly responsible for the massacre of the MacDonalds of Glencoe, a small Jacobite clan much addicted to banditry and erroneously tarnished as popish. However, he actively connived in their exemplary punishment on 13 February 1692, which was masterminded covertly by his Secretary of State for Scotland, Sir James Dalrymple, Master (later 1st Earl) of Stair, and effected with the full co-operation of the military high command in Scotland. William pardoned all involved in the massacre, rather than holding them to account for treason, after the mislaid orders for the massacre were published in the *Paris Gazette*.

[21] F. S. Carney, *The Politics of Johannes Althusius* (London, 1964), pp. 12–21; C. Kidd, 'Religious Realignment Between the Restoration and Union' in Robertson, ed., *A Union for Empire*, pp. 145–68; *Correspondence of Col. N. Hooke*, I, pp. 78–84, 372–428, and II, pp. 22–37, 88–93, 140–3, 230–9, 247–8. Clandestine activities of Jacobites in London were actually castigated as conventicles during the 1690s (Richard Ames, *The Jacobite Conventicle: A Poem* (London, 1692), as also in Glasgow in 1703 (NLS, Wodrow MSS, quarto lxxxii, fols. 91–2).

[22] NAS, Clerk of Penicuik Papers, GD 18/3123, and Bruce of Kinross Papers, GD 29/115; BL, The Scotch Plot, 1702–4, Papers of Simon Fraser, Lord Lovat, Add.MSS 31,250, fols. 1–3; BOU, Carte Papers: Nairn's Papers, vol. II (1689–1706), MS Carte 209/24, /26–7, /71; GCA, Hamilton of Barns Papers, TD 589/918; Anon., *An Historical Account of the Publick Transactions in Christendom. In a Letter to a Friend in the Country* (London, 1694); HL, Huntington Manuscripts, Manuscript Newsletters from London to Tamworth (1690–1704), HM 30,659/23, /30, /55–61, /65, /68, /70, /72, /77, /89.

250　Union and Empire

the Hanoverian Succession. However, the Scottish Jacobites and their associates within the Country Party preferred to exhaust parliamentary means to oppose Union rather than commit to an armed rising, a position sustained until the Union came into operation in May 1707.[23] The holding of extra-parliamentary activities in reserve was not necessarily a misguided strategy, nor a cowed response to the coercive pressures exercised by the English ministry, but a calculated risk based on the strength of their parliamentary position during the legislative war of 1703–5.

Religion and party

Jacobitism in all three kingdoms has been devalued by ready acceptance of Whig propaganda that property, Protestantism and progress, embedded into the constitutional settlements of 1689–91, stood as the bulwark against absolutism, Roman Catholicism and incivility. A re-reading of Scottish Jacobitism free from Whig polemics traces its roots to two interrelated factors, traditionalism and Episcopalianism. The dynastic appeal of Jacobitism was grounded in adherence to the hereditary principle of kingship. The royal house of Stuart was the rightful trustee of Scotland in the same way that Highland chiefs and Lowland heads of families were the customary protectors of their kindreds' patrimonies. Dynastic legitimacy was seen as the source of justice, the basis of government. Moreover, the lawful exercise of government and the maintenance of justice were imperiled by the sundering of genealogical continuity, first by William of Orange in 1689 and then by the prospect of the Hanoverian Succession. In vernacular poetry, Jacobitism was seen as a corrective to political, social and commercial deviations from custom. Jacobitism represented the maintenance of a divinely warranted tradition. However, vernacular

---

[23] *MGC*, I, pp. 197–8, 238–9, 265–6. BL: Negotiations of Col. Hooke in Scotland, 1705–7, Add.MSS 20,858, fols. 79–80, 143–4, 277; Sidney, 1st Earl of Godolphin: Official Correspondence, Home, 1701–10, Add.MSS 28,055, fols. 174–82; Hatton-Finch Papers: Letters to the Earl of Nottingham, Secretary of State, vol. II (1703–25), Add.MSS 29,589, fols. 45–6; BOU, Carte Papers – Nairn's Papers, vol. II (1689–1706), MS Carte 209/11, /50; *Portland*, IV, pp. 273–77, 307–9; Macpherson, *OP*, I, pp. 623–5; *Correspondence of Col. N. Hooke*, II, pp. 262–78. Strategically, the Jacobite plotters directly lifted the game plan adopted by the Covenanting Movement during the Bishops' Wars in 1640: to invade the northern English counties and cut off the coal supply from Newcastle to London. This strategy, first enunciated in 1692, was further refined after the establishment of the Bank of England two years later. By 1705, the strategy of invasion was intended to provoke a stop in English trade and thereby prevent the fiscal–military state supplying its allies with cash. Indeed, the stopping of the coal trade following the invasion of Newcastle would reputedly reduce London to such an extremity that its citizens would rise and sue for peace.

poets were essentially upholding the rightful trusteeship of the Stuarts, not their divine right as monarchs to suspend or dispense with laws.[24]

Traditional support for an organic rather than a contractual polity was reinforced by hierarchical religion. Although the exiled Stuarts consistently promised to maintain Protestantism with parliamentary approval in both Scotland and England, the use of his prerogative powers by James VII & II to set aside penal laws against Roman Catholics was instrumental in his removal from the three kingdoms. However, the cry of Protestantism in danger from the combined forces of the papacy and universal monarchy no longer carried the same political resonance in the British Isles that had fanned the flames of revolution during the Thirty Years' War. The superseding of Habsburg Spain by Bourbon France meant that universal monarchy was no longer in step with the papacy, particularly as Louis XIV promoted Gallican autonomy as a counter to the Ultramontane centralising authority of Rome. James VII & II's favouring of Gallicanism had alienated the papacy and opened up fault-lines among British Catholics. The leading Scottish Catholic, George Gordon, 1st Duke of Gordon, had acquiesced in the Revolution rather than take a stand against William of Orange.[25]

In marked contrast to the situation in Ireland, Roman Catholicism was a minority pursuit in Scotland, even more so than in England. Excluded from parliament, Catholics had a peripheral impact on the political process after the Revolution. Of the 153 nobles eligible to attend the Scottish Estates that Queen Anne summoned for May 1703, only Gordon and another 6 were denied seats as papists. Never the focal point of Jacobite plotting in Scotland, their committed opposition to the abjuration of the royal house in favour of the Hanoverian Succession was taken for granted; but it should not be presumed that they would all have accepted the party line coming from Saint-Germain and opposed political incorporation.[26]

---

[24] HL, Bridgewater & Ellesmere MSS, EL 8770; Alexander Bruce, *A Discourse of a Cavalier Gentleman on the Divine and Human Law, with respect to the Succession* (1706); A. I. Macinnes, *Clanship, Commerce and the House of Stuart*, pp. 188–9; M. G. H. Pittock, *Inventing and Resisting Britain: Cultural Identities in Britain and Ireland, 1685–1789* (Basingstoke, 1997), pp. 108–18.

[25] HL, Bridgewater & Ellesmere MSS, EL 9882; S. Pincus, 'The European Catholic Context of the Revolution of 1688–89: Gallicanism, Innocent XI, and Catholic Opposition' in Macinnes & Williamson, eds., *Shaping the Stuart World*, pp. 79–114.

[26] BOU, Carte Papers – Nairn's Papers, vol. II (1689–1706), MS Carte 209/50, and Carte Papers (1701–19), MS Carte 180/21, /146. In addition to the 7 excluded papists, 14 minors were not eligible to attend, 8 titles were dormant, 16 Englishmen with Scottish titles were absent, as were 26 Scottish peers, leaving 82 nobles in attendance. Of the 3 Catholics who publicly renounced their faith in 1703 in order to participate in the Scottish Estates, only Francis Sempill, Lord Sempill of Glassford, consistently opposed political incorporation. John Meldrum of Urquhart, a burgh commissioner for Dornoch,

More pragmatic than his father in his approach to Gallicanism, James VIII & III remained a staunch Catholic. He reportedly refused suggestions from the Court Party, who sent Lord Belhaven to Paris for three months in 1701, that he should declare himself a Protestant to pave the way for his own succession instead of the Hanoverians'. Although the exiled Stuarts' Catholicism remained a powerful propaganda tool against them throughout their former British and American dominions, their principled refusal to sacrifice their faith for political advantage stiffened the resolve of Episcopalians, as well as Catholics, in Scotland not to be reconciled to the Presbyterian Kirk.[27]

The confessional allegiance of Scottish Jacobites, especially in the heartlands of the Highlands and the north-east, was overwhelmingly Protestant, but Episcopalian. Under episcopal direction, the inculcation of non-resistance and passive obedience from the pulpit bolstered support for James as Duke of Albany & York and later as James VII & II in the 1680s. Throughout all three kingdoms, advocates of non-resistance, particularly from the Exclusion Crisis, became identified with the Tories and those of limited monarchy with the Whigs. Yet both the Tories and Whigs in England, and among the English interest in Ireland, had supported the Revolution. The Tories, however, had sought to justify the armed overthrowing of James without recourse to Whig arguments that he had broken his contract with his people. Tories in England had contented themselves with the fiction that James had deserted his throne and were reassured by the émigré Scottish Whig, Gilbert Burnet, Bishop of Salisbury, that the principle of non-resistance applied only to executive power, not to the total subversion of government. However, as James had never visited Ireland before the Revolution, he could hardly be held to have deserted a country in which he was to fight personally in a war of reclamation. William King, Bishop of Derry, persuasively claimed that resistance was justified when submission to tyranny was more dangerous to the body politic than war, as was evident from James's intended destruction of Protestantism for the benefit of his co-religionists in Ireland. In Scotland, Episcopalians argued that they, not the nonconforming Presbyterians, had the right to resist arbitrary monarchy and that the forfeiture of James for tyrannical actions did not justify the religious change brought about by the Whigs through the Claim of Right. On the distinctly erastian and dubious grounds that they no longer commanded the

and George Ogilvy, Lord Banff, allied with the Court Party in favour of Union, albeit the latter held out for an inducement of £11 2s (£122 Scots) before journeying to Edinburgh for the critical session of 1706–7 (*APS*, XI, pp. 40, 48, 305, 313–15, 404–8; A. I. Macinnes, 'Catholic Recusancy and the Penal Laws, 1603–1707', *RSCHS*, 12 (1987), pp. 27–63).

[27] NAS, Clerk of Penicuik Papers, GD18/3123.

confessional allegiance of the majority of Scots, the Episcopalian clergy had been ousted from the Kirk in favour of the Presbyterians. Thus, Episcopalians could claim to be freed of all obligations to William of Orange by his overthrowing of the establishment in the Kirk, the only instance of this occurring in the three kingdoms at the Revolution. Tories in Scotland, therefore, predominantly identified with Jacobitism.[28]

However, a minority of Episcopalians, particularly career-minded politicians such as the Earl of Cromartie and some merchants engaged in the colonial trade, were prepared to seek an accommodation first with William of Orange and then Queen Anne in order to secure religious toleration. Led by the arrogant and avaricious John Paterson, Archbishop of Glasgow, these Episcopalians, who became known as 'the jurors', avoided direct association with Jacobitism and from 1703 actively lobbied Queen Anne for her protection and material assistance in return for prayers for her preservation. Paterson and his associates argued that, in parishes where most if not all of the landowners and inhabitants were Episcopalian, their clergy should be allowed openly to preach and administer the sacraments in meeting houses, a concession which would not threaten the Presbyterian Kirk's right to exact stipends for their ministers or force them to give up their control of parish churches. Paterson, who was comfortable with the prospect of political incorporation, claimed widespread support in Fife as well as north of the Tay.[29] However, the vast majority of Episcopalians, led by Alexander Rose, Bishop of Edinburgh, consistently refused to abjure the exiled Stuarts as the rightful royal authority. Having rejected an accommodation with the Presbyterian establishment in 1695, they, no less than the Roman Catholic community, were subject to penal laws.[30]

Paterson and Rose had presented a united front after the accession of Queen Anne in lobbying for a nationwide collection to relieve the suffering of the Episcopal clergy denied funding from the state and with no external means of support. But they made separate overtures to Court

---

[28] Macinnes, *Clanship, Commerce and the House of Stuart*, pp. 173–7; T. Harris, 'Incompatible Revolutions? The Established Church and the Revolutions of 1688–9 in Ireland, England and Scotland' in Macinnes & Ohlmeyer, eds., *The Stuart Kingdoms*, pp. 204–25.
[29] T. Clarke, 'The Williamite Episcopalians and the Glorious Revolution in Scotland', *RSCHS*, 24 (1999), pp. 33–51; NLS, Wodrow MSS, folio xxxv, fols. 67, 74; NAS, Mar & Kellie Collection, GD 124/15/279/4, /414/26; *LP*, I, pp. 84–5; [Sinclair], *Some Thoughts on the present State of Affairs*.
[30] B. Lenman, 'The Scottish Episcopal Clergy and the Ideology of Jacobitism' in E. Cruickshanks, ed., *Ideology and Conspiracy: Aspects of Jacobitism, 1689–1759* (Edinburgh, 1982), pp. 36–48; Pittock, *Inventing and Resisting Britain*, pp. 42–4; HL, Huntington Manuscripts, Manuscript Newsletters from London to Tamworth (1690–1704), HM 30,659/15, /19, /21, /62, /64, /66.

in 1703, with the latter claiming that a portion of the episcopal rents appropriated to the Crown at the Revolution should be laid aside for Episcopalian relief. No promises were made either to give up Jacobitism or to support moves towards Union. Queen Anne was not unsympathetic towards relief scaled to clerical rank and she did instruct the Scottish Privy Council to exercise discretion over services held in Episcopalian meeting houses. She did not concede or seek to impose toleration. Her willingness to accord some licence, to those willing to live submissively, towards the Presbyterian establishment was tested in Glasgow in March 1703. A group of prominent Episcopalians, having demanded the protection of dragoons because of disruption to a previous meeting in January, flaunted the open profession of their faith within earshot of Presbyterian congregations. The difficulties encountered by the Presbyterians in establishing themselves in the Jacobite heartlands had enabled non-juring priests to remain in their parishes long after the Revolution. Presbyterian ministers attempting to take over parochial charges were subjected to rabbling organised with the approval of the landed elite. The Kirk, usually through its general assembly, did counter-attack by encouraging presbyteries, as district courts, to bring civil actions to remove non-juring clergy from parishes within their bounds. But selective prosecutions were sporadic rather than sustained. Though making much of Episcopalians 'as friends of the French interest', the Kirk tended to discriminate discreetly rather than fulminate publicly, given the episcopal polity of the Anglican establishment in England and the professed sympathy for Scottish Episcopalians by such leading clerics as William Nicolson, bishop of Carlisle.[31]

The Kirk had further reasons to be cautious. The juring Episcopalians pressing for toleration tended to identify with the Court Party, while non-jurors sided not only with the Jacobites but also with the wider confederated opposition in the Country Party. This latter association was particularly appealing to the younger generation of Jacobites such as George Lockhart of Carnwath, alienated by William of Orange's purported misgovernance of Scotland. Indeed, the prospect of imposing constitutional limitations on monarchy, though problematic for Saint-Germain no less than Queen Anne in the course of the legislative

---

[31] HL, Loudoun Scottish Collection, box 16/LO 7017, box 18/LO 8327, 8333, 8351, and box 42/LO 9345, 9347; DH, Loudoun Papers, unmarked green deed box, bundle 1706/Lord Advocate; NLS, Wodrow MSS, quarto xxviii, 150–3; Orkney Archives, Kirkwall, Town Council Minute Book, 1691–1732, fols. 90–1; *LDN*, p. 135; *LQA*, pp. 113–14, 119, 182–3; GCA, Records of the Maxwells of Pollock, T-PM/109/91, /98; *Laing*, pp. 140–1; *Mar & Kellie*, pp. 264–7. Bishop Rose was also prepared to lobby support from Thomas Tenison, Archbishop of Canterbury, to ensure payments from the royal bounty for Scottish Episcopalians in the run-up to Union (*ibid.*, pp. 142–4).

war, allowed Jacobites as Cavaliers to play more subtle cards than plotting and extra-parliamentary protest. The willingness of Jacobites to promote limitations but not necessarily contractual restrictions on the Stuarts on their return from exile can be traced back to James Graham, 1st Marquess of Montrose and hero of the Royalist campaigns in Scotland for Charles I during the 1640s. Montrose, who had initially supported the binding restrictions on monarchy imposed by the Covenanting Movement in Scotland, came to advocate the maintenance of a constitutional equilibrium in which parliament would be a safeguard, not a permanent check on monarchy – sentiments whose supporters were to resurface in England in the guise of constitutional Royalists and later as Jacobite Whigs.[32] A similar sentiment in favour of a constitutional equilibrium was expressed by Hamilton (then Earl of Arran) during his forlorn endeavours to prevent the replacement of James VII & II by William of Orange in January 1689. Jacobitism, in turn, became attractive to constitutional reformers disillusioned by the Revolution settlement established in Scotland. Thus, Sir James Montgomerie of Skelmorlie, a noted colonial entrepreneur in South Carolina and leader of the Club pressing for radical constitutional change in 1689–90, had become a Jacobite plotter against William of Orange.

As Hamilton struggled to hold together the confederated opposition during the legislative war, Andrew Fletcher of Saltoun, who drew inspiration from the Club, emerged as the forthright spokesman of the constitutional reformers. Although Fletcher of Saltoun actually wished to return to Covenanting limitations on monarchy as achieved in 1640–1, he drew support from prominent Jacobites such as Charles Hay, 13th Earl of Errol, and William Keith, 9th Earl Marischal.[33] Notwithstanding the tensions provoked by the enigmatic Hamilton's leadership of the opposition, Charles Home, 6th Earl of Home, largely kept strains among Jacobites about the future exercise of prerogative powers in check. However, his death in 1706 laid bare the rivalries between Hamilton and John

---

[32] BL, Hanover State Papers, vol. 1 (1692–1706), Stowe MS 222, fo. 216; Macinnes, *The British Revolution*, p. 137; D. L. Smith, *Constitutional Royalism and the Search for Settlement, c. 1640–1649* (Cambridge, 1994), pp. 39–80; M. Goldie, 'John Locke's Circle and James II', *HJ*, 35 (1992), pp. 557–86; Szechi, 'Constructing a Jacobite'.

[33] HL, Loudoun Scottish Collection, box 30/LO 8973, box 37/LO 9085–6, 9088–9; P. A. Hopkins, 'Sir James Montgomerie of Skelmorlie' in Cruickshanks & Corp, eds., *The Stuart Court in Exile and the Jacobites*, pp. 39–59; J. R. Young, 'The Scottish Parliament and the Covenanting Heritage of Constitutional Reform' in Macinnes & Ohlmeyer, eds., *The Stuart Kingdoms*, pp. 226–50; Macinnes, 'Influencing the Vote'. So strong was this association that Fletcher of Saltoun was interned with the same earls and other leading Jacobites once the attempted invasion of Scotland ordered by Louis XIV in 1708 was launched.

Murray, 1st Duke of Atholl, a former careerist politician, lukewarm to the Revolution, which many of his family, friends and tenants had opposed. Atholl, despite his rumoured plotting, made no sustained endeavour to lay claim to Jacobite loyalties until all prospects of office had vanished by 1704.[34]

Links between Jacobitism (in the guise of Cavaliers) and constitutional reform proved not only problematic for the Court in exile at Saint-Germain but also for the Kirk, which was itself divided. A conservative grouping associated with William Carstares, Principal of Edinburgh University, supported the erastian nature of the Revolution settlement in Scotland and favoured the Court Party. As erastians, they had a distinctly more relaxed stance on toleration that was anathema to the more radical grouping galvanised by the likes of Robert Wylie, minister in the town of Hamilton in Lanarkshire, who upheld Covenanting claims for the autonomy of the Kirk and favoured the Country Party. Carstares preferred closet lobbying of English ministers and prominent Presbyterians in the Court Party such as the Earls of Marchmont and Loudoun.[35] But Wylie, with strong backing from Anne, Duchess of Hamilton, believed in mobilising grass-roots support and acting as a pressure group. Wylie worked in tandem with the émigré polemicists Hodges and Ridpath, in drawing on the opinions of two lord advocates – Sir John Nisbet and Sir George MacKenzie, in their response to the abortive Union negotiations of 1670 – that parliament could not alter the fundamental constitution of Scotland to bring about either the Hanoverian Succession or political incorporation without the consent of the people, as expressed through a general election.[36]

---

[34] D. Szechi, *George Lockhart of Carnwath, 1681–1731: A Study in Jacobitism* (East Linton, 2002), pp. 46–70; *LP*, I, pp. 72–4, 158; *MSSM*, pp. 114–15; *MGC*, I, p. 131; P. H. Brown, *The Union of England and Scotland*, pp. 155–73.

[35] *SPC*, pp. 713–14, 717, 719, 721, 739–41, 749–53; *Portland*, VIII, pp. 103–7, 113, 150, 250–1.

[36] Robert Wylie, *A Speech Without Doors, concerning toleration* (Edinburgh, 1703), and *A Letter Concerning the Union, with Sir George Mackenzie's observation and Sir John Nisbet's opinion upon the same subject* (1706). NLS, Wodrow MSS: folio xxv, fols. 71–2, 112–13, 137–8; quarto xvi, fols. 157–66; quarto xl, fols. 71–2; quarto lxxv, fo. 138; quarto lxxxii, fols. 49–51. The radical minister from Lanark, John Bannatyne, in *A Letter from a Presbyterian Minister in the Countrey, to a Member of Parliament; and also of the Commission of the Church concerning toleration and patronages* (Edinburgh, 1703) and *Some Queries Proposed to Consideration, relative to the union now intended* (Edinburgh, 1706), vociferously condemned toleration as a breach of the Claim of Right and argued that it would be the thin end of the wedge to bring in patronage upholding the rights of landed proprietors over their congregations. The radicals were particularly aggrieved that the Covenanting Movement had condemned the Britannic Engagement of 1648, which advocated political incorporation, yet the erastians were prepared to argue for a Union which condemned to the flames any prospect of an autonomous, Covenanted Kirk and a godly State.

The radicals could also call on extra-parliamentary support from militant Cameronians in the south-west of Scotland – now led by John MacMillan, minister of Balmaghie – and a sectarian splinter known as the Hebronites who followed John Hebron, minister of Urr, who even became implicated in Jacobite plotting by 1706.[37] Notwithstanding Daniel Defoe's claims to the contrary as an English dissenter, the radicals could also draw on testimony from ministers in the American colonies and from congregations in Ulster and the north of England, especially from Newcastle which claimed to be the largest congregation for the Scottish diaspora, that the Church of England at home and abroad was not sympathetic to Presbyterianism – a situation that was not expected to change in the event of Union.[38]

In England, Tory-instigated parliamentary divisions on occasional conformity by dissenters, as well as on threats to the national church, proved a clear indicator of party politics that intensified as the Whigs secured control of both houses in the run-up to Union.[39] Toleration for Episcopalians and the preservation of Presbyterianism were not clearly defined party issues in the Scottish Estates. However, religion did have a pronounced party impact in relation to rights of resistance exercised by the political nation against the monarchy. Since the Reformation in the mid sixteenth century, the claimed right to resist an ungodly monarchy clearly differentiated the reception of Calvinism between Scotland and England, a difference perpetuated by first the National Covenant of 1638 and then the Solemn League and Covenant of 1643, which extended this right to the imposition of fundamental limitations on the monarchy in Kirk and State.[40] Although this right was essentially secularised through the Claim of Right in 1689, the Revolution underscored the Scottish preference for a written constitution that prescribed the fundamentals of governance.

---

[37] *Laing*, pp. 101–9; BL, Blenheim Papers, vol. DXXI, Add.MSS 61,631, fo. 18; [ker], *The Memoirs of John Ker of Kersland*, pp. 12–92.

[38] *Scotland and the Americas, c. 1650 – c. 1939*, pp. 254–5; *Journal of the Commons House of Assembly of South Carolina*, XIV (1706), pp. 5–8, 10, and XV (1706–7), p. 15; NLS, Wodrow MSS, folio xxv, fo. 135; Anon., *A Narrative of a New and Unusual American Imprisonment of Two Presbyterian Ministers and prosecution of Mr Francis Makemie. One of them, for preaching one Sermon at the City of New York* (1707); Daniel Defoe, *The Dissenters in England vindicated from some reflections in a late pamphlet, entituled, Lawful prejudices, &c.* (Edinburgh, 1707); James Webster, *Lawful Prejudices Against an Incorporating Union with England* (Edinburgh, 1707); D. Macree, 'Daniel Defoe, the Church of Scotland, and the Union of 1707', *Eighteenth Century Studies*, 7 (1973), pp. 62–77.

[39] *A Complete Collection of the Protests made in the House of Lords*, pp. 142–7; Scuirty & Dewar, *Divisions in the House of Lords*, for session 1702–3 to session 1706–7; Wodrow MSS, folio xxviii, fols. 199–200; Hayton, 'Introductory Survey' to *The Commons 1690–1715*, pp. 222–7, 454–8, 462–6.

[40] Mason, *Kingship and Commonweal*, pp. 139–64; Macinnes, *The British Revolution*, pp. 111–51.

In the course of the legislative war, rival interpretations of the Claim of Right led to the conservative defence of the Revolution settlement by the Court Party and to radical pressure for further limitations from the Country Party, particularly as the English preference for succession through the Lutheran house of Hanover would move the monarchy even further from the Reformed tradition.[41]

Limiting the prerogative

Religious issues appeared to be the most divisive ones from the outset of the Scottish parliament on 6 May 1703. Queensberry, with support from Seafield, Cromartie (then Viscount Tarbat) and Atholl (then Lord Tullibardine) had taken advantage of differences between the Presbyterians and Jacobites during the preceding general election to gain the support of Home and his Cavalier associates. In return for them confirming the queen's right and title to rule Scotland, accepting the legality of the 1702 parliamentary session following William of Orange's death and granting supply to the armed forces, Jacobite exiles were granted an indemnity to return home, financial support was promised for the Episcopalian clergy and leave was given to bring in an overture for toleration. This accommodation was short-lived. Queensberry came under pressure from the erastian Presbyterians in the Court Party, led by Marchmont, to ratify both the Claim of Right and the existing establishment in the Kirk, measures which made it treasonable to contest not only the queen's accession but also the Presbyterian establishment. The coalition promptly sundered when the Cavaliers' overture for toleration failed after a strong admonition from the Commission of the Kirk – charged with overseeing ecclesiastical affairs between the annual

---

[41] Kidd, *Subverting Scotland's Past*, pp. 39–41; Sir John Clerk of Penicuik, *A Short Essay upon the Limitations to prove that they are so far from being of consequence to the nation, that they may tend very much to its prejudice* (Edinburgh, 1703); John Hamilton, Lord Belhaven, *A Speech in Parliament touching limitations* (Edinburgh, 1703); Fletcher of Saltoun, *Speeches by a Member of Parliament*; George Ridpath, *An Historical Account of the Antient Rights and Power of the Parliament of Scotland* (Edinburgh, 1703); James Hodges, *The Rights and Interests of the two British Monarchies, inquir'd into and clear'd; with a special respect to an united or separate state. Treatise I* (London, 1703); Anon., *A Speech Without Doors anent the giving a subsidy before the passing of an Act of Security* (Edinburgh, 1704); Anon., *A Speech Intended to have been Spoken in Parliament by a Member who was necessarily absent* (Edinburgh, 1705); George MacKenzie, Earl of Cromartie, *An Abstract of what was spoke in Parliament by E. C.* (1705), and *A Friendly Return to a letter concerning Sir George Mackenzie's and Sir John Nisbet's Observation on the matter of Union* (1706); Anon., *The Smoaking Flax Unquenchable*; Anon., *An Answer to Some Queries &c Relative to the Union: in a Conference betwixt the Coffee Master and A Country Farmer* (1706); Anon., *The Scotch Echo to the English legion: or, The Union in Danger, from the Principles of some Old and Modern Whigs in both Nations, about the Power of Parliaments* (Edinburgh, 1707).

general assemblies – that any concession to Episcopalianism would threaten the Presbyterian establishment. Hamilton took advantage of this disunity to bring back almost all the Cavaliers into the Country Party to pursue a programme to redress the interference of English ministers in Scottish affairs, to promote the probity and accountability of Scottish officials and judges, and to defend the acclaimed rights and liberties of Scotland.[42] This programme, which caught the English ministry off guard and initiated the legislative war, ironically took inspiration from the Act of Settlement of 1701, which unilaterally proclaimed the Hanoverian Succession. In the process, the Act had proposed limitations on absentee monarchy and on votes cast in the House of Commons by placemen on the government payroll.[43]

There were two key Acts restricting the prerogative powers of the monarchy. The first was the Act anent Peace and War which laid claim not so much to an independent foreign policy as to a binding commitment on Queen Anne's successor, if the common monarchy continued, to gain consent from the Scottish Estates before any war could be declared. Although the sovereign was to be free to take all requisite measures to suppress any insurrection or repel invasion from abroad, any treaties for peace, alliance or commerce also required ratification by the Estates. This desire to prevent a repetition of the dubious dealings by which the English ministry manoeuvred the Scots into the War of the Spanish Succession was also a feature of the second measure, the Act of Security. In this case, however, the presumption was made that the common monarchy would not continue unless, prior to the death of Queen Anne, 'there be condicions of government settled and enacted' which recognised: the honour and sovereignty of the separate crown and kingdom; the freedom, frequency and power of parliaments; and that the religion, liberty and trade of the nation should not be subject to English or any foreign interference. As these conditions were to be in place during the queen's lifetime, they applied not to her successor but to the English ministry. The Scottish Estates were seeking not so much a self-denying ordinance from the English parliament as a communication of trade secured by a federative union. They were insistent on their right to elect for

---

[42] *LP*, I, pp. 51–69; Crossrigg, *DPP*, pp. 95–109; BOU, Carte Papers – Nairn's Papers, vol. II (1689–1706), MS Carte 209/50; P. W. J. Riley, 'The Formation of the Scottish Ministry of 1703', *SHR*, 44 (1965), pp. 112–34.

[43] Macpherson, *OP*, I, pp. 612–19; *ACS*, I, pp. 203–8; *Buccleuch*, p. 663; BL, Sidney, 1st Earl of Godolphin: Official Correspondence, Home, 1701–10, Add.MSS 28,055, fo. 5; NLS, Wodrow MSS, quarto lxxxii, fols. 92–6; HL, Huntington Manuscripts, Manuscript Newsletters from London to Tamworth (1690–1704), HM 30,659/86; Smith, *A History of the Modern British Isles*, pp. 316–17. The Act of 1701 debarred not only the exiled royal house, but a total of fifty-seven Stuart descendants of James I with prior claims.

themselves a hereditary successor from the Stuart line, provided he or she was Protestant, on the twentieth day following Anne's death. Moreover, the new sovereign was committed, within thirty days if resident in Britain or within three months if resident overseas, to accept the limitations prescribed in the coronation oath and any further limitations imposed by the Scottish Estates up to Anne's death and in the twenty days thereafter. To distance themselves further from the English fiscal–military state, all able-bodied men who were Protestants were to be equipped, trained and mobilised as a national militia.[44]

In an attempt to regain control of the parliamentary agenda, the Court Party had promoted a Wine Act that maintained French links despite the current English trade embargo, a measure which both legitimised the current smuggling operations of Scottish commercial networks and brought in money to the customs. While Queensberry, as the queen's commissioner, was prepared to accept the Act anent Peace and War, he deferred giving consent to the Act of Security until he received fresh instructions from London. Notwithstanding a willingness among her English ministry to pass both Acts with a view to rescinding them in a later session, Anne emphatically rejected what she deemed the exorbitant demands of the Scots. Before formal withholding of consent was received, Marchmont endeavoured to facilitate the Hanoverian Succession. But an Abjuration Act disowning the exiled royal family was peremptorily thrown out. The rejection of this measure, which would have brought Scotland into line with England, stood in stark contrast to the wave of British patriotism that had led to Protestant oaths of association abjuring the exiled house, in Scotland as well as England, following the failed assassination plot of 1695.[45] Darien, the dubious manoeuvring of Scotland into the War of the Spanish Succession and, indeed, the failed negotiation of union as a Scottish initiative at the outset of 1703 had taken their political toll. Patriotism now wore a distinctively Scottish guise, with Fletcher of Saltoun singularly deploying his eloquence against the insidious influence of the English ministry. Once the Estates were notified that royal consent was withheld, they declined to vote supply for the Scottish forces in the standing army. Parliament was duly prorogued on 16 September.[46]

---

[44] *APS*, XI, pp. 101–2, 107 c.6, 112, 136 c.3; *A Source Book of Scottish History*, III, pp. 472–7.

[45] HL, Huntington Manuscripts, Manuscript Newsletters from London to Tamworth (1690–1704), HM 30,659/57, /60, /66–7, /88; ACA, Aberdeen Council Register, 57 (1681–1704), p. 513; GCA, Records of the Maxwells of Pollock, T-PM/109/80, /89, 97; Crossrigg, *DPP*, pp. 112–36; *Laing*, pp. 10–41; *A Complete Collection of the Protests made in the House of Lords*, pp. 132–4.

[46] Ridpath, *PPS*; BL, Sidney, 1st Earl of Godolphin: Official Correspondence, Home, 1701–10, Add.MSS 28,055, fols. 7–8, 300–2, and Hatton-Finch Papers: Letters to the Earl of

In the immediate aftermath of the parliament, Queensberry sought to shore up the position of the Court Party by having eight peers promoted (including Tarbat, becoming Earl of Cromartie, and Tullibardine, becoming Duke of Atholl) and four gentry elevated to the peerage. At the same time, the Cavaliers agreed, in response to overtures from Seafield, Cromartie and Atholl, that they and Alexander Montgomery, 9th Earl of Eglinton, should repair to London to mend fences with the English ministry and the Court.[47] However, as forewarned by Stair, Queen Anne, no less than the English ministry, was concerned about the threat posed to the prerogative powers of the monarchy by legislation for limitations in the Scottish Estates, not just because they created a precedent for similar encroachments in the English parliament but because they left the door open to the restoration of the royal house in exile should James, Prince of Wales, convert to Protestantism. Heightened suspicions that Scotland was the back door to an invasion from France were strengthened with the revelations of the putative 'Scotch Plot' whereby Queen Anne was to be replaced by her half-brother with armed assistance from Louis XIV. As these revelations occurred during the visit of the four peers to London and as Atholl was implicated, along with Hamilton, the first casualty of the Plot was the putative accommodation between the Court Party and the Cavaliers.[48]

The Plot was essentially a fabrication of Simon Fraser of Beaufort, a wholly disreputable individual convicted of treason in his absence in 1698 for attempting to acquire the vacant title and estates of the Lord Lovat and the chiefship of Clan Fraser by kidnap, rape, forgery, fraud and extortion. The Court at Saint-Germain initially resisted his deployment as an agent in Scotland, but, after Beaufort turned Roman Catholic on escaping from Scotland into exile in France, he managed to ingratiate

---

Nottingham, Secretary of State, vol. II (1703–25), Add.MSS 29,589, fols. 97, 107–8; NLS, Wodrow MSS, folio xxv, fo. 87; RC, TKUA, England, Akter og Dokumenter nedr Sofart og Handel: Order med Bilag, 1703, A.III/ 207/45, /46, /50, /55–7, /59, /61–3, /65–7. Rosenkrantz, the Danish envoy, actually had the Act anent Peace and War and the Act of Security translated into French and despatched to the royal court at Copenhagen.

[47] *LP*, I, pp. 70–1, 77–94; BOU, Carte Papers (1701–19), MS Carte 180/146. The new patents for peerages were not entirely a political gesture as the Marquess of Douglas, then a minor, was made a duke. Stair and Archibald Primrose, Viscount Rosebery, who were upgraded to earls, were all stalwarts of the Court Party, as was George Boyle, Lord Boyle, who became Earl of Glasgow; so ostensibly were the four gentry created peers, James Steward of Bute as Earl of Bute and Charles Hope of Hopeton as Earl of Hopeton, John Crawford of Kilbirnie as Viscount Garnock and Sir James Primrose of Carrington as Viscount Primrose. However, Bute, Garnock and Primrose did not remain affiliated to the Court in the run-up to Union.

[48] HL, Loudoun Scottish Collection, box 20/LO 9532–3, 9535–7; RC, TKUA, England, Akter og Dokumenter nedr Sofart og Handel: Order med Bilag, 1703–4, A.III/ 207/67, /208/71, /84 and /209/1–2, /10, /17, /20, /27–8.

himself at the Court of Louis XIV at Versailles through the patronage of Cardinal Francesco Gualterio, the papal nuncio. Despite justifiable scepticism at Versailles about Beaufort's claims to be able to mobilise the Highland clans, the Jacobite Court was prevailed upon to support Beaufort's exploratory mission to Scotland. However, they insisted that he was accompanied by a minder, Sir James Murray, who was able to take advantage of the indemnity to Scottish Jacobites to return with Beaufort, via England, during the parliamentary session of 1703. Beaufort made contact with Queensberry who, though extremely doubtful of the agent's sincerity, was certainly intrigued by his purported contacts. Hamilton was a ready target, not only for his leadership of the Country Party, but for his long-suspected association with Saint-Germain. Atholl was viewed as a potential political rival whom Queensberry was not averse to discrediting. As the brother of the Dowager Lady Lovat whom Beaufort had raped, Atholl was instrumental in bringing capital charges and continued to seek judicial redress once he learned of the agent's presence in Scotland. Queensberry had financed and twice given passes to Beaufort to allow him to travel unmolested to the Highlands to take soundings from clan chiefs and thereafter to travel back to England to make contacts with Jacobite networks among the London Scots. Queensberry had also procured from Nottingham other passes under false names to allow Beaufort to make his escape to the continent once his clandestine activities in London were discovered.[49]

Beaufort's scheming was actually exposed by Robert Ferguson. A prolific polemicist, he had earned the soubriquet of 'the plotter' on switching his allegiance from the Whigs to become embroiled in the attempted assassination of William of Orange in 1695, when he was actually subjected to a judicial examination by the future Duke of Atholl. Ferguson made contact with Atholl when he arrived in London with the delegation of the four peers in October 1703. Atholl duly exposed Queensberry's complicity before Queen Anne. Intercepted letters from Beaufort back to his former associates in London proved particularly incriminating. Although revelations of the Plot were also made to members of the

---

[49] BL, The Scotch Plot, 1702–4, Papers of Simon Fraser, Lord Lovat, Add.MSS 31,249, fols. 17, 19–22, 26–7, 29–30, and Add.MSS 31,250, fols. 1–3; NLS, Wodrow MSS, folio xxv, fols. 89–90; *SC*, pp. 367–8; Macpherson, *OP*, I, pp. 666–9. Cromartie, a longstanding antagonist of Beaufort's social aspirations in the Highlands, was also initially targeted by Queensberry as a potential political rival. Cromartie, however, was merely guilty of political ambition not Jacobite plotting. The only chief from whom Beaufort elicited support was Robert Stewart of Appin whose clan was among the most consistent Jacobite stalwarts in Scotland but not in the first rank in terms of territorial interest. Stewart's estate was located in Argyllshire, dominated by the Clan Campbell, whose chief until 1703 was Archibald, 1st Duke of Argyll and patron of Fraser of Beaufort.

Scottish Privy Council then in London, it was their English counterparts who commenced an investigation into Beaufort and his associates with a committee drawn from both Whigs and Tories and including Nottingham as well as Godolphin. In the interim, Sir James Murray had exposed Beaufort as a fraud at Saint-Germain. Claims that he had been turned by Queensberry to act as his agent in France led to Beaufort's imprisonment in the Bastille and served as a cautionary reminder for Saint-Germain only to employ agents who could be assured of the trust of leading Scottish Jacobites who also endorsed Murray's report on Beaufort.[50]

By December, the House of Lords decided to intervene and take control of an investigation that appeared more intent on damage limitation for the ministries in Scotland and England than holding those incriminated to account. A committee of seven lords, all leading Whigs, with the newest member of the party Junto, Charles Spencer, 3rd Earl of Sunderland, to the fore, proceeded not only to investigate the associates of Beaufort based in London but also called to account, without prior clearance from the Scottish Privy Council, contacts Beaufort had made within the military establishment in Scotland. The committee was also instrumental in instigating the prosecution, conviction and actual banishment abroad of David Lindsay, who was at best peripheral to the plot but was seized when returning to Scotland via England on the strength of the Jacobite indemnity which the Lords refused to recognise. This intrusive insensitivity was compounded by an address to the queen claiming that leading Scottish politicians were undoubtedly implicated in plotting, which provoked another bitter round of Anglo-Scottish tensions.[51] Within Scotland, the conduct of the Lords cemented the accord between the Country Party and the Cavaliers, albeit the alliance of Hamilton and Atholl remained uneasy. At the same time, Queensberry's involvement was exploited by

---

[50] BOU, Carte Papers (1701–19), MS Carte 180/11; Macpherson, *OP*, I, pp. 641–56, 663–5, 669–72; *A Collection of Original Papers about the Scots Plot* (1704), part I, pp. 4–5, 7–61; Anon., *An Account of the Scotch Plot in a Letter from a Gentleman in the City to his Friend in the Country* (London, 1704). Simon Fraser of Beaufort, returning to Scotland prior to the Jacobite rising in 1715, secured the title of Lord Lovat on siding with the Whig ministry. He was duly convicted of treason (the only person to be so prosecuted successfully in Scotland and England) and executed in 1747 for his involvement in the last major Jacobite rising in 1745.

[51] BL, Papers of Cardinal F. A. Gualterio; Letters of Queen Mary of Modena and the Princess Louisa 1701–18, Maria, Add.MSS 20,293, fols. 16–17; HL, Loudoun Scottish Collection, box 20/Lo 9532, /Lo 9536–7; ICA, Argyll Papers, bundle 17/3; *Burnet's HHOT*, pp. 746–50; *A Complete Collection of all the Protests made in the House of Lords*, pp. 139–40; *A Collection of Original Papers about the Scots Plot*, part II, pp. 1–22, 32–40, 49–87. Among the London Scots questioned was Thomas Keith, an agent for the Country Party (PRO, Secretaries of State: State Papers Scotland, series 1, 1683–1783, SP 54/1/19–20).

a group drawn mainly from the Country Party, led by Roxburghe, John Leslie, 9th Earl of Rothes, and Sir James Baillie of Jerviswood, who saw opportunities for gaining office at the expense of the highly compromised queen's commissioner, especially as his associate Stair had, in the course of heated discussions on the Plot in the Scottish Privy Council, called for the English army to intervene and to suspend the Scottish Estates for the rest of Queen Anne's reign.

This grouping, never more than thirty from all three estates, which was to form the New Party, later the Squadrone Volante, under the nominal leadership of the Marquess of Tweeddale, were not simply disgruntled Darien investors opportunely seeking office to recoup their losses, and held together by political expediency.[52] They were a tight-knit band drawn mainly from Lothian and the Borders, with ties of kinship reinforcing local association. With limited support from the lesser burghs, they represented landed enterprise rather than overseas trade in their commercial commitments. The reforged alliance between the Country Party and the Cavaliers under Hamilton did not augur well for the Presbyterian Kirk and, indeed, led initially to Hamilton's brother, Charles, Earl of Selkirk, and his kinsman, John, Lord Belhaven, joining the New Party. They were also able to draw support from the Court Party, from such erastian Presbyterians as Marchmont, and initially Annandale and James Graham, 4th Marquess of Montrose, with whom they could agree a common platform in support of the Hanoverian Succession. Above all, this grouping, which relied heavily on the ministerial contacts of James Johnston of Wariston – the former Scottish secretary to William of Orange, now an émigré in London – was notably compliant to the dictates of the English ministry notwithstanding Roxburghe's rhetorical swordplay in favour of the independence of the Scottish Estates in the parliamentary session of 1703.[53] However, the enduring legacy of the Plot in both the Lords and Commons, as in the English ministry, was the tainting of leading Scottish politicians across the party spectrum with Jacobitism.[54]

With Queensberry having lost the confidence of the English ministry, and of the queen, Tweeddale was appointed as commissioner to the reconvened session of the Scottish Estates that commenced on 6 July 1704. In

---

[52] *LP*, I, pp. 85–8, 95–8; W. Ferguson, *Scotland's Relations with England*, pp. 188, 216–18; Riley, *The Union of England and Scotland*, pp. 115–18.
[53] NLS, Wodrow MSS, quarto lxxxii, fols. 49–50; BL, Sidney, 1st Earl of Godolphin: Official Correspondence, Home, 1701–10, Add.MSS 28,055, fols. 140–1, 158–9; *PEM*, III, pp. 263–7.
[54] BL, Hanover State Papers 1692–1710: vol. II (1707–10), Stowe MS 223, fo. 20; W. Ferguson, *Scotland's Relations with England*, pp. 180–253; Riley, *The Union of England and Scotland*, pp. 31–72; Speck, *The Birth of Britain*, pp. 98–158.

this session, which lasted until 28 August, the New Party was comprehensively outmanoeuvred by the Country Party, in alliance not only with the Cavaliers, now reinforced by the attendance of a group of nobles led by John Elphinstone, 4th Earl of Balmerino, who had hitherto absented themselves from parliament rather than take any oath that compromised their Jacobitism. The Country Party could now also count on support from Queenberry's closest friends and followers – led, in his absence, by the Earl of Mar – whose numbers at least equalled that of the New Party.[55]

Tweeddale's remit was to secure the Hanoverian Succession and a vote of supply for the armed forces in return for some moderate, and reversible, limitations on the prerogative powers of monarchy. However, Hamilton, abetted by Fletcher of Saltoun, pressed the necessity of no discussion on the Succession without prior agreement to treat with England for a communication of trade. Rothes proposed a counter motion that discussion of the Succession should be preceded by the consideration of what limitations were necessary to rectify the constitution and secure the sovereignty and independence of the nation. When Sir James Falconer of Phesdo, shire commissioner for Kincardine and a law lord, proposed a composite motion, Hamilton and the associates of the Country Party immediately accepted and effectively forced the Hanoverian Succession off the parliamentary agenda. The New Party attempted to regroup by raising the issue of the Plot and calling for the return to Scotland of relevant papers and persons questioned in the course of the House of Lords' inquiry. Despite the prospect of political capital, Hamilton and Atholl honoured the agreement between the Cavaliers and Queensberry's followers not to push for reprisals against Scottish ministers but to concentrate the ire of the Estates on the Lords. A motion of censure was duly carried, but Fletcher of Saltoun's enthusiasm for a further admonition to the House of Commons was rejected as an unwarranted intrusion into English politics. When the New Party proposed a vote of supply, the Country Party, in conscious imitation of a practice brought into disrepute in the English parliament by 1702, tacked a clause onto this measure calling for Queen Anne to assent to the Act of Security. Tweeddale was powerless to do anything but stall.[56]

---

[55] NLS, Wodrow MSS, folio xxv, fo. 124; BOU, Carte Papers – Nairn's Papers, vol. II (1689–1706), MS Carte 209/53; *Laing*, pp. 47–50, 61–85; *Mar & Kellie*, pp. 227–32; Macpherson, *OP*, I, pp. 684–5; *LQA*, pp. 138–41, 159–61; McKay, 'The Political Life of James Douglas, Second Duke of Queensberry 1662–1711', pp. 142–5, 273–4.

[56] *LP*, I, pp. 99–108; BL, Sidney, 1st Earl of Godolphin: Official Correspondence, Home, 1701–10, Add.MSS 28,055, fols. 88, 111–13; Crossrigg, *DPP*, pp. 136–62; *PEM*, III, pp. 273–81; *A Complete Collection of all the Protests made in the House of Lords,*

Anne was faced with a choice. She could reject the Act of Security and disband the forces in the Scottish establishment or accept limitations on the prerogative that could serve as a precedent for similar action in the English parliament. Godolphin was now convinced the latter option was the lesser risk. News of Marlborough's comprehensive victory over the French and their Bavarian allies at Blenheim on 2 August 1704 arrived too late to dissuade Anne from giving her assent to the Act of Security. Spared a campaign appealing to British patriotism, the Scottish Estates duly consented to vote six months' cess, albeit its levying was delayed for six months. The triumph of the Country Party, however, was far from complete. They had failed to press home their advantage to secure the election of commissioners to negotiate a treaty with their English counterparts, a manoeuvre which would either have restricted negotiations to a federative arrangement or forced their outright collapse. At the same time, the proroguing of parliament denied them the opportunity to carry the fundamental programme of limitations advocated by Fletcher of Saltoun. More significantly, the Scottish Estates, in the eyes of Queen Anne, had strayed onto dangerous constitutional grounds in their discussions on limitations linked to state formation in contemporary Europe.[57]

Coercive persuasion

The debates on union and Empire during the legislative war that spilled over into the final session of the Scottish Estates in 1706–7 were not just matters of polemical and intellectual sparring on political order and state formation.[58] They carried an immediate political resonance with the English ministry and Queen Anne. Scottish politicians arguing in favour of political incorporation were prone to refer to accumulative formations through the absorption of lesser kingdoms and principalities into composite monarchies such as Spain and France. But these were imperial powers with claims to be universal monarchies and a propensity towards absolutism. They were also currently antagonists of England

---

pp. 135–7. During the conflict between the Tory Commons and the Whig Lords, the former, much to the chagrin of the latter, tacked to the bill making provision for Prince George should he survive Queen Anne a clause which exempted him from the penalties imposed upon foreigners in the previous year's Act of Settlement, to enable him to remain an officeholder, a Privy Councillor and a member of the Lords.

[57] DH, Parliamentary Notebook of Colonel William Dalrymple, 1704–5, A 817/1, pp. 2–49; *Burnet's HHOT*, pp. 761–3; *LQA*, pp. 145–7, 17; RC, TKUA, England, Akter og Dokumenter nedr Sofart og Handel: Order med Bilag, 1704, A.III/209/35, /44–5, /47–8, /49, /52–4.

[58] J. Robertson, 'Empire and Union: Two Concepts of the Early Modern European Political Order' in Robertson, ed., *A Union for Empire*, pp. 3–36; Mackinnon, *The Union of England and Scotland: A Study of International History*, pp. 258–72.

in the War of the Spanish Succession. Scottish opponents of Union were not averse to pointing out that Portugal and Sweden, since their respective breaches with Spain in the mid seventeenth century and with Denmark–Norway in the early sixteenth century, had thrived as separate states. Conveniently glossed over was the standing of Portugal and Sweden as imperial powers in which constitutional assemblies no longer limited monarchy. The United Provinces offered a more favourable model for commercial rather than monarchic empire, but concerns remained about the effective division of decision making between the States General and the seven provinces. At the same time, the English were experiencing considerable tensions with their Dutch allies, especially over the latter's greater interest in maintaining commercial links with Spain and France than in making decisive military and fiscal commitments to winning the war. The Swiss Cantons offered an alternative federative exemplar, but they were not geared to commercial overseas expansion, nor were they immune to armed hostilities among themselves.[59]

There was one other European model deemed relevant. The merger of Poland and Lithuania into one Commonwealth from the later sixteenth century was termed a 'real union' through an elective monarchy and a common parliament, but also retained distinctive institutions with regard to regional parliaments and separate armed forces. The Polish-Lithuanian Commonwealth mainly impinged on British consciousness with regards to the need for unanimity before any measure could pass in the common parliament and its contested elections to the monarchy. This latter aspect was given particular notoriety by the tradition of greater and lesser nobility confederating to assert rights of resistance that elevated the Commonwealth over the monarchy. This practice of exercising these rights in a *rokosz* (armed rising), affirmed first in 1608, thereafter in 1662 and contemporaneously in 1704 against the elected monarch, Augustus II (who was also Elector of Saxony), had particular relevance

---

[59] Anon., *A Short Account of the Union betwixt Sweden, Denmark & Norway which commenced about the year 1523. Taken from Puffendorf's History of Sweden* (London, 1702); Anon., *The Dutch Drawn to Life*, pp. 32–42, 114–23; Aglionby, *The Present State of the United Provinces of the Low Countries*, pp. 60–81; Temple, *Observations upon the United Provinces of the Netherlands*, pp. 75–120; Carr, *Travels through Flanders, Holland, Germany, Sweden, and Denmark*, pp. 2–65; Anon., *The History of the Republic of Holland*, II, pp. 169–70; Charles Davenant, *Essays upon Peace at Home and War Abroad* (London, 1704), pp. 32–3; *MGC*, I, pp. 507–8, 554–5, and II, pp. 646–7, 682–3, 714–15; HL, Stowe Papers: Brydges Family Papers, ST 58/ 1, pp. 51–3x; Macpherson, *OP*, II, pp. 61–2, 69, 71–2. British perspectives on the constitution and operation of the Helvetian Confederation were greatly coloured by the unfavourable commentary provided in exile by Gilbert Burnet, the future bishop of Salisbury, and published at the Revolution as *Some Letters, containing an account of what seemed most remarkable in Switzerland, Italy, some parts of Germany, &c.* (London, 1688).

to Scotland. The right of the Scottish commonwealth to resist ungodly monarchy that had established the Reformation between 1560 and 1567 can be viewed as a *rokosz*, as can the fundamental limitations in Kirk and State imposed on Charles I in 1640–1, which were notably appealing to constitutional reformers in the Country Party. Likewise, the Claim of Right, which forfeited James VII in 1689 and laid the basis for the Revolution settlement in Scotland, asserted similar rights.[60] Fletcher of Saltoun, who had been implicated in the abortive Rye House Plot of the Whigs in London in 1683, primarily devised the limitations proposed in the course of the legislative war. His programme of fundamental constitutional checks on monarchy would have required a radical reform of the Revolution Settlement in Scotland, a situation anathema to Queen Anne and her consort, George, Prince of Denmark.[61] Her firm resolve to defend her prerogative powers was bolstered by details of the latest *rokosz* in Poland-Lithuania carried in the newsletters and annual political commentaries. Simultaneously, Whigs ambitious for office were keen to

---

[60] DH, Memorandums of Colonel William Dalrymple, particularly during the debates of 1706–7 in the last parliament of Scotland, A 817/2, pp. 53–4; Algernon Sidney, *Discourses Concerning Government* (London, 1704), p. 68; John Savage, *The Ancient and Present State of Poland* (London, 1697), pp. 11–13; Bernard Connor, *The History of Poland in several letters to persons of quality* (London, 1698), pp. 1–32; Gaspard de Tende, *An Account of Poland* (London, 1698), pp. 1–7, 76–80, 223–9; E. Opalinski, 'The Path Towards the Commonwealth of Two Nations' in Macinnes & Ohlmeyer, eds., *The Stuart Kingdoms*, pp. 49–61; J. R. Young, 'The Scottish Parliament in the Seventeenth Century: European Perspectives' in Macinnes, Riis & Pedersen, eds., *Ships, Guns and Bibles*, pp. 139–72.

[61] LP, I, pp. 122–4; P. H. Scott, *Andrew Fletcher and the Treaty of Union*, pp. 83–4, 227–8; RC, TKUA, England, Akter og Dokumenter nedr Sofart og Handel: Order med Bilag, 1702–5, A.III/207/56, /62–6, and /209/45, /48 and /210/38, /42–3, /45–6. Fletcher of Saltoun's programme of limitations extended to twelve points: (1) there were to be annual elections to parliament which was to sit in the winter term, choose its own president and determine everything by balloting rather than by voting; (2) for every nobleman created there was to be a member of the gentry admitted to parliament; (3) no officials, only nobles and elected members to have a vote in parliament; (4) the monarch was to give assent to all laws offered by the Estates, and the president of parliament was empowered to give the royal assent in the monarch's absence; (5) an elected Committee of Estates, of thirty-one members, to have executive powers and be accountable to parliament, with powers on extraordinary occasions to summon parliament, with all decisions determined by balloting; (6) the monarch to have no power to make peace or war without consent of parliament; (7) all civil and military places and all pensions formerly conferred by the monarchy to be given by parliament; (8) no standing army to be kept in time of peace without the consent of parliament; (9) all able-bodied men, between the ages of sixty and sixteen, to be formed into an armed militia; (10) no general indemnity or pardon for any transgression to be valid without the consent of parliament; (11) the fifteen high court judges to be incapable of being members of parliament, or of holding any other post or pension, but the salary belonging to their position and three presiding judges to be named by parliament; there were to be no extraordinary judges appointed and the central criminal and civil courts were to be separated; (12) a monarch breaking any of these conditions of government was to be declared forfeit by the Estates.

distance themselves from their past associations with a Polish interest since the Exclusion Crisis, when the Earl of Shaftesbury was castigated by Tory polemicists as the 'King of Poland' for his endeavours to prevent the succession of James, Duke of York.[62]

The Whig position was of critical importance in the aftermath of the Scottish parliamentary session of 1704. The party position in Scotland was becoming increasingly fluid. The New Party was confirmed as the leading but not the dominant group on the Scottish Privy Council. By the conclusion of the parliamentary session, Annandale had effectively ended his brief flirtation with the New Party and was attempting to set out his stall as leader-in-waiting for the Court Party. At the same time, the accommodation between the Cavaliers and Queensberry's friends and followers effectively ended when Marischall and Atholl presented, just prior to the adjournment of the Estates, an address to Queen Anne calling for the relevant papers and persons implicated in the Scotch Plot to be returned to Scotland and for the House of Lords to be censured for their unilateral investigation as an encroachment on the prerogative. In England, the political situation was considerably more tense. Nottingham had demitted his post as secretary of state in the spring of 1704, partly in response to attacks on his integrity by the committee of seven investigating the Scotch Plot, but primarily because of his growing frustration at the failure of Godolphin's English ministry to support occasional conformity and cut back on military expenditure. Nottingham and the Tories in the wake of the Scottish parliamentary session mounted a sustained attack on Godolphin for moving the queen to assent to the Act of Security. Godolphin was only spared a motion of censure during a state of the nation debate in late November by the Whig Junto coming to his rescue, their alliance being cemented by

[62] Patrick Gordon, *Geography Anatomiz'd: or, the geographical grammar* (London, 1704), pp. 140–2; David Jones, *A Compleat History of Europe: or, a view of the affairs therein, civil and military for the year 1704* (London, 1705), pp. 85–7; John Toland, *Anglia Libera: or the limitations and succession of the crown of England explain'd and asserted* (London, 1701), pp. 108–9. Prince George came from perhaps the most complete but least admired absolutist regime in Europe, if the published commentary of the former ambassador to Denmark, Robert Molesworth, Viscount Molesworth, was to be believed (*An Account of Denmark as it was in the year 1692* (London, 1694), pp. 258–71). For a flavour of the Tory polemics directed against Shaftesbury, and his abortive plotting against Charles II that led to his flight into exile to Holland where he died in 1683, see the following anonymous pamphlets: *A Modest Vindication of the Earl of S[. . .]y: in a letter to a friend concerning his being elected King of Poland* (London, 1681); Anon., *The Last Will and Testament of Anthony King of Poland* (London, 1682); *The King of Poland's Last Speech to his Countrymen* (London, 1682); *The Case is Alter'd Now: or, The conversion of Anthony King of Poland, published for satisfaction of the sanctifyed brethren* (London, 1683); *A Congratulation of the Protestant-joyner to Anthony King of Poland, upon his arrival in the lower world* (London, 1683).

the rejection in the Lords of a fresh attempt to introduce occasional conformity and continuing support for Marlborough's direction of the war.[63]

Although Harley, now secretary of state, ensured, with the support of Queen Anne, that Sunderland would not be brought into the English ministry, the Whig Junto in the Lords were instrumental in promoting the Alien Act in December 1704, which eventually passed through both houses by February 1705. This Act, which was readily endorsed at Court, represented the English backlash to the Scottish offensive during the legislative war. More importantly, it marked a signal switch in public policy, with the English ministry no longer concentrating on securing the Hanoverian Succession but giving priority to political incorporation as a means both of pre-empting the Scottish programme of limitations and of bringing Scottish commerce at home and abroad under regulation from Westminster. The Scots were invited to treat for Union or face from Christmas 1705 an embargo on commodities specifically targeted at the landed interest, notably with respect to rental income derived from rearing cattle and sheep, from extracting coal, and from spinning and weaving linen. In an extension of transatlantic restrictions and in direct breach of Colvin's Case of 1608, Scots trading to England and Ireland were to face the same tariffs as foreigners and Scottish residents were to be prohibited from inheriting property in either England or the American colonies. At the same time, a clear signal was also given that an agreement to enter into Union as an English initiative would consolidate Scottish prospects for manufacturing through landed enterprise rather than overseas trade. In expectation that the Scots would negotiate on English terms, the Act prescribed that the queen would appoint the commissioners to treat for both kingdoms. The theme of coercive persuasion was furthered by the accompanying instruction that garrisons at Carlisle, Berwick, Newcastle and Hull were to be stepped up to facilitate an invasion of Scotland by land and sea if necessary. The prospect that Scotland was about to face a rerun of the Cromwellian occupation and forced union of the 1650s was not allayed by increased Anglo-Scottish tensions provoked by the affair of the *Worcester*.[64]

---

[63] DH, Parliamentary Notebook of Colonel William Dalrymple, 1704–5, A 817/1, pp. 49–55; NLS, Wodrow MSS, folio xxv, fo. 127; *LP*, I, pp. 105–8; *CBJ*, pp. 12–27; *Burnet's HHOT*, pp. 763–6; RC, TKUA, England, Akter og Dokumenter nedr Sofart og Handel: Order med Bilag, 1704–5, A.III/209/60, /68–72, /75, and 210/1–2, /7; *LDN*, pp. 238–9, 248–51.

[64] *A Source Book of Scottish History*, III, pp. 477–8. The Alien Act was officially entitled 'An Act for the effectual securing the kingdom of England from the apparent dangers that may arise from several acts lately passed by the parliament of Scotland'.

In the summer of 1704, the *Worcester*, on its return from the East Indies, had been berthed at Fraserburgh harbour in Aberdeenshire from where it was given a protective escort to Leith. However, the directors of the Company of Scotland now saw an opportunity to exact reprisals for Darien and subsequent perceived injustices. Once the *Worcester* had been seized and taken across the Firth of Forth to Burntisland, questioning of the crew raised suspicions that they had actually been party to the disappearance of two ships chartered by the Company of Scotland, the *Speedy Return* and the *Content*, in the Indian Ocean off the pirate-infested island of Madagascar in 1701. At the directors' instigation in December 1704, charges of piracy were brought against Captain Thomas Green and seventeen of his crew. Found guilty in March 1705 by the Scottish Court of Admiralty, in which three of the five judicial assessors were prominent investors in Darien, and four were members of the New Party, Green and his crewmen were executed in a series of public hangings that April. Informed opinion in Scotland was not uniformly convinced of their guilt, but there was a clear animosity towards the English East India Companies that spilled onto the streets in the course of their trial and execution. The charges were not without foundation. A more equitable verdict would have been 'not proven' rather than 'guilty'. Tweeddale's conduct as chancellor was also called into question as he chose not to intervene in such a politically charged case, preferring to let the due process of law run its course. English concerns about the exaction of judicial revenge under pressure from the mob, as articulated by Joseph Taylor, a supercilious barrister who arrived in Edinburgh in the aftermath of the executions, have to be set against the flagrant disregard for Scots law exhibited by the House of Lords during the investigations into the Scotch Plot.[65]

[65] Insh, *The Company of Scotland Trading to Africa and the Indies*, pp. 278–312; BL, Sidney, 1st Earl of Godolphin: Official Correspondence, Home, 1701–10, Add.MSS 28,055, fols. 158–9, 162–4; DH, Loudoun Papers, bundle 17/2; *CBJ*, pp. 60, 64–6, 74–5, 77–8; *SC*, pp. 386–93, 397–8, 401–3, 409–10, 419–22; *LRS*, pp. 27–32; Joseph Taylor, *A Journey to Edenborough in Scotland*, ed., W. Cowan (Edinburgh, 1903), pp. 121–5. At the instigation of the joint board of the English East India Companies the *Annandale*, chartered by the Company of Scotland to trade in the East Indies, had been seized in the Downs in January 1704. The ship had clearly been intent on interloping from England rather than voyaging from Scotland. The endeavours of the Company to seek judicial redress had duly foundered in the English Court of Exchequer. The *Worcester* had been seized on the initiative of Mr Roderick MacKenzie as secretary to the Company of Scotland. Of the five judicial assessors in the Admiralty Court – the Earl of Loudoun, Lord Belhaven, Dundas of Arniston, Home of Blackadder and Cockburn of Ormiston – only the former was neither an investor in Darien nor a member of the New Party. The assize which pronounced the guilty verdict was made up of five skippers from the Firth of Forth and nine Edinburgh merchants; its foreman was Sir James Fleming of Rathobyres, also a Darien investor (*List of the several Persons Residenters in Scotland who have subscribed as*

The executions in April served to ratchet up Anglo-Scottish tensions, with the increased manning levels in the Border garrisons actually being implemented at the same time. Thus, when the Scottish Estates were recalled on 28 June, primarily to respond to the Alien Act, they met against a background of coercive persuasion generated by the English ministry – situation notably exploited by George Ridpath, who issued a contentious warning that negotiation not conquest was the only secure means to effect Union, and only then if the English respected Scottish concerns with regard to their religion, liberty and trade.[66]

'Scotland's ruine'?

Following pressure from the Whig Junto and discreet lobbying by Queensberry, the young Duke of Argyll was released from his service with Marlborough to return as queen's commissioner to the recalled Scottish Estates. Despite his impetuousness, Argyll brought a military ruthlessness to his political planning. Never averse to exploiting place and patronage, he insisted on the removal of the leading members of the New Party from the Scottish Privy Council. Argyll was not immediately able to manoeuvre Annandale out of office, but the latter's role as secretary of state was shadowed by the duke's kinsman, Loudoun. Argyll made full use of the managerial skills of Mar, who duly became joint secretary with Loudoun after the conclusion of the parliamentary session on 21 September 1705. Pending the triumphalist return of Queensberry to Edinburgh on 24 July, Mar was particularly adroit in maintaining links with Hamilton and the Country Party while detaching Montrose from his flirtation with the New Party, now renamed the Squadrone Volante, in their declared resolve to treat issues on their merit. The three-month session demonstrated, however, that Queensberry's friends and followers, not the Squadrone, held the balance of power.[67]

Adventurers in the Joynt-Stock of the Company of Scotland). Green's financial needs and legal representation in Edinburgh had actually been serviced through the commercial network of John Watson, in association with William Fraser in London. However, the money advanced to Green on the security of Thomas Hammond, from a merchant house affiliated to the (Old) East India Company, was never fully reimbursed (NAS, Letter and Account Book of John Watson, younger, merchant, Edinburgh, 1696–1713, CS 96/3309; *A List of Names of All the Adventurers in the Stock of the Governour and Company of the Merchants of London Trading into the East Indies, the 4th April, 1700* (London, 1700).

[66] NROB, Berwick Guild Book (1697–1716), B1/14, p. 104; [George Ridpath], *The Reducing of Scotland by Arms, and Annexing it to England as a Province Considered* (Edinburgh, 1705); [William Atwood], *Remarks upon a late Dangerous Pamphlet, Intitled, The Reducing of Scotland by Arms, and annexing it to England as a Province* (London, 1705).

[67] *LP*, I, pp. 108–15; *ISL*, pp. 6–24; *LRS*, pp. 15–26, 32–48; HL, Loudoun Scottish Collection, box 5/LO 7036, box 21/LO 11379; NLS, Wodrow MSS, quarto lxxxii, fols. 49–50;

Initial sparring appeared to confirm the expectation that the 1705 session would be a rerun of that of 1704 with the issue of the Hanoverian Succession subordinated to the composite resolve according priority to limitations and treating for Union or at least a communication of trade. However, Argyll's remit from Court, according to Rosencrantz, the Danish envoy, was to secure an entire Union in return for unfettered Scottish access to England's colonies in the (undifferentiated) Indies and to permit moderate limitations that would not be binding in the event of political incorporation.[68] Argyll duly accorded priority to trade and commerce, which subtly prepared the ground for Union by favouring manufactures developed through landed enterprise rather than overseas trade (see Chapter 8). When the limitations were discussed, Fletcher of Saltoun's programme achieved only piecemeal success while its promoter became increasingly marginalised as a shaper of the political agenda. Indeed, the Country Party gradually lost their controlling influence in the course of these debates. Although the Cavaliers stood solidly within the ambit of the Country Party in terms of the limitations, they equivocated when Hamilton and Atholl attempted to revisit the Scotch Plot. After Queensberry arrived from Court, Argyll revealed that he had received only copies of the papers requested from the House of Lords and that none of the persons implicated had been sent north for questioning. By this juncture, Queensberry's friends and followers were no longer freelancing and firmly aligned themselves with the Court Party, which also benefited from periodic absenteeism among the opposition as the session became protracted.

When the Estates moved from limitations to discuss treating for Union, Mar draughted an overture for a meeting of commissioners that judiciously left out how they were to be chosen. As the mood of the house was clearly in favour of setting a treaty in motion, the Country Party, with the Cavaliers in tow, attempted to impose such restrictions as would render negotiations meaningless. Accordingly, Hamilton took his stance against an incorporating union that would in any way 'derogate from any fundamental laws, ancient privileges, offices, rights, liberties and dignities of this nation'. The Court Party, mindful that the agreed limitations would be made redundant by the incorporation of the Scottish Estates within the English parliament, vigorously and successfully opposed this

---

BL, Sidney, 1st Earl of Godolphin: Official Correspondence, Home, 1701–10, Add.MSS 28,055, fols. 27–8, 41, 238, 241; RC, TKUA, England, Akter og Dokumenter nedr Sofart og Handel: Order med Bilag, 1705, A.III/210/13–14; *MGC*, I, p. 257; *CBJ*, pp. 60–2, 66–70, 75–82, 92–4, 100–5; Riley, *The Union of England and Scotland*, pp. 145–51.

[68] RC, TKUA, England, Akter og Dokumenter nedr Sofart og Handel: Order med Bilag, 1705, A.III/210/26, /29, /31, /33, /38–9, /41–3; *LQA*, pp. 163–4.

clause, which was lost by two votes. The Country Party then moved another clause prohibiting the Scottish commissioners from treating with their English counterparts until England repealed the specific sections of the Alien Act that discriminated against Scottish interests. The Court Party proposed instead that this should be a separate resolve rather than an amendment to the overture to treat with England and then carried the day. As Atholl was mobilising support from the Country Party, with backing from the Squadrone, to protest against this measure late in the evening of 1 September, Hamilton dramatically rose to his feet and proposed to Seafield that the nomination of the commissioners should be left to the queen. This measure, which aborted the prospect of election by the Estates, was adroitly accepted by the chancellor and, with twelve to fifteen members of the Country Party having left the house, was duly carried by eight votes. The Country Party as a whole and the Cavaliers in particular were left distraught by what they conceived as a key betrayal by Hamilton.[69]

Lockhart of Carnwath has perceptively attributed this quixotic behaviour to Mar's covert dealings with Hamilton on the basis that the duke would become a commissioner if he left nominations to the queen. Indeed, Argyll subsequently refused to serve as a commissioner as a point of honour once Queen Anne vetoed Hamilton's nomination. Other explanations remain speculative.[70] However, two key points must be borne in mind. Firstly, Hamilton had become increasingly fatigued with the political infighting within the Scottish Estates in the course of the legislative war. On the one hand, he was concerned that the independence of Scotland was 'now a jest' and, on the other, England was set on war if Union could not be driven through. Despite the profound misgivings of his mother, the Duchess Anne, Hamilton, in the wake of the

---

[69] DH, Parliamentary Notebook of Colonel William Dalrymple, 1704–5, A 817/1, pp. 56–132; *LP*, I, pp. 115–34; ACA, Aberdeen Council Letters (1700–19), 8/96; *Mar & Kellie*, pp. 233–5; *Portland*, IV, pp. 238–9; Crossrigg, *DPP*, pp. 162–72; *CBJ*, pp. 116–20, 124–6; *ISL*, pp. 25–40; *LRS*, pp. 54–91; *Burnet's HHOT*, pp. 780; Taylor, *A Journey to Edenborough in Scotland*, pp. 114–19. If Hamilton had not proposed the queen nominate commissioners, there was, in the eyes of his associates on the Country Party, a meaningful prospect that the English Parliament would have rejected commissioners chosen by the Scottish Estates (NAS, Hamilton Papers, GD 406/1/9745).

[70] *LP*, I, pp. 134–7; NLS, Wodrow MSS, quarto lxxxii, fols. 50–1. As a revival of the old cliché about overmighty subjects in Scottish history, Hamilton has been imputed to have had designs on the Scottish throne should Scotland have abandoned the common monarchy and turned to the noble family next in line to the Stuarts (W. Ferguson, *Scotland's Relations with England*, p. 189). Notwithstanding the duke's descent from Mary Stewart, daughter of James II of Scotland, his regal aspirations rested only on the testimony of the English antiquarian Bishop Nicolson of Carlisle, and the wholly unreliable Simon Fraser of Beaufort (*LDN*, p. 134; Macpherson, *OP*, I, p. 645).

Alien Act, had been contemplating whether the queen should nominate commissioners for Scotland as well as England 'to preserve the peace of Brettan'. Secondly, Argyll had gained considerable political leverage over Hamilton two months before the parliament commenced when, once again, he was specified as the Scottish lynchpin in another Jacobite plot which purportedly involved concerted action in all three kingdoms, supported by France, to dethrone the queen and replace her with her half-brother, the Prince of Wales. That Hamilton sought to retrieve this situation by proposing the nomination of commissioners by the queen is a possibility; that he was further compromised at Court is a certainty.[71]

With nomination by Queen Anne a fait accompli, the parliamentary session of 1705 effectively petered out. Supplies for the forces were voted for fourteen months. An order of the house having been presented at Court for the removal of the specific sections of the Alien Act deemed derogatory to Scotland, the necessary adjustments were duly carried through the English parliament with no more than token demurring on the part of the Tories.[72] Lockhart of Carnwath plaintively dates 'the commencement of Scotland's ruine' to Hamilton's quixotic motion on 1 September.[73] However, this is manifestly a partisan argument leavened generously with hindsight. There was still much to play for before political incorporation became a reality. Negotiations between the commissioners of both kingdoms set for the spring of 1706 had to be carried to a successful conclusion. The agreed Treaty had then to pass through both

---

[71] NAS, Hamilton Papers, GD 406/1/6798, /8071, /10344, /11805; BL, Sidney, 1st Earl of Godolphin: Official Correspondence, Home, 1701–10, Add.MSS 28,055, fols. 174–82; *SC*, p. 405; *LRS*, pp. 35, 41–2, 190–9. The Jacobite Plot, which was ostensibly planned between October 1704 and April 1705, was revealed to Argyll by an Irish participant, James MacDaniell, whose uncle John Mullany, the Roman Catholic Bishop of Killalie, was reputedly a ringleader. His revelations suggested that not only Hamilton and the dukes of Atholl and Gordon were involved, but also leading English Tories, including the Earl of Nottingham and Sir Edward Seymour, had promised support. When French forces amounting to 13,000 men landed in County Cork, there were to be simultaneous risings in England and in Scotland, where another 6,000 French troops were to disembark through Dundee once the Scottish Estates met in June. Key Jacobite agents from Saint-Germain were reputedly in place at the end of April when MacDaniell provided two highly embellished and unsubstantiated narratives of the Plot to Argyll who duly transmitted them through Godolphin to the Court.

[72] *Lords*, new series, VI (1704–6), pp. 318–19; *Laing*, pp. 119–23; *LDN*, pp. 302–3, 312, 331–2; *LP*, I, pp. 137, 139–40; DH, Parliamentary Notebook of Colonel William Dalrymple, 1704–5, A 817/1, pp. 133–53; RC, TKUA, England, Akter og Dokumenter nedr Sofart og Handel: Order med Bilag, 1705, A.III/210/45–6; *A Source Book of Scottish History*, III, pp. 479–80. The Tories were now more concerned to press for the Hanoverian heir presumptive to live in England to facilitate the succession and to resist toleration than to contest Union with Scotland (*A Complete Collection of all the Protests made in the House of Lords*, pp. 140–1; NLS, Wodrow MSS, folio xxviii, fols. 199–200).

[73] *SR*, p. 106.

parliaments. Extra-parliamentary pressures were anticipated in Scotland. While opposition from the Kirk or the Convention of Royal Burghs would undoubtedly be peaceful, that from the Covenanting remnants and the Jacobites could extend to a *coup d'état*. The reaction of Scottish commercial networks at home and abroad remained problematic, especially as the delay between the passage of Union and its actual implementation offered the prospect for a last international fling for Scotland as a rogue nation.

10   Securing the votes, 1706–1707

By the outset of 1706, Union was on course as an English initiative supported both by the ministry and the Whig Junto. Incorporation with Scotland represented the conjunction of political and economic imperatives in the midst of the War of the Spanish Succession. Through Union, England stood to gain much-needed manpower for Empire, manufacturing and war. At the same time, Union offered a meaningful prospect of terminating the disruptive impact of Scottish commercial networks, particularly their carrying trade, on England's transatlantic commerce and woollen industry. By securing the Hanoverian Succession, Union seemingly lessened the prospect of a French invasion through Scotland in the guise of supporting Jacobitism. At Court, the behaviour of the Scots as a rogue nation commercially appeared to be replicated politically by their desire for parliamentary limitations on monarchy. Queen Anne was an enthusiastic advocate of a Union that would terminate the Scottish Estates, as was the Court Party in Scotland, intent on upholding the royal prerogative, conserving the Revolution Settlement in Kirk and State, and securing new avenues for place and profit in the British Empire. Albeit some originally designated were reluctant to serve, Loudoun, as a secretary of state, duly managed the nomination of Scottish commissioners to treat for Union to suit the interests of the Court Party. The Squadrone Volante was accorded a supplementary presence as supporters of the Revolution, erastian Presbyterianism and landed enterprise.[1] Leading members of the Squadrone were simultaneously encouraging in private the pro-Union agenda of the English Whigs, yet maintaining in

---

[1] HL, Loudon Scottish Collection, boxes 5/LO 8081, 14/LO 7811, 16/LO 7984, 18/LO 8334 and 8338, 19/LO 8437, 8440 and 8468, 20/LO 7637, 22/LO 10063, 33/LO 9114, 35/LO 9146, 37/LO 9076, 43/LO 10045, 44/LO 9431, 45/LO 12653; DH, Loudoun Papers, unmarked green deed box, bundle 1706/Stair, /Glasgow, /Montrose, /Leven, /Justice Clerk, /Roseberrie, /Sir James Smollett, /Sutherland, /Lord of Session; *MLP*, p. 158; *SPC*, pp. 737–42, 749–52; *Mar & Kellie*, pp. 242–55. Sir Robert Stuart of Tillicoultry, a law lord, declined to become a commissioner, albeit he subsequently voted in parliament in favour of Union.

public a discreet silence on incorporation to enhance their role as political brokers.[2] Both the Court Party and the Squadrone were mindful that the consent of the Scottish Estates to the Williamite Succession in 1689 had not achieved close political rapport with England in lieu of Union. Accordingly, political incorporation became their price for the Hanoverian Succession.

Notwithstanding the sole presence of Lockhart of Carnwath among the nominated commissioners, the game was far from up for the Country Party.[3] So long as the negotiated Treaty required parliamentary ratification, they were in position to shape it article by article through rejections or by amendments unacceptable to the English parliament. Protests and stalling motions could force the dissolution of the Scottish Estates. The Union could then be contested in a general election. Extra-parliamentary action that mobilised public antipathy towards incorporation with England could even terminate the Treaty. For the Country Party, the most pertinent historical precedent was not the Revolution but the Whiggamore Raid, the *coup d'état* mounted in 1648 against aristocratic endeavours to achieve incorporation through the Britannic Engagement. All parties in Scotland, however, were conscious that England had the military and fiscal resources to rerun the Cromwellian Union of the 1650s.

Negotiating Union

The negotiations for Union between the parliamentary commissioners from England and from Scotland were conducted over three months from 16 April to 22 July. Not only was this duration similar to that in 1702, but the commissioners in 1706 also followed the same procedural rules. There were higher levels of attendance than in 1702, even though the full complement of English and Scottish commissioners was never present at any meeting. While the high continuity of (fourteen English and twelve Scottish) commissioners from 1702 certainly expedited negotiations, the commissioners in 1706 were primarily chosen to reflect party dominance rather than as a balanced representation, in both the English and Scottish parliaments. All prominent Tories, with the exception of John Sharp, Archbishop of York, were absent from the English ranks. Aside from Lockhart of Carnwath, the Scottish commissioners were drawn

---

[2] *PEM*, III, pp. 285–300; *Marchmont*, pp. 157–8; *CBJ*, pp. 134–55.
[3] *SR*, 118–23; Hamilton Papers, GD 406/1/5321–3, /5346. Lockhart attributed his nomination to his being the son-in-law of Lord Wharton, a prominent member of the Whig Junto. Bishop Burnet of Salisbury put Lockhart's participation down to the machinations of Stair who was determined to implicate the Jacobites in the Treaty (*Burnet's HHOT*, pp. 798–9).

predominantly from the Court Party reinforced by the Squadrone. As in 1702, the negotiations were conducted in secret but were subject to more intense lobbying from Scotland. The Company of Scotland pressed for reparations for Darien. But the erastians in the Kirk, led by Carstares, managed to keep the general assembly, which met during the negotiations, from making any demonstrable overture or comment on Union. At the same time, rumours about the course of the negotiations, especially contents subversive to an amicable outcome, circulated with greater venom and velocity than in 1702. However, the greatest difference between the negotiations of 1706 and those of 1702 was that they were now concluded successfully in favour of political incorporation, which was accepted by, rather than imposed upon, Scotland.[4]

Commentaries by two Scottish participants, Sir John Clerk of Penicuik and Lockhart of Carnwath, would appear to support the view that the accomplishment of Union was a foregone conclusion. Ostensibly, other than a far from passive dispute on Scottish representation at Westminster, negotiations were meaningful only in the context of the altered balance and survival of distinct party interests in the first British parliament.[5] However, there are two other key documents – a pamphlet attributed to the English commissioner John, Lord Somers, a leading member of the Whig Junto who had pushed through the Alien Act in 1705 to force the Scots to treat for Union, and a proposition paper prepared subsequently for the English ministry – that suggest the negotiations were indeed purposeful and robust.

Lord Somers in his pamphlet published in 1705 espoused a federative rather than an incorporative union as being more respectful to the national interests and religious and legal traditions of Scotland as well as England. In order to co-ordinate endeavours between the separate parliaments of both countries within a united kingdom, he came up with the ingenious solution of a fixed number of MPs (fifty-six each) from England

---

[4] Dicey & Rait, *Thoughts on the Scottish Union*, pp. 373, 380–3; *Mar & Kellie*, pp. 255–62; PRO, Secretaries of State: State Papers Scotland, series II (1683–1783), SP 54/2/1/; NLS, Wodrow MSS, quarto lxxiii, fo. 263, and lxxxii, fols. 50–1; NAS, Hamilton Papers, GD 406/1/5345; HL, Loudon Scottish Collection, box 3/LO 7171, 14/LO 7819, 19/LO 8478–81; DH, Loudoun Papers, unmarked green deed box, bundle 1706/Glasgow; Anon., *A Letter to one of the Commissioners for the Present Union of England and Scotland, 30 April 1706* (London, 1706). Negotiations were originally scheduled at Somerset House but were moved to the Cockpit, in the more commodious Council Chambers at Whitehall. Negotiations were based on the exchange of written proposals. When one side made a proposal, this was considered separately by the other side who gave their response and counter-proposals in writing.

[5] *LP*, I, pp. 180–8; *MLP*, pp. 158–63; Penicuik, *HUSE*, pp. 85–9; P. W. J. Riley, 'The Union of 1707 as an Episode in English Politics'; P. H. Scott, *Andrew Fletcher and the Treaty of Union*, pp. 148–62.

and Scotland who would sit in both parliaments in order to harmonise common policies. However, Somers was intent on securing economic regulation from Westminster to bring Scottish commercial networks at home and abroad under the control of the English ministry. Westminster would also have final say on foreign as well as fiscal policy to prevent the Scots acting separately on issues of war and peace. Scotland would therefore come under the control of the English fiscal–military state but would secure a communication of trade that would give guaranteed access to colonial markets in America and promote a common market within Britain.[6]

Colonial access, which had been conceded in principle to the Scots during the negotiations of 1702, had been specifically removed from the proposition paper of 1705. Scots were only to be guaranteed a common market in the United Kingdom. By way of compensation, the Scots were to receive generous reparations for Darien, for adjusting to higher rates of taxation and public expenditure, and for the standardisation of the currency on the basis of sterling. While equivalents for all but the former purpose had been agreed in 1702, the negotiations then had broken down on reparations for Darien. A composite equivalent now proposed amounted to £600,000 payable in yearly instalments of £30,000 over twenty years. An amount of £230,000 was to be paid as reparation for Darien, based on a capital sum of £140,000 (£13,000 less than actual losses for the scheme) together with interest at 6.5 per cent over eleven years. The sum of £110,000 was to be apportioned as compensation to offset incorporation in the English National Debt and the standardisation of the coinage. Higher taxes were to be rebated by an allocation of £260,000 for maintenance of the poor, encouragement of manufactures and other commercial improvements. Notwithstanding the equalising of fiscal burdens, Scotland, for a period of years still to be determined, was to pay no more land tax than that usually paid in the six northern counties of England. The Scots were to be represented in the new British parliament by not less than twenty peers in the Lords and not less than forty shire and burgh commissioners in the Commons. The established Churches, the legal systems and local government in both countries were to remain unaffected by political incorporation.[7]

---

[6] [John Somers, Lord Somers], *An Essay upon the Union of the Kingdoms of England and Scotland* (London, 1705), was re-issued anonymously in Scotland as *A Scheme for Uniting the Two Kingdoms of England and Scotland, different from any that has been hitherto laid down* (Edinburgh, 1706). Of the common MPs, no more than twelve in each country's quota were to be peers.

[7] BL, Hanover State Papers, vol. I (1692–1706), Stowe MS 222, fols. 343–4; DH, Loudoun Papers, A240/2.

Given the scope for wide-ranging negotiations, other than on reserved issues, unanimity was not inevitable. The opening speeches on 16 April by William Cowper, Lord Keeper of the Great Seal, for England, and by Seafield in his capacity as Lord Chancellor for Scotland, were effectively pious platitudes. The former proposed a safe and happy Union while the latter responded by wishing Union to secure the Protestant religion, disappoint Jacobite designs and advance commerce. Six days later the negotiations began in earnest. The English presented a united front with no mention of Somers's federative kite-flying. They proposed three key measures. The kingdoms were to be united as 'Great Britain' rather than as an England–Scotland amalgam (on the lines of Denmark–Norway). The 'United Kingdom' was to be represented by one and the same parliament, with its location at Westminster presumed rather than stated. The succession after Queen Anne was to accord with the Act of Settlement that had prescribed the house of Hanover in 1701. Two days later, on 24 April, the Scots agreed to accept the Hanoverian Succession, but specified that the same privileges of citizenship must apply throughout Scotland, England and the dominions. There should also be a communication of trade guaranteeing access for goods and shipping between Scotland, England and the American plantations. Rather than propose or press the issue, the Scots had left open the prospect of a federative Union. But when the English insisted upon an entire Union through political incorporation the Scots offered no resistance. On 25 April, they agreed to meet the three initial English proposals for a 'United Kingdom' with a common parliament and a common monarchy committed to the Hanoverian Succession. In turn, the English accepted free trade throughout the United Kingdom and its overseas dominions.

In response to the proposal of the English commissioners for common fiscal and commercial regulations on 29 April, the Scots deferred answering until a committee of equal numbers from both sides could undertake a detailed review of the respective revenues, income streams and public debts of both kingdoms.[8] The English commissioners duly consented to this proposal on 1 May and four days later the detailed work of negotiation was effectively devolved to twenty-two commissioners who constituted the Committee of Both Kingdoms, a strategy last used in 1644–6 (see Chapter 3), but now in an incorporative rather than a federative context. This Committee was dominated by the political heavyweights on

---

[8] Anon., *Observations on the Fourth Article of Union* (Edinburgh, 1706). As negotiations moved from broad principles to specific measures a committee of ten commissioners, five from each side, was appointed to review the minutes and maintain an accurate record of proceedings. Lawyers predominated on both sides, with Clerk of Penicuik being one of the Scots chosen. Their remit was merely to record, not shape, proceedings.

both sides. In the absence of Godolphin, Harley effectively led for the English, supported by three members of the Whig Junto in the Lords – Sunderland, Wharton and Somers – together with the recently appointed Speaker of the Commons, John Smith, another prominent Whig. On the Scottish side, the Court Party were exclusively represented, with Seafield, Queensberry and Stair to the fore. No shire commissioners were included, meaning that Clerk of Penicuik and Lockhart of Carnwath were not integral to the decision-making process. As the only burgh representative was Sir Patrick Johnston, Lord Provost of Edinburgh, Scottish commercial interests went largely by default. The full body of commissioners were now only required to ratify the decisions made by the Committee of Both Kingdoms. Their discussions for the remainder of the negotiations became formulaic rather than purposeful.

Within the first six days of its deliberations that commenced on 5 May, the Committee of Both Kingdoms had determined that all parts of the United Kingdom were to be under the same common regulations, prohibitions and restrictions. Equal impositions were to be exacted as customs and excise, albeit the Scots had tried to wriggle out of the latter requirement. An equal land tax was also agreed, with the proviso that the Scottish proportion was not to exceed £480,000 when a tax was set at a top rate of 4s (20p) in the pound, according to the valuation of estates (which process was to remain separate in Scotland and England).[9] Scotland was to be exempt from certain common exactions for the duration of the War of the Spanish Succession. But the country fared less well in the detailed negotiations for equivalents and political representation at Westminster (see Chapter 11).

Having conceded the Scots free access to the American colonies, the English negotiators did not concur that the merging East India Companies should be wound up along with the Company of Scotland trading to Africa and the Indies. Reparations for Darien, compensation for augmented public debts and standardised coinage, and encouragement for manufactures were significantly altered from the proposition paper of 1705. Just under £400,000 was offered as a capital sum, which was designated as the greater Equivalent and was to be effected within seven rather than twenty years. Although this represented a higher return

---

[9] Effectively Scotland faced an increase of £12,000 sterling in a land tax usually levied at £36,000 per annum, which represented the largest component in the pre-Union Crown revenues in Scotland, ahead of the customs (£30,000) and the excise (£35,000). The Crown revenues amounted to no more than £110,694. However, Scotland, unlike England, had no substantial national debt (Sinclair, *The History of the Public Revenue of the British Empire*, pp. 333–5). For full details of the accounts and estimates of the respective revenues of England and Scotland, see Bruce, *REC*, pp. dl–dlxxxvi.

in less time than the £340,000 proposed for reparations and compensation in 1705, there was no commitment to pay in instalments and the interest rate for the capital lost at Darien dropped from 6.5 to 5 per cent. The money for manufactures was drastically cut back from £260,000 over twenty years to £14,000 over seven years, in equal annual instalments. Thus, the promotion of fishing and of linen and woollen manufacturing through a rising or accumulating sum was designated the lesser Equivalent and yielded £2,000 yearly, as against £13,000 proposed in 1705. The notion that the Union would serve to boost the Scottish economy was clearly ill served by the Scottish negotiators. In like manner, Scottish political representation was not particularly generous with the number of peers in the Lords being cut back from at least twenty, as proposed in 1705, to sixteen. Albeit the number of shire and burgh commissioners in the Commons was increased to forty-five, the English negotiators had begun from a base figure of thirty-eight, as against the minimum of forty suggested in 1705. The established Kirk, the civil and criminal operation of Scots law in the private sphere, and local government in town and country were not unequivocally reserved. Manifestly, the leading players in the Court Party did not necessarily cut the best deal for Scotland.[10]

Containing dissent

Faced with a sceptical rather than a uniformly hostile reaction to the negotiated Treaty,[11] the principal task facing the leaders of the Court Party, from the presentation of the articles of Union to Queen Anne on 23 July to the opening of what became the final session of the Scottish Estates on 3 October, was news management – a task given a considerable patriotic boost by Marlborough's decisive victory at Ramillies on 23 May, which had removed the threat of a complete French occupation of the Netherlands. Indeed, the polemicist Charles Davenant hailed the victor as not only making a substantive contribution to 'Quieting our Domestic Broils', but ensuring that 'the British Empire will be soon so firmly

---

[10] BL, Hanover State Papers, vol. I (1692–1706), Stowe MS 222, fols. 343–4; DH, Loudoun Papers, A240/2; RC, TKUA England, Akter og Dokumenter nedr Sofart og Handel: Order med Bilag, 1705–6, A.III/ 214, /216; Defoe, *HUGB*, 'Of the Last Treaty', pp. 1–104; Bruce, *REC*, pp. cccl–dxx; *Burnet's HHOT*, pp. 791–2; W. Ferguson, *Scotland's Relations with England*, p. 235. Two Anglo-Scots were prominent in the calculation of the Equivalents – David Gregory, the Saville Professor of Astronomy at Oxford University, and William Paterson, of Darien infamy. The former, a mathematician of note, was duly rewarded with the direction of the Mint in Scotland in July 1707 (ACA, Gregory Family MSS, MS 2206/48/50D/1).

[11] *LP*, I, pp. 150–7; Penicuik, *HUSE*, pp. 93–7.

fix'd as to be out of all Dangers'.[12] Queen Anne was certainly intent on promoting the Union within the context of a victory obtained with divine blessing. The day after she received the Treaty, she had been persuaded to announce that Queensberry would be her commissioner at the next crucial session of the Scottish Estates. Her accompanying letters of instruction made it clear that any attempt by the Estates to promote a federative alternative to political incorporation or to insist upon limitations on the Hanoverian Succession would nullify the Treaty.

In effect, the Estates were only granted scope to determine the method whereby peers and commissioners for the shires and burghs would be returned to the first parliament of Great Britain, and to take any measures necessary to secure the Presbyterian establishment in the Kirk. Queen Anne primarily placed her confidence not in Queensberry but in Seafield, whom she considered to have 'behaved himself the most faithfully of all my Scottish servants'. Seafield, in turn, anticipated the direction, content and limitations of the campaign against Union once the contents of the Treaty were leaked to James Hodges, the émigré polemicist. Hodges duly set the tone for the resurgent polemical debate by broadsheet and pamphlet that prioritised roadblocking issues of sovereignty and religion, as the prospect of free trade was undoubtedly advantageous to the Court Party so long as the details of economic regulation and fiscal expectations remained under wraps.[13] But the roadblocks of religion and sovereignty meant the Country Party resumed their polemical campaign on the defensive. By the time the debate had swung back to issues of political economy, the English ministry, with encouragement from the Whig Junto, had foisted William Paterson and Daniel Defoe on the Court Party, as masters of political spin and polemical rebuttal (see Chapter 8).

Reflecting on the recently negotiated Treaty, Seafield recognised the legitimacy of concerns about the loss of sovereignty from the suppression of the Scottish Estates, and the consequent fear that Scotland would become an English province. However, he held also that Scottish sovereignty had been badly managed by the Estates. Union would incorporate Scotland into a better constitution with real prospects for Scots of meaningful participation in Empire on an equal basis with the English.

[12] HL, Stowe Papers: Brydges Family Papers, ST 58/vol. 1, pp. 63–5; NROB, Berwick Guild Book (1697–1716), B1/14, pp. 124–5; *Mar & Kellie*, pp. 263–4.
[13] *LQA*, pp. 173, 190–2; NLS, Wodrow MSS, folio xxxv, fols. 137–8, and quarto lxxxii, fo. 51; Penicuik, *HUSE*, pp. 93–5; *MGC*, I, p. 556; *Portland*, VIII, pp. 227, 240–1; Anon., *To the Loyal and Religious Hearts in Parliament, Some Few Effects of Union, proposed between Scotland and England* (Edinburgh, 1706); Anon., *Scotland's Speech to her Sons* (Edinburgh, 1706); [William Wright], *The Comical History of the Marriage-Union betwixt Fergusia and Heptarchus* (London, 1706).

The Scottish constitution was capable of internal reformation so long as the Estates remained upon a Revolution footing, but England might act harshly and coercively towards a separate Scotland should a common monarchy be abandoned. He was also sceptical about the real value of English concessions, recognising that the greater Equivalent could be viewed as a bribe, with the indeterminate promise to pay arrears of pensions as well as reparations for Darien being effectively the price of purchasing the Scottish kingdom. But the lesser Equivalent offered a beneficial rebate from higher taxes. Scotland was exempt for the duration of the War of the Spanish Succession from extraordinary impositions laid on England for paying the National Debt. The increased land tax would be levied for no more than eight months in the year. Free trade with England and the plantations removed all prospects of the Scots being treated as aliens, opened up greater scope for a Scottish carrying trade more cost-effective than the English, and gave secure access to colonial markets for coarse cloth and salted fish. Seafield was apprehensive about how soon these purported benefits would be effected. He recognised that the economic basis of the Treaty was primarily in English interests as Scotland could be drained of manpower away from manufactures to the colonies, the precedent having already been set by Scottish migration to Ireland. For all manufactures other than coarse cloth, free trade would open up Scotland to the rigours of English competition and, at the same time, bring any expansion in the fishing trade under the control of English capital. Recession not growth was a more meaningful outcome of Union which 'may indeed enrich and be the advantage of Scottsmen, but that it will enrich that part of Brittain now called Scotland is that which I still doubt'.

Seafield also recognised that the power of the pulpit could be turned against the Union unless the Presbyterian establishment was secured and the Kirk was spared 'the hazard of toleration'. The requirement of the sacramental test for public office, that is the taking of communion according to Anglican rites, would bar Scots from civil and military places of profit in England and the Empire, but not be a barrier to Englishmen holding office in Scotland. While he was convinced that outright rejection of Union 'must infallibly prove Scotland's ruine', he recognised that a just and firm settlement could well be federative and that the case for political incorporation required adroit management.[14] Once the parliamentary

---

[14] *Laing*, pp. 125–35. Seafield deemed it a matter of regret that England would only treat for an incorporating union, whereas Cromartie, in advance of the negotiations, had enthusiastically endorsed the rejection of any federative alternative (NAS, Mar & Kellie Collection, GD 124/15/279/4).

session got underway on 3 October, the leaders of the Court Party were intent on ensuring that the passage of Union should not be derailed by outside forces. They duly accorded priority to the diluting of institutional protests anticipated from the Kirk, the Company of Scotland and the Convention of Royal Burghs, and then to localising extra-parliamentary dissent.

In dealing first with the Commission of the Kirk, which acted as the ecclesiastical executive between general assemblies, the Court Party made full use of not only erastian clergy like Carstares but also supportive politicians attending as ruling elders from 11 October. In particular, the Court Party was represented by the Earl of Glasgow, Adam Cockburn of Ormiston, the lord justice-clerk, and two other lawyers: Sir David Hume of Crossrigg and Mr Francis Montgomerie of Giffen; attending from the Squadrone were the Earl of Marchmont and George Baillie of Jerviswood. Acting in concert they ensured that initiatives and addresses on the part of the Kirk did not work against an incorporating Union even though the radicals and their sympathisers in the Country Party, who promoted these initiatives, had a greater presence among ministers and ruling elders on the Commission. Accordingly, attempts to promote a national fast prior to the discussions on Union in the Scottish Estates were watered down into local initiatives to be taken at the volition of presbyteries. As the Scottish Estates prepared to debate Union, the moderator of the Commission, William Wishart, minister of South Leith, strove diligently to ensure unity of purpose in addresses against the sacramental test and the accompanying abjuration oath that favoured the Church of England, and, in a similar vein, against episcopal influence. The Scottish Estates ignored these addresses but did accede on 9 November to a further unifying address that became the basis for the Act for Securing the Protestant Religion and Presbyterian Church Government, which made no concessions to toleration for Episcopalians. This Act, which was supplementary yet integral to the Treaty of Union, conformed to the parliamentary remit prescribed by Queen Anne and promoted by Seafield. Undoubtedly, the promotion of this unifying address from 17 October did demonstrate the Kirk's capacity to influence debate within the parameters of incorporation and to exert the appropriate amount of pressure to ensure concessions acceptable to the English ministry.[15]

---

[15] J. Stephen, 'The Kirk and the Union, 1706–07: A Reappraisal', *RSCHS*, 31 (2002), pp. 68–96. NLS, Wodrow MSS: folio xxv, fols. 142–4; quarto lxxii, fo. 267; quarto lxxxii, fols. 51–70. DH, Loudoun Papers, unmarked green deed box, bundle 1706/October; Penicuik, *HUSE*, pp. 98–9, 118–21; *SR*, pp. 153–5; Defoe, *HUGB*, 'Of the Carrying on of the Treaty in Scotland', pp. 34–6, 38–40, 51–5; *Portland*, VIII, pp. 250–1.

While the radicals in the Kirk were certainly willing to galvanise protests against Union from the grass-roots, only three presbyteries (less than 5 per cent of the total) and fifty-nine parishes (no more than 6 per cent of the total) actually petitioned against Union. Of the three presbyteries, Lanark and Hamilton came within the spheres of influence of the house of Hamilton, and Dumblane within that of Atholl. Both these ducal houses also influenced the petitions from parishes, which tended to cluster in south-west, west and central Scotland. However, the primary influence outside central Scotland would appear to be the location of the parishes in the Covenanting heartlands which had a long tradition of supplicating in defence of civil and religious liberties. The militant Cameronians in the south-west went so far as to submit their own select petition against Union. Nonetheless, the mainstream of the Kirk, as reflected in the addresses from the Commission, was not intent on outright opposition to Union. Indeed, the Commission was reverting to a stance evident since the Revolution and reiterated by the Kirk's refusal to take a party line over Darien. Its primary mission was not to protect the sovereign independence of Scotland, or to advance the cause of a federative Union or even the Hanoverian, as distinct from a Protestant, Succession. The Kirk stood above all for its own institutional interests as the preferred ecclesiastical establishment in Scotland.[16]

The Court Party and the Squadrone were less in concert in diluting the protests of the Company of Scotland on 27 November that focused on the greater Equivalent rather than a root-and-branch attack on Union. In their internal debates in the course of that month, the General Council was split between those prepared to accept the dissolution of the Company in return for reparations and those holding out for reparations without the need to dissolve as required by the Treaty. Marchmont and his son, Patrick Hume, Earl of Polwarth, were of the latter persuasion. However, Cockburn of Ormiston, supported by Sir David Dalrymple, the solicitor-general, and the Earl of Cromartie – all of whom had been Scottish commissioners to negotiate Union – mounted a successful rearguard action that prevented outright rejection of this aspect of the Treaty. Accordingly, the protest was primarily a factual rather than an emotive statement, built around six key points. The sum offered in reparations was deemed inadequate for taking away trading privileges that were now to accrue to the restructured East India Company. Whereas the English

---

[16] A. I. Macinnes, 'The 1707 Union: Support and Opposition' in McNeill & MacQueen, eds. *Atlas of Scottish History*, pp. 151–3; *PEM*, III, pp. 303–9; NAS, Wodrow MSS, quarto xl, fols. 71–2, and lxxiii, fols. 271, 280–1; HL, Loudoun Scottish Collection, box 13/LO 8314. There were even petitions drafted to commanders in regimental companies to encourage soldiers to dissent from Union.

ministry was claiming a compound interest of 6 per cent for all monies advanced in payment of the Equivalents, the Company of Scotland was only being offered 5 per cent simple interest for sums advanced as capital stock, a rate deemed inequitable. No security was being offered for the timely payment of reparations. The Company was obliged to dissolve before reparations were paid. Even though the Company intended to charter ships up to its dissolution, no security or safe conduct was offered for their trading overseas. It was not inconsistent with the trade of the United Kingdom for the Company to continue, especially as the Union, despite its claims for free trade, denied Scots a presence in the East Indies. No amendment to the Treaty of Union resulted from this representation.[17]

A similar fate had already been meted out to the address from the Convention of Royal Burghs, specially convened at Edinburgh to scrutinise the Treaty of Union on 29 October. The Court Party certainly exercised influence over the lesser burghs whose commissioners in the Estates were often carpet-baggers, such as Clerk of Penicuik, who sat for Whithorn in the south-west though his estate was near Edinburgh. Nevertheless, the Convention came out against political incorporation. The Convention was not implacably opposed to Union with England but would have preferred a federative arrangement as more conducive to the differing branches of Scottish trade. In effect, the Convention was influenced by William Black, the polemicist and advocate from Aberdeen, and his associates among the leading burghs, who argued for the primacy of overseas trade rather than landed enterprise in promoting manufactures.[18] But this was increasingly a minority position within the Scottish Estates, who were no more receptive to individual addresses from twenty-one royal and nine dependent burghs against political incorporation. The petitions of the latter were influenced in part by shared concerns for Scottish trade in the aftermath of Union, in part by Covenanting affinities in the south-west, but also by association with leading members of the Country Party and Cavaliers. The latter were principally responsible for mobilising addresses from the royal burghs, as well as from eighteen shires, which largely followed a set formula that upheld the sovereignty

---

[17] *To His Grace, Her Majesty's High Commissioner, and the Right Honourable Estates of Parliament. The Humble Representation of the Council-General of the Company of Scotland Trading to Africa & the Indies* (Edinburgh, 1706); [MacKenzie], *Proceedings of the Company of Scotland with relation to the Treaty of Union*; *SR*, pp. 155–7.

[18] *To His Grace, Her Majesty's High Commissioner, and the Right Honourable Estates of Parliament. The Address of the Commissioners to the General Convention of the Royal Borrows of this Ancient Kingdom* (Edinburgh, 1706); *SR*, pp. 151–3; ACA, Aberdeen Council Register, 58 (1705–21), p. 57; NLS, Wodrow MSS, quarto lxxxii, fols. 56–7; Defoe, *HUGB*, 'Of the Carrying on of the Treaty in Scotland', pp. 36–7.

and independence of the Crown and kingdom and attacked political incorporation as contrary to the fundamental laws and constitutions of Scotland. These petitions, which respectively represented about a third of the royal burghs and over half of the shires, also amounted to a significant increase – by eleven royal burghs, but only one shire – from the total petitioning for redress as a result of the Darien fiasco six years earlier (see Chapter 4).

The addresses did not, however, lead to any major shift in party allegiances in the Scottish Estates. Indeed, the most identifiable response of the commissioners for the burghs and shires was a blatant disregard for the wishes of their constituents.[19] Although the Court Party's attitude to petitioning from the constituencies was generally dismissive, it was unable, as its opponents commented pointedly, to mobilise any addresses in favour of the Union. The commissioner for the eastern burgh of Montrose was mandated discreetly to vote for political incorporation, an action attempted but not sustained in Ayr and reputedly contemplated, but disclaimed, in Glasgow because of public hostility to Union. Indeed, the perceived threat, as much as the actual occurrence, of civil disturbance led to addresses against Union being subscribed in both these western burghs. The leaders of the Court Party applied their influence, particularly in the Highlands, the Borders and the south-west, to suppress the endeavours of gentry and burgesses to petition against Union. Notwithstanding their picture of partial rather than endemic protest in Scotland, the addresses against Union enabled the confederated opposition to claim that the Treaty lacked public support.[20]

The addresses, moreover, carried the implicit threat that peaceful protest could be replaced by public disorder targeted against the Scottish proponents of Union and the English ministry.[21] The Court Party had anticipated this response, particularly from the Jacobites north of the Tay and the Cameronians and other radical Covenanters in the south-west. In addition, trouble was also expected from Edinburgh, where the rioting during the Green case in 1705 was but part of a long tradition of

---

[19] Macinnes, 'The 1707 Union: Support and Opposition' in McNeill & MacQueen, eds., *Atlas of Scottish History*, pp. 151–3; J. R. Young, 'The Parliamentary Incorporating Union of 1707: Political Management, Anti-Unionism and Foreign Policy' in Devine & Young, eds., *Eighteenth Century Scotland*, pp. 24–52; Penicuik, *HUSE*, p. 118; NLS, Wodrow MSS, quarto lxxv, fo. 142, and lxxxii, fols. 55–6; Crossrigg, *DPP*, pp. 178, 180, 182; *CBJ*, p. 170; *Buccleuch*, p. 718; *Laing*, pp. 139–40.

[20] T. C. Smout, 'The Burgh of Montrose and the Union of 1707 – A Document', *SHR*, 66 (1987), pp. 183–4; *LP*, I, pp. 167–8; *CTB*, XXII part ii, pp. 185–6; *APS*, XI, pp. 396–87.

[21] K. Bowie, 'Public Opinion, Popular Politics and the Union of 1707', *SHR*, 82 (2003), pp. 226–60; *CBJ*, p. 168; BL, Sidney, 1st Earl of Godolphin: Official Correspondence, Home, 1701–10, Add. MSS 28,055, fols. 324–5, 400.

political riots by residents reinforced by migrant protestors; as well as from Glasgow, where tensions between Presbyterians and Episcopalians had spilled over into the streets in 1703; and from Dumfries, where the Hebronites had been threatening violent protests since the parliamentary resolve of 1705 to treat for Union. Once the Scottish Estates moved to debate Union, rioting duly broke out in the streets and was sustained by mass lobbying of the parliament house. The most notorious incident in the capital was on the evening of 23 October when the mob stormed the house of Sir Patrick Johnstone who had been a commissioner negotiating Union when provost and was one of the city's commissioners in parliament. Queensberry himself faced attack from the mob on 18 November. In the interim, the local fast day for contemplation of Union in Glasgow turned into a rabbling of the magistrates to protest against political incorporation. The most theatrical demonstration was reserved for Dumfries on 20 November. John Hebron and around 200 of his followers publicly burned the articles of Union and issued a counter-declaration claiming the consent of the generality of the nation for their resolve to defend fundamental laws, and religious and civil liberties. Having reputedly drawn an audience of many thousands, they then moved along the Solway Firth to take an encore in Kirkcudbright.[22]

The leaders of the Court Party and the English ministry were less concerned with these individual demonstrations than with the possibility that the Jacobites and the militant Covenanting remnant might concert a *coup d'état* that could be exploited by the confederated opposition to terminate Union. This possibility was certainly played up by Daniel Defoe and by John Ker of Kersland, the former to enhance his own importance as a spy for the English ministry and the latter to demonstrate his worth as a Cameronian of repute whose covert liaison with Jacobites merited reward from the Court Party. Yet, neither Defoe nor Kersland made any distinction between the Cameronians who confined their protests to petitioning and the Hebronites who were willing to take armed action.[23] Certainly, Atholl had used the section of the Act for Security empowering local militias in order to muster numerous clansmen (grossly exaggerated at 4,000) on his estates in August, once news of the conclusion of negotiations for the Treaty had reached Scotland.

---

[22] NLS, Wodrow MSS, quarto lxxv, fols. 141, 147–8, and lxxxii, fols. 64, 71–2; DH, Loudoun Papers, unmarked green deed box, bundle 1706/October, /November; Anon., *An Account of the Burning of the Articles of the Union at Dumfries* (Edinburgh, 1706); Crossrigg, *DPP*, pp. 176–7, 184, 187; *SR*, pp. 177–80; *Portland*, VIII, pp. 150, 177, 226; *ISL*, I, pp. 53–7.

[23] Defoe, *HUGB*, 'Of the Carrying on of the Treaty in Scotland', pp. 1–2, 11–23, 27–34, 40–3, 55–74; [Ker], *The Memoirs of John Ker of Kersland*, pp. 27–39; *Portland*, IV, pp. 378–9.

However, the Privy Council had already procured extra armaments for Scottish garrisons before negotiations actually commenced. Localised rioting and reports of concerted militancy in Lanarkshire duly served as the excuse Queensberry needed to move that the militia provision of the Act of Security be suspended. At the same time, he bolstered the armed guards surrounding the Scottish Estates, thereby reversing the situation of intimidation. Whereas the mobs had targeted the leaders of the Court Party, the increased military presence in Edinburgh served to make the Country Party and even the Squadrone uncomfortable. So responsive was the English ministry to the apprehensions of Queensberry and his associates that the parliamentary proceedings might be disrupted that a menacing presence of three regiments of foot were garrisoned on the Borders, and a further three of horse, one of foot and one of dragoons were stationed conveniently in Northern Ireland, when the actual voting on the articles of Union commenced in November.[24]

Queensberry also made judicious use of *agents provocateurs*, such as Major James Cunningham of Aiket. Though a shadowy figure, Cunningham appears to have played a key role in countermanding a rendezvous outside the town of Hamilton at the outset of December by an anticipated force of 7,000–8,000 Jacobite clansmen and militant Covenanters. Extraordinarily bad weather, sustained from October to December, limited both the scope and enthusiasm for extra-parliamentary mobilisation. Nevertheless, disaffected tradesmen from Glasgow were sufficiently resourced to issue a declaration against Union and pay wages to those recruited for the march on the parliament. In the event, considerably fewer than 500 men actually turned up. Even this figure was sufficient for the Duke of Hamilton to take fright at the prospect of the Estates being dissolved by force of arms.[25] A few weeks later, Hamilton again proved the unexpected ally of the Court Party. The Cavaliers, at the urging of

[24] *Mar & Kellie*, p. 315; *MGC*, II, p. 727; *ISL*, I, pp. 57–8; Crossrigg, *DPP*, pp. 187–8; *CBJ*, pp. 170, 174; NAS, Mar & Kellie Collection, GD 124/15/414/2; NLS, Wodrow MSS, quarto lxxiii, fols. 269–70, 282; HL, Loudoun Scottish Collection, box 43/LO 12573; *APS*, XI, p. 309. The arrival of the Dutch fleet off Edinburgh on a recruiting venture facilitated the removal of unruly elements from the capital (*LDD*, p. 166).

[25] *SR*, pp. 180–4; *Orain Iain Luim*, pp. 222–5; BL, Blenheim Papers, vol. DXXI, Add.MSS 61,631, fols. 14–16; DH, Loudoun Papers, unmarked green deed box, bundle 1706/December. Militant proceedings seem to have been instigated by a Glasgow contingent of around fifty men – dismissed merely as a rabble by Defoe (*HUGB*, 'Of the Carrying on of the Treaty in Scotland', pp. 62–70) – who were led by a Captain Finlay. Once they had provisioned themselves with arms in the city on Friday 29 November, they proceeded initially to Kilsyth by way of Kirkintilloch to meet up with a contingent from Stirling where hostility to Union had threatened rioting. But on hearing of the imminent arrival of a troop of dragoons they retraced their steps and made for Hamilton by Monday 2 December, where they were joined by some recruits from Lanarkshire before dispersing and returning in a disorderly manner through Rutherglen to Glasgow. The

Lockhart of Carnwath, had attempted to regain the political initiative by organising a mass-lobby of the parliament by over 500 gentry who were party to the addresses from the shires against Union. They were to demand, as freeholders and parliamentary electors, that the Estates suspend proceedings until Queen Anne be acquainted with the true extent of public antipathy towards the Union. Again unwilling to be compromised by his reputed Jacobitism, Hamilton forestalled this lobby by his insistence that any address to the queen must accept the Hanoverian Succession. The proclamation of 27 December forbidding further meetings of freeholders in Edinburgh was less a prescription than a recognition that extra-parliamentary activism was now exhausted.[26]

Managing proceedings

The three months between the conclusion of negotiations by the parliamentary commissioners and the reconvening of the Scottish Estates were marked by concerted political action involving the Court Party and the English ministry. Loudoun, who had been integral to the increased wheeling and dealing for military commissions and places of profit under the Crown prior to the negotiations, now ratcheted up this activity. Having been notably successful in winning over Alexander Murray, Lord Elibank, Loudoun made strenuous but ultimately fruitless endeavours to secure the commitment of Balmerino. Loudoun's promises and delivery of relatively modest awards were undoubtedly overshadowed by the claims made by his kinsman, Argyll, directly to the English ministry. Before he committed himself irrevocably to the Treaty, Argyll demanded to be indemnified and reimbursed for his past services as queen's commissioner in 1705. He also blatantly claimed over forty-five military and civil places of profit, principally for himself and then for his kinsmen and political associates. By securing an English title, as Baron Chatham, he went directly into the House of Lords rather than having to stand for election as a Scottish peer after Union. He also procured a Scottish peerage for his brother Archibald Campbell, as Earl of Islay. Only when he was assured that his demands were being met did he depart from London in

---

arrival of a further contingent of dragoons ended the protest by Sunday 15 December. Although Finlay and a few ringleaders were arrested, they were released in the aftermath of Union. The Commission of the Kirk had also sent out a circular letter to the presbyteries cautioning against any rising (NLS, Wodrow MSS, quarto lxxxii, fols. 75–6; *SPC*, p. 754).

[26] *SR*, pp. 184–8; *APS*, XI, p. 343; NLS, Wodrow MSS, quarto lxxv, fo. 149, and lxxxii, fols. 72–3.

October 1706; even then Mar remained wary of alienating Argyll through the parliamentary session.²⁷

Godolphin offered further assistance in the wake of the negotiations by authorising the covert advance of £20,000 from the English Treasury, reputedly to meet arrears of salary owed mainly to Scottish politicians holding public office. However, this money, which was channelled through the Earl of Glasgow, was used primarily to shore up potential votes for Union from the Court Party and the Squadrone rather than to persuade members of the Country Party to abandon their opposition.²⁸ Thus, preferential treatment was accorded to Montrose and Eglinton among the waverers in the Court Party, and to Tweeddale, Roxburghe and Marchmont as leaders of the Squadrone. Payments were also used to bring lukewarm supporters of Union back into line. William Cunningham, 11th Earl of Glencairn, initially received £100 from recorded arrears in excess of £4,886. Having initially registered his opposition when voting for Union commenced in November, Glencairn subsequently followed the party line in twenty-eight further divisions after the Court leadership threatened to 'debauch' prospects of further repayments of arrears and to withhold confirmation of his pension of £700 from the civil list. Queensberry, who had already been advanced £1,500 yearly from the Scottish customs and excise to reimburse him for past services, received the bulk of this covert funding – £12,325 – which he seemingly used as a discretionary fund as well as to meet his own legitimate expenses as queen's commissioner.²⁹ Queensberry was influential in persuading the former recusant George Ogilvy, Lord Banff, to accept the oaths affirming Protestantism and to attend parliament, for a rather modest inducement of little more than £11. He may also have assisted with the expenses of James Hamilton, 6th Earl of Abercorn, an Irish resident and member of the Irish Privy Council, whom he also persuaded to attend the final

---

²⁷ ICA, Argyll Papers, bundles 69/1, 144/1. HL, Loudoun Scottish Collection: boxes 2/LO 10796, 10805; 4/LO 7259, 7846; 10/LO 8265; 23/LO 8815; 31/LO 8998; 33/LO 8675; 39/LO 12370. DH, Loudoun Papers, unmarked green deed box, bundle 1706/Stair, /Argyll, /Lord Rankillor, /Lord Treasurer, /Marlborough, //August–December; *Mar & Kellie*, I, pp. 284–91, 373–5; *MGC*, II, pp. 651, 655, 659, 662, 682.
²⁸ Macinnes, 'Influencing the Vote'; Riley, *The Union of England and Scotland*, pp. 256–9, 336–8; P. H. Brown, *The Union of England and Scotland*, pp. 200–1; NAS, Dalhousie MSS, GD 45/1/175; *CBJ*, pp. 156–7, 160–1; *Portland*, VIII, p. 283.
²⁹ *Mar & Kellie*, pp. 312–13, 321; NLS, Wodrow MSS, quarto lxxxii, fo. 57; ICA, Argyll Papers, bundle 88/103. Although the only money that can be itemised against extra-parliamentary activity was the £100 granted, for no specified arrears, to Cunningham of Aiket, this serves as an indicator, not as a final account of monies paid to spies and *agents provocateurs* to enhance the aura of menace surrounding the final session of the Scottish Estates.

Table 2. *Party office profile*[30]

	All	Court	Squadrone	Country
Office	111	75	7	29
Arrears	69	48	5	16
Unpaid	50	35	1	14
Paid	27	20	5	2

session in support of the Court Party. But as table 2 demonstrates, there were significant numbers in all three parties who claimed, but did not receive, arrears for their civil and military offices, albeit the 48 members of the Court Party and the five in the Squadrone with recorded arrears were more open to managerial manipulation than the 16 in the Country Party. Discrepancies arise from those officeholders with recorded arrears who were unpaid and those who actually received selective payments. That 10 out of the 27 members from all parties who were paid monies had no recorded arrears certainly supports a prima facie case for bribery. But only 5 of these with no recorded arrears were not officeholders; the others may well have had arrears of salary that were not itemised in the public accounts prised from the British parliament by Lockhart of Carnwath in 1711. The sums involved, which range from just over £11 to almost £1,105, though of relatively greater significance when converted into £133 to £12,160 Scots, are hardly indicative of the widespread bribery popularly assumed to have influenced the 242 attending members of the Scottish Estates in favour of Union.[31] Despite the covert endeavours of the Court

---

[30] *LP*, I, pp. 262–72; *CTB*, XXI part ii, pp. 36, 300–1, 352, and XXII part ii, pp. 78–9, 112–19; *Calendar of State Papers, Domestic Series of the Reign of Anne*, ed. R. P. Mahaffy vols. I–II (London, 1916 and 1924), I (1702–3), pp. 454–82, 571–2, and II (1703–4), pp. 399–436; NAS, Kennedy of Dalquharran Papers, GD 27/6/2.

[31] *LP*, I, pp. 222–3; *Orain Iain Luim*, pp. 222–9; T. Crawford, 'Political and Protest Songs in 18th century Scotland I: Jacobite and Anti-Jacobite', *Scottish Studies*, 14 (1970), pp. 1–33. Indeed, Seafield's dismissive remark at the formal ratification of political incorporation, 'Now there's an end of ane old song', has lived on in popular imagination as the conclusion of a fiddlers' rally rather than an orchestrated rhapsody. Montrose and Roxburghe had no arrears recorded and received respectively £200 and £500; however, both had held office. Elibank and Sir Kenneth MacKenzie of Cromartie, who received respectively £50 and £100 without recorded arrears or any evidence of officeholding, appear to have been two former associates of the Country Party who had been bribed to vote for Union. Elibank had been won over by Loudoun before any funding became available from the English Treasury and MacKenzie of Cromartie was actually the son of the Earl of Cromartie who had lined up with the Court Party long before the final session of the Scottish Estates. In addition to Elibank, the other member of the Country Party to receive money was Atholl, who was given £1,000 from arrears of £1,500, but this was not a serious or successful endeavour to subvert his attested opposition to Union as he was

Party leadership to secure the firm commitment of the Squadrone to political incorporation, there was no guaranteed majority in favour of the negotiated Treaty before the Scottish Estates came to vote on the actual articles of Union.[32]

While the Court Party was seeking to shore up its commitment to Union and bring in such backwoodsmen as Banff and Abercorn, the Country Party failed to maximise their support. Ten Jacobite peers who were not infirm, financially embarrassed or exiled overseas failed to come to parliament as they refused to take the necessary oaths to recognise the legitimacy of Queen Anne as monarch. This was the largest category of able-bodied Protestant peers resident in Scotland who absented themselves from the Scottish Estates.[33] The Jacobites in the guise of Cavaliers, along with their associates in the Country Party, also overestimated the strength of the anti-Unionist support that could be mobilised. The view of the Cavaliers that a pro-Union standpoint was still a minority position appeared to be reinforced by a military and political survey of Scotland undertaken by the resident Jacobite agent in Edinburgh, Captain Henry Straton, which he personally delivered to Saint-Germain in July 1706 after Lockhart of Carnwath returned with his account of the Treaty negotiations in London. According to Straton, the forces available for the defence of Scotland in field and in garrison amounted to no more than 2,860 men, a figure that could certainly be matched by Jacobite forces raised in the Lowlands and easily outnumbered by 8,000 clansmen mobilised from the Highlands. Moreover, within the high command of the government forces, as within the six regiments of foot, the two troops of horseguards, the three independent Highland companies and the four castle garrisons, there were well-placed officers who were reputed to be loyal or

---

owed even greater sums for past military offices that remained unpaid, although some of this may have been offset in the £200 paid to his brother, Charles Murray, 1st Earl of Dunmore, a stalwart of the Country Party with no stated arrears.

[32] DH, Loudoun Papers, unmarked green deed box, bundle 1706/September; NAS, Mar & Kellie Collection, GD 124/15/449/19; *CBJ*, pp. 159–63; *MGC*, II, pp. 703, 717; *Portland*, VIII, pp. 202–8.

[33] PRO, Secretaries of State: State Papers Scotland, series II, SP 54/13/143; BOU, Carte Papers (1701–19), MS Carte 180/146; *An Exact List of the Peers of Scotland at the Time of the Union* (London, 1719); *Scots Peerage*. Superficially, there appears to be little difference between the 71 out of 153 peers who failed to attend in 1703 and the 72 out of 157 who failed to attend in 1706. Discounting 8 peerages which remained extinct, the 23 minors, females and attainted who were ineligible to attend were only increased by 1 in 1706, while the number of papists barred was reduced from 7 to 6 by the defection of Banff. The attendance of Abercorn also reduced from 16 to 15 the number of English peers with honorary Scottish titles, and Scottish peers permanently resident in England or Ireland, who remained absentees. The actual absence of others increased from 17 to 19, the main body of whom were the 10 Jacobites; another 3 peers were indisposed or infirm, 2 were financially embarrassed and 4 were overseas, either in exile or in military service.

well-affected or would take no action to resist the restoration of James VIII & III.

However, Straton had operated mainly in the central Lowlands and, other than a cursory visit to Aberdeen, had not set foot in the Jacobite heartlands of the north-east and the Highlands. His political survey was no less marked by misplaced optimism. With the notable exception of Argyll, he reckoned that the majority of shire and burgh commissioners were committed to the Country Party and he was fully persuaded 'that the far greatest part of the nation is well affected' to the Jacobite interest. In leading burghs such as Edinburgh, where 'the magistracy was in Whig hands, the most of the merchants and tradesmen are well affected'. Indeed, Dundee had recently turned out such a magistracy. The only ill-affected were those under the pernicious influence of the Presbyterian ministry. Even in Fife and in the western 'and most Whiggish Shyres', a substantial number of the gentry were supportive, and the Cameronians in the south-west were reputedly prepared to mobilise for the Court in exile. Notwithstanding the considerable influence exercised by the Squadrone in East Lothian and the Border shires of Berwick and Roxburgh, Straton confidently reported that they would be against the Union though they favoured the house of Hanover.[34] Yet James Hodges had warned Hamilton in February 1705, following conversations in London with Tweeddale, that the Squadrone was primarily intent on securing the Hanoverian Succession and, while they preferred a federative union, they were 'rather for an Incorporating Union than none at all'.[35]

The Squadrone eventually declared their hand after the initial reading of the articles of Union on 12 October. Their stance exposed the fragility of the Country Party that was now united only in their opposition to political incorporation, not on any alternative system of governance.[36] But the Country Party still retained the capacity to negate, alter and delay the passage of Union. Moreover, it should not be presumed that the Court Party was wholly bound together by the bonds of officeholding, pensions and places of profit. Thomas Hay, 6th Viscount Dupplin, privately supported, and duly lobbied the English ministry for, a recess to consider the articles and allow members to consult their constituents:

---

[34] BOU, Carte Papers (1701–19), MS Carte 180/146; Macpherson, *OP*, II, pp. 4–22; *SR*, pp. 124–6.
[35] NAS, Hamilton Papers, GD 406/1/5195.
[36] NLS, Wodrow MSS, quarto lxxv, fols. 138–40; *CBJ*, p. 164; W. Ferguson, *Scotland's Relations with England*, pp. 187–95; P. H. Scott, *1707: The Union of Scotland and England*, pp. 22–6. After the articles of Union were read, there was an unusual silence that was broken by Seton of Pitmedden's request that the Treaty be printed in full, which Seafield acceded to without recourse to a vote.

the same plea made in the house by the Country Party after the initial reading. However, this plea had been rejected by Seafield, as was the Country Party's next motion for a fast day for national humiliation and prayer. Instead, the parliament moved for a detailed consideration of the articles of the Treaty, which was carried by sixty-six votes on 15 October. The debates on the articles in the last two weeks of that month revealed the genuine quandary in which those opponents of Union who were not prepared to countenance a Jacobite restoration found themselves.[37]

Thus Annandale, notwithstanding his maverick party associations that had seen him move from the Court in 1703 to the Squadrone in 1704 and now to the Country, warned on 29 October of the inherent dangers of the succession remaining unsettled. Simultaneously, he countered aspersions that those who opposed an incorporating Union were Jacobites and against a Protestant establishment. Annandale wanted the Hanoverian Succession and a federative rather than an incorporative Union. So did the Court Party stalwart, John Gordon, 15th Earl of Sutherland, who, though he had been a commissioner to negotiate the Treaty, was assiduously making private overtures to this effect to the Whig Junto as well as the English ministry – albeit he only passed this information to Hamilton in secret on 23 November.[38] Despite intemperate language from Fletcher of Saltoun, endorsed by Belhaven, to the effect that the Scottish commissioners had negotiated not as treaters but as traitors, the Country Party was so distrustful of its own strength that its leadership did not propose an anti-Union initiative until 25 October. Errol then mounted a protest against Queensberry's bringing in a party of foot ostensibly to guard, but essentially to intimidate, parliament. This gesture to test the political waters secured the commitment of no more than fifty-two members. Even though Queensberry had actually contemplated a temporary adjournment of parliament because of the hostility of the mob, Hamilton headed off the threat by Errol and his associates to follow up their protest with a walk-out of parliament. Hamilton was at one with Stair and Argyll

[37] BL, Sidney, 1st Earl of Godolphin: Official Correspondence, Home, 1701–10, Add. MSS 28,055, fols. 142–3, 324–5; DH, Loudoun Papers, unmarked green deed box, bundle 1706/October; Crossrigg, *DPP*, pp. 173–4; *MGC*, II, pp. 719, 721; Levack, *The Formation of the British State*, pp. 155–6.

[38] DH, Memorandums of Colonel William Dalrymple, particularly during the debates of 1706–7 in the last parliament of Scotland, A 817/2, pp. 27–8; NAS, Hamilton Papers, GD 406/1/9730. Sutherland's intermediary was his son John, Lord Strathnaver, who commanded a regiment of foot that was maintained on the Scottish establishment. In order to consolidate his own position at Court, Mar was intent on blackening Annandale as a Jacobite, a charge which Annandale had never been averse from using against his opponents when in office (*Mar & Kellie*, pp. 296, 304, 314, 330, 336, 352; *LP*, I, pp. 137–8, 159).

in the Court Party that the Estates must take a stand against rebellion.[39] Nine subsequent protests against key articles in the Treaty or the management of proceedings served primarily to expose that the Country Party was a lame confederacy. Its lack of cohesion when protesting was thrown into sharp relief by the sixty-four members of the Court Party and the Squadrone who mounted a single counter-protest on 7 January 1707, at the desultory blocking tactics of the Country Party.[40]

The capacity of the Country Party to make amendments of substance was largely forestalled by the creation of a Committee to examine the calculation of the greater Equivalent on 23 October. This initiative, which played a key role in the sophisticated management of the parliamentary proceedings by the leaders of the Court Party, enabled the two parties that had negotiated the Treaty to continue to shape its actual ratification. On 28 November, when votes were due on the more controversial economic aspects of the Treaty, the nine original members were joined by another six, with equal representation for each Estate. Of the fifteen members on the enhanced committee, all were members of the Court Party and the Squadrone. Of the six who attended irregularly, three had a questionable commitment to Union and occasionally voted in divisions with the Country Party. Nevertheless, the heat was taken out of debates by referring back contentious issues to this Committee or its three associated sub-committees for articles to be amended or redrafted.[41]

---

[39] NLS, Wodrow MSS, quarto lxxv, fols. 40–2; *APS*, XI, p. 309; DH, Loudoun Papers, unmarked green deed box, bundle 1706/October.

[40] Only eighty members (35 per cent of the Estates) failed to participate in protesting, albeit seventy-eight members (34 per cent) protested on only one occasion, the vast majority in the counter-protest (A. I. Macinnes, 'Treaty of Union: Voting Patterns and Political Influence', *Historical Social Research: Historische Sozialforschung*, 14 (1989), pp. 53–61).

[41] NAS, Supplementary Parliamentary Papers, PA 7/20/4 & Home of Marchmont MSS, GD 158/937; DH, Loudoun Papers, unmarked green deed box, bundle 1706/October; *Mar & Kellie*, pp. 278, 336–7; Crossrigg, *DPP*, pp. 175–6, 186; *ISL*, I, pp. 48–53. The three irregular attenders were Argyll, Cromartie and Sir Thomas Burnet of Leys. Sir Gilbert Elliot of Minto, shire commissioner for Roxburgh, Robert Inglis and Hugh Montgomery, burgh commissioners respectively for Edinburgh and Glasgow, broke ranks occasionally, with the latter voting more with the Country than with the Court Party. The three sub-committees were for, respectively, apportioning the Equivalent and adjusting trade and customs; for debts of the Company of Scotland; and for adjusting public debts and coin. Referral of the sixth article, on the equalisation of commercial regulations and fiscal rates, provides an example of the sophistry applied by the committee. Comparison was drawn between the Scottish and English tariffs imposed on tar, tobacco, iron and deals of timber. The Scottish customs were deemed to belong to the Crown in perpetuity, but the English were held to terminate after a fixed number of years, and 11/15ths of current exactions by 1710. Accordingly, the current tariff paid in Scotland for the specified commodities was just under £19,599 (£235,185 Scots), whereas the English equivalent tariff that came into play after the Union was over £34,446; but this would be reduced in 1710 to £10,803. At the same time, the Union removed tariffs on linen and cattle exported to England that currently exacted £22,719. Accordingly, the committee argued

Even though Mar's support for the Hanoverian Succession was suspect in the eyes of the English ministry, his commitment to the attainment of Union was borne out by his energy and zeal as effective leader of the house. Together with Chancellor Seafield, who acted as a far from impartial speaker, they maintained a firm grip on procedural business, especially on the length and frequency of speeches and the order of voting for articles and amendments.[42]

Voting Union

The Court Party did have one tangible success prior to the voting on Union that commenced on 4 November, when they moved successfully that the votes on both sides should be marked and printed with the minutes as a permanent reckoning for future generations.[43] This decision, which led to 30 recorded divisions, provides a clear indicator of party cohesion as well as the importance of cross-voting on key articles of the Treaty. It is too restrictive to view voting in this last session as being cast for and against the Court Party rather than for or against the Union.[44] Undoubtedly, votes were cast for and against the Court Party as collaborators with the English ministry. But cross-voting and abstentions were recorded as a mark of disapproval of the leadership in all three parties in economic and political, as well as constitutional, divisions (see appendix). In addition to the ten Jacobite peers who excluded themselves, fourteen members from all three Estates who were eligible to attend failed to appear and were not replaced by another shire or burgh commissioner. Of the remainder, only eight members failed to vote in any division. At least

---

that the tax burden not only eased but came round to Scotland's advantage after 1710, blithely ignoring their almost certain renewal in that year even if the War of the Spanish Succession had been brought to a conclusion (NAS, Home of Marchmont MSS, GD 158/937).

[42] *Mar & Kellie*, pp. 284–366; *ISL*, I, pp. 41–4; *LRS*, pp. 171–7, 182–4; DH, Loudoun Papers, unmarked green deed box, bundle 1706/October; BL, Hanover State Papers 1692–1710: vol. II (1707–10), Stowe MS 223, fo. 20. Mar and Seafield were particularly adroit at calling to order those in the Court Party depicted as 'the Queen's servants', the seventy-five members holding pensions and places of profit under the Crown. Following the initial reading and reasoning on the twenty-five articles of Union and the incorporated Act for Securing the Protestant Religion and Presbyterian Church Government, which commenced on 12 October and took up the rest of the month, all were subjected to two detailed readings in addition to the amendments to the notably contentious on the floor of the house, prior to their inclusion in the ratification of the Treaty on 16 January 1707. The ratification served as a formal fourth reading. Only six articles were approved without amendments or voting divisions. There were thirty voting divisions, for fifteen articles, thirteen amendments and two proclamations against convocations of potentially riotous and armed opponents of Union.

[43] NLS, Wodrow MSS, quarto lxxv, fo. 145.

[44] Riley, *The Union of England and Scotland*, p. 273.

Table 3. *Party voting profile*[45]

	Court	Squadrone	Country
Nominal strength	113	26	103
Non-voting	10	1	11
Crossed floor to	8	0	6
Actual strength	111	25	98
Solid party, 15+ votes	67	18	28
Party elite, 27+ votes	42	14	5
Cross-voting	29	7	46

three non-voters were present throughout the parliamentary session, two being constrained by office from voting.[46] As table 3 demonstrates, the party affiliations of the twenty-two non-voters effectively cancelled each other out. Although nine members abstained in the critical first votes on the Union and on its ratification on 16 January 1707, they did participate fitfully in interim voting divisions. The salient point about the voting record of the Scottish Estates was the high degree of participation, which certainly negates the suggestion that the last session of parliament was a political charade.[47] Almost half the voting members (49 per cent) entered more than fifteen divisions. An elite band of 61 voted in over twenty-seven divisions, but only five consistently supported the Country Party. In voting, as in protesting, the Country Party manifestly lacked cohesion.

The lack of an absolute majority in the house for any one party clearly stimulated high participation in voting in all three Estates. Notwithstanding their minority position, the voting strength of the Squadrone was vital to securing Union. By throwing in their lot with the Court Party, they consistently secured majorities that prevented amendments to all but one

---

[45] *APS*, XI, pp. 307–414. Ties of kinship and local association were important in all three parties, but least significant in the Country Party. However, these ties were secondary influences on voting, as was evident from the strained relationship between Hamilton and his brother-in-law Atholl (cf. NAS, Hamilton Papers, GD 406/1/10344).

[46] As queen's commissioner, Queensberry was precluded from voting. As lord chancellor, Seafield was obliged to seek special parliamentary dispensation for his vote to be recorded after divisions on key issues; he did so on eleven occasions. The most prominent non-voter in attendance was the lord advocate, Sir James Stewart of Goodtrees, who was opposed to the loss of Scottish sovereignty and unconvinced that the Union was the best guarantee of the Presbyterian Kirk. By not voting against Union, he retained his office (NAS, Mar & Kellie Collection, GD 124/15/449/19).

[47] T. C. Smout, 'The Road to Union' in Holmes, ed., *Britain after the Glorious Revolution*, pp. 455–67.

of the fifteen articles contested by the division of the house.⁴⁸ Yet their actual voting strength of 25 was only decisive in securing the majority in two divisions – in rejecting amendments to customs duties and to Scottish representation at Westminster. Even with their combined strength, the Court Party and the Squadrone only achieved an outright majority in the house, that is 118 or more votes from attending members, on four occasions – for free trade, against amending the Equivalents (twice) and for the initial proclamation discharging unlawful meetings following rioting against the Union. The latter testifies to the capacity of Queensberry to make the vote against or for rebellion. The former confirms the general attractiveness of free trade and the votes both for this article and for the Equivalents belie the dismissal of commercial considerations as not having significant influence in promoting Union.⁴⁹

Undoubtedly, the promise of reparations for Darien – at just over £232,884, that is about 58 per cent of the sum awarded as the greater Equivalent – smoothed the passage of Union. However, no more than 100 out of the 234 members who voted had a financial interest in the Company of Scotland. Only the Squadrone had the majority of their members (19) as voting investors, and the Court Party had almost as many (39) as the Country Party (42). The claim that reparations amounted to 'a swingeing bribe' to buy off opposition to Union must remain not proven in the absence of extant detailed accounts to set actual losses against eventual reimbursements.⁵⁰ There was an expectation that members who had opposed Union would be accorded a low-to-nil priority when reparations were eventually paid. Moreover, 17 members of the Scottish Estates who actively promoted Union were among the commissioners for the Equivalent charged to apportion reparations. Nevertheless, reparations were not detailed until 10 March 1707, almost two months after the conclusion of voting, and the commissioners were not appointed until 2 June, the month after the Union was formally implemented.⁵¹

The leadership of the Court Party adroitly managed the voting to build up a head of steam in favour of Union before proceeding to the more contentious and most keenly contested economic issues. A comfortable

---

[48] NAS, Home of Marchmont MSS, GD 158/938; *PEM*, III, pp. 327–30.
[49] Mitchison, *Lordship to Patronage*, pp. 131–2; Riley, *The Union of England and Scotland*, pp. 210–15, 281. Lockhart of Carnwath voted against the Country Party three times on these issues.
[50] *LP*, I, pp. 157, 193; *Mar & Kellie*, p. 364; *PEM*, III, pp. 321–4; *List of the several persons Residenters in Scotland who have subscribed as Adventurers in the Joynt-Stock of the Company of Scotland*.
[51] NAS, Exchequer Papers: Warrants of the Exchequer Register 1707, E8/66, and Letters of W. & R. Fraser, London, RH 15/13/30; *APS*, XI, p. 439; *CTB*, XXI part ii, pp. 26, 300–1, 352, and XXII part ii, pp. 78–9.

majority of 33 was secured on the first article for a United Kingdom on 4 November with 116 *for* and 83 *against*, after the leadership made it known that this vote would not be binding if subsequent divisions went against Union. A winning momentum was then maintained by the intrusion into the voting agenda of the Act for Securing the Protestant Religion and the Presbyterian Church Government, which was carried by a majority of 75. The leadership then returned to the specific articles, securing the Hanoverian Succession by a majority of 59 and then a unified British parliament by 30.[52]

The alliance of the Court Party and the Squadrone more than held its own in the debates on these articles. Lord Belhaven's celebrated, but apocalyptic, musing on the fate of Scotland post-Union was countered by a no less partial, but reasoned, prospectus offered by William Seton of Pitmedden on Scotland's commercial opportunities in a global partnership with England. In rejecting both a federative arrangement and the continuance of regal union with limitations on Queen Anne's successor, he also pushed the Country Party on to the defensive in the debate on the second article, with Annandale, Hamilton and Belhaven unable to demonstrate convincingly that a federal union would suffice to secure peace and prosperity in Britain. Roxburghe and Stair also made substantive contributions to the debates on the initial articles, which turned the tables on Fletcher of Saltoun by affirming that Scotland must come to terms with political realities. If the country was not to continue as a satellite state, partnership with, rather than separation from, England was both the gateway to Empire and the guarantor of freedom. Having weighed up the advantages and disadvantages of political incorporation, Roxburghe in particular was convinced that Union with England was the only secure path to riches and liberty. In the process, he set the scene for the alliance's resounding victory in the division on free trade, which was carried easily with a majority of 135.[53]

Nevertheless, the leadership of the Court Party was justifiably apprehensive about the unpopularity of certain economic articles, especially an equalised malt tax mainly levied on the brewing of beer. An amendment

[52] Crossrigg, *DPP*, pp. 178–93; NLS, Wodrow MSS, quarto lxxv, fols. 143–5, 147–8; DH, Loudoun Papers, unmarked green deed box, bundle 1706/November.
[53] DH, Memorandums of Colonel William Dalrymple, particularly during the debates of 1706–7 in the last parliament of Scotland, A 817/2, pp. 27–62; Penicuik, *HUSE*, pp. 106–17, 121–37; *PEM*, III, pp. 303–9, 311; John Hamilton, Lord Belhaven, *The Lord Beilhaven's Speech in Parliament the second day of November 1706* (Edinburgh, 1706), and *The Lord Belhaven's Speech in Parliament, the 15th day of November, on the Second Article of the Treaty* (Edinburgh, 1706); William Seton of Pitmedden, *A Speech in the Parliament of Scotland. The Second Day of November, 1706. On the First Article of the Treaty of Union* (Edinburgh, 1706).

to article XIII on the malt tax proposed by the Committee for examining the calculation of the Equivalent, claiming that Scotland should be granted a temporary exemption pending the conclusion of the War of the Spanish Succession, was only carried by the casting vote of Seafield – albeit there was no recorded division. The subsequent inclusion of an explanation underwriting Scotland's exemption from English fiscal measures unless specified in the Treaty of Union was also deemed prudent to secure the comfortable passage of article XIV on equalised customs duties. Writing to Sunderland, the recently appointed English secretary of state on 10 December, Mar was confident of the capacity of 'the friends to the Union' to withstand any explanation, addition or amendments not deemed absolutely necessary. But he was concerned about article VIII on salt tariffs, which had been referred to the Committee after it ran into a barrage of protests on the floor of the house. The leadership was fearful that a series of defeats on this basic commodity would threaten the further passage of Union. Accordingly, debates were adjourned, and potential waverers identified and subjected to concerted lobbying. In the event, the Country Party mustered sufficient support merely to carry a single amendment on 20 December that insisted domestically produced Scottish salt should not carry the same duties as the English, over two-thirds of which was used to repay East India Company loans to the Crown. The Court Party subsequently rallied to control the rate and duration of the lower duties on Scottish salt for domestic consumption. Increased drawbacks on the export of herrings, beef and pork cured with foreign salt were also conceded. Domestic salt from the British Isles was not deemed suitable for this process.[54]

Although the English ministry had become increasingly confident during December that the Union would carry relatively unscathed through the Scottish Estates,[55] the leadership of the Court Party did face one final hurdle. Future Scottish participation in the Lords and the Commons provoked five divisions of the house at the outset of 1707 and occasioned notably fiery clashes between Hamilton and Seafield. The Country Party gained considerable mileage from the seemingly low level of

---

[54] *APS*, XI, pp. 358–68; *Mar & Kellie*, I, pp. 348–9, 356–63; *Laing*, pp. 135–9; *LDD*, pp. 165–6, 178–80; DH, Loudoun Papers, unmarked green deed box, bundle 1706/November–December; NAS, Mar & Kellie Collection, GD 124/15/179; Whatley, *The Scottish Salt Industry*, pp. 1, 87–8. Though a stalwart of the Court Party, William Dalrymple recorded that an equalising of salt tariffs 'would have been a very great burden': 2s 4d out of 3s 4d per bushel levied on salt went towards loan repayments (DH, Memorandums of Colonel William Dalrymple, particularly during the debates of 1706–7 in the last parliament of Scotland, A 817/2, p. 98).

[55] HL, Stowe Papers: Brydges Family Papers, ST 57/vol. 1, p. 62; DH, Loudoun Papers, bundle 17/8.

representation for Scotland at little more than a twelfth of the total membership of the new British parliament, and from the associated requirement that the Scottish members would be required to take the sacramental test and the abjuration oath according to the English formula. Nevertheless, article XXII passed without substantive amendment by 9 January. A decisive majority favoured the ratification of Union, which was duly carried on 16 January 1707, when 110 voted *for* and 68 *against*.[56]

However, as is evident from table 3 and the appendix, there was a demonstrable indulgence in cross-voting in all three parties, which was particularly pronounced in economic divisions. The persistence of such cross-voting counteracts claims of even a rough correlation between economic self-interest and voting on articles primarily concerned with economic issues.[57] At the same time, the Court and the Squadrone outperformed the Country by maintaining higher party discipline, by consistently supporting their party position in fifteen or more divisions, and by securing a higher proportion of members in the elite voting category. Part of the success of Mar and his managerial associates was their capacity to recognise, involve and reward the reservoir of support not only within their own party and the Squadrone, but also among the former members of the Country Party who crossed the floor to support Union. Rather than concentrate political rewards on powerful nobles and rely on their territorial influence over shire and burgh commissioners,[58] the leadership of the Court Party sustained their alliance with the Squadrone by spreading around the spoils of office, a practice that continued even after party strains re-emerged once the Union was ratified in the Scottish Estates.[59] The selective distribution of rewards after the ratification of

---

[56] Crossrigg, *DPP*, pp. 194–6; Penicuik, *HUSE*, pp. 158–74; *PEM*, III, pp. 312–21; DH, Memorandums of Colonel William Dalrymple, particularly during 1706–7 debates in the last parliament of Scotland, A 817/2, pp. 125–44; NLS, Wodrow MSS, quarto lxxv, fols. 152–5; NAS, Clerk of Penicuik Papers, GD 18/3136. The success of the leadership of the Court Party in piloting Union through the Scottish Estates was somewhat tempered by the death of the Earl of Stair, from apoplexy, on Wednesday 8 January.

[57] Smout, *Scottish Trade on the Eve of Union*, pp. 270–5; *The Treaty of Union of Scotland and England 1707*, pp. 26–8.

[58] W. Ferguson, 'The Making of the Treaty of Union of 1707'.

[59] *APS*, XI, p. 431; *Mar & Kellie*, pp. 304, 325, 336, 366, 373–5; *CBJ*, pp. 183–9; MSH, Loudoun Papers, bundle IND/5; Riley, *The Union of England and Scotland*, pp. 292–8. Thus, the Court Party and the Squadrone monopolised the selection of sixteen representative peers who were to sit in the Lords from 1 May until the first British general election. All but four of the forty-five shire and burgh commissioners also selected on 13 February to sit in the Commons came from the alliance, and of the four nominally affiliated to the Country Party, three had effectively crossed the floor in the course of the voting divisions on Union. The choosing of representative peers and MPs by the Scottish Estates on 13 February entailed the setting aside of article XXII of the Treaty of Union with respect both to the election of MPs by their constituents and to the grouping

Union certainly bears out the complaints from the confederated opposition that the Court leadership was more concerned with accountability to party than to parliament.[60] Nevertheless, thirteen members of the Scottish Estates can be identified as having supported the Union consistently without benefit of office, financial inducement, committee service or even ties of kinship to party leaders. Although all but two were rewarded after the ratification, it would seem rather dismissive to presume that these proponents of Union – 15 per cent of solid party activists and 10 per cent of the allied votes of the Court Party and the Squadrone – were merely lobby fodder or placemen devoid of principled commitment.[61]

Conversely, the opposition of the Country Party to the passage of Union was not marked by an unsullied commitment to principle. The component strengths of the confederated opposition became increasingly apparent as Hamilton struggled to hold together his disappointed placemen, the constitutional reformers and the Cavaliers. Only the constitutional reformers were not prone to cross-voting. Under the leadership of Fletcher of Saltoun, the one member of the Scottish Estates to participate in all ten protests mounted by the opposition, they have been identified as a principled, anti-aristocratic grouping.[62] But these radicals who opposed Union as a constitutional impediment to political and social reform, were but a rump of fifteen members out of the ninety-eight voting members of the Country Party. The constitutional reformers were actually outperformed by eleven nobles led by Errol and Marischal, who composed the Jacobite element inclined to support limitations on monarchy.

The rest of the Cavaliers, however, were notably less consistent in their opposition. A group of nineteen, led by Atholl, became increasingly exasperated with Hamilton's misdirection of the confederated opposition. Taking up a suggestion privately mooted in Sutherland's covert letter of

---

of shires and burghs in electoral sets, provisions deemed only to come into operation at the first British general election (in 1708). The immediate presence of Scots in the Lords and the Commons once the British parliament was instituted on 1 May was deemed, by the Squadrone no less than the Court Party, as vital to the consolidation of Union (*PEM*, III, pp. 325–6). In proportion to their voting strength, the Squadrone subsequently did as well as the Court in gaining peerages, military commissions, places on the commission for the Equivalent and membership of the purged commissions for the Exchequer and Treasury. Again, the members of the Country Party who shared in the spoils of office usually had a compromised voting record or had diplomatically absented themselves from the parliament during the voting divisions (NAS, Exchequer Papers, E 8/66; DH, Loudoun Papers, A27/3 and A1131/3–4).

[60] *LP*, I, pp. 146–7; *Burnet's HHOT*, p. 803.
[61] W. Ferguson, *Scotland's Relations with England*, pp. 186–8; Riley, *The Union of England and Scotland*, pp. 274–81.
[62] W. Ferguson, *Scotland's Relations with England*, pp. 190–2; J. Robertson, 'Andrew Fletcher's Vision of Union' in Mason, ed., *Scotland and England, 1286–1815*, pp. 203–25.

23 November, Hamilton, during the debate on article XXII, proposed that the Country Party submit an address to the queen stating their fundamental opposition to an incorporating Union. Once this address was drawn up, Hamilton was to lead the Country Party out of parliament and attempt to force a general election, a manoeuvre that had been successfully accomplished in 1702. This was less a declaration of independence than an endeavour to persuade the Crown and English ministry to support renegotiation for a federative union.[63] However, Hamilton stymied all prospect of concerted action by again insisting that all subscribers must accept the Hanoverian Succession. This was the breaking point for Atholl's Cavaliers, who, in protest, abstained in the vote on ratification. Accordingly, despite a slight drop in numbers in those supporting Union when the first vote is compared with the ratification (see appendix), the more significant deficit was that among those opposing. Indeed, the margin in favour rose from thirty-three to forty-one largely because of Cavalier abstentions.[64]

The price of Union

Whereas the Treaty of Union took over four months to pass through the Scottish Estates, its ratification in both the Commons and the Lords was achieved within five weeks. However, this was not accomplished without rigorous management between 1 February and 4 March 1707.[65] Harley had become particularly concerned about the seemingly negative attitude of the Kirk towards Episcopacy once its own establishment had been secured. At the ratification of the Union through the Scottish Estates, the Commission of the Kirk had submitted an address against a similar establishment being conferred on the Church of England and continued to snipe at the sacramental test and the abjuration oath required for civil and military office.[66] At the same time, much to the displeasure

---

[63] Szechi, *George Lockhart of Carnwath, 1681–1731*, pp. 46–70; *SR*, pp. 188–204; NAS, Hamilton Papers, GD 406/1/9730; DH, Loudoun Papers, unmarked green deed box, bundle 1706/October–December; *Mar & Kellie*, pp. 284–375; P. H. Scott, *Andrew Fletcher and the Treaty of Union*, pp. 204–6.

[64] Macinnes, 'Influencing the Vote'; Whatley, *Bought and Sold for English Gold?* p. 44; Devine, *The Scottish Nation, 1700–2000*, pp. 14–15.

[65] Hoppit, *A Land of Liberty?* p. 253; Speck, *The Birth of Britain*, pp. 114–16; Riley, *The Union of England and Scotland*, pp. 302–5.

[66] NLS, Wodrow MSS: folio xxviii, fols. 208–10; quarto lxxxii, fols. 74–5; quarto lxxv, fols. 153, 155–6. DH, Memorandums of Colonel William Dalrymple, particularly during the debates of 1706–7 in the last parliament of Scotland, A 817/2, pp. 134–8; NAS, Mar & Kellie Collection, GD 124/15.485/2; *SPC*, p. 754; *Unto His Grace Her Majesties High Commissioner and the most Honourable Estates of Parliament, Edinburgh January 16, 1707. The Representation and Petition of the Commission of the General Assembly of the National Church of Scotland* (Edinburgh, 1707).

of Marlborough, Godolphin had come under renewed attack from the Tories who again took up the cudgels on behalf of an allegedly endangered Church of England. Tories, outside as well as within the English parliament, were arguing for a federative rather than an incorporative Union in order to keep Scotland from interfering in English ecclesiastical affairs and to prevent the political balance at Westminster being tilted further in favour of the Whigs. However, the hierarchy of the Church of England, led by Archbishop Tenison of Canterbury, came to the aid of the English ministry by agreeing the format for an Act to secure the Anglican establishment that paralleled that for the Presbyterian establishment in Scotland and served as the English prelude to Union. Moreover, having concerted this measure, they refused to call a Convocation that would have provided a platform for anti-Scottish sentiment within the Church of England.[67]

Harley duly drove the Union through the Commons from 1 February by having all possible amendments taken in a committee of the full house, a task accomplished within eleven days after some Tories walked out on failing to have voting on the first article postponed until the others were discussed. Notwithstanding continuing Tory opposition on the floor led by William Bromley, the member for Oxford University, the ratified Treaty passed unscathed through the house on 28 February, having passed its third reading by 274 votes to 116. The Whig Junto, who were more than a touch disdainful that the Scots had not negotiated a tougher deal, were the principal promoters of the Union through the Lords from 15 February. The Tories, led by Nottingham and Rochester, were particularly vocal in their opposition, with John Thompson, Lord Haversham, having his speech against Union published. Like Belhaven in Scotland, Haversham had a flair for self-publicity. He wished to draw to the attention of the wider British public his preference for a federal solution, which would secure the Hanoverian Succession and not imbalance the proven excellence 'of the good old English Constitution'.[68]

The bill for Union had been considered by the full house sitting as a general committee; its ratification by the Commons was set to be approved in the Lords with little or no scope for debate on 4 March. However, nineteen Tories then staged a series of seven protests against

---

[67] *MGC*, II, pp. 705, 709; *LDN*, pp. 390–3, 414; *Buccleuch*, pp. 716–7; *Burnet's HHOT*, pp. 798–805; HMC, *Lords*, new series, VII (1706–8), pp. 22–3.
[68] [John Thompson, Baron Haversham], *The Lord Haversham's speech in the House of Peers on Saturday, February 15, 1707* (London, 1707). Haversham had incurred the wrath of Queen Anne in 1705 when he had called for the Electress Sophia to be invited to England. His proposal claimed to strengthen the prospects of the Hanoverian Succession, but was primarily intended to embarrass the English ministry.

specific articles and the Treaty as a whole. Their ire was notably directed against Presbyterianism, the greater Equivalent, the capacity of Scots to pay the land tax and other public dues, and Scottish representation by sixteen peers, which they deemed too generous. Only the turbulent Haversham and two associates, Henry Somerset, 2nd Duke of Beaufort, and George Granville, Lord Granville, made futile protests against every article in the Treaty. Two days later, Queen Anne gave her assent to the Treaty of Union as a matter of prime importance for the prosperity, strength and security that it would give to the whole island of Great Britain.[69]

However, the Union promptly came under threat before it came into force on 1 May. From the beginning of January, once Union seemed to be well underway in the Scottish Estates, Scottish commercial networks at home and abroad sought to profiteer from two fiscal circumventions facilitated by the timetable for implementing the Treaty. The first involved the exploitation of drawbacks on customs granted in England on colonial products like tobacco that were subsequently re-exported. Accordingly, Scottish networks imported tobacco wholesale from England prior to 1 May with a view to earning a further drawback after the Union when the tobacco was exported to continental markets. The second entailed the importing into Scotland of industrial quantities of whalebone from Holland, brandy, claret and salt from France and further salt from Spain, which were to be brought into England customs-free after the Union. Not only were Scots paying less customs duty on these commodities before Union, but salt had added value for the curing of fish, and whalebone stimulated considerable manufacturing of bodices and stays for colonial as well as domestic markets.

News of this activity provoked a backlash in the English parliament which, in turn, gained momentum from disquiet about the rigorous management of the Union. Harley had attempted to defuse this situation on 7 April by prescribing drawbacks earned by Scots on colonial goods. He also proposed that unless the Scots paid full English duties in addition to those already paid in Scotland, the re-export of goods and produce

---

[69] BL, Hanover State Papers 1692–1710: vol. II (1707–10), Stowe, MS 223, fols. 17–19; *LDN*, pp. 393–6; *SPC*, p. 759; *MSSM*, pp. 69–70, 78; *CBJ*, pp. 186, 189–90; RC, TKUA, England, Akter og Dokumenter nedr Sofart og Handel: Order med Bilag, 1707, A.III/217; *Lords*, new series, VII (1706–8), pp. 19–21; *A Complete Collection of the Protests made in the House of Lords*, pp. 146–9. According to the analytical list of Sainty & Dewar, *Divisions in the House of Lords*, there were four divisions on the ordering and content of articles between 15 and 24 February, which were carried comfortably, with three similar results, 71–21, 70–23 and 71–22, and a less decisive 58 to 21. The only means the Tories had to force a vote on the ratification in the Lords was on the appended act of security for the Kirk. They lost two divisions on 3 and 4 March, by 55 to 19 on each occasion.

acquired since February would be banned after 1 May. But he did so without the support of the Whig Junto who were subjected to ferocious lobbying by Scottish politicians and merchants. Even the relatively placid under-secretary for Scottish affairs at Court, Sir David Nairn, was moved to claim these prescriptive measures were in direct breach of Union. The Scottish furore and the resultant tension between the Lords and the Commons was only resolved by Queen Anne proroguing parliament on 30 April before the prescriptions could be enacted. An increasingly sharp correspondence between James Brydges, the paymaster-general for Marlborough's forces, and his financial associate John Drummond, the Amsterdam-based, Scottish entrepreneur, revealed not only the intensity of Scottish lobbying, but the actual price of Union. Drummond, who claimed his commitment to Union was being sorely tested, admitted that the circumvention by double drawbacks was scandalous. But he fully supported the importing and manufacturing of continental commodities, in which he specified that £300,000 had been invested by far-from-impoverished Scottish commercial networks in the first four months of 1707: this was in addition to the normal commercial exchange with the continent and in spite of the increased risk from privateers. Thus, the true price of the Union was not the £20,000 advanced to cover arrears of salary or even the £232,888 promised as reparations for Darien, but that of removing the prescriptions, at £300,000 in Scotland's favour.[70]

[70] HL, Stowe Papers: Brydges Family Papers, ST 57/vol. 1, pp. 81–2, 93, 94–6, 110–11, 126, and ST 58/vol.1, pp. 115–16, 144–5, 149–52, 175–7. NAS: Mar & Kellie Collection, GD 124/15/491/2; Journal of William Fraser, merchant, London, 1699–1711, CS 96/524; Letter and account book of John Watson, younger, merchant, Edinburgh, 1696–1713, CS 96/3309. BL, Blenheim Papers, vol. DXXI, Add. MSS 61, 631, fo. 19; *GMC*, II, pp. 749–50, 754–6; *Lords*, new series, VII (1706–8), pp. 91–6; Speck, *The Birth of Britain*, pp. 117–18. The Scottish tariff on whalebones was 90 per cent lower than in England. Drummond, who had three ships involved in the circumvention of continental import duties, claimed that the rumoured £400,000 invested by Scots in whalebone alone was the fabrication of a few scoundrel customs officers who had gleaned their information in an Amsterdam brandy shop where some English bankrupts resorted. He knew from the Dutch director of the Greenland trade that there was not the equivalent of £150,000 of whalebone in all seven of the United Provinces.

Part V

Conclusion

11 The Treaty of Union

The two kingdoms may have been united, but the reaction to the implementation of the Treaty of Union on 1 May 1707 was markedly different in England from in Scotland. Queen Anne, accompanied by her English ministry and the members of the Houses of Lords and Commons in the newly proclaimed British parliament, attended a service of thanksgiving in St Paul's Cathedral, a service which was replicated from London to Berwick-upon-Tweed and served to affirm imperial monarchy and the consolidated fiscal–military state, if not Protestant solidarity. Also in attendance was Queensberry (soon to be given a British peerage as the Duke of Dover) and the full contingent of sixteen representative Scottish peers but only a handful of Scottish MPs, the absentees being more in tune with the muted response to Union in Scotland. Whereas there were celebratory bonfires and the ringing of bells throughout England, the only commemorative sounds heard north of Berwick were the precautionary movement of an additional company of guards into Edinburgh and plaintive laments played on the church bells of the city, commencing with 'Why should I be sad on my wedding day?'.[1] Elsewhere in Scotland nobody protested and nobody celebrated the day of Union. Indeed, the day seems to have gone unrecorded in the minutes of town-councils, in the journals and account books of merchants, as well as in the registers of local government and the Kirk. Neither Presbyterian nor Episcopalian clergy issued sermons of celebration or condemnation.[2]

---

[1] *Mar & Kellie*, p. 389; RC, TKUA, England, Akter og Dokumenter nedr Sofart og Handel: Order med Bilag, 1707, A.III/217; *MLP*, pp. 68–9. Whereas a royal order for dissolving the Scottish Estates was prepared in the aftermath of the queen's assent to Union on 6 March and duly effected on 29 April, the English parliament, without the necessity of a dissolution, was declared to be the British parliament in the House of Lords on 1 May.

[2] There are twenty-three sermons of thanksgiving purportedly delivered on 1 May (see McLeod & Mcleod, *Anglo-Scottish Tracts, 1701–1714*, pp. 42–3, 51, 77, 82, 111–15, 131, 149–50). All are from England but none surpassed the case for Union eloquently made by the London Scot, John Arbuthnot, a doctor and an Episcopalian, whose *A Sermon preach'd to the people, at the Mercat Cross of Edinburgh in December* (Edinburgh, 1706) was never delivered nor indeed intended to be delivered, being based on an apocryphal text

Yet Queensberry, at the opening of the last session of the Scottish Estates, had claimed that the Treaty would secure a perpetual union 'upon just and equall terms advantageous to both the Kingdoms' and in his concluding remarks had claimed that the Treaty would prove a visionary act of statesmanship. He duly embarked on his triumphalist journey south on 2 April, being notably feted from his crossing the Border until his arrival in London, where the queen and the English ministry again lauded him.[3] However, in anticipation of the arrival of Queensberry and the other leaders of the Court Party and the Squadrone, Godolphin had made the rather curmudgeonly comment to Marlborough on 4 April that 'The Scots are all expected next week. They will bring with them a great deal of pretensions and create us a good deal of trouble'. Yet this can also be deemed a more realistic reading of the Treaty of Union which, from its conception to its delivery, primarily served the interests of England, notwithstanding the hopes and ambitions of its Scottish backers.[4]

The articles

The Treaty of Union can be divided into three components – the articles for constitutional arrangements, those for economic issues and those for preserved Scottish institutions.[5] The Revolution of 1688–91 had represented a triumph for the Gothic perspective of the English parliament over the Britannic one of Stuart monarchy, a triumph that had marginalised the Irish and threatened to do the same for the Scottish. Accordingly, article I can be viewed as an accommodation between the Gothic and the Scottish perspectives in so far as the newly created 'United Kingdom' was to be called 'Great Britain'. Thus, Scotland was not incorporated into England, but with England in Great Britain. However, English views of parliamentary supremacy, legislative precedent and the common law continued to take precedence over Scottish claims for a written constitution as an aspect of fundamental law, to wit the National Covenant of 1638, the Solemn League and Covenant of 1643 and the Claim of Right of

---

to reveal the maxims of wisdom relating to political economy. Scotland should be content with the standing and privileges of Wales as growth in trade and manufactures was to be stimulated mainly through landed enterprise. No mention was made of Ireland though the tract was also published in Dublin in 1706 and subsequently was re-issued in Dublin and London during the passage of Union at Westminster.
[3] DH, Loudoun Papers, A 1131/8; *APS*, XI, p. 491; *MLP*, pp. 68–9.   [4] *MGC*, II, p. 745.
[5] *APS*, XI, pp. 406–13, c.7; *The Treaty of Union of Scotland and England 1707*, pp. 81–107; *A Source Book of Scottish History*, III, pp. 480–9. A particularly helpful copy of the Treaty with italicised amendments is to be found in Whatley, *Bought and Sold for English Gold?* pp. 101–17.

1689. Thus, the Hanoverian Succession as prescribed in the English Act of Settlement of 1701 was reaffirmed by article II, and the unified British parliament specified in article III was the continuation of the Houses of Lords and Commons, with the addition of sixteen peers in the former and forty-five shire and burgh commissioners to the latter by article XXII.[6]

The drastic restriction in the number of Scottish peers participating in the parliamentary process was especially insisted upon by Whigs as well as Tories in England. The eighty-three nobles attending the last session of the Scottish Estates numbered not far behind the ninety-nine who entered the division lists of the House of Lords during the passage of Union, and usually matched those who entered the division lists since the accession of Queen Anne once proxy votes were discounted.[7] This reduction was partially ameliorated by article XXIII, which conceded that the sixteen representative peers would have all the parliamentary privileges that the peers of England enjoyed, especially the right of sitting in the trial of fellow peers. All the peers of Scotland, and their successors, were to be peers of Great Britain and have rank and precedence after the English peers and before all peers of Great Britain created after the Union. The Scottish nobility had reluctantly accepted this article in the belief that many of them would be rewarded for their services to Union by being created peers of Great Britain; but this expectation did not materialise immediately after 1707. They had to suffer a further indignity in 1708 when the British parliament ruled that their elder sons could not sit as MPs, a prospect which they had viewed as partial compensation for their reduced numbers.[8]

---

[6] According to article XXII, and subsequently worked out by a separate complementary enactment (*APS*, XI, pp. 425–6, c.8; *The Treaty of Union of Scotland and England 1707*, pp. 115–19; NAS, Supplementary Parliamentary Papers, PA 7/20/97), an individual MP was to be returned for each of twenty-seven shires at every general election, while six smaller shires were grouped randomly in three sets of two – notably, Bute and Caithness, Nairn and Cromarty, and Clackmannan and Kinross. The shires in these sets were to return an MP at alternate elections. Only Edinburgh among the burghs was to return an MP at every general election. The remaining sixty-five royal burghs were apportioned into fourteen electoral sets – nine of five burghs and five of four burghs – primarily on geographic grounds with little respect to trading activity or fiscal standing.

[7] Sainty & Dewar, *Divisions in the House of Lords*, see analytical lists for 1702–7. The highest number in any division in the session of 1702–3 was 128, but if proxies are discounted this was reduced to 104; for the session of 1703–4 the figure was 130 reduced to 101 by the removal of proxies; for the session of 1704–5, the figure was 125 reduced to 88 without proxies; and for 1705–6, the highest voting division (without any proxies) had 99 peers participating.

[8] NAS, Home of Marchmont MSS, GD 158/941; DH, Notes of Colonel William Dalrymple, first parliament of Great Britain 1707–8, A 817/3, pp. 5–6; Penicuik, *HUSE*, pp. 196–7. Although Queensberry was admitted to the Lords as Duke of Dover in 1708, he was

Any temptation to view the Anglo-Scottish Union as a triumph for the Britannic vision of James VI & I must consider the scale of representation accorded to Scotland in the House of Commons, which further underscored that a federative arrangement had lost out to an incorporation that was explicitly imperial and commercial. Scottish representation was less than that for the counties of Devon and Cornwall, a tangible indication that Union marked the culmination of England's intrusive hegemony throughout the seventeenth century. Nevertheless, William Paterson, in spinning the case for political incorporation at the opening of the last session of the Scottish Estates, was adamant that the sparse representation of Scotland was justified. In proportion to its land tax, Scotland was to have a more generous representation in the new British parliament than Wales or any other district of England except Cornwall, whose representation was linked to its former wealth from tin mining. Paterson's case was duly elaborated in the house on 7 January 1707, when the leaders of the Court Party who had served as commissioners for the negotiation of the Treaty claimed that Scottish representation was 'greater then we could pretend to have it by any rule' whether based proportionally on land tax, customs and excise or population.[9]

Nevertheless, the subordinate Scottish representation at Westminster, the sacrifice of Scottish sovereignty, however tenuous, and the monopolising of places of profit by Scottish politicians favoured by the predominantly English ministries, ensured that Jacobitism remained viable as a political cause if not a sustained movement. Indeed, Scottish Jacobitism acquired not only new impetus but also new direction from the Union. Before 1707, Jacobitism had sought to alter the Scottish political agenda. After 1707, this objective was submerged in the struggle to reassert and retain the political identity of Scotland. Patriotism, no less than dynasticism, became its driving force. Far from securing peace within the British Isles, the Union provoked two major risings in 1715 and 1745, and two minor ones in 1708 and 1719, albeit Scotland not England bore the brunt of combat. The succession of the Elector of Hanover as George I in 1714

---

not allowed to vote directly for the representative peers, who duly included Hamilton. Made Duke of Brandon in 1711, presumably in recognition of his pusillanimous ineptitude in opposing Union, his sitting in parliament as a British peer was contested on the grounds that this privilege was exclusive to English peers and the sixteen peers chosen for Scotland.

[9] J. Robertson, 'Empire and Union: Two Concepts of the Early Modern European Political Order' in Robertson, ed., *A Union for Empire*, pp. 3–37; BL, W. Paterson, Treatises on the Union, Add. MS 10403, third letter, pp. 28–30; DH, Colonel Dalrymple's Memorandums, particularly during 1706–7 debates in the last Parliament of Scotland, A 817/2, pp. 125–6.

having terminated his ministerial career, the first major rising was led by Mar, the political manager of the passage of Union through the Scottish Estates.[10]

Jacobitism also benefited from the inevitable political recession that followed on from the concession of free trade (article IV), which created a common market in which Scotland was comparatively under-resourced and under-capitalised and lacking a competitive edge in manufacturing and skilled labour. Nevertheless, this article ended all prospects of a renewal of the tariff war that had culminated in the Alien Act of 1705, and had two major and enduring benefits. In the first place, it allowed for the free flow of capital across the Borders. No longer could English investors be prevented from investing in Scottish ventures, as had been the case at Darien. In the second place, the Scots were now guaranteed access to the American colonies of the Crown. The operations of their commercial networks no longer required the circumvention of the English Navigation Acts. Although the Scots could now trade legally in the West Indies, the East Indies remained a monopoly of the merging East India Companies based in London, which was the only English trading concern able to exclude rival companies or restrict the active participation of anyone wishing to engage in commerce overseas. This monopoly was effectively underwritten by the Union even though writers on political economy were becoming 'Sufficiently Convinced that Monopolies, or Exclusive Companies are in all Cases prejudicial unto, and most Inconsistent with the growth and Encrease of Trade'. There was no question of the 'English' becoming the 'British' East India Company.[11]

Scottish commercial networks were brought under further commercial regulation in article V, which allowed Scottish-built ships to come within the scope of the English Navigation Acts. Scottish ships built abroad, the vast majority in 1707, were also deemed as British, with one important proviso. Scots who were part-owners of these ships were given twelve months to buy over or sell vessels that were held with a majority foreign shareholding. Daniel Defoe claimed that he actually suggested this year of grace to the Scottish Estates to give sufficient notice for Scots to dissolve mainly Dutch partnerships. This article did not necessarily work to the benefit of Scots engaged in commercial networks that were dominated by merchants of other countries. But it did allow Scottish networks, with minority foreign participants, to operate as British commercial entities. However, the major assertion of English control over Scottish trading

---

[10] A. I. Macinnes, 'Jacobitism in Scotland: Episodic Cause or National Movement?' *SHR*, 86 (2007), pp. 225–52.
[11] HL, Loudoun Scottish Collection, box 48/LO 10102; Mackillop, 'Accessing Empire'.

operations occurred with article VI. Henceforth, all parts of the United Kingdom were to be under the same trading regulations and liable to the same customs and duties. This article offered two immediate benefits. Scottish cattle drovers were no longer to be liable to local taxes and customs that had proved particularly irksome when levied at Carlisle along with import duties to England. Scottish exporters of the staple crops of oats and barley were to enjoy the higher English premium or bounties awarded to exporters of grain. Article VII carried this regulation further by imposing the same rates of excise.[12]

Nevertheless, there were several inherent disadvantages in the Scots having to adjust to English commercial regulation and meet higher duties for customs and excise. In the first place, the Scottish carrying trade was specifically targeted with respect to exports of wool from England, a practice that was now proscribed throughout the United Kingdom. Until the negotiations on Union, it was declared illicit only by the English parliament, as in the legislation accompanying the Alien Act of 1705, and duly disregarded by Scottish commercial networks. Although Scottish wool-masters, particularly those landowners from the Borders affiliated to the Squadrone, supported this measure as an encouragement to manufacturing through landed enterprise, the immediate beneficiaries were English not Scottish manufacturers. In the second place, higher duties of customs and excise made smuggling an attractive option for Scottish commercial networks who did not abandon their circumvention of the Navigation Acts once they became British regulations.

Unrestricted access to the American colonies after 1707 enabled Glasgow merchants to secure dominance in the tobacco trade, primarily by expanding the store system in which the merchant rather than the planter bore the risk of transatlantic shipping. Whitehaven, hitherto third after Bristol and Liverpool in the Atlantic trade, was so eclipsed by Glasgow merchants' use of the store system, in tandem with smuggling, mainly through the Isle of Man, that the Cumbrian town actually petitioned for repeal of the Treaty of Union in 1710. The Glasgow merchants took advantage of drawbacks of customs for re-export by shipping out huge quantities of tobacco to the Isle of Man and then bringing small amounts back illicitly to ports in the south-west of Scotland. Likewise, Scottish entrepreneurs duly extended the store system perfected by the Glasgow tobacco lords into the Caribbean in order to enhance

---

[12] Daniel Defoe, *Observations on the Fifth Article of the Treaty of Union, humbly offered to the Consideration of the Parliament, relating to Foreign Ships* (Edinburgh, 1706); Penicuik, *HUSE*, pp. 190–2.

profits from sugar and rum.[13] As smuggling developed nationwide in the wake of Union, Jacobites were certainly to the fore in the illicit importation of wines and brandy from France. While successive British governments feared the association of Jacobitism with this clandestine pursuit in Scotland, political capital for the exiled Stuarts rarely if ever accumulated outside the Highlands and the north-east.[14]

In Scotland, salt produced from solar evaporation of seawater in France and Spain had long been considered more suitable for curing of perishable commodities for export than the domestic salt produced from the fuelling of saltpans by coal. Accordingly, article VIII served to curtail the smuggling of vast quantities of foreign salt by allowing delayed payments of higher import duties and by drawbacks raised to English rates on foreign salt used exclusively in the curing of herring, beef and pork for export. However, the main substance of this article was to ensure, for Scottish salt used for domestic consumption, a rolling seven-year exemption from the higher rates paid in England to meet the Crown loans to the East India Company. The exemption of Scotland from other current English duties such as stamp duty on paper, vellum and parchment (article X), the tax on windows and lights (article XI), the duties on coals, ashes and cinders (article XII) and that on malt (article XIII), can be regarded as economic palliatives, which were further confirmed by article XIV, that specified the malt tax would not be levied on beer produced and consumed in Scotland for the duration of the War of the Spanish Succession. Article IX can also be regarded as a palliative to smooth Scotland's accession into the United Kingdom in confirming that the land tax on the country was not to exceed £480,000. This sum was deemed equitable in relation to the highest taxes ever raised in Scotland and the highest rates ever levied in England before the Union. Moreover, Scottish landlords had to bear the brunt of the expenses in collecting the land tax, which in England was a charge borne by the government and could amount to a deduction of up to a twentieth of all tax collected. This article, therefore, allowed a measure of protection to the landed interest in Scotland and removed an impediment to landed enterprise.[15]

---

[13] Somerville, *The History of Great Britain*, pp. 598–600; *Lords*, original series (1689–90), pp. 168–9; *Calendar of Treasury Papers (1557–1728)*, ed. J. Reddington, 6 vols. (London, 1868–89), pp. 117, 170, 229, 241, 252–3, 261; T. M. Devine, *The Tobacco Lords* (Edinburgh, 1975), pp. 55–71; A. I. Macinnes, 'Scottish Gaeldom from Clanship to Commercial Landlordism' in Foster, Macinnes & MacInnes, eds., *Scottish Power Centres*, pp. 162–90.
[14] Whatley, *Scottish Society*, pp. 171, 194–7; *Historical Papers Relating to the Jacobite Period, 1699–1750*, I, pp. 1–27, 131–65; HL, Loudoun Scottish Collection, box 15/LO 7973 and box 46/LO 12761.
[15] Penicuik, *HUSE*, pp. 192–3; Somerville, *The History of Great Britain*, pp. 600–1.

As Sir John Clerk of Penicuik made clear in his exposition upon article XV, the Equivalents were perhaps 'more talked of, and less understood' than any other aspect of the Treaty of Union. Because Scotland had been guaranteed access to English domestic and colonial trade under article IV, it was not unreasonable to expect that Scotland should pay a share of the English National Debt after 1707. However, this debt had been magnified by the War of the Spanish Succession and stood at around £20 million when the Union was negotiated in 1706. Moreover, there was a shortfall of £3 million in the funds provided to service the National Debt. Accordingly, it was deemed equitable that Scotland should be indemnified by a greater Equivalent totalling £398,085 10s (50p) that was to be paid over seven years from the customs and excise as recompense for higher public burdens, for the standardisation of the coinage and as reparations for Darien. In exchange for reparations the Company of Scotland trading to Africa and the Indies was dissolved. A lesser Equivalent of £2,000 per annum was also to be paid out of the customs and excise, initially to promote the manufacture of coarse woollens and then to fishing and other manufactures such as linen, which actually became the principal beneficiary of this fund.

William Paterson, as one of the calculators of the Equivalents, had claimed that the Scots were to benefit greatly from this article, particularly as reparations for Darien would claim the major share of the monies allocated. His further promotion of the commercial advantages that would accrue to Scotland from free trade were somewhat tempered when it became evident, by 3 December 1706, that the customs and excise to be raised in Scotland in the first year after the Union was not likely to amount to more than £123,000 – less than that raised in 1700 and less than a third of the greater Equivalent. It was also admitted that foreign trade was not likely to advance more than £40,000 per annum in the first seven years of Union. Neither Clerk of Penicuik nor Paterson spelled out the full implications of article XV. As the Equivalents were to be raised by higher levels of customs and excise on Scotland after 1707, the Scots were effectively paying for their own compensation, reparations and investment in manufacturing. It took twenty years for the Equivalents to be implemented. Article XV was not so much a Union dividend as a testimony to inept Scottish negotiation.[16]

---

[16] Sir John Clerk of Penicuik, *An Essay upon the Fifteenth Article of the Treaty of Union* (Edinburgh, 1706); BL, W. Paterson, Treatises on the Union, Add. MS 10403, fourth letter, pp. 37–8, 41–3, and fifth letter, pp. 45–8, 53–4; *A State of the Publick Revenues and Debts of England, Together with a Scheme of the Sums of Money Allowed to Scotland by the Treaty of Union in name of Equivalent* (Edinburgh, 1706).

There were two other articles relating to economic issues. The standardisation of the coinage to sterling was duly specified in article XVI, which undoubtedly facilitated both the supply of money and the stability of exchange rates, features that were notably deficient in Scotland prior to 1707. However, it also removed the option for Scots to use Dutch currency as the standard for commercial exchange, a practice which had produced a measure of stability throughout the seventeenth century and had indeed cushioned Scots against swings in the value of sterling, especially in times of war. Like article V concerning shipping, this was a clear indication that Scottish commercial networks should operate within a British framework rather than continuing to favour association with the Dutch. Also to be standardised were weights and measures. Although the Convention of Royal Burghs regularly received notice of the standards in use in England, article XVII remained largely inoperative in bringing the Scots into line until the nineteenth century.[17] In terms of political economy, the Treaty of Union removed impediments, redressed grievances and gave guaranteed access to colonial markets in the interests of equal opportunity for growth. But the Treaty neither gave nor guaranteed economic security for Scotland any more than for England.

The importance of commercial and fiscal regulation in the making of Union was underlined by article XVIII, which specified that Scots law in this area was to be brought into line with that of England. The article went on to draw a distinction between laws concerning public policy and civil government, which were to be the same throughout the United Kingdom, and those concerning private rights, which were to be unaltered in Scotland unless the British parliament should legislate for the evident utility of the Scottish subjects of the Crown. Notwithstanding this distinction between public and private law, the whole apparatus of Scots law was effectively alterable by the parliament of Great Britain. Article XXV appeared even handed in declaring void statutes and laws of both England and Scotland that were inconsistent with or contrary to the Treaty. But article XIX spelled out that the preservation of Scots law was not unconditional, which, in turn, served notice that other preserved institutions in local government or even the Kirk were not guaranteed unalterable status. The Court of Session and the College of Justice (or Court of Justiciary), as the supreme Scottish courts for hearing, respectively, civil and criminal cases, were to remain as constituted by statute in Scotland, but subject to regulation by the British parliament

---

[17] Penicuik, *HUSE*, p. 195; R. E. Zupko, 'The Weights and Measures of Scotland before the Union', *SHR*, 55 (1977), pp. 124–39.

for the better administration of justice. Cromartie, as a staunch advocate of political incorporation, had been adamant that no appeals should be allowed from the supreme Scottish courts to the House of Lords because appeals would derogate from their status as the last vestiges of Scottish sovereignty, because of the prevailing ignorance of Scots law in the British parliament, and because of the great expense attendant on appeals from Edinburgh to London. However, the matter of appeals was left open rather than excluded in the Treaty.[18]

The first Scot to bring an appeal from Scotland to the Lords was Cromartie's fellow member of the Court Party, Archibald Primrose, 1st Earl of Rosebery, over fishing rights in the water of Cramond near Edinburgh, in February 1708. The more celebrated case was that of the Episcopalian clergyman James Greenshields, an Ulster Scot whose preaching and use of an Anglican liturgy in Edinburgh in defiance of the local presbytery led to his imprisonment by the town council, a decision upheld in the Court of Session but lost on appeal to the House of Lords in 1711. This decision paved the way in the following year for the first substantive breach in the Act for securing the Protestant Religion and Presbyterian Church Government as embodied within the Treaty of Union. By the Toleration Act, Episcopalian congregations which were prepared to recognise Queen Anne as the rightful monarch secured the right, as jurors, to worship according to the Anglican liturgy. By the Patronage Act, the right of leading landowners to nominate ministers to serve in vacant parishes was restored, but if a majority of a congregation dissented the matter was left to the resolution of the presbytery. The first Act confirmed the split between the jurors and the Jacobite-adhering, non-jurors among Scottish Episcopalians. The second solidified existing divisions between erastian and radical Presbyterians and paved the way for schisms throughout the eighteenth and into the nineteenth century. Schisms, in turn, lessened the grip of the established Kirk on education and poor relief which had been confirmed by the Union.[19]

However understated it was on appeals, article XIX was far more prescriptive in restructuring and subordinating other aspects of the judicial process in Scotland. The Court of Admiralty in Scotland and heritable admiralty jurisdictions were continued but brought into conformity with English practice, and made subject to the Lord High Admiral or the

---

[18] George MacKenzie, Earl of Cromartie, *A Letter to a Member of Parliament upon the 19th Article of the Treaty of Union between the two Kingdoms of Scotland and England* (Edinburgh, 1706).

[19] *Lords*, new series, VII (1706–8), p. 554; HL, Loudoun Scottish Collection, box 18/LO 8351 and box 45/LO 9439; *APS*, XI, pp. 402–3, c.6; Devine, *The Scottish Nation, 1700–2000*, pp. 18–19.

Commissioners of the Admiralty for Great Britain and ultimately to the regulation of the British parliament. More strikingly, the Scottish Court of Exchequer was not only to be brought into conformity with English practice: the first British parliament decided the Scottish Court should be superseded in deciding all questions concerning the revenues accruing from customs and excise by a new court that followed mainly English law and procedures and was presided over initially by an English judge, with at least one of its four judges throughout the eighteenth century being an English lawyer. The changes brought about under this article undoubtedly had a positive, long term effect in familiarising Scottish lawyers with the workings of a more developed legal system, attuned to commerce, legislative reform and due process, that produced precedents of authority and clarity.[20]

Nevertheless, three important political qualifications are required. Firstly, the judicial changes were wholly consistent with the Treaty's containment of the rogue behaviour of Scottish commercial networks evident in the articles on economic issues. Secondly, the foisting of the English treason law on Scotland in the wake of the abortive Jacobite rising of 1708 was not done to improve justice but rather to expedite easier convictions. Moreover, this treason law was a breach in the spirit, if not the letter, of Union in foisting on Scotland the alien concept of attainting the blood that condemned not just errant parents, but innocent children and even subsequent generations to forfeit their titles and property. Thirdly, article XIX left open the question of whether the Scottish Privy Council was to be continued, even though this Council had played a vital role in securing Union by monitoring dissent within Scotland, by holding troops reinforcing the Borders and in Northern Ireland in reserve, and by intimidating Episcopalian clergy north of the Firth of Tay as Jacobites opposed to the Hanoverian Succession. Ostensibly abolished by the first British parliament to integrate local government throughout the United Kingdom, the Privy Council was sacrificed for electoral appeasement. With the first British general election looming in 1708, the Squadrone did not wish the Court Party to gain any managerial advantage from their continuing control of the Council. With the removal of the country's central intelligence agency, the main beneficiaries, as was borne out in the risings of 1715 and 1745, were the Scottish Jacobites.[21]

---

[20] J. W. Cairns, 'Scottish Law, Scottish Lawyers and the Status of the Union' in Robertson, ed., *A Union for Empire*, pp. 243–68; *Lords*, new series, VII (1706–8), pp. 573–9.

[21] DH, Notes of Colonel William Dalrymple, First Parliament of Great Britain 1707–8, A 817/3, pp. 3, 38–43, 88–92, and Loudoun Papers, unmarked green deed box, bundle 1706/October–December; HL, Loudoun Scottish Collection.

The inherently conservative, if not reactionary, nature of the Treaty of Union was manifested in relation to local government. Heritable jurisdictions as part of feudal rights to property (article XX) were retained, as were the rights and privileges of the royal burghs (article XXI). The latter was a result of the royal burghs' ongoing campaign not to accommodate the commercial aspirations of dependent burghs. The former article was roundly condemned by radicals within the Kirk and by constitutional reformers as 'scandalous & ancient badges of the Scots slavery to their Lords', and was even regretted by more reflective members of the Court Party. In reality, justices of the peace and commissioners of supply were assuming increasing responsibility for administration and fiscal exactions in the shires with full encouragement from the first British parliament. Heritable jurisdictions, other than estate management in baronial courts equivalent to that of manorial courts in England, had become anachronistic and were no longer fit for purpose by the time of their abolition in 1747, in the wake of the last Jacobite rising.[22] The final article (XXIV) to be considered appeared on the one hand to be a continuation of the qualified but subordinated continuation of Scottish institutions: that is, the Great Seal of Scotland was to be retained but the Great Seal of England was to assume responsibility for authenticating government records in the United Kingdom. On the other hand, the retention of the Scottish seal warranted the creation of the Royal Bank of Scotland in 1727 to manage the eventual funding for the greater and lesser Equivalents. In the longer term, the associated requirement of this article that all public and private records of Scotland should be retained there, notwithstanding the Union, laid the foundation for archivally based Scottish history within an imperial context.

The aftermath

The immediate reaction to Union in Scotland, as in England, was far from favourable. Scottish politicians at Westminster were increasingly seen as venal pawns of the ruling ministry. Breaches in both the spirit and the letter of the Treaty with respect to reserved areas in the Kirk and Scots law, administrative dismantling and delays in honouring the Equivalents occasioned growing resentment at the governance of Scotland. A premature endeavour to bring about parity in the malt tax led to a concerted effort

---

[22] NLS, Wodrow MSS, quarto lxxv, fo. 150; DH, Notes of Colonel William Dalrymple, First Parliament of Great Britain 1707–8, A 817/3, pp. 56–63; Penicuik, *HUSE*, p. 196.

by the Scottish contingent at Westminster to terminate the Union in 1713. This effort was marshalled by Seafield (now 4th Earl of Findlater) who had presided over the passage of the Treaty in the Scottish Estates. The motion to terminate lost narrowly in the House of Lords, by four votes exercised through proxies.[23] The Union not only survived and endured, but actually thrived from the mid eighteenth century with the crushing of Jacobitism. The Scottish landed elite, merchants and professional classes came to realise that Empire presented them with a golden opportunity for personal and family advancement, and the burgeoning fiscal–military state learned to cultivate their evangelical capacity for enterprise and exploitation.[24]

The making of the United Kingdom in 1707 was the product of power, control and negotiation. England had the military power to coerce and the fiscal power to persuade. The English ministry was intent on controlling through political incorporation what had become a rogue state in terms of commercial exchange. In return, Scottish manpower, Scottish enterprise and ultimately Scottish intellectual endeavour were harnessed in service of Empire. The Union gave Scotland free access to the largest commercial market then on offer. The unrestricted movement of capital and skilled labour within that market stimulated and fructified native entrepreneurship both domestically and imperially. However, given that England was as much, if not more, in need of a stable political association, the question remains whether Scottish politicians made best use of their negotiating options. The landed elite, backed up institutionally by the Kirk, opted to conserve their privileged position within Scotland rather than to continue the Scottish Estates for the promotion of political and social reform. Association with England was a more feasible, though not necessarily less bloody or more commercially sound, option than an alliance with the United Provinces, at least until Jacobitism was crushed and Empire expanded. An association with England, on the other hand, was less religiously fractious than one with France. In uniting with England, the Scots prioritised the attainment of sustainable prosperity through manufacturing stimulated by landed enterprise rather than by overseas trade. The former option was also reinforced by territorial acquisitiveness through Empire that opened up opportunities for Scots, if not necessarily Scotland, through colonies, manufactures and war.

[23] Holmes, *Politics, Religion and Society in England*, pp. 109–38. HL, Loudoun Scottish Collection: box 23/LO 8831, /LO 8868; box 33/LO 9116; box 42/LO 9347; box 43/LO12573. Anon., *Reasons for Dissolving the Treaty of Union Betwixt Scotland and England In a Letter to a Scots Member of Parliament, from one of his Electors* (London, 1713).
[24] Devine, *Scotland's Empire*, pp. 62–8.

Political incorporation, however, was not an end in itself. The fortunes of the Union have been umbilically linked to the Empire. As the British Empire has declined in the twentieth century, Union has moved from a constitutional fixture to a constitutional option, particularly within the context of a European Community that continues to expand at the outset of the twenty-first century.

Appendix. Recorded voting divisions in the Scottish Estates

Category	Content	For/Against*	Majority
1. *Constitutional*			
First vote	Principle of Union	116/83	33
Ratification	Treaty of Union	110/69	41
Securing religion	Presbyterian establishment	113/38	75
Vote 2	Hanoverian Succession	116/57	59
Vote 3	British parliament	113/83	30
Vote 21a	Burgh privileges	104/22	82
Vote 21b	Burgh privileges	105/8	97
Vote 23	Peers' privileges	88/50	38
2. *Economic*			
Vote 4	Free trade	154/19	135
Vote 7	Exciseable liquors	114/78	36
Vote 14a	Customs duties	107/88	19
Vote 14b	Customs duties	105/66	39
Vote 15a	Equivalents	121/50	71
Vote 15b	Equivalents	138/27	111
Vote 8a	Salt tax	92/93	(1)
Vote 8b	Salt tax	110/82	28
Vote 8c	Salt tax	114/39	75
Vote 8d	Salt tax	112/86	26
Vote 15c	Equivalents	112/71	41
Vote 15d	Equivalents	112/55	57
Vote 18a	Regulation of trade	103/72	31
Vote 18b	Regulation of trade	103/52	51
3. *Political*			
Procedural order	Voting sequence	112/84	28
Proclamation I	Unlawful meetings	145/04	141
Proclamation II	Unlawful meetings	110/62	48
Vote 22a	Scottish representation	114/73	41
Vote 22b	Scottish representation	101/59	42
Vote 22c	Scottish representation	105/54	51
Vote 22d	Scottish representation	83/65	18
Vote 22e	Scottish representation	94/63	31

*'Votes for' are those of the supporters of Union regardless of whether they were voting against amendments proposed by the opponents of Union.

Bibliography

PRIMARY SOURCES

ARCHIVAL MATERIAL

Aberdeen City Archives
  Aberdeen Council Letters, vols. 7–8 (1682–1719)
  Aberdeen Council Register, vols. 57–8 (1681–1721)
  Aberdeenshire Commissioners of Supply, Valuation Book & Rolls, c. 1685–1741, 1/10 and 1/15
  Transcript of Propinquity Books, 1 (1706–22)
Aberdeen University Library
  Crathes Papers (Burnet of Leys), MS 3661
  Duff House (Montcoffer Papers), MS 3175
  Duff of Meldrum Collection, MS 2778
  Gregory Family MSS, MS 2206
  Leith Ross MS 3346
Bodleian Library, Oxford University
  Carte Papers (1701–19), MS Carte 180
  Nairn's Papers, vol. II (1689–1706), MS Carte 209
  Memorandum of Meetings relating to land in New England 1635–8, Bodl.MS Bankes 23
British Library, London
  Abstract of Decrees of the Court of Claims, 1662, Egerton MS 789
  An Abstract of Every Rent per annum in every Barony in Each County in the Kingdom of Ireland, 1678, Add.MSS 15,899
  Blenheim Papers, vol. DXXI, Add.MSS 61,631
  Collection of Historical and Parliamentary Papers 1620–60, Egerton MS 1048
  Edmondes Papers, Stowe MS 172
  Fees, Crown Grants Etc., Stowe MS 597
  Hanover State Papers, vols. I–II, 1692–1710, Stowe MSS 222–3
  Hardwicke Papers, vol. DXVI, Add.MSS 35,864
  Hatton-Finch Papers: Letters to the Earl of Nottingham, Secretary of State, vols. I–II (1694–1725), Add.MSS 29,588–9
  India Office Records, Court Minutes, 1702–5, B/47
  Lauderdale Papers, Add.MSS 23,234

Leeds Papers, vol. XVII, Egerton MS 3340
Letters and State Papers: Birch Collection, Add.MSS 4158
Maitland and Lauderdale Papers, 1532–1688, Add.MSS 35,125
Negotiations of Col. Hooke in Scotland, 1705–7, Add.MSS 20,858
Nicholas Papers, Egerton MSS 2533, 2542
Original Documents relating to Scotland, the Borders & Ireland, 16th and 17th centuries, Add.MSS 5754
Papers of Cardinal F. A. Gualterio; Letters of Queen Mary of Modena and the Princess Louisa Maria, 1701–18, Add.MSS 20,293
Papers Relating to English Colonies in America and the West Indies, 1627–99, Egerton MS 2395
Papers Relating to Ireland, vol. II (1691–1700), Add.MSS 21,136
Papers Relating to Trade etc., Sloane MS 2902
Petitions, 1648–54, Add.MSS 34,326
Scotch Plot, 1702–4. Papers of Simon Fraser, Lord Lovat, Add.MSS 31,249
Sidney, 1st Earl of Godolphin: Official Correspondence, Home, 1701–10, Add.MSS 28,055
T. Astle, Historical Collections, Add.MSS 34,713
The Scotch Plot, 1702–4, Papers of Simon Fraser, Lord Lovat, Add.MSS 31,249–50
W. Paterson, Treatises on the Union (transcribed London, 1708), Add. MSS 10403

Centre historique des Archives Nationales, Paris
Affaires Estrangers (consulats) Etates Unis: Etats de commerce et de navigation des ports 1697–1830, B/III/444

Dumfries House, Cumnock, Ayrshire
Loudoun Papers & Deeds
Parliamentary Memorandums & Notes of Colonel William Dalrymple, 1704–8

Dundee City Archives
Dundee Council Book, vols. IV–VIII (1613–1715)
Dundee Register of Ships, 1612–81

Edinburgh City Archives
Convention of Royal Burghs, Moses Collection, SL 30

Glasgow City Archives
Campbell of Succoth MSS, TD 219
Dunlop of Garnkirk Papers, D 12
Hamilton of Barns Papers, TD 589
Records of the Maxwells of Pollock, T-PM
Research Papers and Notes compiled by R. F. Dell, TD 1022/11
Register of Deeds B.10.15

Huntington Library, San Marino, California
Blathwayt Papers
Bridgewater & Ellesmere MSS
Hastings Irish Papers
Huntington Manuscripts

Manuscript Newsletters from London to Tamworth (1690–1704), HM 30,659

HM 1264, [Nehemiah] Grew, 'The Meanes of a most Ample Encrease of the Wealth and Strength of England in a few years humbly presented to Her Majesty in the 5th Year of Her Reign'

Loudoun Scottish Collection

Robert Alonzo Brock Collection

Stowe Papers

    Brydges Family Papers

    Greville Papers

    Temple Papers

Inveraray Castle Archives, Inveraray, Argyllshire

    Argyll Papers

Mount Stuart House, Rothesay, Isle of Bute

    Loudoun Papers

National Archives of Scotland, Edinburgh

    Account book of James Lawson, merchant, Anstruther Easter, 1688–98, CS 96/3263

    Advertisement: Emigration to New Jersey 1688, RH 18/1/93

    Andrew Russell Papers, GD 1/885 and RH 15/106

    Biel MSS, GD 6

    Breadalbane Collection, GD 112

    Bruce of Kinross Papers, GD 29

    Campbell of Barcaldine Papers, GD 170

    Clerk of Penicuik Papers, GD 18

    Commission book, James Ramsay, merchant, Rotterdam, 1691–4, CS 96/1337

    Cromartie MSS, GD 305

    Dalhousie MSS, GD 45/14/335

    Douglas of Strathendry MSS, GD 446

    Eglinton MSS, GD 3

    Exchequer Papers: Warrants of the Exchequer Register 1707, E8

    Hamilton Papers, GD406

    Hay of Haystoun Papers, GD 34

    Home of Marchmont MSS, GD 258

    John McGregor Collection, GD 50

    Journal of William Fraser, merchant, London, 1699–1711, CS 96/524

    Kennedy of Dalquharran Papers, GD 27

    Kinross House Papers, 1668–85, GD29

    Letter and account book of John Watson, younger, merchant, Edinburgh, 1696–1713, CS 96/3309

    Letter book of Gilbert Robertson, merchant, Edinburgh, 1690–4, CS 96/1726

    Letter book of John Swinton of that Ilk, merchant, London, 1673–7, CS 96/3264

    Letters and Papers of Thomas Bannatyne, RH 15/14

    Letters of W. & R. Fraser, London, RH 15/13

    Leven & Melville MSS, GD 26

    Macpherson of Cluny Papers, GD 80/868

Mar & Kellie Collection, GD 124
Memorandum, account and letter book of William and John Cowan, merchants, Stirling, 1697–1754, CS 96/1944
Miscellaneous Foreign Papers RH 9/5/23
Miscellaneous Papers of Charles Mitchell of Pitteadie, Writer in Edinburgh, RH 15/19
Montrose MSS, GD 220
Ogilvie of Inverquharity Papers, GD 205
Papers pertaining to the Argyll Family, GD 1/1158
Scarth of Breckness MSS, GD 217
Scott of Ancrum MSS, GD 259
Seafield Papers, GD 248
Society of Antiquaries Papers, GD103
Supplementary Parliamentary Papers, PA 2 and PA 7
Titles to Lands in East New Jersey, RH 15/131/1
Trinity House Leith, GD 226
Waste book, Leith, 1675–8, CS 96/157

National Library of Scotland, Edinburgh
Dunlop Papers, MS 9250
Saltoun Papers, MS 17498
Wodrow MSS,
folio, xxv, xxviii, xxxiii, xxxv
octavo, ix
quarto, ix, xvi, xxv, xxvi, xxviii, xxxiv, xxxvi, xl, lxxiii, lxxv, lxxxii

Newberry Library, Chicago
Edward E. Ayer Manuscript Collection
George Martin, 'An Essay on Barbados' (1651), Ayer MS 276
Memoranda on French colonies in America, including Canada, Louisiana, and the Caribbean (1702–50), 4 vols., Ayer MS 293
Sir Richard Dutton, 'The State of Barbados' (1684), Ayer MS 827

New England Historic Genealogical Society, Boston
Biographical Sketches of the Founders of the Scots Charitable Society MSS B 536/V.12

Northumberland Record Office, Berwick-upon-Tweed
Berwick Guild Books (1659–1716), B 1/12–14

Orkney Archives, Kirkwall
Balfour of Balfour and Trenaky, D2
Kirkwall Town Council Minute Book, 1691–1732
Papers relating to the family of Moodie of Milsetter, SC 11/86

Public Record Office, London (also National Archives)
Anglo-Scottish Committee of Parliament appointed to confer with the deputies from Scotland: minute book, 1652 October 14 – 1653 April 8, SP 25/138
Prussia – State Papers, 1706–8, SP 90/4
Secretaries of State: State Papers Scotland, series II, SP 54/1–4, /18

Rigsarkivet, Copenhagen
Danske Kancelli, diverse breve, documenter og akter, C.63 III, 'Den af Isack Holmes Fuldmaglig, Seneca Torsen holdte Journal paa alle engelske og

skotske Skippere saavel fra Vestersoen som fra Østersoen, der har passeret Øresund, 23 April 1681 – January 15, 1684'

TKUA, England, A I, 3–4, Breve, til Vels med Bilag fra Medlemmer af det engelske Kongehus til medlemmer af det danske, 1613–1726

TKUA, England, A II, 12, Breve fra forskellige engelske Stats og Hofembedsumamd til Kong Christian IV, 1588–1644

TKUA, England, A II, 14, Akter og Dokumenter vedrgrende det politiske Forhold til England, 1631–40

TKUA, England, A II, 33–7, Politiske Forhold, 1679–1701: State Papers Denmark – Greg's Diplomatic Papers (1694–9)

TKUA, England, Akter og Dokumenter nedr Sofart og Handel: Order med Bilag, 1702–7, A.III/ 207–10, /214–17.

Vestindisk-guineisk Kampagne, 1671–1755, A 4/465–7, Direktionens correspondence – Supplikationskopibøger (1690–1712)

Shetland Archives,
  Bruce of Sunburgh Papers, D8
Tollemache Family Archives, Buckminster, Grantham, Lincolnshire
  Papers, TD 3758–60

PAMPHLETS AND TRACTS

Abercromby, Patrick. *The Advantages of the Act of Security Compared with these of the Intended Union Founded on the Revolution Principles Publish'd by Mr Daniel De Foe* (1706)

A Brief Account of the Province of East-Jersey in America Published by the present proprietors thereof (London, 1682)

A Brief Account of the Province of East-New-Jersey in America: published by the Scottish Proprietors having interest there (Edinburgh, 1683)

A declaration of the state of the colony and affaires in Virginia. With the names of the adventurors, and sums adventured in that action (London, 1620)

Aglionby, William. *The Present State of the United Provinces of the Low Countries* (London, 1667)

A Letter Concerning Trade from several Scots Gentlemen that are Merchants in England, to their Countrymen that are Merchants in Scotland (London, 1706)

A Letter from the Commission of the General Assembly of the Church of Scotland met at Glasgow, July 21, 1699 (Edinburgh, 1699)

Alexander, Sir William. *An Encouragement to Colonies* (London, 1624)

The mapp and description of New England, together with a discourse of plantation and colonies; also a relation of the nature of the climate, and how it agrees with our owne-countrey England (London, 1630)

Ames, Richard. *The Jacobite Conventicle: A Poem* (London, 1692)

Amy, Thomas. *Carolina: or, A brief description of the present state of that country, and the natural excellencies thereof* (London, 1682)

An Abstract of the Laws of New England as they are now established (London, 1641)

[An American.] *An Essay upon the Government of the English Plantations on the Continent of America* (London, 1701)

Anderson, James. *An Historical Essay shewing that the Crown and Kingdom of Scotland, is Imperial and Independent* (Edinburgh, 1705)
Andrew Fletcher of Saltoun: Selected Political Writings and Speeches, ed. D. Daiches (Cambridge, 1979)
Anon. *A Brief Description of the Province of Carolina on the coasts of Floreda* (London, 1666)
  A Call to Scotland for threatening famine (Edinburgh, 1698)
  A Congratulation of the Protestant-joyner to Anthony King of Poland, upon his arrival in the lower world (London, 1683)
  Advice to Great Britain &c. A Poem by a hearty Lover of his Country (London, 1701)
  A Familiar Discourse between George, a true-hearted English gentleman and Hans a Dutch merchant: concerning the present state of England (London, 1672)
  A Letter Concerning the Consequence of an Incorporating Union in Relation to Trade (Edinburgh, 1706)
  A letter from a gentleman in the country to his friend in Edinburgh wherein it is clearly proved, that the Scottish African and Indian Company is exactly calculated for the interest of Scotland (Edinburgh, 1696)
  A Letter to one of the Commissioners for the Present Union of England and Scotland, 30 April 1706 (London, 1706)
  A Letter to Sir J. P. Bart., A Member for the ensuing parliament, relating to the Union of England and Scotland (London, 1702)
  A Modest Vindication of the Earl of S[. . .]y: in a letter to a friend concerning his being elected King of Poland (London, 1681)
  An Account of the Burning of the Articles of the Union at Dumfries (Edinburgh, 1706)
  An Account of the Scotch Plot in a Letter from a Gentleman in the City to his Friend in the Country (London, 1704)
  An Answer to Some Queries &c Relative to the Union: in a Conference betwixt the Coffee Master and A Country Farmer (1706)
  A Narrative of a New and Unusual American Imprisonment of Two Presbyterian Ministers and prosecution of Mr Francis Makemie. One of them, for preaching one Sermon at the City of New York (1707)
  An essay against the transportation and selling of men to the plantations of foreigners with special regard to the manufactories, and other domestick improvements of the kingdom of Scotland (Edinburgh, 1699)
  An Historical Account of the Publick Transactions in Christendom. In a Letter to a Friend in the Country (London, 1694)
  A proper project for Scotland to startle fools, and frighten knaves, but to make wisemen happy (Edinburgh, 1699)
  A Seasonable Warning or the Pope and King of France Unmasked (1706)
  A Short Account of the Union betwixt Sweden, Denmark & Norway which commenced about the year 1523. Taken from Puffendorf's History of Sweden (London, 1702)
  A Speech Intended to have been Spoken in Parliament by a Member who was necessarily absent (Edinburgh, 1705)

A Speech Without Doors anent the giving a subsidy before the passing of an Act of Security (Edinburgh, 1704)
A True Account of the Horrid Conspiracy against the Life of His Sacred Majesty William III (Edinburgh, 1692)
Britannia's Triumph (London, 1697)
Caledonia; or, the Pedlar turn'd Merchant. A Tragi-Comedy, as it was acted by His Majesty's Subjects of Scotland in the King of Spain's Provinces of Darien (London, 1700)
Carolina described more fully than heretofore (Dublin, 1684)
Certaine Inducements to Well Minded People (London, 1643)
Essay upon the Union (London, 1706)
Impartial history of the plots and conspiracies against the life of King William III contrived by the devices of our enemies at the Court of France (London, 1696)
In the act for raising two million, and for settling the trade to the East-Indies are the following clauses (Edinburgh, 1698)
More Excellent Observations of the Estate and Affairs of Holland (London, 1622)
Nova Britannia: offering most excellent fruits by planting in Virginia. Exciting all such as be well affected to further the same (London, 1609)
Observations on the Fourth Article of Union (Edinburgh, 1706)
Reasons for Dissolving the Treaty of Union Betwixt Scotland and England In a Letter to a Scots Member of Parliament, from one of his Electors (London, 1713)
Scotland's Speech to her Sons (Edinburgh, 1706)
Some considerations concerning the prejudice which the Scotch act establishing a company to trade to the East and West-Indies (with large priviledges, and on easie terms) may bring to the English sugar plantations, and the manufactury of refining sugar in England, and some means to prevent the same from Scotland and other nations (London, 1696)
Some considerations upon the late act of the Parliament of Scotland, for constituting an Indian company in a letter to a friend (London, 1695)
The Antiquity of Englands Superiority over Scotland and The Equity of Incorporating Scotland or other Conquered Nations, into the Commonwealth of England (London, 1652)
The art of assassinating kings taught Louis XIV and James II by the Jesuits (London, 1696)
The Case is Alter'd Now: or, The conversion of Anthony King of Poland, published for satisfaction of the sanctifyed brethren (London, 1683)
The Conduct of the Dutch relating to the Breach of Treaties with England (London, 1760)
The Dutch Drawn to Life (London, 1660)
The Funeral of the Good Old Cause, or A Covenant of Both Houses of parliament against the Solemn League and Covenant (London, 1661)
The King of Poland's Last Speech to his Countrymen (London, 1682)
The Last Will and Testament of Anthony King of Poland (London, 1682)
The Miraculous and Happie Union of England & Scotland (Edinburgh, 1604)
The Profit and Loss of the East-India-trade, stated, and humbly offer'd to the consideration of the present Parliament (London, 1700)

The Scotch Echo to the English legion: or, The Union in Danger, from the Principles of some Old and Modern Whigs in both Nations, about the Power of Parliaments (Edinburgh, 1707)

The Smoaking Flax Unquenchable: where the union betwixt the two kingdoms is dissecated, anatomized, confuted and annulled (1706)

The True Picture of a Modern Tory (London, 1702)

To the Loyal and Religious Hearts in Parliament, Some Few Effects of Union, proposed between Scotland and England (Edinburgh, 1706)

Arbuthnot, John. *A Sermon preach'd to the people, at the Mercat Cross of Edinburgh in December* (Edinburgh, 1706)

A State of the Publick Revenues and Debts of England, Together with a Scheme of the Sums of Money Allowed to Scotland by the Treaty of Union in name of Equivalent (Edinburgh, 1706)

[Atwood, William.] *Remarks upon a late Dangerous Pamphlet, Intitled, The Reducing of Scotland by Arms, and annexing it to England as a Province* (London, 1705)

Atwood, William. *The Scotch Patriot Unmask'd* (London, 1705)

  The Superiority and Direct Dominion of the Imperial Crown of England over the Crown and Kingdom of Scotland, the True Foundation of a Compleat Union, reasserted (London, 1705)

[B., A., a diligent observer of the Times], *A Brief Relation of the beginning and ending of the Troubles in the Barbados; with the True Causes thereof* (London, 1653)

[Bacon, Sir Francis.] *Three speeches of the Right Honourable, Sir Francis Bacon Knight, then his Majesties Sollicitor Generall, after Lord Verulam, Viscount Saint Alban. Concerning the post-nati naturalization of the Scotch in England, Union of the lawes of the kingdomes of England and Scotland* (London, 1641)

Baillie, Robert. *A Dissuasive from the Errours of the Times* (London, 1645)

Baker, Richard. *The Marchants Humble Petition and Remonstrance to his Late Highenesse, with an accompt of the losses of their shipping, and estate, since the war with Spain* (London, 1659)

Bannatyne, John. *A Letter from a Presbyterian Minister in the Countrey, to a Member of Parliament; and also of the Commission of the Church concerning toleration and patronages* (Edinburgh, 1703)

  Some Queries Proposed to Consideration, relative to the union now intended (Edinburgh, 1706)

[Barclay, David & Forbes, Arthur.] *An Advertisement concerning the Province of East-New-Jersey in America* (Edinburgh, 1685)

Battie, John. *The Merchants Remonstrance. Wherein is set forth the inevitable miseries which may suddenly befall this kingdome by want of trade, and decay of manufacture* (London, 1644 and 1648)

B[emde], J[ohn.] *A Memorial Briefly pointing out some Advantages of the Union of the Two Kingdoms: Humbly offered to the Consideration of the Commissioners appointed to that end* (London, 1702)

Black, David. *An Essay upon Industry & Trade shewing the Necessity of the One, the Conveniency and Usefulness of the Other and the Advantages of Both* (Edinburgh, 1706)

Black, William. *A Letter Concerning the Remarks upon the Consideration of Trade* (1706)
  Answer to a Letter concerning Trade sent from several Scots Gentlemen, that are Merchants in England to their Countrymen that are Merchants in Scotland (Edinburgh, 1706)
  A Short View of the Trade and Taxes of Scotland (1706)
  Some Considerations in Relation to Trade (Edinburgh, 1706)
  Some Few Remarks Upon the State of the Excise after the Union, compar'd with what it is now (1706)
  Some Overtures and Cautions in Relation to Trade and Taxes (1707)
  The Preface to the Fifth Essay, at removing national prejudices (Edinburgh, 1707)
  Wednesday 18th December 1706. Remarks upon a pamphlet intitul'd, The Considerations in Relation to Trade Considered, and a short view of our present trade and taxes reviewed (1706)
Blackmore, Sir Richard. *A true and impartial history of the conspiracy against the person and government of King William III of glorious memory, in the year 1695* (London, 1723)
Bland, John. *Trade Revived, or, A way proposed to restore, increase, inrich, strengthen and preserve the decayed and even dying trade of this our English nation* (London, 1659 and 1660)
Blith, W. *The English improver improved or the survey of husbandry surveyed discovering the improveableness of all lands* (London, 1652)
Bowles, Edward. *The Mysterie of Iniquity, Yet Working in the Kingdomes of England, Scotland, and Ireland, for the Destruction of Religion Truly Protestant* (London, 1643)
Brewster, Sir Francis. *New Essays on Trade* (London, 1702)
Brown, Andrew *An Essay on the Project for a Land-Mint* (1705)
  A Scheme Proposing a True Touch-Stone for the due trial of a proper union betwixt Scotland & England (Edinburgh, 1706)
  Some Very Weighty and Seasonable Considerations tending to dispose, excite and qualify the nation, for the more effectual treating with England in relation to an union of confederacy (Edinburgh, 1703)
Bruce, Alexander. *A Discourse of a Cavalier Gentleman on the Divine and Human Law, with respect to the Succession* (1706)
Budd, Thomas. *Good Order established in Pennsilvania & East New Jersey in America, being a true account of the country* (Philadelphia, 1685)
Burnet, Gilbert. *Some Letters, containing an account of what seemed most remarkable in Switzerland, Italy, some parts of Germany, &c.* (London, 1688)
B[urton], R[ichard]. *A View of the English Acquisitions in Guinea, and the East-Indies* (London, 1686)
  The English Empire in America: or a prospect of His Majesties dominions in the West-Indies (London, 1685)
  The history of the Kingdom of Scotland, containing an account of the original of that nation, and of the most remarkable transactions and revolutions during the reigns of seventy two kings and queens to the seventh year of William III (London, 1696)

Cant, A[ndrew]. *A Sermon preached on the XXX Day of January 1702/3 at Edinburgh, by one of the Suffering Clergy in the Kingdom of Scotland* (Edinburgh, 1703)
Carr, William. *Travels through Flanders, Holland, Germany, Sweden and Denmark* (London, 1691)
Cary, John. *A Discourse concerning the Trade of Ireland and Scotland as they stand in Competition with the Trade of England* (Bristol, 1695, and London, 1696)
[Castell, William.] *A Petition of W. C. exhibited to the High Court of Parliament now assembled, for the propagating of the Gospel in America and the West Indies* (London, 1641)
  A Short Discoverie of the Coasts and Continent of America, from the equinoctiall northward and the adjacent isles (London, 1644)
[Chamberlen, Hugh.] *Dr Chamberlen's Petitions and Proposals for a Land Bank to Increase Trade, humbly offered to the House of Commons* (London, 1693)
  Papers relating to a Bank of Credit upon Land Security proposed to the Parliament of Scotland (Edinburgh, 1693)
Child, John. *New England's Jonas cast up in London* (London, 1647)
Child, Sir Josiah. *A Discourse about Trade* (London, 1690)
  A treatise wherein it is demonstrated . . . That the East-India trade is more profitable and necessary to the kingdom of England, than to any other kingdom or nation in Europe (London, 1681)
Clerk of Penicuik, Sir John. *A Letter to a Friend, giving an account how the Treaty of Union has been received here* (Edinburgh, 1706)
  An Essay upon the Fifteenth Article of the Treaty of Union (Edinburgh, 1706)
  A Short Essay upon the Limitations to prove that they are so far from being of consequence to the nation, that they may tend very much to its prejudice (Edinburgh, 1703)
Cleveland, John. *The Character of a London-diurnall with severall poems* (London, 1647)
[Codrington, Robert.] *His Majesties Propriety, and dominion on the British Seas asserted: together with a true account of the Neatherlanders insupportable insolencies, and injuries, they have committed; and the inestimable benefits they have gained in their fishing on the English Seas* (London, 1665 and 1672)
[Cooke, Edward.] *Arguments for and against an union, between Great Britain and Ireland, considered* (Dublin, 1798)
Coke, Roger. *A Discourse of Trade: in two parts . . . The latter of the growth and increase of the Dutch trade above the English* (London, 1670)
  A Discourse of Trade in two parts (London, 1675)
  England's improvements in two parts: in the former is discoursed how the kingdom of England may be improved; in the latter is discoursed how the navigation of England may be increased and the sovereignty of the British Seas more secured to the crown of England (London, 1675)
Copland, Patrick. *A Declaration of Monies* (London, 1622)
  Virginia's God be Thanked (London, 1622)
Craig, Alexander. *The Political Recreations of Mr Alexander Craig of Rose-Craig, Scoto-Britan* (Aberdeen, 1623)

Craig, Sir Thomas, *Scotland's Soveraignty Asserted*, trans. from Latin by George Ridpath (London, 1695)

Crofton, Zachary. *Excise Anatomiz'd, and Trade Epitomiz'd: declaring, that the unequall imposition of excise, to be the only cause of the ruine of trade, and universall impoverishment of this whole nation* (London, 1659)

Davenant, Charles. *Discourses on the Publick Revenues, and on the Trade of England: Part I – Of the Use of Political Arithmetick, in all Considerations about the Revenues and Trade* (London, 1698)

Essays upon Peace at Home and War Abroad (London, 1704)

The true picture of an ancient Tory in a dialogue between Vassal a Tory and Freeman a Whig (London, 1702)

Day, J. *A publication of Guiana's plantation newly undertaken* (London, 1630)

de Britaine, William. *The Dutch Usurpation or, a brief view of the behaviour of the States General of the United Provinces, towards the Kings of Great Britain: with some of their cruelties and injustices exercised upon the subjects of the English nation* (London, 1672)

[Defoe, Daniel.] *A Fourth Essay at removing national prejudices* (Edinburgh 1706)

A Fifth Essay, at removing national prejudices (Edinburgh, 1707)

An Essay at Removing National Prejudices against a Union with Scotland. Part I & Part II (London, 1706), *Part III* (Edinburgh, 1706)

Considerations in Relation to Trade Considered, and a short view of our present trade and taxes (Edinburgh, 1706)

Memoirs of John, duke of Melfort; being an account of the secret intrigues of the Chevalier de S. George, particularly relating to the present times (London, 1714)

Observations on the Fifth Article of the Treaty of Union, humbly offered to the Consideration of the Parliament, relating to Foreign Ships (Edinburgh, 1706)

The Advantages of Scotland by an Incorporating Union with England, Compar'd with these of a Coalition with the Dutch or League with the French (1706)

The Dissenters in England vindicated from some reflections in a late pamphlet, entituled, Lawful prejudices, &c. (Edinburgh, 1707)

The State of the Excise after the Union, compared with what it is now (Edinburgh, 1706)

The State of the Excise &c, Vindicated (Edinburgh, 1706)

Denton, Daniel. *A Brief Description of New York formerly called New Netherlands* (London, 1670)

De Unione Regnorum Britanniae Tractatus by Sir Thomas Craig, ed. C. S. Terry (Edinburgh, 1909)

Donaldson, James. *Husbandry anatomized* (Edinburgh, 1697)

Douglas of Glenbervie, Sylvester. *Speech of the Right Honourable Sylvester Douglas: in the House of Commons on Tuesday, April 23, 1799; on seconding the motion of the Right Honourable Chancellor of the Exchequer, for the House to agree with the Lords in an address to His Majesty, relative to a Union with Ireland* (Dublin, 1799)

Drake, John. *Historia Anglo-Scotica* (London, 1703)

Dundas, Henry. *Substance of the speech of the Right Hon. Henry Dundas, in the House of Commons, Thursday, February 7, 1799, on the subject of legislative union with Ireland* (London, 1799)

Eburne, Richard. *A plaine pathway to plantations* (London, 1624)
Edit du roy pour l'establisement de la Compagne des Indes occidentals. Verifié en Parlement le unziéme jour de iullet 1664 (Paris, 1664)
Elliot, Gilbert, Earl of Minto. *The speech of the Lord Milton, in the House of Peers, April 11, 1799, on a motion for an address to His Majesty, to communicate the resolution of the two houses of Parliament, respecting an union between Great Britain and Ireland* (London, 1799)
Emeris, [M]. *A Panegyrick upon William II* (Edinburgh, 1699)
[F., R.] *The Present State of Carolina with Advice to the Settlers* (London, 1682)
[Fairfax, Blackerby.] *A Discourse upon the Uniting Scotland with England* (London, 1702)
Ferguson, Mr Adam. *Chaplain to the Regiment, A Sermon preached in the Ersh Language to his Majesty's First Highland Regiment of Foot commanded by Lord John Murray at the Containment at Camberwell on 18 December 1745* (London, 1746)
Ferguson, Robert. *A Brief Account of some of the late incroachments and depredations of the Dutch upon the English* (London, 1695)
Fletcher of Saltoun, Andrew. *Selected Political Writings and Speeches*, ed. D. Daiches (Edinburgh, 1979)
  Speeches by a Member of Parliament, which began at Edinburgh the 6th of May 1703 (Edinburgh, 1703)
  State of the Controversy betwixt United and Separate Parliaments (1706)
For the Colony in Virginia Britannia. Lawes Divine, Morall and Martiall &c. (London, 1612)
Gentleman, Tobias. *England's Way to Win Wealth and to Employ Ships and Mariners* (London, 1614)
[Gildon, Charles.] *The Post-Boy Robb'd of his Mail: or, The Pacquet Broke Open* (London, 1706)
Gordon, John. *Elizabethae Reginae Manes De Religione Et Regno Ad Iacobum Magnum Brittaniarum Regem, Per Ionnem Gordonium Britanno-Scotum* (London, 1604)
Grant, Francis. *The Patriot Resolved* (1707)
Hamilton, John, Lord Belhaven. *A Speech in Parliament touching limitations* (Edinburgh, 1703)
  The Lord Beilhaven's Speech in Parliament the second day of November 1706. On the subject-matter of an union betwixt the two Kingdoms of Scotland and England (Edinburgh, 1706)
  The Lord Belhaven's Speech in Parliament, the 15th day of November, on the Second Article of the Treaty (Edinburgh, 1706)
Hayman, Robert. *Quodlibets, lately come over from New Britaniola, old New-foundland. Epigrams and other small parcels, both morall and divine* (London, 1628)
Herries, Walter. *An Enquiry into the Caledonian Project, with a defence of England's procedure (in point of equity) in relation thereunto* (London, 1701)
  A New Darien Artifice Laid Open (London, 1701)
  The Defence of the Scots Settlement at Darien answer'd paragraph by paragraph (London, 1699)

[Hill, Joseph.] *The Interests of these United Provinces Being a Defence of the Zeelanders Choice* (Middleburgh, 1673)
Hilton, William. *A Relation of a Discovery lately made on the Coast of Florida* (London, 1664)
Hodges, James. *The Rights and Interests of the two British Monarchies, inquir'd into and clear'd; with a special respect to an united or separate state. Treatise I* (London, 1703)
   The Rights and Interests of the Two British Monarchies with a Special Respect to An United or Separate States. Treatise III (London, 1706)
[Holland, John.] *A short discourse on the present temper of the nation with respect to the Indian and African Company, and of the Bank of Scotland also, of Mr Paterson's pretended fund of credit* (Edinburgh, 1696)
Howard, E. *A pastoral poem upon the discovery of a late horrid conspiracy against the sacred person of William III, King of England* (London, 1696)
Howell, James. *Londinopolis, an historical discourse or perlustration of the city of London, the imperial chamber, and chief emporium of Great Britain* (London, 1657)
Hutchison, Francis. *Sermon preached at St. Edmund's-Bury on the First of May 1707 being the day of Thanksgiving for the Union of Scotland and England* (London, 1707)
Jervis, Sir John Jervis White. *A letter addressed to the gentlemen of England and Ireland, on the inexpediency of a federal union between the two kingdoms* (Dublin, 1798)
[Johnson, Robert.] *The New Life of Virginia: Declaring the former successe and present estate of that plantation, being the second part of Nova Britannia* (London, 1612)
Johnson, Thomas. *A Discourse Consisting of Motives for the Enlargement and Freedom of Trade, Especially that of cloth, and other woollen manufactures, engrossed at present contrary to the law of nature, the law of nations and the lawes of this kingdom* (London, 1645)
Johnson, William. *Reasons for adopting an union, between Ireland and Great Britain* (Dublin, 1799)
Kerr, Captain Charles. *Strictures upon the union betwixt Great Britain and Ireland... Particularly detailing the advantage derived to Scotland from her union with England* (Dublin, 1799)
Lawton, Charles. *The Jacobite Principles vindicated; in Answer to a Letter sent to the Author* (London, 1693)
Lewes, Robert. *The Merchants Mappe of Commerce wherein, the universall maner and matter of trade is compenduously handled* (London, 1638)
Lithgow, William. *Scotlands welcome to her native sonne, and sovereign lord, King Charles* (Edinburgh, 1633)
MacKenzie, George, Earl of Cromartie. *A Friendly Return to a letter concerning Sir George Mackenzie's and Sir John Nisbet's Observation on the matter of Union* (1706)
   A Letter from E[arl of] C[romartie] to E[arl of] W[harton] Concerning the Union (Edinburgh, 1706)
   A Letter to a Member of Parliament upon the 19th Article of the Treaty of Union between the two Kingdoms of Scotland and England (Edinburgh, 1706)

Bibliography 341

An Abstract of what was spoke in Parliament by E. C. (1705)
A Second Letter, on the British Union (Edinburgh, 1706)
A Speech in Parliament, concerning the exportation of wool (Edinburgh, 1704)
My Lord Chancellor, it was my humble opinion on the beginning of this session of Parliament, that the interest of this kingdom and the posture of publick affairs, did invite upon us on several accounts to have begun with an act and commission for a treaty with England (Edinburgh, 1703)
Parainesis Pacifica, or, A persuasive to the union of Britain (Edinburgh, 1702)
[MacKenzie, Roderick.] *A Full and Exact Account of the Proceedings of the Court of Directors and Council-General of the Company of Scotland Trading to Africa and the Indies, with relation to the Treaty of Union now under the Parliament's Consideration* (Edinburgh, 1706)
Maddison, Sir Ralph. *Englands looking in and out presented to the High Court of Parliament now assembled* (London, 1640)
Marius, John. *Advice Concerning Bills of Exchange* (London, 1655)
Markham, Gervaise. *A Way to Get Wealth: containing the Sixe Principal Vocations or Callings, in which everie good Husband or House-Wife may lawfully employ themselves* (London, 1631 and 1648)
[Maxwell, Henry.] *An Essay upon an Union of Ireland with England* (London, 1703, and Dublin, 1704)
[Meston, William.] *Old Mother Grim's Tale: Decade I* (London, 1737)
The Poetical Works of the Ingenious and Learned William Meston: sometime Professor of Philosophy in the Marshal College of Aberdeen (Edinburgh, 1767)
Morton, Thomas. *New English Canaan or New Canaan* (Amsterdam, 1637)
Murray, Sir David. *The Tragicall Death of Sophinisba. Written by David Murray, Scoto-Brittaine* (London, 1611)
Murray, Robert. *A proposal for a national bank consisting of land, or any other valuable securities or depositions, with a grand cash for returns of money* (London, 1695)
National Association for the Vindication of Scottish Rights. *Address to the People of Scotland, and statement of grievances* (Edinburgh, 1853)
Orain Iain Luim: Songs of John MacDonald, Bard of Keppoch, ed. A. M. MacKenzie (Edinburgh, 1973)
Order of Charles I empowering Company of Adventurers for the Plantation of the Island of Eleuthera (London, 1647)
Orr, Robert. *An address to the people of Ireland, against an union* (Dublin, 1799)
Parker, Henry. *The Generall Junto, or The Councell of Union: chosen equally out of England, Scotland and Ireland, for the Better Compacting of Three Nations into One Monarchy* (London, 1642)
Parker, Henry. *Of a Free Trade. A discourse seriously recommending to our nation the wonderful benefits of trade, especially of a rightly governed and ordered trade* (London, 1648)
[Paterson, William, alias Midway, Lewis.] *An Inquiry into the Reasonableness and consequences of an Union with Scotland* (London, 1706)
Paterson, William, alias 'Philopatris'. *An Essay Concerning Inland and Foreign, Publick and Private Trade; together with some Overtures, shewing how a Company*

of National Trade, may be constituted in Scotland, with the Advantages which will result therefrom (1704)

Paterson, William. *The Writings of William Paterson*, ed. S. Banister, 3 vols. (London, 1859)

Paxton, Peter. *A Scheme of Union Betwixt England and Scotland with Advantages to both Kingdoms* (London, 1705)

Penn, William. *A letter . . . to the Committee of the Free Society of Traders of that province [Pennsylvania], residing in London* (London, 1683)

Percival, Thomas. *The Rye-house travestie, or, A true account and declaration of the horrid and execrable conspiracy against His Majesty King William III* (London, 1696)

[Person of Quality.] *Great Britain's Union and the Security of the Hanoverian Succession Considered* (London, 1705)

Petty, Sir William. *Britannia Languens, or a Discourse of Trade* (London, 1680)
Political Arithmetick (London, 1690)
The Political Anatomy of Ireland, 1672 (Dublin, 1691)

[Philo-Caledon.] *A defence of the Scots settlement at Darien. With an answer to the Spanish memorial against it. And arguments to prove that it is in the interest of England to join with the Scots and protect it* (Edinburgh, 1699)

Plantagenet, Beauchamp. *A description of the province of New Albion and a direction for adventurers with small stock to get two for one, and good land freely and for gentlemen and all servants, labourers and artificers to live plentifully* (London, 1641, 1648 and 1650)

P[ollexfen], J[ohn]. *Of Trade* (London, 1700)

Potter, William. *Humble proposals to the honourable Councell for Trade and all merchants and others who desire to improve their estates* (London, 1651)
The Key of Wealth: or, A new way, for improving trade (London, 1650)
The Trades-man's jewel: or a safe, easie, speedy and effectual means for the incredible advancement of trade, and multiplication of riches (London, 1650)

Proposals by the Proprietors of East-Jersey in America, for the building of a town on Ambo-point (London, 1682)

Prynne, William. *The first tome of an exact chronological vindication and historical demonstration of our British, Roman, Saxon, Danish, Norman, English kings supreme ecclesiastical jurisdiction, in, over all spiritual, or religious affairs, causes, persons, as well as temporal within their realms of England, Scotland, Ireland, and other dominions* (London, 1665)

Pym, John. *A Most Learned and Religious Speech spoken by Mr. Pym, at a Conference of both Houses of Parliament the 23 of . . . September. Declaring unto them the Necessity and Benefit of the Union of his Majesties three kingdomes, England, Scotland, and Ireland in matters of Religion and Church-Government* (London, 1642)

Reynell, Carew. *The True English Interest, or an Account of the Chief National Improvement* (London, 1674)

[Ridpath, George.] *A Discourse upon the Union of England and Scotland* (Edinburgh, 1702)
An Historical Account of the Antient Rights and Power of the Parliament of Scotland (Edinburgh, 1703)

Considerations upon the Union of the Two Kingdoms (London, 1706)
The Case of Scots-men residing in England and in the English Plantations (Edinburgh, 1703)
The Proceedings of the Parliament of Scotland begun at Edinburgh 6 May 1703 (Edinburgh, 1704)
The Reducing of Scotland by Arms, and Annexing it to England as a Province Considered (Edinburgh, 1705)
The Scots Episcopal Innocence (London, 1694)
Robertson of Struan, Alexander. *Poems on Various Subjects and Occasions* (Edinburgh, 1749)
Robinson, Henry. *Brief Considerations, concerning the advancement of trade and navigation is humbly tendered unto all ingenious patriots* (London, 1649)
Certain proposals in order to the peoples freedome and accommodation in some particulars with the advancement of trade and navigation in this commonwealth in general (London, 1652)
Rutherford, Samuel. *Lex Rex or the Law and the Prince* (Edinburgh, 1848)
Scotland, Company of, Trading to Africa and the Indies. *Scotland's right to Caledonia (formerly called Darien) and the legality of the settlement asserted in three several memorials presented to His Majesty in May 1699* (Edinburgh, 1700)
Scot of Pitlochy, George. *A Brief Advertisement Concerning East-New-Jersey in America* (Edinburgh, 1685)
The Model of Government of the Province of East-New-Jersey in America (1685)
[Scott, Thomas.] *A Relation of Some Points concerning the State of Holland* (London, 1621)
The Spaniards Cruelty and Treachery to the English in the time of peace and war (London, 1654)
Scott, Sir Walter. *The Letters of Malachi Malagrowther*, ed. P. H. Scott ed. (Edinburgh, 1981)
Seton of Pitmedden, William. *A Speech in the Parliament of Scotland. The Second Day of November, 1706. On the First Article of the Treaty of Union* (Edinburgh, 1706)
Scotland's Great Advantages by an Union with England: shown in a letter from the country to a Member of Parliament (1706)
Some Thoughts, on ways and means for making this nation a gainer in foreign commerce (Edinburgh, 1705)
The Interest of Scotland in three essays (London, 1700)
Sibbald, Sir Robert. *Provision for the Poor in Time of Dearth and Scarcity* (Edinburgh, 1699)
Sidney, Algernon. *Discourses Concerning Government* (London, 1704)
[Sinclair, Sir Archibald.] *Some Thoughts on the present State of Affairs* (1703)
Smith, John. *Advertisements for the inexperienced planters of New England or anywhere* (London, 1631)
Smith, Captain John. *The Trade & Fishing of Great-Britain displayed with a description of the islands of Orkney and Shetland* (London, 1662)
Smith, Sir Thomas. *The Defence of Trade* (London, 1615)

[Somers, John, Lord Somers.] *An Essay upon the Union of the Kingdoms of England and Scotland* (London, 1705)
A Scheme for Uniting the Two Kingdoms of England and Scotland, different from any that has been hitherto laid down (Edinburgh, 1706)
Spotiswood, John. *A Speech of one of the Barons of the Shire of B[erwick] at a meeting of the Barons and Freeholders of that shire, for choosing commissioners to represent them in the ensuing Parliament, summoned to convene at Edinburgh the 12th day of November* (Edinburgh, 1702)
The Trimmer: or some necessary cautions concerning the union of the kingdoms of Scotland and England (Edinburgh, 1706)
Spreull, John. *An Account Current betwixt Scotland & England balanced together with An Essay of a Scheme of the Product of Scotland, and a few Remarks on each* (Edinburgh, 1705)
Temple, Sir William. *Observations upon the United Provinces of the Netherlands* (London, 1673)
The British Union: A Critical Edition and Translation of David Hume of Godscroft's De Unione Insulae Britannicae, ed. P. J. McGinnis & A. Williamson (Aldershot, 2002)
The Declaration of the British in the North of Ireland, With some queries of Colonel Moncke, and the answers of the British to the queries (London, 1649)
The Perfect Diurnall (London, 1650 and 1652)
The Petty Papers, ed. Marquis of Landsdowne, 2 vols. (New York, 1967)
The Political and Commercial Works of Charles D'Avenant, ed. C. Whitworth, 5 vols. (London, 1771; reprinted 1968)
Thomas, Sir Dalby. *An Historical Account of the Rise and Growth of the West-India Colonies and of the great advantage they are to England in respect of Trade* (London, 1690)
[Thompson, John, Baron Haversham.] *The Lord Haversham's speech in the House of Peers on Saturday, February 15, 1707* (London, 1707)
Thornborough, John, Bishop of Bristol. *A Discourse Shewing the Great Happiness that hath and may still accrue to his Majesties Kingdomes of England and Scotland By re-Uniting them into ane Great Britain* (London, 1604 and 1641)
Tittler, Colonel. *Ireland profiting by example: or, the question, whether Scotland has gained, or lost, by an union with England, fairly discussed. In a letter, from a gentleman in Edinburgh, to his friend in Dublin* (Dublin, 1799)
To His Grace, Her Majesty's High Commissioner, and the Right Honourable Estates of Parliament. The Address of the Commissioners to the General Convention of the Royal Borrows of this Ancient Kingdom (Edinburgh, 1706)
To His Grace, Her Majesty's High Commissioner, and the Right Honourable Estates of Parliament. The Humble Representation of the Council-General of the Company of Scotland Trading to Africa & the Indies (Edinburgh, 1706)
To His Grace Her Majesties High Commissioner and the Honourable Estates of Parliament, the humble petition of the peer shank workers and fingren spinners of Aberdeen and places thereabout (Aberdeen, 1706)
Toland, John. *Anglia Libera: or the limitations and succession of the crown of England explain'd and asserted* (London, 1701)
Two Tracts by Gregory King, ed. G. E. Barnett (Baltimore, 1936)

Unto His Grace Her Majesties High Commissioner and the most Honourable Estates of Parliament, Edinburgh January 16, 1707. The Representation and Petition of the Commission of the General Assembly of the National Church of Scotland (Edinburgh, 1707)

[Verax, Philanax.] *A letter from a member of the Parliament of Scotland to his friend at London concerning their late act for establishing a company of that kingdom tradeing to Africa and the Indies* (London, 1695)

Violet, Thomas. *The Advancement of Merchandize: or, Certain propositions for the improvement of trade of this Common-wealth, humbly presented to the right honourable the Council of State* (London, 1651)

Virginia and Maryland. Or, the Lord Baltimore's printed Case, uncased and answered. Shewing the illegality of his Patent and usurpation of Royal Jurisdiction and Dominion there (London, 1848)

Ward, Edward. *A Journey to Scotland giving a character of that country, the people and their manners* (London, 1699)

Webster, James. *Lawful Prejudices Against an Incorporating Union with England* (Edinburgh, 1707)

Whittel, John. *Constantinus Redivivus, or, A full account of the wonderful providences and unparallell'd successes that have all along attended the glorious enterprises of the heroical prince, William the 3rd, now King of Great Britain* (London, 1693)

Willsford, Thomas. *The Scales of Commerce and Trade* (London, 1660)

Wilson, Samuel. *An Account of the Province of Carolina in America* (London, 1682)

Wood, William. *New England Prospects* (London, 1634)

[Wright, William.] *The Comical History of the Marriage-Union betwixt Fergusia and Heptarchus* (London, 1706)

Wylie, Robert. *A Letter Concerning the Union, with Sir George Mackenzie's observation and Sir John Nisbet's opinion upon the same subject* (1706)

A Speech Without Doors, concerning toleration (Edinburgh, 1703)

COMMENTARIES AND MEMOIRS

Abercromby, Patrick. *The Martial Achievements of the Scottish Nation*, 2 vols. (Edinburgh, 1711–15)

Adair, Patrick. *A True Narrative of the Rise and Progress of the Presbyterian Church in Ireland (1623–1670)*, ed. W. D. Killen (Belfast, 1866)

Anon. *Britanniae Speculum: or a Short View of the Ancient and Modern State of Great Britain and the adjacent Isles, and of all other the Dominions and Territories, now in the actual possession of His present Sacred Majesty, King Charles II* (London, 1683)

The History of the Republick of Holland from its First Foundations to the Death of King William, 2 vols. (London, 1705)

Boyer, Abel. *The History of the Life and Reign of Queen Anne* (London, 1722)

Bruce, John. *Report on the Events and Circumstances which produced the Union of England and Scotland*, 2 vols. (London, 1799)

Burnet, Gilbert. *Bishop Burnet's History of His Own Time*, 2 vols. (London, 1724–34)

Bishop Burnet's History of His Own Time: from the Restoration of King Charles the Second to the Treaty of Peace at Utrecht, in the reign of Queen Anne (London, 1857)

Burnet, Gilbert. *The Memoirs of the Lives and Actions of James and William, Dukes of Hamilton and Castleherald* (London, 1838)

Campbell, John. *A Political Survey of Britain: Being a Series of Reflections on the Situation, Lands, Inhabitants, Revenues, Colonies and Commerce of this Island*, 2 vols. (London, 1774)

Chalmers, George. *Caledonia, or, A Historical and Topographical Account of North Britain, from the most ancient to the present times*, 8 vols. (Paisley, 1887–1902)

Clerk of Penicuik, Sir John. *History of the Union of Scotland and England*, ed. D. Duncan (Edinburgh, 1993)

Connor, Bernard. *The History of Poland in several letters to persons of quality* (London, 1698)

Craufurd, George. *The Lives and Characters, of the Officers of the Crown, and of the State in Scotland, from the beginnings of the reign of King David I to the Union of the Two Kingdoms* (London, 1726)

Cunningham, Alexander. *The History of Great Britain from the Revolution in 1688 to the Accession of George the First*, ed. T. Hollingberry, 2 vols. (London, 1787)

Dalrymple, Sir John. *Memoirs of Great Britain and Ireland from the dissolution of the last Parliament of Charles II until the sea-battle of La Hogue*, 2 vols. (London, 1771–88)

[Defoe, Daniel.] *The History of England from the beginning of the reign of Queen Anne, to the conclusion of the Glorious Treaty of Union between England and Scotland* (London, 1707)

The history of the union between England and Scotland (London, 1786)

The History of the Union of Great Britain (Edinburgh, 1709)

de Tende, Gaspard. *An Account of Poland* (London, 1698)

[Elzevirus, Bonaventure & Elzevirus, Abraham.] *Respublica, sive Status Regni Scotiae et Hiberniae* (Leiden, 1627)

Ferguson, Adam. *An Essay on the History of Civil Society 1767*, ed. D. Forbes (Edinburgh, 1966)

Hamilton, Charles. *Transactions during the reign of Queen Anne: from the union to the death of the princess* (Edinburgh, 1790)

Hermannides, Rutgerius. *Britannia Magna* (Amsterdam, 1661)

[Hooke, Nathaniel.] *Secret History of Colonel Hooke's Negotiations in Scotland in 1707* (Edinburgh, 1760)

Jones, David. *A Compleat History of Europe: or, a view of the affairs therein, civil and military for the year 1704* (London, 1705)

[Ker, John.] *The Memoirs of John Ker of Kersland in North Britain, Esq., Relating Politicks, Trade and History* (London, 1727)

Knox, John. *A View of the British Empire, more especially Scotland; with some proposals for the improvement of that country, the extension of its fisheries, and the relief of the people* (London, 1784)

Lewis de Lolme, John. *The British Empire in Europe* (London, 1787)

Bibliography 347

[Lockhart of Carnwath, George.] *Memoirs concerning the Affairs of Scotland, from Queen Anne's Accession to the Throne, to the Commencement of the Union of the Two Kingdoms of Scotland and England in May 1707* (London, 1714)

Macintosh, Daniel. *The History of Scotland from the invasion of the Romans till the Union with England, with a supplementary narrative of the rebellions in 1715 and 1745* (London, 1822)

Mackenzie, George. *The Lives and Characters of the Most Eminent Writers of the Scottish Nation*, 3 vols. (Edinburgh, 1708–22)

Macpherson, James. *The History of Great Britain, from the Restoration to the Accession of Power of the House of Hannover* (London, 1775)

Marshal, Ebenezer. *The history of the union of Scotland and England: Stating the circumstances which brought it to a conclusion, and the advantages resulting from it to the Scots* (Edinburgh, 1799)

Mémoires Du Comte De Forbin (1656–1733), ed. M. Cuénin (Paris, 1993)

Memoirs of the Life of Sir John Clerk of Penicuik, ed. J. M. Gray (Edinburgh, 1892)

Memoirs of the Secret Services of John Macky, esq., during the reign of King William, Queen Anne and King George I, ed. J. M. Gray (London, 1895)

Molesworth, Robert, Viscount Molesworth. *An Account of Denmark as it was in the year 1692* (London, 1694)

Murray, Sir Alexander. *The true interest of Great Britain, Ireland and our plantations: or, A proposal for making such an union between Great Britain and Ireland, and all our plantations, as that already made betwixt Scotland and England* (London, 1740)

Oldmixon, John. *The British Empire in America, containing The History of the Discovery, Settlement, Progress and present State of all the British Colonies on the Continent and Islands of America*, 2 vols. (London, 1708)

Oldmixon, John. *The History of England, during the reigns of King William and Queen Mary, Queen Anne, King George I* (London, 1735)

Postelthwayt, Malachy. *Britain's commercial interest explained and improved, in a series of dissertations on several important branches of her trade and police . . . Also the great advantage which would accrue to this kingdom from an union with Ireland* (London, 1757)

Robertson, William. *History of Scotland during the Reigns of Queen Mary and of King James VI till his accession to the throne of England*, 3 vols. (London, 1812 edition)

Savage, John. *The Ancient and Present State of Poland* (London, 1697)

'Scotland's Ruine': Lockhart of Carnwath's Memoirs of the Union, ed. D. Szechi (Aberdeen, 1995)

Scott, David. *The History of Scotland: Containing All the Historical Transactions of the Nation, from the Year of the World 3619, to the Year of Christ 1726* (Westminster, 1728)

Scott, Sir Walter. *Tales of a Grandfather; being stories taken from Scottish History* (Edinburgh, 1828), and new edition, *The Tales of a Grandfather: being the History of Scotland from the earliest period to the close of the rebellion 1745–46* (London, 1898)

Sinclair, Sir John. *The History of the Public Revenue of the British Empire* (London, 1790)

Smith, Adam. *An Inquiry into the Nature and Causes of the Wealth of Nations*, ed. R. H. Campbell & A. S. Skinner (Indianapolis, 1981)

Smollett, Tobias. *The History of England from the Revolution to the death of George the Second*, 4 vols. (London, 1758–60; new edition London, 1841)

Somerville, Thomas. *The History of Great Britain during the reign of Queen Anne* (London, 1798)

Struthers, John. *The History of Scotland from the Union to the abolition of the heritable jurisdictions*, 2 vols. (Glasgow, 1827–8)

Stuart, Gilbert. *Observations concerning the Public Law, and the Constitutional History of Scotland: with occasional remarks concerning English antiquity* (Edinburgh, 1779)

The Lockhart Papers: Memoirs and Correspondence upon the Affairs of Scotland from 1702 to 1715, ed. A. Aufrere, 2 vols. (London, 1817)

Tindal, Nicholas. *The History of England, by Mr Rapin de Thoyras; continued from the Revolution to the Accession of King George II*, 10 vols. (London, 1744–6)

Verstegan, Richard. *Restitution of Decayed Intelligence* (Antwerp, 1605)

[von] Puffendorf, Samuel. *An Introduction to the History of the Principal Kingdoms and States of Europe* (London, 1699)

Wallace, James. *The History of the Lives and Reigns of the Kings of Scotland from Fergus the first King, continued to the commencement of the Union of the Two Kingdoms of Scotland and England in the year of the reign of our late Sovereign Queen Anne, Anno Domini, 1707* (Dublin, 1722)

Wodrow, Robert. *The History of the Sufferings of the Church of Scotland from the Restoration to the Revolution*, ed. R. Burns, 4 vols. (Glasgow, 1829–30)

Wright, Alexander. *A Treatise on the Laws concerning the Election of the Different Representatives sent from Scotland to the Parliament of Great Britain* (Edinburgh, 1773)

PUBLISHED RECORDS

Aberdeen Council Letters, 1552–1681, ed. L. B. Taylor, 6 vols. (Oxford, 1942–61)

A Collection of Original Papers about the Scots Plot (London, 1704)

A Complete Collection of the Protests made in the House of Lords from 1641 to the dissolution of the last Parliament, June 1747 (London, 1747)

Acts of Assembly passed in the Colony of Virginia from 1662 to 1715 (London, 1727)

Acts of the Parliament of Scotland, ed. T. Thomson & C. Innes, 12 vols. (Edinburgh, 1814–72)

Acts of the Privy Council Colonial Series, ed. W. L. Grant & J. Munro, 2 vols. (London, 1908–10)

A List of Names of All the Adventures in the Stock of the Governor and Company of the Merchants of London Trading into the East Indies, the 4th April, 1700 (London, 1700)

An Account of the Proceedings of the Estates in Scotland, 1689–1690, ed. E. W. H. Balfour-Melville, 2 vols. (Edinburgh, 1954)

An Exact List of the Peers of Scotland at the Time of the Union (London, 1719)

Annals and Correspondence of the Viscount and the First and Second Earls of Stair, ed. J. M. Graham, 2vols. (Edinburgh, 1875)

Bibliography

A Selection from the Papers of the Earls of Marchmont illustrative of events from 1685–1750, ed. G. H. Rose, 3 vols. (London, 1831)

A Source Book of Scottish History, vol. III, ed. W. C. Dickinson & G. Donaldson (Edinburgh, 1961)

A Treaty for the Composing of Differences and Establishing of Peace in America between the Crowns of Great Britain and Spain (London, 1670)

Blaeu, Johannes. *Scotiae Quae Est Europae, Liber XII* (Amsterdam, 1654 and 1662)

Bristol and America: a record of the first settlers in the colonies of North America, 1654–1865, ed. W. D. Bowan (London, 1929)

Burns, Robert. *The Canongate Burns*, ed. A. Noble & P. S. Hogg (Edinburgh, 2001)

Calendar of Records in the Office of the Secretary of State, 1664–1703, ed. W. Nelson (Paterson, NJ, 1899)

Calendar of State Papers, Domestic Series of the Reign of Anne, ed. R. P. Mahaffy, vols. I–II (London, 1916 and 1924)

Calendar of State Papers Domestic Series, of the reign of Charles I, ed. J. Bruce & W. D. Hamilton, 17 vols. (London, 1858–82)

Calendar of Treasury Books (1706–8), ed. W. A. Shaw, vols XXI–XXII (1950–2)

Calendar of Treasury Papers (1557–1728), ed. J. Reddington, 6 vols. (London, 1868–9)

Calendars of State Papers, Colonial: America and the West Indies, ed. W. M. Sainsbury, J. W. Fortescue & C. Headlam, 17 vols. (London, 1880–1916).

Camden, William. *Britain, or A Chronological description of the most flourishing kingdomes, England, Scotland and Ireland, and the islands adjoining, out of the depth of antiquity* (London, 1610 and 1637)

[Charles I.] *By the King a proclamation for the better encouragement, and advancement of the trade of the East-Indie Companie, and for the prevention of excesse of private trade* (London, 1632)

Childrey, Joshua. *Britannia Baconica: Or, the Natural Rarities of England, Scotland and Wales as they are to be found in every shire* (London, 1661)

Collections of the New York Historical Society for 1869 (New York, 1870)

Collins, Greenville. *Great Britain's coasting-pilot, being a new and exact survey of the sea-coast of England* (London, 1693)

Colonial Records of North Carolina, second series X. The Church of England in North Carolina: Documents 1699–1741, ed. R. J. Cain (Raleigh, NC, 1999)

Commission of King James The Second to Sir Edmund Andros June 3, 1686 (London, 1686)

Correspondence of Colonel N. Hooke, Agent from the Court of France to the Scottish Jacobites in the years 1703–1707, ed. W. D. MacRay, 2 vols. (London, 1870–1)

Correspondence of George Baillie of Jerviswood, MDCCII–MDCVIII, ed. George Elliot, Earl of Minto (Edinburgh, 1842)

Curson, H. *A Companion of the Laws and Government Ecclesiastical, Civil and Military of England, Scotland and Ireland, and Dominions, Plantations and Territories thereunto belonging* (London, 1699)

Extracts from the Records of the Burgh of Glasgow, 1666–1690, ed. J. D. Marwick (Glasgow, 1905)

Extracts from the Records of the Convention of the Royal Burghs of Scotland, 1677–1711, ed. J. D. Marwick (Edinburgh, 1880)
General Meeting of the Company of Scotland, Trading to Africa and the Indies, Edinburgh, April 3 1696 (Edinburgh, 1696)
General Meeting of the Company of Scotland trading to Africa and the Indies, Edinburgh, 12 May 1696 (Edinburgh, 1696)
Gordon, Patrick. *Geography Anatomiz'd: or, the geographical grammar* (London, 1704)
Goss, J. *World Historical Atlas, 1662* (London, 1990)
Graham, E. M. *The Oliphants of Gask: Records of a Jacobite Family* (London, 1910)
Historical Papers relating to the Jacobite Period, 1699–1750, ed. J. Allardyce, 2 vols. (Aberdeen, 1895)
HMC, *10th Report, Appendix part iv*, Lord Braye's MSS, ed. H. C. M. Lyte & F. H. B. Daniell (London, 1887)
   Appendix to Third Report, Manuscripts of John Webster, Esquire, advocate in Aberdeen, ed. J. Stuart (London, 1872)
   Calendar of the Manuscripts of the Marquess of Ormonde K. P. preserved at Kilkenny Castle, new series, vol. VIII (London, 1920)
   Manuscripts of the House of Lords, original series, 3 vols. (1689–93), ed. E. F. Taylor & F. Skene (London, 1889–94); new series, 7 vols. (1693–1708), ed. C. L. Anstruther, J. P. St John, C. Headlam, J. B. Hotham, F. W. Lascelles & C. K. Davidson (London, 1900–21)
   Report on the Laing Manuscripts preserved in the University of Edinburgh, vol. II, ed. H. Paton (London, 1925)
   Report on the Manuscripts of the Duke of Buccleuch & Queensberry preserved at Montague House, Whitehall, vol. II, part 2 (London, 1903)
   Report on the Manuscripts of the Earl of Mar and Kellie preserved at Alloa House, ed. H. Paton (London, 1904)
   The Manuscripts of His Grace the Duke of Portland, preserved at Welbeck Abbey, vol. IV, ed. J. J. Cartwright (London, 1897), and vol. VIII, ed. S. C. Lomas (London, 1907)
   The Manuscripts of the Duke of Roxburghe; Sir H. H. Campbell, bart.; the Earl of Strathmore; and the Countess Dowager of Seafield (London, 1894)
Hume of Crossrigg, Sir David. *A Diary of the Proceedings in the Parliament and Privy Council of Scotland, May 21* MDCC – *March 7*, MDCCVII, ed. J. Hope (Edinburgh, 1828)
Intimate Society Letters of the Eighteenth Century, ed. Duke of Argyll, 2 vols. (London, 1910)
[James VII.] *His Majesties most gracious declaration to his good people of his ancient kingdom of Scotland commanding their assistance against the Prince and Princess of Orange, and their adherents* (Edinburgh, 1692)
Journal of the Commons House of Assembly of South Carolina (1692–1708), ed. A. S. Salley, 16 vols. (1907–34)
Journal of the Courts of Common Right and Chancery of East New Jersey, 1683–1702, ed. P. W. Edsall (Philadelphia, 1937)
Journal of the House of Commons, 9 (1667–87) and 13 (1699–1702)

Journals of the House of Lords, 12 (1666–75) and 15 (1691–6)
Journals of Sir John Lauder of Fountainhall with his observations on public affairs and other memoranda, 1665–1676, ed. D. Crawford (Edinburgh, 1900)
Lauder of Fountainhall, Sir John. *Historical Notices of Scottish Affairs (1661–1688)*, 2 vols. (Edinburgh, 1848)
Legislative Journals of the Council of Virginia (1680–1721), ed. H. R. McIlwaine, 3 vols. (Richmond, VA, 1925–8)
Letters Relating to Scotland in the Reign of Queen Anne by James Ogilvy, First Earl of Seafield and others, ed. P. H. Brown (Edinburgh, 1915)
List of the several persons Residenters in Scotland who have subscribed as Adventurers in the Joynt-Stock of the Company of Scotland Trading to Africa and the Indies (Edinburgh, 1696)
Macpherson, James. *Original Papers, containing the secret history of Great Britain from the Restoration, to the accession of the House of Hanover*, 2 vols. (London, 1775)
Magnus, Joannus & Magnus, Olaus. *De Omnibus Gothorum Sic Numque Regibus, qui unquam ab initio nationis extitere* (Rome, 1554 and 1567)
Maryland, http://www.mdarchives.state.md.us/ Proceedings and Acts of the General Assembly, vols. 2–27 (1666–1710); Proceedings of the Council of Maryland, vols. 2–25 (1636–1731); Proceedings of Maryland Court of Appeals vol. 77 (1695–1729); Proceedings of the Provincial Court, vols. 41–69 (1658–80); Proceedings of the County Court of Charles County, vol. 60 (1666–74); Somerset County Judicial Records, vol. 89 (1675–7)
Minutes of the Council and General Court of Colonial Virginia (1622–76), ed. H. R. McIlwaine (Richmond, VA, 1979)
Minutes of the Court of Albany, Rensselaerswych and Schenectady (1668–1680), ed. A. J. F. Canhaer, 3 vols. (Albany, 1926–32)
Minutes of the Provincial Council of Pennsylvania, 1683–1775, ed. S. Hazard, 10 vols. (1851–2)
Miscellany of the Maitland Club, vol. III, ed. J. Dennistoun & A. Macdonald (Edinburgh, 1843)
Miscellany of the Scottish Burghs Record Society, ed. J. D. Marwick (Glasgow, 1880)
Narratives of New Netherlands, ed. J. F. Jameson (New York, 1909)
North Carolina Higher Court Records 1670–1696, ed. M. E. E. Parker (Raleigh, NC, 1968)
North Carolina Higher Court Records, 1697–1701, ed. M. E. E. Parker (Raleigh, NC, 1971)
North Carolina Higher Court Records, 1702–1708, ed. W. S. Price (Raleigh, NC, 1974)
Ó Buachalla, B. *Foras Feasa ar Éirinn, History of Ireland: Foreword* (Dublin, 1987)
O'Flaherty, Roderic. *Ogygia; or, a Chronological Account of Irish Events Collected from very Ancient Documents faithfully compared with each other, and supported by the Genealogical and Chronological Aid of the Sacred and Prophane Writings of the First Nations of the Globe*, 2 vols. (Dublin, 1793)
Province and Court Records of Maine, ed. C. T. Libby, R. E. Moody & N. W. Allan, 6 vols. (Portland, ME, 1928–75)

Record of the Court of Assistants of the Colony of Massachusetts Bay, 1630–1692, ed. J. Noble, 3 vols. (Boston, 1901–28)

Records of the Court of Chancery of South Carolina, 1671–1779, ed. A. K. Gregorie (Washington, DC, 1950)

Records of the Court of New Castle on Delaware, 2 vols. (Lancaster, PA, 1904–35)

Records of the Courts of Sussex County, Delaware, 1677–1710, ed. C. W. Horle, 2 vols. (Philadelphia, 1991)

Registers of the Privy Council of Scotland, first series, ed. D. Masson, 14 vols. (Edinburgh, 1877–98); second series, ed. D. Masson & P. H. Brown, 8 vols. (Edinburgh, 1899–1908); third series, ed. P. H. Brown, H. Paton & E. W. M. Balfour-Melville, 16 vols. (Edinburgh, 1908–70)

Sainty, J.C. & Dewar, D. *Divisions in the House of Lords: an analytical list, 1685–1857* (London, 1976)

[Saltonstall, Wye.] *Historia Mundi: Or Mercator's Atlas* (London, 1635)

Scotland and the Americas, c. 1650 – c. 1939: A Documentary Source Book, ed. A. I. Macinnes, M. D. Harper & L. G. Fryer (Edinburgh, 2002)

Scotland and the Commonwealth 1651–53, ed. C. H. Firth (Edinburgh, 1895)

Seafield Correspondence from 1685 to 1708, ed. J. Grant (Edinburgh, 1912)

Seller, John. *Atlas Minimus or a Book of Geography showing all the Empires, Monarchies, Kingdomes, Regions, Dominions, Principalities and Countries in the whole World* (London, 1679)

Speed, John. *The Theatre of the Empire of Great Britain: presenting an exact geography of the kingdomes of England, Scotland, Ireland and the isle adjoyning* (London, 1616 and 1627)

State Papers and Letters addressed to William Carstares, Secretary to King William, relating to public affairs in Great Britain, but more particularly in Scotland, during the reign of K[ing] William and Q[ueen] Anne, J. McCormick ed. (Edinburgh, 1774)

Tabeller over Skibsfart og Varetransport gennem Oresund, 1492–1660, ed. N. E. Bang & K. Korst, 3 vols. (Copenhagen, 1906–22)

Tabeller over Skibsfart og Varetransport gennem Oresund, 1661–1783 og gennem Storebaelt, 1701–1748, ed. N. E. Bang & K. Korst, 4 vols. (Copenhagen, 1930–53)

Taylor, Joseph. *A Journey to Edenborough in Scotland*, ed. W. Cowan (Edinburgh, 1903)

The Bannatyne Miscellany, vol. III, ed. D. Laing (Edinburgh, 1855)

The Colonial Records of North Carolina, vol. I (1662–1712), ed. W. L. Saunders (Raleigh, NC, 1886; reprinted Wilmington, NC, 1993)

The Covenants and the Covenanters, ed. J. Kerr (Edinburgh, 1896)

The Cromwellian Union 1651–52, ed. C. S. Terry (Edinburgh, 1902)

The Darien Papers: being a selection of original letters and official documents relating to the establishment of a colony at Darien by the Company of Scotland trading to Africa and the Indies, 1695–1700, ed. J. H. Burton (Edinburgh, 1849)

The Dongan Papers, 1683–1688, ed. P. R. Christoph, 2 vols. (Syracuse, NY, 1993–6)

The Earl of Stirling's Register of Royal Letters, Relative to the Affairs of Scotland and Nova Scotia from 1615 to 1635, ed. C. Rogers, 2 vols. (Edinburgh, 1873)

The Earl of Strafforde's Letters and Dispatches, ed. W. Knowler, 2 vols. (London, 1739)

The Jacobite Threat: A Source Book, ed. B. P. Lenman & G. S. Gibson (Edinburgh, 1990)
The Journal of John Winthrop, 1630–1649, ed. R. S. Dunn, J. Savage & L. Yeandle (Cambridge, MA, 1996)
The Letters and Diplomatic Instructions of Queen Anne, ed. B. C. Brown (London, 1968)
The Letters of Daniel Defoe, ed. G. H. Healey (Oxford, 1955)
The London Diaries of William Nicolson, Bishop of Carlisle 1702–1718, ed. C. Jones & G. Holmes (Oxford, 1985)
The Marlborough–Godolphin Correspondence, ed. H. L. Snyder, 3 vols. (Oxford, 1975)
The Nicholas Papers, Correspondence of Sir Edward Nicholas, Secretary of State, ed. G. F. Warner, 2 vols. (London, 1886)
The Treaty of Union of Scotland and England 1707, ed. G. S. Pryde (London, 1950)
The Whole Prophecies of Scotland, England, France, Ireland and Denmarke (Edinburgh, 1617)
Walker, Patrick. *Six Saints of the Covenant*, ed. D. H. Fleming, 2 vols. (London, 1901)
Wharton, Walter. *Land Survey Register, 1675–1679, West Side Delaware River*, ed. A. C. Myers (Wilmington, DE, 1955)
William, R. *His Majesties most gracious letter to the Parliament of Scotland* (Edinburgh, 1700)
Williams, E. N. *The Eighteenth Century Constitution: Documents and Commentary* (Cambridge, 1960)
Wingate & Washington, Messrs. *An Abridgement of the laws in force and use in Her Majesty's plantations* (London, 1704)

WORKS OF REFERENCE

ELECTRONIC

Early English Books online – http://eebo.chadwyck.com/home?ath
Eighteenth Century Collections online – http://galenet.galegroup.com/servlet/ECCO
Grosjean, A. & Murdoch, S. 'Scotland, Scandinavia and Northern Europe, 1580–1707' (SSNE: computer database, University of St Andrews 2006–7): http//www.st-andrews.ac.uk/history/ssne
Oxford Dictionary of National Biography – http://www.oxforddnb.com

HARD COPY

Coldham, P. W. *The Complete Book of Emigrants 1607–1660* (Baltimore, 1987)
Dobson, D. *Scottish Emigration to Colonial America, 1607–1785* (Athens, GA, 1994).
Ghirelli, M. *List of Emigrants from England to America, 1682–92* (Baltimore, 1968)
McLeod, W. R. & McLeod V. B. *Anglo-Scottish Tracts, 1701–1714* (Kansas, 1979)

Moreland, C. & Bannister, D. *Antique Maps* (London, 2000)
Passengers to America, ed. M. Tepping (Baltimore, 1978)
Rabb, T. K. *Enterprise & Empire: Merchants and Gentry Investment in the Expansion of England, 1575–1630* (Cambridge, MA, 1967)
Scots Peerage, ed. Sir J. Balfour-Paul, 9 vols. (Edinburgh, 1904–14)
Stevenson, D. & Stevenson, W. B. *Scottish Text and Calendars: An Analytical Guide to Serial Publications* (Edinburgh, 1987)
The House of Commons 1690–1715, ed. D. W. Hayton, E. Cruickshanks & S. Handley, 5 vols. (Cambridge, 2002)
The Parliaments of Scotland: Burgh and Shire Commissioners, ed. M. D. Young, 2 vols. (Edinburgh, 1993)
Van Mingroot, E. & Van Ermen, E. *Scandinavia in Old Maps and Prints* (Knokke, 1987)

SECONDARY SOURCES

THESES

Dobson, L. D. S. 'Scottish Trade with Colonial Charlestown, 1683–1783' (University of Aberdeen, Ph.D. thesis, 2005)
McAlister, K. F. 'James VII and the Conduct of Scottish Politics, c. 1679 – c. 1686' (University of Strathclyde, Ph.D. thesis, 2003)
McKay, C. 'The Political Life of James Douglas, Second Duke of Queensberry, 1662–1711' (University of Strathclyde, Ph.D. thesis, 2005)
Vance, J. 'Constitutional Radicalism in Scotland and Ireland in the Era of the American Revolution, c. 1760–1789' (Aberdeen University, Ph.D. thesis, 1998)

MONOGRAPHS

Adams, I. & Somerville, M. *Cargoes of Despair and Hope: Scottish Emigration to North America 1603–1803* (Edinburgh, 1993)
Allan, D. *Philosophy and Politics in Later Stuart Scotland* (East Linton, 2000)
 Scotland in the Eighteenth Century: Union and Enlightenment (Harlow, 2002)
 Virtue, Learning and the Scottish Enlightenment: Ideas of Scholarship in Early Modern History (Edinburgh, 1993)
Andrews, C. M. *The Colonial Period of American History: England's Commercial and Colonial Policy* (New Haven, 1943)
Appleby, J. *Economic Thought and Ideology in Seventeenth-Century England* (Princeton, 1978)
Armitage, D. *The Ideological Origins of the British Empire* (Cambridge, 2000)
Arnold, M. *The Study of Celtic Literature* (London, 1867)
Ash, M. *The Strange Death of Scottish History* (Edinburgh, 1980)
Barclay, T. & Graham, E. J. *The Early Transatlantic Trade of Ayr, 1640–1730* (Ayr, 2005)
Barnard, T. C. *Cromwellian Ireland: English Government and Reform in Ireland, 1649–1660* (Oxford, 1975)

Beresford, M. *New Towns of the Middle Ages: Town Plantation in England, Wales and Gascony* (London, 1967)

Bliss, R. M. *Revolution and Empire: English Politics and the American Colonies in the Seventeenth Century* (Manchester, 1990)

Braddick, M. J. *State Formation in Early Modern England, c. 1550–1700* (Cambridge, 2000)

  The Nerves of State: taxation and the financing of the English State, 1558–1714 (Manchester, 1996)

Brenner, R. *Merchants and Revolution: Commercial Change, Political Conflict, and London's Overseas Traders, 1550–1653* (Princeton, 1993)

Brewer, J. *The Sinews of Power: War, Money and the English State, 1688–1783* (London, 1989)

Brock, W. R. *Scotus Americanus: A Survey of the Sources for Links Between Scotland and America in the Eighteenth Century* (Edinburgh, 1982)

Brown, K. M. *Kingdom or Province? Scotland and the Regal Union, 1603–1715* (Basingstoke, 1992)

  Noble Society in Scotland. Wealth, Family and Culture from Reformation to Revolution (Edinburgh, 2000)

Brown, P. H. *The Legislative Union of England and Scotland: The Ford Lectures Delivered in Hilary Term, 1914* (Oxford, 1914)

Burgess, G. *The Politics of the Ancient Constitution: An Introduction to English Political Thought, 1603–1641* (University Park, PA, 1992)

Burns, J. H. *The True Law of Kingship: Concepts of Monarchy in Early Modern Scotland* (Oxford, 1996)

Burton, J. H. *History of Scotland, from the Revolution to the Extinction of the last Jacobite Rebellion (1689–1746)*, 2 vols. (London, 1853)

Calder, A. *Revolutionary Empire: The Rise of the English-Speaking Empires from the Fifteenth Century to the 1780s* (London, revised 1998)

Campbell, R. H. *Scotland Since 1707: The Rise of an Industrial Society* (Oxford, 1965)

Canny, N. *Kingdom and Colony: Ireland in the Atlantic World* (Baltimore and London, 1988)

  Making Ireland British, 1580–1650 (Oxford, 2003)

Carney, F. S. *The Politics of Johannes Althusius* (London, 1964)

Chaudhuri, K. N. *The Trading World of Asia and the English East India Company, 1660–1760* (Cambridge, 1975)

Checkland, S. G. *Scottish Banking: A History, 1695–1973* (Glasgow and London, 1975)

Clark, G. N. *The Later Stuarts, 1660–1714* (Oxford, 1934)

Clark, J. C. D. *Revolution and Rebellion: State and Society in England in the Seventeenth and Eighteenth Centuries* (Cambridge, 1986)

Clark, P. *British Clubs and Societies, 1580–1800: The Origins of an Associational World* (Oxford, 2000)

Clarke, A. *Prelude to Restoration in Ireland: The End of the Commonwealth, 1659–1660* (Cambridge, 1999)

Cowan, I. B. *The Scottish Covenanters, 1660–88* (London, 1976)

Cunningham, B. *The World of Geoffrey Keating* (Dublin, 2000)

Daiches, D. *Scotland and the Union* (London, 1977)
Dalhede, C. *Handelsfamiljer på Stormakstidens Europamarknad*, 2 vols. (Stockholm, 2001)
Davidson, N. *Discovering the Scottish Revolution, 1692–1746* (London, 2003)
Davis, R. *The Rise of Atlantic Economies* (London, 1973)
Devine, T. M. *Scotland's Empire, 1600–1815* (London, 2003)
  The Scottish Nation, 1700–2000 (London, 1999)
  The Tobacco Lords (Edinburgh, 1975)
Dicey, A. C. & Rait, R. S. *Thoughts on the Union between England and Scotland* (London, 1920)
Donaldson, G. *Scotland: James V – James VII* (Edinburgh, 1978)
Dow, F. D. *Cromwellian Scotland, 1651–1660* (Edinburgh, 1979)
Dunn, R. S. *Sugar and Slaves: The Rise of the Planter Class in the English West Indies, 1624–1713* (Chapel Hill, 1992)
Eggerton, H. E. *Federations and Unions within the British Empire* (Oxford, 1911)
Eriksonas, L. *National Heroes and National Identities: Scotland, Norway and Lithuania* (Brussels, 2004)
Ferguson, N. *Empire: How Britain Made the Modern World* (London, 2004)
Ferguson, W. *Scotland: 1689 to the Present* (Edinburgh, 1978)
  Scotland's Relations with England: A Survey to 1707 (Edinburgh, 1977)
  The Identity of the Scottish Nation: An Historic Quest (Edinburgh, 1998)
Flinn, M. *Scottish Population History from the 17th Century to the 1930s* (Cambridge, 1977)
Fry, M. *The Scottish Empire* (Edinburgh, 2001)
Fulton, T. W. *The Sovereignty of the Sea: An Historical Account of the Claims for Dominion of the British Seas* (Edinburgh, 1911)
Furber, H. *Rival Empires of Trade in the Orient, 1600–1800* (Oxford, 2004)
Galloway, B. *The Union of England and Scotland 1606–1608* (Edinburgh, 1986)
Games, A. *Migration and the Origins of the English Atlantic World* (Cambridge, MA, 1999)
Gentles, I. *The New Model Army in England, Ireland and Scotland, 1645–1653* (Oxford, 1992)
Glendinning, M., MacInnes, R. & MacKechnie, A. *A History of Scottish Architecture, from the Renaissance to the Present Day* (Edinburgh, 1996)
Graham, E. J. *Maritime History of Scotland, 1650–1790* (East Linton, 2002)
Graham, I. C. C. *Colonists from Scotland: Emigration to North America, 1707–1783* (Ithaca, NY, 1956)
Greene, J. P. *Peripheries and Center: Constitutional Developments in the Extended Politics of the British Empire and the United States, 1607–1688* (Atlanta, 1986)
  Pursuits of Happiness: The Social Development of Early Modern British Colonies and the Formation of American Culture (Chapel Hill, 1988)
Grosjean, A. *An Unofficial Alliance: Scotland and Sweden, 1569–1654* (Leiden, 2003)
Harris, T. *Restoration: Charles II and His Kingdoms, 1660–1685* (London, 2005)
Harris-Sax, D. *The Widening Gate: Bristol and the Atlantic Economy, 1450–1700* (Berkeley, 1991)
Hawke, E. G. *The British Empire and its History* (London, 1911)

Hayton, D. W. *Ruling Ireland, 1685–1742: Politics, Politicians and Parties* (Woodbridge, 2004)
Holmes, G. *Politics, Religion and Society in England, 1679–1742* (London, 1986)
  The Making of a Great Power: Late Stuart and Early Georgian Britain, 1660–1722 (Harlow, 1993)
Hopkins, P. *Glencoe and the End of the Highland War* (Edinburgh, 1986)
Hoppit, J. *A Land of Liberty? England 1689–1727* (Oxford, 2000)
Hutton, R. *The Restoration: A Political & Religious History of England and Wales, 1658–1667* (Oxford, 1985)
Insh, G. P. *Scottish Colonial Schemes, 1620–1686* (Glasgow, 1922)
  The Company of Scotland Trading to Africa and the Indies (London, 1932)
Israel, J. I. *Dutch Primacy in World Trade, 1585–1740* (Oxford, 1990)
  Radical Enlightenment: Philosophy and the Making of Modernity, 1650–1750 (Oxford, 2001)
  The Dutch Republic: Its Rise, Greatness and Fall, 1477–1806 (Oxford, 1995)
Jackson, C. *Restoration Scotland, 1660–1690: Royalist Politics, Religion and Ideas* (Woodbridge, 2004)
Johnson, A. *The Swedish Settlements on the Delaware: The History and Relation to the Indians, Dutch and English, 1638–1664*, 2 vols. (New York, 1911)
Jones, D. W. *War and Economy in the Age of William III and Marlborough* (Oxford, 1988)
Kamen, H. *Empire: How Spain Became a World Power 1492–1763* (New York, 2003)
Kamen, M. *Empire and Interest: The American Colonies and the Politics of Mercantilism* (New York, 1970)
Kearney, H. *Strafford in Ireland, 1633–41: A Study in Absolutism* (Manchester, 1959, 2nd edition Cambridge, 1989)
Keeble, N. H. *The Restoration: England in the 1660s* (Oxford, 2002)
Keith, T. *Commercial Relations of England and Scotland, 1603–1707* (Cambridge, 1910)
Kelly, J. *Prelude to Union: Anglo-Irish Politics in the 1780s* (Cork, 1992)
Kettner, J. H. *The Development of American Citizenship 1608–1870* (Chapel Hill, NC, 1978)
Kidd, C. *British Identities before Nationalism: Ethnicity and Nationhood in the Atlantic World, 1600–1800* (Cambridge, 1999)
  Subverting Scotland's Past: Scottish Whig Historians and the Creation of an Anglo-British Identity, 1689 – c. 1830 (Cambridge, 1993)
Kishlansky, M. *A Monarchy Transformed: Britain 1603–1714* (London, 1996)
Kliger, S. *The Goths in England: A Study in Seventeenth and Eighteenth Century Thought* (New York, 1952)
Kulikoff, A. *From British Peasants to Colonial American Farmers* (Chapel Hill, 2000)
Kupperman, K. O. *Providence Island 1630–1641: The Other Puritan Colony* (Cambridge, 1993)
Landsman, N. *Scotland and its first American Colony, 1683–1760* (Princeton, 1985)
Lang, A. *History of Scotland from the Roman Occupation*, 4 vols. (New York, 1907)

Lenihan, P. *Confederate Catholics at War, 1641–49* (Cork, 2001)
Lenman, B. *Britain's Colonial Wars 1688–1783* (Harlow, 2001)
  England's Colonial Wars 1550–1688: Conflicts, Empire and National Identity (Harlow, 2001)
  The Jacobite Risings in Britain, 1689–1746 (London, 1980)
Levack, B. P. *The Formation of the British State: England, Scotland and the Union, 1603–1707* (Oxford, 1987)
Lounsbury, R. G. *The British Fishery at Newfoundland, 1634–1763* (New Haven, 1934)
Macaulay, T. B., Lord Macaulay, *The History of England from the Accession of James II*, 6 vols. (London, 1849–61)
MacDonald, A. R. *The Jacobean Kirk, 1567–1625: Sovereignty, Polity and Liturgy* (Aldershot, 1998)
McIlvanney, L. *Burns the Radical: Poetry and Politics in Late Eighteenth-Century Scotland* (East Linton, 2002)
Macinnes, A. I. *Charles I and the Making of the Covenanting Movement, 1625–41* (Edinburgh, 1991)
  Clanship, Commerce and the House of Stuart, 1603–1788 (East Linton, 1996)
  The British Revolution, 1629–1660 (Basingstoke, 2004)
Mackinnon, J. *The Union of England and Scotland: A Study of International History* (London, 1896)
McLynn, F. *The Jacobites* (London, 1985)
MacRae, Revd A., *Scotland from the Treaty of Union with England to the Present Time (1707–1907)* (London, 1908)
Marshall, G. *Presbyteries and Profits: Calvinism and the Development of Capitalism in Scotland, 1560–1707* (Oxford, 1980)
Mason, R. A. *Kingship and the Commonweal: Political Thought in Renaissance and Reformation Scotland* (East Linton, 1998)
Mathieson, W. L. *Scotland and the Union: A History of Scotland from 1695 to 1747* (Glasgow, 1905)
Merriman, M. *The Rough Wooings: Mary Queen of Scots, 1542–1551* (East Linton, 2001)
Mitchison, R. *A History of Scotland* (London, 1977)
  Lordship to Patronage: Scotland, 1603–1746 (London, 1983)
Monod, P. K. *Jacobitism and the English People, 1688–1788* (Cambridge, 1995)
Morison, S. E. *The Oxford History of the American People, vol. 1: Prehistory to 1789* (New York, 1994)
Morton, G. *Unionist-Nationalism: Governing Urban Scotland, 1830–1860* (East Linton, 1999)
Murdoch, A. *British History, 1660–1832: National Identity and Local Culture* (Basingstoke, 1998)
Murdoch, S. *Britain, Denmark–Norway and the House of Stuart, 1603–1660* (East Linton, 2000)
  Network North: Scottish Kin, Commercial and Covert Associations in Northern Europe, 1603–1746 (Leiden and Boston, 2006)
Nicholls, A. D. *The Jacobean Union: A Reconsideration of British Civil Policies under the Early Stuarts* (Westport, CT, 1999)

Ó Buachalla, B. *Aisling Ghearr: Na Stiobhartaigh Agus an tAos Leinn, 1603–1788* (Dublin, 1996)
Ó Ciardha, É. *Ireland and the Jacobite Cause, 1685–1766: A Fatal Attachment* (Dublin, 2002)
O'Gorman, F. *The Long Eighteenth Century: British Political & Social History, 1688–1832* (London, 1997)
Ó Siochrú, M. *Confederate Ireland, 1642–9: A Constitutional and Political Analysis* (Dublin, 1999)
Pagden, A. *Lords of all the World: Ideologies of Empire in Spain, Britain and France c. 1500 – c. 1800* (New Haven, 1995)
Pawlisch, H. S. *Sir John Davies and the Conquest of Ireland: A Study in Legal Imperialism* (Cambridge, 1985)
Perceval-Maxwell, M. *The Outbreak of the Irish Rebellion of 1641* (Montreal, 1994)
The Scottish Migration to Ulster in the Reign of James I (London, 1973)
Petrie, Sir C. *The Jacobite Movement: The First Phase, 1688–1716* (London, 1950)
Pincus, S. *England's Glorious Revolution 1688–1689: A Brief History with Documents* (Boston, 2006)
Protestantism and Patriotism: Ideologies and the Making of English Foreign Policy, 1650–1668 (Cambridge, 1996)
Pittock, M. G. H. *Inventing and Resisting Britain: Cultural Identities in Britain and Ireland, 1685–1789* (Basingstoke, 1997)
Pocock, J. G. A. *The Machiavellian Moment: Florentine Political Thought and the Atlantic Republican Tradition* (Princeton, 1975)
Prowse, D. W. *A History of Newfoundland from the English, Colonial, and Foreign Records* (New York, 1895)
Reid, J. G. *Acadia, Maine and New England: Marginal Colonies in the Seventeenth Century* (Toronto, 1981)
Rendall, J. *The Origins of the Scottish Enlightenment* (London, 1978)
Riley, P. W. J. *King William and the Scottish Politicians* (Edinburgh, 1979)
The Union of England and Scotland: A Study in Anglo-Scottish Politics of the Eighteenth Century (Manchester, 1978)
Robert, R. *Chartered Companies: Their Role in the Development of Overseas Trade* (London, 1969)
Robertson, J. *The Scottish Enlightenment and the Militia Issue* (Edinburgh, 1985)
Robinson, P. *The Plantation of Ulster* (Belfast, 2000)
Schama, S. *The Embarrassment of Riches: an Interpretation of Dutch Culture in the Golden Age* (London, 1991)
Scott, D. *Politics and War in the Three Stuart Kingdoms, 1637–49* (Basingstoke, 2004)
Scott, P. H. *1707: The Union of Scotland and England in Contemporary Documents with a Commentary* (Edinburgh, 1979)
Andrew Fletcher and The Treaty of Union (Edinburgh, 1992)
'The Boasted Advantages': The Consequences of the Union of 1707 (Edinburgh, 1999)
Scott, W. R. *The Constitution and Finance of English, Scottish and Irish Joint-Stock Companies to 1720*, 3 vols. (Cambridge, 1911–12)
Seeley, Sir J. R. *The Expansion of England: Two Courses of Lectures* (London, 1891)

Sher, R. *Church and University in the Scottish Enlightenment: The Moderate Literati of Edinburgh* (Edinburgh, 1985)
Sheridan, R. B. *Sugar and Slavery: An Economic History of the British West Indies, 1623–1775* (Barbados, 1974)
Sirmans, M. E. *Colonial South Carolina: A Political History, 1663–1763* (Williamsburg, VA, 1966)
Slafter, E. F. *Sir William Alexander and American Colonization* (Boston, 1873)
Smith, D. L. *A History of the Modern British Isles, 1603–1707: The Double Crown* (Oxford, 1998)
— *Constitutional Royalism and the Search for Settlement, c. 1640–1649* (Cambridge, 1994)
Smout, T. C. *A History of the Scottish People, 1560–1830* (Glasgow, 1969)
— *Scottish Trade on the Eve of Union, 1660–1707* (Edinburgh and London, 1963)
Smyth, J. *The Making of the United Kingdom, 1660–1800* (Harlow, 2001)
Soisin, J. M. *English America and Imperial Inconstancy: The Rise of Provincial Autonomy 1696–1715* (London, 1985)
— *English America and the Restoration Monarchy of Charles II: Transatlantic Politics, Commerce and Kinship* (London, 1980)
— *English America and the Revolution of 1688* (London, 1982)
Somerville, J. P. *Politics and Ideology in England, 1603–1640* (London, 1986)
Speck, W. A. *The Birth of Britain: A New Nation, 1700–1710* (Oxford, 1994)
Stanhope, P. H., Earl of Stanhope, *History of England, Comprising the Reign of Queen Anne until the Peace of Utrecht, 1701–1713* (London, 1871)
Stevenson, D. *Revolution and Counter-Revolution in Scotland, 1644–1651* (London, 1977)
— *Scottish Covenanters and Irish Confederates* (Belfast, 1981)
— *The Covenanters: The National Covenant and Scotland* (Edinburgh, 1988)
Szechi, D. *George Lockhart of Carnwath, 1681–1731: A Study in Jacobitism* (East Linton, 2002)
— *The Jacobites: Britain and Europe, 1688–1714* (Manchester, 1994)
Taylor, J. *A Cup of Kindness: The History of the Royal Scottish Corporation, a London Charity, 1603–2003* (East Linton, 2003)
Trevelyan, G. M. *England under Queen Anne*, 3 vols. (London, 1930–2)
— *The Parliamentary Union of England and Scotland 1707* (London, 1929)
Trevor-Roper, Hugh, Lord Dacre. *From Counter-Reformation to Glorious Revolution* (London, 1992)
Troost, W. *William III, the Stadholder-King: A Political Biography* (Aldershot, 2005)
Vallance, E. *Revolutionary England and the National Covenant: State Oaths, Protestantism and the Political Nation, 1553–1682* (Woodbridge, 2005)
Vergé-Franceschi, M. *Colbert: La politique du bon sens* (Paris, 2003)
Ward, H. M. *The United Colonies of New England, 1634–90* (New York, 1961)
Webb, S. S. *The Governors-General: The English Army and the Definition of Empire, 1569–1681* (Chapel Hill, 1979)
Whatley, C. A. *Bought and Sold for English Gold? Explaining the Union of 1707* (East Linton, 1994; 2nd edition, 2001)

Scottish Society, 1707–1830: Beyond Jacobitism Towards Industrialisation (Manchester, 2000)
The Scottish Salt Industry, 1570–1860: An Economic and Social History (Aberdeen, 1987)
Wheeler, J. S. *The Irish and British Wars, 1637–1654* (London, 2002)
Whyte, I. D. *Scotland's Society and Economy in Transition, c. 1500 – c. 1760* (Basingstoke, 1977)
Woolf, D. R. *The Idea of History in Early Stuart England: Erudition, Ideology, and 'The Light of Truth' from the Accession of James I to the Civil War* (Toronto, 1990)
Woolrych, A. *Britain in Revolution, 1625–1660* (Oxford, 2002)
Wormald, B. H. G. *Francis Bacon: History, Politics and Science, 1561–1626* (Cambridge, 1993)
Wright, T. *The History of Scotland from the Earliest Period to the Present Time*, 3 vols. (London, 1852–5)
Wrightson, K. *Earthly Necessities: Economic Lives in Early Modern Britain* (New Haven, 2000)
Wrigley, E. A. & Schofield, R. S. *The Population History of England, 1541–1871: A Reconstruction* (London, 1981)
Wyon, F. W. *The History of Great Britain During the Reign of Queen Anne* (London, 1876)
Young, J. R. *The Scottish Parliament 1639–1661: A Political and Constitutional Analysis* (Edinburgh, 1996)

EDITED BOOKS

Adamson, J., ed., *The Civil Wars: Rebellion and Revolution in the Kingdoms of Charles I* (London, 2007, forthcoming)
Armitage, D. & Braddick, M. J., eds., *The British Atlantic World, 1500–1800* (Basingstoke, 2002)
Asch, R. G., ed., *Der europäische Adel im Ancien Régime: Von der Krise der ständischen Monarchien bis zur Revolution (ca. 1600–1789)* (Böhlau, 2001)
Three Nations – A Common History? England, Scotland, Ireland & British History, c. 1600–1920 (Bochum, 1993)
Bailyn, B. & Morgan, P. D., eds., *Strangers Within the Realm: Cultural Margins of the First British Empire* (Chapel Hill, 1991)
Bernard, T. & Fenlon, J., eds., *The Dukes of Ormonde, 1610–1745* (Woodbridge, 2000)
Borschberg, P. & Krieger, M., eds., *Water and State in Europe and Asia* (Delhi, 2007) forthcoming
Bradshaw, B. & Morrill, J., eds., *The British Problem, c. 1534–1707: State Formation in the Atlantic Archipelago* (Basingstoke, 1996)
Bradshaw, B. & Roberts, P., eds., *British Consciousness and Identity: The Making of Britain, 1533–1707* (Cambridge, 1998)
Brady, C. & Ohlmeyer, J., eds., *British Interventions in Early Modern Ireland* (Cambridge, 2005)

Brown, K. M. & Mann, A. J., eds., *The History of the Scottish Parliament, vol. II: Parliament and Politics in Scotland, 1567–1707* (Edinburgh, 2005)
Burgess, G., ed., *The New British History: Founding a Modern State, 1603–1715* (London, 1999)
Canny, N., ed., *Europeans on the Move: Studies on Migration, 1500–1800* (Oxford, 1994)
   The Oxford History of the British Empire, vol. 1: The Origins of Empire: British Overseas Empire to the Close of the Seventeenth Century (Oxford, 1998)
Connolly, S. J., ed., *Kingdoms United? Great Britain and Ireland since 1500: Integration and Diversity* (Dublin, 1999)
Coward, B., ed., *The Blackwell Companion to Stuart Britain* (Oxford, 2002)
Cruickshanks, E., ed., *Ideology and Conspiracy: Aspects of Jacobitism, 1689–1759* (Edinburgh, 1982)
Cruickshanks, E. & Corp, E., eds., *The Stuart Court in Exile and the Jacobites* (Rio Grande, OH, 1995)
Cullen, L. M. & Smout, T. C., eds., *Comparative Aspects of Scottish and Irish Economic and Social History, 1600–1900* (Edinburgh, 1977)
Devine, T. M. & Young, J. R., eds., *Eighteenth Century Scotland: New Perspectives* (East Linton, 1999)
Dyrvik, S., Mykland, K. & Oldervoll, J., eds., *The Satellite State in the 17th and 18th Centuries* (Oslo, 1979)
Ellis, S. G. & Barber, S., eds., *Conquest and Union: Fashioning a British State, 1485–1725* (London, 1995)
Ellis, S. G. & Esser, R., eds., *Frontiers and the Writing of History, 1500–1850* (Hannover-Laatzen, 2006)
Evans, R. J. W. & Thomas, T. V., eds., *Crown, Church and Estates: Central European Politics in the Sixteenth and Seventeenth Centuries* (London, 1991)
Foster, S., Macinnes, A. I. & MacInnes, R., eds., *Scottish Power Centres from the Early Middle Ages to the Twentieth Century* (Glasgow, 1998)
Fouquet, G., Hansen, M., Jahnke, C. & Schlürmann, J., eds., *Von Menschen, Ländern, Meeren: Festschrift für Thomas Riis* (Tönning, 2006)
Graham, B. J. & Proudfoot, L. J., eds., *An Historical Geography of Ireland* (London, 1993)
Greene, J. P. & Pole, J. R., eds., *Colonial British America: Essays in the New History of the Early Modern Era* (Baltimore, 1984)
Greengrass, M., ed., *Conquest and Coalescence: the Shaping of the State in Early Modern Europe* (London, 1991)
Grosjean, A. & Murdoch, S., eds., *Scottish Communities Abroad in the Early Modern Period* (Leiden, 2005)
Holmes, G., ed., *Britain After the Glorious Revolution* (London, 1969)
Houston, A. & Pincus, S., eds., *A Nation Transformed: England after the Restoration* (Cambridge, 2001)
Jackson, G. & Lythe, S. G. E., eds., *The Port of Montrose: A History of its Harbour, Trade and Shipping* (New York and Tayport)
Jones, C., ed., *Britain in the First Age of Party, 1680–1750: Essays Presented to Geoffrey Holmes* (London, 1987)
   The Scots and Parliament (Edinburgh, 1996)

Katz, S. N., Murrin, J. M. & Greenberg, D., eds., *Colonial America: Essays in Politics and Social Development* (New York, 1993)
Kenyon, J. & Ohlmeyer, J. H., eds., *The Civil Wars: A Military History of England, Scotland and Ireland 1638–1660* (Oxford, 1998)
Keogh, D. & Whelan, K., eds., *Acts of Union: The Causes, Contexts and Consequences of the Act of Union* (Dublin, 2001)
Kupperman, K. O., ed., *America in European Consciousness, 1493–1750* (Chapel Hill, 1995)
Kyle, C. R. & Peacey, J., eds., *Parliament at Work: Parliamentary Committees, Political Power & Public Access in Early Modern England* (Woodbridge, 2002)
Lenihan, P., ed., *Conquest and Resistance: War in Seventeenth Century Ireland* (Leiden, 2001)
Levene, M. & Roberts, P., eds., *The Massacre in History* (Oxford, 1999)
MacCuarta, B., ed., *Ulster 1641: Aspects of the Rising* (Belfast, 1997)
Macinnes, A. I. & Ohlmeyer, J., eds., *The Stuart Kingdoms in the Seventeenth Century: Awkward Neighbours* (Dublin, 2002)
Macinnes, A. I., Riis, T. & Pedersen, F. G., eds., *Ships, Guns and Bibles in the North Sea and Baltic States, c. 1350 – c. 1700* (East Linton, 2000)
Macinnes, A. I. & Williamson, A. H., eds., *Shaping the Stuart World, 1603–1714: The American Connection* (Leiden and Boston, 2006)
Mackillop, A. & Murdoch, S., eds., *Military Governors and Imperial Frontiers c. 1600–1800: A Study of Scotland and Empires* (Leiden, 2003)
McNeill, P. G. B. & MacQueen, H. L., eds., *Atlas of Scottish History to 1707* (Edinburgh, 1996)
Mason, R. A., ed., *Scotland and England, 1286–1815* (Edinburgh, 1987)
  Scots and Britons: Scottish Political Thought and the Union of 1603 (Cambridge, 1994)
Mijers, E. & Onnekink, D., eds., *Redefining William III: The Impact of the King-Stadholder in its International Context* (Aldershot, 2007)
Merritt, J. F., ed., *The Political World of Thomas Wentworth, Earl of Strafford 1621–1641* (Cambridge, 1996)
Moody, T. W., ed., *Nationality and the Pursuit of National Independence* (Belfast, 1978)
Moody, T. W. & Vaughan, W. E., eds., *A New History of Ireland*, vol. IV (Oxford, 1986)
Morrill, J., ed., *The Scottish National Covenant in its British Context, 1638–51* (Edinburgh, 1990)
Murdoch, S., ed., *Scotland and the Thirty Years' War, 1618–1648* (Leiden, 2001)
Ó Baoill, C. & McGuire, N. R., eds., *Rannsachadh na Gàidhlig 2000* (Aberdeen, 2002)
Ohlmeyer, J. H., ed., *Ireland from Independence to Occupation* (Cambridge, 1995)
  Political Thought in Seventeenth-Century Ireland: Kingdom or Colony (Cambridge, 2000)
Ó Siochrú, M., ed., *Kingdoms in Crisis: Ireland in the 1640s* (Dublin, 2000)
Peck, L. L., ed., *The Mental World of the Jacobean Court* (Cambridge, 1991)
Philipson, N. T. & Mitchison, R., eds., *Scotland in the Age of Improvement* (Edinburgh, 1970)

Pocock, J. G. A., ed., *The Varieties of British Political Thought, 1500–1800* (Cambridge, 1996)
Rae, T. I., ed., *The Union of 1707: Its Impact on Scotland* (Glasgow, 1974)
Robertson, J., ed. *A Union for Empire: Political Thought and the British Union* (Cambridge, 1995)
Simpson, G. G., ed., *Scotland and Scandinavia 800–1800* (Edinburgh, 1990)
Smout, T. C., ed., *Anglo-Scottish Relations from 1603 to 1900* (Oxford, 2005)
Stone, L., ed., *An Imperial State at War: Britain from 1689–1815* (London, 1994
Wormald, J., ed., *Scotland Revisited* (London, 1991)
Young, J. R., ed., *Celtic Dimensions of the British Civil Wars* (Edinburgh, 1997)

JOURNAL ARTICLES

Armitage, D. 'Making the Empire British: Scotland in the Atlantic World 1542–1717', *Past & Present*, 155 (1997), pp. 34–63
Arnold, L. J. 'The Irish Court of Claims of 1663', *IHS*, 24 (1985), pp. 417–30
Bowie, K. 'Public Opinion, Popular Politics and the Union of 1707', *SHR*, 82 (2003), pp. 226–60
Buckroyd, J. M. 'Bridging the Gap: Scotland 1659–1660', *SHR*, 66 (1987), pp. 1–25
Campbell, R. H. 'The Anglo-Scottish Union of 1707. II: The Economic Consequences', *Economic History Review*, new series, 16 (1964), pp. 468–77
Canny, N. 'Writing Atlantic History; or, Reconfiguring the History of Colonial British America', *Journal of American History*, 86 (1999), pp. 1093–114
Carstairs, A. M. 'Some Economic Aspects of the Union of Parliaments', *Scottish Journal of Political Economy*, 2 (1955), pp. 64–72
Clarke, A. 'The History of Poynings' Law, 1615–1641', *IHS*, 18 (1972), pp. 207–22
Clarke, T. 'The Williamite Episcopalians and the Glorious Revolution in Scotland', *RSCHS*, 24 (1999), pp. 33–51
Crawford, T. 'Political and Protest Songs in 18th century Scotland I: Jacobite and Anti-Jacobite', *Scottish Studies*, 14 (1970), pp. 1–33
  'Political and Protest Songs in Eighteenth Century Scotland, II: Songs of the Left', *Scottish Studies*, 14 (1971), pp. 105–31
Cruickshanks, E. 'Jacobites, Tories and "James III"', *PH*, 21 (2002), pp. 247–54
Devine, T. M. & Lythe, S. G. E. 'The Economy of Scotland under James VI: A Revision Article', *SHR*, 50 (1971), pp. 91–106
Elliot, J. H. 'A Europe of Composite Monarchies', *Past & Present*, 137 (1992), 48–71
Ferguson, W. 'Imperial Crowns: A Neglected Facet of the Background to the Treaty of Union of 1707', *SHR*, 53 (1974), pp. 22–44
  'The Making of the Treaty of Union of 1707', *SHR*, 43 (1964), pp. 89–110
Fox, C. 'Swift's Scotophobia', *Bullán: An Irish Studies Journal*, 6 (2002), pp. 43–65
Fryer, L. G. 'Documents Relating to the Formation of the Carolina Company in Scotland, 1682', *South Carolina Historical Magazine*, 99 (1998), pp. 110–34

'Robert Barclay of Urie and East New Jersey', *Northern Scotland*, 15 (1995), pp. 1–17
Geiter, M. K. 'The Restoration Crisis and the Launching of Pennsylvania, 1679–81', *EHR*, 112 (1997), pp. 300–18
Goldie, M. 'John Locke's Circle and James II', *HJ*, 35 (1992), pp. 557–86
Graham, E. J. 'In Defence of the Scottish Maritime Interest, 1681–1713', *SHR*, 71 (1992), pp. 88–109
Gregg, E. 'Was Queen Anne a Jacobite?', *History*, 57 (1972), pp. 358–75
Griffiths, N. E. S. & Reid, J. G. 'New Evidence on New Scotland, 1629', *William and Mary Quarterly*, third series, 39 (1992), pp. 492–508
Halliday, J. 'The Club and the Revolution in Scotland 1689–90', *SHR*, 45 (1966), pp. 143–59
Hamilton, C. L. 'The Anglo-Scottish Negotiations of 1640–41', *SHR*, 41 (1962), pp. 84–6
Hanham, A. '"So Few Facts": Jacobites, Tories and the Pretender', *PH*, 19 (2000), pp. 233–57
Harris, T. 'Tories and the Rule of Law in the Reign of Charles II', *Seventeenth Century*, 8 (1993), pp. 9–27
Hayton, D. 'Traces of Party Politics in Early Eighteenth-Century Scottish Elections', *PH*, 15 (1996), pp. 74–99
Horwitz, H. 'The East India Trade, the Politicians and the Constitution: 1689–1702', *Journal of British Studies*, 17 (1978), pp. 1–18
Hughes, E. 'The Negotiations for a Commercial Union between England and Scotland in 1668', *SHR*, 24 (1927), pp. 30–47
Israel, J. L. 'A Conflict of Empires: Spain and the Netherlands 1618–1648', *Past & Present*, 76 (1977), pp. 34–74
Jones, W. D. '"The Bold Adventurers": A Quantitative Analysis of the Darien Subscription Lists (1696)', *Scottish Economic & Social History*, 21 (2001), pp. 22–42
Karsten, P. 'Plotters and Proprietaries, 1682–83: The "Council of Six" and the Colonies', *Historian*, 38 (1976), pp. 474–84
Keith, T. 'The Economic Case for the Scottish Union', *EHR*, 21 (1909), pp. 44–66
Kelly, J. 'The Origins of the Act of Union: An Examination of Unionist Opinion in Britain and Ireland, 1650–1800', *IHS*, 25 (1987), pp. 236–63
Kidd, C. 'North Britishness and the Nature of Eighteenth-Century British Patriotisms', *HJ*, 39 (1996), pp. 361–82
Landsman, N. C. 'Nation, Migration, and the Province in the First British Empire: Scotland and the Americas, 1600–1800', *AHR*, 104 (1999), pp. 463–75
Lewis, C. 'Some Extracts Relating to Sir Edmund Plowden and Some Others from the Lost Minutes of the Virginia Council and General Court, 1642–45', *William & Mary Quarterly*, second series, 20 (1940), pp. 62–78
MacCuarta, B. 'The Plantation of Leitrim, 1620–41', *IHS*, 32 (2001), pp. 297–320
Macinnes, A. I. 'Catholic Recusancy and the Penal Laws, 1603–1707', *RSCHS*, 12 (1987), pp. 27–63

'Early Modern History: The Current State of Play', *SHR*, 53 (1994), pp. 30–46

'Influencing the Vote: The Scottish Estates and the Treaty of Union, 1706–07', *History Microcomputer Review*, 2 (1990), pp. 11–25

'Jacobitism in Scotland: Episodic Cause or National Movement?' *SHR*, 86 (2007), pp. 225–52

'Le jacobitisme en Écosse, cause épisodique ou mouvement national?' *L'évolution des mondes modernes, Séminaire de D. E. A. De l'Institut de Recherches sur les Civilisations de l'Occident Moderne, Université Paris Sorbonne*, 2 (2004–5), pp. 1–28

'Repression and Conciliation: The Highland Dimension, 1660–1688', *SHR*, 65 (1986), pp. 167–95

'The First Scottish Tories?' *SHR*, 67 (1988), pp. 56–66

'Treaty of Union: Voting Patterns and Political Influence', *Historical Social Research: Historische Sozialforschung*, 14 (1989), pp. 53–61

McKenny, K. 'Charles II's Irish Cavaliers: The 1649 Officers and the Restoration Land Settlement', *IHS*, 28 (1993), pp. 409–25

Mackillop, A. 'Accessing Empire: Scotland, Europe, Britain and the Asia Trade, 1695 – c. 1750', *Itinerario*, 19 (2005), pp. 7–30

Macree, D. 'Daniel Defoe, the Church of Scotland, and the Union of 1707', *Eighteenth Century Studies*, 7 (1973), pp. 62–77

Murdoch, S. 'The Good, the Bad and the Anonymous: A Preliminary Survey of the Scots in the Dutch East Indies 1612–1707', *Northern Scotland*, 22 (2002), pp. 63–76

Murdoch, S., Little, A. & Forte, A. D. M. 'Scottish Privateering, Swedish Neutrality and Prize Law in the Third Anglo-Dutch War, 1672–1674', *Forum Navale*, 59 (2003), pp. 37–65

Netzloff, M. 'Forgetting the Ulster Plantation: John Speed's The Theatre of the Empire of Great Britain (1611) and the Colonial Archive', *Journal of Medieval and Early Modern Studies*, 31 (2001), pp. 313–48

Ohlmeyer, J. H. 'Seventeenth-Century Ireland and the New British and Atlantic Histories', *AHR*, 104 (1999), pp. 446–62

Perceval-Maxwell, M. 'Ireland and the Monarchy in the Early Stuart Multiple Kingdom' *HJ*, 34 (1991), pp. 279–95

Pincus, S. 'Neither Machiavellian Moment nor Possessive Individualism: Commercial Society and the Defenders of the English Commonwealth', *AHR*, 103 (1998), pp. 705–36

Pocock, J. G. A. 'The Limits and Divisions of British History: In Search of an Unknown Subject', *AHR*, 87 (1982), pp. 311–36

Riley, P. W. J. 'The Formation of the Scottish Ministry of 1703', *SHR*, 44 (1965), pp. 112–34

'The Union of 1707 as an Episode in English Politics', *EHR*, 84 (1969), pp. 498–527

Rusche, H. 'Prophecies and Propaganda, 1641 to 1651', *EHR*, 84 (1969), pp. 752–70

Smout, T. C. 'The Anglo-Scottish Union of 1707. 1: The Economic Background', *Economic History Review*, new series, 16 (1964), pp. 498–527

'The Burgh of Montrose and the Union of 1707 – A Document', *SHR*, 66 (1987), pp. 183–4

'The Development and Enterprise of Glasgow, 1560–1707', *Scottish Journal of Political Economy*, 7 (1960), pp. 194–212

'The Early Scottish Sugar Houses, 1660–1720', *Economic History Review*, new series, 14 (1961), pp. 240–53

Smyth, J. '"Like Amphibious Animals": Irish Protestants, Ancient Britons, 1691–1707', *HJ*, 34 (1993), pp. 785–96

Stephen, J. 'The Kirk and the Union, 1706–07: A Reappraisal', *RSCHS*, 31 (2002), pp. 68–96

Storrs, C. 'Disaster at Darien (1698–1700)? The Persistence of Spanish Imperial Power on the Eve of the Demise of the Spanish Habsburgs', *European History Quarterly*, 29 (1999), pp. 5–38

Szechi, D. 'Constructing a Jacobite: The Social and Intellectual Origins of George Lockhart of Carnwath', *HJ*, 40 (1997), pp. 977–96

Watt, D. 'The Management of Capital by the Company of Scotland 1696–1707', *Journal of Scottish Historical Studies*, 25 (2006), pp. 97–118

Whatley, C. A. 'Economic Causes and Consequences of the Union of 1707', *SHR*, 68 (1989), pp. 150–81

Whyte, I. D. 'Poverty or Prosperity? Rural Society in Lowland Scotland in the Late Sixteenth and Early Seventeenth Centuries', *Scottish Economic & Social History*, 18 (1998), pp. 19–31

Williamson, A. H. 'Scots, Indians and Empire: The Scottish Politics of Civilization, 1519–1609', *Past & Present*, 150 (1996), pp. 46–83

'Union with England Traditional, Union with England Radical: Sir James Hope and the Mid-Seventeenth Century British State', *EHR*, 110 (1995), pp. 303–12

Zupko, R. E. 'The Weights and Measures of Scotland Before the Union', *SHR*, 55 (1977), pp. 124–39

Index

Abercorn, Charles Hamilton, 5th Earl of (Viscount Strabane) 129
Abercorn, James Hamilton, 6th Earl of 293–4, 295
Abercromby, Patrick 17–18, 235
Aberdeen 209, 218–19, 223, 224, 225
civic improvements 223–4
Act anent Peace and War (1704) 39, 129, 259, 260–1
Act for Securing the Protestant Religion and Presbyterian Church Government (1707) 286, 302, 322
Act for the Settling of Ireland (1652) 119
Act of Explanation (1665) 120
Act of Security (1703) 39, 129, 259–61, 265–6, 290
Act of Settlement (1662) 120
Act of Settlement (1701) 39, 90–1, 128, 129, 259
Admiralty, Court of 322–3
Adventurers Act (1642) 115
agriculture 213
see also famine
Alexander, William, of Menstrie (Jr) 145
Alexander, William, of Menstrie (Sr) *see* Stirling
Alien Act (1705) 39, 130, 185, 198, 228, 230, 270, 272, 317, 318
Allardyce, John 101
Althusius, Johannes 249
America *see* colonies
Anderson, James 127
Annandale (ship) 271–2
Annandale, William Johnston, 1st Marquess of 97–8, 131, 264, 269, 272, 297, 302
Anne, Princess, of Denmark 90
Anne, Queen 10–11, 13, 15, 34, 49, 196, 229, 270, 286, 307
accession 8, 129, 239
attitudes to monarchy 243–4

concern for royal prerogative 97, 240, 261, 268
dealings with Darien scheme 181
dealings with parliament 91–2, 94–5, 98–9, 265–6
Episcopalian approaches to 253–4
pro-Union stance 15, 277, 284
provisions for succession 39, 259–60, 265–6, 281
and Treaty of Union 274–5, 292, 308, 309, 313
appeals *see under* law
Arbuthnot, John 313–14
Argyll, Archibald Campbell, 8th Earl / Marquess of 70, 73, 74, 78
execution 82–94
Argyll, Archibald Campbell, 9th Earl of 167
Argyll, Archibald Campbell, 10th Earl / 1st Duke of 262
Argyll, Elizabeth Campbell, Dowager Duchess of 90
Argyll, John Campbell, 2nd Duke of 26, 98, 272–3, 274–5, 292–3, 296, 297–9
Armitage, David 45
army
increase in size/expense 221–2
personnel 193–4
provisioning 194
Arthur, King 55
Ashley Cooper *see* Shaftesbury
Atholl, John Murray, 1st Duke of 13–14, 90, 255–6, 262, 275, 290
and Union negotiations / Treaty 258, 260–1, 263, 265, 269, 273, 274, 294–5, 300, 305–6
Atwood, William 127
Augustus II of Poland 267

Bacon, Sir Francis 63–4
Bacon, Nathaniel 162
Baillie, George, of Jerviswood 286

Baillie, Sir James, of Jerviswood 264
Balmerino, John Elphinstone, 4th Earl of 265, 292
Balthazar, Malthias 10
Baltic, trade with Scotland 211, 214, 215, 224
  decline 216
Baltimore, Cecil Calvert, 2nd Baron 140
Baltimore, George Calvert, 1st Baron 140–1
Banff, George Ogilvy, Lord 251–2, 293, 295
Bank of England 194, 227, 237
Bank of Scotland 174, 175, 177, 226–7
Bannatyne, John 8, 256
Bannatyne Club 34–5
Barbados 161
Barclay, Robert, of Urie 167
'Barebones Parliament' 78
baronetcies, creation/sale of 144
Beaufort, Henry Somerset, 2nd Duke of 308
Beaufort *see* Fraser, Simon
Bede (the Venerable) 57
Belhaven, John Hamilton, Lord 33, 90, 180, 233, 252, 264, 271–2, 297, 302, 307
Benbow, John, Admiral 178–9
Bende, John 101
Bible, Authorised Version 56
Bishops' Wars (1639–40) 68, 117, 151, 250
  see also London, Treaty of
Black, David 232, 234–5
Black, William 234, 236–7, 288
'black oath' 113
Blaeu, Joan 59
Blaeu, Willem 55
Blair, James 185
Blathwayt, William 170, 178
Bloome, Richard 82
Board of Trade (and Plantations) 184–5, 188–90, 192, 195, 197, 199–200, 231
Boece, Hector 57–8, 59, 107
Bo'ness 211
Boston 152–3
Boyer, Abel 14
Boyle, David *see* Glasgow
Boyle, Roger *see* Orrery
Brandon, Duke of *see* Hamilton, James Douglas-Hamilton
Breda, Treaty of 162
Brewer, John 48
Brewster, Sir Francis 128
Britannic Engagement 74

Britannic perspective (on state formation) 54–5, 57, 81–3, 117, 157–9, 315–16
  impact on colonial affairs 138–42, 185
  objections to 65
Bromley, William 307
Brown, Andrew 233
Brown, P. Hume 38–9, 41
Browne, John 157, 165
Bruce, Alexander, of Broomhall (later Earl of Kincardine) 92
Bruce, John 27
Brydges, John 234, 309
Buchanan, George 18, 20, 58–9, 67, 107
Burnet, Gilbert, Bishop 14–15, 16, 32, 40, 93, 99, 252, 267, 278
Burnet, Sir Thomas, of Leys 298–9
Burnett, John 147
Burns, Robert 29
Burton, J. Hill 36
Bute, James Stuart, 1st Earl of 104, 261
Butler *see* Ormond

Cabot, Sebastian 155
Camden, William 54–5, 58, 59
Cameronians *see* Covenanters, radical wing
Campbell, Alexander, Colonel 179
Campbell, Archibald *see* Argyll; Islay
Campbell, John (historian) 22–3
Campbell, John (politician) *see* Argyll
Campbell, Roy 43
Canada *see* France, colonial conflicts with; Newfoundland; Nova Scotia
Cardross, Lord 166–7
Carey *see* Falkland
Caribbean, British enterprises in 140, 142, 146–7
  military vulnerability 191
  see also names of islands
Carlisle, James Hay, 1st Earl of 146–7
Carlisle, James Hay, 2nd Earl of 149
carrying trade *see* tramp trading
Carstairs, A. M. 42
Carstares, William 32, 44, 98–9, 167, 256, 286
Cary, John 190, 192
Catherine of Braganza 159
Catholic Church / Catholicism
  in Ireland 108–9
  plans to wipe out 116
  in Scotland 251–2
  toleration *see* James II
  see also Catholic Confederation
Catholic Confederation 108, 115–18, 120
  military capabilities 117
Cavendish *see* Devonshire

Cavendish-Bentinck *see* Portland
Céitinn, Séathrún *see* Keating, Geoffrey
Chalmers, George 25–6
Chamberlen, Hugh 173, 229–30
Charlemagne 57
Charles I 65–7, 205, 268
　and Bishops' Wars 68
　and Civil War 73–4
　common fishing scheme 66, 111, 141, 208
　dealings with Covenanters 68, 69–70, 114–15
　dealings with Ireland 108, 112, 116–18, 122
　dissatisfaction with 66–7, 115
　economic policy 141–2, 220
　execution 74, 151–4
　foreign policy/relations 64, 145
Charles II 83, 85, 164, 165, 178
　foreign/colonial policy 82–3, 157–8, 169
　marriage 159
　proclamation in Scotland 74–5, 151–2
　Restoration 79, 80, 81–2, 120
　stance on Union 84–5, 155–8
Child, Sir Josiah 170
Christian IV of Denmark 65
Church of England 306–7
Churchill *see* Marlborough
Civil War
　colonial impact 147–8, 151–2
　military progress 72–3
　outbreak 70
　in Scotland 73–5, 255
Claim of Right (1689) 87, 92, 131, 257–8, 268, 314
Clark, G. N. 41
Claybourne, William 146
Claypoole, Norton 163–4
Clerk, Sir John, of Penicuik 30–1, 232–3, 279, 282, 288, 320
Clifford, Jeronimy 162
Clotworthy, Sir John (later Viscount Massarene) 115, 116, 121
'Club the' 87–91
co-partneries, governmental encouragement 209–10, 228
Cobbe, Walsall 162–3
Cockburn, Adam, of Ormiston 271–2, 286, 287
Coke, Roger 170
Colbert, Jean-Baptiste 206
colonies
　calls for inclusion in Union 22–3
　compensation for loss of 155–6

English jurisdiction over 148–9
grant/sale of titles 147
(*see also* baronetcies)
hereditary control 146–7
illegal trade in 186–8
Irish 110
legal systems/practices 164, 168–9
opening up of trade with 280, 318–19
policy switch 169–71, 185
Scottish involvement in 137–8, 142–7, 149, 152–3, 157–8, 161–3, 164, 172–3, 196–7; restrictions on 153–4, 185, 197
Scottish owned/occupied 85, 164–9; (*see also* Darien; East New Jersey; Nova Scotia; South Carolina)
Scottish trade with 147, 219
sources of manpower 195–7
trade with 122
transportation of criminals/undesirables to 152, 168
see also servitor colonialism; *names of territories*
Colquhoun, William 165
Colvin's Case (1608) 63, 83, 111, 143, 185–6
commissioners, parliamentary 75–6, 281
　appointment 62, 78, 92, 273–4, 275
　continuity of personnel 95
　distribution by party 277–9
Committee for Both Kingdoms 72–3, 281–3
Committee of Trade 206, 207, 209–10, 213, 217
Commonwealth
　continuance of methods post-Restoration 156–7
　electoral system 77
　Scottish collaboration with 78–9
　see also incorporation; Ireland; Scotland
Company of Scotland 174, 179–80, 181, 182, 183–4, 198, 199, 226–7, 271, 282, 287–8, 301
Company of the Royal Fishery (of England / Scotland / Great Britain and Ireland) 208–9
compensation payments *see* colonies
confederation
　arguments/demands for 69–72
　economic, projected 124
　models 71
　projected expansion 70
Connacht, resistance to Cromwellian forces 118, 119
consignment system (of trading) 187
Constantine, Emperor 55, 56

Index

constitution, written, (un)desirability of 314
convoys, merchants' use of 222
Conway, Edward Conway, 1st Earl of 121–2
Copland, Patrick 139
Cornwall, incorporation into Union 4, 131–2
Council for Trade and Plantations (England) *see* Board of Trade
Council of Trade (Scotland) 229, 231
Country Party 89, 92–4, 98, 100, 180, 181, 229, 233, 240, 249–50, 254, 263–6, 273–4
  and Treaty of Union 278, 286, 295–9, 300, 301, 303–5, 306
Court Party 87–8, 92–3, 97–100, 106, 129, 132, 181, 229, 232, 237, 254, 273–5
  and Treaty of Union 277–8, 283, 285–6, 287, 289, 292–4, 297, 298–9, 304–5
Courten, Sir William 147
Covenanters
  colonial involvement 149, 151–2, 165, 203
  demands for political reform 69–72
  elimination 82
  governmental moves against 112–13, 247
  internal divisions 70, 73–5, 78–9
  political/military gains 68
  protest activity 121, 249
  radical wing 93–4, 256, 287, 290
  relations with Ireland 114–15
  role in Civil War 72–5
Cowper, William 280–1
Craig, Sir Thomas, of Riccarton 62
Craufurd, George 15
Cromartie, George Mackenzie, 1st Earl of (formerly Viscount Tarbat) 45, 97, 98, 99–100, 127, 232, 233, 253, 262
  and Union negotiations / Treaty 258, 260–1, 284–5, 287, 298–9, 322
Cromwell, Oliver 73, 74–5, 77, 78, 82–3, 118–19, 126, 151
  death 78, 79
Cromwell, Richard 78, 84
cross-voting (in Treaty deliberations) 304–5
Crouch, Nathaniel *see* Bloome, Richard
Cumming, Alexander 230–1
Cunningham, Alexander 26–7, 32, 240
Cunningham, James, Major, of Aiket 291, 293
Cunningham, William *see* Glencairn

Dacre, Lord *see* Trevor-Roper, Hugh
Daiches, David 43

Dalrymple, Sir David, of Hailes 103–4, 287
Dalrymple, George, of Dalmahoy 103–4
Dalrymple, Sir Hew, of North Berwick 103–4
Dalrymple, Sir James *see* Stair
Dalrymple, Sir John 21–2
Dalrymple, William, Col., of Glenmure 8, 9, 103–4, 202, 303
Danish West Indian and Guinea Company 177–8
Darcy, Patrick 114
Darien (colonial venture) 15, 30, 33, 36, 38, 42, 45, 130–1, 172, 181, 231–2
  (calls for) reparations 172, 198, 279, 280, 282–3, 301, 320; (*see also* Equivalent(s))
  economic impact 181, 190–1, 198, 199, 234
  English attitudes to 128, 176–7, 178–9, 182, 183–4
  founding 175–6
  funding 176, 181
  political impact 88–9, 91, 216
  precedents 143
  reasons for failure 176–9
  Scottish commentaries on 179–80
Davenant, Charles 95, 192, 194–5, 283–4
Davidson, Neil 46–7
Davies, Sir John 63–4, 107
de Lolme, John Lewis 25–6
Declaratory Act (1720) 106
deficit financing 221–2
Defoe, Daniel 12–13, 25–6, 32, 36, 37, 235–6, 238, 257, 284, 290, 317
Delaware 163
Denmark 83
deputies
  absence 77
  election 76, 78
Devine, Tom 46
devolution, (modern) movement for 3, 46
Devonshire, William Cavendish, 1st Duke of 91
Dicey, Albert, and Robert Rait, *Thoughts on the Union Between England and Scotland* 39–40, 41
divine right, theory of 56–7
Donaldson, James 219
Douglas, Archibald Douglas, 3rd Marquess / 1st Duke of 261
Douglas, James *see* Queensberry
Douglas-Hamilton *see* Hamilton, James Douglas-Hamilton; Orkney, George; Ruglen; Selkirk
Dover, Duke of *see* Queensberry

Drake, John 127
drawbacks (on customs dues) 308–9
Drummond, James *see* Perth
Drummond, John (businessman) 234, 309
Drummond, John (politician) *see* Melfort
Drummond, William, Governor 161–2
Dudley, Joseph, Governor 197
Dunbar, battle of 75
Dundas, Henry 28–9, 31
Dundas, Robert, of Arniston 271–2
Dundee 223
Dunlop, William 166–7, 228
Dunmore, Charles Murray, 1st Earl of 294–5
Dupplin, Thomas Hay, 6th Viscount 296–7
Dutch Wars *see* Netherlands

East India Company/ies 50, 92, 128–9, 141–2, 177, 192, 199, 271
   merged under Treaty of Union 282, 317
East New Jersey, Scottish colony in 165, 167–8, 169, 172, 175–6, 206, 224, 232
   investors 175–6
economy / commercial life, Scottish 24–5, 42–3, 46–7, 50, 64, 100, 101–2
   adaptations prior to Union 197–200
   commentaries 202–4, 232
   crises (1696-1704) 226
   currency 226–7, 320–1
   dealings with England 228–31
   dealings with Ireland 123–4, 129–30
   fluctuations 103
   inward investment 228
   proposals for improvement 229–31
   recovery (following famine/crisis) 218, 226–7
   role in Empire 190–1, 196
   scope for expansion 228
   strength of 190, 207–8, 215, 219–20, 225–6
   see also officials; taxation; trade
Edinburgh 218, 220
education, governmental prioritisation 218
Edward I of England 53
Edward III of England 53
Edward VI of England 53
Eglinton, Alexander Montgomery, 9th Earl of 261, 293
Elibank, Alexander Murray, Lord 292, 294–5
Elizabeth I of England 53
Elizabeth of Bohemia 90
Elling, Jens 10
Elliot, Sir Gilbert, of Minto 298–9

Elphinstone *see* Balmerino
Elzevirus, Bonaventure/Abraham 59
emigration
   numbers 141, 160
   planning 195
'Empire, British,' first use of term 16
England
   economic policy/priorities 188–9
   global status 5
   government policy on Union 25
   motivations for Union 7
   overseas trade 189–90, 192–5
   statistics 190, 199–200
   party politics 95–7, 257, 269–70; (*see also* Tory Party; Whig Party)
   political/economic dominance 5, 81–2, 198–9, 215
   population 191–2
   social desirability of contact with 239
ennoblement 103
   see also baronetcies
entrepreneurialism 159–64
Episcopalianism
   attempts to enforce 66–7, 80
   relationship with Jacobitism 252–4
Equivalent(s) (sum paid in compensation) 282–3, 301, 320
   Committee for calculation of 298
   objections to 287–8
Errol, Charles Hay, 13th Earl of 255, 297, 305
European Community/Union 49, 326
exchange rates 226, 227
Exchequer, Court of 323
Exclusion Crisis 85–6, 125, 268–9
export laws 159–60
exports *see* trade

Fairfax, Blackerby 96
Falconer, Sir James, of Phaedo 265
Falkland, Henry Carey, Viscount 141
famine (1690s) 217–19
   attempted remedies 218–19
Farrett, James 146
Fearne, David 236
federative union 71–2
   calls for 83–5, 100, 127, 279–80
   defined 5
Fergus MacEarc, King 57, 58, 108, 125
Ferguson, Adam 11, 18–19, 22
Ferguson, George 216
Ferguson, Robert 262
Ferguson, William 43–4
Finch *see* Nottingham
Finlay, Captain 291–2

Index   373

fishing 66, 101–2, 111–12, 141, 208–9, 210, 212, 223–4, 227
Fleming, Sir James 271–2
Fletcher, Andrew, of Saltoun 105, 127–8, 129, 130, 132, 219
  later commentators' view of 17, 28, 41, 43, 44, 45, 48–9, 106
  proposals for constitutional monarchy 266, 268, 273
  role in Treaty debates 255, 265, 297, 302, 305
  stance on Union 13–14, 233, 255, 260
Forbes, Sir Arthur, of Corse *see* Granard
Forrester, Andrew, Captain 146
Foulis, James 167, 184
France
  colonial conflicts with 144, 145, 171, 196–7
  economy 206
  émigrés from 195
  recognition of Jacobite claims 244; (*see also* Louis XIV; Wales, James Francis Edward Stuart, Prince of)
  relationship with England/Scotland 15, 26, 66, 190, 200, 238–9, 325
  see also French Revolution; Napoleonic Wars
Fraser, Simon, of Beaufort 261–2, 263, 274
Fraser, William 225–6, 234, 271–2
Frederick I of Prussia 130
Free Kirk 7
free trade 153
  role in Treaty of Union 281–2, 285, 301, 317
French Revolution, Scottish/Irish responses to 28–9

Gael, role in Irish tradition 107–8
Garnock, John Crawford, Viscount 261
George, Prince, of Denmark (consort of Anne) 10, 49, 265–6, 268, 269
George I 15, 26, 90, 316–17
George II 16
George IV 34
Gerard, Sir Digby, Lord Gerard 89
Gerrard, Robert (Jr) 224
Gerrard, Robert (Sr) 224
Gibson, Walter 157, 165–6
Glasgow 153, 157, 183, 209, 211–12, 219, 220, 318–19
Glasgow, David Boyle of Kelburn, 1st Earl of 97, 261, 286, 293
Glencairn, William Cunningham, 11th Earl of 293
Glencoe, Massacre of 88, 174, 248–9

'Glorious Revolution' *see* Revolution
Godolphin, Sidney Godolphin, 1st Earl of 26, 30, 34, 36, 89, 91–2, 97, 130, 170, 191, 194, 198, 239, 263, 266, 269–70, 282, 293–4, 306–7, 314
Gordon, George Gordon, 1st Duke of 251, 275
Gordon, Sir John, of Lochinvar (colonist) 144–5
Gordon, John (politician) *see* Strathnaver; Sutherland
Gordon, Patrick 224–5
Gordon, Sir Robert 59
Gothic perspective (on state formation) 54, 60–1, 74, 82–3, 86, 120, 126, 148, 154, 155–7, 173, 185, 197, 205, 314
Graham *see* Montrose
Granard, Arthur Forbes, 1st Earl of 121, 123
Grant, Francis (later Lord Cullen) 232–3
Granville, George Granville, Lord 308
Green, Thomas, Captain 271–2, 289
Greenshields, James 322
Greg, William 236
Gregory, David 283
Grew, Nehemiah 196
Gualtiero, Francesco, Cardinal 261–2

Hamilton, Anne, Duchess of 89, 180, 256, 274–5
Hamilton, Andrew, Governor 185–6
Hamilton, Charles (historian) 31
Halifax, Charles Montague, Lord 96, 170
Hamilton, Charles (politician) *see* Abercorn
Hamilton, Elizabeth, Duchess of 89
Hamilton, Gustavus 184
Hamilton, James, of Boghall (entrepreneur) 148–9
Hamilton, James Douglas-Hamilton, 4th Duke of (later Duke of Brandon) 13–14, 16, 31, 33, 44, 89–90, 92–3, 97, 104, 129, 180, 184, 198, 249, 255–6, 275
  role in 'Scotch Plot' 261, 262
  and Union negotiations / Treaty 259, 263, 264, 265, 273–4, 275, 291–2, 296, 297–8, 300, 302, 303, 305–6, 315–16
Hamilton, James Hamilton, 3rd Marquess / 1st Duke of 70, 73, 141
Hamilton, James (politician) *see* Abercorn
Hamilton, John, Lord Belhaven *see* Belhaven
Hammond, Thomas 271–2
Handasyd, Thomas, Governor 197

374   Index

Hanoverian Succession 94, 240, 265–6, 275, 302
  opposition to 14, 250
  see also Act of Settlement
Harley, Robert 26, 91–2, 130, 198, 235, 236, 270, 282, 306, 307, 308–9
Haversham, John Thomson, Lord 307, 308
Hay, Charles *see* Errol
Hay, James *see* Carlisle
Hay, John *see* Tweeddale
Hay, Peter, of Haystoun 147
Hay, Thomas *see* Dupplin
Hay, William *see* Kinnoull
Hebron, John 256–7, 290
Hebronites *see* Covenanters, radical wing
Henderson, Alexander 148
Henry VII of England 155
Hermannides, Rutgerius 82
Herries, William 179
historiography 11, 12
Hodges, James 229, 232, 235, 256, 284, 296
Hodges, Robert 127
Holy Roman Empire 71
Home, Charles Home, 6th Earl of 255–6, 258
Home, Sir John, Baronet Home of Blackadder 271–2
Home Rule, call for 7
Hooke, Nathaniel, Captain 244
Hope, Sir James, of Hopetoun 204
Hopeton, Charles Hope, 1st Earl of 261
house building 213
Howard *see* Nottingham
Hume, Sir David, of Crossrigg (lawyer/politician) 286
Hume, David, of Godscroft (writer/political commentator) 58–9
Hume, Sir David (politician/diarist) 202
Hume, Patrick *see* Marchmont
Huntington Library, San Marino, CA 9, 10
Hutchinson, Francis 132–3

imports *see* trade
incorporation
  acceptance 281
  bodies of opinion undecided on 101–2
  calls for 83–5, 89–91, 98–100, 128, 130–2, 235–7, 266–7, 284–5
  under Commonwealth 75–9
  opposition to 233, 288–9
indentured servants *see* servitor colonialism
independence, arguments against 43
Inglis, Robert 298–9

Ireland
  arguments for/against Union 22–3, 26–8, 126–8
  (attempted) enforcement of Protestantism 112–13, 115–20
  civil war 116
  colonial involvement 142–3, 195; (*see also* colonies; New Albion)
  dependent status 106–7, 109, 114, 118–20, 125
  economy/trade 121–2, 132, 190, 199
  English attitudes to 124–5
  English political agenda in 120
  forfeiture of estates 126
  governance 114
  parliament, position on British succession 128–9
  political aspirations 125
  position under Commonwealth 75, 118–20
  rebellion (1641) 70, 114–18
  rejection of Union 4, 6, 106
  relationship with England 25
  relationship with Scots nobility 122–3
  as warning to Scots 106–7, 112–13
Irish perspective (on state formation) 107–9
iron/steel trade 212–13
Islay, Archibald Campbell, 1st Earl of 292
ius imperium, concept of 61–2, 81

Jacobites/Jacobitism
  activities post-Union 316–17, 319
  (alleged) plots 275; (*see also* 'Scotch Plot')
  armed risings 26, 223, 250, 316–17, 323
  cellular structure 248–9
  Court in exile 244–5
  in England 245, 249
  fears of 48–9, 238–9, 240
  internal differences 255–8
  involvement in commercial enterprise 20–1
  in Ireland 245
  movement of funds 246–7
  poetry 250–1
  polarising impact 245–6
  political ideology 13–14, 15, 243–4, 250–1
  redefinition 17–19
  refusal to recognise Anne 295–6
  religious leanings 252–8
  Scottish focus 249–50
  (verbal) attacks on 14, 15–16

Jamaica 153
James II of Scotland 274
James IV of Scotland 53, 58
James VI of Scotland / I of England 4, 17, 66, 74, 76, 108, 109, 146
  foreign policy 64
  implementation of policy 62, 64
  religious policy 66
  theory of monarchy/statehood 53–8, 60, 61–2, 138, 315–16
James VII of Scotland / II of England 35, 97, 120, 156, 208–9, 221, 244
  armed conflict with William III 125
  colonial policy 164, 165, 169–70
  death 90
  deposition 10, 13, 21, 87, 201, 268
  economic policy 141–2, 206, 215
  Irish responses to 124–5
  plans for restoration 296
  policy of religious toleration 85–6, 168, 251
  qualities as ruler 243, 246–8
  Scottish support for 21–2, 252
  stance on Union / Anglo-Scottish relations 85–6, 158–9
'James VIII/III' see Wales, James Francis Edward Stuart, Prince of
Johnston, Adam 163–4
Johnston, Archibald 88
Johnston, James, of Warriston 88, 264
Johnston, Sir Patrick 282, 290
Johnston, William see Annandale
joint-stock ventures 142

Keating, Geoffrey 107–9
Keith, Theodora 38
Keith, Thomas 263
Keith, William see Marischal
Kenneth MacAlpine, King 57
Ker, John, of Kersland (government agent) 14, 290
Ker, John (politician) see Roxburghe
Kincardine, Earl of see Bruce
King, Gregory 191–2
King, William, Bishop 252
Kinnoull, William Hay, 4th Earl of 155–6
Kirk, (Sir) David 141, 145
Kirk, Lewis 145
Kirk of Scotland
  (calls for) retention under Union 97–8
  comment on Darien scheme 180, 181
  handling of religious differences 254, 256
  influence for peace 31

  overthrow of leaders 252–3
  political importance 21
  position under Treaty of Union 285–7, 306
Knox, John 24, 58

la Tour, Claud St Stephen, Seigneur de 155
landed enterprise, role in national economy 231–4
Lang, Andrew 38–9
Laud, William, Archbishop 66, 112
Lauderdale, John Maitland, 2nd Earl (later Duke) of 73–4, 80–1, 83–5, 121, 124, 155, 164, 247
Law, John 230
law, Scottish
  appeals 322
  applicability in Ireland 117–22
  brought under English control 321–3
  common vs civil 61–2, 63–4
  maintenance within Union 76–8, 84–5
Leeward Islands 149
Leopold I, Emperor 191
Leslie, John see Rothes
Leven, David Melville, 3rd Earl of 98
Limerick, Treaty of (1691) 125
Lindsay, David 263
Lithgow, William 203
Livingstone, Robert 158
local government 223–5, 323–4
Locke, John 126, 166
Lockhart, George, of Carnwath (politician) 13–14, 16, 32, 33, 44, 104–5, 202, 254, 274, 275
  and Treaty of Union 278, 279, 282, 291, 294, 295, 301
Lockhart, George (merchant/surgeon) 162–3
London
  population / economic importance 141, 191
  Scottish community 153, 228–9, 233–5
London, Treaty of (1641) 69–70, 114, 148, 151
Long Parliament 69, 115, 203
Loudoun, Hugh Campbell, 3rd Earl of / Loudoun Papers 8, 97, 256, 271–2, 277, 292
Louis XIII of France 145
Louis XIV of France 10, 12, 15, 83, 84, 86, 90, 92, 125, 177, 191, 238, 243, 244, 247–8, 251, 261–2
Lovat, Dowager Lady 262
Low Countries see Netherlands

Macaulay, Thomas Babington (Lord) 35–6, 45–6
Macaulay, Zachary, Revd 35
MacDaniell, James 275
Macintosh, Daniel 32–3
Mackenzie, Sir George, of Rosehaugh (lawyer) 84, 256
Mackenzie, George (historian) 17–18
Mackenzie, George (politician) *see* Cromartie
Mackenzie, Sir Kenneth, of Cromartie 294–5
Mackenzie, Roderick 271–2
Mackillop, Andrew 50
Mackinnon, James 37–8
Mackintosh, Henry 162
Mackleir, Hans (John Maclean) 151
Macky, John 14
Maclean, John *see* Mackleir, Hans
MacMillan, John 256–7
Macpherson, James 23, 24, 33, 240
MacRae, Alexander, Revd 38–9
Maddison, Sir Ralph 203
Madrid, Treaty of 164, 178
Magnus, Joannus/Olaus 60–1
Mair, John 58
Maitland *see* Lauderdale
Man, Isle of 187
manufacturing industries
    expansion 216–17
    investment in 226, 227–8
    quality control 230–1
    see also landed enterprise
Mar, John Erskine, 6th Earl of 9, 97, 226, 237, 316–17
    management of Union negotiations 265, 272, 273–4, 292–3, 297, 298–9, 303, 304
Marchmont, Patrick Hume, 1st Earl of 93, 97, 129, 256, 264
    and Union negotiations / Treaty 258, 260, 286, 287, 293
Margaret Tudor, Queen (of James IV) 53, 58
Marischal, William Keith, 9th Earl 255, 269, 305
Markham, Gervaise 203
Marlborough, John Churchill, 1st Duke of 12, 30, 91–2, 97, 191, 193, 199, 239, 266, 283–4, 306–7
Marlborough, Sarah Churchill, Duchess of 97
Marshal, Ebenezer 31–2, 36
Marxist analyses 46–7
Mary, Queen of Scots 53

Mary II (of Orange), Queen 86–7, 88
Maryland 140
Mason, John, Captain 141
Massachusetts Bay Company 139–40
Massarene, Viscount *see* Clotworthy
Mathieson, William 38
Maxwell, Henry, of Finaboge 128
Maxwell, Sir John, of Nether Pollock 101–2
Meldrum, John, of Urquhart 251–2
Melfort, William Drummond, 1st Earl of 168
Melville, Andrew 58
Melville, Viscount *see* Dundas, Henry
Menstrie *see* Stirling
mercantilism 156, 205–7, 209
Mercator, Gerard 55–6
Militia Act (1757) 22
Miller (emissary from Ireland) 133
mining 228
Minuit, Peter 151
Miraculous and Happie Union of England and Scotland, The (Anon.) 56
Mitchison, Rosalind 43
Molesworth, Robert Molesworth, Viscount 128, 269
Molyneux, William 106, 126–7, 130, 131, 190
monarchy
    contractual 87
    (proposed) constitutional limitations 254–7, 259–60, 268, 305
    right of resistance to 58–9, 257–8
Montgomerie, Francis, of Giffen 286
Montgomerie, Sir James, of Skelmorlie 255
Montgomery *see* Eglinton
Montgomery, Hugh 298–9
Montrose, James Graham, 1st Marquess of 255
Montrose, James Graham, 4th Marquess of 264, 272, 293, 294–5
Mullany, John 275
Murdoch, Steve 47
Murray, Alexander, Lord Elibank *see* Elibank
Murray, Sir Alexander, of Stanhope 22
Murray, Charles *see* Dunmore
Murray, Sir James 262, 263
Murray, John *see* Atholl
Musgrave, Sir Christopher 127

Nairn, Sir David 8, 9, 309
Namier, Sir Lewis 44
Napoleonic Wars 26–7
National Association for the Vindication of Scottish Rights 35

Index 377

National Covenant (1638) 67–8, 148, 257, 314
  see also Covenanters
National Debt (English) 188, 194
  creation of 48
  shared with Scotland 94–5, 320
Navigation Acts (1650–73) 42, 81–2, 83, 94, 156, 160, 163, 168, 204, 233, 317
  adjustments to 198–9
  circumvention 47, 159, 172, 183–4, 186–8, 196–7, 205, 210, 221
  exemptions 86, 159
  impact on Scots trade 154, 156–7, 206–7
  objections to 121–2, 173
  reassertion 86, 177, 185, 216
  relaxation/non-enforcement 124, 158, 164, 183–4
Netherlands 6, 26, 45, 291
  cartography 55, 59
  consideration of union with 237–8, 325
  currency, use of 321
  as economic model 201, 214, 234–5, 267
  fishing expertise 209
  hostilities with England 76, 158, 162, 201, 204, 207–8, 222
  plans for inclusion in Confederation 70
  political alliances 83
  Scottish competition with 225
  trading links with Scotland 83, 84, 101, 150, 151, 154, 158, 162, 172, 177–8, 190, 200, 202, 224, 227, 239
networks (commercial), Scottish 172, 182, 213–14, 225–6, 227
  advantaged by loopholes in Treaty 308–9
  English fears of 196, 197
  illegal methods 186–8
  regulation under Treaty of Union 317–19, 323
  rivalries between 162–3
  rivalry with English 189–90
  trading practices 160–4
New Albion (colony) 110, 143
New England 140, 146
  Confederation of 151
  Dominion of 169–70
  disintegration 182
  United Colonies of 71
New Jersey see East New Jersey
New Model Army 117, 119
New Party (later Squadrone Volante) 180, 264–5, 269
New Sweden 150–1
Newfoundland 140–1, 156
Nicolson, William, Bishop 99, 254, 274

Nine Years' War 177, 182, 184, 187, 188, 191, 193–4, 201, 216, 222, 248–9
Nisbet, Sir John, of Dirleton 84, 93–4, 256
nobility (Scottish)
  dealings with Ireland 122–3
  representation at Westminster 303–4, 315, 316
  role in national opinion/activities 19, 102–5
nonconformism 121
Northampton, Treaty of (1328) 69
Nottingham, Charles Howard, 1st Earl of 65
Nottingham, Daniel Finch, 2nd Earl of 91–2, 95–6, 262, 263, 269–70, 275, 307
Nova Scotia 143–7, 154

oaths of allegiance 246, 295
  see also 'black oath'
O'Bruadair, David 125
officials, role in national economy 221–2
O'Flaherty, Roderic 125
Ogilvie, James see Seafield
Ogilvie, William 25
Ogilvy, George see Banff
'Old Pretender' see Wales, James Francis Edward Stuart, Prince of
Oldmixon, John 15–16
Øresund see Baltic
Orkney, George Douglas-Hamilton, 6th Earl of 104
Orkney and Shetland 76–7
Ormond, James Butler, 2nd Duke of 133
Ormond, James Butler, Marquis / 1st Duke of 118, 120
Orr, Robert 28
Orrery, Roger Boyle, 1st Earl of 120

Pakington, Sir John 96
papacy
  recognition of Jacobite claims 244
  relationship with Irish Catholicism 118
  relationship with Stuart monarchy 251
paper money 230
Parker, Henry 68, 203
Parks, Daniel 197
parliament (British, post-Union) 313
  Scottish representation 280, 283, 303–4, 315, 316
parliament (Scottish)
  (alleged) corruption 24, 29
  elections to 78, 92, 93–4
  plans to co-ordinate with English 279–80
  positive achievements 40
  publication of proceedings 30–1

parliament (Scottish) (*cont.*)
  religious divisions 258–9
  walk-out from 92, 93
Parliamentarian Party/army
  alliance with Covenanters 72
  military successes 73, 74–5
Paterson, John, Archbishop 253–4
Paterson, William 45–6, 130–2, 174–5, 229, 232, 236, 283, 284, 316, 320
patriotism, Scottish expressions of 17–19, 21–2, 239–40, 260
Patronage Act (1711) 322
Paxton, Peter 236
Penn, William 163, 167, 186
Pennsylvania 164
Perth, James Drummond, 4th Earl of 168
Petty, Sir William 59, 123–4
Philip of Anjou 191
Philiphaugh, battle of 73
Pitt, William (the younger) 28
plantation(s) 102, 124, 194–5
  English vs Scottish interests 111–12
  in Ireland 109–14, 119–20; undermining 112–14
Plowden, Sir Edmund 110
Pocock, John (J. G. A.) 49
Poland-Lithuania, Commonwealth of 97, 267–9
Pollexfen, John 192
Polwarth, Patrick Hume, Earl of 287
Port Royal 145
Portland, William Cavendish-Bentinck, 3rd Duke of 25, 27
ports, role in trade networks 161, 207–8
Portugal 267
Postelthwayt, Malachi 22
Potter, William 203
Poynings' Law (1494) 109, 112, 113
Presbyterianism, public profile 121
Primrose, Archibald *see* Rosebery
Primrose, James Primrose, Viscount 261
privateers 188, 194, 198, 207, 222–3
Privy Council, abolition of 323
Providence Island Company 140
Prowse, Valentine 182
Pryde, George S. 41–2
Pufendorf, Samuel von 82–3
Puritanism 140, 149
Pym, John 68

Queensberry, James Douglas, 2nd Duke of 13–14, 16, 26, 31, 32, 43, 92–3, 95, 97, 98, 106, 181, 185, 226, 291
  discredited by 'Scotch Plot' 262–3, 264–5

and Union negotiations / Treaty 258, 260–1, 272–3, 282, 284, 290, 293–4, 297, 300, 301, 313, 314, 315–16

Rait, Robert *see* Dicey, Albert
Ramillies, battle of 239, 283–4
Randolph, Edward 170, 183–4
religious toleration, negotiations for 253–4
Restoration *see* Charles II; Scotland
Revolution (1688)
  economic impact 216
  impact in Scotland 13, 21–2, 86–91, 173–4
  Settlements (1688–91) 10, 106, 243
  Whig view of 20
Reynell, Carew 170
Rich *see* Warwick
Richier, Isaac, Governor 179
Ridpath, George 100–1, 229, 232, 256, 272
Riley, R. W. J. 44
Rinuccini, Giovanni Battista, Bishop 118
Robertson, John 45
Robertson, William 19, 21, 24, 30, 32
Rochester, Lawrence Hyde, 1st Earl of 91, 95–6, 170, 307
Rose, Alexander, Bishop 253–4
Rosebery, Archibald Primrose, 1st Earl 261, 322
Rosenkrantz, Iver 10, 202, 260–1, 273
Rothes, John Leslie, 9th Earl of 264, 265
Roxburghe, John Ker, 5th Earl / 1st Duke of 127, 132, 264, 293, 294–5, 302
royal burghs 206–8
  Convention of, responses to Union proposals 288–9, 321
  financial manoeuvring 220
  and overseas trade 216
Royal Navy 160–1, 193, 194
Royal Scottish Corporation 174
Ruglen, John Douglas-Hamilton, 1st Earl of 104
Rump Parliament 78
Rutherford, Samuel 70
Rycaut, Sir Paul 178
Rye House Plot 165
Ryswick, Peace of 238–9

Saint-Germain-en-Laye *see* Jacobites, Court in exile
salt, tariffs on 303, 319
Sandelin, Jacob Evertsen (James Sandilands) 151
Scot, George, of Pitlochy 167–8, 169
Scot, Sir John, of Scotsarvit 168
'Scotch Plot' 261–4, 269, 271

Scotland
  compared with Ireland 127
  constitutional reform 68, 70
  contribution to Empire 325; (see also under colonies)
  cultural standing 20
  English attitudes to 124–5, 231
  English discrimination against 99–100, 143, 156, 185–6, 216
  English recognition of 69
  impact of Union on 5–6
  institutions 5, 321–4
  internal religious disputes 7
  international standing 137–8
  military contribution to Empire 34, 161
  objections to English policies 92–4, 109
  parliament see separate main heading
  party politics 13–14, 41–2, 87, 97–100, 264–6, 269, 272–6, 289, 292–306; (see also Country Party; Court Party; New Party; Squadrone Volante)
  political relationships 6
  population 217
  position under Commonwealth 75–6, 79
  rivalry with England 20
  status under Restoration 80–2, 156–7
  status within Empire 143
  Unionist politics 10–11
Scott, David 18
Scott, Paul 44–5
Scott, W. R. 38–9
Scott, Sir Walter 33–5, 36
  Letters of Malachi Malagrowther 35
  Tales of a Grandfather 34
Scottish Charitable Society 152–3
Scottish Company for Africa and India 184–5
Scottish perspective (on state formation) 54, 57, 59, 314
Seafield, James Ogilvie, 1st Earl of 44, 88, 97, 104, 131, 325
  and Union negotiations / Treaty 258, 261, 280–1, 282, 284–5, 286, 294–5, 296, 297, 298–9, 300, 303
seals (national) 324
Seeley, J. R. 37
Selden, John 60
Selkirk, Charles Douglas-Hamilton, 2nd Earl of 104, 264
Sempill, Francis, Lord Sempill of Glassford 251–2
servitor colonialism 142, 152

Seton, William, of Pitmedden 90–1, 105, 232, 296, 302
Seymour, Charles see Somerset
Seymour, Sir Edward 89, 91–2, 127, 275
Shaftesbury, Anthony Ashley Cooper, 1st Earl of 124, 165, 166, 269
Sharp, John, Archbishop 99, 278
Shetland Islands 225
  see also Orkney and Shetland
ships
  building 213
  trading regulations 317
Sibbald, Sir Robert 217–18
Sinclair, Sir John, of Ulbster 29–30
Skene, Alexander 185
Smith, Adam, *The Wealth of Nations* 23
Smith, English 162–3
Smith, John 282
Smith, John, Captain 141
Smollett, Sir James, of Bonhill 93
Smollett, Tobias 16–17
Smout, Christopher 42–3, 46
smuggling 318–19
Solemn League and Covenant (1643) 61, 70–2, 116, 151, 257, 314
  authorship 148
  condemnation/burning 82, 121
Somers, John, Lord Somers 96, 130, 279–80, 281, 282
Somerset, Charles Seymour, 6th Duke of 91
Somerset, Henry see Beaufort
Somerville, Thomas 30–1
Sophia, Electress of Hanover 90, 307
sources, published/manuscript 7–11
South Carolina, Scottish colony in 161–2, 165–8, 172, 175–6, 206
  investors 175–6
  reasons for failure 166–7
Spain
  agreements with see Madrid, Treaty of
  rivalry with Britain in New World 138, 166, 178–9, 188
Spanish Succession, War of the 10, 12, 14, 90, 91, 92, 172, 191, 196, 201, 238–9, 243, 248–50, 259
  economic impact 187, 192–5, 222–3
  influence on Union 277
  taxes suspended for duration of 285, 302–3
Speck, Bill 49
Speed, John 55, 59
Spelman, Sir Henry 60
Spotiswood, John 233

Spreull, John 228–9, 230
Squadrone Volante (Flying Squad) 14, 16, 132, 272
  and Treaty of Union 277–8, 286, 287, 293–4, 296, 300–2, 304–5, 323
  see also New Party
St Vincent 165
Stair, James Dalrymple, 2nd Viscount / 1st Earl of 87–8, 97, 103–4, 129, 304
  and Glencoe Massacre 248–9
  and Union negotiations / Treaty 261, 264, 278, 282, 297–8, 302
Stanhope, Philip Stanhope, Earl of 36
state formation, methods/theories 4–5, 49–50, 53–67, 80–1, 107–9
  compromises between 101, 314
  continental models 266–9
  see also Britannic perspective; Gothic perspective; Scottish perspective
Stewart, Sir James, of Goodtrees 300
Stewart, Mary (daughter of James II of Scotland) 274
Stewart, Robert, of Appin 262
Stewart, Walter, of Pardovan 8
Stirling, William Alexander of Menstrie, 1st Earl of 141, 144–6, 155–6, 168, 197
store system (of trading) 187
Strabane, Viscount see Abercorn
Strafford, Thomas Wentworth, 1st Earl of 66, 110, 112–14
Strathnaver, John Gordon, Lord 297
Straton, Henry, Captain 295–6
Struthers, John 33, 240
Stuart, Gilbert 19
Stuart, Sir James, of Ardmaleish see Bute
Stuart, James Francis Edward see Wales, Prince of
Stuart, Sir Robert, of Tillicoultry 277
Sunderland, Charles Spencer, 3rd Earl of 263, 270, 282, 303
Sutherland, John Gordon, 15th Earl of 297
Sweden
  as model of state formation 267
  New World colonies see New Sweden
  plans for inclusion in Confederation 70
  political alliances 83
  trading links with Scotland 150, 151, 212–13
Swift, Jonathan 133
Switzerland 267

Tables 67–8
Tacitus 60–1
Tarbat, Viscount see Cromartie
taxation 206–8, 210, 220, 221, 223
  in Treaty of Union 280, 282, 285, 319;
  exemptions favouring Scotland 319
Taylor, Joseph 271
Tenison, Thomas, Archbishop 99, 254, 307
textile trade/industry 102, 210, 212, 213, 217, 227, 228, 237, 318
Thirty Years' War 64
Thomas, Sir Dalby 173
Thomas, David 146
Thomas the Rhymer 57
Thomson, John see Haversham
Thornborough, John, Bishop 56
timber trade 213
Tindal, Nicholas 16
titles, sale of see baronetcies; colonies
TKUA (Tyske Kancellis Udensrigske Afdeling, Copenhagen) 10
tobacco trade 210, 318–19
Toleration Act (1689) 322
Tory Party/ideology 28–9, 91, 95–6, 252–3, 306–8
  involvement in commercial enterprise 20–1
trade (international)
  balance of payments 230
  decline 216
  England–Scotland 199–200, 217, 236–7
  excess time spent 215
  exports 230–1
  flexibility of commodities 215
  importance to Scottish economy 137–8, 199, 231–2, 234–5
  imports 212–13, 230–1
  maritime protection 222
  national drive to increase 205–6
  opening up 208
  standardisation of regulations 317–18
  see also Baltic; Board of Trade; Committee of Trade; Council of Trade; economy; England; free trade; Ireland; Navigation Acts; Netherlands; networks; names of commodities
tramp trading 160, 214–15, 222–3
transportation see colonies
treason, law of 323
Treaty of Union (1707) 3, 6, 172–3, 197
  constitutional content 284–5, 301, 314–17
  economic content/implications 198–9, 281–3, 285, 287–8, 298–9, 301, 302–3, 308–9, 317–21
  favouring of English interests 282–3, 285, 314–16, 320

Index

fears of armed response 290–2
financial incentives for support 293, 294–5, 301, 304–5
formal implementation 17
formal objections to 286–92
guiding principles 6–7, 10–11
institutional content 321–4
later commentaries 38
non-Jacobite opponents 297–8
non-negotiable areas 284
passage through English parliament 306–8, 309
passage through Scottish Estates 230, 295, 299–306
preliminary negotiations 197–8, 231–9, 272–6, 278–9, 283, 292–9; procedure 278–9; secrecy 279
protests against 289–90, 291–2, 298, 307–8
reaction to draft form 283
reception in Ireland 132–3
religious content/implications 285–7, 306–7, 322
responses to implementation 313–14, 324–5
Trevelyan, G. M. 40–1
Trevor, Thomas 185–6
Trevor-Roper, Hugh, Lord Dacre 46–7
Tubuganti, battle of 179
Tucker, Thomas 205, 206
Tullibardine, Earl of *see* Atholl
Tweeddale, John Hay, 2nd Marquis of 14, 90, 180, 264–5, 271, 293, 296–8

Ulster, plantation of 110–12, 138–9
 influence in New World 144
Union
 (alleged) benefits to Scotland 19–20, 30–3, 130–3, 325
 alternatives to 237–9
 benefits to England 277
 breakaways from 235
 calls for equality within 24–5, 27–8, 29–30, 34–5, 148
 Committee on 77–8
 controversy over 3
 debates on (just prior to Union Treaty) 266–9
 English coercive methods 270–2
 as international model 40–1
 modern views of 48–50
 moves to terminate 324–5
 nature of process 4–5; as ideological 45–6; as political 43–5

 objections to 267–9
 preliminary negotiations/manoeuvres 23–4, 29, 40, 62–7, 94–5
 rejections of 4–5
 relative representations under 124
 salient factors 325–6
 suggested extension 22–3
 see also Treaty of Union
United Irishmen 28
United Provinces *see* Netherlands

Vanderheiden, (Jasper) 234
Vaughan, William, Dr 141
Veere (Zeeland) 207–8, 222, 238
Vernon, James 179
Verstegan, Richard 60–1
Violet, Thomas 203–4
Virginia 139, 140, 142, 146
volunteer forces 25

Wales, incorporation into Union 4, 128, 131–2
Wales, James Francis Edward Stuart, Prince of ('the Old Pretender') 244, 261, 275
 recognition as 'James VIII/III' 10, 90, 243
 religious standpoint 252
Walker, George 223
Walker, Patrick 217–18
Wallace, James 15
Wallace, William 17, 34
Warwick, Robert Rich, 1st Earl of 148–9
Watson, John 225–6, 271–2
weights and measures, standardisation of 321
Wentworth *see* Strafford
West Indian Company 150–1, 154
'Western Design' 153, 154, 204
Wharton, Thomas, Lord Wharton 96, 278, 282
Whatley, Christopher 46
Whig Party/ideology 30–3, 35–7, 86, 95–7, 124–5, 126–7, 248, 252, 268–70, 307
 adjustments to 37–42
 anti-Jacobite rhetoric 245–6, 250
 fragmentation 42–5
 political/social reforms 32
 in Scotland 19–22
Whitehaven 183, 187, 318
Whole Prophecies of Scotland, England, France, Ireland and Denmarke, The (Anon.) 56–7

Whyte, Ian D. 46
William III (of Orange) 10, 13, 21–2, 97, 98, 221, 222
  accession 15, 86–7, 201, 250
  attempted assassination 89, 248, 260, 262
  dealings with Darien scheme 15, 174, 176–8, 179, 181–2
  death 35, 90, 92, 94, 96, 258
  economic policy 21, 232
  and Glencoe Massacre 248–9
  hostilities with Jacobites 125, 182
  policy on Union 88–9
  unpopularity in Scotland 217, 243, 247–8, 249, 253, 254

Willoughby, William, Lord Willoughby of Parham 149, 152, 154
wine/spirit trade 210, 228
  legislation 260
Wishart, William 286
Wodrow, Robert 8
Worcester (ship) 270–2
Worcester, battle of 75
Wright, Thomas 36
Wylie, Robert 8, 256
Wyon, Frederick 36–7

Yeaman, George, Captain 223
York, Duke of *see* James VII/II
Young, John 48–9